FAREWELL TO INNOCENCE

Sigmund Freud

FAREWELL TO INNOCENCE

Freud and Psychoanalysis

by

Dr. Milton Robin

A.S.P.
Associated Science Publishers
New York, N.Y.

Farewell To Innocence

ISBN: 0-935016-73-2

Typesetting, engraving and layouts by:
Excelsior Typographers and Engravers, Unltd.
(A Division of Excelsior Music Publishing Co.)

First Edition

Published by:
Associated Science Publishers
15 West 44th Street
New York, N.Y. 10036

Distributed by:
Scientific and Technical Book Service
50 West 23rd Street, New York, N.Y. 10010

Printed in U.S.A.

Library of Congress Cataloging-in-Publication Data

Robin, Milton, 1920-
Farewell to innocence : Freud and psychoanalysis / by Milton Robin. -- 1st ed.
p. cm.
Includes biblographical references and index.
ISBN 0-935016-73-2. ISBN 0-935016-72-4 (pbk.)
1. Freud, Sigmund, 1856-1939. 2. Psychoanalysts--Austria--Biography.
3. Psychoanalysis--History. I. Title.
BF173.F85R636 1988
150.19'52--dc19

88-21850
CIP

Acknowledgments

A special thanks to Carol Conklin whose initial stimulation started the project, and to George and Sherry Bellak who were there from the beginning and gave most willingly of their expertise. Also a word of appreciation to Shelley Robin, and Joy and Hoyt Hobbs. Their readings of the manuscript and their valuable comments provided important support and encouragement. I was privileged to have the support of Lydia Sarney, a more than able secretary, who checked the material with the library, made sure that all the Ts were properly crossed and kept the manuscript together.

An honorable mention for creativity is due David Zinn for laboriously and tastefully converting the manuscript into a book.

Finally, I am deeply indepted to Letty Grierson. Her patience, strength and kind persuasion transformed my labored English into real writing. Letty's steady editing hand kept the raw material on course and insured it a safe journey.

CONTENTS

INTRODUCTION

"What does a woman want?" asks Sigmund Freud.

What kind of question is that? Common sense tells us that women want essentially what men want: happiness, love, security, well-being, recognition.

His answer? Even more outrageous than his question:

> It is an envy for the penis that gives the analyst an unusual amount of trouble...A positive striving to possess a male genital...a repudiation of femininity...the striving to be masculine...the female's wish for a penis is a source of severe outbreaks of depression in her...Nothing can be done to help her.
>
> (Sigmund Freud, *'Analysis Terminable and Interminable,'* 1937, Standard Edition XXIII, P. 250)

And this man claims to be a scientist? How can such nonsense have given rise to an international psychiatric and psychological movement? A movement, moreover, in which women psychiatrists and psychologists enjoyed a prominent place? How could psychoanalysis, espousing such absurdity, influence the artists, intellectuals, and scientists of the world?

Perhaps Freud sounds more reasonable when he discusses men? Not at all; he says that no civilized man can be fully potent, that the very nature of the sex drive precludes the possibility of full gratification.

> The sexual life of civilized man is...severely impaired; it sometimes gives the impression of being in a process of becoming atrophied...Its importance as a source...of happiness has...diminished...Something in the nature of the function itself...denies us full satisfaction.
>
> (*'Civilization and Its Discontents,'* 1930, S.E. XII p.105)

Note what Freud has to say about marriage.

> This brings us to the question whether sexual intercourse in legal marriage can offer full compensation for the restriction imposed before marriage. There is such an abundance of material supporting a reply in the negative that we can give only the briefest summary of it...satisfying sexual intercourse in marriage takes place only for a few

> years; after three, four or five years, the marriage becomes a failure insofar as it has promised the satisfaction of sexual needs.
> (*'Civilized Sexual Morality and Modern Nervous Illness,'* 1908, S.E. IX, p.183)

Are we dealing with a misanthrope? And he goes further to state that no one can enjoy full sexual pleasure who loves his partner but feels respect for her at the same time.

> The man almost always feels his respect for the woman acting as a restriction on his sexual activity and only develops full potency when he is with a debased sexual object.
> (*'On The Universal Tendency to Debasement in the Sphere of Love,'* 1912, S.E. XI, p.184)

A man must debase his partner? Love, concern, respect, these feelings dilute sexual satisfaction? Was Professor Freud crazy? No wonder his writings were considered unfit even for medical journals.

As though he hasn't said enough, he goes on to judge our highest emotions, those which distinguish us from animals, our religious sense, our reverence for God, in the following way: "The whole thing is so patently infantile, so foreign to reality...it is humiliating to discover how large a number of people...try to defend it."[1] And then he proceeds to assert that the noblest accomplishments of man: science and art, morality and esthetics, are founded on his renunciation of sexual satisfaction.

But if we persist, we find out something else about Sigmund Freud: it was he alone who obliged the world to recognize that women have the same sexual feelings as men do. It is he who fought for a woman's right to decent, humane treatment for her neurosis, rather than be subjected, as she was earlier, to various forms of brutality, from surgical removal of the clitoris to being smeared with repugnant-smelling valerian. For maintaining that ground he was maligned, ostracized, insulted in the streets, at times rendered almost unable to earn a living.

Freud's contention was that man is not master in his own house; that human behavior is determined by a force outside of awareness—the unconscious. Moreover, the unconscious is crazy, out of touch with reality. But: make the unconscious conscious and patterns of behavior that are self-destructive will change, symptoms will disappear, sickness will give way to health. Bizarre? Perhaps. But medical literature is replete with histories of individual suffering that was overcome by psychoanalysis. Until Freud's day, the medical profession would not deign to treat "imaginary" illnesses. Freud alone studied the condition and finally understood the origin of the disease.

At Freud's memorial, September 1939, Ludwig Jekels, one of the oldest and most philosophical of his students, spoke:

> This man's entire being was devoted to the noblest principles of humanism....Thirst for the truth, and love are the fundamentals of humanism.....His

[1] S.E. IX, p.74

great need to love was an obstacle to his work.

The Humanist of whom Jekels spoke had been regarded throughout the world as an enemy of civilization. Every country from the capitalist United States to the socialist Soviet Union had rejected his theories. Medical groups, religious organizations, Marxist political revolutionaries, women's rights groups, universities, all agreed: Freud and his theories were unacceptable. Pope Paul VI has gone so far as to blame him for our modern sexual libertinism. Even the majority of his own followers refused to go along with his later theories—and these men and women were psychoanalysts who had in the past themselves withstood ridicule, even loss of professional positions. He was too radical for them. At one point Freud lamented: "I am a commander-in-chief without an army."

In order that we may fully understand psychoanalytic psychology, the author prefers we retrace the steps Freud trod; that we share the problems he faced and some of the truths as well as errors he is responsible for. By following his steps we shall be better able to separate what he actually said from the misrepresentations of his theories that he had to contend with throughout his life. Many textbooks are devoted to this subject. But this is not a textbook, it is an adventure. Let us go to the beginning. Freud's story is unique. It is the story of a man whose work shook the world.

CHAPTER I

The Happiest Years

At the time when Darwin's work was exciting every country of Europe, and was pointing the way to new explorations of nature and man, seventeen-year-old Freud graduated from high school. The uneasy problem of choosing a career had to be faced. Given his particular circumstances, his choice lay between business, medicine, or law. Many years later he wrote that it was hearing Goethe's essay on Nature read aloud at a popular lecture that led him to choose medicine. The essay depicts Nature as a beautiful and bountiful mother who permits her favorite children to explore her secrets.

There is a myth that persons of genius are poor students in school. The list claims Einstein, Darwin, Schweitzer, Edison, and others. Freud was an outstanding exception to that myth. He was an extraordinary student. He once remarked that he had a "photographic" memory, and that he would answer examination questions in the teachers' own words. Few teachers can resist such appreciation.

Medical school was the same. In his second year he was awarded a grant to spend the summer in Trieste, where his teacher, Carl Claus, had set up a zoological experimental station. He was to try to solve a problem which had been puzzling scientists since the days of Aristotle. The gonadic structure of male eels had never been fully determined. As Freud wrote: "No one has ever found a mature male eel. No one has yet seen the testes of the eel, in spite of innumerable attempts for centuries." To a twenty-year-old student, not only was the recognition by his teacher rewarding, the opportunity of spending Easter vacation on the shores of the Adriatic doing research was also relished. And after painstakingly dissecting some four hundred eels, Freud found the answer within the histological structure in the eel's abdominal cavity. The paper was presented before the Academy of Science by Carl Claus and published in their bulletin. It was Freud's first publication.

Ernest Jones wryly remarked that the future discoverer of the castration complex must have been disappointed at not being able to find the testes of the eel.

Freud now turned his full attention to research. He transferred to the Physiological Institute under the tutelage of the eminent Dr. Wilhelm von Brucke. Brucke was a par-excellence example of a professional scientist. He was well-disciplined, conscientious, and a tireless worker. The standards he set for himself, he also exacted from his assistants and students. A student had written in one of his papers: "Superficial observation reveals...." Brucke returned the paper, the objectionable line crossed out and his own comment on the margin: "One is not to observe superficially."

This short, red-headed, blue-eyed man, who Freud said influenced him more than any man in his life, had a reputation for being cold, impersonal, and purely rational. (In truth, Brucke was a very compassionate man.) There are those who feel that any display of emotions is a sign of weakness. Indeed, there are many cultures which express this attitude. Open expressions of feelings are considered bad form, and a great deal of energy is expended maintaining this facade. And so with Brucke. When his son died, he forbade his family and friends to mention his son's name. He removed any trace, any reminder of the boy: photographs, clothes, etc., from his house. It was as though even the thought of his child would be more than he could bear, that he would break down and behave in a way he considered bad taste.

It was said of Brucke that no one who ever worked with him felt anything but loyalty and devotion. He was free of vanity and the need for power; he encouraged original work in his students and respected fresh ideas, even if they differed from his own; his reputation was impeccable. Over the years he proved to be a most important benefactor and a most loyal friend to Freud. In fact, we shall see, at times his help and support were indispensable.

Freud held Brucke in awe. Years later he said that Brucke, forty years his senior (exactly his father's age), was the greatest authority I ever met.

Brucke and Hermann Helmholtz led a new "antivitalistic" school of physiology which claims that everything has a natural, material base. There is no supernatural, no spiritual essence, or divine plan. All phenomena can ultimately be traced to physical—chemical forces. Freud embraced the philosophy of materialism with his characteristic intensity and extremism.

One can imagine Brucke's astonishment could he have known that one day one of his most dedicated pupils, and his favorite, would bring forth a theory of the mind using concepts such as "wish," "intention," "purpose," "aim," words the antivitalists had just abolished from scientific thinking.

To whatever extent he identified with the old master, Freud dedicated himself with unswerving commitment to his scientific and intellectual integrity, and his ethical values. And for the rest of his life he remained loyal to that commitment even at the price of rejection and ostracism.

As time went by Freud became addicted to two things: work and cigars. He felt he needed nicotine during his creative periods. His smoking probably played a significant part in the developing cancer of the jaw from which he was to die. He tried many times to give up his "vice," usually at the insistence of his physicians, but he couldn't do it.

> I have gained the insight that masturbation is the one great habit that is a "primary addiction," (Freud is referring to the masturbation of infancy which is invariably repressed and requires a psychoanalysis to bring to memory, not the masturbation of adolescence and adulthood) and that the other addictions, for example, alcohol, morphine, tobacco, etc., enter into life only as a substitute for and a withdrawal (symptom) from it...The doubt of course arises whether such an addiction is curable or whether analysis and therapy must stop short at this point and remain content with transforming a hysteria into a neur-

> asthenia.
> (Letter to Fliess, December 22, 1897 '*S. Freud's Letters,*' p.239)

His other addiction was in the tradition of his revered Ernst Wilhelm von Brucke; the application of the scientific method to the pursuit of truth. No comforting illusions stand in the way of discovery. And indeed, he was to discover some of the most profound and disquieting truths concerning the human condition.

> That is all I had to say to you about femininity. It is certainly incomplete and fragmentary and does not always sound friendly....If you want to know more about femininity, inquire from your own experiences of life, or turn to the poets, or wait until science can give you deeper and more coherent information.
> ('*New Introductory Lectures,*' 1933, XXII, p. 135)

We are far ahead of our story. To return to the Physiological Institute, on one occasion Freud's extreme involvement with his new hero and his conviction that antivitalism is the whole truth, led him to behave badly in an argument in a German students' club. The discussion was on the relation of philosophy to the natural sciences. Freud "thrust himself forward" and argued from an "extremely one-sided point of view." Through a play on words involving his opponent's name, he rudely insulted him, implying that the man was a swine. He refused to apologize and there was even talk of a duel. "There was a general uproar and I was called upon from many sides to withdraw my remarks, but I refused to do so. The man I had insulted was too sensible to look upon the incident as a 'challenge' and let the affair drop."[1]

The opponent was the formidable Victor Adler who went on to enjoy international prominence as a leader of the Austrian Social Democrats.

Research in histology is not without its own drama. Freud was at the Institute at a time when the man with the microscope was trying to answer universal questions about God, evolution, nature, and the aims of life. (For example, are the structures and elements of nerve cells different for higher and lower animals? Or, are both based on the same units?) Is the human different from an oyster in kind or is it correlative to the number of cells and complications of their respective fibers? Are human cells qualitatively different from a monkey's cells? Or do they fit into a continuum in a line of development? Freud was fascinated by the search and did spectacular work. (He demonstrated that higher forms of life do, indeed, evolve from lower forms.)

He spent six years (1876-1882) at the Physiological Institute and would refer to that period as the happiest years of his youth.

> At length, in Ernst Brucke's physiological laboratory, I found rest and full satisfaction, and men too, whom I could respect and take as my

[1] '*Sigmund Freud His Life in Pictures and Words.*' K.R. Eissler, Harcourt Brace Jovanovich, N.Y. 1978, p.84.

> models: the great Brucke himself, and his assistants, Sigmund Exner and Ernst Fleischl von Marxow. With the last of these, a brilliant man, I was priviledged to be upon terms of friendship.
> (*'An Autobiographical Study,'* 1925, S.E. XX p.10)

Exner was a scientist of first quality. He had a friendly and humorous manner, but he was ambitious, proud, and authoritative. Fleischl was one among the very rare. Brilliant, enthusiastic, handsome, athletic, very wealthy' this charming, amiable, gifted man was destined to suffer incredible pain from an infection contracted while conducting research in pathological anatomy. More of this, however, in a later chapter.

At the Institute he also met Dr. Josef Breuer. It is not unusual in psychoanalysis that an important theme makes its appearance prematurely: enjoys a light airing, recedes, and returns later. This is the case with Breuer for the Freud-Breuer episode is a major part of the story of Freud and psychoanalysis. For the moment, however, we shall touch upon it lightly; later it will be discussed in full detail.

Breuer confided to Freud that he had successfully treated a hysteric. Furthermore, he had used hypnosis! Freud was fascinated. At that time respectable physicians would not treat hysterics. Dr. Josef Breuer was fourteen years older than Freud, and enjoyed a prestigious and lucrative private practice. A very kind man, his interests extended far beyond medicine and science. He was at home in the world of literature, art, and music. Freud and he were attracted to each other at once and were to share a deep friendship that lasted fifteen years. The medical establishment considered hysterics as malingerers who wished to make their doctors look foolish. The profession's attitude toward such patients was punitive and different form of "treatment" were devised to deal with them.

Hysteria as we know it today, if one can describe it simply, is a condition in both men and women, the symtoms of which can mimic any disease. Its uniqueness lies in the fact that these symptoms have no organic base. On examination a paralyzed limb would prove to be neurologically intact; a blind eye equally so. The condition has been reported throughout history and has always been an enigma. Further, it had been considered to affect women almost exclusively. In fact, its name, hysteria, is derived from the Greek word for the womb. Today, thanks to Freud's work, hysteria is appreciated as a serious condition which can be helped through psychotherapy.

A review of the literature on medical history shows that the great clinicians sensed a relationship between hysteria and sex.

CHAPTER II

■ *Physicians For Unknown Diseases*

There is a silent moment between the dark of night and the first stirrings that accompany the rising sun. Slowly, one can make out through the mist, the silouette of an isolated building. It's a bit lighter now. The silhouette is familiar: it is the Temple of Imhotep, who was the father of Egyptian medicine. The streaks of morning sun are just reaching out; the view of the Temple becomes clearer and the level stone pavement in front of the Temple has begun to reflect the new day's light. There is no sound, no movement, not even from the trees that surround the Temple. Suddenly the outline of a huddled form, a woman's, seated with her back against the Temple wall, comes into view. Was she there asleep all night? The sun has come up from below the horizon. She is awake now. If she sees anyone, she pays no attention.

Her name is Shah. She is in her late twenties. She seems of medium height, perhaps a shade on the plump side. The rust-colored, coarsely woven dress that falls into soft folds as it reaches her ankles looks comfortable. A brownish shawl over her head and shoulders barely covers two strands of green clay beads around her neck as she fingers them nervously. Leather thong sandals, worn thin, protect her feet. She seems mildly distressed. Yesterday the doctor told her that her womb had "wandered" from its natural location and that was why she had been nervous, weepy, and forgetful, and also why she had pain in her right ear.

Shah's marriage to Ipy was arranged for her by her father and the local priests. Ipy is a sailor and is away for months at a time. Each time she looks forward to his return, but festive as Ipy's return from the sea is, something about it is disappointing. It would be better if she were to have a child, but Isis does not respond to her offerings and her prayers. She lives with Ipy's mother, Senna. Shah's mother-in-law lost her husband in a mine accident years ago and she has not remarried. Senna is a good-looking woman, energetic, easily moved to laughter, and well liked in the village. She is fond of Shah and kind to her. She knows Ipy's absences are hard on Shah and that barrenness adds to her daughter-in-law's difficulties. She has noticed the symptoms that Shah has shown in the last weeks.

A few days ago Senna took Shah to a doctor who was referred by their own local doctor/priest. Shah's condition required the skill of a specialist, and this man fortunately resided in the next village. They had to wait at the Temple, with others, because the doctor was conducting special prayers with another priest, something having to do with the receding waters.

When their turn came, Senna and Shah entered the doctor's office. It was one of the side rooms of the Temple, not large, sparsely furnished but the sun streaming in from the light shafts made it altogether pleasant. Standing to greet them was a rather short man. His head was shaved and he was wearing a loose-fitting, white linen garment that fell to his mid-calf. A twisted leather rope encircled his waist. Three-quarter-length sleeves seemed to hide thick arms. A slit down the front of the bodice exposed a portion of his chest on which hung a falcon-shaped pendant on a chain (the symbol of Ra). There was a soft scraping sound from his leather sandals as he approached to shake their hands. His manner was serious but not unfriendly. Senna described Shah's recent behavior and symptoms and the doctor paid close attention, from time to time turning his eyes to Shah. He directed a few questions to Senna and asked her to wait outside while he spoke to Shah alone. How are you and your husband doing? How does it feel not being able to have children? What is it like living with your mother-in-law, an obviously attractive and vital woman? Shah answered softly, an occasional quiver in her voice betraying her feelings. The doctor seemed to be concentrating on every word. Now he spoke softly: "My dear, your womb has slipped from its natural place. You are uncomfortable and not yourself because it has strayed too high. We must get it down to where it belongs. Do not be alarmed; it is not a difficult task. After tomorrow's sunset, come here and make you offerings to Khons. Do not go home; sleep outside on the patio. Bring with you whatever will make you comfortable. At this time of year a shawl may be necessary during the night. At daybreak I will come here with my assistants. We will bring with us the necessary medicines for your condition. Those with a strong aroma you will have to squat over. The few that have to be burned you will straddle over, standing upright so that the smoke may enter your body. There is no pain involved in this procedure. Go now; do as I have told you; I shall see you two days from now.

The above scene took place in Egypt about five thousand years B.C.[1]

To be sure our knowledge of primitive psychiatries is fragmentary. One can be certain that primitive man was often frightened; means and agencies were evolved to deal with his fear. Indeed, in every known society there exist religious rituals, special prayers to special deities, and medicine men, priests, and doctors, whose function is to deal with man's fears both internal and external. The aim of treatment was to get rid of uncertainty and fear concerning the illness rather than to study the illness itself. There is an Egyptian stela in the Bibliotheque Nationale in Paris which tells the story of a princess of the Twentieth Dynasty Pharaohs, who, afflicted with what they call a demoniacal possession, was cured by the Egyptian god Khons.

There are several striking things about the above example of Egyptian medicine: there is no clear distinction between religion and medicine, so that some priests are trained to be physicians. It was noted that physicians tended to be specialists: "Some are physicians for the eyes, others for the head, teeth, abdomen, and for unknown diseases."[2]

Linking hysterical symptoms to conflicts around sexuality was remarkable in itself. In fact, the outstanding impression ancient Egyptian medicine gives is of its

---

[1] *'Ebers papyrus,' 'Kahoun papyrus,' 'Herodotus,' personal communication with Carol Jean Conklin.*

[2] *'Herodotus II,'* 84.

humanism. In the literature discovered by archeologists, one learns that the relationship between patient and doctor was one of mutual sympathy and respect; an attitude not consistent in the history of medicine.

Hippocrates (fifth century B. C.) was not what we today would call a research scientist. But he was a great clinician and some of his observations are still useful in present-day surgery. He recognized hysteria not as a mental disease, but as a physical affliction. He believed the condition was limited to woman and caused by a disturbance of the uterus, intuitively sensing the sexual factor in the disorder. He recommended marriage as the best remedy for hysteria.

The great Galen (second century B. C.) found that medication was of no avail in hysteria and on occasion advised stimulation of the clitoris. Even today that sounds like a radical prescription. Galen's intuition was awesome; it was not until the twentieth century that the scientific connection between emotional disorders and sexuality was established.

The above examples of ancient medicine demonstrate again a benign attitude toward the patient. One may question the treatment of hysteria, but cannot deny that the feelings of the patient are being given kind consideration.

History, that written record of mankind, cannot claim to be kind or consistent. The present author suggests that when the social climate is unkind, it is more unkind to women than to men. The period between Galen and today is as full of contrasts and inconsistencies as is man himself.

After the age of Galen, demonology, the belief that the Devil could possess and afflict a person, was to rule medical psychology for sixteen hundred years. The Dark Ages. Emotional disorders became the province of the Church. Physical illness was considered to be natural, but mental illness was believed to be supernatural. An important question was posed. Can supernatural diseases be treated by natural methods? What today would be recognized as hysterical symptoms were called *stigmata diaboli*. The very existence of man as man was due to an original sin. The goal became religious salvation.

The Prince of Darkness, the Devil, was the enemy. His chief purpose was to triumph over the Lord. His means was the contamination of the human soul. He would enter people's bodies with or without their knowledge or consent, and compel them to commit un-Christian acts. Thus, the sin-laden soul would be lost to heaven and Satan would have triumphed over God. An anxious society believed that the danger had to be faced and overcome, or the world would go to Hell.

And next to the Devil, of course, the woman was seen as the root of all evil. Eve was the source of sin and the witch was her representative on earth. Mental illness was equated with the Unclean Spirit, and the major preoccupation of the Devil—Sex. "All witchcraft come from carnal lust, which is in women insatiable....Wherefore for the sake of fulfilling their lusts they consort even with devils."[1]

The witch was blamed for everything. The official position was that whatever was wrong in one's life, even if one was unaware, was the consequence of having been "bewitched." "Witchcraft" in the mouth of the pious, could explain anything

[1] '*Malleus Maleficarum,*' English edition, p.47

and was often exploited by the powerful. For example, when Henry VIII decided to get rid of Anne Boleyn, he had no difficulty explaining to church authorities that he had been seduced into marriage by witchcraft. His proof? The good Lord had not allowed them a male issue.

Pope Innocent VIII on December 9, 1484, issued a bull:

> Witches....have slain infants yet in the mother's womb, as also the offspring of cattle, have blasted the produce of the earth, the grapes of the vine, the fruit of trees....they hinder men from performing the sexual act and women from conceiving....

To destroy the witch who brings evil to the land is perhaps justifiable, but when she is persecuted for her good and helpful acts, how can it be justified? Incomprehensible as it may seem the "crimes" committed by witches included ministering to the sick. The ability to relieve suffering through herbs and drugs, to ease the pain of labor, to provide information about contraception, to heal, etc., this was proof of being possessed by an alien spirit.

> For this must always be remembered, as a conclusion, that by Witches we understand not only those which kill and torment, but all Diviners, Charmers, Jugglers, all Wizards, commonly called wise men and wise women....we reckon all good Witches, which do no hurt but good, which do not spoil and destroy, but save and deliver....It were a thousand times better for the land if all Witches, but especially the blessing Witch, might suffer death.
>
> (Thomas S. Szasz, '*The Manufacture of Madness,*' N.Y. Dell Publishing Co, 1970, p.89)

Is there no end to the madness. Is anyone safe when hatred for women is given full rein? "For they who resort to such witches are thinking more of their bodily health then of God...."[1]

When accused, how could a witch defend herself?

In the name of saving mankind, an official witchhunt was blessed before it was launched. Two theologians wrote *Malleus Maleficarum (The Witches' Hammer).* This book is the most horrible, anti-erotic, cruel, misogynous, and yet the most authoritative document of the age. It is simply mad with fear and hatred of women.

The mutterings and the fantasies of the mentally ill seemed like corroboration of the principles of demonology. The credibility of self-confessed sinners or witnesses never came into question. The sole authority in these matters was the lawyer, not the physician. It is incredible today that someone could be accused of traveling hundreds of miles through the air on a broomstick and consorting with the Devil. But such accusations were considered sufficient evidence for a burning. A witch was any-

---

[1] '*Malleus*' p.150

one who was called a witch or who claimed the title herself (the delusions of the mentally ill were taken at face value). If even a well-educated and sophisticated person suffering from hysteria is prone to suggestion, imagine the plight of an illiterate peasant woman caught up in the official madness. The attention suddenly paid to her by the church and town authorities must have been overwhelming. Add further the fearful reaction of the villagers and townspeople. Imagine her fear and at the same time her sense of importance when told she possessed magical powers. But, it was not necessary for her to agree that, yes indeed, she soured her neighbors' milk or helped her sick neighbor. Once she was accused she had to stand trial.

Accusations were easy to come by. Many believed in the reality of witchcraft and were quick to blame any mishap on the first female at hand. In that respect no woman was safe. Many accusers were thrill seekers, many were spiteful, some were paid by the courts to find the Devil's helpers, and of course there were some who were just crazy. In some instances even children were encouraged to act as though they were bewitched and make nonsensical accusations.

Mental illness was puzzling and at the same time frightening. The sick were not pitied; they were dreaded. They were considered to be possessed by the forces of darkness and even their own families would disown them. These unfortunates, nearly always women, were literally thrown out of their homes. They would wander through the woods and along roads, helpless, unable to care for themselves. They lived in stables and eventually lost any vestige of human appearance. The very sight of them would corroborate popular superstition.

Now our poor peasant woman is carted off to court. She is asked questions about her genitals! Has she "known" Satan? What spells has she worked? Etc. An important question would be the names of other women she knows to be witches. But suppose she refuses to confess to being a witch? Ah! Does she really think we officials are so easily deceived? We have no choice; force must be used to get her to admit her passion for the Devil.

She might be forced to take purgatives, or simply whipped. If she still doesn't confess, and we all know how clever and stubborn the Devil is, then she may be forced to eat huge quantities of salted meat while drink is withheld from her. Ah, this is a stubborn one. We turn to thumbscrews, leg vises. Still no confession? We cut off her fingers. We put her in stocks whose nails eat into her flesh, we dump her into scalding water mixed with lime....Even a list of tortures can become tedious, so let us turn to the final challenge to Satan. We put her on a spit and turn her slowly over a fire. The record shows that practically all of the accused confessed.

Even when the woman pleaded love and devotion to God and disavowed any traffic with the Devil, it was of no avail. "We have often learned from the confession of those whom we have caused to be burned that they have not been willing agents of witchcraft."[1]

And now the trial begins. She is brought into the courtroom where "of her own free will" she repeats her confession. But, suppose our victim manages to stay in touch with reality and changes her mind? She claims that she was forced to confess, that she could no longer stand the pain? My God, dealing with Satan isn't

---

[1]'*Malleus,*' p.103

easy. He's clever and elusive, but his pretended innocence doesn't fool us. It's back to the torture chamber. The end of the whole procedure is an execution.

In all societies women suffer from some form of discrimination, a phenomenon we shall try to explain. But in this period of history it was as though the whole world rose up against the female as testimony to its own insanity. Society allowed its horror, suspicion, and terror of women full expression.

Let us return to our peasant woman. It was not enough to torture her, to break her spirit, and literally break her body; she was not granted the right to face her judges. Stripped naked, her head and genitals shaved so the Devil would have no place to hide, her marks of torture and her wounds exposed, she would be led into the court backwards, so that she could not bewitch the innocent onlookers! The judges? They were proud, convinced they were carrying out the good Lord's wishes. Demonology, the systematic degradation and torture of women, was paying Eve back for the original fall.

In this atmosphere no one was safe. Not everyone accused of being a sorcerer or a witch was mentally sick, but practically everyone who was mentally ill was considered a witch. Even girls and boys of nine or ten were found guilty and punished.

Tradition can be a good thing if used to preserve values in times of abrupt change and revolutionary upheaval. But tradition that clings stubbornly to dogma builds up an impassable barrier against change and growth.

Medical history can boast that here and there a voice would be raised in reason, but it was quickly labeled heretical and easily silenced.

> Those err who say that there is no such thing as witchcraft, but that it is purely imaginary, even although they do not believe that devils exist except in the imagination of the ignorant and vulgar....But this is contrary to true faith which teaches us that certain angels fell from heaven and are now devils....And because infidelity in a person who has been baptized is technically called heresy, therefore such persons are plainly heretics.
> (Ibid. pp.2,3)

With stunning simplicity, two monks (Johann Sprenger and Heinrich Kramer) brushed aside any enlightenment from the past and any careful medical examination of the accused in the present. After all, how does one object to "this is contrary to true faith"? The medical man was now completely excluded; insanity, heresy, and witchcraft were fused into a single concept. If the public execution of heretics and witches, especially by burning, seems macabre to us today, in those days it was an act of mercy. The body had to be burned to deliver the soul from evil and darkness. Despite the unspeakable torture of hundreds of human beings, the stake was symbol of ecstasy and of communion with God.

The struggle between science and superstition is dramatic and difficult. It persists even into our own time—in Freud's the stake might have become obsolete (the last witch to be executed was in Switzerland in 1782), but confinement in mental asylums, surgery of the genitals, and other forms of cruelty were still in use. Freud's discoveries put an end to all that! Hysterics are no longer subjected to clitorectomies or smeared with valerian, or have their wombs packed in ice. His fight against this barbarism, and the vilification he suffered therefrom, are important themes in our story.

At that time, 1882, when the subject of hypnotism was discussed in Brucke's Institute, neither Breuer nor the twenty-six-year-old Freud would have dreamed that four years later, one of them would be telling his colleagues that hysterical women were not malingerers, but were sick. And more than that, that it was probably the poor sexual performance, the sexual inadequacy of their husbands that caused the illness. Stated simply: when husbands do not satisfy their wives in bed, the wives become ill. One can imagine how much favor that message found in a male-dominated culture at the turn of the century. One can also imagine what society wished to do to him.

But again, we are ahead of our story and must return to Freud as he worked with a microscope at the Institute.

CHAPTER III

■ *Hook, Line, and Sinker*

One evening, on his return from work, Freud was introduced to Martha and Minna Bernays, friends of his sister Anna, who were visiting her. Much to the surprise of his family, instead of as usual retreating to his room and his studies, Freud joined the festivities at the family table. One glance at Martha had been enough: Sigmund Freud had fallen in love, as the saying goes, hook, line and sinker! "The sweet girl of whom everyone speaks with admiration....despite all my resistance, captivated my heart at our first meeting."[1]

For several weeks after that first fateful glimpse of Martha, he retreated behind his unsociable and rather eccentric demeanor. Then, unable to suppress his feelings any longer, he declared himself, "because any suggestion of artificiality towards such a girl would have been unbearable."[2]

Every day she was sent a red rose accompanied by a calling card with a message in Spanish, Latin, or German. In one he asked an important question: which fell from her lips more frequently—expressions of good sense or of kindness?

Three months later they were secretly engaged. Why secretly? Why couldn't they announce their love to the world? Because he had no money and no prospects. Her family would have found him "not eligible," and his friends would have considered him irresponsible.

As a student his needs had been modest: books seemed to be the best thing money could buy. But once he met Martha his poverty became a serious matter indeed. Whatever money he could spare, he sent to her, and she saved it in a common fund. If his situation demanded it, he would borrow from this fund and pay it back when he was able. From time to time, Martha would feel shy about receiving money from him, and he would challenge her with questions like: "Do we belong together or don't we?" or, "Do you wish me to address you as Fraulein and you to address me as Herr Doktor?"

Upon hearing that her daughter was engaged (so much for secrets), Martha's mother whisked her away from Vienna to Wandsbeck, a suburb of Hamburg (about 500 miles from Vienna), where the Bernays family lived. Mrs. Bernays, a widow and solely responsible for her daughters' well-being, felt that if an engagement was to be a long one, the couple had better be apart. So for the next five years, except for an occasional meeting, the relationship was reduced to an exchange of letters.

He saw her on both days prior to her departure, and noted that he had given her more kisses in those two days than he had given his sisters in a lifetime of twen-

---

[1] '*The Letters of S. Freud,*' Basic Books, N.Y. 1975, p.25

[2] '*The Life and Work of Sigmund Freud,*' Vol. I, Ernest Jones, 1953, Basic books, Inc., N.Y. p.103

ty-six years.

As we said, Martha's move to Wandsbeck presented problems. They both still believed they were secretly engaged, so how could he write to her without raising her family's suspicion?

> My sweet darling girl:
> ....the little intrigues and plans your absence in Hamburg call for....how you have changed my life....You are leaving and you must put up with my writing to you. How shall we arrange that no one know about it?....A little plan has occurred to me. If a man's handwriting would appear strange in your uncle's house, Martha could address a number of envelopes with her own tender hand, and I would fill the precious shell with a beggarly content.
> (Ibid. p. 105)

Martha got an old friend of hers, Fritz Wahle, to address a number of envelopes with a code, so she would know whom they were really from. And her letters were not sent directly to Freud's home, but to a laboratory assistant at Brucke's Institute. Still, keeping their secret was not easy. They feared that the few close friends who knew would betray it to the many who did not. When asked by his sister Rosa if he were writing to Martha he denied it "like a statesman grown gray with lying." Naturally, it was not long before everyone knew.

He was pleased to learn from her letters that he resembled her father. It was quite clear that she had loved him deeply.

Freud's attraction to Martha was not simply boy meets girl; it was nothing short of an authentic grand passion. His intense nature made him feel the full power of love with all of its worst jealousies, raptures, fears, and sufferings.

One cannot know the core of a man, his inner life, without some knowledge of his attitude toward love. This, Freud usually kept strictly private. His feelings of love and tenderness were well known to his family and friends, but not to the general public. This view of him was almost denied us: after his death Martha several times expressed the wish to burn the letters but her daughters would not let her sacrifice that testimony of his love and devotion.

Unless one has read his letters to Martha, one cannot appreciate Freud's intense passion for her. He kept this side of his nature strictly reserved and it was not until the death of Martha twelve years later that the outside world was able to read their correspondence. And what a correspondence it was. His innate self comes to the surface; we see at last the private Sigmund Freud. He describes the entire gamut of emotions: despair and bliss. Whatever he feels, he feels intensely. We are confronted with a man of a complicated and intense passion. The style of the letters is his own; an extraordinary range of vocabulary, the turn of a phrase, distinction and profundity of thought, delicate tenderness, and in lighter moments a delightful sense of humor. The letters can stand among the great love literature of the world.

He wrote more than nine hundred of these letters to his sweetheart. They wrote to each other daily, not simply brief notes, but voluminous letters, seven to eight pages was about average. One letter ran to twenty-two pages. They were not merely love letters, bu much more. The lovers discussed all sorts of topics: their daily activities, family gossip (Martha's brother Eli was engaged to Freud's sister Anna); ideas on art, literature, philosophy; Freud's work; important personalities; issues of the day; and so forth. Of particular interest is a letter dated November 5, 1883, which reveals Freud's views of women.

In 1879, before he met Martha, he was called up for his year's national service. Military duty for medical students was far less demanding then than it is today. Medical students continued to live at home and their duties consisted chiefly of standing around in hospitals. The main hazard was boredom.

So what does young Sigmund do to cope with boredom? He translates the work of John Stuart Mill. He was a specially gifted translator who, instead of translating word for word, would read a passage, close the book, and figure out how one would say the same thing in German. He worked quickly and his translations were brilliant.

One of Mill's most famous essays was on the enfranchisement of women. He dedicated it to his wife.

In a discussion of Mill, twenty-four-year-old Sigmund Freud discloses his ideas and feelings about women.

> Dear Martha:
>
> I railed at the time at his lifeless style and at not being able to find a sentence or phrase that one could commit to memory....He was perhaps the man of the century who best managed to free himself from the domination of customary prejudices. On the other hand—and that always goes together with it—he lacked in many matters the sense of the absurd; for example, in that of female emancipation and in the woman's question altogether....A prominent argument was that a married woman could learn as much as her husband. We surely agree that the management of a house, the care and bringing up of children, demands the whole of a human being and almost excludes any earning, even if a simplified household relieved her of dusting, cleaning and cooking, etc. He had simply forgotten all that, like everything else concerning the relationship between the sexes....In his whole presentation it never emerges that women are different beings—we will not say lesser, rather the opposite from men....He finds the suppression of women an analogy to that of negroes. Any girl....whose hand a man kisses and for whose love he is prepared to dare all, could have set him right. It is really a stillborn thought to send women into the struggle for existence exactly as men....It is possible that changes in upbringing may suppress all a woman's tender attributes....and that she can earn a livelihood like men....It is also possible that in such an event one would not be justified in mourning the passing away of the most delightful thing the world can

> offer us—our ideal of womanhood....Nature has determined woman's destiny through beauty, charm and sweetness. Law and customs have much to give women that has been withheld from them, but the position of women will surely be what it is: in youth an adored darling, and in mature years, a loved wife.
>
> (Ibid. p.176)

Whatever one may think about young Freud's views on women, certainly there is nothing scientific about them. Was he reflecting a cultural ideal of the time? Or was this the dream of a particular postadolescent idealist? Shortly after the above was written, Freud plunged into a deep study of the human mind and behavior. Would his view of women and men and life change?

It is a most unusual correspondence with a sweetheart. Above all, their daily letters contained the most exquisite concern for each other.

> Dear Martha: June 19, 1882
>
> ....I knew it was only after you had gone that I would realize the full extent of my happiness and, also the degree of my loss as well. I still cannot grasp it, and if....that sweet picture were not lying in front of me, I would think it was all a beguiling dream and be afraid to wake up. Yet friends tell me it's true, and I myself can remember details more charming, more mysteriously enchanting than any dream-phantasy could create. It must be true, Martha is mine....the girl I feared to court and who comes toward me with high-minded confidence, who strengthened the faith in my own value and gave me new hope and energy to work when I needed it most....Do please try to steal from your fond relations all the photos of you as a child....

> Dear Martha: June 19,1884
>
> ....after all, you know the key of my life, that I can work only when spurred on by great hopes for things uppermost in my mind. Before I met you I didn't know the joy of living, and now that "in principle" you are mine, to have you completely is the one condition I make to life, which I otherwise don't set any great store by. I am very stubborn and very reckless and need great challenges, I have done a number of things which any sensible person would be bound to consider very rash. For example, to take up science as a poverty-stricken man, to capture a poor girl—but this must continue to be my way of life: risking a lot, hoping a lot, working a lot. To average bourgeois common sense I have been lost long ago....

Freud was an avid reader and he was eager to share his interests with Martha. He wrote a general introduction to philosophy for her which he called a "Philosophical ABC." That was followed by Huxley's "Introduction to Science." However, that turned out not to be her area of interest. At the time his chief pleasure was English literature, but he could not persuade his beloved to master English. He referred to it as his favorite wish. On the other hand, she was well acquainted with German classics and they had lively discussions of the great novels. Quotes from the poets, especially Goethe and Heine, found their way into their letters. Freud's quotes often came from an even more extended literature:

Had we never loved so kindly
Had we never loved so blindly
Never met, or never parted
We had ne'er been broken-hearted.

(A verse from Burns he had found in a volume of Byron)

Freud loved to send books, both to Martha and her sister. These ranged from Dickens to Homer, from history to philosophy. His comments on the books were like a review of a whole library. One wonders when he found time to read so much.

Like a typical Viennese he frequented the theater—at times it was more important than food—and on occasion the opera. The opera had to be Mozart. "Carmen" was an exception: he felt the Bizet opera to be especially beautiful. Martha would get a detailed critique of the performances. After seeing "The Magic Flute" he wrote:

> Some of the arias are wonderfully beautiful, but the whole thing rather drags, without any really individual melodies. The action is very stupid, the libretto quite crazy, and it is simply not to be compared with 'Don Giovanni.''
>
> (Ibid. p.178)

Martha's temperament and her views on how life should be lived were much more normal than his. She was sure of his love. She needed less reassurance. She knew that she had no reason whatsoever to be jealous. She understood that couples have adjustments to make and she felt that it was the man's place to lead the way. Sometimes she had doubts. When she couldn't please him or make the desired changes as quickly as he wished, she wondered whether she was worthy of him. But when pressed she displayed a toughness of spirit that could stand up to him. In fact she was tougher than he; his bark was worse than his bite. His innate gentleness came sooner or later to the surface and triumphed.

What was Martha's attitude toward her mother's taking her away to Wandsbeck? Years later she expressed admiration for her mother's resolute behavior. She was in fact attached to her mother and remained so—this Martha who in the end of her life (she lived to be ninety) could only read in the evening. She had been brought up to think that daytime was a time for work. Reading was a relaxation reserved for after work was done.

Martha's family did not approve of her engagement to Freud. He had no money, no status, and above all, from a religious point of view, was practically a heathen.

Martha, five years younger, came from a family quite distinguished in Jewish culture. Her grandfather had been Chief Rabbi of Hamburg, and was related to Heinrich Heine. His name is often mentioned in Heine's letters, where he is referred to as "a man of high intelligence." His brother again was the editor of a newpaper in Paris and one of his sons became a professor of German at the University of Munich and later an official reader to King Ludwig of Bavaria. Another brother taught Latin and Greek at the University of Heidelberg. To the Bernays family Freud was a nobody and an impoverished one at that. The men in the family were particularly annoyed that Freud had never asked their permission to woo Martha; a petition that would have been immediately denied. "They would prefer you to marry an old Rabbi or a Schochet." (A butcher who follows Jewish rules)[1]

Martha was deeply attached to her family and Freud resented this. He was very demanding and insisted that he be the dominant figure in her life. Not infrequently he put her in an awkward position. He charged that her family was going to be his "most dangerous rival." A source of friction was her adherence to the strict rules of orthodox Judaism. He loathed what he considered superstition and called her "weak" for making Mamma's wish law. He was concerned about her health and blamed her foolish, superstitious, kosher diet. Her sister Minna fought the family and was frank in her criticisms of their beliefs. "You don't love her (mother) very much and are as considerate as possible to her; Minna loves her, but doesn't spare her."[2]

One gets the impression of a young man looking for trouble. For instance, his resentment of the Bernays family was such that when Martha's brother Eli Bernays married his sister Anna, Freud did not attend the wedding. It was a formal affair, full-dress and accompanied by rituals and ceremonies that he reffered to as "simply loathsome." We shall see later what he had in mind for his own wedding.

Of course, Martha was influenced by her Husband. But more often than not, she stood her ground and proved to be the stronger. Later, he was to express his appreciation of the resistance she offered. The last thing he wanted was a shallow, complaisant doll.

If one day the world was to see him as an authority on love, he surely went through a fiery apprenticeship. Only one week after their engagement, he worked himself into a jealous fit. He had learned that before Martha met him, she had had fond feelings for Max Mayer, a cousin. His senseless jealousy was maliciously fed by one of his sisters, who told him how Martha loved some songs Max had composed for her. Freud was so upset that he forbade Martha to refer to her cousin as Max, and only as Herr Mayer. Characteristically, when he got over this mood, he felt ashamed.

> Can there be anything crazier I said to myself. You have won the dearest girl quite without any merit of your own, and you know no better than only a week later to reproach her....and torment her with jealousy....When a girl like Martha is fond of me how can I fear a Max Mayer or a legion of

---

[1]Ibid. p.134.
[2]Ibid. p.117

> Max Mayers?....It was an expression of my clumsy, self-tormenting kind of deeply rooted love....The feeling I had about Max Mayer came from a distrust of myself not of you.
> (Ibid. p.110)

But Freud couldn't maintain this kind of wisdom, and on more than one occasion his jealousy flared up and made him suffer. His next jealous episode involved their close friend, Fritz Wahle. Fritz and Martha were like brother and sister although there was at least one occasion when she permitted him to kiss her. When she and Freud became engaged, Fritz assumed that his old relationship with Martha would remain unchanged and she did nothing to contradict his assumption. Freud found their correspondence puzzling, almost inappropriate.

It should be added that both Fritz Wahle and Max Mayer were artists and for Freud this was disquieting. He believed that artists had a special capacity to attract women. In fact, he had been told that Fritz in particular had the reputation for being able to steal any woman from another man.

> I think there is a general enmity between artists and those engaged in the details of scientific work....We know that they possess in their art a master key to open with ease all female hearts, whereas we stand helpless at the strange design of the lock and have first to torment ourselves to discover a suitable key to fit.
> (Ibid. III)

Schonberg, a friend of both, noticed that Fritz's behavior was strange: when he heard of Martha's engagement, he burst into tears. Then he began to complain that Martha's letters were cold and he felt neglected. Schonberg arranged to meet with his two friends in a cafe to discuss the matter, settle things, and reestablish the friendship. Fritz was sullen and certainly odd. He muttered that if Freud did not make Martha happy he would shoot him and then himself. The surprised and innocent Freud could only laugh. Fritz in a fury further hinted that if he were to instruct Martha to break her relationship with Freud she would obey him. Freud continued to laugh. Whereupon Fritz seized pen and paper and wrote a letter immediately. Freud insisted upon reading it and when he saw ''Beloved Martha'' and ''undying love' he was outraged. Schonberg also read it and was shocked. Freud tore the letter into shreds, at which Fritz, stunned, left. They followed him, reassuring and trying to make light of the entire episode. Then Fritz broke down and wept. Freud was deeply moved; his own eyes became moist. He took him by the arm and escorted him home.

The next day Freud thought he had behaved like a weakling and felt ashamed:

> The man who brings tears to my eyes must do a great deal before I forgive him. He is no longer my friend, and woe to him if he becomes my enemy. I am made of harder stuff than he is, and when we match each other he will find he is not my equal....

(Ibid. p.112)

So we get a glimpse of the postadolescent, twenty-six-year-old Sigmund Freud.

CHAPTER IV

■ *Medulla Oblongata*

Freud desperately wanted to marry and rasie a family, but to undertake such responsibility was out of the question. Then as now, "theoretical research doesn't pay." In view of Freud's financial position, Brucke, his venerated teacher, advised him to give up his career in theoretical research, pointing out that the salary of a research worker could hardly support him, let alone a wife.

> The turning point came in 1882, when my teacher, for whom I felt the highest possible esteem, corrected my father's generous improvidence by strongly advising me, in view of my bad financial position, to abandon my theoretical career. I followed his advice, left the physiological laboratory and entered the General Hospital as an Aspirant (clinical assistant).
>
> (The Standard Edition of the *'The Complete Psychological Works of Sigmund Freud,'* hereafter known as *'S.E. An Autobiographical Study,'* 1925, S.E. XX, p.10)

He was not attracted to the practice of medicine, but had no choice, now that he had to earn a living. He thought that if he had an all-round medical training, was able to pull a tooth, to assist in childbirth, to set a broken leg, he could support a wife and family. One month after his engagement to Martha, he entered the Vienna General Hospital. He had no wish to specialize and he was to spend the next three years at the hospital acquiring clinical experience.

No one need make a case against poverty, but the inevitable pettiness that accompanies it is always offensive. For a person of Freud's character it was particularly irksome. To illustrate: one day, long after he had left the ranks of the poor, and was dining with colleagues from England, the waiter, after dessert, began to make minute inquiries as to how much bread each guest had eaten. Freud spoke to him very sharply. "You make us ashamed in front of foreigners," he said.

Freud had always believed there was a close connection between a good appearance and self-respect; so now clothes presented a problem. His tailor, a friend of the family, was a patient man, but at times he had to be paid by installment. Someone told the tailor that Freud was one of the cleverest doctors in the hospital. When the tailor repeated this, Freud's comment was: "The good opinion of my tailor matters to me as much as that of my professor."

Martha and he would discuss how their money should be spent. Should they invest their capitol in a new suit or shoes? She once gave him a neckie and for the first time he owned two good ties. On two occasions he mentions having to borrow a coat from Fleischl so that he could visit someone he looked up to.

Freud's own family lived in a state of chronic poverty. His father, Jakob, Freud, was a wool merchant, but the manufacture of textiles, the town of Freiberg's principal source of income, had been in a decline for twenty years. The introduction of machines threatened handwork and all of Central Europe felt the effect. In addition, in the forties, the new Northern Railway bypassed Freiberg, further reducing business and leading to unemployment.

Czech nationalism grew as a result of the 1848-49 revolution, fanning the feelings of hatred against the German-Austrians who had been the ruling class in Moravia. The Jews, who were German in education and language, found themselves in the role of scapegoat. In fact the revolution had started with riots against the Jewish textile merchants and manufacturers, whom the Czechs considered responsible for their plight. Feeling for these reasons that there was no future for him in Freiberg, Jakob moved with his family to Leipzig, and a year later to Vienna. Sigmund was four years old.

Jakob married three times. From his first marriage (at the age of seventeen) there were two sons, Emanuel and Phillip. Little is known of his second marriage, but at forty he married a third time. Amalie Nathansohn, the nineteen-year-old bride, was described as beautiful. A year after her marriage she gave birth to Sigmund. At the time of his third marriage, Jakob was a grandfather; his elder son was himself the father of a one-year-old son. So Sigmund was born an uncle and for three years his chief playmate was his nephew John. This was one of many paradoxes young Sigmund had to ponder. Amalie subsequently gave birth to five daughters and two other sons, one of whom died at the age of eight months.

His stepbrothers, Emanuel, with his wife and two children, and Phillip, did not go to Vienna. They migrated to Manchester, England, where their knowledge of the textile business stood them in good stead and brought them some success.

What kind of person was Jakob Freud? The following anecdote gives us a glimpse of him in relation to his son. Moritz Rosenthal (later a famous concert pianist) was once at six years of age, speaking disrespectfully to his father in Jakob Freud's presence. Laughingly, but also reprovingly, Jakob said, "What? You are talking back to your father? My Sigie's little toe is cleverer than my head but he would never talk to me like that."[1]

Jakob and young Sigmund would take walks together and discuss views of the world. On one such talk, when Freud was about twelve years old, Jakob told a story to show how much better things were now than they had been in his day.

> "When I was a young man," he said, "I went for a walk one Saturday in the streets of your birthplace; I was well dressed, and had a new fur cap on my head. A Christian came up to me and with a single blow knocked off my cap into the mud and shouted: 'Jew! Get off the pavement.' "And what did you do?" I asked. "I went into the roadway and picked up my cap," was his quiet reply. This struck me as unheroic conduct on the part of the big, strong man who was holding the little

> boy by the hand. I contrasted this situation with another which suited my feelings better: the scene in which Hannibal's father, Hamilcar Barca, made his boy swear before the household altar to take vengeance on the Romans. Ever since that time Hannibal had had a place in my phantasies.
> (*'The Interpretation of Dreams'* 1900 S.E. IV p.197)

Years later (at the age of twenty-seven) Freud was to triumph where Jakob had failed. He opened the window on a train and someone objected and insisted that he close it. Freud refused. A discussion ensued and they were about to arrive at a compromise—to open the ventilation slit instead of the window—when from the background came a shout, "He's a dirty Jew." The whole situation changed. The first opponent took up the theme and declared that Christians are considerate of other people but Jews, etc. The voice from the rear announced that he was going to climb over the seats and teach Freud a lesson. Freud told the first man to keep his remarks to himself since they inspired no respect, and told the other to step up and take what he deserved. Both antagonists backed down. Freud related the story proudly to Martha in a letter (December 16, 1883).

After telling the story of the cap Jakob never quite regained the place he once held in the esteem of his young son. More than thirty years later Freud reported the incident in *The Interpretation of Dreams.*

Despite the family's desperate financial circumstances, Jakob never suggested to Freud that he be practical and help support them. Instead he encouraged and sustained his son in whatever direction his "golden head" chose.

When Jakob died at the age of eighty-one Freud wrote to Fleiss: "....my father's death has affected me profoundly. I treasured him highly and had understood him exactly. With his peculiar mixture of deep wisdom and fantastic lightness he had meant very much in my life....Now I feel quite uprooted."[1]

To return to his poverty: in two areas Freud felt his deprivation keenly—in his inability to give his sweetheart gifts, much less visit her, and in the plight of his family. His father, now seventy years old, earned practically nothing. It is hard to figure out what the family lived on. Freud recalled that his mother was given to complaining and no wonder—she had tuberculosis of the lung. In 1884, he wrote that they were hoping she would remain alive a little longer. As it turned out, she lived to the age of ninety-five in full possession of her faculties.

On occasion Freud would get a pupil, mostly referred by Fleischl, and he would send the extra money to his mother. He was really concerned about their having enough to eat. His sisters could not go out to work. The only work available would have been menial and that would impair their chances for marriage. When Anna married Eli Bernays, the new son-in-law helped very considerably. Emanuel too sent some money regularly from Manchester.

Freud undertook hospital responsibilities for a somewhat unorthodox reason: for the sake of money in order to marry. Perhaps it is not surprising that he became a somewhat unorthodox physician.

---

[1]Jones I, p.19
[2]Jones I, p.324

He had kept one tool, his microscope, and he could not resist his passion for research. In a short time he was once more involved in neurology, and even lecturing on the subject. "In a certain sense I nevertheless remained faithful to the line of work upon which I had originally started. The subject which Brucke had proposed....I now passed on to the human central nervous system."[1]

In a letter to a friend, Knopfmacher, he seriously doubts whether he will ever wish to be a physician: "I have moved to another laboratory and am preparing myself for my proper profession—mutilating animals or tormenting human beings—and I decide more and more in favor of the former alternative."[2]

The only lectures that Freud found interesting were by Meynert on psychiatry. Theodor Meynert, the world's leading authority on brain anatomy, was impressed with Freud and offered him an appointment in his department of psychiatry and permission to work in the lab. He was soon involved in brain anatomy, working on the newborn brain, in order to discover something about brain structure before it grew too complex. Freud hoped that the research would bring him a *docentur* (university lectureship) and advance his career.

> I gradually became familiar with the ground; I was able to localize the site of a lesion in the medulla oblongata so accurately that the pathological anatomist had no further information to add; I was the first person in Vienna to send a case for autopsy with a diagnosis of polyneuritis acuta. The fame of my diagnoses and of their post-mortem confirmation brought me an influx of American physicians, to which I lectured in a sort of pidgin-English. About the neuroses I understood nothing. On one occasion I introduced to my audience a neurotic, suffering from a persistent headache, as a case of chronic localized meningitis; they all quite rightly rose in revolt and deserted me, and my premature activities as a teacher came to an end. By the way of excuse I may add that this happened at a time when greater authorities than myself in Vienna were in the habit of diagnosing neurasthenia as cerebral tumour.
> (Auto. p.12)

Freud saw himself turning more and more to neurology. He concentrated on the medulla, the nervous tissue at the base of the brain, and during two years of research, published three papers. The work required great patience, dexterity, and precision. The following excerpt is submitted merely to give the reader a taste of what the work was like. It's from the first of his papers and is concerned with the roots and connection of the acoustic nerve.

> ....There are three roots, or groups of fibers, all of which end in nuclei on the side on

---

[1]Auto. S.E. XX, p.10
[2]Jones I, p.53

> which they enter; the outer fibers in an anterior nucleus, the middle and a portion of the inner fibers in the inner nucleus. Various bundles of fibers then radiate in the medulla from these nuclei, e.g., to the decussation in the nucleus tegmenti of the cerebellum. Some, issuing from the anterior nucleus, make up the corpus trapezoides and pass through the upper olivar nucleus; after crossing the interolivary tract....
> (Jones I, p.206)

Many years later he wrote about it more amusingly:

> The medulla oblongata is a very serious and beautiful thing. I remember very well how much time and trouble I devoted to the study of it years ago. Today, however, I must say I do not know of anything that seems to me more irrelevant for the psychological understanding of anxiety than a knowledge of the nervous paths its excitations follow.
> (Ibid. p.204)

By the time Freud went to study with Charcot, he was considered one of the leading neurologists and neuropathologists in Europe.[1]

Freud was still very eager to get married. The ingenuity he showed in laboratory techniques led Brucke to say that his new methods alone would bring him fame. In fact, a gold-staining method he worked out for tracing nerve endings under a microscope almost became accepted lab procedure, which would have established his name professionally. The technique, however, proved too difficult for most practioners. Brucke's words stayed with him nonetheless. He never stopped looking for a scientific breakthrough that would lead to a reputation, a sucessful private practice, and Martha. "I am not finding it easy to wrest attention from the world, for it is thick-skinned and hard of hearing."[1]

---

[1]*Depth Psychology,* Dieter Wyss, 1966, W.W. Norton Inc. N.Y. p.46
[2]Jones I, p.195

CHAPTER V

■ *Grave Reproaches*

The subject of cocaine was first mentioned in a letter to Martha, April 21, 1884:

> I am also toying now with a project and a hope which I will tell you about; perhaps nothing will come of this either. It is a therapeutic experiment of coca leaves, which some Indian tribes chew in order to make themselves resistant to privation and fatigue. A German has tested this stuff on soldiers and reported that it has really rendered them strong and capable of endurance. I have now ordered some of it and for obvious reasons am going to try it out on cases of heart disease, then on nervous exhaustion, particularly in the awful condition following withdrawal of morphine (as in the case of Dr. Fleischl). There may be any number of other people experimenting on it already, perhaps it won't work. But I am certainly going to try it and, as you know, if one tries something often enough and goes on wanting it, one day it may succeed. We need no more than one stroke of luck of this kind to consider setting up house. But, my little woman, do not be too convinced that it will come off this time. As you know an explorer's temperament requires two basic qualities: optimism in attempt, criticism in work....
>
> ('*The Psychoanalytic Revolution,*' Marthe Robert, Harcourt Brace, and World, Inc., N.Y. 1966, p.46)

The first obstacle was the cost of the cocaine. He was dismayed to find it cost three gulden, thirty-three kreuzers ($1.27). (Although Freud never thought of himself as poor, he had in fact at this time practically no money.) He boldly ordered a gram from the Merck Chemical Co. and tried the effect of a twentieth of a gram on himself. He found that his mood became cheerful without his energy for work being sapped. He also observed that the drug acted as a gastric anesthetic, quelling any feelings of hunger. It occurred to him that cocaine might be used to check vomiting from various causes. He decided to try the drug on his friend Fleischl.

Ernst von Marxow-Fleischl was a physicist and a physiologist, and was Brucke's assistant at the Institute. At the age of twenty-five, he had contracted an infection while conducting research in pathological anatomy. The amputation of his right thumb may have saved his life, but continued growth of neuromas required a series of painful operations. He awaited his slowly approaching death in a state of intolerable pain. Unable to sleep, he concentrated his attention on the study of mathematics and physics. When he felt he had exhausted this diversion he would study Sanskrit.

Freud had always admired Fleischl from a distance but it was not until after Freud left the Institute that they became personal friends.

> He is a throughly excellent person in whom nature and education have combined to do their best. Rich, trained in all physical exercises, with the stamp of genius in his manly features, good-looking, refined, endowed with many talents and capable of forming an original judgment about most things, he has always been my ideal and I could not rest till we became friends and I could experience a pure joy in his ability and reputation.
> (*'Letters of S. Freud,'* Basic Books, N.Y. 1960, p.11)

On another occasion he wrote:

> I admire and love him with an intellectual passion, if you will allow such a phrase. His destruction (referring to his terrible disease and approaching death) will move me as the destruction of a sacred and famous temple would have affected an ancient Greek. I love him not so much as a human being, but as one of Creation's precious achievements. And you needn't be at all jealous.
> (Letter to Martha, October 28, 1883)

Fleischl of course knew of Freud's poverty and urged him to borrow whatever he needed without any reluctance: "Within a small and select circle of men who are in accord over the most important things it would be just as wrong for one of them not to share his opinions with the others as for one of them to be unwilling to accept any help."[1]

And Fleischl had been suffering this unbearable pain for ten years. His strength was worn down and periodically even his mind would be affected. Perhaps it was his desperation that led him to take too much morphine, and now he was suffering an additional affliction—morphine addiction.

> I asked him quite disconsolately where all this was going to lead to. He said that his parents regarded him as a great savant and he would try to keep at his work as long as they lived. Once they were dead, he would shoot himself, for he thought it

---

[1]Jones I, p.161

> quite impossible to hold out for long. It would be senseless to try to console a man who sees his situation so clearly....He is not the sort of man you can approach with empty words of consolation. His state is as desperate as he says, and one cannot contradict him....
> (Ibid. I, p.90)

Freud hoped that the use of cocaine would allow them to dispense with morphine. At first it was very successful. "Fleischl clutched at the new drug like a drowning man." And cocaine did indeed enable him to break the addiction. But in spite of this success, his condition worsened. One evening he did not answer his door when his friends called. Freud, Exner, and Obersteiner forced their way in and found him lying almost senseless with pain. Several operations and electrical treatments revealed later that his state was worse than ever.

However Fleischl actually continued to share Freud's view of the value of the new drug. When Freud published an article in the St. Louis Medical and Surgical Journal (December 1884), Fleischl added a note describing his own favorable experiences with it. He expressed the view that cocaine and morphine were antithetical and that cocaine was the antidote to morphine addiction.

On one occasion Freud sat up all night with him while Fleischl lay in a warm bath. The experience was unnerving. "Every note of the profoundest despair was sounded." That was the first of many such nights he spent with him, and Freud noted that Fleischl was now taking enormous doses of cocaine, a full gram a day. This was one hundred times the quantity that Freud took for depression and indigestion, and that only occasionally. Freud came to realize that irreparable damage had been done to his friend.

> Every time I ask myself if I shall ever in my life experience anything so agitating or exciting as these nights....His talk, his explanations of all possible obscure things, his judgments on the persons in our circle, his manifold activity interrupted by states of the completest exhaustion relieved by morphine and cocaine: all that makes an ensemble that cannot be described.
> Ibid., p.91)

So even under such conditions, Fleischl was able to fascinate Freud with his brilliance, erudition, and creativity. On the other hand the worst night of his life was witnessing Fleischl's intoxication from cocaine, his delerium tremors, and his screaming that white snakes were creeping over his skin.

Fleischl's relatives finally took him to St. Gilgen where they could look after him. Freud consented to accompany him, but at the last minute Fleischl preferred to be alone. Freud was convinced that his friend could not last for more than six months, but the wretched man was destined to suffer for six more years.

It is no surprise that the Fleischl experience left its mark on Freud. In "The Interpretation of Dreams," the famous Irma dream led to associations with Fleischl and to self-reproach.

When Freud had first mentioned cocaine in his letter to Martha he had talked of "a therapeutic project and a hope." But the cocaine episode proved to be another bitter disappointment.

The original positive results from his experiments had left him very optimistic. He made no secret of his discovery. He sent some to Martha "to make her strong and give her cheeks a red color." He sent some to his sisters; he urged his friends and colleagues to experience his "magical drug."

He had a spectacular success with a colleague who suffered from an acute case of gastric catarrh.

> One day I was standing in the courtyard with a group of colleagues of whom Carl Koller was one, when another interne passed us showing signs of intense pain. I said to him: "I think I can help you," and we all went to my room, where I applied a few drops of a medicine which made the pain disappear instantly. I explained to my friends that this drug was the extract of a South American plant, the coca, which seemed to have powerful qualities for relieving pain and about which I was preparing a publication. The man with the permanent interest in the eye (Koller was an ophthalmologist) did not say anything.
>
> (Hans Sachs, *'Freud, Master and Friend,'* 1944, Harvard University, p.71)

Koller and Freud collaborated on tests with a dynamometer to see whether the apparent increase of muscular strength following the use of the drug was subjective or whether it could be objectively verified.

There were also discussions with Leopold Konigstein, an ophthalmologist like Koller, about the numbing powers of cocaine. Freud suggested to Konigstein who, incidentally, was a friend of long standing, that he use it to alleviate the pain of certain eye disorders.

But Freud was impatient. He and Martha had not seen each other for a year and he was eager to join her in Wandsbeck. As a result, he did not use his customary thoroughness. He hurriedly finished his paper on cocaine, and left his projects with Koller and Konigstein until his return from vacation.

We can see that his activities, looked at from today's vantage point, were dangerous. He of course was innocent—he had seen no side effects, no signs of craving the drug, in himself. Nowadays we know that to develop a drug addiction needs a special disposition, which Freud, fortunately or unfortunately, did not have.

The essay on cocaine, although a comprehensive review of the subject, may be regarded as more of a literary exercise than a scientific contribution. It was written in his best style—simple, lively, and distinct. There is no doubt about his emotional involvement with the subject, an involvement that never appeared in his subsequent writings. He used phrases that one does not associate with scientific style. For instance, an animal, after an injection of cocaine, responds with "the most gorgeous excitement." Literature that questioned the drug's effectiveness he referred to as "slander." The literary presentation must undoubtedly have played a role in the monograph's popularity.

He began by tracing the history and use of cocaine by South American Indians.

He described it botanically and went into detail about the methods of its preparation. He even made reference to the mythical Manco Capac, the Royal Son of the Sun god who had sent it as a gift from the gods "to satisfy the hungry, fortify the weary and make the unfortunate forget their sorrows."

He told how the plant reached Spain in 1569 and England in 1596. He reported a number of self-observations of the drug's effects on sleep, hunger, and fatigue.

> Exhilaration and lasting euphoria, which in no way differs from the normal euphoria of the healthy person....You perceive an increase of self-control and possess more vitality and capacity for work....Long intensive mental or physical work is performed without any fatigue....This result is enjoyed without any of the unpleasant after-effects that follow exhilaration brought about by alcohol....Absolutely no craving for further use of cocaine appears after the first or even repeated taking of the drug....

In the final paragraph, which is central to our story, he said:

> The capacity of cocaine and its salts, when applied in concentrated solutions, to anesthetize cutaneous and mucous membranes suggests a possible future use....some additional uses of cocaine based on this anesthetic property are likely to be developed in the near future.
>
> (*'Life in Pictures,'* Kurt Eissler, Harcourt, Brace Jovanovich, p.110, 1978)

Then, having met his publisher's deadline, he raced off to Wandsbeck. The Last month had been an "eternal wait":

> While it is the privilege of the Lord that in his sight a thousand years are but yesterday, we poor humans have to delight in the opposite; for us a day can be a thousand years. It is an invention of the devil that suffering lengthens time and joy shortens it.
>
> (Ibid. I, 130)

The month in Wandsbeck was like a fantasy come true. He arrived at the station at six in the morning, and there was Martha waiting for him. He gathered her to him "as in a dream." He and Mamma got on well and became friends, and this was to last. The joyous visit was a turning point in their relationship. He discovered that Mamma was really human and, except for an occasional lapse, he no longer doubted Martha's love. It was a happy time.

Four weeks later when he returned from Hamburg, he learned that something very important had happened. Carl Koller had become world-famous overnight.

He had used cocaine as a local anesthesia, and had performed successful surgery on the eye.

So Freud had missed fame and fortune and Martha and everything he longed for by the narrowest of margins.

One might charge Koller with acting in undue haste. His paper was read and practical demonstrations were given at the Ophthalmological Congress at Heidelberg on September 15, two weeks before Freud was due to return to Vienna. It did contain this one reference: "Cocaine has been prominently brought to the notice of Viennese physicians by the thorough compilation and interesting therapeutic paper of my hospital colleague Dr. Sigmund Freud."

How had Konigstein come to fail in his examination of the anesthetizing properties of cocaine? What had happened?

In a letter to Josef Meller Freud wrote:

> August 28, 1884
>
> Cocaine gave at the time an opalescent solution. Konigstein, disturbed by this totally irrelevant circumstance, requested from his pharmacist that he prepare a clear solution. The pharmacist, not knowing the intended use of the fluid, added a drop of hydrochloric acid, and the patient screamed in pain when a drop of the clear fluid was instilled into them (his eyes). Thereupon Konigstein desisted from further experiments.
>
> (*'Talent and Genius,'* K.R. Eissler, Quadrangle Books, N.Y. 1971, p.158)

His letters to Konigstein and Koller exhibit no lapse in his friendly feelings, not the slightest suggestion of reproach. In fact, his letters express concern, care, and affection for his two fellow scientists.

Seven months later (April 1885), Freud's father called upon him complaining of something amiss in the vision of one of his eyes. Koller happened to be there and made a diagnosis of glaucoma. The next day, with Koller administering the anesthetic and with Freud's assistance, Konigstein successfully performed the necessary surgery. Koller graciously remarked that the three people associated with the introduction of cocaine were all present together.

Years later, in his autobiography, Freud wrote:

> ....It was the fault of my fiancee that I was not already famous at that youthful age. A side interest, though it was a deep one, had led me in 1884 to obtain from Merck some of what was then the little-known alkaloid cocaine and to study its physiological action. While I was in the middle of this work an opportunity arose for making a journey to visit my fiancee, from whom I had been parted for two years. I hastily wound up my investigation of cocaine and contented myself in my monograph on the subject with prophesying that further uses for it would soon be found. I suggested, however, to my friend Konigstein, the

> ophthalmologist, that he should investigate the question of how far the anesthetizing properties of cocaine were applicable in diseases of the eye. When I returned from my holiday I found that not he, but another of my friends, Carl Koller (now in New York), whom I had also spoken to about cocaine, had made the decisive experiments upon animals' eyes and had demonstrated them at the Ophthalmological Congress in Heidelberg. Koller is therefore rightly regarded as the discoverer of local anaesthesia by cocaine, which has become as important in minor surgery; but I bore my fiancee no grudge for the interruption.
> ('*Autobiography*,' 1925, E.E. XX,14)

The monograph brought Freud many congratulations and considerable recognition from his colleagues. A popular article on the monograph appeared in the press and that in turn was copied in the American press. Freud was soon plagued with letters asking for help and further information and with invitations to lecture on the subject. Cocaine was popular. However, within two years, reports concerning cocaine addiction came in from all parts of the world. Freud found himself subjected to severe criticism. Having tried to find a cure that would benefit society, he was now accused of being a criminal and of unleashing a new evil, "the third scourge of humanity." On the other hand, many people rallied to his side, among them the distinguished physician and writer Arthur Schnitzler. All Freud ever said of the experience later was, it led to "grave reproaches."

CHAPTER VI

■ *Silk Hat and White Gloves*

An outstanding feature of freud's life was the high quality and status of his friends. It seems that whoever worked with him held him in high esteem. He enjoyed the affection and support of some of the most important and influential professional men of the day. The list was headed by three men, the inestimable Brucke, Hermann Nothnagel, professor of internal medicine at the University of Vienna, and Theodor Meynert, professor of psychiatry at the University. Their support and interest enabled him to get the appointments, scholarships, and grants that are so essential in academic life. And so with the position of *Privatdocent* (this highly prized position has no exact counterpart in American schools). A *Privatdocent* does not have to attend faculty meetings or receive a salary, but he is permitted to hold classes and be paid for them on topics outside the curriculum. The holder of the position enjoys a high prestige with the public, as well as with the profession. Few of these positions are granted, so the small group is elite. The requirements are extremely demanding and necessitate the publication of independent, original work. "From the beginning of his medical career, Freud had this goal well in mind."[1]

> Dear Martha March 29, 1884
> ....one more word about the *Dozentur.* There are two kinds of advantages. First the right (actually the only duty) to give lectures on which, if they are well attended....I could manage to live....Secondly, one rises to a higher social level in the medical world and in the eyes of the public, has more prospects not only of getting patients but of better paying ones—in short, it helps one to build up a certain reputation....

Brucke closed a careful, detailed evaluation of Freud's publications with the following recommendation:

> Dr. Freud is a man with a good general education, of quiet and serious character, an excellent worker in the field of neuro-anatomy, of fine dexterity, clear vision, comprehensive knowledge, and a cautious method of deduction, with the gift for

[1]Jones I, p.70

> well-organized written expression. His findings enjoy recognition and confirmation, his style of lecturing is transparent and secure. In him the qualities of a scientific researcher and of a well-qualified teacher are so well united that the committee submits the suggestion that the Honorable College resolve on his admission to the further habilitation tests.

Three months later Freud had to acquire a silk hat, white gloves, and a full evening suit for the oral examinations. He passed the exams and two weeks later he was invited to give a public lecture in the theater of Brucke's Institute. He spoke on The Medullary Tracts of the Brain. The lecture was an instant success. Two months later he was called to police headquarters to ascertain if his character and record were worthy of the honor. He jokingly added, "I was resolved to divulge nothing." A month later, September 5, 1885, the Ministry ratified the appointment: a *Privatdocent* in neurology.

The *Privatdocentur* didn't have immediate practical significance: Freud was still too impoverished to marry. He decided to leave the Meynert clinic to work in a private mental hospital just outside Vienna. There he would receive board and lodging and one hundred gulden ($40) a month. It was an institution for the wealthy and the socially superior, and Freud was required to wear a silk hat and white gloves when on duty.

> ....I arrived here yesterday at 8 a.m. with a walking stick for luggage and became a member of this very mixed community....There are 60 patients in the house, mental cases of every shade from light feeble-mindedness, which the layman wouldn't detect, to the final stages of withdrawal. The medical treatment is of course negligible, confined to their secondary surgical and internal complaints; the rest consists of supervision, nursing, diet, and non-interference. The kitchen of course is in the (big) house. The mildest cases lunch with the director, the doctor and the inspector. Needless to say, they are all rich people, counts, countesses, barons, etc. The piece de resistance are two Highnesses, Prince S. and Prince M. The latter, as you may remember, is a son of Marie Louise, wife of Napoleon, and thus, like our Emperor, a grandson of Emperor Franz. You cannot imagine how dissipated these princes and counts look, although they are not actually feebleminded, rather a mixture of feebleminded and eccentric.
>
> (*'Freud,'* Eissler p.111)

While he was at the hospital news arrived that was to change the course of his life. He was notified that a travel scholarship he had applied for had been granted. Once again his superiors, led by Brucke, had stood up, fought, and won for him the cherished University Jubilee Travel Scholarship. This meant he was now to spend six months in Paris with the legendary Charcot, at the Salpetriere, the most famous clinic in the world, and he was to be paid the sum of six hundred gulden. Fleischl told him that what brought him success had been "Brucke's passionate intercession, which had caused a general sensation."[1]

A jubilant letter followed:

> Princess, my little princess, oh, how wonderful it will be! I am coming with money and staying a long time and bringing something beautiful for you and then go on to Paris and become a great scholar and then come back to Vienna for a huge enormous halo, and then we will soon get married, and I will cure all the incurable nervous cases and through you shall be healthy and I will go on kissing you till you are strong and gay and happy....and they lived happily ever after.
>
> (*'Freud,'* Eissler, p.112)

Freud spent six weeks in Wandsbeck with Martha before going on to Paris.

---

[1]Jones I, p.76

CHAPTER VII

■ *Standing Room Only*

Brucke's words "Your methods alone will make you famous yet" were still with him. And he knew that only a breakthrough in research could bring him fame and financial independence—and Martha. However for the moment, studying under Charcot at the Salpetriere was a solution. French science in general enjoyed the highest reputation so that merely being known to be studying in Paris was a proof of distinction in Vienna. Furthermore, Charcot was known to be a member of the scientific elite. So Freud went to Paris to study with Jean Martin Charcot, the leading neurologist and neuropathologist in the world, and to work in the laboratory of the world-famous Salpetriere clinic.

Besides that there was an important reason for studying with Charcot. Freud was interested in treating nervous disorders and for that purpose he had to study hypnosis. At the time hypnosis was one of the few weapons in the therapeutic arsenal even though it was ridiculed as a serious medical tool in Vienna. Freud however had as a student had an opportunity to assess its validity. He had witnessed an exhibition in which he saw the subject grow deathly pale, and he became convinced of the genuineness of the phenomenon. Anyway there was no other way to study and treat nervous disease. Charcot was the grand master of hypnosis.

Freud arrived in Paris in October 1885. "Paris itself had for many long years been another goal of my longings; and the blissful feelings with which I first set foot on its pavement seemed to me a guarantee the others of my wishes would be fulfilled as well."[1] This was how Freud wrote of Paris about fifteen years after that actual first visit. He had completely forgotten what his initial impressions and experiences were like. The man who was to study memory, its function and its distortions, could have used himself as one of the illustrations.

Because in fact he felt like a country bumpkin in the big city. He was bewildered by the crowds, intimidated by the Parisians, by the complexity and pace of the city. And he was very lonely.

> Dear Martha
> I am here as if marooned on an island in the ocean and long for the hours when the ship is due that re-establishes my communication with the world. For you are my whole world, and the ship sometimes fails to appear.

---

[1] '*The Interpretation of Dreams,*' 1900 S.E. IV, p.195

Add to the loneliness the fact that at the time there was an anti-German spirit in France which made Freud prefer not to speak German if he could avoid it. He was self-conscious about his accent in French. All he had been able to afford before leaving Vienna was four lessons. So he spoke English or Spanish whenever possible.

He met few people not connected with the hospital, because of his shyness. Martha had two cousins in Paris whom he visited a few times and there were two old cronies from Vienna. One was a Russian nobleman, Darkschewitsch, whom he had worked with on the medulla. The other was an Austrian couple, Dr. and Mrs. Richetti. The husband had a successful practice. He once got Freud excited by offering him his house for his honeymoon, but the offer was never repeated. Like Freud, he was attending Charcot's demonstrations. He knew Charcot personally and Freud owed his invitation to Charcot's house to Dr. Richetti.

The Richettis had no children and evidently became very fond of Freud. They were a delightful and amusing couple. Freud tells how on one occasion the three of them went out to dine in a fancy restaurant. Imagine the shock when they discovered it was a fancy brothel they were in. Freud confesses that he was apt to indulge in his *Schnorrer's** fantasies about them: he would dream of their passing away and leaving him all their money. Years later he confessed to another *Schnorrer* fantasy. He fantasized that he had stopped a runaway horse. A great man, very rich, stepped from the carriage, shaken but full of gratitude for his courage. "You are my savior—I owe my life to you. What can I do for you?" he would say.

As time passed he found Paris "magnificent and charming." He even felt a certain "local patriotism" for it and spoke of its "magic." He was most impressed of all by Notre Dame.

> ....I am under the full impact of Paris and, waxing very poetical, could compare it to a vast, overdressed Sphinx who gobbles up every foreigner unable to solve her riddles...The tradespeople cheat one with a cool smiling shamelessness. Everyone is polite but hostile. I don't believe there are many decent people here. Anyhow I am one of the few, and that makes me feel isolated....The town and the people are uncanny; they seem to be of another species from us. I believe they are all possessed of a thousand demons. Instead of "Monsieur" and "Voila l'echo de Paris" I hear them screaming "A la lanterne" (hang on a lamp-post) or "A bas dieser und jener" (down with this one and that one). They are people of psychical epidemics, of historical mass convulsions. The ugliness of Paris women can hardly be exaggerated: not a decent pretty face.
>
> (Martha December 3, 1885, *'Freud,'* Eissler p.120)

His choice of a souvenir of Paris was a photograph of Notre Dame. He wrote:

**Schnorrer:* an ingratiating beggar

> My first impression on entering was a sensation I have never had before; "this is a church"....I have never seen anything so movingly serious and sombre, quite unadorned and very narrow, which is no doubt partly responsible for the general impression. I really must read Victor Hugo's novel here, for this is the place properly to understand it.
> (Martha, Nov. 19, 1885, Ibid. 120)

On two occasions he climbed the tower and in a statement years later said it was his favorite resort.

One of the temptations that Freud found irresistible in Paris was the theater.

> ....I had been to the Port St. Martine Theater to see Sarah Bernhardt. I am still rather tired and ravaged by the heat and blood and thunder melodrama which lasted from 8 to 12:30, but it was worth it....I really cannot praise the play. Victorien Sardou's Theodora....a pompous trifle....But how this Sarah can act! After the first few words uttered in an intimate, endearing voice, I felt I had known her all my life. I have never seen an actress who surprised me so little; I at once believed everything about her. She was almost never off the stage. In the first scene, she is seen giving audience, lying on a "throne" sofa, with a bored, arrogant expression.
> (Martha, Nov. 8, 1885, Ibid. 122)

> They wrote me from home that the wife of our family physician, Dr. Kreisler, is in Paris....The unfortunate woman has a 10-year old son who, after two years in the Vienna Concervatorium, won the great prize there and is said to be highy gifted. Now instead of secretly throttling the prodigy, the wretched father, who is overworked and has a house full of children, has sent the boy with his mother to Paris to study at the conservatoire and try for another prize. Just imagine the expense, the separation, the dispersal of the household!....Little wonder that parents grow vain about their children, and even less that such children grow vain themselves....The prodigy is pale, plain, but looks pretty intelligent.
> (Martha No. 26, 1885, Ibid. 122)

By the way, the name of the youth who failed to win Freud's approval was Fritz Kreisler! Two years later he was playing at Steinway Hall in New York.

Self-conscious about his accent, socially timid, practically without funds, torn between his desperate wish for recognition and his actual lack of status, Freud as usual turned to Martha for reassurance.

> Dear Martha Feb. 2, 1886
> Do you really find my appearance so attractive? Well, this I very much doubt. I believe people see something alien in me and the real reason for this is that in my youth I was never young and now that I am entering the age of maturity I cannot mature properly. There was a time when I was all ambition and eager to learn, when day after day I felt aggrieved that Nature in a benevolent mood hadn't stamped my face with that mark of genius which now and again she bestows on men. Now for a long time I have known that I am not a genius and cannot understand how I ever could have wanted to be one. I am not even very gifted; my whole capacity for work probaby springs from my character and from the absence of outstanding intellectual weaknesses. But I know that this combination is very conducive to slow success, and that given favourable conditions I could achieve more than Nothnagel, to whom I consider myself superior and might possibly reach the level of Charcot. By which I don't mean to say that I will get as far as that, for these favourable conditions no longer come my way. Oh how I run on! I really wanted to say something quite different. I wanted to explain the reason for my inaccessibility to and gruffness with strangers, which you mentioned. It is simply the result of suspicion due to my having learned that common or bad people treat me badly, but this is bound to disappear to the extent to which I grow stronger and more independent and don't have to fear them anymore. I always comfort myself with the fact that people subordinate to or on a par with me have never considered me unpleasant, only superiors or people otherwise above me....
> (M. Robert p.55)

The importance of Freud's stay in Paris was not his journalistic impressions of the city; it was his contact with Charcot. Salpetriere was no longer merely a giant insane asylum. Under Charcot's direction, it had become the finest neurological clinic in the world. The five thousand patients, the feebleminded, prostitutes, the senile, hysterics, etc., were no longer lumped together. Now there was a procedure for classifying, diagnosing, and examining the former dregs of French society. Charcot transformed a rubbish heap into a hospital, a laboratory, and a place to study the mentally ill.

Freud was so overwhelmed by Charcot that his own work would never be the same. The experience marked the end of his use of the microscope.

Every Tuesday morning there would be a long line at the door of the Salpetriere clinic. One would think that one of the great theatrical figures of the day was performing there; Bernhardt or Nijinsky. No, it was merely Charcot's Tuesday morning lecture and demonstration. Not only doctors and students attended, but anyone who could get hold of a letter of admission. There was always standing room only.

The lights dim. The great man walks on stage. The amphitheater which is equipped with footlights comes to life. The noise dies down; there is silence. The personality and the appearance of the man is electrifying: black frock coat and flowing tie, long black hair pushed behind his ears, barrel-chested, thick-necked, his lofty manner and cold objectivity create the very impression he tries to avoid—sensationalism. He experiences himself as a scientist, not an entertainer, but he cannot keep his personality out of it. He puts on the best show in town.

He begins in a deep rhythmic voice. The Institute contains every type of mental disorder, but our limited knowledge makes clear classification impossible. However, one group has been isolated....

The subject today is hysteria. This particular group of patients manifest the symptoms of almost any disease, but the origin of their disability is not organic. It is mental. They are not impostors, neither are they true epileptics, or true paralytics, and so forth. But, they are ill.

"Now let us hypnotise a few of these hysterics." The audience stirs, the show is about to begin. Attendants bring in three women and seat them on chairs close to the footlights. The three patients stare at Charcot.

Jeanne Bonnard. Age forty-six. Seamstress. Subject to epileptic seizures, she has been in Salpetriere for twelve years. He rapidly describes the condition of the other patients. He then returns to Jeanne Bonnard and places a magnet on her chest. He announces that in a few moments this woman will be in a hypnotic trance. He does not even speak to her; the magnet by itself will induce the trance. The woman sleeps. This poor, ignorant, peasant woman will now put on the most spectacular show in Paris.

Charcot runs through his repertoire. At a sign or gesture from him she goes into catalepsy and assumes the classic catatonic postures, the bizarre poses commonly seen in mental hospitals. Charcot has names for the various positions. His authoritative voice calls out: "The Attitude of Supplication," "The Attitude of Crucifixion," "The Attitude of Ecstatic Waiting," and so on, including the spectacular *arc de cercle!* The audience is stunned. Charcot's running comment is precise, scientific, medical, informative; he comments on how the hysteric can simulate a physiological disease.

Again, center stage for Mademoiselle Bonnard. A sign from Charcot and her hand begins to swell. It grows to twice its normal size. It turns blue. It becomes extremely cold. He has produced a case of *l'oedeme bleu.*[1] He goes on to speak of how hysterics can take on the stigmata of the crucifixion, blindness, seizures, and so forth....

Freud was dumbfounded. He never recovered from the impact of this experience. Do the answers lie not so much in neuroanatomy but in the human mind? Had Charcot just established a link between physical symptoms and the state of the mind?

> Dear Martha October 21, 1885
> ....I think I am changing a great deal....Charcot, who is one of the greatest of physicians and a man whose common sense borders on genius, is simply wrecking all my aims and opinions. I sometimes

[1].l'oedeme bleu: edema

> come out of his lectures as from out of Notre Dame, with an entirely new idea about perfection. But he exhausts me; when I come away from him I no longer have any desire to work at my own silly things;....My brain is sated as after an evening in the theatre. Whether the seed will ever bear fruit I do not know; but what I do know is that no other human being has ever affected me in the same way.

Freud's first meeting with Charcot was formal and polite. Freud was just one of many foreign students and the great man paid him little attention. The third volume of Charcot's *Lecons* had not yet been translated and it occurred to Freud to ask for permission to do the translation. Mme. Richetti composed the letter.

> My dear Professor,
> As for the past two months I have been fascinated by your eloquence and immensely interested by the subject with which you deal in a masterly manner, it has occurred to me to offer you my services for the translation into German of the third volume of your "Lessons"....
>
> By translating the first part of the third volume of the "Lessons" which takes up these new questions which have been raised and elucidated by you, Sir, I am certain of rendering a service to my compatriots to whom this part of your investigations is less accessible than the others and of introducing myself to advantage to the German doctors.
>
> It remains for me to explain to you, Sir, why I take the liberty of writing to you when I am fortunate enough to speak to you, having permission to be present when you visit the Salpetriere....it is very possible....that some reason decides you to refuse it. In this case you have only not to mention it to me and I hope that you will be willing to excuse this request and to believe me to be, with the most sincere admiration,
>
> Your completely devoted,
> Dr. Sigm. Freud

But Charcot did consent and Freud was overjoyed. In fact, when the translation was complete Charcot was so pleased that he presented Freud with a set of his complete works bound in leather. "I was admitted to the circle of his personal acquaintances, and from that time forward I took full part in all that went on at the clinic."[1]

---

[1]Auto. p.12

Freud, in a letter, had spoken of Charcot's warm and keen interest in his patients, in contrast to the "serene superficiality" of the Viennese physician. He visited Charcot at his palatial residence socially, and professionally discussed the details of the translation.

> Madame Charcot is small, rotund, vivacious, hair powdered white, amiable, in appearance, not very distinguished. The wealth comes from her; Charcot started out quite poor; her father is rumored to be worth countless millions.
> (Freud, Eissler, p. 119)

At the Charcot soirees evening dress had to be worn. Freud discovered that he couldn't tie the white tie he bought for the occasion and he had to resort to the ready-made black one he brought with him from Hamburg. Later, he was delighted to hear that Charcot had the same problem and depended on his wife to perform the task.

> The study is as large as the whole of our future home, a room worthy of the magic palace he dwells in.... When you enter you look through a triple window to the garden; the plain panes are separated by pieces of stained glass.... The other compartment has a fireplace, a table, and closets containing Indian and Chinese antiques. The walls are covered with Gobelins and pictures....
> (Jones I, p. 187)

The soirees were attended by the outstanding figures of the day in science, letters, arts, and academia. Freud felt a little less than comfortable at being in such distinguished company.

> My appearance was immaculate.... This was my tails first appearance. I bought myself a new shirt and white gloves.... I had my hair set and rather wild beard trimmed in the French style; altogether I spent 14 francs on the evening. As a result I looked very fine and made a favorable impression on myself.... And now you will be anxious to know how I fared.... Very well. I approached Lepine, whose work I knew and had a long conversation with him, then I talked to Strauss and Geles de la Tourette and accepted a cup of coffee from Mme. Charcot, later on I drank beer, smoked like a chimney, and felt very much at ease without the slightest mishap occurring.
> (M. Roberts, p. 57)

Charcot's research had revealed to the world that hysterical symptoms could be

---

[1] Auto. p. 12

reproduced and also removed by means of hypnosis. Symptoms were a psychic phenomenon. Charcot had added something new to medical theory: hysterical symptoms can be approached through the mind. The weight of his personality, and his prestige made the medical profession accept hypnosis as a means of investigation. Classification was no longer confined to sane or insane. Charcot's leap went way beyond the mechanism of the Helmholtz school. A new thought forced its way upon medicine: ideas, mental events, can influence physical processes in the body. The vista that this concept opened up seemed unlimited.

When Freud left Paris, he parted from Charcot on the best of terms. They never met again. Freud managed a visit to Paris in July 1889, but Charcot was on a holiday, and when Charcot visited Vienna in August 1891, on his way back from a consultation in Moscow, Freud was away.

Freud left Paris in February 1886. He was to return three times. In 1889 to explore new concepts in hypnotism; in 1910 to attend a psychoanalytic convention; and in 1938, to escape the Nazis.

CHAPTER VIII

■ *The Last of the Microscope*

Still concerned about finances, Freud spent a few weeks in Berlin before returning to Vienna. He studied at the Adolph Baginsky Clinic while in Berlin, to learn about the general diseases of childhood.

> What appeals to me.... are the children in the clinic.... As long as their brains are free of disease, these little creatures are really charming and so touching when they suffer. I think I would find my way about in a children's practice in no time.
> (Freud, Eissler, p. 123)

Being an authority on childhood diseases would ensure his making a living as a physician. The pediatrist Max Kassowitz offered him the post of director of a new neurological department at the public institute for children's diseases. Freud worked there three times a week for several years (without pay).

Vienna at that time was ruled by Burgermeister Lueger, who was openly anti-Semitic. In fact this attitude prevailed in professional, academic, and government circles. An appointment in the University Psychiatric-Neurological Clinic was out of the question for "racial" reasons. Freud was never offered a position by the university even long after he had achieved international fame.

He had a deeply ambivalent feeling about Vienna and at times he used strong language to describe his attitude toward the city: it "disgusted" him, it was "physically repulsive," and so on.

Ernest Jones wrote:

> In the early years of my acquaintanceship with Freud, before I knew of that dislike, I innocently remarked on how interesting it must be to live in a town so full of new ideas. To my surprise he started up and barked at me: "I have lived here for fifty years and have never come across a new idea here."
> (Jones I, p. 293)

Yet he could never bring himself to leave Vienna. For the sake of earning a living he considered moving to England "with its sober industriousness, its general devotion to the public weal." America, where many german scientists were finding a home, was also considered. Martha wrote: "I have heard that the Americans have no superfluity of brain anatomists."

Nothnagel offered him references in Madrid and Buenos Aires. On his thirtieth birthday, Freud wrote: "Dear Martha:.... if only you would wake me with a morning kiss I should be indifferent to where we were, in America, Australia, or anywhere else." An earlier letter stated: "I feel full of fight and am not thinking of giving up my future in Vienna."

Finally, in 1939, he promised his family he would leave if the Nazis entered Vienna.

> ....when I got there in March 1939, the day after Hitler's triumphant entry, he was still adamant, saying, "This is my post and I can never leave it." The image of a captain not leaving his ship gave me the idea of telling him the story of the officer who had been blown to the surface by the boiler explosion when the Titanic went down. On being sternly interrogated: "At which moment did you leave the ship?" he proudly answered: "I never left the ship, Sir, she left me." Freud saw that this was the case, that Austria had ceased to exist, and so consented to depart for England, the land of his early dreams.
> (Jones I, p. 294)

Freud published his first book *Aphasia* in 1891, and dedicated it to Breuer. Most students of his works agree with Freud's own judgment—that it is the most valuable of his neurological writings. It was radical work that upset the world of neurology. It showed that he was still under the influence of the Helmholtz school, but slowly emancipating himself from its more mechanical aspects. His severest criticism was of Meynert's doctrine of the cortex containing".... a projection of the various parts of the body." Freud demonstrated the errors in the histological anatomy on which it was based. His book was ignored by his colleagues. Nine years later only two hundred fifty-seven copies had been sold. Today, *Aphasia* is considered a masterpiece.

Now we come to the last of Freud's work with the microscope. He had already published nine papers on pathoneurological diseases of children, and these had brought his name into public recognition among the neurologists of the world. By 1885 he had become the leading authority on children's paralysis. Nothnagel, in preparing his great encyclopedia of medicine, commissioned Freud to write the section on Infantile Cerebral Paralysis. By now Freud was interested in psychology and the writing of this section proved a laborious undertaking. He was a year late in finishing it. The Swiss neurologist Brun in a review written in 1936 said:

> Freud's monograph is the most thorough and complete exposition that has yet been written on the cerebral paralysis of children.... One gets an idea of the superb mastery of the enormous clinical material here brought together and critically worked through from the fact that the bibliography alone occupies fourteen and a half pages. It was a superb achievement and alone would suffice to

> assure Freud's name a permanent place in clinical neurology.
>
> (Ibid. p. 219)

Before we take leave of Freud the neurologist and move on to Freud the psychologist and especially to his slowly developing theories of female psychology, it seems fitting to mark the end of his neurological period with some excerpts from his obituary of Charcot.

> While he was still a student he happened to engage a maid-servant who suffered a peculiar tremor and could not find a situation on account of her clumsiness. Charcot recognized her condition as a *paralysie choreiforme,* a disease which had already been described by Duchenne, but whose basis was unknown. Charcot kept this interesting servant, although in the course of the years she cost him a small fortune in dishes and plates. When at last she died he was able to demonstrate from her case that *paralysie choreiforme* was the clinical expression of multiple cerebro-spinal sclerosis....
>
> He took personal charge in what were known as his "Lecons du Mardi." There he took up cases which were completely unknown to him; he exposed himself to all the chances of an examination, all the errors of a first investigation, he would put aside his authority on occasion and admit, in one case that he could arrive at no diagnosis and in another that he had been deceived by appearances; and he never appeared greater to his audience than when, by giving the most detailed account of his processes of thought and by showing the greatest frankness about his doubts and hesitations, he had thus sought to narrow the gulf between teacher and pupil.... a change occurred in the direction of Charcot's scientific pursuits, and to this we owe the finest of his work. He now pronounced that the theory of organic nervous illnesses was for the time being fairly complete, and he began to turn his attention almost exclusively to hysteria, which thus all at once became the focus of general interest. This, the most enigmatic of all nervous diseases, for the evaluation of which medicine had not yet found a serviceable angle of approach, had just then fallen into thorough discredit; and this discredit extended not only to the patients but to the physicians who concerned themselves with the neurosis.... The first thing that Charcot's work did was to restore dignity to the topic. Little by little, people gave up the scornful smile with which the patient could at that time

feel certain of being met. She was no longer necessarily a malingerer, for Charcot had thrown the whole weight of his authority on the side of the genuineness and objectivity of hysterical phenomena.

He treated hysteria as just another topic in neuropathology; he gave a complete description of its phenomena, demonstrated that these had their own laws and uniformities.... a number of surprising discoveries were made. Hysteria in males, and especially in men of the working class, was found far more often than had been expected; it was convincingly shown that certain conditions which had been put down to alcoholic intoxication or lead-poisoning were of a hysterical nature; it was possible to subsume under hysteria a whole number of affections which had hitherto not been understood and which had remained unclassified....

The construction of this great edifice was naturally not achieved without violent opposition. But it was the sterile opposition of an old generation who did not want to have their views changed.... When it was objected that.... hysteria in men, and so on, were not observable outside France, he pointed out how long he himself had overlooked these things, and he said once more that hysteria was the same in all places and at every time....

It is inevitable that the advance of our science, as it increases our knowledge, must at the same time lessen the value of a number of things that Charcot taught us; but neither changing times nor changing views can diminish the fame of the man whom—in France and elsewhere—we are mourning today.

Vienna, August, 1893 (Charcot S.E. III, 11-23)

CHAPTER IX

■ *Feelings of a Conqueror*

Freud finally returned to Vienna in April 1886. The time had come to start a private practice and much of the first week was spent looking for a suitable office. Also, after having been away so long, there were many people to visit. Breuer was among the first and Breuer received him warmly, embraced and kissed him. But he was pessimistic about Freud's professional chances.

Freud was as fond of Mathilde, Breuer's young and pretty wife, as he was of Breuer, and the feelings were mutual. Freud could not help speaking of his approaching marriage, and Mathilde entered into the subject with interest. Breuer got upset: "For God's sake don't egg him on to get married." He said Freud should not consider it for at least another two years. He went on to advise him to see many patients gratis, and count on earning about five gulden ($2) a day for the first two years. Freud was dismayed. Thirty years old, bursting with energy, completely monogamous, he felt he could no longer put off marrying. He had estimated that he had to earn at least twenty-five hundred gulden a year ($1,000) to make marriage possible (he had promised his own family $2,000 a year). A few days later he got over his discouragement and thought that Breuer's advice was right.

Freud's letters express his warm regard for and appreciation of Breuer's qualities. The latter had an extraordinarily wide range of knowledge, was very intelligent, and at the same time practical. Above all he was a man of wisdom. As well as all this, he again and again displayed a subtle understanding of Freud's more subjective judgments.

Freud was a constant visitor in the home of these "dear, good, understanding people." Talking with Breuer was like sitting in the sun; he radiated light and warmth. "I don't know what he sees in me to be so kind. He is a man who always understands one. One does not adequately characterize him by only saying good things about him; one has also to emphasize the absence of so much badness."

Freud would often turn to Breuer for advice—as to what he should specialize in, what travel grants he should apply for, for help in the problems that arose between Minna and Schonberg.

Before leaving for his trip to Wandsbeck, Freud had asked him for an extra fifty gulden. Breuer calmly replied, "My dear fellow, I'm not going to lend it to you. You would only come back from Wandsbeck without a penny, with debts to your tailor, and frightfully crapulent after the debauch." A few days later Breuer called on him to say he had only wanted to give Freud some sense of restraint and had no intention of refusing him the necessary funds.

Freud often accompanied Breuer when he visited his patients. At times this meant having to spend the night away from Vienna. On one occasion Breuer entered Freud's name as his brother, so that Freud would not have to tip the waiter.

One evening the Breuers were entertaining and there was dancing for the young people. Freud described the party:

> Dear Martha:
> You can imagine how furious so much youth, beauty, happiness, and merriment made me, after my painful headache and our long hard separation. I am ashamed to say that on such occasions I am very envious; I am really disagreeable and unable to enjoy anything. The occasion itself was very pleasant: there were mostly girls of from fifteen to eighteen, and some very pretty ones. I fitted in no better than the cholera would have.
> (Jones I, 171)

Although he was earning very little money, he was as always very busy. Every morning he worked in Meynert's laboratory on his anatomical research and wrote papers about it, which were afterwards published. He continued the translation of four large works, two by Charcot and two by Bernheim, and he was preparing his lecture on hysteria for the Medical Society. The last pertained to his travel scholarship. There was also the work at the Kassowitz Institute and of course his own practice. A full day's work for anyone but typical of the schedule he maintained for the rest of his life.

Those of Freud's patients who did pay were usually referred by Breuer. Those who came directly came mostly gratis. Nothnagel referred the Portuguese ambassador, who proved a little less than scrupulous when it came to paying his bill. Nevertheless things began to improve and by June he had earned three hundred eighty-seven gulden, more than the daily $4.00 that he needed to live on.

Freud had little confidence in his medical abilities and complained of a sense of inadequacy as a practitioner. He found the responsibility of private practice a different experience from the communal hospital work he was accustomed to. On one occasion he performed minor surgery on Hugo Themig, a well-known actor. The patient wrote him a polite letter of thanks but did not come back. Assuming that the patient was dissatisfied, Freud returned the fee. He wrote to Martha about the incident, adding that fortunately his sense of humor had saved him from feeling "ashamed of his ignorance, embarrassment, and helplessness."

Freud's first consultation was with Pollitzer, a world-renowned ear specialist. A week after the consultation he was called in by Pollitzer who paid him fifteen gulden. Then, through Fleischl, Pollitzer heard that Freud was planning to marry a girl as penniless as himself. And what was more, that he had turned down an opportunity to marry a girl with a dowry of one hundred thousand gulden. Pollitzer's opinion of Freud's common sense and judgment dropped sharply.

Even though he was still unsure of being able to earn a living in Vienna, Freud felt he could no longer put off being with Martha:

> Society and the law cannot in my eyes bestow on my love more gravity and benediction than it already possesses.... and when you are my dear wife before all the world and bear my name we will pass our life in calm happiness for ourselves

> and earnest work for mankind.... all we need is two or three little rooms.... a little world of happiness....
> (Ibid. p. 139)

This letter asked why they shouldn't marry now, when they were in the best years of their youth, said that two rooms and dry bread would be sufficient; why didn't she borrow money from her relatives as a dowry? "You know it is only poor people who are embarrassed at being given anything; the rich never are."[1] Their correspondence was full of financial calculations, wedding plans, and controversy regarding the kind of marriage ceremony they should have.

When his friend Paneth married Sophie Schwab, Freud witnessed a Jewish wedding for the first time. He found the proceedings so horrifying that he wrote Martha a sixteen-page letter ridiculing the whole thing. Considering Martha's background it was bound to become a burning issue between them. Freud so detested ceremony, especially religious ceremony, that the thought of such a wedding was anathema to him. He wanted a wedding that would be as small, natural, and quiet as possible. In an earlier letter he had asked, "Would you willingly do without the ring, the presents, congratulations, the being stared at and criticized, even the wedding dress and carriage, that everyone gazes at and even the "aah" of admiration when you appear? You must of course have your own way in the matter."[2]

Now that he felt the promised day was within reach, he tried to borrow more money from his friends. He even went to his future mother-in-law suggesting that she should arrange a loan from her wealthy sister.

After four years of privation his impatience could no longer be contained:

> ....if sometimes we have to rack our brains to know where this or that is coming from what will it matter? After all we should be together.... How long does one stay young, how long healthy, how long does one stay pliable enough to adapt oneself to the changing mood of the other? You would be an old maid if I let you wait until I could save up enough to pay for everything and you would have forgotten how to laugh.... I hardly live like a decent human being. I have taken you to myself in every respect, as sweetheart, as wife, as comrade, as working companion and I have to live in the most painful privation.... I do not enjoy anything.
> (Ibid. 146)

At this time (1886) Freud was unexpectedly called up for a month's military service. Not only did it mean an added expense for his own uniforms but for a month he would not earn anything.

As a senior army surgeon he quickly rose from first lieutenant to captain. It

---

[1] Ibid. p. 162
[2] Ibid. p. 140

was strenuous duty. Up at 3:30 in the morning, he was subjected to drill and marching till noon. Afternoons were devoted to medical assignments. Freud was thirty years old and solidly built. He still found the work taxing.

Martha advised that he not march when it was too hot and in any event not to march too rapidly. In *Man and Father,* by Martin Freud, we read:

> A few weeks before his marriage was eventually arranged in 1886, my father had to serve for a month in the Austrian army during maneuvers held at Olmuetz in Moravia.... There is a letter preserved written from this place to.... Dr. Josef Breuer, which might be quoted to show that.... human attitudes to soldiering have not changed very much....

Olmuetz would seem to have at least one attraction, a first-class cafe....

> When two or three generals sit down together, I can't help it, but they always remind me of parakeets, for mammals don't usually dress in such colours (save for the back parts of baboons). The whole troop of waiters surround them and nobody else would seem to exist for the waiters. Once, in despair, I grabbed a waiter by the coat-tails and shouted, "Look here, I may be a general some time, so fetch me a glass of water!"
>
> (Sigmund Freud: Man and Father by Martin Freud. The Vanguard Press, N.Y. 1958, p. 22)

> "An officer," he wrote, still in the letter to Dr. Breuer, "is a miserable creature. Each officer envies his equals in rank, bullies his subordinates and fears his superiors. The higher he rises, the more he fears them." Showing how he himself felt, he adds, "I detest the idea of having inscribed on my collar how much I am worth.... The commanding officer.... went into the swimming pool. I was astonished to note that his swimming trunks carried no marks of distinction."
>
> (Ibid. p. 23)

Even though the exact calculations had to be changed, Freud was resolved that nothing should interfere with his general plans. He was firm on going through with the wedding.

Frau Bernays, Martha's mother, who herself had lived through an engagement of nine years, was deeply upset that they should go forward under such conditions.

> Dear Sigi:
>
> Your letter astonished me not a little and the only sensible passage in it was, "I am once more prepared to give up our wedding plans." That you could for a single moment in the present circum-

stances, when you have to interrupt your practice for almost two months, think of marrying in September is in my opinion an abysmally irresponsible piece of recklessness. Another word would be more fitting, but I will not use it. I shall not give my consent to such an idea. As you know from my letter of the twenty-third, I had already taken steps to obtain money for your marriage and had this unhappy military business not come in between I should certainly have been in favor of not postponing the wedding any longer. But since through this calamity your livelihood is completely endangered, the plan has become in a word impossible and impracticable.

When a man without means or prospect gets engaged to a poor girl he tacitly shoulders a heavy burden for years to come, but he cannot make anyone else responsible for it. He cannot, however, increase this burden by in the end marrying out of despair, which is just what you are doing. If one has waited for four years, then a few months more or less hardly matter, and on calm reflection you must certainly admit that.

To take a flat in August, just before you are going away for five or six weeks, is literally to throw away money (which unfortunately is rare enough) out of the window. So what I think is this. You keep your present flat till November, or if you think it is a pity for the money you can give it up and rent another on your return. You then begin your practice over again, and if it turns out to be possible you can arrange for the wedding at the end of the year. That makes a difference of three months, which is surely unimportant. Don't think I can't imagine how uncomfortable your present life is, but to run a household without the means for it is a curse. It is one I have myself borne for years, so I can judge. I beg and implore you not to do it. Do not let my warning go unheeded and wait quietly until you have a settled means of existence. First regain some calmness and peace of mind which at present is so entirely wrecked. You have no reason whatever for your ill-humor and despondence, which borders on the pathological. Dismiss all these calculations, and first of all become once more a sensible man. At this moment you are like a spoiled child who can't get his own way and cries, in the belief that in that way he can get everything.

Don't mind the last sentence, but it is really true.

> Take to heart these truly well-meant words and don't think badly of
>
> Your faithful Mother
> (Ibid. p.147)

Emmeline Bernays was an intelligent, well-educated, courageous woman, who upon her husband's death assumed the responsibilities of head of the family.

It might be mentioned that Freud's mother, Amalie, was also a personality in her own right. She enjoyed socializing and card playing at an hour when most old ladies would be in bed. When she was ninety she was given a beautiful shawl as a gift. Her comment was that it would "make her look too old." Six weeks before she died, at the age of ninety-five, her photograph appeared in the newspaper. Her comment? "A bad reproduction; it makes me look a hundred." Visitors to Herr Professor found it odd to hear her refer to him as "mein goldener Sigi."

Years later he wrote: "A man who had been the indisputable favorite of his mother keeps for life the feelings of a conqueror, that confidence of success that often induces real success."[1]

It is not known if Freud answered Frau Bernay's letter. The directness and even eloquence of her plea in any case did not affect his decision. All that remained was to find suitable quarters and furnish them.

In July a telegram from Martha joyfully carried the latest news. Aunt lea had sent her twelve hundred fifty gulden for a wedding gift and Uncle louie from London also sent a present of eight hundred marks. So now they could go ahead with their plans. The following letters discussed in detail color schemes, curtains and all matter of furnishings.

Sigmund Freud spent busy evenings looking for a suitable apartment, which he discovered to be in short supply. There seemed simply none to be had. It was fustrating since he wanted so much to have everything settled and waiting for his bride before he left for the military maneuvers.

On the night of December 8, 1881, a disastrous fire at the Ring theater had taken over six hundred lives. A newly built apartment house had just been erected on the ill-fated site by the Emperor's orders. The new building was being referred to as the House of Atonement and few were willing to live in a place with such morbid associations. Freud asked Martha if she shared the popular superstition. She telegraphed her willingness to take the apartment and Freud rented it at once. The rent was six hundred forty dollars a year, more than they had budgeted for, but Freud's characteristic optimism and boldness overrode his doubts.

There was one final disappointment before the fulfillment of his cherished wish. Since they were to be married in Germany, Freud had comforted himself with the thought that only a civil ceremony would be necessary. But Martha informed him although a civil marriage was valid in Germany, in Austria, where they would be living, they would not be considered married unless a religious ceremony had also been held. There was mothing to be done about it. Martha made it as easy as possible for him by arranging the wedding for a weekday, when few could attend. It was also to be held in her mother's house so that formal evening dress would be unnecessary. Freud spent two nights with Uncle Elias Philip, who was to be his tutor

---

[1]Ibid. 5

in the Hebrew Broche (prayers) he would have to recite during the ceremony. The marriage took place on September 13, 1886.

As we mentioned before, prior to 1951, when his letters could be studied, the world knew practically nothing of Freud's private love life. The man who taught the world the importance of the sex drive, how diverse it is and how incalculable the role it plays in the development of character, this man never revealed his own passion and how he dealt with his private frustrations. He was totally silent on his own sex life.

To illustrate his theory he spoke of himself in two works, *The Interpretation of Dreams* and *The Psychopathology of Everyday Life.* He freely revealed feelings of envy, covetousness, jealousy, death wishes toward rivals and friends, and so forth. But he never alluded to his own sexuality, even though where else but in his own experience could he have discovered the importance of Eros and the Libido? From where but himself could his optimism have come?

There is in his writing one slight reference to his sexual experience. In 1915, when he was sixty years old, he wrote to James Putnam, an American psychiatrist: "Sexual morality as defined by society, in its most extreme form, that of America, strikes me as very contemptible. I stand for an infinitely freer sexual life, although I myself have made very little use of such freedom."[1] The man who "profaned" everything led an exemplary life himself from the moralistic point of view.

Freud could not prevent the onslaught (he was a pervert, an enemy of civilization, etc.), but his absolute silence concerning his private life protected his family and friends from the curiosity of the public.

In 1930 he received the Goethe Prize for Literature. In his address to the society that met to honor the great man, he said, "Goethe was not only, as a poet, a great self-revealer, but also, in spite of the abundance of autobiographical records, a careful concealer."[2] Can there be any doubt that Freud was also talking about himself? He closed his address with the words of Mephistopheles: "The best of what you know may not, after all, be told to boys."[3]

The picture the world had of Freud during his lifetime is put into words by Stefan Zweig in "Mental Healers":

> For half a century Sigmund Freud shut his private life away behind the severe-looking door of a Vienna apartment. One would be almost tempted to say he had no private life, since it went on so modestly in the background. An almost unseen official figure, a mode of life of almost bourgeois regularity, unbroken by any startling changes or happenings (the exceptions all took place in the intellectual sphere) and never a single personal statement which might lend itself to anecdote or raise an eyebrow. Seventy years in the same city, more than forty years in the same house. Consulta-

---

[1]*Letters of Sigmund Freud,* N.Y., Basic Books Inc., 1960 p. 308
[2]S.E. XXI 212
[3]*Faust,* Part 1, Scene 4

> tions always in the same study. Father of six children, a man who had no personal needs, his only love his profession and his vocation. A man who never gave a minute of his time to seeking worldly vanities, position or honours, who never put the creator above his creation, and in whom the rhythm of life was subordinated absolutely and exclusively to that of never-ending, patient work.
> (M. Roberts 62)

Martha was a twenty-five-year old bride and her groom was thirty. Freud was a handsome man, 5'7'', slender. They must have made a good-looking couple. During the honeymoon they wrote joint letters to Mamma in Wandsbeck, each taking turns writing a line. Freud concluded with: ''Here at our present residence at Lubeck on the first day of what we hope will prove a thirty years war between Sigmund and Martha.'' No war took place and the thirty years stretched to fifty-three.

Freud had at last won his heart's desire and every indication pointed to an unusually successful marriage. Martha proved to be a loving wife and mother and a good housekeeper; (she kept her servants indefinitely). In the early years Freud would discuss his theories and cases with her. Later on, she could not have followed the flight of his ideas any more than his colleagues could.

After a while she came to be known as Frau Professor. She never quite adopted the easy-going ways of the Viennese and she retained her precise Hamburg speech. Freud weaned her away from Jewish orthodoxy, and religion had no part in their household. Much later, after her husband's death, she enjoyed discussing Jewish festivals and customs with the children and with anyone who had similar feelings.

They had six children, three boys and three girls. They named their children after important and cherished people in their lives. They lived together for fifty-three years. Freud would on occasion travel without Martha, but only rarely were they separated from each other. Martha suffered only one rival, his work.

CHAPTER X

■ *A Good Man Gone Wrong*

From then on, Freud was to lead a double life. At home he enjoyed the comfort and security of a man who loves his family and friends, who on their side are devoted to him.

> We live pretty happily in steadily increasing unassumingness. When we hear the baby laugh we imagine it is the loveliest thing that can happen to us. I am not ambitious and do not work very hard.
>
> (Jones I, p. 152)

His public life, however, was something else. His name was still associated with the "third scourge of humanity," cocaine, an association which gave rise to attacks in the press. Dr. Albrecht Erlenmayer attacked him personally in a paper which warned the world that Freud was dangerous. His use of hypnotism was even more bitterly criticized. In the eyes of many, Freud was a dangerous, irresponsible quack. Amid this atmosphere of disquiet the thirty-year-old Freud was trying to establish a private practice and to earn a living.

At the same time, he insisted on fighting for the right of women suffering from hysteria to receive humane treatment. Only women were punished for being neurotic. Men with similar symptoms would not be castrated, packed in ice, or subjected to myriad forms of humiliation. The medical establishment would not forgive Freud. Not only did his colleagues deny him referrals but he was subjected to insults and frequently even cut in the street!

Freud was alone in his mission. Even those who should have known better would not stand up and be counted. Breuer, who certainly knew better, allowed himself very reluctantly to be drawn into the battle, and when he saw where it was leading, finally split with his friend. Meynert knew that Freud was right, that hysteria was an emotional disorder; but for personal reasons he was embarrassed, and would not stand by Freud's side. In fact, Meynert was the one to lead the opposition. If a Josef Breuer and a Theodor Meynert would not take up this fight, one can imagine how isolated Freud felt professionally.

But few men have the courage and integrity Freud had. Few men, embarking on a difficult career, desperate for security, would give up the patronage and support of the leading figures in the profession—let alone antagonize them. Freud antagonized them.

The relationship with Meynert was a classic case and a tragic one: classic in that we have the story of an old master having to give way to a young challenger; tragic in that the outcome was inevitable.

Theodor Meynert, with his prominent forked beard and large, powerful, intimidating head, was recognized as the world's leading neurologist and psychiatrist. No mean achievement. Implied is dedication, hours of extremely delicate work with microscope and scalpel. In medical school, Freud had found Meynert's lectures on psychiatry fascinating, in fact the only lectures worth listening to. Meynert seemed to be trying to apply the knowledge of physics and chemistry to human behavior. Freud continued to hold Meynert in the highest esteem, and spoke of "the great Meynert in whose footsteps I follow with such veneration," but as a psychiatrist he had a less lofty opinion of Meynert.

Freud's own psychiatric training had consisted of one hour a day for five months in Meynert's Psychiatric Clinic, two months in the men's ward, and three months in the women's, and much reading. He had learned how little psychiatrists understood their subject.

Meynert at the time was quite taken with young Freud. He encouraged him and even put his own laboratory at his disposal. He publicly supported Freud's candidacy for *Privatdocent* and interceded with Nothnagel in his favor. It was thus that Freud got the assignment of a salaried assistant at the clinic.

Meynert passionately adhered to the Helmholtz view: that everything is material and that all behavior can be understood only through physiology, chemistry, and physics. Yet this brilliant man, like his medical colleagues, would not go near a woman who was suffering from hysteria. Why? The reasons given were that the diversity of the symptomatology proved that these women were malingerers whose aims were to make the physician look foolish.

In his autobiography Freud has told us that it was a condition of his travel scholarship to Paris that he report to the Medical Society everything he learned at Salpetriere. He titled the paper he wrote "On Male Hysteria." This was hardly a tactful approach under the circumstances. Science systematically collects data, studies, classifies, and tries to understand it. Freud was presenting detailed information that seriously questioned prevailing concepts. For instance he described a traumatic hysteria a man suffered after a fall from a scaffold. Freud had followed the case at Salpetriere, and he asserted there was no difference between the manifestations of male and female hysterical symptoms. They follow the same patterns, although the patterns may appear to us imprecise at the time. He suggested that some cases of "railway spine" for instance might be hysterical. Neurologists who had a vested interest in injuries to the nervous system (they frequently led to legal battles and court cases) could hardly be pleased with such interpretations. The storm broke. Reactions bordered from "there's nothing really new here," to out-and-out skepticism.

> The duty devolved upon me of giving a report before the *Gesellschaft der Aerzte* (Society of Physicians) upon what I had seen and learned with Charcot. But I met with a bad reception. Persons of authority... declared that which I said was incredible. Meynert challenged me to find some cases in Vienna similar to those which I had described and to present them before the Society. I tried to do so; but the senior physicians in whose departments I found any such cases refused to allow me to observe them or to work at them.

> One of them, an old surgeon, actually broke out with the exclamation, "But my dear sir, how can you talk such nonsense? Hysteron (sic) means the uterus so how can a man be hysterical?" I objected in vain that what I wanted was not to have my diagnosis approved but to have the case put at my disposal...."
>
> (Auto. p. 15)

Meynert was upset. He admired Charcot the great neurologist, but Charcot's interest in hysteria and, further, his use of hypnotism meant, in Meynert's view, "a good man gone wrong": a man who resorted to theatrics and quackery. How could the brilliant Freud be involved in such garbage? How could he possibly side with Charcot against his own loyal friend?

> At length, outside the hospital, I came upon a case of a classical hysterical hemi-anaesthesia in a man, and demonstrated it before the *Gesellschaft der Aerzte.* This time I was applauded, but no further interest was taken in me. The impression that the high authorities had rejected my innovations remained unshaken; and, with my hysteria in men and my production of hysterical paralyses by suggestion I found myself forced into the opposition. As I was soon afterwards excluded from the laboratory of cerebral anatomy and for terms on end had nowhere to deliver my lectures, I withdrew from academic life and ceased to attend the learned societies. It is a whole generation since I have visited the *Gesellschaft der Aertze.*
>
> (Ibid. p. 15)

Freud had been deeply hurt and on a number of occasions referred to the "bad reception." He found it impossible to gain a sympathetic hearing for the idea of male hysteria, despite his firsthand observations of such cases.

In point of fact, Freud was not the first to recognize male hysteria. Only five years earlier a paper had been presented to the Society on the subject, and there had been others since. Freud, however, was the first to assert that hysteria was not a malevolent female stunt, but in fact a pathology that affected women and men alike. Furthermore that the dynamics were similar for both sexes.

A year later Freud's sins had mounted too high to be forgivable. With the publication of *On Aphasia* he really drew blood. Meynert had always taught that the cortex contained "a projection of the various parts of the body. Freud demonstrated the errors in histological anatomy on which this was based. The fibers entering the cord nuclei are more numerous than those passing on from there to the cortex, so there could be no continuity between the perifery and the brain."[1] Meynert could only feel uneasiness at Freud's growing superiority in the field of

---

[1](Jones I p. 215)

brain anatomy. Their relationship became more and more strained. Freud was not only fighting to extend the concept of hysteria from females to males, but also insisting that the offensive hypnosis could be used in the treatment. Meynert disappointed Freud. He had expected more from Meynert. He was puzzled at Meynert's unscientific, emotional attitude. The great researcher was actually refusing to look at data.

What Freud did not know was that Meynert himself was an hysteric. He suffered from attacks of aphasia and paralysis of the right arm. He couldn't face the possibility that the symptoms were psychological. His self-esteem demanded that there be a physiological basis for his condition. Brilliant as he may have been, in his youth he had been quite unstable. His grandfather, a police surgeon, repeatedly had him arrested and put in jail for being drunk. Meynert feared his own suppressed feelings and the role they might be playing in his life.

By the time Freud returned to Vienna, Meynert was past his prime. He found it increasingly difficult to keep up with the new ideas and methods which young Freud mastered so easily. He was losing his preeminence. Oddly enough, if Meynert had dared to look at the information that Freud was offering and had stood by him, he would have ended up a noble warrior in the forefront of a lively battle. But as it was, he regressed. He took to drink. The once great man had difficulty maintaining self-control.

Freud visited Meynert during his final illness and Meynert confessed that he was a classic case of male hysteria, but that he had kept it a secret all these years.

What was all the fuss about? The issue would seem to be whether or not symptomatology in females that did not follow the regular rules of the nervous system was a valid area for study. At the time, women who displayed such symptoms were confined to insane asylums, subjected to surgery, or other forms of punishment, because they were merely malingerers and shamming, in the attempt to avoid work and their real duties. The irony of course was that many, perhaps most, of the complaints and problems brought to physicians were basically neurotic, and that physicians were treating neurotic patients all the time.

Freud won. Women whose difficulties take the form of symptoms that do not follow conventional neurological pathways are no longer burned at the stake, or subjected to any other forms of brutality, at least not formally and officially. Today they are given the therapeutic agents available. To be sure Freud was a humanist. But that was not his fight. He was fighting for the recognition of scientific facts; anyone's prejudices notwithstanding. He dedicated his life to the relentless pursuit of scientific truth.

Freud's passion for the truth may be illustrated by the following anecdote. In 1923 during a visit to Freud, Felix Deutsch was asked to examine a troublesome lesion in the former's palate, for which he had already undergone surgery. "At the very first glance," Deutsch saw that he was dealing with an advanced cancer. Rather than tell the truth to his venerable friend he pronounced it as a bad leukoplakia. However, he did tell the truth to the Committee. The Committee consisted of a group of Freud's most intimate and trusted colleagues. The Committee "decided" not to tell Freud, but to allow him to enjoy a planned two-week vacation in Rome with his daughter Anna. During the last year of Freud's life, Jones mentioned the Committee's decision fifteen years earlier. According to Jones, Freud's eyes were ablaze with anger as he asked *"Mit welchem recht?* (With what right?) Freud was furious that others should decide that anything but the truth was acceptable to him."[1]

Freud's passion led to the discovery of some of the most profoundly disturbing truths about the human condition. Not the least was that man is not master in his own house; dark unknown forces play a role in his decisions.

---

[1]Freud: *Living and Dying*. Schur Int. U. Press, N.Y. 1972, p. 361)

CHAPTER XI

■ *Breuer's Baby*

The next thread in our story connects us directly with psychology, male and female, and the beginnings of psychoanalysis. Freud met Breuer, who was fourteen years his senior, at the Brucke Institute in the late seventies. Dr. Josef Breuer was not simply an established physician; he was a symbol of the establishment. He was a man of considerable scientific understanding who had made many permanent contributions to scientific knowledge. "He had produced several works of permanent value upon the physiology of respiration and upon the organ of equilibrium."[1] He was a Corresponding Member of the Vienna Academy of Sciences; his sponsors being Exner, Hering, and Ernst Mach, all men with international reputations. He was besides the family physician to Brucke, Exner, Brentano, and others of their status.

From the first he and Freud were drawn to each other and spent much time together discussing all manner of subjects. "He became my friend and helper in my difficult circumstances. We grew accustomed to share all our scientific interests with each other. In the relationship the gain was naturally mine." Breuer was among those devoted friends of Freud who help support him financially. He regularly sent Freud a much needed "loan" and would not ever deign to refer to it.

In later years when he no longer needed financial support from his friends, Freud proved to be himself quite generous. He often gave financial aid to colleagues and to students who were in need.

In 1922 the son of an old servant of Freud's shot his father, who was attempting to rape the youth's half-sister. Although he did not know this young man, Freud engaged a lawyer and paid all legal expenses. The youth was found not guilty.

Another example of Freud's generosity was revealed almost a half-century after the event. In an English publication, in 1952, a Bruno Goetz recalled that he had once consulted Freud concerning headaches he suffered from. As Goetz left the office, Freud slipped an envelope containing 200 kronen into his hand, a sum which amounted to about a full day of Freud's earnings.[2]

But to return to our story, Breuer confided to Freud that he had been treating a hysterical female, and furthermore that he had used hypnosis with considerable success. Freud was fascinated. In 1880 the medical attitude toward hysterics was "hands off." He and Breuer discussed the details of the case over and over again. The treatment had lasted about eighteen months and had been terminated six months earlier. Breuer's work made a deep impression on him. So deep, that three years later when he went to Paris, he told Charcot of the remarkable work that a colleague in Vienna had done with a hysteric. Oddly enough, Charcot didn't at the time show

---

[1]Autobiographical Study, p. 19

[2]Talent and Genius. Eissler, K.R. Quadrangel Books, N.Y. 1971, p. 10

much interest. "Charcot's thoughts seemed to be elsewhere." Perhaps it was because Freud was so much under the influence of the great man, widening his horizons every day that his own interest in Breuer's discovery subsided at the time.

When Freud returned to Vienna, he had once more to make a living and he set up as a specialist in "nervous illnesses." Patients appeared in his office whose problems had clearly no organic basis. For example, although a patient complained that her arm was paralyzed, examination would prove that neurologically and physiologically the patient was sound. In short, the patient was an hysteric.

> Anyone who wants to make a living from the treatment of nervous patients must clearly be able to do something to help them. My therapeutic arsenal contained only two weapons, electrotherapy and hypnotism.... My knowledge of electrotherapy was derived from W. Erb's textbook (1882), which provided detailed instructions for the treatment of all the symptoms of nervous diseases. Unluckily I was soon driven to see that following these instructions was of no help whatever, and that what I had taken for an epitome of exact observations was merely the construction of phantasy.... So I put my electrical apparatus aside, even before Moebius had saved the situation by explaining that the successes of electric treatment in nervous disorders (insofar as there were any) were the effect of suggestion on the part of the physician.
>
> (Autobiography, p. 16)

All Freud's interest in Breuer's discoveries and success with his hysteric was rekindled. Breuer, good scientist that he was, had practically written the case up. Freud studied it, and discussed with Breuer the theoretical and technical implications of the work. Strangely, Breuer seemed unwilling to go back to the case; he only reluctantly went along with Freud's enthusiasm.

The patient, later to be famous as Anna O., was a remarkably intelligent and attractive woman of twenty-one. Her father was very ill and while nursing him, she had developed a variety of symptoms, among which were severe disturbances of speech, cross-eyedness, paralysis of three of her limbs, partial paralysis of her neck muscles, persistent somnambulism, inability to feed herself, and severe headaches. Later she developed a severe and painful cough, which brought Breuer into the picture.

Little wonder that the medical establishment, given its level of knowledge at the time, did what it could to avoid such cases. And little wonder that Freud was regarded as a tiresome crank, a thorn in their side. The irrefutable fact is that pre-Freudian therapists did not have the wherewithal, the knowledge, do deal with such conditions. The treatment of a hysterical neurosis requires an understanding of the unconscious. For such an understanding the world had to wait for Freud. Freud and Freud alone has taught us what a neurosis is and how to treat it.

During the treatment, Anna O. spoke of having two selves, a real one and an evil one, which last forced her to behave badly. She would become abusive, throw things, smash windows and so on. New symptoms appeared. She complained that the walls of the room were collapsing, that she saw black snakes, death heads, skeletons. For two weeks she became mute although she made constant efforts to speak.

Breuer found himself dealing with a double personality, with two states of consciousness. One was normal, the other childish, belligerent, troublesome. Transition from one state to the other took place very rapidly and seemed to be brought on by a kind of autohypnosis.

Every evening, she would tell Dr. Breuer about her horrifying hallucinations, the disagreeable thoughts and events of the day; after telling which she would feel better. On one occasion she related the details and circumstances associated with the first appearance of a particular symptom. To Breuer's astonishment, the symptom then completely disappeared. Anna O., whose intelligence may have been near genius, immediately saw the value of her "talking cure" and she continued to explore the original circumstances that had surrounded each symptom. She referred to the whole procedure as "chimney sweeping." Today the method is still called what Breuer called it, catharsis, and it is still used extensively and often affords a measure of relief. For this we are indebted to Anna O.

During the treatment, Anna forgot how to speak German, her mother tongue. She could only speak English. Breuer would ask her to read aloud from a French or Italian text and she would do so, translating without effort into English.

Breuer's work was brilliant; the case has to be studied in detail to be appreciated. For example, after two weeks during which she was mute, Breuer told her she was clearly offended about something and had determined not to speak about it. The inhibition immediately disappeared.

Given the exciting new discoveries he was making, Breuer's reticence puzzled Freud. He seemed unwilling to get involved with the case even though their discussions led to lively theoretical speculation. After much persuasion, Breuer finally agreed to write up the complete case.

In those days devoting hours every day to a single patient for more than a year was unheardof. Breuer's heroic patience is as remarkable as his insight. Nonetheless he gave up treating hysteria after the Anna O. case. In addition to our now knowing he had personal reasons for this decision, we must remember that his time was in great demand. Freud, on the other hand, had lots of time. He was delighted to accept Breuer's referrals. Having patients come to him over a long period of time provided him with a much-needed living.

By this time the material from Anna had become massive and thus overwhelming. In order to narrow its scope, to sharpen its focus, Breuer took to hypnotizing Anna every morning and then returned to her in the evening when she was lucid and normal. He also explored the effect of hypnotizing her in the evenings as well, and carefully observed and meticulously documented the efficacy of each method. For example, she sometimes failed to hear someone's entrance into the room, a most unusual symptom. He recorded in detail 100 separate instances that might have contributed to her pseudo-deafness.

The evening hypnosis led to a new method of treatment. Breuer would put Anna under a deep hypnosis and insist that she tell him what was oppressing her mind. This procedure succeeded in removing her inhibitions and at the same time the physical symptoms, which was, after all, the purpose of the tratment. In her normal waking state she could describe no better than other patients the connection between her symptoms and any life experience. In hypnosis, she would connect her symptoms with earlier events of her life.

> It turned out that all her symptoms went back to moving events she had experienced while nursing her father; that is to say, her symptoms had a meaning and were residues or reminiscences of those emotional situations.
>
> (Autobiographical Study, p. 20)

> Breuers' final, complete version of the case stated:

> In this way too, the whole illness was brought to a close.... She was moreover free from the innumerable disturbances which she had previously exhibited.... but it was some time before she regained her mental health entirely.
>
> (Studies in Hysteria, 1893, S.E. II, p. 40)

Breuer's report of the case contains certain obscurities and omissions of detail. Particularly sketchy is a description of the termination, which seems to have been rather sudden. This paucity of detail stands in marked contrast to the plenitude in regard to her early symptoms. In view of the promising discoveries, Breuer's aversion to the subject, the hasty ending, and the sudden lack of detail left Freud puzzled.

Later, Freud discovered what had happened, but out of consideration for an old and loved friend, he kept the secret. The events are common knowledge among psychoanalysts today.

> Freud has related to me a fuller account than he described in his writing of the peculiar circumstances surrounding the end of this novel treatment. It would seem that Breuer had developed what we should nowadays call a strong counter-transference to his interesting patient. At all events he was so engrossed that his wife became bored at listening to no other topic and before long jealous. She did not display this openly, but became unhappy and morose. It was a long time before Breuer, with his thoughts elsewhere, divined the meaning of her state of mind. It provoked a violent reaction in him, perhaps compounded of love and guilt, and he decided to bring the treatment to an end.... He announced this to Anna O., who was by now much better, and bade her goodbye. But that evening he was fetched back to find her in a greatly excited state, apparently as ill as ever. The patient, who according to him had appeared to be an asexual being and had never made any allusion to such a forbidden topic throughout the treatment, was now in the throes of an hysterical childbirth (pseudocyses), the logic-

> al termination of a phantom pregnancy that had been invisibly developing in response to Breuer's ministrations. Though profoundly shocked, he managed to calm her down by hypnotizing her, and fled the house in a cold sweat. The next day he and his wife left for Venice to spend a second honeymoon, which resulted in the conception of a daughter....
>
> (Jones, VI. 1, p. 224)

Anna O., whose real name was Bertha Pappenheim, didn't do quite as well as Breuer's published account might imply. Relapses occurred, and on one occasion she was placed in an institution, where the psychiatrist in charge fell in love with her. By the age of thirty she had become a woman of serious purpose. She became one of the first social workers in the world, the actual first in Germany. She founded several institutes where she trained students, and she published a periodical. She devoted a major part of her life's work to women's emancipation causes. She organized expeditions to Russia, Poland, and Roumania, to rescue children whose parents were victims of pogroms. She died in 1936 at the age of 77. She never married. She was deeply religious to the very end.

We are profoundly indebted to the massive collaboration of Bertha Pappenheim and Josef Breuer. In that spirit of gratitude let us generalize about some of what they have taught us. They taught us that there are two mental states: a conscious and an unconscious. They taught us that our thoughts, feelings, attitudes, perceptions, and even points of view are determined by forces within the unconscious. This is the bedrock of psychoanalysis: that our thoughts, feelings, and behavior are in large measure related to unconscious determinants. One may agree or disagree with this concept, but it is fundamental to psychoanalysis. Take, as a simple example, the difference between an optimist and a pessimist. If asked to substantiate their opposing views, both would resort to philosophical and existential explanations. Psychoanalytic investigation however reveals that there are determinants of which they are entirely unaware. In analysis we discover that the optimist feels that, no matter what, "Mamma's tit will always be there." The pessimist? He knows better!

The famous collaboration of Breuer and Anna O. also taught us that hysterical symptoms have a history: they are substitutes for repressed feelings and when one goes back to their first appearance and succeeds in linking them to the feeling experienced at the time, there can be therapeutic results.

Negative, unacceptable thoughts and feelings cannot be released normally; therefore their emotional energy is damned up. The inhibited feelings are converted into the symptoms we see in our hysterical patients. If the damned-up energy is relieved by being reexperienced, the symptom may disappear. This came to be known as the Theory of Strangulated Affects.

Breuer's work with Anna O. presented Freud with an immediate question: is it possible to generalize from one case?

> The state of things which he had discovered seemed to me to be of so fundamental a nature that I could not believe it could fail to be present in any case of hysteria.... I therefore began to repeat Breuer's investigations with my own patients....

> After observing for several years that his findings were invariably confirmed in every case of hysteria.... I proposed to him that we should issue a joint publication.
> (Autobiography, 1925, S.E. XX,21)

From the time of his talk on Male Hysteria, Freud had found that he and his colleagues were in growing opposition. He seemed to them to be leading a crusade against accepted and conventional medicine. Freud at first eagerly accepted this challenge. But he also knew he needed all the help he could muster, and it was natural to turn to the man who had introduced him to the mystifying field of hysteria, Josef Breuer.

Freud was in any case bent on reviving Breuer's interest in hysteria, or at least to have him make his discoveries known to the world. He couldn't understand why he met such resistance. Breuer was the older man but Freud was clearly the driving force and the leader in this undertaking. It occurred to him that Breuer's reluctance might be due to his unpleasant experience with the patient. When Breuer saw Anna writing with pain and announcing "Dr. Breuer's baby is coming," he must have been quite shaken. Freud told Breuer of an experience of his own with a patient who quite suddenly threw her arms around him and expressed erotic affection. The two doctors then discussed the phenomenon of transference which refers to feelings the patient directs toward the therapist, feelings based on no real relation between them. They derive from fantasies which have become unconscious. The part of the patient's emotional life which he can no longer recall is re-experienced by him in his relation to the therapist. He "transfers" old unconscious fantasies onto the therapist. Transference arises spontaneously during all human relationships, and resembles what occurs between a patient and a therapist.[1] The discussion had a calming effect on Breuer, who evidently was suffering from self-reproach regarding the episode with Anna O. As a result Freud succeeded at last in getting Breuer's cooperation. It was agreed that they would keep the theme of sexuality as much as possible in the background. Two years later they published the famous *Studies in Hysteria,* from which we can date the beginning of psychoanalysis. During the preparation of the book Breuer remarked that the transference phenomenon "is the most important thing we both have to make to the world."

The book was poorly received and Breuer felt discouraged. "Breuer's self-confidence and powers of resistance were not developed as fully as the rest of his mental organization."[2] Freud says that he himself was able to laugh at the critics' lack of comprehension. At the end of thirteen years, 626 copies had been sold.

Breuer seems to have resented Freud's dragging him into the affair and their relationship began to deteriorate. The clearer it became that there is a sexual aetiology in hysteria, the more uncomfortable Breuer became. Freud disliked the way that Breuer became full of doubt and insecurity concerning his conclusions. He was ambivalent on the subject, would vacillate between one side and the other. He would defend Freud publicly and disagree with him privately. At a meeting of the College of Physicians, Breuer spoke favorably of Freud's work, particularly expressing his

---

[1]Five Lectures, 1910, S.E. XI, p. 51
[2]Autobiography XX, 23

agreement with his view of sexual aetiology. After the meeting Freud thanked him. To his surprise, Breuer responded with "I don't believe a word of it," and abruptly turned away. He presented the picture of a man half afraid of his own discoveries.

The relationship cooled and a friendship of twenty years was practically ended. After the summer of 1894 they never collaborated again.

Previously one heard constantly of Breuer's generosity, cheerfulness, sympathy, and intellectual stimulation. Now surprisingly, in Freud's correspondence with Fliess, we hear of Breuer's weak personality. His presence is irritating, he's difficult to get along with, he cannot take a definite stand on controversial issues, he focuses on detail for purposes of debate rather than understanding. Hanna, Breuer's daughter, reported that on one occasion Freud even walked by her father on the street and pretended not to see him.

Disagreement about the aetiology of hysteria alone does not account for Freud's bitterness. The explanation lies in his own history and psychology.

As we know when Freud's father, Jakob, married Amalie Nathansohn, Freud's mother, Jakob had sons from a previous marriage and was a grandfather. Sigmund Freud therefore, was born an uncle, with a nephew a year older than he. When he was ten months of age his brother Julius was born. Julius died at the age of eight months. Nephew John and Freud were constant companions. According to Freud:

> My present-day anger, which was only slight... received reinforcements from sources in the depth of my mind and thus swelled into a current of hostile feelings against persons of whom I was in reality fond. The source of this reinforcement flowed from my childhood... my warm friendships as well as my enmities with contemporaries went back to my relations in childhood with a nephew who was a year my senior... according to the testimony of our elders, we sometimes fought with each other and made complaints to them about each other. All my friends have in a certain sense been reincarnations of this first figure... My emotional life has always insisted that I should have an intimate friend and a hated enemy. I have always been able to provide myself afresh with both, and it has not infrequently happened that the ideal situation of childhood has been so completely reproduced that friend and enemy have come together in a single individual...
> (Int. Dreams S.E. V p. 483)

Again in a letter to Fliess he writes:

> I greeted my one-year-younger brother (who died within a few months) with evil wishes and genuine infantile jealousy, so that his death implanted a seed of self-reproach in me... This nephew and this younger brother now determine the neurotic element, but also the intensity of all my friendships.

(L. 70 Vienna, 3. 10. 97)

Once again Freud's scientific researches took him into areas that others found objectionable and threatening. Breuer had meant a great deal to him. His old friend had been his chief source of encouragement and gratification. He admitted that it was painful to think that Breuer was no longer part of his life. On occasion Freud would express bitterness and disappointment concerning his old benefactor.

In the tradition of his teacher, the great Brucke, Freud was bound to go where the data took him, regardless of other considerations. Whether it meant fighting against discrimination and for the proper treatment for women who were suffering from a neurosis, or making it clear that men also suffered from such neuroses, or proving that hypnosis can be useful in the treatment of hysteria, or that sexual factors play a role in the formation of symptoms, one stated it simply and clearly, regardless of the objections of friends, the rejection by patrons, and malevolence of the public.

Promising as Breuer's hypnotic method was, Freud found that he himself was not always able to induce hypnosis in the patient. Furthermore, the patient frequently relapsed which Freud attributed to the lack of depth in the hypnotic trance. He visited Bernheim and Leibault in France to improve his technique, only to discover that these two doctors felt similar limitations. They also, like himself, were more successful with poor and uneducated patients than with the educated middle-class.

The four cases that Freud presented in *Studies in Hysteria* enable us to trace the evolution of his technique. We see the steps he took to substitute for hypnosis when the tecnhique proved ineffective. In fact he gradually gave up his attempts to "put patients under" and urged them to concentrate on a particular symptom. The abandonment of hypnosis brought new insights into mental processes. He became aware of the presence of an obstacle: the patients' own resistance to treatment, their reluctance to cooperate in their own therapy. "One gets the impression of a demon striving not to come to the light of day because he knows that will be his end."[1]

It is always interesting to read Freud's writing; his case studies read like novels. His first case was Frau Emmy von N., reputed to be the wealthiest woman in Europe.

> On May 1, 1889, I took on the case of a lady of about forty years of age....
>
> This lady, when I first saw her, was lying on a sofa bed with her head resting on a leather cushion. She still looked young and had finely-cut features, full of character. Her face bore a strained and painful expression, her eyelids were drawn together and her eyes cast down.... She kept her fingers, which exhibited a ceaseless agitation resembling athetosis, tightly clasped together....
>
> What she told me was perfectly coherent and revealed an unusual degree of education and intelligence. This made it seem all the more strange when every two or three minutes she suddenly broke off, contorted her face into an expression of horror and disgust....
>
> She clenched and unclenched her hand sev-

> eral times. "Keep still!-Don't say anything!-Don't touch me!-Supposing a creature like that was in the bed! Only think, when it's unpacked! There's a dead rat in among them-one that's been gn-aw-aw-ed at!"
>
> (Studies in Hysteria, 1893, S.E. II p. 48-51)

Elisabeth von N. was married to a business man who had accumulated a fortune. At the time of the marriage he was sixty-five years of age, his bride was twenty-three. Four years later he died. When the children of his first wife discovered that he had left his entire estate to Elisabeth, they accused her of poisoning their father. The body was disinterred, an autopsy performed, and the young widow exonerated. Fifteen years later she came to Vienna for treatment with Breuer. Her symptoms included facial tics, stammering, and delusions. Breuer worked with her for six weeks and then referred her to Freud. After seven weeks with Freud she went home, reportedly very much improved. Then a year later she returned to Vienna for a second treatment which was to last two months. Once again her symptoms disappeared but again only temporarily.

> The therapeutic success on the whole was considerable; but it was not a lasting one. The patient's tendency to fall ill in a similar way under the impact of fresh trauma was not got rid of. Anyone who wanted to undertake the definitive cure of a case of hysteria such as this would have to enter more thoroughly into the complex of phenomena than I attempted to do.
>
> (Hysteria p. 101)

Frau Emmy von N. was a good example of how hysteria is quite compatible with an unblemished character and a respected mode of life, whatever the doctors might say of "malingering."

> The woman we came to know was an admirable one. The moral seriousness with which she viewed her duties, her intelligence and energy, which were no less than a man's, and her high degree of education and love of truth impressed both of us greatly; while her benevolent care for the welfare of all her dependents, her humility of mind and the refinement of her manners revealed her qualities as a true lady as well. To describe such a woman as a "degenerate" would be to distort the meaning of that word out of all recognition.
>
> (Hysteria p. 103-104)

The above statement was the answer of Breuer and Freud to the prevailing medical concept that hysteria is the result of a "genetic degeneracy."

---

[1]Jones, Vol. 1, 275)

An investigation of the resistance itself, rather than any attempt to shout it down or suggest it away, led Freud straight into the then uncharted world of the mind. He was to spend the rest of his life exploring that strange territory.

His work on clinical psychopathology, the neurosis and the psychosis, is fascinating and important, but his interest went far beyond curing the sick. He sought a comprehensive theory of neurosis, and beyond that he hoped to throw light on how the mind worked, its structure and its function in general. There lay his genius. Whereas others regarded neuroses merely as diseases, or abnormalities, Freud saw that they represented a variety of mental functioning and opened the way to the deepest layers of the "mind," of all minds.

Freud's fourth case in the book was resistant to hypnosis; the case of Fraulein Elisabeth was the first in which he dispensed entirely with hypnotism and used the new "concentration" technique.

This was the method. The patient would be asked to lie down, close her eyes, and concentrate on a particular symptom. If nothing were forthcoming, Freud would press her forehead with his hand and assure her that thoughts and memories would come. On realizing that patients censor their thoughts, Freud issued a strict injunction that no matter how irrelevant, trivial, or unpleasant the thought might be, there was to be no censorship. This was the first step toward the "free association method." On one occasion, Frl. Elisabeth expressed annoyance at his interrupting her with his questions. Freud took the hint and another step was taken toward free association, the methods psychoanalysis employs today.

It was not however until four years later, that Freud finally renounced hypnotism as a viable technique, and came to rely entirely upon free association. Deeply imbued as he was in the Helmholtz school of causality and determinism, he believed that mental events follow the same laws as all other events, and that therefore the "free association" were not accidental. They followed rather the laws of cause and effect; but in this case the cause was unconscious. Today's psychoanalysts still adhere to this principle.

From the very first Freud detected an unwillingness on the part of the patient to reveal memories that were unpleasant or painful. This unwillingness he called resistance, and he soon connected it with repression: thoughts blocked from the conscious mind. *Repressed memories were replaced by symptoms.* Both resistance and repression are theoretical inferences drawn from direct observation of many patients.

At this time in medical history, a hereditary predisposition was considered a necessary aspect of illness, particularly mental illness. However in Freud's efforts to trace the patient's memories back to the origin of the symptom or the "traumatic event," he noted that the patients didn't stop there, but insisted on going much further back into childhood itself. He soon realized that early experiences, with or without heredity, were a fundamental part of predisposition. The importance of this formulation is not to be overlooked. If hereditary factors were of prime importance in the formation of a neurosis, what development could one hope for in the study of the disease?

Freud's researches terminated Charcot's theory of heredity as the basis for neurosis. Neurotic behavior was not just tissue change in the neurologic system, but the product of repression. Thoughts and feelings not available to the conscious mind found expression in neurotic symptoms and behavior. The task was to study these complex mental processes.

Freud also noted that a striking number of significant memories concerned sexual experiences. He was astonished. He had not been prepared for this, and it left him uncomfortable. Neverthteles, he turned his attention resolutely in this dubious direction and explored his patient's sexual activities. With what consequences? His practice, his income, and his reputation took a sharp drop. Once more his public image was dragged through the mud of Vienna.

Yet, when studying Freud's "sexual" writings, one gets the impression of an almost puritanical detachment. He seems to display little personal interest in what is to many an engrossing topic. Indeed, he seems almost naive. He is genuinely surprised that his discoveries meet with a cold reception.

> I did not at first perceive the peculiar nature of what I had discovered. I unhesitatingly sacrificed my growing popularity as a doctor, and the increase in attendance during my consulting hours, by making a systematic enquiry into the sexual factors involved in the causation of my patients' neuroses; and this brought me a great many new facts which finally confirmed my conviction of the practical importance of the sexual factor. I innocently addressed a meeting of the Vienna Society for Psychiatry and Neurology with Krafft-Ebing in the chair, expecting that the material losses I had willingly undergone would be made up for by the interest and recognition of my colleagues. I treated my discoveries as ordinary contributions to science and hoped they would be received in the same spirit. But the silence which my communications met with, the void which formed itself about me, the hints that were conveyed to me, gradually made me realize that assertions on the part played by sexuality in the aetiology of the neuroses cannot count upon meeting with the same kind of treatment as other communications. I understood that from now onwards I was one of these who have disturbed the "sleep of the world" as Hebbel says, and that I could not reckon upon objectivity and tolerance. Since, however, my conviction of the general accuracy of my observations and conclusions grew even stronger.... the outcome of the situation could not be in doubt. I made up my mind to believe that it had been my fortune to discover some particularly important facts and connections, and I was prepared to accept the fate that sometimes accompanies such discoveries.
>
> (A History of the Psychoanalytic Movement, 1914, S.E. XIV, p. 21)

But Freud was sure that he was on to something important, and an accumulation of information about the role played by sexual factors in pathology increased his conviction. Breuer had once remarked about the neurotic behavior of one of his patients that such matters were always related to the marriage bed. Also, Freud had once overheard Charcot exclaim to his assistant that certain nervous disorders were always a question of "la chose genitale." Again, when he was a young medical student, Chrobak, "perhaps the most distinguished of the Viennese physicians," reporting on a patient whose husband was impotent, said that the only cure cannot be prescribed: "repeated doses of a normal penis."

> There was some consolation for the bad reception accorded to my contention of a sexual aetiology in the neuroses, even by my intimate circle of friends—for a vacuum formed itself about my person.... The idea for which I was being made responsible had by no means originated with me. It had been imparted to me by three people whose opinion had commanded my deepest respect.... Two of them later denied having done so when I reminded them of the fact, the third, the great Charcot, would probably have done the same if it had been granted to me to see him again.
> (Ibid. p. 12)

Freud says that at the time he was shocked at these cynical remarks, but did not take them seriously and forgot about it.

> I have not, of course, disclosed the illustrious parentage of this scandalous idea in order to saddle other people with the responsibility of it. I am well aware that it is one thing to give utterence to an idea once or twice in the form of a passing *apercu,* and quite another to mean it seriously—to take it literally and pursue it in the face of every contradictory detail and win it a place among accepted truths. It is the difference between a casual flirtation and a legal marriage with all its duties and difficulties.
> (Ibid. p. 15)

Freud maintained that whenever a thorough investigation of a patient was carried out, sexual aetiological factors would be found. Further, that when sexual tension arising in the body finds insufficient discharge and gratification, the tension is transformed into anxiety. One can see the bias of his early training. He was still thinking in terms of physical energies as explanations for everything. Freud was not to change this theory of anxiety until thirty years later.

CHAPTER XII

A Modest Proposal

After four years of research with patients regarding the importance of sexual factors in neuroses, Freud published *Neuro-Psychoses of Defense* (1894 S.E. III). He presented his ideas modestly. In hysteric patients, particularly in women, there are sexual thoughts and sensations that the woman herself finds unacceptable. She tries to repress them and if the repression is unsuccessful, a symptom is formed.

Why did the above diagnosis cause a furor? Why did it appear so revolutionary? What was the conventional medical approach to cases of this kind at that time?

As recently as the early nineteenth century, medical theory was comparatively undeveloped. For example, the role of germs in causing disease had yet to find its way into common medical practice. The sick were kept in dark, poorly ventilated rooms in order to avoid ''drafts.'' Moisture, air, and water were regarded as sources of disease; even fresh drinking water was frequently withheld from patients. Also, although doctors knew that blood circulated, they didn't know why. (Miguel Servetus, who discovered the pulmonary circulation of blood, was burned at the stake!) ''Healers'' and midwives were as popular as physicians and, too often, just as effective. The midwife or the healer was usually a member of the community who earned his or her real living as a farmer, boot maker, and so forth. The physician, on the other hand, practiced his profession full-time. He depended on his practice for a living. Perhaps because of this, his methods were more dramatic and attracted more attention. Healers tended to use herbs, fresh air, sunshine, and diet, while the doctor sought remedies often more powerful than the disease itself. He resorted to enemas, vomiting, leeches, drugs, and bloodletting, not always to the patient's advantage. Eventually, through licensing laws, the medical doctor triumphed over the healers, homeopaths, hydropaths, botanicists, and eclectics. By the middle of the century, the AMA could boast of a membership of 40,000. Women were not welcome in the profession and only a very few courageous, very bright, and determined women managed to overcome the prejudice against them. In the late nineteenth century Harvard Medical College had to dismiss a woman student because the other students threatened to riot if she were a member of their class. In fact women physicians were not accepted for membership in the AMA until 1915.

The same period also saw the rise of a new savior, a new religion: Science. Through the door of science came Darwin's theory of evolution. All scientific theories sooner or later became popularized, enabling prejudice to bend the new ones to their own ends. Popularized Darwinism claimed that everything could be explained by evolution, including society itself. Since man evolved from ''lower'' forms of life, social hierarchy and economic class was said to develop on the basis of ''natural law.'' Popular literature spoke of ''advanced races,'' ''advanced classes,'' ''advanced individuals.'' For the religious, it was understood as part of the ''Divine Plan.''

The scientist himself was, of course, the most advanced evolutionary type, not only intellectually but also morally. As the physician came more and more to be identified as a scientist, his status rose. The medical profession came to assume the responsibility of moral and spiritual as well as physical public health. Science was associated with laboratories and research, and indeed, as medicine became more scientific, the education and training of physicians vastly improved.

Measurement in numbers, science's favorite method, was now at the service of Social Darwinism. Head sizes, cranial proportions, facial features, brain weight were measured and placed on a scale of progress. The conclusions? Whites were superior to Negroes and Males were superior to Females. Within these categories more specific classifications were developed. Northern Europeans were superior to Slavs, Italians, Jews, etc. And, obviously, the rich had better, "more advanced" adaptive mechanisms than the poor. Everything was assigned its place in the natural order of evolution.

> Anthropometry of Race and Sex
> ....Analyses of skull capacity, facial angle, and body dimensions.... support the Caucasian's claim of racial superiority. These early examinations included statistics on women, and evidence amassed from the very beginning tended to relegate the female, with the Negro, to a subordinate position in race and sex development....
>
> Nineteenth-century medical science indicated that women's inferiority was clearly evident in almost every analysis of the brain and its functions....
>
> The remark by Carl Vogt, professor of natural history at the University of Geneva, for example, that the grown-up Negro partakes, as regards his intellectual faculties, of the nature of the child, the female and the senile White....
>
> (*The Physician and Sexuality in Victorian America,* Haller & Haller, W.W. Norton & Co., N.Y., 1974, p. 48-51)

Does one dare consider where a black woman would be placed? According to Darwin, evolution proceeds from the simple to the complex. Formless protozoa evolve into dinosaurs, or beetles, or eventually any known form of life. As the organism becomes biologically more complex there is greater variation, greater differentiation and, more to the point, greater specialization. Specialization was seen as the great design of evolution, a prerequisite for the survival of the fittest. Among the original protozoa there is no sexual distinction. It is only as we ascend the evolutionary ladder and as organisms become biologically more complex, that differences in sexual function emerge. The higher on the scale, the greater the sexual differentiation. And, as civilization and evolution progress, the divergence between the sexes increases. The conclusion? Males were developed to be capable of performing a variety of tasks for the maintenance of life. Females were developed merely to reproduce. The distinctions between different men in society was the product of evolution and natural selection. Women on the other hand were incapable of such differentiation and specialization. Their function, clearly, was to have babies.

> Just as her sexual organs restricted her activities, so they dictated the pattern and purpose of her life. Her reproductive system came to be seen as a sacred trust, one that she must constantly guard in the interest of the race. The uterus, considered the controlling organ in the female body, took on an importance which reduced woman to simply a vessel, an organ bearer.
>
> (Female Complaints. Sarah Stage, W.W. Norton Co. 1979, p. 69)

Dr. M. L. Holbrook, addressing a medical society in 1880 said: ".... it was as if the Almighty in creating the female sex, had taken the uterus and built up a woman around it.[1]

Almost any symptom a woman produced led to a medical attack on the sexual organs. Why? Because, since the ovaries were the controlling organ of the female, any abnormality, from headache to sore feet, might be traced to some ovarian malfunction. If the reproductive organs were the source of the illness, they were the focal point of the treatment.

> .... although not every case went through all four (stages); a manual investigation, leeching, injection and cauterization.... Bennet, a famous English gynecologist.... advocated placing the leeches right on the vulva or the neck of the uterus, although Bennet cautioned the doctor to count them as they dropped off when satiated, lest he "lose" some. Bennet had known adventurous leeches to advance into the cervical cavity of the uterus itself, and he noted, "I think I have scarcely ever seen more acute pain than that experienced by several of my patients under these circumstances.".... the "injections" into the uterus advocated by these doctors. The uterus became a kind of catch-all.... water, milk and water, linseed tea, and "decoction of marshmallow.... tepid or cold" found their way inside of nervous women patients. The final step, performed at this time, one must remember, with no anesthetic but a little opium or alcohol, was cauterization.... in cases of more severe infection, through the use of much stronger hydrate of potassa, or even the "actual cautery," a "white-hot iron" instrument.
>
> (quoted in "For Her Own Good." Ehrenreich & English, Anchor Press, Garden City, N.Y., p. 123)

---

[1]Ibid. p. 69

The above techniques were gradually replaced by a new fad: surgery. The latter part of the nineteenth century saw the advancement of clitoridectomy (removal of the clitoris) as the solution to women's complaints.

Amorous thoughts or just heavy thinking could upset the female physiology. So it became the duty of nineteenth century gynecologists to enter the war between the brain and the uterus for control of the women's character. Each person contained a limited amount of "energy" and the uterus and the brain were in competition for the vital flow. Men for their part were encouraged to side with the brain in the struggle and not to waste their precious seed on excessive marital relations, on masturbation, or on unworthy women. Women for theirs were urged not to think! Not to read! Their vital fluids should be spent to develop the reproductive function and not the brain. In fact, too much mental stimulation could cause damage to the reproductive system and produce babies who were weak, irritable, and inferior.

> Manly pursuits by women, such as higher education, lessened those sexual and maternal instincts so important to the perpetuation of the species. The duties of motherhood were direct rivals of brain work, for they both require for their performance an exclusive and plentiful supply of phosphates.
>
> (Haller, p. 61)

After all, who could argue with scientific terms like phosphates? Who would dare to deprive an unborn child of the most vital nutrients? Who can muster an argument against "nerve molecules," "conductibility of the neurones," "fluid theory," and "molecular perturbation"? What resulted? A widespread use of electrical gadgetry for physical and emotional problems. Take for example the case of 'exhausted sexual organs"...

> One electrode was inserted in the rectum and the other in the urethra.... External applications of electricity were given along.... the nerves connected to the genital organs.... the physician, applying a variety of electrodes, made "frequent use of electric wind" in treating the bankrupt nervous system.

One could dwell on this area of medical history, but the point has been made. The prejudice against women found its full expression in nineteenth century scientific medicine. And the rationalizations for that mysterious prejudice were couched in pseudoscientific terminology.

What does one do when surgery, emetics, leeches, bullying, and all the available means of dealing with women's complaints fail, as for instance in hysteria, where every variety of symptom can be found? The doctors abandoned everything but their punitive attitude. Employ humiliating, painful, and even inhumane techniques, or, better still, do what most respectable doctors did, refuse to treat them at all. Such was the status quo when Freud appeared on the scene.

"If the repression is unsuccessful a symptom is formed" was followed later that year, 1894, by the following pronouncement in an address to the College of

Physicians: "With previously healthy men, an anxiety neurosis is rooted in abstinence; with women it occurs mostly through coitus interruptus."[1] A simple, moderate, direct statement. Direct yes. Simple, moderate? Absolutely not! It's about as moderate as an explosive. He had just said, in black and white, for all the world to hear: Women have sexual feelings! Moreover, women have sexual feelings just like men! What's more, when their men do not satisfy them sexually, they get sick! The doctor form Vienna has just planted a bomb at the very center of the structure of our society.

What is that Dr. Freud trying to do? Upset the community? Undo the mores of our culture? Bring down our civilization? Our moral code is predicated on the belief that only men are sexual. We have a sharp and clear division of labor. Women are confined to the home, the kitchen, and the nursery (or prostitution.) Men are the providers. What does this scourge of humanity think he's doing? Does this pervert intend to make women's sexual feelings legitimate? Something for us to approve? Acceptable? Something must be done to this traitor to civilization. And what, just suppose, if we do accept it? Does that mean that women, young and old, can do what men, young and old, can do? It's much, much too much.

Freud continued modestly: "....every hyseria is founded in repression, always with a sexual content."[2] In his paper he also announced for the first time that the use of hypnosis can be dispensed with in the treatment of neurosis.

Freud had observed that among his newly married patients, where woman tended to be young, her symptoms were often a product of her husband's potency disturbance. Her anxiety was usually caused by a partial arousal and incomplete release, as a result of her husband's premature ejaculation.

Women aged thirty-three to forty-three years, who by this time usually have as many children as they wish for, suffered from attempts to prevent further pregnancies. The practice of coitus interruptus supplied only partial arousal and gratification; they became ill because their need for orgasm was ignored. Freud added that when the husband failed to elicit pleasurable anticipation in his wife, more complex symtomatology occurred. Once again he was assuming that neuroses are acquired, and not inherited, and that they can respond to proper treatment.

Freud was astonished to hear from his women patients that their fathers had molested them in childhood. Small wonder that Breuer had taken flight. Practically everyone else did, too. Freud was finally forced to conclude that in hysteria the cause is a passive sexual experience, a "traumatic seduction," before puberty. This conclusion was based on thirteen fully analysed cases. The critical age was three to four years and the seducation in each case was experienced with indifference or with some degree of disgust and fear. With the obsessional neuroses, of which he cites six fully analysed cases, the predisposing childhood sexual experience was active and pleasurable.

These findings, amplified and with fuller detail, were presented in an address to the Society of Psychiatry and Neurology. According to Freud it was poorly received. "The donkeys gave it an icy reception." Krafft-Ebing, who was in the chair remarked, "It sounds like a scientific fairy tale."[3] It was practically the last paper Freud was to present in Vienna.

---

[1]Jones I, p. 262
[2]Ibid. 262
[3]Aetiology of Hysteria, 1896, S.E. III, p. 189

Freud's belief in the reality of the seductions shows less insight than we are accustomed to expect from him. Where was his scientific skepticism? In all fairness to him it must be remembered that at times one must suspend judgment and adopt an almost naive receptivity in order to see something new. Freud was struck with the fact that the patient would recall an early sexual contact and immediately try to deny it. She would be reluctant to reproduce the early scenes. She would state that she didn't really believe it, even though the material had come up spontaneously. She stressed that she had no "feelings" about the subject, in contrast to her feelings about other forgotten material. Freud wrote, "Now this last attitude on their part seems absolutely decisive. Why should patients assure me so emphatically of their unbelief, if from any motive they had invented the very things that they wish to discredit?"[1] It was not long before Freud found the answer to this question and it proved to be a watershed for psychoanalysis.

Freud's next paper pleads the justification for and the importance of investigating the sex life of neurotic patients. He also makes the first pronouncement concerning infantile sexuality.

> We do entirely wrong to ignore the sexual life of children; in my experience children are capable of all the mental and many of the physical activities. Just as the whole sexual apparatus of man is not comprised in the external genital organs and the two reproductive glands, so his sexual life does not begin only with the onset of puberty, as to casual observation it may appear to do.
>
> (Sexual Aetiology of the Neuroses, 1898, S.E. III, p. 280)

He went on to illustrate some of the consequences traceable to early sexual contact between child and grown-up.

A young man suffered a hysterical paraplegia, a complete paralysis of the lower body, including both legs. His analysis revealed that as a child he had been required to stimulate the genitals of a grown-up woman with his foot. In another case, a woman suffered from anxiety attacks at certain hours of the day and only the presence of a particular sister could calm her. Psychoanalysis solved the riddle. The man who had assaulted her inquired at every visit whether the sister was at home. He feared she would interrupt him.

One of the baffling characteristics of the neurotic is that he or she reacts to innocuous events with seemingly exaggerated emotional behavior. Freud understood that the "hysterial reaction" was relative to an earlier event.

> Or again, let us take the instance of young girl who blames herself most frightfully for having allowed a boy to stroke her hand in secret.... You can, of course, answer the puzzle by pronouncing her an abnormal, eccentrically disposed and

---

[1]Jones I, 264

> over-sensitive person; but you will think differently when analysis shows you that the touching of her hand reminded her of another similar touching, which had happened very early in her childhood and which formed part of a less innocent whole, so that her self-reproaches were actually reproaches about the old occasion.
> (Ibid. p. 218)

Here Freud inserts an observation about men patients. These tend to be more aggressive than women and tend therefore to develop obsessional neuroses rather than hysteria. In obsessional cases the symptoms are "self-reproaches about acts of sexual aggression in childhood.... From this I might conclude that the character of the infantile scenes.... had a determining influence on the choice of the later neurosis."[1]

> I have now come to the end of what I have to say today. Prepared as I am to meet with contradiction and disbelief, I should like to say one thing more in support of my position. Whatever you may think about the conclusions I have come to, I must ask you not to regard them as the fruit of idle speculation. They are based on a laborious individual examination of patients which has in most cases taken up a hundred or more hours of work. What is even more important to me than the value you put on my results is the attention you give to the procedure I have employed. This procedure is new and difficult to handle, but it is nevertheless irreplaceable for scientific and therapeutic purposes... it inspires us with the hope of a new and better understanding of all functional psychical disturbances. I cannot believe that psychiatry will long hold back from making use of this new pathway to knowledge.
> (Ibid., 220-221)

So, a word from Freud the optimist.

There is no mention here of the seduction theory. Something very important must have taken place. Indeed it had: an event unique in human history was in process: Freud's own self-analysis.

Quite unexpectedly in a letter to Fliess he wrote "The great secret of something that in the past few months had gradually dawned on me."

The terrible truth: his whole theory of hysteria was built on something that had never occurred. Most, though not all, of the childhood seductions which the patients had reported NEVER HAPPENED!

> I believed these stories, and consequently supposed that I had discovered the roots of the subse-

[1]Ibid. p. 220

> quent neurosis in these experiences of sexual seduction in childhood. My confidence was strengthened by a few cases in which relations of this kind with a father, uncle, or elder brother had continued up to an age at which memory was to be trusted. If the reader feels inclined to shake his head at my credulity, I cannot altogether blame him; though I may plead that this was at a time when I was intentionally keeping my critical faculty in abeyance so as to preserve an unprejudiced and receptive attitude towards the many novelties which were coming to my notice every day. When, however, I was at last obliged to recognize that these scenes of seduction had never taken place, and that they were only phantasies which my patients had made up or which I myself had perhaps forced on them, I was for some time completely at a loss. My confidence alike in my technique and in its results suffered a severe blow; it could not be disputed that I have arrived at these scenes by a technical method which I considered correct...
> (Autobiography, p. 34)

It was a turning point in his scientific career and a test of his fortitude and integrity. Was the psychological method on which his entire theory rested trustworthy?

In a letter to Fleiss he gave four reasons for questioning his conclusions. First his disappointment with analysis itself, and his inability to bring every case to a proper completion. Secondly, how could he have possibly believed that so many fathers were sexual perverts! Thirdly, and perhaps most importantly, his sudden clear realization that the unconscious could not distinguish between truth and emotional fiction. In the unconscious there is no criterion of reality (later to be known as primary process thinking). Fourthly, that such memories never emerge in the deliria of even the most regressed psychotics.

For four years, on this issue alone, he had been the laughing stock of Vienna. Publicly to renounce his belief in the reality of the seductions and to admit his error, required the ultimate in scientific integrity. The letter to Fliess continues:

> The expectation of lasting fame, the certainty of wealth and complete independence, the thought of travel, of sparing my children the heavy cares that robbed me of my own youth; it was such a fair prospect. All that depended on the problems of hysteria being resolved. Now I can once more resign myself modestly to daily cares and economics.
>
> There follows a poetic, captivating passage:
>
> Tell it not in Gath, publish it not in the streets of Askalon, in the land of the Philistines, but between you and me I have the feeling of a victory rather than a defeat.

80. *A Modest Proposal*

(Fleiss, Sept. 21, 1897)

Not without reason might he feel optimistic: he was now on the verge of exploring the whole scope of infantile sexuality; and his investigation of dream psychology had just begun taking wing.

CHAPTER XIII

■ *Marriage Amortized*

Freud was now ready to take the giant steps towards the study of infantile sexuality and the theory of dreams. He wrote a letter to Fleiss that contained a curious reference:

> My dear Wilhelm 31.10.97
> ....As I have time on my hands, I have decided to take on two cases without fee. That, including my own, makes three analyses which bring in nothing.
>
> My own analysis is going on, and it remains my chief interest.... Also sexual excitation is of no more use to a person like me....
>
> Forgive today's chatter, which is only intended to keep our correspondence alive.
>
> Cordially your
> Sigm.

"Sexual excitation is of no more use to a person like me," it taken literally, could only mean that Freud was practicing abstinence. Earlier correspondence would tend to support this conclusion. To Fleiss (April 19, 1894) "....you are more competent than anyone else to make the differential diagnosis.... The libido has long since been subdued." For the sake of his work the reticent Freud was prepared to reveal more of himself than most men do.

> And here I may be allowed to break off these autobiographical notes. The public has no claim to learn any more of my personal affairs—of my struggles, my disappointments, and my successes. I have in any case been more open and frank in some of my writings (Such as "The Interpretation of Dreams" and "The Psychopathology of Everyday Life") than people usually are who describe their lives for their contemporaries or for posterity. I have had small thanks for it, and from my experience I cannot recommend anyone to follow my example.
>
> (Auto. p. 73)

His sexual life, however, he kept secret. He could withstand the barbs aimed at himself but he was determined to protect his family from any invasion of their privacy.

But no such privacy is possible for a man who is in the process of making his place in history—nor for his family.

Freud was later to write:

> Sexual love is undoubtedly one of the chief things in life, and the union of mental and bodily satisfaction in the enjoyment of love is one of its culminating peaks. Apart from a few queer fanatics, all the world knows this and conducts its life accordingly; science alone is too delicate to admit it.
>
> (Further Recommendations on Technique, 1924 S.E. XII p. 169-70)

Would the same man who wrote this voluntarily refrain from sexual love?

There is no doubt that Martha in his eye had no peer: she was the only woman in Freud's life. During the courtship he had pursued her single-mindedly and with passion. He was possessive and jealous, on occasion forcing Martha to choose between her family and himself. He knew that his doubts about Martha's love for him stemmed entirely from his uncertainty about his own lovableness. He would apologize to her for his doubts but it did not help. Sooner or later jealousy would return with all its torture: "When the memory of your letter to Fritz and our day on the Kahlenberg comes back to me I lose all control of myself, and had I the power to destroy the world, ourselves included, to let it start all over again—even at the risk that it might not create Martha and myself—I would do so without hesitation."[1]

Freud was mad with love.

But, nevertheless, the passionate side of his marriage may have subsided much earlier than with most men. "Indeed we know this in so many words."[2] This quote is from a letter to Freud from Emma Jung.

> Kusnacht, 6 Nov. 1911
>
> My Dear Professor Freud,
>
> Your nice kind letter has relieved me of anxious doubts, for I was afraid that in the end I had done something stupid. Now I am naturally very glad.... for the goodwill you show to all of us...
>
> The second reason was provided by the conversation.... when you told me about your family. You said then that your marriage had long been "amortized," now there was nothing more except to die....
>
> Please don't be angry with me if I venture to speak again about the "manifest content" of your talk....
>
> With warm love and veneration,
> Emma Jung

---

[1]Jones I p. 114
[2]Jones 2 p. 386

What is a marriage that has been amortized? A marriage that no longer yields a profit? The financial term "amortize" becomes clearer if we look at its Latin root: ad-mortis, unattested, dead. And the phrase "nothing more except to die," where does that come from?

In the "The Psychical Mechanism of Forgetfulness" Freud noted the overriding importance that Turks attach to sexual enjoyment.

> Herr, you must know, that if *that* comes to an end then life is of no value.... that this was really true.... I have plenty of evidence, which I need not bring up here, derived from my own self-investigation.
>
> (1898 S.S. p. 292-294)

Throughout their courtship Freud had been unnecessarily anxious about Martha's health. He railed against her kosher diet, he sent her cocaine, he insisted on her taking Blaud's pills and drinking wine; if he kept her up too late he would blame himself the next day. Martha dutifully followed his recommendations. He would often write that she had only two duties: "To keep well and love him."[1]

In the first eight years of their marriage they had six children. Unfortunately, Martha's pregnancies left her ill. Even after the birth of their first child, which went well, Freud wrote "My daughter is flourishing and my wife is slowly getting better."[2] The phlebitis brought me back once more to my wife, who had suffered from thrombosis during one of her pregnancies...."[3] During Martha's sixth pregnancy they planned to name the child Wilhelm (after Fliess) if a son, or Anna (after a family friend), if a daughter. "Wilhelm" or "Anna" is behaving very badly and should see the light in November."[4] "Martha is already suffering pretty badly. I wish it were over."[5]

Freud's concern for Martha's health continued through their courtship, their marriage, indeed, until the very end. His sexual love threatened damage: Martha's health suffered because of his embraces.

One might deduce from Freud's writings that his jealous nature allowed him only with reluctance to share Martha with the children. (The reader may recall his recommendation that the twelve-year-old Fritz Kreissler be throttled.) Considering Freud's low income, which was to provide for a wife, six children, a sister-in-law, and partially at least for a mother and several sisters, it is not surprising that he was not eager to have more children.

Freud's views on coitus interruptus, masturbation, and the condom are set forth in "Sexuality in the Aetiology of the Neuroses" (1898 S.E. III p. 263-287). He considered all such alternatives to naked and direct intercourse as deleterious to the emotional health of both partners.

Condoms, prior to the discovery of the latex process in the early thirties, were

---

[1]Jones I p. 102
[2]Origins p. 52
[3]Dreams p. 118
[4]Origins p. 132
[5]Ibid. p. 134

very clumsy. Perhaps Madame de Sevigne's description, "a gossamer against infection and steel against love" could be applied to them. In "Civilized Sexual Morality" we read:

> As a consequence of this consideration (pregnancy), satisfying sexual intercourse in marriage takes place only for a few years; and we must subtract from this, of course, the intervals of abstention necessitated by regard for the wife's health.... For all the devices hitherto invented for preventing conception impair sexual enjoyment, hurt the fine susceptibilities of both partners and even cause illness. Fear of the consequences of sexual intercourse first brings the married couple's physical affection to an end; and then, as a remoter result, it usually puts a stop as well to the mental sympathy between them, which should have been the successor to their original passionate love.
> (1908 S.E. IX p. 194)

If Freud did renounce sexual pleasure with Martha, he should have received support from one of his own theories: that of sublimation. Sublimation was the process whereby unacceptable drives (pre-oedipal) were transformed into socially acceptable activities. Sublimation was a means of rising above primitive instincts. In "Leonardo da Vinci" he wrote:

> Few details are known about the sexual behaviour of the great artist and scientist, but we may place confidence in the probability that the assertions of his contemporaries were not grossly erroneous. In the light of these traditions, then, he appears as a man whose sexual need and activity were exceptionally reduced, as if a higher aspiration had raised him above the common animal need of mankind.
> (1910 S.S. XI p. 101)

If Freud was able to see a connection between reduced sexuality and creativity and genius, that connection would certainly have appealed to him.

Did Freud's alleged abstinence have a role in the development of his psychoanalytic theory? Probably not—although it is of interest that from the period of his self-analysis (after Martha's sixth pregnancy), he emphasized the traumatic experience as a determinant in neurosis less, and the conflict between natural drives and social restraints more.

Thus the man who "saw sex everywhere," who was associated with the abandonment of civilized restraints on sexual conduct, whom even Pope Paul VI has blamed for our modern sexual licentiousness, may have lived all the mature years of his life in saintly abstinence.

On the other hand, those close to the family have reported that Martha hoped for an early menopause and that soon after the birth of Anna her wish was fulfilled. Martha's menopause apparently occurred prematurely when she was in her late thirties

(Roazen p. 52). And there are indications that Freud's libido was still alive and active. He described a moment when, while reaching for a chair, quite by "accident," he put his arms around the waist of a pretty girl who, at the last moment, had slipped in before him to reach for the same chair. "I naturally got out of the situation as rapidly as it had arisen."[1] He observed that the young woman was very attractive, "aroused a feeling of pleasure" in him, and that his "clumsy movement" was really the expression of a sexual wish from his unconscious. At a meeting of the Vienna Society (1908) he mentioned that he was thinking about writing on the psychology of love but that he had decided to delay the project until his own libido had been extinguished. His first essay "The Psychology of Love" did not appear until two years later. The project was never completed. "The Taboo of Virginity," his last essay, written in 1918, was only the third essay in the series.

The private lives of the historically significant become part of the public domain. Whatever the truth of Freud and Martha's physical relationship was, they keenly disliked being separated from each other, even for a single night. On more than one occasion, during vacations, they shared a tiny room rather than be apart. And in none of Freud's writings is voluntary celibacy offered as a worthwhile goal nor any suggestion made that it represents an admirable sublimation. It would seem that the man who preferred to sleep with his wife, even if the bed were too narrow, had hardly renounced his sensuality or embraced the philosophy of celibacy.

[1]The Psychopathology of Everyday Life 1907 ed. S.E. VI p. 176

CHAPTER XIV

■ *Freud Did It*

Freud was prone to philosophic theorizing, but he didn't trust his intellectual flights. He needed the presence of someone whom he admired, whom he felt close to, who would not ridicule his ideas, and who would both stimulate and enforce scientific thinking. He was dependent on such a person: one who would help him maintain scientific discipline. It was an unusual kind of "dependency." It was not the familiar dependence which results in clinging and weakness, but rather a need for help in controlling imagination, keep it from soaring too high and losing contact with solid scientific ground. He needed a reliable feedback.

There had been the excellent Ernst von Fleischl, the inestimable Ernst Brucke (after whom Freud named a son), and there had been Theodor Meynert. Meynert had given him high hopes that turned to disappointment when Freud got interested in the topic of hysteria and the use of hypnosis. Then there was the brilliant and gentle Breuer, after whose wife he named a daughter. Now there was a vacancy just at a time when his imagination was soaring. Freud complained of the isolation he felt "since the scientific intercourse with Breuer has ceased." The new personality who came now into his life was Wilhelm Fliess.

He appeared to be the perfect collaborator and scientific support for Freud. He was grounded in physiological medicine, and a follower of the Helmholtz school. His goal was to understand biology and medicine in terms of physics and ultimately of mathematics. But beyond this he had a special advantage: far from being apprehensive about sexual matters, he had made them the center of his own work. Freud needed Fliess to listen to his latest findings and theoretical speculations and to pass judgment on them and Fliess did.[1]

The Fliess episode and the story of how the world came to know about it is dramatic. Although Freud destroyed the letters he received from Fliess, Fliess saved everything Freud wrote. After Fliess's death in 1928, his widow sold a packet of private letters, along with scientific notes and manuscripts, to a bookseller in Berlin. She sold them under strict orders that they were not to fall into Freud's hands, because she knew he would destroy them. When the bookseller, Reinhold Stahl, fled to France to escape the Nazis, he offered the documents to Marie Bonaparte who bought them at once for L1001 ($480). She had been a former analysand of Freud and was now his student and a friend of the Freud family. She took them with her to Vienna where she was doing post-graduate work, and spoke of them to Freud. He was indignant about the sale and told her, in the form of a Jewish anecdote, what to do with the documents. It was how to cook a peacock.

---

[1]See Volume I of Ernest Jones's "The Life and Work of Sigmund Freud" for an excellent description of Fliess's theories.

> You first bury it in the earth for a week, and then
> dig it up again.
> And then?
> And then you throw it away.
> (Ibid. 288)

He offered to buy them from her, but she stoutly refused. Before returning to France she deposited them in the Rothschild Bank in Vienna during the winter of 1937-1938, with the intention of studying them on her return the following summer.

Hitler invaded Austria in March, and Marie Bonaparte, fearing that a Jewish bank might be ransacked, went at once to Vienna. Since she was a princess of Greece and Denmark, she was permitted to withdraw the contents of her safe deposit box under the watchful eye of a Gestapo guard. She brought them secretly to Paris and deposited them at the Danish Legation. After the war she sent them to England. The letters survived the final peril of the mines that were still in the English Channel and arrived safely in London. They had been wrapped in waterproof and buoyant material to give them a chance of survival should the ship be blown up en route.

The correspondence both provides important information about Freud's life, and enables us to observe the development of his ideas, at a time when Fliess was his sole public. He had no one else with whom he could discuss his work. Fliess could not have had a very deep comprehension of Freud's theories, but he accepted them, praised them, and encouraged Freud to continue his pursuits. Freud's acceptance of Fliess's mathematical conjectures had to be on the same level since Freud was not well versed in mathematics. Nevertheless, the relationship was of primary importance as it emboldened him to continue his journey across this uncharted universe.

"Know Thyself," the counsel of the Delphic oracle, has always appealed to our best minds. Heraclitus' injunction came closer to reality: "The soul of man is a far country, which cannot be approached or explored."[1] Throughout history men have tried to explore the "far country." Now and then, there have been flashes of insight, but they are mere flickers of light in a void, leaving us as unknowing as we were before.

But Freud did it! He was the first person to explore the inner reaches of his own mind. His experience was unique. He had one advantage over all the philosophers, poets, and writers who had come before him: he was acquainted with and had studied the phenomenon of resistance. What he had learned from his patients about blocking, avoiding, rationalizing, and repressing, he used and applied to himself. The result was one of the most remarkable achievements in human history.

---

[1]Ibid. 319

CHAPTER XV

Even Jacob Freud

Freud's primary interest was to discover how the mind works. His genius lay in his ability to take the particular and see it as a universal. If a patient's mind contained a conscious and an unconscious, then this characterized the mind of everybody, including his own. If all patients revealed a sexual history that went back to early childhood, then everyone had such a sexual history, including himself.

The need to investigate his own mind had been slowly building up and Freud's self-analysis was not the result of a clear, dramatic decision: there was no "aha" experience. The need to study himself emerged out of the ongoing circumstances as a necessity.

Freud's father died at the age of eighty-one in October, 1896. Freud was unexpectedly, painfully, profoundly shaken. One mourns the death of one's father, but a fathers' death at eighty-one years does not usually evoke an extreme emotional reaction in a man of forty. A man who has his own home, a wife, and a family. Freud knew that his reaction to his father's death was out of proportion and therefore neurotic—that is, in proportion to an earlier unconscious event. It was then that it occurred to him to use his own methods of investigation on himself.

There were other matters of the mind to be cleared up too. Since 1893 he had become aware of the improbability of his seduction theory. The number of fathers reported as having made sexual assaults on their children was becoming more and more suspect. Taking notice of hysterical symptoms in his own sisters and brother (but not in himself) would indict even his own father, Jacob Freud. Doubts now pressed and crowded into his mind. How much longer could he postpone the discovery of whether he too had such wishes and feelings?

It is impossible today to appreciate the magnitude of the task of self-analysis. Only one who has undergone psychoanalysis can sense what must have been Freud's feelings as he approached his own unconscious, especially as he was completely on his own, without the help of an objective, well-trained professional. One of his favorite authors had always been Goethe whom he often quoted: "The first and last thing required of genius is love of truth."[1]

In a letter to Fliess he wrote "To describe it in writing is far more difficult than anything else, and besides it is far too extensive.... I cannot give you any idea of the intellectual beauty of the work."[2]

The self-analysis began in July 1897; Freud was forty-one years old. The chief method he relied on was observing and studying the material most readily available—his own dreams. He drew heavily on them for the sources of a book he had begun.

---

[1]Ibid. p. 320

[2]The Origins of Psychoanalysis, 1954, Basic Books N.Y., p. 219

In analyzing and reporting his dreams he exposed himself far more than most men would be willing to do.

Only four months into his analysis he demonstrated his powers of self-criticism. The seduction theory was dead. In the letter to Fliess already referred to he wrote, "Let me tell you straight away the great secret which has been slowly dawning on me in recent months. I no longer believe in my neurotica." Perverse acts by the father was no longer a credible explanation. What really took place?

In analyzing his own current dreams, he had discovered in himself jealousy of his father and sexual passion for his mother. He also grasped that he had projected his own desires onto his father. This made him see at once what a general human characteristic it is. The early suductions of his patients may not have been historical truth, but he saw now that it was a psychological truth. The child's incestuous fantasies were projected onto the father. (Thirty-four years later he would write that prior to the projections onto the father, there were projections onto the mother.)

What a giant step. Psychological truth lay in the patient's fantasies. No concept, before or since, is more important to psychoanalytic theory.

A long-range view reveals how he gradually acquired his insights. What today appears to be obvious was quite obscure then. He, naturally, began his investigations with the conventional sentiment of childhood innocence. Seduction by adults aroused a precocious sexual stimulation in the child victim. This led to Freud's interest in the organic basis of sexual stimulation. For more than four years he believed that a neurotic was one who had been the victim of precocious stimulation by an adult; robbed of innocence, the child developed a neurosis. Normal people did not experience sexual feelings until puberty.

Freud was perplexed that so large a number of fathers made incestuous assaults. Even more incredible, their sexual practices usually focused on the mouth and the anus! It passed belief that so many fathers were perverse, but the information from patients was not to be denied.

Then, finally, Freud discovered the truth of the matter in himself: regardless of what incestuous wishes a parent might feel, the incestuous feelings of children toward their parents (particularly the parent of the opposite sex), and the related fantasies, were what he had to deal with.

Freud saw also that the sexual excitation of early childhood is "pre-genital," the organs concerned were the two alimentary orifices, the mouth and anus.

> My dear Wilhelm:
> My self-analysis is the most important thing I have in hand, and promises to be of greatest value to me, when it is finished.... I have found love of mother and jealousy of the father in my own case, too, and now believe it to be a general phenomenon of early childhood.... If that is the case, the gripping power of Oedipus Rex...becomes intelligible.... The Greek myth seizes on a compulsion which everyone recognizes because he has felt traces of it in himself. Every member of the audience was once a budding Oedipus in phantasy.... The idea has passed through my head that the same thing may lie at the root of Hamlet. I am not thinking of

> Shakespeare's conscious intentions.
> (Ibid. p. 223)

This letter may mark the beginning of a sympathetic relationship between psychoanalysis and the arts. Psychoanalysis was always well received by artists, itellectuals, and scientists (particularly physicists who were at home with the concept of unseen forces), whereas the medical profession at large, which tends to be conservative, rejected it.

Freud's new finding, namely, the importance of fantasies in the life of a neurotic, cannot be over-emphasized. It is a watershed in the maturation of psychoanalysis. The unconscious contains what was and is in the mind of the child. The normal adult preceives and reacts to reality. The neurotic perceives and defends himself from his infantile perception of the world and it is the intrusion of his early belief system that forces him into unrealistic, neurotic behavior.

From then on, Freud examined infantile sexuality from a fresh perspective. Deeper penetration into the dynamics of infantile sexuality was leading to an appreciation of the difference in the experience of males and females.

His relentless pursuit of the truth in himself during analysis did not protect him from the personal pain involved in the exploration of the unconscious. For four or five years, he was subject to the same disturbances that he had observed in his patients—depression, physical symptoms, anxiety and confusion, as well as moments of elation, enthusiasm, and a sense of mastery and growth.

Self-analysis certainly did not cure Freud of all his neurotic characteristics; it was far too incomplete. However, he did emerge from his unique ordeal feeling stronger and more peaceful than before. He said he felt that he could now pursue his work with serenity and composure.

Ernest Jones has written that Freud told him he never ceased analyzing himself; that he put aside the last half-hour of his day for that purpose.

CHAPTER XVI

The Royal Road

The Interpretation of Dreams was published in 1900, when Freud was forty-three years old. He had withheld its publication for five years, feeling that this was his magnum opus, the work by which he would be remembered. "Insight such as this falls to one's lot but once in a lifetime."[1]

General judgment agrees that this is Freud's most original work. It is one of the most solid props of psychoanalysis. The book contains the germs of all his later research, his theories and conclusions. He himself referred to dreams as the "*via regia*" (the royal road) to the unconscious. He held that dreams have meaning, and that the meaning pertains to the dreamer himself.

The first one hundred pages are devoted to a survey of the scientific literature on the problem of dreams. It contains references and suggestions in the fields of mythology, symbolism, education, and literature which have given rise to many special studies. It is a very technical book. Psychoanalyzing dreams requires considerable technical knowledge. For example, distinctions are made between the manifest dream, which is a mechanism, and the latent dream. The "dream work" involves processes like condensation, displacement, symbols, primary process, and so forth. These operations are strikingly similar to the mechanisms that contribute to neurotic symptoms.

Freud noted that patients, while free-associating, would recall dreams and relate to them. After a while it became clear to him that just as daydreams are wish fulfillments, so are night dreams, however distorted. There was also a resemblance to hallucinatory states, which as Meynert had pointed out were also expressions of wishes. The analysis of his own dreams confirmed his theory that the motivation of a dream is the fulfillment of a hidden wish.

Stated very simply, the psychoanalytic theory of dreams is as follows: a conflict or a problem during the day gives rise to a wish for an unconscious, infantile solution. The infantile solution-wish is expressed in a dream that night. Because the solution is regressive, primordial, taboo, it is threatening to the dreamer. Therefore in order to get by the dreamer's censor and not awaken him, it must disguise itself. The "dream work" is responsible for the disguise: the confusion and nonsense within the dream (people flying, the dead speaking, and so on) to prevent the censor from taking it seriously. If the censor is not deceived, the dreamer will feel anxious and wake up, thereby ending the fulfillment of the inadmissible wish. Analyzing a dream is a very technical procedure that attempts to strip off the disguise and reveal the latent, regressive wish. "Dreams contain the psychology of the neuroses in a nutshell."

[1]Preface, Third Edition

> Psycho-analysis, then, has demonstrated the following facts. All dreams have a meaning. Their strangeness is due to distortions that have been made in the expression of their meaning. Their absurdity is deliberate and expresses derision, ridicule and contradiction. Their incoherence is a matter of indifference for their interpretation. The dream is described by us as its "manifest content." In the process of interpreting this we are led to the "latent dream-thoughts," which lie hidden behind the manifest content and which are represented by it. These latent dream-thoughts are no longer strange, incoherent or absurd; they are completely valid constituents of our waking thought.
>
> (The Claims of Psycho-Analysis to Scientific Interest, 1913, S.E. XIII, p. 170)

If dreams have a secret meaning, so do neurotic symptoms. The dream work, the mechanism that the mind employs to deceive the dreamer, was quickly recognized by Freud to be connected to the mechanisms that neurotics employ to support their symptoms.

By this work, psychoanalysis grew from a method of treating hysterics into an exploration of the human mind.

The Oedipus complex, one of the core concepts of psychoanalysis, makes its first appearance in this book. At a particular phase of development (phallic) a child is in love erotically, with the parent of the opposite sex and wishes to eliminate the parent of the same sex. The little boy, fearful of repercussions for his murderous feelings toward his father, and his incestuous feelings toward his mother fears that his guilty member, his penis, will be taken away. He develops castration anxiety, a basic factor in the psychology of males.

The essential substance of the child's passion is to be found in the Greek legend of King Oedipus. Oedipus killed his father and took his mother to wife. That he did so without knowing that they were his parents, represents the acting out of an unconscious wish. Freud never changed his mind about the importance of the Oedipus in the human drama, the nucleus of the neurosis.

At that time, 1900, Freud felt that the little girl's development, although less clear than the boy's, essentially followed the same pattern. She, too, suffered an Oedipus complex; however the repercussion she feared for her incestuous wishes and her hostility to her mother, was not castration, but rejection and abandonment. Freud held this view of parallel development for boys and girls for more than thirty years. Then in 1931, presented with new information about female development, he changed his mind. New data provided by women psychoanalysts enabled him to modify his original theory and bring it closer to observed facts.

Studying the mechanisms and drives that give rise to dreams and symptoms, gave Freud insight into the dynamics of many other things—slips of the tongue, errors, humor, forgetfulness, and in fact, all the mental processes in which a latent wish forces itself upon actual behavior. Throughout his career, when he felt besieged by doubts, he would think about "The Interpretation of Dreams," and feel reassured that his work was valid. He devoted the rest of his life to extending this study in minute detail.

Six hundred copies of the book were printed. It took eight years to sell them. In other words, the book was practically ignored. A Professor Raimann wrote a book to disprove Freud's theories, but didn't bother to read Freud's book because his colleagues assured him it was not worth his time. He concluded: "You see that these sick people have the inclination to unburden their minds. A colleague in this town has used this circumstance to construct a theory about this simple fact so that he can fill his pockets adequately."[1]

[1]Jones I, p. 361

CHAPTER XVII

■ *2467 Mistakes*

The year of the publication *Dreams,* 1900, Freud had had only one new case in eight months. He was paying dearly for his ideas—financially which he could ill afford, but also professionally by being isolated. He himself said that for ten years there was no one at all with whom he could discuss his novel concepts and theories. He referred to this period of his life as "splendid isolation." His only intellectual companions were Minna Bernays, his warm and bright sister-in-law, and Fliess, with whom he corresponded and occasionally met.

Freud's "splendid isolation" refers only to his professional life. He had a wide circle of friends and acquaintances. Saturday nights were religiously devoted to a card game at Professor Konigstein's home. They played *tarock,* an old Viennese game, which usually ran into the wee hours. He gave up chess; there simply was not enough time for both *tarock* and chess. Alternate Tuesday nights were spent at the B'nai B'rith, a Jewish club known for its intellectual, cultural, and social gatherings. In response to their honoring his seventieth birthday he spoke:

> ....In my loneliness I was seized with a longing to find a circle of picked men of high character who would receive me in a friendly spirit in spite of my temerity. Your society was pointed out to me as the place where such men were to be found....
>
> So it was that I became one of you.... There was no question whatever of my convincing you of my new theories; but at a time when no one in Europe listened to me and I still had no disciples even in Vienna, you gave me your kindly attention. You were my first audience....
>
> (Address to the Society of B'nai B'rith, 1926, S.E. XX, p. 273)

Years later the Nazis declared the B'nai B'rith an "underground political group" and used it as a pretext to seize the publishing house (*Verlag*) Freud was associated with.

Freud always enjoyed social companionship. Before his marriage he was part of a group who met regularly at the Cafe Kurzweil for chess, cards, and conversation. They called themselves the *Bund* (Union) and Freud would speak of them as old school companions. They would enjoy strolling accompanied by their girlfriends, or often, sisters.

His closest friend was Ignaz Schonberg. Schonberg was engaged to Martha's sister Minna and they looked forward to becoming a happy quartet. Freud once remarked that the quartet was made up of two good people and two bad people. He and Minna were wild and passionate and wanted their own way and that was bad; Martha and Schonberg were thoroughly lovable and that was good. "That is why we get on better in a crisscross arrangement; why two similar people like Minna and myself don't suit each other specially; why the two good-natured ones don't attract each other."

Schonberg suffered from pulmonary tuberculosis. In April 1884 he took a position in Oxford to assist in the preparation of a Sanskrit Dictionary, but his health deteriorated and he had to leave England after a year. He traveled to Hamburg to see Minna for the last time and break off their engagement; he did not wish to tie her down. Freud's reaction was that he himself would have behaved differently in the situation; that only death would separate him from Martha.

Freud examined him in June, saw that his larynx was already affected and considered his case hopeless. Schonberg died in February 1886. Minna never married.

In regard to Freud's "splendid isolation," perhaps the loneliness of a genius is inevitable. He represents intellectual innovations to an uncomprehending world which, unprepared to accept the new doctrines, feels threatened and hostile. What is left but isolation? In his centenary address commemorating the one hundredth anniversary of the birth of Sigmund Freud, Ernest Jones claimed that Freud's ability to bear loneliness was a measure of his revolutionary originality and the courage necessary for such a quality. Nevertheless, in his "An Autobiographical Study" and in much of his correspondence, it is clear that Freud yearned for recognition and companionship, and when fame finally came to him was delighted. Although living in the center of an academic vacuum such as Vienna, he was compensated throughout his life by many lasting warm and personal friendships with disciples and followers from all over the world. There were many who were deeply devoted to him and whom he deeply appreciated and loved.

In central Europe at that time there was not the general interest in sports and athletics that has grown up since. Freud's main exercise was hiking, particularly on mountains. During his student days his chief pleasure was walking alone. (He was also a good swimmer and he took advantage of every opportunity to swim in lakes or the sea.) Jones mentions a later walking tour in the Harz Mountains with a half-dozen colleagues who were a quarter of a century younger than the sixty-five-year old Freud. "He excelled all of us both in speed and in endurance."[1]

Freud didn't seem to be aware that from the beginning interest in his methods was growing, chiefly in the Anglo-Saxon countries. More and more abstracts of his writings appeared in the psychiatric journals, and, by 1910, there were many reviews, some several hundred pages long. Eventually "The Interpretation of Dreams" was to be translated into English, Russian, Spanish, French, Swedish, Japanese, Hungarian, and Czech.

Freud worked on. He believed that whatever he could discover about the mind of the neurotic would apply to normal people too. He grew interested in how the deeper layers of the mind found expression in fantasy, in neuroses, customs, folklore, legend and myth. As a physician he had to treat patients who were mentally disturb-

---

[1]Ibid. 18

ed, but his interests went far beyond direct medical application. His interests were heterogeneous.

At this time he was still very far from any development as fine as discerning differences in male and female psychology. His focus was on the discovery that everyone has a conscious and an unconscious mind and that emotional and mental difficulties are the result of conflict between the two.

As early as 1898 (August 26), he wrote to Fliess of having "at last grasped a little thing that I have long suspected...." He was referring to ordinary slips of memory, slips of the tongue, the pen, and so forth. It is a curious fact that until then, the concept was unknown in psychology and there was no word for it. He called the phenomena "parapraxis," "faulty function."

Freud was fond of using parapraxis in his lectures. They lent themselves, along with dreams, to the extension of his discoveries from the mentally disturbed to normal mental lives. The material was simple, unobjectionable on the surface, and lay within the experience of every normal person. Common slips of the tongue allowed him to explain easily and simply the fundamental theses established in "Dreams," and demonstrate the existence of the primary and secondary processes of mental functioning. Another fundamental belief of his which could be supported by an examination of everyday errors, was the universal application of determinism to mental phenomena.

In a letter to Fliess he related how he couldn't recall the name of a well-known author. Analysis showed this was not accidental—the repression was determined by personal reasons. The determinants were connected to infantile experiences and the names that occurred to him as substitutes were compromises similar to neurotic symptoms.

He published his findings on errors as *The Psychopathology of Everyday Life.* Its main theme was the influence of unconscious processes on ordinary conscious functions. All errors, slips of the tongue, the pen, forgetting, misplacing things, etc., are a compromise between the intention and a repressed thought. There are occasions when the "unintentional" slip carries an obvious meaning.

A patient reported an embarrassing slip he had made during a dinner party. He had addressed his fiancee by his former girl-friend's name. For a moment everyone at the table was stunned, the patient muttered some lame excuse for his error. His fiancee's dismay showed that she understood the "meaning" of the slip very well. A short time later their engagement was broken and he married his former girlfriend.

Prior to his work, such forgetting and slips of the tongue had no significance, they were merely regarded as part of the absurdity of life. Although dramatists and novelists instinctively use parapraxis as a means of giving us a glimpse into the hero's secret feelings, officialdom was more comfortable with phrases like "confusion of thought," fatigue, or momentary lapse.

To follow Freud in such matters is not difficult, but he warns the reader he is taking a serious step. He is acknowledging nothing less than the existence of unconscious mental processes, which, moreover, are at odds with the conscious ones.

The book explores the problem of determinism versus free will. Freud shows how decisions which seem to be entirely spontaneous and "uncaused" are nevertheless the result of deeper motives outside direct awareness.

In a letter to Fliess (August 27, 1899), referring to his work on his *Dream* book, he had written:

> The psychologists will have enough to rail at in any case, but a thing like this must take its own course. Any attempt to make it better than it is in itself only gives it a forced quality. So it will contain 2,467 mistakes which I shall leave in it....

In the twelfth chapter of *The Psychopathology of Everyday Life,* where he dealt with determinism and superstition, he wrote:

> In a letter to a friend I informed him I had just then finished correcting the proofs of "The Interpretation of Dreams" and did not intend to make any more changes in the work, even if it contains 2,467 mistakes....

Freud was obviously making a rough estimate of the number of mistakes he made in the book and chose any large number at random. Now to show that "certain seemingly unintentional performances prove, if psycho-analytic methods of investigation are applied to them, to have valid motives and to be determined by motives unknown to consciousness"[1], he attempts to discover why he chose the number 2,467.

> I had read in the newspaper that a General E.M. had retired from the post of Master of Ordnance. I should explain that I am interested in this man. While I was serving as a medical officer-cadet he came to the sick quarter one day (he was then a colonel) and said to the medical officer: "You must make me well in a week, because I have some work to do for which the Emperor is waiting." After that episode I decided to follow his career, and lo and behold! now he has reached the end of it, having become Master of Ordnance, and is already (1899) on the retired list....
>
> (Ibid. 242)

He mentioned the newspaper article to Martha who realizing that it was a contemporary of his who was retiring remarked, "Oughtn't you to be on the retired list too, then?" "Heaven forbid" he exclaimed.

Now to connect the two events, the number with the news of the retired General.

> I celebrated my twenty-fourth birthday under military arrest (having been absent without leave).... That gives you the "24" in the 2467. Now take my present age—43—add 24, and you have 67. In other words, in answer to the question whether I meant to retire too, my wish gave me another twenty-four years work. I was obviously annoyed at having failed to get very far myself during the period in which I had followed Colonel

[1]The Psychopathology of Everyday Life, S.E. VI, p. 239

> M's career; yet I was celebrating a kind of triumph over his career being at an end, while I still have everthing in front of me. So one can say with justice that not even the number 2467 which I threw out unthinkingly was without its determinants from the unconscious.
> (Ibid. 243)

By 1901 there were very few analysts but they made up in commitment and devotion what they lacked in numbers. What Freud had done was to erase the line between normal and abnormal mental functioning, and establish that normal behavior may reveal the unconscious. The "Freudians" became a most self-conscious group. One could not pause in conversation, pick up the wrong spoon, or mispronounce a word without being subjected to "analysis." Colleagues knowingly looked at one another if one of their members coughed while another was speaking. " "What did he mean by that?" was the phrase of the day. Analysts "analysed" one another's dreams over coffee and pastry. It was fascinating and it was fun. The spirit of the time was the pursuit of truth.

The Psychopathology of Everyday Life was more favorably received than most of Freud's work. In fact it became probably his most popular book, running through ten editions in his own lifetime, and being translated into twelve languages, including Serbian and Japanese. New examples were added with each edition, so that the last edition stretched out to nearly four times the length of the original one.

CHAPTER XVIII

■ *Like Other Men*

At the turn of the century, Freud's financial straits were as bad as ever. He wrote to Fliess that he had three patients, two of whom he had accepted without a fee. The third was himself. Responsibility for a wife and six children, for his sister-in-law Minna Bernays who had come to live with them after the death of her fiance, for his own mother and sisters, all this left him desperate. His colleagues would not refer patients to him; after all, who could send a lady to someone who employed such questionable methods?

Viennese society was ruled by a snobbery to be found nowhere else. Respect for titles of which there was a whole hierarchy, outweighed any other consideration in social commerce. Hiring anyone who was not a *Privatdocent* was to lower oneself socially, especially in medical circles. In an honest attempt to improve his financial condition, Freud submitted his name for promotion to associate professor. His name did not appear on the annual lists of promotion in 1897, 1898, and 1899. In 1900 all the names submitted were ratified except his. Two reasons account for this: anti-semitism was practically official and would have been reason enough in itself, but in addition, Freud's reputed association with sexual matters was hardly in his favor. After four years of doing little to promote his own cause, he decided to "become like other men" and exert what influence he might have. No doubt his dignified aloofness had given him a private feeling of superiority, but that was a luxury he could no longer afford. On a visit to his old teacher Exner he found that the Minister of Public instruction, Wilhelm von Hartel, was being influenced by someone and that he would have to find a counterinfluence. He turned to an old friend and patient, Elsie Gomperz. It was her husband who, twenty years before, had engaged Freud to translate the John Stuart Mill Essays. He had been a co-professor of philology with von Hartel. Frau Gomperz went to see the Minister who pretended to be ignorant of the subject, made promises, but did nothing further. In the meantime, Frau Marie Ferstel, who was in treatment with Freud, heard of the situation. She at once entered into competition with Frau Gomperz. Baroness Ferstel, whose husband was a diplomat, made sure she met the Minister personally. She learned that he was eager to obtain a painting by Bocklin for the new Modern Gallery in Vienna and the owner of the painting happened to be her aunt. A deal was made: a painting in exchange for an appointment. It took Frau Ferstel three months to wrest the painting from her aunt but finally, at a dinner party, the Minister told the Baroness he wanted her to be the first to hear that he had submitted the necessary document to the Emperor to sign. The next day she rushed into Freud's office with the cry, *"Ich hab's gemacht* (I've done it)."

He wrote to Fliess an amusing account of the bargain:

> dinner at her house that the appointment had gone to the Emperor for signature....
>
> The population is participating extensively.
>
> Congratulations and bouquets are just now raining on me as if His Majesty had officially recognized the role of sexuality, the Council of Ministers had confirmed the importance of dreams, and the necessity of a psychoanalytic treatment of hysteria had been passed in Parliament with a two-thirds majority.
>
> (March 11, 1902)

Acquaintances who had looked away when they passed him on the street now bowed when they saw him, even at a distance. Incredible as it may seem, even his children's schoolmates behaved differently to them and expressed their envy. But the most important thing was that now his age-old concern about his practice and how to earn a living was over. A change for the better had taken place, a turning point in his life. From then on, to the end of his life, he was known simply as *Herr Professor.*

In a letter to Fliess he said that he felt like an ass. Knowing the ways of the world, and particularly of Vienna, he should have taken these steps years ago and spared his family and himself much deprivation.

Freud had to appear before the Emperor to thank him for this symbol of distinction. For the occasion it was necessary to wear his military service medal and it had long been lost. So his friend Herzig lent him his, but warned him that the moment he entered the Audience Chamber the keen-eyed Emperor would call out, "Isn't that Herzig's medal?"[1]

Freud became a professor in 1902, and coincidental with his attaining this status, he found himself more and more surrounded by a band of disciples and followers that eventually grew into an international psychoanalytic association. In addition, while he still was looked upon as a charlatan by his medical colleagues, his ideas were gaining ground among the intellectuals, artists, and scientists of the world.

---

[1]Jones I, 341

CHAPTER XIX

■ *All The Lurid Details*

We have traced the development of Freud's work, following assiduously the chronological events of his life. Now we're in the twentieth century, and it gets harder to be chronological. The biographical material for study is much greater than for the earlier period. There are many eye-witness accounts such as by Freud's family, his pupils, his friends, and there are also some five thousand letters of his correspondence. Furthermore, his writings begin to take many directions: the fields of religion, anthropology, and sociology are now invaded by his thinking.

Self-analysis did not resolve his deepest unconscious conflicts, but it gave him insight and knowledge and it integrated his personality. The result was a mental harmony that enabled him to follow where his curiosity led him and also to face the many stresses that lay ahead.

Freud's intellectual record up to this point is impressive. In the twenty-five years that he had been a professional scientist, he had made noteworthy contributions. Under the influence of Brucke and Meynert, he had done outstanding work in establishing difficult and controversial points in the microscopic anatomy of the brain. But, more importantly, he had made contributions to the theory of evolution by determining how the sensory and spinal nerve ganglia emerge from the central nervous system. Ironically, although he noted the unitary nature of the neurone, which is the foundation of modern neuro-physiology, it was another neurologist, Waldeyer, who coined the name for it and is therefore associated with its discovery. Freud's work on cocaine brought to the attention of the medical profession the value of the drug in medicine.

So it was that, on two occasions, while he was still in his twenties, he narrowly missed fame. His wish to earn a living and marry drove him into private practice as a neurologist. He was not attracted to the work, but in one aspect of it, children's paralysis, he became the leading authority in Europe. Freud's patients were mostly neurotic. After giving up on the conventional therapies of the time he tried hypnosis. A few months later he became bored by this monotonous method and more and more, his interest turned to the meaning and source of his patient's symptoms. Recalling Breuer's account of his cathartic treatment of symptoms, some seven years before, Freud arranged the collaboration of himself and Breuer on "Studies in Hysteria." However, as the sexual aetiology of the neurosis became more apparent, Breuer became resistant and the two friends parted. In spite of his own puritanical leanings, Freud was to discover more and more material to corroborate the role of sexuality in the origins of the neurosis. It was only gradually that he was forced to accept the significance of sexual factors and the extent to which they are buried in our mental life. The essentially incestuous nature of infantile sexuality, and his belief in the reality of his patient's seduction fantasies, brought on a storm of abuse against his work. He was seen as an enemy of civilization itself. Nonetheless, the further Freud went into "The Interpretation of Dreams," the more he recognized the similarity of the mental processes in dreams and in neuroses. Both neuroses and dreams had their origins in early childhood, and both used similar mechanisms.

In a letter to Fliess he mentioned that he had a new patient, a girl of eighteen years. She was to become the famous "Case of Dora," which for discretionary reasons, (her brother was a well-known political figure) Freud did not publish for five years. After eleven weeks Dora had terminated the treatment and Freud told Fliess it was a "fragment of an analysis." When it was published Freud chose that phrase for the title.

"Fragment of an Analysis of a Case of Hysteria" is really a continuation of "The Interpretation of Dreams." The focus is on two dreams which are discussed in such a way that the reader can see clearly the link between the content of the dreams and the patient's symptoms. We now see Freud at work. We are allowed to watch the way he deals with various situations in the analysis, how and when he employs interpretation, and how he works with a patient's dreams. He says that Dora left the treatment because he did not adequately deal with the transference, and a close examination of the case tends to substantiate this view. With his usual frankness, he points out errors he made in technique. It might be added, however, that not only was this case analyzed before the development of techniques to deal with transference, but by the time Dora terminated the treatment all her symptoms had cleared up.

The Dora case reads like a novel, and Freud was to remark how much more complicated life is than art. If he were creating a novel from the material, for reasons of taste he would have omitted some of the disturbing issues, a prerogative that an artist enjoys. Freud however had to report all the lurid details. The story is about two unhappily married couples, one being Dora's parents. We get a detailed picture of sexual intrigues and wife-swapping and an attempt to get eighteen-year-old Dora to stand in for her mother. The other couple Freud called Herr and Frau K. Dora's father and Frau K. established a warm, loving, sexual relationship. Dora and Frau K. enjoyed each other's company and were good friends. Herr K. meantime was enamored of Dora. After paying attention to her for several years, and buying her gifts, he one afternoon declared his love for her and his hope of obtaining a divorce and marrying her. Dora struck him in the face. She raced off into the woods and later complained that Herr K. had behaved improperly, and insisted that the two families stop seeing each other. Angry scenes ensued. Dora's father and uncle accused Herr K. of improprieties which he vehemently denied and Frau K. announced that Dora had no interest in anything but sexual matters. Shortly after the incident of Herr K.'s advances and Dora's hysterical reaction, Dora's parents discovered a suicide note she had written and her father brought her to see Freud.

> No doubt this case history, as I have so far outlined it, does not upon the whole seem worth recording. It is merely a case of "petite hysterie" with the commonest of all somatic and mental symptoms: dyspnoea, tussis nervose, aphonia, and possible migraines, together with depression, hysterical unsociability and a taedium vitae which was probably not entirely genuine....

(Fragment of an Analysis of a Case of Hysteria, 1905 (1901) S.E. VII, p. 24)

Freud's chief object in publishing the case was to show the importance of dream interpretation in analytic treatment. He asserted that unless one had learned the art of dream interpretation, one could not penetrate into the structure of the neurosis. Two dreams are presented and analysed as far as the patient's resistance will permit. The analysis of the dreams disclosed feelings and wishes that Dora had repressed: sexual love for her father, for Herr K., and for Frau K. also. She was of course totally unaware of these feelings. In addition, the dream analysis revealed a very complicated interplay of emotions, especially hostility, disgust, and jealousy.

In a letter to Fliess we read: "Anyhow, it is the most subtle thing I have yet written and will produce an even more horrifying effect than usual. One does one's duty, however, and what one writes is not for the passing day."[1]

Until now (1905), Freud's writings had been quietly ignored or, if they were mentioned, it was with condemnation. But with the appearance of the Dora analysis, the silence ended in a furor. Freud had to be stopped. Imputing to a girl of eighteen years tendencies toward sexual perversion was not to be tolerated. Even more intolerable was the publication of such intimate details about a patient without her permission. Now the public had him; how dare he break the ethical code and reveal a confidence that existed between a patient and her doctor? He was seen as a pervert, a menace to society. "Something must be done about this man."

In his "Prefatory Remarks," Freud had written that he felt awkward about publishing his findings without other workers' checking and testing his conclusions. Whereas until now he had been accused of giving no information about his patients, now he expected to be charged with giving information that ought not be given. "I can resign in advance any possibility of ever removing their objections."[2]

Freud shared the difficulty he felt in presenting this case histories. It it is true that hysterical disorders are the expression of a patient's most secret wishes, then a complete elucidation of a case of hysteria must betray the intimacies revealed to the analyst. But this poses a question: to whom is the analyst responsible? The individual patient? Science? The many other patients who suffer or will some day suffer from the same disorder?

> Thus it becomes the physician's duty to publish what he believes he knows of the causes and structure of hysteria, and it becomes a disgraceful piece of cowardice on his part to neglect doing so, as long as he can avoid causing direct personal injury to the single patient concerned. I think I have taken every precaution to prevent my patient from suffering any such injury.
>
> (Ibid. p. 8)

Dora did not live in Vienna. Furthermore, no one (except Fliess who lived in Berlin) knew she was in treatment with Freud. In addition, he withheld publication

---

[1]Ibid. p.4
[2]Ibid. p.7

until such changes occurred in the patient's life that''...her own interest in the occurrences and psychological events which are to be related here may now have grown faint.''[1]

Actually, Freud waited until Dora married and was a mother. He then nublished the case in a purely scientific and technical periodical which should afford a guarantee against non-professional and unauthorized readers.

Freud let it be known that sexual matters would be discussed with all frankness.

> ....the organs and function of sexual life will be called by their proper names and the pure-minded reader can convince himself from my description that I have not hesitated to converse upon such subjects in such language even with a young woman. Am I then to defend myself upon this score as well?...
>
> And anyone who has hitherto been unwilling to believe that a psychosexual aetiology holds good generally and without exception for hysteria...would do better to suspend his judgment until his work has earned him the right to a conviction.
>
> (Ibid. p. 9-13)

Freud's professional, scientific, and also humane plea for an objective reading of his work did not quiet the critics. Friedlander, a psychiatrist, wrote a scathing review, full of gross misunderstandings, many of them obviously biased. So angry was Friedlander with Freud for discussing sexual matters with an adolescent girl, so busy was he at establishing Freud's wickedness, that he makes an error in favor of his bias. He gives Dora's age as fourteen.

Freud could well remark, ''It rains abuse from Germany.'' Later, he added ''It needs a good stomach.''[2]

The fault of the opposition was not their rejection of psychoanalysis or the decisive way in which they expressed their views: what is unforgivable is their arrogance, their coarseness, and the bad taste of their attacks.

Why were his colleagues so angry? Why was the world outraged? What terrible thing had he said? Simply, that women have sexual feelings! That the repression of their sexual drives gives rise to physical symptoms. And, in this particular case, that an eighteen-year-old woman had heterosexual and homosexual desires in her unconscious, that accounted for her symptoms and her behavior.

Today we can see that the society had to feel threatened by Freud's revelation; their culture and mores were in large measure predicated upon the very denial of female sexuality.

As a postscript it might interest the reader to learn that in 1909, before his break with Freud, Jung expressed his own difficulty with patients dwelling on ''disgusting'' details. He told Ernest Jones that discussing sexual matters with patients made meeting them afterwards very unpleasant. Better to touch on these

---

[1]Ibid. p. 8.

[2]Jones I, p. 118

matters lightly; the patient would understand and the doctor would not have to speak crudely.

CHAPTER XX

■ *The Full Account*

In 1905 Freud published his *Three Essays on the Theory of Sexuality.* A very technical book, it has become one of the pillars of psychoanalysis and along with "Dreams," is his most original and important contribution. In it he set down for the first time all that he had learned about the development of the sexual drive from its beginnings in infancy. Whereas "Dreams" had been hailed as merely preposterous, the *Essays* brought him more opprobrium than any of his other writings. it was considered a shocking attack on the innocence of the nursery. The assertion that children have sexual urges from the time of infancy—urges that undergo a complicated development before they attain the familiar mature form, and further, that the first sexual objects of these children are the parents—all could only be the product of an obscene mind. An attack upon children was unforgivable. Freud was to suffer from such reactions throughout his life. Today were anyone to assert that sexuality does not undergo a process of development, he would be looked upon as naive.

Freud stated that his conclusions were based entirely on his everyday observation of patients and that they are to be regarded only as contributions to a complex subject which needed to be enlarged upon by other disciplines: Sociology, Physiology, and Biology.

He went on to say that since few people can remember much from the first three years of life, the very existence of infantile sexuality has been overlooked. Resistance in adults, lack of observation, distaste, or ignorance, have kept its existence from consciousness. Nevertheless, during these years the child does experience and display very strong and complicated emotions. And how a child experiences any particular stage of development, is a major determinant for his character and mental health. There is a correlation between specific pathology and specific psychosexual stages. Schizophrenia is associated with an arrested development at the early oral stage, melancholia and depression with later oral development, paranoia with late oral and early anal phases, and so forth.

It was Freud who put forward the view, now widely accepted but seeming bizarre at that time, that the infant's erotic sensations undergo a process of development until about the age of four. From four until puberty no psychosexual growth takes place and this phase is called the "latency" period. Freud did not mean that there are no erotic sensations during this period; the fact is that sexual sensations are present during latency but the reproductive function of sex being delayed, the sensations undergo no further development. The pregenital phases are known as oral and anal, which refer to bodily functions that the child experiences as auto-erotic.

The first part of the book deals with deviations of the sex drives. Such practices are often so far removed from any possibility of reproduction or even of genital activity, that their mere existence justifies extending the meaning of the word "sexual" beyond its popular use.

Homosexuality, which Freud preferred to call "inversion," is discussed fully. "It has been found that all human beings are capable of making a homosexual object choice and have in fact made one in their unconscious.[1] Freud insisted on making the reader uncomfortable. If everyone is capable of a homosexual choice and indeed, has made one in his unconscious, is anyone normal? It was very unsettling. His earlier writings had erased the line between crazy and normal in favor of degrees on a continuum. Now he claimed to have evidence that there was no clear line between normal and abnormal sexual behavior—that normal "eccentricities" merge into perversions. And he said this in a professional, objective, unemotional manner. He added that it was mostly perverse sexual wishes that contributed to the formation of a neurosis. This is what he meant by "neuroses are the negative of the perversions." "The conclusion now presents itself to us that there is indeed something innate lying behind the perversions but that it is something innate in everyone."[2]

The problem of acquired or hereditary factors in homosexuàlity are explored, and Freud warned against a tendency to be one-sided in the matter. Most "deviations" are present in a mild form in normal life. They are termed perversions when they are characterized by exclusiveness and fixation.

The focus is on development. Genital maturity is reached only through complex evolutionary changes in the basic features from which the drives emanate from the very beginning of life. Many of the early needs should and do find expression in adult life, for instance, the "forepleasure," which Freud distinguished from "end pleasure," the complete gratification. The early drives are gratified in looking, touching, kissing, hugging, etc.

He examined the significance of these experiences as far as the parents were concerned. Harm can be done if the child is over-stimulated. Since the child has no outlet, over-stimulation may affect sexual attitudes later in life. In discussing the Oedipus complex, he remarked: "Recognition of it has become the shibboleth that distinguishes supporters of psycho-analysis from their opponents."[3] Abberations that may be taking place during the developmental process are manifested in problem behavior and, or, symptoms; in short, pathology.

And so the dynamic that lies behind hysteria and other forms of neurosis turns out to be infantile sexuality. It seemed as though Freud's attack upon the innocence of our children was relentless. He said that his theory of perversion was "only demonstrable in children" and he proceeded to turn his attention in that direction. He examined the course of development of these innate, universal drives, to see whether the outcome would be normal, neurotic, or perverse; and why. No previous work had ever been done on the subject of infantile sexuality; so once again Freud found himself a pioneer, exploring uncharted territory.

Freud examined the sex drive itself. He divided it in two: an aim and an object. The aim is discharge of accumulated tension, which discharge is experienced as pleasurable. The object is that which attracts the organism and elicits the discharge. We are accustomed to think of the object as a member of the opposite sex. However, investigation uncovers a variety of objects. For a considerable number of people the

---

[1]Three Essays on the Theory of Sexuality, 1905, S.E. VII, p. 145

[2]Ibid. p. 171

[3]Ibid. p. 226

object turns out to be a member of the same sex. There are cases in which children are chosen as sex objects. Animals, too, not rarely among rural people, can be objects of sexual intercourse. Moreover, a material object such as a lock of hair, or a shoe, can in some cases evoke sexual discharge.

> The most striking distinction between the erotic life of antiquity and our own no doubt lies in the fact that the ancients laid the stress upon the instinct itself, whereas we emphasize its object. The ancients glorified the instinct and were prepared on its account to honour even an inferior object; while we despise the instinctual activity itself and find excuses for it only in the merits of the object.
> (Ibid. p. 149)

The aim of the drives of course is the same: pleasurable discharge of tension. In the first phase of development the source of the discharge is the mouth. The object is the mother, or more specifically, the breast. Eventually, however, the mother as a whole person is perceived and taken as a love object.

Because at this stage the erotic zone is primarily the mouth it is called the "oral stage." The pleasures that the child enjoys at this time, sucking, being held, being cuddled, being warm, eating, rocking motions, being looked at and admired, and so forth, are known as oral pleasures and form part of the normal human repertoire for sensual gratification.

Oral pleasure yes, but oral eroticism? Should these activities be included under the heading "sexual"?

> I shall take thumb sucking as a sample of the sexual manifestations of childhood.... There is no question of the purpose of this procedure being the taking of nourishment.... even the big toe may be taken as the object upon which this sucking is carried out.... Sensual sucking involves a complete absorption of the attention and leads either to sleep or even to a motor reaction in the nature of an orgasm. Thus we find at this early stage, what holds good all through life, that sexual satisfaction is the best soporific.... Most cases of nervous insomnia can be traced back to lack of sexual satisfaction. It is well known that unscrupulous nurses put crying children to sleep by stroking their genitals.... In the nursery, sucking is often classed along with other kinds of sexual "naughtiness" of children.
> (Ibid. p. 180)

Far from priding himself on his originality Freud sought eagerly for corroboration of his views in the writing of others. In a footnote added in 1920 he observes:

> In 1919, a Dr. Galant published, under the title of *Das Lutscherli,* the confession of a grown-up

> girl who had never given up this infantile sexual activity and who represents the satisfaction to be gained from sucking as something completely analogous to sexual satisfaction, particularly when this is obtained from a lover's kiss. "Not every kiss is equal to a *Lutscherli*—no, not by any means. It is impossible to describe what a lovely feeling goes through your whole body when you suck; you are right away from this world. You are absolutely satisfied, and happy beyond desire. It is a wonderful feeling; you long for nothing but peace—uninterrupted peace. It is just unspeakably lovely: you feel no pain and no sorrow, and ah! you are carried into another world."

The most striking aspect of this sexuality is that it is not directed toward other people, it is auto-erotic. The wish is to renew the original pleasure, sucking at mother's breast. The child's lips are an erotogenic zone. At first erotic activity attaches itself to functions serving the purpose of self-preservation. Later it becomes independent of them.

> No one who has seen a baby sinking back satiated from the breast and falling asleep with flushed cheeks and a blissful smile can escape the reflection that this picture is a prototype of the expression of sexual satisfaction in later life. The need for repeating the sexual satisfaction now becomes detached from the need for taking nourishment.
> (Ibid. p. 182)

Freud, characteristically, emphasizes the uniqueness of each person. He makes clear that it is not every child who sucks in this way. In those children who do, perhaps it is a constitutional factor that contributes to the erotic significance of the labial region. If that persists, these children, when they grow up, will become epicures of kissing. We might anticipate a powerful motive for smoking, drinking, and eating. If however the oral sensuality is repressed, we will have a person who is easily disgusted and may produce hysterical vomiting. "Many of my women patients who suffer from disturbances of eating, globus hystericus, constriction of the throat and vomiting, have indulged energetically in sucking during their childhood."[1]

It is customary to think of character as the result of an interplay between heredity and environment, with particular emphasis on family upbringing. Psychoanalytic investigation discovered that elements of infantile sexuality which cease to be employed in the sexual life of the adult, undergo a transformation into certain character traits. Thus we can speak of oral, anal, and genital sources of character formation.

Intense pleasure in sucking is never completely abandoned but persists during the whole of life under all kinds of disguises. Nevertheless, as the child matures he significantly renounces a portion of his original pleasure in sucking. Analysts know

---

[1]Ibid. p. 182

that every renunciation takes place only on the basis of an exchange.

The stage of teething causes a considerable amount of the pleasure in sucking to be replaced by pleasure in biting. During the same period the child begins to feel ambivalent to external objects and everything it puts into its mouth it tries to bite into pieces. Observation shows that the child takes as much pleasure in his aggressive attitude as he does in his loving one. A displacement of pleasurable sensations to other parts of the body and bodily functions then takes place. Psychosexual development is a gradual process and the oral and anal phases may overlap. Therefore, many character traits can be understood as arising from two different sources; in fact, the destiny of anal eroticism is closely connected with its history in the oral phase.

At the height of the infant's experience with oral pleasure, it is demanded of him that he acquire the social habits of cleanliness. Paradise has ended! From now on he is subjected to social demands and social criticism. The "battle of the pot" has begun. It is always traumatic.

The success of the toilet-training process rests on the gradual strengthening of the anal and urethral sphincter muscles. The action of these muscles is similar to that of the lips in sucking and is modeled after it. The child soon learns that retaining his excretions also gets to be pleasurable. The pleasurable sensations of this process are the foundation of the mental pleasure arising from the retention of every kind of possession. Pleasure in all forms of property is established.

The child has now experienced three kinds of pleasure: taking in, expelling, and the added pleasure in retention. If the relation of these three sources of physical and mental pleasure are kept in favorable balance, an exceedingly important step has been taken in the individual's social development, and in his ability to overcome the ambivalence of his emotional life.

The first and perhaps the most important step however toward attaining normal social and sexual relationships lies in dealing successfully with oral eroticism. Pleasure in sucking is essentially pleasure in taking in, and any divergence from the usual quantity of sucking pleasure can result in disturbances. For instance the child may be insufficiently gratified, or on the contrary may be overindulged in sucking pleasure. In either case the effect will be the same. The child will have difficulty leaving the sucking stage and the pleasure of the next stage will be approached with excessive intensity. The inevitable disappointment in the new stage, which the normal child can overcome, will more readily result in regression to the earlier stage in children whose sucking experience was outside normal limits. Furthermore, the child whose sucking was either disappointed or overindulged, will take pleasure in biting; and the most primitive form of sadism will appear. Such a disturbance of development becomes manifested in pronounced hostility or overdeveloped envy. The formation of character begins under the influence of strong ambivalence.

In certain cases, where the sucking pleasure has been either withheld or overindulged, the entire character seems to be under oral influence. An attitude toward life develops based on an expectation that a kind person will take care of them, as though mother's breast will eternally flow. This unrealistic optimism results in a life of inactivity and passive dependency; they make no real effort and in some cases even disdain any bread-winning activity. By contrast, some children who emerge from their oral phase unimpaired, carry with them a lighthearted conviction that everything will work out well for them. And their optimism does indeed help them achieve their aims.

Again, those who experienced disappointment of oral cravings in the early years often show a melancholic seriousness or even a marked pessimism. Not only is optimistic belief in life absent, but an apprehensive attitude is consistently shown. They expect the worst, and manage to find difficulties in the simplest undertakings. Such a person renounces all ideas of personal success and seeks security in a regular income. We find them among civil servants who choose a modest but secure living and abandon any path that could lead to more success but would incur risk.

One patient, a physician by profession, took a relatively unimportant job examining people who applied for life insurance. In medical school he had shown an aptitude for research, but "It's too risky." Thus his orality, his tendency to seek guarantees of sustenance for life, influenced his choice of work. "They have a good pension plan, Doc."

A middle-aged man related to people in a way that suggested he was always asking for something, either making a modest request or, at times, an aggressive demand. His analyst guessed that those who knew him regarded him as a "leech" and his behavior also expressed an element of cruelty, (suggesting the presence of oral-sadistic qualities). This man had a tendency to be impatient with the presence of other people and yet couldn't stand being alone. He also displayed a compulsive need to give by way of the mouth: he talked incessantly. Analysis revealed that he felt his thoughts were inexhaustible and had unusual value. He related to others by way of oral discharge. Analytic work traced the source of his behavior to a long period of ungratified desire to suck.

In certain neurotics whose character formation belongs to the oral-sadistic stage, the hostile purpose of speech is especially noticeable. In such cases, analysis has shown that speaking is a mild form of aggression, in place of biting and devouring. It serves the purpose of killing the person who is fustrating them. Actually, speaking may be used to express the entire range of instinctual tendencies, hostile or friendly, asocial or social. In some patients, speaking signifies craving as well as attacking and represents every kind of bodily evacuation, including the act of fertilization.

A well-educated man had been told, during the course of his life, that he talked too much. He was surprised, in his analysis, to discover that his compulsive speech represented to him escape from toilet training. He experienced the listener who indulged him as expressing acceptance of his wish to regress and be free of all social constraints.

The varieties that exist within the character formation of the oral neurotic depends upon whether the source is the early or later oral stage, in other words, whether the tendency is to suck or to bite. If the character feature is based on the biting phase, marked symptoms of ambivalence will be found; positive and negative instinctual desires. The character traits based on the earliest stage, sucking, are not yet subject to ambivalence; the desires are still free from the tendency to destroy the object. This lack of ambivalence makes character formations that originate in the earliest stage resemble the formations derived from the final genital stage. This is explicable in that these two phases are the least open to ambivalent feelings.

The orally gratified person is usually bright, sociable, and accessible to new ideas. He tends to identify with the nurturing parent and has an abundance of generosity.

Things are quite different in the oral-sadistic stage. Here we find envy and hostility.

Many oral characters are impatient, restless, and tending to be hasty. Those oral impulses which have escaped social modification may be manifested as an intense interest in food and an inclination to oral perversions.

Pleasure in sucking is pleasure in taking in and when elevated to the intellectual sphere, can have practical significance. Persons with an inclination to observe nature possess the curiosity necessary for a variety of branches of scientific investigation. The scientific personality enables us to appreciate how impulses from different erotic zones must support each other if the most favorable results are to be obtained. Scientific research combines observations with enough tenacity and ability to "digest" the collected facts, and without undue haste, give them back to the world.

It is important to understand that in normal character development, we will find derivatives from all the original instinctual sources combined with one another.

> Sometimes we may feel dismayed in face of the mass of phenomena which meets us in the wide field of human mentality, from the play of children and other typical products of the early activity of phantasy, through the first development of the child's interests and talents, up to the most highly valued achievements of mature human beings and the most extreme individual differentiations. But then we must remember that Freud has given us in the practice and theory of psychoanalysis an instrument with which to investigate this wide subject and to open up the road to infantile sexuality, that inexhaustive source of life.
>
> (Selected Papers of Karl Abraham, Basic Books, N.Y. 1927, p. 406)

The succession of psychosexual stages result from normal physiological and maturational processes. For example, before there can be control of the musculature, mylenization of the nerve fibers has to take place. Freud's interest is in the psychological factors of the process. The next stage is the "anal phase."

CHAPTER XXI

I Will Not

No part of psychoanalytic theory has been subject to as much ridicule as that of anal eroticism. The whole idea that character traits should be connected with the humble anus and the erotic excitability of that lowly organ is grotesque. Critics at the time claimed that Freud's theories were becoming beastly. Ernest Jones has written that he was working at Kraeplin's Psychiatric Clinic in Munich when his colleagues first heard about "anal eroticism"—they broke out into jeers and vied with one another in making obscene remarks.

The anal phase is the most complicated of all the psycho-sexual stages. Because it involves the musculature, it is the organic substructure of a person's character. When Freud published "Character and Anal Erotism," he made no use of his persuasive powers but presented the theme quite bluntly. In his analytical experience, patients who recalled strong sensations of pleasure in the anus during infancy, were apt in later life to develop what he termed the anal triad: stubbornness, orderliness, and miserliness.

That excitations experienced by the infant in the region of the anal canal can lead to certain character traits may seem unbelievable; nevertheless anyone who has seriously studied psychoanalytic psychology can have no doubt about the truth of that very fact.

The erotic zones, the mouth and skin, now spread to include the anus. This usually happens at about one and a half years of age; the child now has muscular control and can regulate the discharge from the bowel. Many children hold back their stool until its accumulation builds up tension which is at once painful and pleasurable. Since the greater the tension, the greater the pleasure at release, the normal process of evacuation may be used for purposes other than simple elimination.

The infant's endeavor to get as much pleasure as possible out of his performance introduces a second aspect: the struggle to control the process. The character trait Freud described as obstinacy now appears. When a baby refuses to empty his bowels until he himself decides, his mother is right when she calls him "naughty." By producing the feces he can express his compliance with parental demands or, by withholding it, his active disobedience. He experiences relationships as essentially submissive-dominant and in that dichotomy lies one of the roots of masochism and sadism. The lowly anus is indeed a factor in character formation.

As he grows older the child may be extremely disobedient or unusually docile if he later develops a reaction-formation against his defiance. Reaction-formation is an unconscious process whereby an unacceptable impulse is repressed and replaced with its opposite—hate with love, activity with passivity, and so on. A woman was overly clean, fussy and stubborn and in analysis discovered that these traits were a defense against her wish to play with feces. She had absorbed her mother's prohibition as "I must be very clean and please her." Another patient was the middle one of three sisters. When she was born her eldest sister was still under one year old and her mother had not quite succeeded in toilet training the older child. She had therefore a double amount of washing imposed on her. Then when the patient was a few months old, her mother became pregnant for a third time. She decided to hasten the training of her second child, so that she would not be too busy when the baby arrived. She forcefully trained her, earlier than usual, and reinforced her words with smacking when necessary. She was pleased with the results: her second child had become a model of cleanliness abnormally early, and was also wonderfully submissive. However when she was grown-up the patient was in such conflict between her conscious attitude of docility and her anger and desire for vengeance that she had difficulty in social situations and in relationships.

There are also character traits that derive from the excretory product itself. One must understand that the primary attitude the infant has to his own fecal material is very positive. He regards his product as part of himself; it's valuable and he feels a strong sense of possession. Eventually he perceives mother's pleasure when he presents her with this part of himself, especially where and when she wants him to. He senses her joy. Indeed it is the first "thing" he gives to her; his first "gift."

In order for the child to be socialized and civilized he has to be taught to experience fecal matter as something disgusting. Prior to training, he will produce and smear his excreta with an expression of pleasure and affection. Adults do not always appreciate this delightful game. The infant has to be taught not to soil itself and its surroundings, and has to be educated to perform at regular times. In this his own feelings are ignored, which he experiences as a narcissistic injury.

The child undergoes a trauma. He has been free to give in to every impulse immediately and absolutely no demands have been made on him. In other words, he has lived entirely by the "pleasure principle." His mere presence is a joy and if he as much as smiles, those around him are delighted. But now a traumatic change takes place. He must face the facts of life: a place for everything and everything in its place. We have entered the phase of toilet training! The pleasure principle no longer exists. You do your duty no matter what you may be feeling. Coming as it does at a time when the child is entirely vulnerable, the impact of the new order cannot be exaggerated. He must conform or perish. His Majesty doesn't know what hit him. His primary narcissism has been injured and forever afterwards, something in him longs for a return to the days before the demands were made, before the conflicts began, before he was cast out of the Garden of Eden.

> Lou Andreas Salome (1916)...has shown how...the first prohibition which a child comes across—the prohibition against getting pleasure from anal activity and its product...must be the first glimpse of an environment hostile to his instinctual impulses...he learns to separate his own entity from this alien one...he carries out the first repression of his possibilities for pleasure. From that time on, what is "anal" remains the symbol for everything that is to be repudiated and excluded from life.
>
> (Essays, p. 187, footnote added 1920)

Although all children are not equally successful in being trained, the majority sooner or later adapt themselves to the demands. When things go well, the child makes a virtue of necessity; he becomes proud of his attainment. Parental praise for "being good" compensates for the primary injury to his narcissism. Indeed analytic investigation has discovered the importance to later sadism of the conflict between the infant and the demands made upon him for cleanliness.

The gratifications in the anal phase are more complex than in the previous stage. Some pleasures are derivative of the act itself, some from the product of the act. Those satisfactions related to control pertain to the act, and may determine how one relates to others later on. The product itself may give rise to an emotional investment in "things." Within normal limits anal pleasure not only lead to feelings of enjoyment, they tend to adapt one to social mores.

But we must proceed cautiously, for nothing is more alien to the minds of normal adults than the unconscious thoughts and feelings associated with the anal phase of psychosexual development.

For example, later, the bowel content comes to acquire the meaning of "baby." How can the mind of a mere child possibly connect the birth of children with feces? The child's earliest belief about the origin of babies is that they come from the mother's abdomen. Children have not yet learned the mystery of semen, so they conclude that the baby comes from eating a particular thing and leaves the body through the same opening that other solid material does, namely, the anus. They feel that in some special way the baby was created out of feces. The germ of truth in this idea is that the body can create only two solid things—feces and children.

Freud found that the pleasure of emptying the bowels is particularly strong in some people. It may be repressed very early in life and the sensations related to the anus deflected in other directions. If the new direction is socially acceptable, we call it "sublimation." Sublimation is a change of the original infantile instinctual aim into a socially acceptable act which thereby avoids damming up instinctual energy and which allows a mature gratification in place of the original infantile pleasure. An example would be found in a person who becomes a physician, thereby sublimating his sadistic strivings into caring for others.

In Freud's anal triad, obstinacy is related to the act itself, whereas cleanliness would seem to refer to the product. But stinginess seems to be instilled by both.

Those infants who postpone the act of defecation as long as possible may later be procrastinators. They compulsively delay what has to be done until the very last moment and then plunge into the task with a desperate intensity. Any interference is keenly resented: "Let me finish" is their slogan.

Women who are afflicted with what is known in German as *hausfraupsychose* (housewife psychosis) allow routine tasks to pile up until an accumulated energy breaks forth into an orgy of cleaning. These outbursts are followed by a marked sense of satisfaction and then succeeded by another period of inactivity. With this type there is considerable variation of the two phases: with some the phase of persistence, thoroughness, and general energy is predominant; whereas with others it is postponement, inactivity, brooding, and delay which may even appear like a temporary paralysis.

Of course these attributes can also be very positive: some tasks require thoroughness and persistence. People who have these attributes often show an extraordinary capacity for getting things done despite apparent obstacles. They are convinced that no one can do things as well as they, or be relied upon to do them properly. They do not make good colleagues and are bad managers, because they are unable to allocate work even though nothing is getting done and the situation is urgent.

"Time is money" and many neurotics worry about wasting time. Only time spent alone and at work seems proper. They cannot tolerate disturbance in their work schedule nor inactivity and "idle pleasure." Ferenczi describes people who exhibit a "Sunday neurosis"; when they are not productive they feel anxious. This type often saves time in small amounts and wastes it on a grand scale. They have been known on occasion to react to interference with outbursts of anger.

The pride and primitive sense of power a child experiences in evacuation, enables us to understand the feelings of helplessness we find in neurotically constipated patients. Their libido has been displaced from the genital to the anal zone and they endure the inhibition of bowel function as though it were genital impotence or frigidity.

To continue with our incredible subject, the two most remarkable symbols for feces are money and children. Naturally everyone who hears this for the first time is shocked. Concerning the money symbol, Freud wrote:

> Wherever the archaic mode of thought has prevailed or still prevails, in the older civilizations, in myths, fairy-tales, superstition, in unconscious thinking, in dreams, and in neuroses, money has been brought into the closest connection with filth. It is well known how the gold with which the devil presented his admirers changed into filth on his departure, and surely the devil is nothing other than the personification of the repressed unconscious impulses...and everyone is familiar with the figure of the "goose that lays the golden eggs." Indeed, even in ancient Babylonia gold was regarded as the dung of hell.
>
> (Quoted by Jones, Papers on Psychoanalysis London, 1950, 425)

Freud offers the opinion that the association of money with feces is the association of opposites, between the most valuable substance that man possesses and the least valuable. There is an even more direct link. The infant retains his sense of the value of his product and attaches it to money even though the primary feeling of pleasure and pride has been turned into its opposite, disgust and loathing.

Popular expressions point to the same association. We speak of a "filthy miser," "he's loaded," "he's rolling in it," "he smells of money," and so on. Examples from literature are endless: "I hate equality on a money basis. It is the equality of dirt."[1] Even Milton in "Paradise Lost" refers to "grooms besmear'd with gold."

Sandor Ferenczi in a brilliant paper, "The Ontogenesis of the Interest in Money,"[2] presents in detail the stages a child passes through from the original idea

---

[1]D.H. Lawrence, The Rainbow, 1915 p. 431

[2]Sex in Psychoanalysis, Basic Books, Inc. 1950, 333

of excrement to the remote one of money. The child first represses his attraction to the smell of his product and plays with something similar but ordorless: mud pies. He still clings to moisture, stickiness, and consistency. From this he passes on to sand. Cleaner and dryer; nevertheless he takes great pleasure in filling sand holes with water. Next, hardness replaces consistency. He collects pebbles, then artificial objects like marbles and buttons. Then, something purer: money; shining coins with their bright color and clinking sounds. Finally, even paper money signifies anything of value. A curious copro-symbol is one's last will and testament. The association is that something of exceptional value and importance is being left behind.

One of the most typical anal character traits is parsimony. There are cases in which the connection between the need to retain feces and habitual thriftiness is clear. A very rich but frugal businessman used to tell his children that they should retain their feces as long as possible in order to extract every bit of nutrition out of what they ate. He was known to be penny-wise and dollar-foolish.

A patient who was quite well-to-do complained of the cost of laundry. In order to diminish her laundry bill she would not change her underclothing more than she felt was absolutely necessary. Consciously she disliked parting with money, but unconsciously she discovered she disliked parting with bodily dirt. When "forced to do so, she would react with extreme annoyance.

Some neurotics limit their parsimony or avarice to certain kinds of expenditures and are surprisingly liberal in other respects. For example, one patient would avoid spending money on anything that "didn't last." He practically refused to attend the theater, to travel, to entertain, and so on, because they were "passing things" and "you had nothing to show for it." This same man did not hesitate to buy his wife jewelry and other finery.

There is a perversion characterized by an impulse to stain or contaminate. This compulsion leads to defiling people by throwing ink or other chemicals over them. The same tendency makes uneducated people carve or write their names on something beautiful and thereby injure it. The sublimation or the positive manifestation of the wish to smear? An interest in painting, art, and printing—in other words, leaving one's mark on some substance.

The libidinal overemphasis on possession explains the difficulties of those patients who cannot separate themselves from objects of all kinds, even those without monetary value or practical use. Under the pretext of possible future use, they collect in the attic all sorts of broken objects. Sooner or later they will get rid of the whole lot at once, after which they feel relieved.

All collectors are basically analerotic. They take a special pleasure in surveying their possessions. Closely related are those who enjoy looking at their own mental creations such as letters, manuscripts, and completed works of all kinds. The origin of this tendency is looking at one's own feces. This ever-new source of pleasure is, in some neurotics, an irresistible compulsion. The sublimation of this complex is the fond care lavished on a given collection in museums and libraries.

Extravagance and generosity, the opposite of parsimony, can be another anal trait. A young woman would spend her entire salary within a few days. When dining with friends she would pick up the check despite their protests, buy expensive gifts and clothes and so on until her money account was depleted. During the next two weeks she behaved sensibly. In analysis she recalled suffering from constipation at about five years of age. It was a cause for concern in the family, a time of enemas, but she remembered that both she and her mother would feel good after she had a large movement and was "empty." After analysis she still tended to be generous but without the self-destructive compulsion to give away her money and "be empty."

If "dirt is matter in the wrong place," then if it is in the right place, presumably, it is no longer dirt. When this thinking is exaggerated into neurotic compulsion there is a restlessness and an uncontrollable need to arrange various objects in a room until everything is exactly in its "right place." Such people are intolerant of any disorder. A patient was incapable of conducting an ordinary conversation if she noticed that a picture was slightly askew. A useful development of this may be seen in those who have a high capacity for organization.

Orderliness is one of the characteristics of the anal triad; it's an extension of cleanliness. We find that the conduct of our patients with regard to cleanliness and order is just as contradictory as it is with spending money. They may be well groomed on the outside but their underclothing and the covered parts of their body are dirty. These same people may maintain scrupulous order in their homes. For example, on the desk every object will be carefully and neatly placed. On the other hand, the drawers of the desk will be a mess.

Neurotic orderliness transferred to the field of thought commonly leads to pedantry with an emphasis on definitions and exactitude that results in boredom for the listener. The valuable variety of this trait would be a "dislike for muddled thinking" and an appreciation of lucidity of thought. Such persons can make matters quite clear and they make good teachers.

What are we to say about those people who have a tendency to be occupied with the reverse side of various things and situations? Also, what about those who are "different" in that they wear clothes that are dissimilar from the prevailing fashion, or work when others play? And of course there are those whose eating habits are "different." Duke Ellington was said to order dessert before the rest of dinner: "I love ice cream and I want it before I get full on that other stuff."

The appreciation that the libido from the genital may be displaced to the anal zone may enable us to understand the behavior of many people who are considered eccentric.

> The anal character sometimes seems to stamp itself on the physiognomy of its possessor. It seems particularly to show itself in a morose expression. Persons who are deprived of normal genital gratifications tend to surliness as a rule.
>
> (Ibid. 301)

Karl Abraham goes on to say that many of these people give the impression that they are constantly sniffing at something. This introduces a phenomenon which we will not explore, namely, the infant's interest in his production of intestinal gas and its psychological derivatives.

The phenomenon of anal eroticism is nothing less than incredible and limitless. The psychological richness of the second psychosexual stage will never be exhausted.

The publication of "Character and Anal Erotism" (1908) increased the contempt in which Freud was held. Since then research has established the correlation between the anal phase and the formation of character. The data pertaining to this stage has become immense. Diagnosis and treatment of neurotic forms of anal eroticism make up a large share of psychoanalytic literature and go far beyond the scope of this account.

CHAPTER XXII

■ *My Love, My Enemy, My Fate*

The Genital or Oedipal is the next and final psychosexual stage. The child's erotic life has up till now consisted of himself and one other: mother (or a mother surrogate). From his point of view they are a perfect couple. Undoubtedly she has everything he needs. He's past three years old now and his awareness of others is more developed. He knows he has a rival: father. In fact he's "put down" every night while his beloved goes off with that stranger. He finds himself in a triangle. Furthermore his erotic zones now include the penis. His wish? To get rid of his competition and contact mother with his new libidinally charged member.

The little girl in the Oedipus phase is in the same situation: attraction to the parent of the opposite sex and a wish to remove the parent of the same gender.

Until now there has been no apparent difference in the libidinal development of boys and girls. But, we have now stumbled on a very puzzling difference. In the oral and anal stages mother was the love object. Now we see that the girl has turned from mother to father. How did it happen? When? Are we sure she prefers father? Sometimes it would seem obvious that she needs mother. Father? Mother? What does the little girl want?

This question is not directed to a normal woman. Rather, we are addressing what is in the mind of a very young child: what is in the mind of the unconscious.

Freud discovered that there are, in fact, two principles of mental functioning: "primary process" and "secondary process." "Primary process" refers to the first stages of mental life before the development of the sense of reality. Such thinking is characterized by the absence of logic, reality, coherence. Dreams are examples of primary process: one may fly in a dream or appear naked in public, and so on. Contradictions may exist side by side; none of it makes sense; it is non-sense. One of Freud's most far-reaching discoveries is that the unconscious is governed by the primary process.

Secondary-process thinking is logical, oriented to reality, and belongs to later stages of development. One of Freud's not-so-pleasant messages is that human thought contains both modes: primary and secondary, two systems in conflict. (If, after childhood, primary process tends to dominate one's thinking, severe pathology is the result.)

The genital phase for the male is relatively simple. He has only one genital organ, the penis, and his love object is still the mother. He continues to wish to undo the separation and join her in eternal bliss. The intensity and the sublime aim of his drive results in a mighty, almost mystical overevaluation of his connecting link to her, his male member. He cannot conceive that a person could exist without one. This conviction is obstinately defended when he finds out that the little girl doesn't have a penis. The discovery can be traumatic, and he must deny what he sees. After all, if she doesn't have one, then he can lose his! His hope and the means to achieve the mystical union with the eternal goddess would be gone. He forms a theory that "women no less than men originally had a penis, but that they lost it by castration. The conviction which is finally reached by males that women have no penis often leads them to an enduringly low opinion of the other sex."[1]

The male develops a castration complex which affects his character, may underlie a neurosis, and in analytic treatment becomes a stubborn resistance.

Freud discovered that in the mind of the child, the purpose of his "instrument" is to undo the separation between him and mother!

> Anxiety of the newborn baby and the anxiety of the infant-in-arms are both conditioned by separation from the mother....
> ....castration anxiety...is also a fear of separation....The high degree of narcissistic value which the penis possesses...is a guarantee to its owner that he can be once more united to his mother—i.e. to a substitute for her—in the act of copulation....It may be added that for a man who is impotent (that is, who is inhibited by the threat of castration) the substitute for copulation is a phantasy of returning into his mother's womb...by using his genital organ to represent him, he is now (in his phantasy) replacing that organ regressively by his whole person.
> (Inhibition, Symptoms and Anxiety S.E. XX p. 138, 1926)

So long as the girl child took her mother as her love object, and strove to undo the separation between them, Freud believed that psychologically there was no difference between boys and girls. However, whereas the male organ is relatively simple, the female genital is complex: it consists of a clitoris and a vagina. Her processes are therefore much more complicated. When she yearns for contact with her love object, which part of her genital comes into play? If she is striving toward mother, we are not surprised when she tells us it's the clitoris that is the active member. But when she longs for the father which member plays the principle role? When she tells us that her fantasy is to have a baby with father, she is talking about her biologically receptive organ, the vagina. What then is the role of the clitoris in the final phase of development? This important question has suffered from popular misunderstanding. When excitement originating in the clitoris extends successfully to include the vaginal orifice, the woman is in the process of entering her final psychological phase. The repression at puberty puts aside her childish masculinity, the exclusiveness of the clitoris as it were, her attention to mother, and predisposes the young woman toward her adult role. In the process she turns to father, the male, the object necessary for the completion of her biological destiny.

In girls puberty is marked by an increase of repression. Freud felt that modesty and shyness resulting from this mechanism presented an especial attraction for men.

---

[1]Essays, p. 195

> What is thus overtaken by repression is a piece of masculine sexuality.... When at last the sexual act is permitted and the clitoris itself becomes excited, it still retains a function: the task, namely, of transmitting the excitation to the adjacent female sexual parts, just as, to use a simile, pine shavings can be kindled in order to set a log of harder wood on fire.
>
> (Ibid. p. 221)

The clitoris is not renounced, or repressed, or made anaesthetic, when the transfer to the vagina takes place. Quite the contrary, it has a most important function to perform, to help incite, sensualize, and sexualize the vagina.

The child wishes to undo the separation between herself and mother, and enjoy a union that once seemed to exist in a dim idyllic past. But what can serve as a bridge to this promised land? It seems that once there was a connection but now it's missing. When finally, the recognition of the anatomical differences between the sexes occurs, she reacts quite differently from the boy. She does not resort to denial. She acknowledges the unwelcome situation.

The male is viewed as bigger, more powerful, and better. She feels inferior and wishes she were a boy. Instead of denial and a castration complex, she experiences envy. In some inexplicable way her connection to mother was taken away from her. She even fantasizes that another one will grow. She suffers from penis envy.

The persistent wish for a magic link, a powerful organ, may later in life play a prominent role in her self-image, her attitude toward sexuality in general, and therefore her character.

Let it be stated outright: penis envy in a woman does not mean that she wishes she were a man. She does not wish to marry a woman and raise a family. The wish to change one's gender goes far beyond the scope and meaning of unconscious envy of the penis. Nor does penis envy imply that she does not like men.

Frustrations and disappointments in the analysand's current life, unconsciously recall similar feelings from the distant past. The patient, like all neurotics, suffers from re-experiencing rather then recollecting. As a child she endured aloneness, frustration, and disappointment. Her longing is to be reunited with mother and her powerlessness to bring it about was sorely felt. Exactly as the boy did, she too uses information that comes later to answer earlier questions. The recognition of the anatomical differences between the sexes affords an answer to the mystery: "It looks like he has what I once had that could connect her and me. Mine must have been taken away. I am being punished. I am not as good as he is. If I had it I would be powerful. I would join her forever and never suffer again." All this lies in the mind of a child, long repressed, long forgotten, unconscious. What men have makes them better than women, all women, mother too! "Mother's is the same as mine, she too lacks a penis, she cannot give me a proper genital."

According to Freud herein lies the dynamic that lets the child take a momentous step in the resolution of her Oedipal complex. The emotional attachment to her original love object, mother, is given up and replaced by identification. The depreciation of females has taken root. The way is paved for turning to father, the bearer of the magic wand.

> The path to the development of femininity now lies open to the girl, to the extent to which it is not restricted by the remains of the pre-Oedipus attachment to her mother which she has surmounted.
>
> (Female Sexuality, p. 239, S.E. XXI 1931)

How ironic that penis envy and the disdainful attitude toward mother should facilitate the adoption of a feminine attitude toward father.

> Renunciation of the penis is not tolerated by the girl without some attempt at compensation. She slips—along the line of a symbolic equation, one might say—from the penis to a baby. Her Oedipus complex culminates in a desire, which is long retained, to receive a baby from her father as a gift—to bear him a child.... It must be admitted, however, that in general our insight into these developmental processes in girls is unsatisfactory, incomplete and vague.
>
> (Dissolution of the Oedipus Complex, p. 178-179 S.E. XIX 1924)

Everyone who undergoes a psychoanalysis discovers the presence of penis envy. In males it invariably take the form of feelings of inadequacy. No man's penis is ever big enough, powerful enough or contains the magic he seeks. The Garden of Eden beckons eternally, but he always fails to reach it: the permanent union never takes place. No matter how "big" a man he becomes, no matter how much money, power, and fame he achieves, he doesn't make it.

There is a substratum of bisexuality that gets reinforced through idenification and adds to the complexity of the genital stage. "If I cannot have mother and everything I need, then I will be her." The little boy suffers from Venus envy. There is the possibility that identification with the mother may lead to homosexuality; however as a rule, Venus envy is not eroticized. Generally, it provides men with the capacity for friendships with men and women, and the ability to be tender and nurturing. There is some suggestion that identification with mother is associated with artistic creativity. Moreover, men who accept this aspect of their character are comfortable with women, enjoy fore-play, and make good lovers.

Analysis reveals in the child thoughts and feelings that at night mother and father gave to each other everything he needed. Why was he left out? Why was he excluded? One day the little boy sees father's penis. The boy never gets over it! The question has been answered. Mother prefers father because he is bigger. The universal solution is to acquire the giant penis by castrating father.

In this stage there is no difference in the psychology of little boys and little girls. Frequent erections of the clitoris enable the girl to understand, without any instruction, the sexual manifestations of the opposite sex: she merely transfers the sensations she has experienced to boys. Indeed her inferences are correct. Both sexes feel the same inferiority in the presence of a superior organ. Freud says that the boy's solution is identification with father. "You may love me too because I'm just like him." The boy knows that he must wait. "When I'm big and powerful I'll

> The path to the development of femininity now lies open to the girl, to the extent to which it is not restricted by the remains of the pre-Oedipus attachment to her mother which she has surmounted.
>
> (Female Sexuality, p. 239, S.E. XXI 1931)

How ironic that penis envy and the disdainful attitude toward mother should facilitate the adoption of a feminine attitude toward father.

> Renunciation of the penis is not tolerated by the girl without some attempt at compensation. She slips—along the line of a symbolic equation, one might say—from the penis to a baby. Her Oedipus complex culminates in a desire, which is long retained, to receive a baby from her father as a gift—to hear him a child.... It must be admitted, however, that in general our insight into these developmental processes in girls is unsatisfactory, incomplete and vague.
>
> (Dissolution of the Oedipus Complex, p. 178-179 S.E. XIX 1924)

Everyone who undergoes a psychoanalysis discovers the presence of penis envy. In males it invariably takes the form of feelings of inadequacy. No man's penis is ever big enough, powerful enough or contains the magic he seeks. The Garden of Eden beckons eternally, but he always fails to reach it: the permanent union never takes place. No matter how "big" a man he becomes, no matter how much money, power, and fame he achieves, he doesn't make it.

There is a substratum of bisexuality that gets reinforced through identification and adds to the complexity of the genital stage. "If I cannot have mother and everything I need, then I will be her." The little boy suffers from Venus envy. There is the possibility that identification with the mother may lead to homosexuality; however as a rule, Venus envy is not eroticized. Generally. it provides men with the capacity for friendships with men and women, and the ability to be tender and nurturing. There is some suggestion that identification with mother is associated with artistic creativity. Moreover, men who accept this aspect of their character are comfortable with women, enjoy fore-play, and make good lovers.

Analysis reveals in the child thoughts and feelings that at night mother and father gave to each other everything he needed. Why was he left out? Why was he excluded? One day the little boy sees father's penis. The boy never gets over it! The question has been answered. Mother prefers father because he is bigger The universal solution is to acquire the giant penis by castrating father.

In this stage there is no difference in the psychology of little boys and little girls. Frequent erections of the clitoris enable the girl to understand, without any instruction, the sexual manifestations of the opposite sex: she merely transfers the sensations she has experienced to boys. Indeed her inferences are correct. Both sexes feel the same inferiority in the presence of a superior organ. Freud says that the boy's solution is identification with father. "You may love me too because I'm just like him." The boy knows that he must wait. "When I'm big and powerful I'll have her."

Our inherent bisexuality, as Freud called it, confuses children and makes them anxious. At the same time that father is the boy's rival, he is attracted to him and mother is a rival. So what does masculine and feminine mean? As stated earlier, Freud had objections to these terms.

> It is essential to understand clearly that the concepts of "masculine" and "feminine" whose meaning seems so unambiguous to ordinary people, are among the most confused that occur in science. It is possible to distinguish at least three uses. "Masculine" and "feminine" are used sometimes in the sense of activity and passivity, sometimes in a biological, and sometimes, again, in a sociological sense.
> (Essays p. 219)

The most serviceable meaning in psychoanalysis is the association of masculine-feminine with active-passive.

> It would appear, therefore, that in both sexes the relative strength of the masculine and feminine sexual dispositions is what determines whether the outcome of the Oedipus situation shall be an identification with the father or with the mother.
> (The Ego and the Id, S.E. XIX 1923, p. 33)

Every individual displays a mixture of characteristics belonging to his own and to the opposite sex.

The task in analysis is to enable the analysand to make conscious what has been repressed. Psychoanalysis has discovered that there is truth in the child's persistence that there was once a connection to paradise: THE UMBILICAL CORD. There you have it. The envied magic penis is a screen for the umbilical cord. Penis envy for men and women proves to be the same: a construct to recreate the past, the time before the separation, the time before the demands, the time of the "pleasure principle," the time before we were cast out of Eden. What was overwhelming to the child, the adult deals with realistically and as simply as possible. The infantile solution gives way to adult judgment.

Infantile sexuality is the foundation of psychoanalytic theory of sexuality, but it was not developed from direct observation of children. Rather, the theory was constructed on the memories and retrospection of adult patients. Freud wished for more direct proof of his theories but the limitation was real: one could not ask a child if he wishes to incorporate his mother, or use his feces as a bridge to her, or submit to father sexually and have a baby from him.

> Surely there must be a possibility of observing in children at first hand and in all the freshness of life the sexual impulses and wishes which we dig out so laboriously in adults from among their own debris—especially as it is also our belief that they

> are the common property of all men, a part of the human constitution, and merely exaggerated or distorted in the case of neurotics.
> (Analysis of a Phobia in a Five-Year-Old Boy, 1909, S.E. X, p. 6)

With this end in view, Freud for many years had been urging his friends and pupils to collect observations of the sexual life of children. Then came a stroke of luck; the opportunity to corroborate directly some of the theory was at hand.

A five-year-old boy had developed a phobia; it was impossible for him to go out of doors for fear that he would be bitten by a horse. (In those days, automobiles were rare; on the other hand, there were hundreds of horses on the streets.) The boy's mother had been in analysis with Freud before she was married, and his father was a physician who had attended Freud's lectures. The situation was practically tailor-made. Freud had one interview with the boy, and the father, with Freud's help, conducted the analysis. It was the first therapeutic application of psychoanalysis to a child, and the first opportunity to check by direct observation some of the conclusions Freud had reached about child development. The case was published as "Analysis of a Phobia in a Five-Year-Old Boy." (1909 S.E. X) "Little Hans" as the case was commonly referred to became famous.

The first reports of Hans show that, although not quite three years old, he had a strikingly lively interest in his penis, which he referred to as his "widdler." His curiosity, his thirst for knowledge, was directed at his parents.

> Hans: Mummy, have you got a widdler too?
>
> Mother: Of course. Why?
>
> Hans: I was only thinking.
>
> (Ibid. p. 7)

At three-and-a -half years, Hans realized that an essential difference between animate and inanimate objects was the presence of a widdler. At the zoo he called out in an excited and joyful voice: "I saw the lion's widdler." later he reflected, "a dog and a horse have widdlers; a table and a chair haven't."[1]

The great event in Hans's life at the time was the birth of his baby sister. He was extremely excited by the new arrival but also jealous. During the first few days after the event, he was taken ill with a sore throat. In his fever he was heard saying, "But I don't want a baby sister." Watching his seven-day-old sister being given a bath, he remarked: "But her widdler's still quite small." Then he added, "When she grows up it will get bigger all right."

Hans's interest in his widdler was not entirely theoretical; as might be expected he was impelled to touch it. When seen masturbating he was threatened with castration by his mother. "If you do that, I shall send for Dr. A. to cut off your widdler."

Another time while his mother was undressing before going to bed, she asked Hans why he was staring.

---

[1]Ibid. p. 7

Hans: "I thought you were so big you'd have a widdler like a horse."[1]

After an attack of influenza, his fear of being bitten by a horse increased so much that he was afraid to leave his house. Hans also expressed the fear that a horse would come into his room. At this time Hans's affection for his mother was quite intense. He repeatedly asked if he could sleep with her and "coax" (caress). (Hans quite unashamedly announced that he masturbated regularly before going to sleep.) Mother would indulge him by taking him into her bed. Hans was a little Oedipus: he wanted his father out of the way so he could sleep with his mother. He repeatedly expressed his wish to marry his beautiful mother and have innumerable children whom he would look after in his own way.

The father used the nonanalytic method of questioning in detail and often had to help the child find the words he was seeking to express. Critics immediately used this to claim that the conclusions reached were due to the father's suggestions. What the critics did not know, and in fact no one knew, was that Freud was conducting an experiment: he deliberately withheld information from the father. Thus, certain connections which Freud had foreseen had not been passed on to the father who had to flounder until the child himself made them clear. There were times, too, when the child brought out important ideas which surprised both Freud and the father.

The case of "Little Hans" runs to about one hundred fifty pages. Hans "seems to be a positive paragon of all the vices." The report is replete with Hans's corroboration of much of what Freud set down in the "Three Essays."

> I arranged with Hans's father that he should tell the boy that all this business about horses was a piece of nonsense and nothing more. The truth was, his father was to say, that he was very fond of his mother and wanted to be taken into her bed.
>
> (Ibid. p. 28)

Freud had the father explain that Hans was afraid of horses because he had taken so much interest in their widdlers. Freud further suggested that the father should enlighten Hans in the matter of anatomical differences.

> The child's past behavior justified us in assuming that his libido was attached to a wish to see his mother's widdler; so I proposed to his father that he should take away this aim from Hans by informing him that his mother and all other female beings (as he could see from Hanna) had no widdler at all. This last piece of enlightenment was to be given him on a suitable occasion when it had been led up to by some question or some chance remark on Hans's part.
>
> (Ibid. p. 28)

The therapeutic results were excellent. The fact that Hans was an attractive,

---

[1]Ibid. p. 10

bright child, basically healthy-minded, no doubt favored the outcome of the treatment. Fourteen years later, Freud enjoyed a most pleasant surprise. A tall, sturdy young man called on him and introduced himself with: "Ich bin der kleiner Hans." He added that he was in perfect health but that he had absolutely no recall of his analysis. He was on his way to America where he did indeed establish a successful career as an opera director in Philadelphia and New York.

The case of "Little Hans" was hailed as an extraordinary insight into the mind of a child. But, oddly enough, Freud's usual alertness deserted him. The brilliant success of the case did not suggest the possibilities of child analysis! He saw the Little Hans case as an exception.

> The treatment itself was carried out by the child's father.... No one else, in my opinion, could possibly have prevailed on the child to make any such avowals; the special knowledge by means of which he was able to interpret the remarks made by his five-year-old son was indispensable, and without it the technical difficulties in the way of conducting a psychoanalysis upon so young a child would have been insuperable. It was only because the authority of a father and of a physician were united in a single person, and because in him both affectionate care and scientific interest were combined, that it was possible in this one instance to apply the method to a use to which it would not otherwise have lent itself.
>
> (Ibid. p. 5)

There is a determinant that transcends the complications of the genital stage and generally leads to a familiar solution to the Oedipus complex. One cannot overstate the primitive qualities of the Oedipal child's passions: his wish to castrate and murder his father, commit incest with his mother, and cannibalistically devour both of them: to take into himself the body and spirit of his idealized love objects. His untamed wish generates his deepest fear: father will castrate him. In fact, the basic constituent in the psychology of males is castration anxiety. "For his wolf phobia had broken out when he found himself faced by the fact that such a thing as castration was possible; and he clearly classed his gonorrhoea as castration."[1] Such precivilized wishes must give way to the process of socialization and be repressed.

The final course of development that is customarily regarded as normal, barring deviations, fixations, and serious neurotic conflicts, is that the person in question "identifies" with the parent of the same sex, and takes the opposite sex for a love object. The aim is sexual union; as though biology must have its way and the species continue.

The human species considers itself unique. We are different from all other forms of life in that we alone have a "conscience." What is a conscience? Where does it come from? For centuries the answer had been "God." The pious consider this higher agent as one of God's masterpieces, something he has placed "within us."

---

[1]An Infantile Neurosis, S.E. XVII p. 100, 1918

Nevertheless, it was not within the child before the resolution of his Oedipus complex. The sexual drive, by contrast, is within us from the beginning of life.

We know that young children do not understand right from wrong. Their drive for pleasure knows no inhibitions; they are amoral and their behavior is guided by parental authority. Given the child's total vulnerability and dependence, he must submit to survive. Fear of parental disapproval is fear of death. From a psychological point of view it would appear that a conscience is a successful internalization of the feared, watchful, loving parent.

The abandonment of the Oedipus complex requires that the child give up his parents as love-objects. As a compensation for this loss, he makes a strong identification with them. The parental agency that observed and evaluated him has become internalized. The Ego now has a judge: a Superego. A moral agency is developing within the mind. In the course of this development the Superego will be influenced by those whom the Ego takes as his ideal models—teachers, outstanding personalities, and so on. The new agency imposes upon us moral restrictions, seeks ever higher standards of performance, and is the representative of the higher aspect of human beings. Not meeting Superego standards makes us feel inferior and guilty. An exploration of why the Superego tends to be so severe led Freud to discover that the Superego is not constructed on the model of the parents, but rather on the parent's Superego.

Since its earliest beginnings, psychoanalysis has been reproached for concentrating upon and emphasizing the animal in man and ignoring the higher side of human nature.

> Very true.... we have the higher nature in the ego ideal or superego.... when we were little children we knew their higher nature, we admired them and feared them; and later we took them into ourselves.
>
> (Ego and Id, S.E. XIX p. 36, 1923)

Thus the values, traditions, and idologies of past peoples live on in the Superego and influence the continuity of past and present. The Superego, heir to the Oedipus complex, plays a profound role in the life of man.

CHAPTER XXIII

■ *Alternate Monologues*

The early years of this century were for Freud a peaceful and successful interlude between the difficulties of the past and the storms that were soon to follow. His professional life was firmly supported by his publications that were to become classics: *The Interpretation of Dreams, The Psychopathology of Everyday Life,* and more recently, *Three Essays on the Theory of Sexuality.* He was emerging from his self-analysis with feelings of confidence, independence of the judgment of others, and a sense of being in harmony with himself. A small group was meeting with him weekly, who soon were to grow into the Vienna Psycho-Analytic Society. And to his great delight, the prestigious Burgholzli Clinic in Switzerland had written that their researches corroborated his theories! In fact, he and psychoanalysis were on the threshold of becoming well known far beyond the limits of Vienna. The years that Wilhelm Fliess called Freud's splendid isolation had gradually come to an end. This period also marked the end of his friendship with Fliess, a friendship that was clearly a reflection of Freud's own neurosis.

That Freud, happily married, with six children, and by then approaching middle age, should have treasured a friendship with someone who was his intellectual inferior, and submitted to that man's judgment and ideas, may have been the most unwonted experience of his life. And no doubt his freeing himself from that relationship by examination of his own unconscious is unique.

The preceding decade had been a time when Freud was particularly vulnerable. He was struggling to build a practice and make a living by the use of controversial methods, methods that were ridiculed by the medical profession. He was able to withstand the social ostracism, but the intellectual isolation was harder to bear. He needed sorely the support of a man of Fliess's stature, who not only did not reject the theory of the role of sexuality in behavior, but made it the basis of his own approach. Fliess was the indispensable friend and collaborator that Freud required.

Fliess did not have the same need. Whereas Freud was striving to establish himself as a practitioner and a provider, Fliess had a successful practice in Berlin. Vienna, at that time, was governed by Burgermeister Karl Leuger, who publicly proclaimed his antisemitism. Later, in "Mein Kampf," Hitler praised him as his memorable teacher. The restricted atmosphere of Vienna was in sharp contrast to the lively and liberal spirit of Berlin. Moreover, Fliess had married a wealthy Viennese woman, a former patient of Breuer's. This provided much occasion to visit Vienna. He fixed his emotional needs on his wife. Indeed, he was so extraordinarily possessive of her that her friends and even her family complained.

Fliess was a man of exceptional scientific knowledge, culture, and self-assurance. The two men had met in the fall of 1887 following Breuer's advice to Fliess to attend the lectures on anatomy and the central nervous system which Freud was giving. Fliess and Freud soon became friends. No doubt Freud was gratified to find that many of Fliess's hypotheses were based on the therapeutic effect of local applications of cocaine, which Freud himself had discovered. That this fascinating man, whom he considered to be superior to himself, should invite and foster a friendship and an exchange of ideas was a blessing. "For me you remain the healer, the prototype of the man into whose hands one confidently entrusts one's life and that of one's family.[1] Freud believed that Fliess was a genius and decided, were he to have another son, he would name him Wilhelm. His next and last child turned out to be his beloved Anna.

Hindsight makes it obvious that his feelings for Fliess were unrealistic. At that time in Vienna, psychoanalysis was considered to be "Jewish," just as in the 1930's in Germany physics was known as the "Jewish Science." That Fliess was also a Jew allowed him and Freud to discuss personal problems, exchange ideas, and connect theories of physiology with psychology. A correspondence began which quickly grew into a personal as well as intellectual exchange.

Both men suffered from migraine and indulged in long discussions concerning the origin and treatment of the condition. Fliess had consulted many specialists in the field. He himself attributed his condition to pathology of the nose and sinuses and he underwent a number of operations, some quite extensive. This worried Freud and he urged him not to subject himself to more surgery. Intimate personal details and concern for each other mingled with their latest hypotheses. Such was their correspondence.

On two occasions Freud suffered from nasal infection and Fliess, who was a rhinologist, a specialist on the nose and throat, performed the necessary surgery. Some time previously an attack of influenza had left Freud with an arhythmia (irregular heartbeat). Fliess attributed the condition to nicotine poisoning and ordered Freud to abstain from smoking. Freud, who averaged about twenty cigars a day, stopped for a while. But soon he flatly refused to take his friend's advice. He maintained that if he could not smoke cigars, he might live longer but he would be miserable.

Freud's letters contain numerous references to his anxieties about sex, money, and his health, anxieties with which he would not burden his wife. A variety of subjects such as politics, the Dreyfus case and Zola's fight for justice, for instance, medieval writings, dramatic art, anthropology, folklore, and so forth, were also touched on. Their letters are written with affection and without fear of criticism. Above all, they document Freud's personal trials with the birth and slow growth of the psychoanalytic theory. Of particular interest is Freud's revelation, drawn from his self-analysis, that after years of profound doubt and bewilderment he was finally forced to abandon his theory of seduction. He announced to Fliess that he no longer considered sexual seduction as the only origin of a neurosis. His new theory, which he maintained for the rest of his life, was that mere fantasies of sexual encounters could produce a neurosis.

Fliess, on his side, had a theory that many illnesses were related to the nose. He discovered that he could remove symptoms like neuralgic pain, headache, menstrual bleeding, difficulties with respiration and digestion by brushing cocaine

---

[1]Schur p. 66

on the mucuous membrane of the nose. He considered the nose to be important for diagnosis and he introduced a new clinical concept: "nasal reflex neurosis." His hope was that Freud's work would corroborate his theories.

Fliess further believed that human behavior, health, and even death were governed by a biological numerology. There was a twenty-eight day feminine cycle, and a twenty-three-day masculine one, which were active in both sexes. The numbers five and fifty-one were factors and he theorized that rhythms were part of a fundamental law that applied to all living things, indeed to the whole universe. The proper understanding of the periodic laws would enable one to predict the date of conception, birth, illness, and death. The arbitrary way in which he juggled numbers and the mystical features in his writings had led subsequent students of his work to regard it as the product of madness. However, science so violates common sense that it is not inconceivable that one day Fliess's work may prove to be valid.

Did Sigmund Freud take Wilhelm Fliess's theories seriously? Yes. At first, aware how bizarre his own theories had sounded, he was sympathetic to and uncritical of Fliess's ideas. He would keep accounts of his own health, moods, and the various events in his life, such as the death of his father, in an attempt to verify the theories of periodicity. He even used the theory to predict the time of his own death. Based on Fliess's calculations, Freud believed that he would die of heart failure when he was fifty-one years old. (He outlived his prediction by thirty-two years.) He also had surgery performed on his nose by his esteemed friend in order to cure his migraine headaches. The results were disappointing.

Every culture has its own idiomatic language which finds expression in jokes, folktales, and superstitions. Freud's European-Jewish background may have made him responsive to Fliess's numerology. He was raised in a tradition that made him feel that he was one of the "people of the Book," the Bible. Among many generations of Jews, the most important class distinction was between the "learned ones," namely, those who studied the Bible, and those who "did not know." A particular belief that is linked to the Bible is that the Hebrew alphabet is both an orthographic and a numerical system. One studies the alphabet not only to master correct spelling and the established usage of words, but also to learn the meaning of numbers. For example, "eighteen" could be spelled like the Hebrew word for "life," and "seventeen" like the Hebrew word for "good." "Fifty-two" could be spelled like "dog" (a bad number), and so forth.

Freud had told Martha that as a boy he had drawn the number seventeen in a lottery that was supposed to reveal one's character, and out came the word "constancy." He and she became engaged on the seventeenth of the month, which he considered a good omen, and for years they celebrated the seventeenth of every month as an anniversary. So, an old Jewish superstition found its way into Freud's feelings; but was he really serious about Fliess's bionumerology?

On one occasion Ernest Jones, who at that time did not know of the friendship between the two men, asked Freud how Fliess would have explained a case of appendicitis where the attacks occurred irregularly. "Freud looked at me half-quizzically and said: 'That wouldn't have bothered Fliess. He was an expert mathematician, and by multiplying twenty-three and twenty-eight by the difference between them and adding or subtracting the results, or by an even more complicated process, he would always arrive at the number he wanted.'"[1] Freud called Fliess the "Kepler

---

[1]Jones I, p. 291

of biology."[1]

In the early stages of their friendship, Freud tended to submit to his gifted friend. For example, on one occasion, Lowenfeld criticized Freud's theory of anxiety neurosis. Freud responded by referring to the multiplicity of factors in a neurosis and their varying strength. Fliess, on the other hand, thought that Freud should have stressed the role of periodic law and he wrote a separate reply to Lowenfeld. Freud passively accepted Fliess's correction. However, it appears that later Freud would humor his friend. For example, Fliess was developing a theory of left-handedness. Freud's hesitancy to accept the ideas was seen by Fliess as showing doubt about his theory of bisexuality which was connected with ideas on left-handedness. He turned on Freud and accused him of being left-handed. Freud replied that for as long as he could remember he had had two left hands, but he always preferred the one on the right. Fliess, who unlike Freud, had married a very wealthy woman, considered Freud's interest in antiquities and archeology an expensive hobby which Freud could not afford. Freud accepted the criticism with his characteristic charm and wit.

Freud and Fliess's correspondence with each other lasted for seventeen years (1887-1904). Unfortunately, we have only the letters to Fliess, not from him. Freud never saved letters. 'I don't know till this very day whether I destroyed them, or only hid them ingeniously."[2] Fliess was apparently lavish with his praise of Freud's work and made suggestions for his writings in matters of style and syntax which were gratefully accepted and put to use. However, since Fliess's letters were not preserved, the degree of his understanding of Freud's ideas is not clear. But his brilliance is undeniable. It was he who came up with the concept that all human beings are bisexual. Freud thought this over and slowly absorbed it into his own theoretical system. Further, Freud gave Fliess credit for having been the first to perceive the link between paranoia and repressed homosexuality.[3] In addition, Freud said it was Fliess who introduced the terms "latency period" and "sublimation." Nevertheless, later it turned out that Fliess no more really understood Freud's work than Freud understood Fliess's mathematical conjectures. However at the time they held each other in highest esteem and gave each other much needed support. So, rather than being dialogues, the talks about their theories were alternate monologues.

Freud was not alone in his admiration of Fliess. Fliess's friends and patients were impressed with the wealth of his knowledge, his lively imagination, and his unflagging confidence in himself. (Note that so sound and sober a scientist as Karl Abraham chose Fliess to be his physician during the terminal phase of his illness.) Even a patient who was a victim of an almost fatal error commited by Fliess remained loyal to him. Emma, a young woman, was in treatment with Freud for what had been diagnosed as hysterical abdominal symptoms. Freud consulted Fliess, as he had done frequently with other cases, and even suggested that Fliess come to Vienna

---

[1]Roberts p. 90

[2]Schur p. 70

[3]Paranoia is a psychosis characterized by delusions of persecution and megalomania. The predominant defense mechanism is projection, thus an internal perception is experienced as coming from without. Freud derived the formula: I love him (homosexual) is denied and turned into its opposite: I hate and wish to destroy him. The agression is then projected (usually on the love object) and perceived as he hates me and wishes to destroy me.

(Further Remarks on the Neuro-Psychoses of Defense, 1896, S.E. 3 174-182)

and examine the patient for any pathology of the nose and sinuses that might be contributing to her condition. Fliess did so and made a diagnosis. He suggested surgery. He performed the operation, assigned the aftercare to others, and returned to Berlin. Malodorous secretions, pain, and some bleeding persisted in the patient. At first Freud saw the symptoms as hysterical, but soon concern for the patient's suffering made him consult a local specialist. It was discovered that Fliess had left a half-meter strip of gauze in the cavity that the surgery created.

> Attending the patient, Dr. M suddenly pulled out something resembling a thread...a good half of gauze had been withdrawn from the cavity. Immediately there was a flow of blood, the girl turned white, her eyes bulged and her pulse almost stopped...I felt sick...(the nurse) then brought me a small glass of cognac and I felt better.
> (Clark, p. 150)

Subsequently the patient had more hemorrhages and had to undergo further surgery. It was about a month before she was out of danger.

Freud put off informing Fliess until the following day when he described the cause of the persistent symptoms. He then added that his trust in Fliess was unshaken and that no one could possibly blame him for the incident. The specialist from Vienna was in fact responsible for the hemorrhage! The patient should have been taken to the hospital where the wound could have been widened before the gauze was removed, a procedure impossible to attempt in her home.[1]

We see a neurosis at work: Freud could no more be objective toward Fliess than an infant can evaluate his mother objectively. Later letters indicate that unconsciously Freud knew very well what Fliess's responsibility was in the matter. But his emotional dependence of Fliess at the time made it impossible for him to examine the relationship.

Freud was clinging to Fliess in the way a child who fears abandonment clings to his mother. His work would soon shock the world. He knew he was in the process of making epochal decisions which were about to take unknown directions. Fliess represented a strong protector who would be at his side in this anxious time. He hoped that Fliess would help him find a solid basis in physiology for his psychological explanations of clinical material. "I have no desire at all to leave psychology hanging in the air with no organic basis."[2] Fliess, himself a spellbinder, unafraid of grandiose speculation, made it possible for Freud to explore his own implausible, even scandalous theories of infantile sexuality. He exerted no limits on Freud and was ever an encouraging audience. "Breuer would have clipped Freud's wings."[3]

Freud had a dream inspired by the Emma episode. Later he was to demonstrate his integrity by giving the dream a prominent place in "The Interpretation of Dreams" (1900). Today it is known as the famous Irma dream. Its main theme, according to Freud's interpretation, was his wish to be cleared of any guilt and

---

[1]For the medical details of the case see Schur p. 79-81

[2]Psychoamalysis: The First Ten Years, Stewart, Macmillan N.Y. p. 30

[3]Ibid. p. 20

responsibility for his patient's recurring symptoms. Max Schur, Freud's personal physician, offers a deeper interpretation—that Freud's main wish was not clear himself, but to exculpate Fliess; that the infantile wish in the dream was not to jeopardize his transference to Fliess.

Freud's self-analysis led him eventually to understand that his idealization of Fliess was a transference, a piece of his own neurosis. The intensity of his feelings was an unconscious replay of earlier experiences with his parents, before the development of his sense of reality, before he saw them objectively, at a time when he was totally vulnerable. To say that he was emotionally dependent on Fliess is an understatement.

> People like you should not die out, my dear friend; we others need the like of you too much. How much have I to thank you for in consolation, understanding, stimulation in my loneliness...your example...enabled me to gain the intellectual strength to trust my own judgment.
>
> (Roberts, p. 90)

Freud's unconscious and therefore infantile attachment to his idealized authority figure made it necessary for him to preserve the relationship at any cost; even to the point of repressing his scientific objectivity.

However, the more Freud changed as a result of his self-analysis, and the more confidence he gained in his own theories, the less he felt dependent on his colleague from Berlin. In fact, one can recognize hints of a change in Freud's attitude in the course of their correspondence. He draws attention to conflicts in their ideas, and he refers to going through inner struggles which no one can help him with (not even Fliess) but which he has to overcome by himself. Freud's letters indicate that he gradually sensed that a break would be inevitable and that this was painful to him. His self-analysis sharpened his objectivity and also his critical view of Fliess's theories. He would no longer permit himself to accept hypotheses in which he could not believe. Once he could say that at a time in life when it is difficult to make new friends, he had found one "whom I shall ever retain"; now Fliess's personality was beginning to prove incompatible with his own. The letters also convey that Fliess, on his side, was experiencing increasing emotional difficulties as well as a growing rivalry with Freud.

As each man's need for the other diminished, their ways were bound to come to a gradual parting, but a particular meeting hastened the end of the twelve-year friendship. The last time they saw each other was at Achensee in the summer of 1900. Freud was fourty-four, Fliess forty-two years of age. We do not know exactly what happened at Achensee. Fliess later accused Freud of stealing his ideas of bisexuality and not "giving him a by-line." Freud on his side had claimed that the concept of bisexuality as a means of understanding homosexuality was his own. Upon being reminded by Fliess of a particular conversation Freud admitted that he had forgotten. How curious that neither of the men seemed to have been aware that

[1]Talent and Genius, Eissler p. 165

the idea of bisexuality was not new; it had come to the attention of other minds long before. For example, Plato's "Symposium" clearly states the case for bisexuality in man.[1]

Characteristically, instead of covering up his error, Freud used it to shed light on the subject of forgetting. In "The Psychopathology of Everyday Life" (1901) he analyzes this strange case of forgetting a matter of such importance.

Continued misunderstandings arose, each charging the other of behaving badly. According to Fliess's published version, he was showing how periodic processes were at work in the psyche when Freud made a violent attack upon him, which he believed was based on envy. Freud claimed that he was astonished when Fliess called him a "mind reader" and what was worse, asserted that he, Freud, projected his own thoughts on to his patients.

Fliess said that after the meeting at Achensee he decided to withdraw from the relationship. They never met again. Freud could not believe that their valuable friendship was over and for the next two years he tried to mend matters. But his self-analysis had done its work. He now saw that his attachment to his only "audience" was rooted in infantile longings. Furthermore, that his "indispensable" friend from Berlin did not really accept or truly comprehend his own deepest convictions. So in the name of personal growth he accepted the end of a relationship which had meant so much to him. The remaining correspondence avoided scientific intercourse and confined iself to personal and family news. It ended with a card Freud sent from Italy in 1902 (a picture postcard of the Temple of Neptune, Paestum). "Cordial greetings from the culminating point of the Journey. Yours, Sigmund".

But the story doesn't end there. The final break was shocking, arising as it did from an issue very important to Fliess, that of originality. Fliess wanted to be acknowledged and recognized for his discoveries. Freud on the other hand found it encouraging when others before him had said something similar to what he had observed.

On July 20, 1904, Freud received a letter from Fliess. A brilliant Viennese youth, Otto Weininger, had published a book "Sex and Character," which stressed the role of bisexuality. Fliess had heard that Weininger was a close friend of a pupil of Freud's, a young psychologist named Herman Swoboda. He therefore was certain that his great secret had been revealed by Freud to Swoboda. What did Freud have to say about it?

Freud must have been most eager to pacify Fliess because this incident marks one very rare occasion on which he was not completely straightforward.

At first he tried to pass over the incident lightly. He answered that Swoboda was not a student but a patient and admitted that he had said in an analytic session that bisexuality was a universal phenomenon. Swoboda might have made the same remark casually to Weininger. But Weininger could easily have picked up the idea elsewhere, since there were many references to it in medical literature. "That's all I know about the matter."

Fliess was not satisfied. He reminded Freud that he had previously referred to Swoboda as his pupil, not his patient. Furthermore, Weininger could not have gotten the idea elsewhere because the concept of the bisexuality of each cell was Fliess's own discovery and had not, in fact, been suggested before. How strange that no one referred to *The Relationship Between the Nose and the Female Sex Organ* (1897), a book by Fliess in which he presented his theories and which Weininger had read.

There should have been no need to implicate Freud in the matter, but only to berate Weininger for not citing Fliess's authorship sufficiently, because Weininger had mentioned Fliess briefly. Fliess had heard that Weininger interviewed Freud and left a copy of his manuscript with him. Was that true? Freud was in a tough spot. He frankly admitted that in passing on the information he must have been influenced by an infantile wish to undermine Fliess' claim to orginality. Actually, Freud and Weininger met only once. Freud had read Weininger's manuscript and recommended that it not be published because it was unintelligible. Freud, always conscientious, had only recently learned about the power of the unconscious. In fact, for the rest of his life, in his effort to be honest, he too frequently pleaded guilty to acting out an unconscious wish. He knew that a psychological explanation would not satisfy or even interest Fliess. He ended the letter with a tactless remark. He regretted that Fliess had no time to write to him except about such trivial matters as priority. Fliess never wrote to him again. Two years later Fliess published some of their most private letters.

Fliess also published a pamphlet attacking Freud for divulging his discoveries to Swoboda, who, in the meantime, had written a book on periodicity in biology and psychology. The pamphlet accused both Swoboda and Weininger of plagiarism and claimed that the formulations of both authors were the result of Freud's betrayal of him. To this Freud responded at once. He wrote to Karl Klaus, editor of a local newspaper, defending both young men.

> What we are here concerned with is a defense against the overbearing presumption of a brutal personality and the banning of petty personal ambition from the temple of science.
> (Jones I, p. 316)

He also wrote to Magnus Hirschfeld of Berlin, editor of the "Yearbook for Sexual Borderline Cases":

> It is a disgusting scribble...actually we have to do with the fantasy of an ambitious man who in his loneliness has lost the capacity to judge what is right and what is permissible.... It is not pleasant for me to utter harsh words in public about someone with whom I have for twelve years been associated in the most intimate friendship, and thereby provoke him to further insults.
> (Ibid. p. 316)

Swoboda wrote a caustic book attacking Fliess's grandiose conceptions and then initiated legal proceedings against him. Weininger, a "sick genius and greatly misguided by what I was teaching,"[1] was said to be undergoing a kind of self-analysis. In 1903 he committed suicide by shooting himself. He was twenty-three years old.

Despite the bitter ending to their friendship, Freud continued to keep a portrait of Fliess on a wall in his apartment. For the rest of his life he referred to Fliess

[1]Kardiner, "Freud and the Twentieth Century" Ed. B. Nelson

as "a remarkable and indeed fascinating man,"[1] and admired his imagination and courage.

Freud used his idealized transference productively. It had been at a time that he needed someone to help him get through a period when his imagination was flying with very far-reaching and confusing speculations. One can appreciate the temptation to turn from his bewildering and dangerous observations to a more conservative position of comfort and security. Fliess enabled Freud to fly.

> ...if one may be permitted to draw the briefest thumbnail sketch of the friendship as it emerges in these pages, it began with passionate courtship on Freud's part, gradually subsided into gentile patronization...and finally collapsed because Freud had outgrown his friend.
>
> (The Complete Letters of Sigmund Freud to Wilhelm Fliess" Ed. Masson. Reviewed by Christopher Lehmann-Haupt, The New York Times, Thursday April 4, 1985)

---

[1]Eisler p. 170

CHAPTER XXIV

■ *A Little Discussion Group*

Freud's splendid isolation was coming to an end. His work was steadily gaining the attention of professional journals and medical colleagues. For a small select group, it was an exciting time: a revolutionary discovery had been made that would change the world. Freud would often be approached by someone who had read his writings, with whom he would arrange to meet to discuss the subject further. Wilhelm Stekel's autobiography catches the flavor of the day:

> (I read) "The Interpretation of Dreams"....I was enraptured. I wrote a long paper....emphasized the importance of this book which was inaugurating a new science.... The books and my talks with Freud were like sunshine after rain. At last I had learned the right method of curing neurotics. Many obscure cases in practice ceased to be enigmas....I wrote numerous articles about Freud and was one of the first to recognize the greatness of this genius. I was the apostle of Freud who was my Christ....
>
> I gave him the suggestion of founding a little discussion group; he accepted the idea, and every Wednesday evening after supper we met in Freud's home....
>
> These first evenings were inspiring....everybody participated in a real discussion. On the first night we spoke about the psychological implication of smoking.... We were like pioneers in a newly discovered land, and Freud was the leader. Every evening was like a revelation. We were so enthralled by these meetings that we decided new members could be added to our circle only by unanimous consent.
>
> (The Autobiography of Wilhelm Stekel, 1950 Liveright Publishing Corp. N.Y. p. 105-116)

This group grew into the famous Vienna Psycho-Analytical Society. By 1910, they had added so many new members they had to move to larger quarters.

Jones has described his own introduction to the Vienna Wednesday night group:

> Jung had told me in Zurich what a pity it was that

> Freud had no followers of any weight in Vienna, and that he was surrounded there by a "degenerate and Bohemian crowd" who did him little credit, so I was curious to see them. I soon found that Jung's description was a highly colored one, to put it mildly. None of the painters and poets he had imagined existed, and the members of the Vienna Psycho-Analytical Society....were much what one might have expected them to be. I was obliged to ask myself whether his account had proceeded from anything more than simple anti-Semitism, for it is true that they were all Jews; so for many years were all European psychoanalysts except those in Switzerland and England. They were all practicing physicians, for the most part very sober ones, and if their cloaks were more flowing and their hats broader than what one saw in Zurich, London, or Berlin...that was a general Viennese characteristic. They were decidedly middle-class, and lacked the social manners and distinction I had been accustomed to in London. On the other hand, they were more cultivated and better educated; the theatre, opera, and concert hall meant much to them, and they were at home in both German and classical literature.
>
> (Free Associations, Ernest Jones, Basic Books, N.Y. 1959, p. 167)

Members presented papers, followed by an open discussion. One was free to disagree with a given viewpoint, but hard debate was not permitted in the meeting. Freud insisted that the members listen and think, and keep argument to a minimum. The following letter illuminates his sensitivity and consideration for the members of the society:

> I wish to inform you that I propose at the beginning of this new working year to dissolve the little Society...a short note sent before October 1st to our secretary, Otto Rank, will suffice to insure a renewal of your membership....
>
> Allow me to give the reason for this action which may well seem to you to be superfluous. We are only taking into account the natural changes in human relationships if we assume that to one or another member in our group membership no longer signifies what it did years earlier, whether because his interest in the subject is exhausted, or his leisure time and mode of life are no longer compatible with attendance, or that personal associations threaten to keep him away. Presumably he would still remain a member, fearing lest his resignation be regarded as an unfriend-

> ly action....
> (Jones II, p. 10)

This delicate means of accepting resignations was made use of by other societies in later years.

CHAPTER XXV

■ *My Heir, My Aryan, My Friend*

In the autumn of 1904, Freud heard from Eugen Bleuler, Professor of Psychiatry in Zurich, that he and his staff had been following Freud's work for the past few years and that their own researches corroborated his ideas. Furthermore, they were finding new applications for psychoanalytic psychology. Bleuler, a recognized authority on dementia praecox (schizophrenia), at the instigation of his chief assistant, Jung, was applying his theories to the field of psychosis. Freud couldn't believe it! He was elated. His work, neglected for so long everywhere, was being warmly received in the most famous psychiatric clinic in the world. He must have felt like a starving artist who has lived and worked in isolation, and then one day receives word from the world's richest patron that he had been following his career and he would like to arrange an exhibition of his work in the world's most famous museum.

Freud had urged psychiatrists to go beyond mere classification and simple descriptions. It was not enough to say "the patient was quiet today," "she doesn't wash," "she just stares at the wall; dementia praecox." Freud insisted that there was meaning in behavior, all behavior, and a proper study of mental processes could bring about a proper understanding of the patient, and possibly, a therapeutic intervention. His efforts in this direction had only led to his being alienated from the medical scene in Vienna.

Freud knew that he had made a great discovery and that it would open up a new world of psychiatry. He feared however that it might die with its handful of followers and perhaps not be discovered again for a long time. Keeping his brainchild alive, seeing it grow and get out into the world was imperative. He was ambitious in the sense that Moses was ambitious: he had a purpose, a mission that transcended any individual consideration. But like Moses, he felt that he was destined to see the promised land only from a distance. Jung would be his Joshua and explore the new land of psychiatry.

Carl Gustav Jung (1875-1961) was a well-known and respected member of the world of psychiatry. He was a staff member of the most prestigious center for training, the Burgholzli in Zurich, Switzerland. He and his chief of staff, Eugen Bleuler, represented psychiatry at its best.

The Burgholzli, a huge network of buildings, was the psychiatric clinic of the University of Zurich. Although fundamentally a Swiss institution, the university clinic opened its doors to many foreign doctors and students for training in psychiatry. Every variety and every stage of mental disorder could be observed among its three thousand patients, and Jung and his students conducted laboratory experiments in order to approach psychopathology scientifically. Freud, in the spirit of his teacher, Ernst Brucke, felt that a science must have an experimental base and that the Burgholzli was vital to making psychoanalysis scientific and therefore respectable.

The Viennese doctor in private practice could not possibly conduct experiments and build an experimental base for the new science: psychoanalysis. Freud further hoped that the Swiss would form a group similar to the Viennese psycho-Analytic Society, which would give rise to other groups, particularly in England. The gospel must be spread.

> 8 December 1907
>
> Dear Friend and colleague,
> ....The Congress in Salzburg in spring 1908 would make me very proud;...I believe that once the English have become acquainted with our ideas they will never let them go. I have less confidence in the French....
>
> (The Freud/Jung Letters, Princeton University Press, 1974, p. 102)

In 1906, the year that marked his final break with Fliess, Freud recieved a letter from Jung expressing his appreciation of his work and Jung added that when he applied psychoanalytic psychology to his newly developed word-association test, even bizarre psychotic behavior became comprehensible. Freud was overjoyed.

Jung and Freud met on February 27, 1907. (That year Freud also met Abraham and Ferenczi.) Jung later gave Jones a lively account of his first interview. He had much to discuss with Freud and with his characteristic intense animation, Jung held forth for three hours. At that point, Freud, the patient listener, interrupted him. Jung said he could hardly believe his ears when Freud proceeded to organize all that Jung had been talking about under several precise headings which enabled them to continue the discussion with a more profitable give-and-take. Jung's enthusiasm and admiration for Freud and his theories seemed unlimited. He considered his meeting Freud the high point of his life. He said that whoever acquired a knowledge of psychoanalysis had the kind of vision that only comes with having eaten of the fruit of the tree of knowledge.

At that time, to support psychoanalytic theory publicly meant to risk one's reputation. Freud was dazzled and deeply grateful that Jung had brought his work to the attention of his famous chief, Bleuler. He was even more impressed with the young psychiatrist's courage. Jung's brilliant intellect, wide range of interests, and culture made him irresistible. Freud expressed the opinion that Jung had a truly original mind and he was grateful for such support from distant Switzerland. He decided that Jung, nineteen years his junior and whom he felt he could influence, would succeed him as leader of the psycho-analytic movement as his "son and heir."

Erudite, young, imaginative, Christian, Jung belonged to the world of European science. He inhabited a world that suffered no race discrimination, no frontiers, a world that was intellectually free. Under Jung's protection, psychoanalysis would be free from racial attacks and would find its rightful place in the world of science. Freud's emotional involvement with Jung never reached the heights that it had with Fliess. It has been suggested that the more mature Freud was a product of his own self-analysis.

After so much rejection and abuse, it was natural for Freud to be joyous when the world-renowned university professors from a foreign country offered their wholehearted support for his work. Of course, he would make much of his new adherent, his first from abroad, and a Gentile. Psychoanalysis could become something more than a Jewish sect in Vienna charged with pornography. Under the leadership of the tall, blond, robust Carl Gustav Jung, the personification of exalted Aryan manhood, psychoanalysis would become part of the science of the West.

How did Jung respond to his role as Crown Prince, heir to the psychoanalytic throne? In his enthusiasm for psychoanalysis he embraced the role Freud had chosen for him. It seemed only proper that he should one day take over the leadership of the new science of the mind.

Freud's Viennese colleagues, who had rallied around him when he stood alone, felt neglected. They became jealous of Jung. Their feelings were all the stronger because they anticipated anti-Semitism from him. Freud himself shared this fear, but he suppressed it for the sake of the baby: psychoanalysis. Some of the Viennese predicted even then that Jung would not long remain in the psychoanalytic camp.

(Jung could be charming and witty. Jones once asked him if he thought that Dadaism, just then taking hold in Zurich, had a psychotic base. Jung replied: "It's too idiotic for any decent insanity.")[1]

In 1907 Jung organized a group to study psychoanalysis. It was called the "Freud Group." Jung was the leader and the members made useful contributions to analytic knowledge. Jones attended one of their meetings at the Burgholzli Mental Hospital.

> ....I made a detour to visit Jung at Zurich....Jung was already a man of international fame in psychiatry.... At that time I could best describe Jung as a breezy personality. He had a restlessly active and quick brain, was forceful or even domineering in temperament, and exuded vitality and laughter; he was certainly a very attractive person. He cherished the notion, rightly or wrongly, that his descent owed something to one of Goethe's love affairs, and I feel sure his career was influenced by a medley of scientific, literary, and philosophical pretensions in which he tried to emulate his great ancestor. With all his intelligence and learning, however, Jung lacked both clarity and stability in his thinking.... My first observation of this was his attempt to combine his important discoveries in the psychology of dementia praecox with the pathological findings...whereby the mind poisoned the brain. His grasp of philosophical principles was so insecure that it was little wonder that they later degenerated into mystical obscurantism....
>
> I...discussed with him our plans for organising the first Psycho-Analytical Congress. I remember vainly protesting against his wish to call it a Congress for Freudian Psychology, a term which offended my ideas of objectivity in scien-

[1]Jones 2, p. 39

> tific work. Jung, Brill and I then went on to Salzburg, where the Congress was to take place on April 26, 1908, and there I first met Freud.
> (Free Associations, Ernest Jones Basic Books Inc. N.Y. p. 164-166)

The occasion was international in the true sense, with representatives from America, Austria, England, Germany, Hungary, and Switzerland, and it was the first public recognition of psychoanalysis. Freud in an effort to avoid the role of chairman, insisted that the Chair be held by Bleuler, the senior and most authoritative of the Swiss psychiatrists. Jung was so sure that Bleuler would refuse that he did not even ask him. The Congress therefore differed from all subsequent ones in that there was no chairman, no council, no secretary, and no kind of subcommittee. The meeting completed its work in one day.

Jung had urged Freud to present a case history and Freud did so by describing the analysis of an obsessisonal neurosis. Afterwards the patient became known as the "Rat Man." In his soft tone and distinct, conversational style, Freud began at eight in the morning and at eleven he stopped, suggesting that his audience had had enough. But his listeners had been held in rapt attention; they insisted that he continue, which he did until one o'clock. He had spoken for five hours to a group fully engrossed in the case material. The novelty of the content and the extraordinary gift for organized presentation of the speaker, held them spellbound.

The patient, aged twenty-nine, had been a well-known lawyer from Vienna. Since childhood he had suffered from obsessional impulses. At present he was plagued by thoughts of the death of his father and fiancee; also, that he would do something terrible such as cut his own throat.

While on army maneuvers earlier in the year a fellow officer told him of an Oriental punishment in which a pot that contained live rats was strapped to a man's buttocks. The compulsive thoughts of its happening to himself was so agitating, that he turned to psychoanalysis for relief. The peculiar symptom led to his being referred to as the "Rat Man."

Freud explained how the patient's observation of parental intercourse played an important role in the aetiology of the neurosis. He described the difficulty of distinguishing the facts of the patient's recollections from fantasies and distortions. He emphasized that a patient only fears what he wishes, hence ambivalence—the compulsive doubting, the doing and the undoing, so characteristic of the obsessional neuroses. The patient felt that if he were to think of someone he would surely meet that person immediately afterwards or if he were to inquire about someone's health he would hear that the person had just died. It was the "Rat Man" himself who coined the phrase "The Principle of the Omnipotence of Thought." Freud added that obsessional neurotics are superstitious in this way, even against their better judgment.

Freud presented much more than a case histry during those five hours. He discussed at length the complexities and the mystery of the obsessional neurosis.

To Jung:

> 20 June 1909 Vienna
>
> Dear Friend,
>
> ....My energy is pretty well exhausted, except for

> one undertaking.... This one undertaking is my paper about the Rat Man. I am finding it very difficult; it is almost beyond my powers of presentation; the paper will probably be intelligible to no one outside our immediate circle. How bungled our reproductions are, how wretchedly we dissect the great art works of psychic nature! Unfortunately this paper in turn is becoming too bulky. It just pours out of me, and even so it's inadequate, incomplete and therefore untrue. A wretched business. I am determined to finish it before leaving...for America....
>
> Sincerely yours, Freud
>
> (Freud/Jung Letters p. 238)

> Kusnach bei Zurich 14 Oct. 1909
>
> Dear Professor Freud
>
> Occasionally a spasm of homesickness for you comes over me but only occasionally; otherwise I am back in my stride.... Your Rat man has filled me with delight, it is written with awesome intelligence and full of the most subtle reality. Most people though, will be too dumb to understand it in depth. Splendid ingenuities! I regret from the bottom of my heart that I didn't write it.... As I have frequently observed with my students.... They are incapable of following logical trains of thought and stand there glumly, ears drooping. It will be just the same with the Rat Man, you'll see, although every sentence is made to measure and fits reality to a T...
>
> Yours sincerely, Jung
>
> (Ibid. p. 251)

The analysis of the Rat Man began in October 1907 and was terminated within eleven months. The results were exceptional; the patient enjoyed much success in his work and his private life. He was killed in World War I.

The Salzburg Congress was a success. The members felt confident that psychoanalysis was no longer vulnerable and that its future was assured. That evening, after hearing more papers, they celebrated at a lively banquet. Nevertheless, several months later Freud wrote to Jung:

> 29 November 1908 Vienna, IX Berggasse 19
>
> Dear Friend,
>
> No, the dawn is not yet. We must carefully tend our little lamp, for the night will be long.... But I am quite used to irresponsible statements by my followers. Not long ago one of my Wednesday people screwed up his courage and read a paper on the nature of the perversions; it sounded as if I had never said a word about them in the Three Essays, and friend Stekel backed him

> up....
> I am quite ready to believe that the agitation against you does you no harm. From all this hostility we may infer that we have made much more of an impression than we thought. Moral: Go on slaving.
> With kind regards and congratulations on the blessed event.
> Yours Freud,
> (Ibid. p. 181)

An incident occurred that cast a shadow on the jubilant group and was a harbinger of things to come. Jung had presented a paper "On Dementia Praecox" (today known as schizophrenia). He described the work done at the Burgholzli and put forth the view held by his chief, Bleuler, that dementia praecox is due to an organic condition; a hypothetical toxin's effects on the brain. Abraham took issue with Jung's nonpsychoanalytic position in his own presentation of "The Psychosexual Differences between Hysteria and Dementia Praecox."

Karl Abraham, an analyst from Berlin, did not like Jung. He had worked with him at the Burgholzli and didn't trust Jung's attachment to religion, mysticism, and other "unscientific nonsense." A clash between them took place over the dynamics of dementia praecox. Abraham upheld Freud's view of mental illness; namely that the condition involves massive blocking of thoughts and feelings rather than the destruction of the brain. Jung was outraged. Freud was upset. He wrote to Abraham urging him to adopt a more conciliatory attitude toward Jung:

> Lieber und geehrter Herr Kollege,
> ....I would make a request to you on the fulfillment of which all sorts of things may depend. I recollect that your paper led to some conflict between you and Jung, or so at least I gathered from a few words you said to me afterwards....In the matter at issue itself I unhesitatingly thought you were in the right and I attributed Jung's sensitiveness to his own vacillation....It is also important for us that Jung should find his way back to the views he has just forsaken....I believe there is some prospect of that, and Jung himself writes to me that...(he is) almost inclined to abandon...the organic nature of dementia praecox. So you would do me a personal favor if you would communicate with Jung before publishing your paper and ask him to discuss his objections with you so that you can take them into account. A friendly gesture of that kind will assuredly put an end to the nascent disagreement between you....
> Be tolerant and don't forget that really it is easier for you to follow my thoughts than for Jung, since to begin with you are completely independent, and then racial relationship brings you closer

> to my intellectual constitution, whereas he, being a Christian and the son of a pastor, can only find his way to me against great resistances. His adherence is therefore all the more valuable. I was almost going to say it was only his emergence on the scene that has removed from psychoanalysis the danger of becoming a Jewish national affair.
>
> I hope you will give your attention to my request and I greet you warmly.
>
> Yours,
> Freud
>
> (Jones 2, p. 47)

Karl Abraham, a sensible man, appreciated Freud's concern and took his advice in the proper spirit. However, his friendly overture was ignored; there was no response from Jung. Whereupon, Abraham resumed his critical attitude, prompting another letter from Freud:

> Do not misunderstand: I have nothing to reproach you for. I surmise that the repressed anti-Semitism of the Swiss, from which I am to be spared, has been directed against you in increased force. But my opinion is that we Jews, if we want to cooperate with other people, have to develop a little masochism and be prepared to endure a certain amount of injustice. There is no other way of working together. You may be sure that if my name were Oberhuber my new ideas would, despite all the other factors, have met with far less resistance.
>
> (Ibid. p. 49)

Abraham did what Freud asked of him but with little enthusiasm. In his opinion it was only a matter of time before Jung would leave the psychoanalytic movement. Karl Abraham, brilliant to the point of genius, throughout his life remained cooperative and devoted to his old mentor.

It was at the Salzburg Congress that Jones first met Freud. When introduced by Jung, Freud remarked that from the shape of his head he could not be English and must be Welsh! Jones was astonished. Not only because of Freud's observation, but because so few on the Continent even knew of the existence of Wales. Given the situation, one can easily understand the overwhelming impression Freud made on Jones with his casual remark about the shape of his skull. Only years later did Jones learn that Jung had mentioned to Freud that Jones was Welsh.

Ernest Jones, twenty-six years old, working as a neurologist in London's University Hospital, had read some reviews of Freud's papers. He was so impressed that he, together with his brother-in-law Wilfred Trotter (who was to become one of the world's leading surgeons) studied German so that they could read Freud in the original. For fifty years Jones was in the vanguard of the psychoanalytic struggles, within and without the movement. He fought, worked, and lived for the "cause." He once wrote to Freud that he owed his career, his livelihood, his status, even his capacity for happiness in marriage, to the work Freud had done. Jones was loyal, dedicated, and devoted to Freud, but he was not a passive and docile follower. A fiery, waspish fighter, he has been accused of being tactless and imperious with colleagues who disagreed with him at professional meetings. And whoever rejected psychoanalytic theory at psychiatric conventions found himself confronted by an aggressive opponent with a sharp eye for a soft spot in an argument and a devastating tongue. No wonder, then, that Jones had his share of enemies. It is amusing to read in his autobiography that he views himself as a tactful fellow, as a devotee of chess and figure skating, as a man who easily strikes up acquaintances.

Jones was erudite and brilliant and could write, a precious talent in any field. His clear expository style served as a superb promotion for the "cause." More than anyone else, Jones was responsible for whatever popularity Freud's theories enjoyed among an English reading public. Today all students of psychoanalysis are grateful to him for his incomparable three-volume biography of Freud.

Celebrating Jones's fiftieth birthday, Freud closed with these words:

> ...the admission that he cannot think of Ernest Jones, even after his fiftieth birthday as other than before: zealous and energetic, combative and devoted to the cause.
>
> (Dr. Ernest Jones, 1929, S.E. p. 249)

Years later, when Freud's life was threatened by the Nazis, at the risk of personal danger, Jones made an all-out effort to save Freud. Typical of Jones, he succeeded.

CHAPTER XXVI

■ *Who Divined The Famed Riddle?*

In 1906 a group of Freud's colleagues presented him with a medallion designed by a well-known sculptor, Karl Maria Schwerdtner. On one side was his portrait in profile and on the other was a Greek design of Oedipus answering the sphinx. Around it was a line from Sophocles: "Who divined the famed riddle and was a man most mighty?" When Freud read the inscription he turned deathly pale and in a strangled voice asked who had thought of it. Paul Federn identified himself as the man who had chosen the passage. Freud disclosed that when he was a young student at the University he often strolled through the great court inspecting the busts of former professors. He used to fantasize that his bust would be among the celebrated professors and with the IDENTICAL words carved on the medallion. In 1955, Ernest Jones fulfilled Freud's youthful wish. He presented the University of Vienna with a bust of Freud made by the sculptor Konigsberger.

Freud now enjoyed more than a full-time private practice. His patients came, not so much from Vienna as from all parts of Europe. Freud's own rooms consisted of a waiting room, spacious enough to hold the Wednesday meetings, a consulting room with the famous analytic couch, and an inner sanctum, his study proper. He sat upright in a chair behind the couch facing the window and a garden. In later years he added a footstool.

Comfortable, but a char's nightmare, the room overflowed with many books and antiques, on his desk, in cabinets, on tables. He was a passionate collector of Greek, Assyrian, and Egyptian artifacts. His interest in antiques enhanced the pleasure and appreciation he had in traveling. Seldom would he return from his travels without a new acquisition for his collection. In 1910, a Hungarian farmer discovered a Roman cemetery on his property. Sandor Ferenczi, a psychoanalyst from Budapest, made good use of this opportunity and from time to time sent Freud various objects. Freud took pleasure in giving his precious artifacts as gifts to favorite friends and colleagues. The esthetic qualities of the pieces were not as important to him as their historical and mythological significance. In later years, friends and pupils, when they heard of his hobby, made their own contributions.

At eight in the morning he saw his first patient, which meant rising at seven. It was said that this was difficult for him. He worked so long into the night that he always yearned for more rest than he allotted to himself. A cold morning shower refreshed him. His barber appeared every morning to trim his beard, breakfast followed, and a glance at the morning newspaper. Each patient was given fifty-five minutes precisely; he reserved five minutes to clear his head. He insisted on punctuality for his patients and himself.

At one o'clock he took lunch with the whole family. Dinner was often too late for the younger members, who had already retired to bed. He tended to say very little during meals, which sometimes made it difficult for visitors who were forced to manage a conversation with the family without him. He had one habit that the family jocularly commented on. If any of the children were absent from the table, he would silently point at the empty chair with his knife or fork and look questionably to Martha. She would explain why the child was not present, whereupon Freud without saying a word, would now proceed with his meal.

> My father was not fussy over food, but like most people he had his likes and dislikes. He was particularly fond of Italian artichokes...he was not fond of chicken. "One should not kill chickens," he sometimes said. "Let them stay alive and lay eggs."
>
> My father's favourite dish was *Rindfleisch*, boiled beef as it is called in England; and we had this three or four times a week but never with the same sauce. Our *herrschaftskoechin* could produce at least seven different kinds and all of them delicious.
>
> (Ibid. p. 33)

When possible, he would stay free until three o'clock. His constitutional walk was an important part of his schedule. It was a time for shopping, checking proofs with publishers, and so on. Not the least in importance was a visit to the Tabak Trafik shop near the Michaeler Church to examine the latest shipment of cigars. Theodore Reik recalls that he met Freud one afternoon hurrying along and carrying a package. After exchanging greetings Freud remarked that a patient had given him a book, so he had to run out and get the patient a book. Back at his office at three and into his frockcoat, he would work until nine or ten in the evening. Freud's day included twelve ot thirteen analytic hours.

Lunch at one and dinner at nine or ten is a long run without food, but not until he was sixty-five did he allow himself the luxury of a five o'clock cup of coffee. The after-dinner schedule called for another walk, this time with Martha, sister-in-law Minna, or with a daughter. On these occasions they usually stopped at a cafe; in the summer the Cafe Landmann, in the winter the Cafe Central. When his daughters went to the theater, he always met them at a particular lamppost and escorted them home.

Mathilde, his eldest daughter, was fourteen years old when Freud invited her to walk on his right side during their strolls. A school friend saw them and later told her it was not right for a girl to be on her father's right side. She proudly replied, "That is not so with my father. With him I am always the lady."[1]

On returning home he would retire to his study to work on his correspondence, a book, a paper, prepare new editions, correct proof, not only of his own writings, but of the journals and periodicals of which he was editor. He was never in bed before one and usually later.

Saturday evenings were special, he practically never missed his beloved card game of tarok. In his earlier years he had played a good deal of chess in the coffee

[1]Ibid. p. 384

houses, but later he found the concentration more of a strain than a recreation. An evening at the theater or concert hall required the stature of a Shakespeare or a Mozart, otherwise he preferred to work. Sunday was a holiday; usually he saw no patients. In the morning, accompanied by some members of his family, he always visited his mother. With mother and one or two sisters, there would be much family gossip. He was involved in his family's affairs, gave advice and would discuss financial problems with his brother Alexander who still lived at home.

> Alexander, ten years younger than my father...at a comparatively early age he had to abandon his studies to earn a living; but even without a university degree and consequent disadvantages, he went far. He became Austria's leading expert on transport. He was the consultant to the Vienna Chamber of Commerce on this subject and a professor at several academies....He won the approbation of the Government for his services on two transport problems during the First World War.
>
> Two brothers, my father and Alexander could not have been more different in their outlook on life, but were always good friends. In great contrast to Sigmund, Alexander was highly musical....In addition, he was an excellent storyteller who could imitate the various accents of the characters in his stories....He came often to the Bergasse, and before he had a son of his own he spent many Sundays with the sons of his brother.
>
> (Sigmund Freud: Man and Father by Martin Freud, The Vanguard press N.Y. 1958, p. 18)

Sunday afternoon was devoted to the occasional visitor. It was Ferenczi's favorite day for visiting; they would spend hours together in Freud's study. Jones reports visiting with Freud on Sunday evenings until three in the morning. Neither man was able to bring their conversation to an end.

Sunday evening the entire family had dinner together, mother, sisters, Alexander, plus Martha and their six children. Freud would go to his study shortly afterwards. Sunday evening was a time for writing.

Freud was fond of taking his children to the various galleries in Vienna. His knowledge of art and ancient civilizations, and his own traveling must have made him an extraordinary guide.

Freud was not a habitual smoker, he was an addict. Twenty cigars a day. He had no inclination to drink to excess and at home he did not drink at all. The few bottles of wine which were received as Christmas presents were put away for special occasions. The wines that Ferenczi would bring from the Royal cellars of Hungary would simply be added to the collection. Freud had a distinct dislike for anything that clouded his thinking; he always preferred to be clear-minded.

Freud's dress was neat and correct, rather than fashionable and smart. He wore a dark lounge suit, a stiff white low collar, and a readymade black bowtie. He could be seen wearing the broad black hat that was customary in Vienna.

Unquestionably, the only woman in Freud's love life was Martha. They seemed to enjoy an unshakable devotion and a harmony of understanding. In his letters to her when away on holidays, it is made clear that she is first among all mortals. In his later years much of his dependence on Martha was shifted to his daughter Anna, heir to the deep involvement he had shared with Martha. During his illness it was Anna who tended him rather than Martha.

As for Martha's life, there was, after her husband, her sister Minna, who came to live with the family (1896) and stayed until her death. The sisters shared family responsibilities and were so close that on occasion the children complained that they felt excluded. Martha was a competent housekeeper with the high standards of tradition. The household (after Freud was appointed professor) had several servants: a charwoman who came daily to do the heavy work, a housemaid who was both a waitress for the family meals and a receptionist for Freud's patients, a cook whose duties were confined entirely to the kitchen, a nanny for the younger children, and a governess for the elder ones. Martha supervised the servants, did the shopping, and cared for six children, a full time occupation. However, those who knew her agreed that family came before housework.

> My mother knew how to manage servants. They loved and respected her and gave of their best. It is true that she kept the same servants for years on end; and even in those days this was most exceptional in Vienna.
>
> (Ibid. p. 33)

Martha was an educated, cultured woman. She devoted evenings to her reading. She kept abreast of current literature until the end of her long life; and she lived to be ninety years old. It was a special pleasure for her when famous authors came to visit: for instance she was delighted to share Thomas Mann's visit with her husband. From Freud's letters one gets the impression that Martha was familiar with his nonclinical writings. She knew her husband was a great man, and concern for his professional life took priority. She arranged the family life in the apartment to be as quiet as possible so as not to disturb him. Freud himself took his dependency on Martha for granted.

Freud has been described as a severe patriarch whose children held him in awe. One can perhaps criticize his education of his children: in those days it was very rare to allow a child's personality to develop freely with the minimum restraint or reprimand. Freud may have been too lenient. This was true of his sons as well as his daughters. Fortunately, the results were happy. Jones recalls one of Freud's daughters "then a big schoolgirl, cuddling on his lap in a manner that showed no doubt at all of his affection or his readiness to show it."[1] In an early letter to Martha, he once remarked that it was important for a child's self-respect to be dressed well. He loved to share in his children's amusements and on holidays he spent his only spare time with them. He was blessed; his children loved him.

Tante Minna lived with them for forty-two years and it has been said that she deserves her own biography. Freud said that in the lonely nineties she and Fliess were the only people to sympathize with his work. She had more time for reading and study than had Martha, but mostly Minna was famous for her caustic tongue

[1]Jones 2, p. 387

and her epigrams. The latter were considered a family treasure.

Freud was determined to spare his children the anxiety about money that marred his own early life. His plan was that they should have everything they needed for their education and pleasure. However, once they were old enough to earn their own living, they were not to expect anything. In his eagerness to protect his children from anxiety about money, he went far in the opposite direction. Fortunately, there were no bad consequences.

His eldest daughter told a story to illustrate the point. She once saw her aunt paying one of the servants. When she discovered that the servants worked for money, she broke into tears. She insisted that above all, her Nanny worked for love.

Freud would say that there are some things in which one does not economize: health, education, and travel.

Since Freud gave his children all the money they wanted, it speaks well for them that they never abused his generosity. But he was not insensitive to the needs of their friends. For example, his eldest son, Martin, was off on a mountain tour with a friend whose financial circumstances were bad. Freud made Martin inquire how much money his friend was bringing for the journey, and he gave Martin the same amount so as not to embarrass the friend.

Freud loved to give presents. But his impatient nature made it difficult for him to wait until the appropriate time. Despite Martha's protests, the children's birthday gifts always arrived a day early.

In those days, Austrian citizens were meticulously exact in reporting their income tax returns. In 1913 the Tax Department wrote to Freud expressing their astonishment that his income was not larger "since everyone knows that his reputation extends far beyond the frontier of Austria." He replied: "Professor Freud is very honored at receiving a communication from the Government. It is the first time the Government has taken any notice of him and he acknowledges it....There is one point in which he cannot agree with the communication: that his reputation extends far beyond the frontier of Austria. It begins at the frontier."

> From the moment my father became internationally famous, he was continuously photographed until the end of his life....For these posed photographs he used what his children called his *Photographier Gesicht,* his photographing face, rather a stern serious face which did not for a moment reflect his kindly and friendly nature, not severe and reserved, as the world must regard him if they judge him by posed photographs. Sigmund Freud was a very nice grandfather and his true nature is always shown when he is photographed with a grandchild or two.
> (Martin Freud, p. 192)

Freud never invested in the stock market. His savings went into government bonds and insurance policies. The inflation that followed the war completely wiped him out. Later Martin, who became a banker, took charge of his finances and Freud left the matter entirely in Martin's hands. Despite years of poverty, his attitude toward money was quite normal. He acknowledged its importance in the real world, but beyond that it had no emotional meaning.

Fliess's periodic calculations gave Freud fifty-one years to live. This fitted in very well with Freud's preoccupation with his own death. In his letters he often wrote about the significance of fear, and later, of a wish for death. When the appointed time passed without the final event taking place, Freud simply chose another date, February 1918; he would be sixty-two years of age. He told Ferenczi that he had held this "for a long time." In the dark days of the war, he looked forward to the date with resignation and welcome. When he discovered that he was not dead and February had passed, he remarked, "That shows what little trust one can place in the supernatural."[1]

Holidays were important to the Freud family. The discussions would begin months before vacation time. Often Freud would make exploratory expeditions at Easter, and his reports were usually amusing and would be read aloud before the entire family. They were connoisseurs in this matter. The requirements were specific: a comfortable house with a room for Freud to write in if he so chose, pine forests for walks, a certain altitude for air and sun, a good supply of mushrooms, scenery, but above all, quiet. Their choice had to be far from bandstands or other tourist attractions. Martha and the children would leave for the chosen spot in advance, and Freud would follow later. His arrival was a signal that fun was to begin: mushroom hunting, walks, search for wildflowers, and so forth, with prizes for the collectors of the best specimens. Quite often it was Freud himself who won the prize. Many colleagues and students would have been surprised to see the austere professor on vacation, at play with his family.

> Unhappily towards the end of our holiday there was an ugly and depressing incident which remains strongly marked in my memory. My brother Oliver and I were fishing one morning...a few yards from the high-road which ran somewhat above the lake's level. A number of men had been watching us from the road, something which meant little to us....We were shocked and considerably surprised when the men began abusing us, shouting that we were Israelites—which was true—that we were stealing fish—which was untrue—and being very offensive indeed.
>
> We ignored them, refusing to reply, and we went on with our fishing. After a time, the men were met by other people with whom they marched off. Nevertheless, the joy in our fishing had gone....We told father about it all, and he became very serious for a few moments, remarking that kind of thing could happen to us again, and that we should be prepared for it.
>
> That same afternoon father had to go to Reichenhall and as usual Oliver and I rowed him across the lake to the highway to save him part of the walk. The men who had abused Oliver and me that morning were now reinforced by a number of other people, including women, and

[1]Ferenczi, May 9, 1918

> stood on the road near the primitive landing place, apparently prepared to block the way to Reichenhall. As we moored the boat, they began shouting anti-Semitic abuse.
>
> Father, without the slightest hesitation, jumped out of the boat and, keeping to the middle of the road, marched towards the hostile crowd. When he saw me following him, he commanded me in so angry a voice to stay where I was that I dared not disobey. My mild-mannered father had never spoken to me in any but kindly tones; this display of anger, as I thought it, upset me more than all the abuse of the strangers....They numbered about ten men, and all were armed with sticks and umbrellas. The women remained in the background, but cheered on their men-folk with shouts and gestures.
>
> In the meantime, father, swinging his stick, charged the hostile crowd, which gave way before him and promptly dispersed, allowing him a free passage. This was the last we saw of these unpleasant strangers. We never found out from where they came nor what their object had been in waylaying my father.
>
> This unpleasant incident made a deep impression on me...after more than fifty-five years I can still recall the faces of these crusaders in racial hatred....He (father) never recalled the incident at home, and I am not aware that he ever mentioned it in any of his letters to our family or friends.
>
> (Martin Freud p. 71)

Freud had an uncanny flair for guessing where mushrooms might be. In front of the children, he would sneak up on a mushroom and suddenly pounce upon the fungus with his hat as though it were a bird or a butterfly. His boyish humor never failed to delight the youngsters. His latest acquisition of an antique would be placed before him on the dinner table as though it were a guest. Afterwards, it would be put away in its proper place. A day or two later, it would appear again. The children loved it.

According to one of his daughters, Freud was interested in teaching his children three things: the technique of the card game *tarok,* the art of finding mushrooms, and a knowledge of wildflowers. They learned all three lessons very well.

Evidently Freud had a very poor sense of direction. His sons have reported that they would be astonished how after a long walk, he would head for home in the wrong direction. Very early in life he accepted this defect and allowed his sons to be his guides.

Freud felt an almost religious appreciation for fine scenery the vista of mountains and forests. Max Schur wrote that he was surprised to see Freud, at the age of seventy-three, weighed down by cancer, still showing an enthusiastic appreciation of nature. His suffering had not impaired his capacity to enjoy a view of mountains, a meadow, a flower.

Before the war, on holidays, Freud could be seen in Tyrolese costume, shorts, suspenders, and a green hat with a little chamois brush in the band. A thick walking stick and an Alpine cape for wet weather completed the outfit. He had an aversion to umbrellas. He once asked Jones in an irritated tone, ''Why ever do you carry an umbrella?'' Jones replied that it probably was a habit acquired from having to wear a silk hat. Freud answered, ''Then try to give up the habit.'' To Jone's wife he said that all an umbrella did was to keep its own stick dry.

Martha and he did not particularly enjoy parties, and in that sense did very little entertaining. However, there was always a stream of guests to enjoy their hospitality, and if Martha was not the ''perfect'' hostess, she was a thoroughly gracious one. Eventually they set aside a room for guests.

> My parents had many friends, most of them Jewish and members of the upper middle classes, and thus few afternoons passed without the appearance of at least one visitor and often more. While mother was entertaining guests we children would be left in the charge of the reigning governess or perhaps the nanny.
> (Ibid. p. 34)

> Father was not a bit unsocial: he liked company and it was usual to see him at summer resorts in animated conversation walking up and down with newly won friends. These were educated people, not highbrow, leading men in commerce or industry and perhaps an old newspaper editor, an artist or politician.
> (Ibid. p. 48)

Martha and her eldest daughter, Mathilda, were concerned about foreign pupils, especially women. They helped them find apartments and made themselves available to the new person until he or she became acclimated.

Freud's family revolved around him. Martha saw to it that the apartment was quiet, no small achievement with six children. It has been said that she even laid out his clothes every morning and put toothpaste on his toothbrush. His pupils and colleagues joked that they too would be more productive if they had such a wife. Her devotion went even beyond what was expected from a wife at that time.

Daughter Anna bought a dog to accompany her on walks through the forests of the Semmering. In no time at all, Wolf, an Alsatian, became a member of the family. Freud's behavior towards the animal became a family joke: he treated him with all the courtesy that is usually reserved for human beings. He would feed Wolf from his own plate, even though Martha objected, but what brought laughter from the family was Freud's habit of turning on the light if Wolf were lying in a dark room. The family joked that Freud expected Wolf to read if he were not busy with anything else.

Ernst Simmel, a psychoanalyst, has said that he would never forget an incident when he and Freud were walking in the grounds of Schloss Tegel and saw a chained police dog. Simmel warned Freud not to touch the animal because it was vicious. Freud disregarded him, unchained the dog, accepted licks in response to friendly pats, and remarked, "If you had been chained up all your life, you'd be vicious too."[1]

To a patient who had described his own dog, Freud was to say: "The feeling for dogs is the same as we have for our children; it is of the same quality. But do you know in what way it differs?...There is no ambivalence, no element of hostility."[2]

The family dog became part of Freud's life and was frequently present during sessions with patients. Martin Freud claimed that his father did not have to consult the clock. "When Jofi got up and yawned, the time was up; she was never late in announcing the end of a session, although father did admit that she was capable of an error of perhaps a minute, at the expense of the patient."[3]

---

[1]Freud, the Man and the Cause. Ronald Clark, Random House N.Y. 1980, p. 403
[2]Ibid. p. 484
[3]Ibid. p. 484

CHAPTER XXVII

To Find One's Porcupine

This was a lively time for Freud, now fifty-two years old, and for the psychoanalytic movement. In December 1908, he was invited to the United States. Stanley Hall, President of Clark University, Worcester, Massachusetts, asked him to give a series of lectures at the University, as part of the celebration of the twentieth anniversary of its foundation.

The year had been a productive one. Psychoanalysis had been introduced to a far wider and more distant audience, and Freud had published five papers.

He accepted Stanley Hall's invitation, but adopted a casual attitude concerning his visit to America. Afterwards he confided to his friends that he had been anxious about the reception he would receive. To minimize his fear about the entry of psychoanalysis into the New World, he persuaded himself that the real reason for his going to America was to see a wild porcupine. While there he would incidentally give a few lectures. Ferenczi, on the other hand, whom he had invited to join him, was very excited. Ferenczi bought books on the mysterious country and began to learn English. Freud happened to be reading a book on Cyprus and when he learned that the best collection of Cypriot antiquities was in New York, he felt a little more enthusiasm for the trip. He was disinclined to prepare ahead for his lectures, declaring that he would do so aboard ship. Ferenczi asked whether he would bring a silk hat with him, and Freud told him that his plan was to buy one in America and heave it into the sea on the way back.

Freud then heard that Jung had also been invited and that changed his attitude.

> 18 June 1909, Vienna, IX Berggasse 19
>
> Dear Friend,
>
> Your being invited to America is the best thing that has happened to us since Salzburg....What am I to say to those people?...We can think about it on shipboard, on our long walks round the deck....The invitation is the main thing, that the audience is now at our mercy, under obligation to applaud whatever we bring them.

More good news. In the spring his eldest daughter, Mathilde, became engaged and shortly after married to a young Viennese gentleman. Freud was very happy. In response to Ferenczi's congratulations, he confessed that he had hoped that Ferenczi would be the lucky man.

He stayed with his family, who were vacationing in a remote valley close to the Bavarian Alps, until it was time for his trip. As planned, he met Ferenczi and Jung in Bremen. The following day he wrote four long letters to Martha, three from Bremen and one from Southhampton which they reached that evening.

In Bremen Freud was host to his two traveling companions at a luncheon. Jung was a teetotaler. He had been brought up on a fanatical anti-alcohol tradition which was reinforced by the similar views of the Burgholzli. Freud found this attitude on wine somewhat amusing and tried to laugh Jung out of it. And indeed Jung did drink a glass of wine with lunch, whereupon Freud slumped to the ground in a faint.

Freud explained his fainting spell as the effect of his exhausted physical condition, a sleepless night, severe migraine, and some alcohol—as well as the psychic victory over Jung. Freud on occasion suffered from neurotic anxiety when he experienced a triumph over another man. He traced this symptom to the death of his brother Julius when Freud was two years old. His ''triumph'' over Julius left him with feelings that he deserved to be punished. Fainting protected him from feeling guilt.

Jung in ''Memories, Dreams, Reflections'' offered another version of the episode. Jung had been expounding at length the subject of mummified corpses from prehistoric times being recently found in Germany. Freud interrupted him with the charge that Jung had death wishes toward him. Freud then fainted. Jung wrote that he was surprised and alarmed at the intensity of Freud's fantasies.

That evening Jung was the dinner host and the three companions shared a lively exchange of ideas. The following morning they boarded the George Washington for New York.

Years later Bleuler was to charge Freud with having driven Jung to drink.

Freud wrote long letters to Martha every day to be posted later. He described a delightful voyage, with interesting discussions and pleasant laughter throughout each day. Freud claimed that of the three he was clearly the best sailor. He found his steward reading ''The Psychopathology of Everyday Life,'' and at that moment it occurred to him for the first time that he might someday be famous.

A daily activity was analyzing one another's dreams. Jung told Jones that Freud's dreams expressed concern for the future of his family and his work.

In New York they stayed at the Hotel Manhattan, paying two-and-a-half dollars a day. Brill, an analyst practicing in New York, was their host and showed them around the city. The next morning was spent at the Metropolitan Museum of Art; Freud was particularly interested in the Grecian antiquities. Jones joined the party the next day from Toronto. There was dinner at Hammerstein's Roof Garden, followed by a movie. It was the first film they had seen. In the early Hollywood style, it was full of wild chases, and the boyish Ferenczi found it exciting. Freud however was only mildly amused. More museums and much dining had its effect. They agreed it was time for a rest and a day's fast from America's rich food. The trip to Worcester was an overnight journey that included a curious combination of ship and hotel, and finally a train. The next morning Freud was to deliver his first lecture.

What should he talk about? Jung suggested that he devote his lectures to the subject of dreams. Freud replied that the Americans might regard the subject as impractical if not downright frivolous. At Jones's suggestion that he choose a wider subject, he decided on a general view of psychoanalysis. Each lecture was prepared in Ferenczi's company during their half-hour walk to the auditorium.

> In the morning, before the time had come for my lecture to begin, we would walk together in front of the University building and I would ask him to

> suggest what I should talk about that day. He thereupon gave me a sketch of what, half an hour later, I improvised in my lecture. In this way he had a share in the origins of the "Five Lectures."
> (Sandor Ferenczi, 1932, S.E. XXII, p. 227)

This extemporaneous style proved to be an advantage. The "Five Lectures" are easy to read, they are considered among the best general outlines of psychoanalysis, and they have become a favorite of students and laymen alike. They have since been translated into ten languages.

The opening lines of the series give us another look into the man.

> Ladies and Gentlemen
> It is with novel and bewildering feelings that I find myself in the New World lecturing before an audience of expectant enquirers. No doubt I owe this honor only to the fact that my name is linked with the topic of psychoanalysis....
>
> If it is a merit to have brought psychoanalysis into being, that merit is not mine. I had no share in its earliest beginnings. I was a student and working for my final examinations at the time when another Viennese physician, Dr. Josef Breuer, first made use of this procedure on a girl who was suffering from hysteria.
> (Five Lectures on Psychoanalysis, 1909 S.E. XI, 9)

Freud followed his introduction with an account of Breuer and Anna O. Then came comments about the problem of hysteria:

> The enigmatic condition which, from the ancient Greek medicine, had been known as "hysteria" and which has the power of producing illusory pictures of a whole number of serious diseases....Medical skill is in most cases powerless against severe diseases of the brain, but neither can the doctor do anything against hysterical disorders....
>
> Thus the recognition of the illness as hysteria makes little difference to the patient. But to the doctor quite the reverse. It is noticeable that his attitude towards hysterical patients is quite other than towards sufferers from organic diseases. He does not have the same sympathy for the former as for the latter....But all his knowledge—his training in anatomy, in physiology and in pathology—leaves him in the lurch when he is confronted by the details of hysterical phenomena. He cannot understand hysteria, and in the face of it he is himself a layman. This is not a pleasant

> situation for anyone who as a rule sets so much store by his knowledge. So it comes about that hysterical patients forfeit his sympathy. He regards them as people who are transgressing the laws of his science—like heretics in the eyes of the orthodox. He attributes every kind of wickedness to them, accuses them of exaggeration, of deliberate deceit, of malingering. And he punishes them by withdrawing his interest from them.
> (Ibid. 10-12)

Next came an example from a case he himself treated which he concluded with the now famous line "our hysterical patients suffer from reminiscences."

Freud reminded his listeners that the death of Eleanor of Aquitaine in the thirteenth century is commemorated by a carved gothic column at Charing Cross in London. The great Fire of 1666 is commemorated by a towering and more modern column, which is simply known as the Monument. Now, what would one think of a Londoner who shed tears whenever he passed the Monument, or became depressed when he went by Charing Cross?

> Yet every single hysteric and neurotic behaves like these two unpractical Londoners. Not only do they remember painful experiences of the remote past, but they still cling to them emotionally; they cannot get free of the past and for its sake they neglect what is real and immediate. This fixation of mental life to the pathogenic traumas is one of the most significant and practically important characteristics of neurosis.
> (Ibid. 16-17)

The second Lecture was taken up with how the development of psychoanalytic technique grew out of his dissappointment with hypnotism. Using a case from *Studies in Hysteria* he gave the audience an account of resistance and repression.

The third Lecture showed how ordinary everyday errors, forgetfulness, slips of the tongue, and even jokes and humor, led to an understanding of the unconscious. He also expounded the concept and importance of "free association" for a psychoanalysis. He went on:

> I must admit, Ladies and Gentlemen, that I hesitated for a long time...to present you with a detailed account of dream-interpretation. I was held back by a purely subjective and seemingly secondary motive. It seemed to me almost indecent in a country which is devoted to practical aims to make my appearance as a "dream interpreter," before you could possibly know the importance that can attach to that antiquated and derided art. The interpretation of dreams is in fact the royal road to a knowledge of the unconscious....
> (Ibid. p. 33)

He referred to critics who stumbled on the concept of dream interpretation; their objections always revealed their ignorance of the subject. His exposition of the psychoanalytic view of the dream was masterfully simple, concise and complete.

In the fourth Lecture, he came to the tricky question of sex and infantile sexuality in particular. He stated that his research "with surprising regularity" traced the patients' symptoms to their erotic life.

> I am aware that this assertion of mine will not be willingly believed. Even workers who are ready to follow my psychological studies are inclined to think that I overestimate the part played by sexual factors; they meet me with the question why other mental excitations should not lead to the phenomena I have described of repression and the formation of substitutes. I can only answer that I do not know why they should not, and that I have no objection to their doing so.
>
> (Ibid. p. 40)

Further exposition of the subject show the audience that neurotic illness has a history, that psychoanalysis discovered that the unconscious conflicts have their origin in early childhood. Furthermore: "...these powerful wishful impulses of childhood may without exception be described as sexual."

> And now at last I am quite certain that I have surprised you. "Is there such a thing, then, as infantile sexuality?" you will ask, "Is not childhood on the contrary the period of life that is marked by the absence of the sexual instincy?" No, Gentlemen, it is certainly not the case that the sexual instinct enters into children at the age of puberty in the way in which, in the Gospel the devil entered into the swine. A child has its sexual instincts and activities from the first; it comes into the world with them; and, after an important course of development through many stages, they lead to what is known as the normal sexuality of the adult. There is even no difficulty in observing the manifestations of these sexual activities in children; on the contrary, it calls for some skill to overlook them or explain them away.
>
> By a lucky chance I am in a position to call a witness in favour of my assertions from your very midst.
>
> (Ibid. 41-42)

He referred to the work of Dr. Sanford Bell, a Fellow of Clark University, who had published a paper dealing with infantile sexuality in the American Journal of Psychology in 1902. "The author says exactly what I have just told you."

His last Lecture was rather broad and general. He explained how civilization itself contributes to a reality which is unsatisfying, thereby encouraging flight into fantasy. There are various outcomes of fantasies and this raises the problem of adaptation to reality or its alternative, the creation of neurotic symptoms. The exception may be the artist, who may sublimate his fantasies into artistic endeavors rather than developing a neurosis. After a brief account of transference, the phenomenon of displacing feelings from the past onto the analyst, he dealt with certain fears and criticism of psychoanalysis. It is commonly believed that if a forbidden impulse is admitted into consciousness, the instinct will run riot. He explained why the opposite is true; why and how consciousness contributes to the control of antisocial impulses.

That was it. He had presented an honest exposition of psychoanalysis and he felt that he had offended only a few of his listeners.

The five lectures were delivered in German, without notes. His serious conversational tone held his audience in rapt attention. He once remarked that whenever he attended a lecture in which the speaker read from a paper, he had the feeling that they were on a bicycle and that he was running alongside to catch up. Very early in his career he decided never to address an audience by reading. Sink or swim, better to talk extemporaneously without a paper.

The lectures had been open to the public and many important personalities of the profession attended. Afterwards he was surrounded and congratulated by members of the audience.

The reviews of the lectures were mixed. According to the Dean of the University of Toronto: "An ordinary reader would gather that Freud advocates free love, removal of all restraints, and a relapse into savagery."[1]

An Honorary Doctorate was conferred upon him at the close of the ceremonies. When he stood to thank the University he was visibly moved to have it recognized at last, after so many years of abuse, insult, and public contempt, that psychoanalysis was not the expression of a wild imagination, but a reality. Eminent responsible professionals considered it to be valuable, accepted and even honored it. All this was overwhelming. The opening line of his short speech was "This is the first official recognition of our endeavors."

William James, then terminally ill, was in the audience. He knew German well and was able to follow the lectures closely. He was most congenial and with his arm around Jone's shoulder said, "The future of psychology belongs to your work." Incidentally, Freud once said that William James was the only true genius he had ever met.

In his autobiography Freud wrote:

> ...Another event of this time which made a lasting impression upon me was a meeting with William James, the philosopher. I shall never forget one little scene that occurred as we were on a walk together. He stopped suddenly, handed me a bag he was carrying and asked me to walk on, saying that he would catch me up as soon as he had got through an attack of angina pectoris which was just coming on. He died of that disease a year later; and I have always wished that I might be

[1]Ibid. 57

> as fearless as he was in the face of approaching death.
> (Autobiography, S.E. XX, 51-2)

Stanley Hall, their host, stood among the first rank of psychologists. He was openly enthusiastic and appreciative of both Freud and Jung. Freud wrote to Pfister:

> It is one of the pleasantest phantasies to imagine that somewhere far off, without one's having a glimmering of it, there are decent people finding their way into our thoughts and efforts, who after all suddenly make their appearance. That is what happened to me with Stanley Hall. Who could have known that over there in America....there was a respectable old gentleman waiting impatiently for the next number of the Jahrbuch (journal) reading and understanding it all....
> (Jones, II, 57)

A few years later Stanley Hall turned to Adler's school, with its emphasis on social problems as the cause of neurotic conflicts. It is interesting that the Adlerians, with their emphasis on power, enjoyed their greatest success in the United States. When Freud heard what direction Hall's interest had taken, he was very disappointed.

There is a little anecdote that is worth reporting, since it may be the root of an extraordinary rumor that Freud sometimes advocated parricide. Stanley Hall had referred to Freud a friend who was suffering from agoraphobia. The poor man was so afraid to venture out onto the street alone that he could not earn a living. It turned out that one of the reasons for his condition was his unconscious longing to be supported by his father, an angry unsympathetic man. When Stanley Hall asked Freud what he could do for his friend, Freud jestingly replied "Kill his father." Hall was so shocked that Freud had to assure him that he had not made that recommendation to the patient.

J.J. Putnam, the Professor of Neurology at Harvard, attended the lectures. This most distinguished man, in his sixties at the time, was unusually openminded. It was on this occasion that he and Freud met and established a friendship that proved to be permanent. A collection of Putnam's writings was the first volume in the International PsychoAnalytical Library series.

The three travelers visited Niagara Falls which Freud found grander than he had expected. However, when a guide held other visitors back calling out: "Let the old fellow go first," his feelings were hurt. Years later, referring to the trip to the New World, he remarked, "In those days I was a young man, I was only in my fifties."

Having crossed briefly into Canada, which pleased Freud, they proceeded to the Adirondack Mountains near Lake Placid, where they stayed for four days as Putnam's guests. Unfortunately Freud had a mild attack of appendicitis, but not wishing to bother his host or make Ferenczi anxious, he did not mention it to anyone.

In addition to appendicitis, he suffered from prostitis. The latter was particularly bothersome. All his life he had been accustomed to street-side *Pissoirs.* In Europe, facilities for urination by men were quite ample; not so in America. Freud's discription was that in the United States you walked for miles in an underground corridor and then, at the last moment, you suddenly came to a marble palace.

On a walk, to his great surprise and satisfaction, they did actually sight a wild porcupine, and in the inner psychoanalytic circle, "to find one's porcupine" became a recognized saying. Before Freud left, he took with him a souvenir that he kept on his desk for the rest of his life; the Putnams had given him a gift, a small, metal porcupine paperweight.[1]

He never had a favorable impression of America, much of his aversion being unfair prejudice. He attributed his dislike of the country to a lasting intestinal difficulty which he blamed on American cooking, obviously an unconvincing rationalization.

Why was he displeased with America? "The absence of any deep-rooted scientific tradition in America and the much less stringent rule of official authority" (History p. 32), added to the country's traditional puritanism, gave Freud pause. As a European he was accustomed to a slower pace and a sense of dignity and respect for learning. In a culture in which "time is money," these qualities are not very prominent. Even today, many Europeans object to the pace and rhythm of New York.

America, young, brimming with success, enthusiastic, with a dash of arrogance, practical, had no time to explore anything in depth. Freud complained that Americans tended to read popular summaries and reviews of science and philosophy rather than the original source material. They expressed themselves in fads. In the United States, what was popular became a "craze." A "psychoanalytic craze" would use his name and a few terms which would become the "real thing." Amateurs and charlatans would quickly move in and "make a business of it." Freud feared that if psychoanalysis were to find a place in America, it would be sold on every street corner with orange juice and hot dogs.

> Psycho-analysis...has not lost ground in America since our visit; it is extremely popular among the lay public and is recognized by a number of official psychiatrists as an important element in medical training. Unfortunately, however it has suffered a great deal from being watered down. Moreover, many abuses which have no relation to it find a cover under its name....In America, too, it has come in conflict with Behaviourism, a theory which is naive enough to boast that it has put the whole problem of psychology completely out of court.
>
> (Autobiographical Study, p. 52)

It may have seemed to Freud that Americans lacked a sense of tradition, and their free and easy manners made him a little less than comfortable. He used the term "Americanized" for shallow, gaudy, brazen. Furthermore, his difficulty with the English language was a source of frustration to him; he was very sensitive about understanding and being understood by others. On one occasion an American asked another to repeat a statement and Freud turned to Jung and remarked that they couldn't even understand one another. In one of his whimsical moods he predicted that white Americans would get into serious trouble with Blacks. "America is already

[1]Clark, p. 275

threatened by the Black race. And it serves her right. A country without even wild strawberries!''[1]

Over the years, close contact with Americans visiting Vienna softened his attitude. In 1930 Dr. Feigenbaum, editor of an American Medical Review, asked Freud to write something for a special issue on psychopathology. Freud wrote:

> ...I often hear that psycho-analysis is very popular in the United States and that it does not come up against the same stubborn resistance there as it does in Europe. My satisfaction over this is, however, clouded by several circumstances... Quite particularly, often we find in Ameican physicians and writers a very insufficient familiarity with psycho-analysis, so that they know only its terms and a few catchwords...And these same men lump psychoanalysis with other systems of thought, which may have developed out of it but are incompatible with it today. Or they make a hotch-potch out of psycho-analysis and other elements and quote this procedure as evidence of their ''broadmindedness'' whereas it only proves their lack of judgment.
>
> Many of these evils which I have mentioned with regret no doubt arise from the fact that there is a general tendency in America to shorten study and preparation and to proceed as fast as possible to practical application. There is a preference, too, for studying a subject like psycho-analysis not from the original sources but from second-hand and often inferior accounts. Thoroughness is bound to suffer from this.
>
> (Introduction, Medical Review of Reviews, 1930, S.E. XXI, 254)

On the other hand, Americans who were serious and wished to study, found Freud to be very supportive and generous.

---

[1]Jones 2, p. 60

CHAPTER XXVIII

Where Do I Come From?

Psychoanalysis continued to grow and become internationally recognized. However, Freud did not rest; indeed, he pursued with vigor and continued interest his work as clinician and investigator of the minds of patients. Throughout his life, despite what went on outside his consulting room, he carried on his exploration of the human mind.

In 1908 he published ''On the Sexual Theories of Children.'' Unostentatiously, he presented to the world a set of new ideas. Concepts of oral fertilization, birth through the anus, parental intercourse viewed as something sadistic, and the idea that both sexes possessed a penis, were dropped casually before the incredulous eyes of the reader almost without warning.

The material was derived from the conscious memory of adults in psychoanalytic treatment and from the direct observation of what children say and do.

> In consequence of unfavourable circumstances...the following observations apply chiefly to the sexual development of one sex only—that is of males.
> (On the Sexual Theories of Children, 1908, S.E. IX, p. 211)

It should be mentioned that Freud, like his readers, was a bit overwhelmed by the bizarreness of what came from the minds of his patients. As a thorough scientist he appreciated that the sexual life of ''men alone has become accessible to research.'' Nonetheless, he proceeded as though there were a complete likeness between the two sexes. Later in his career, when psychoanalytic research had gathered more information, he was to write: ''The expectation of there being a complete parallel was mistaken.''

The first grand problem in a child's life is, ''Where do babies come from?'' More specifically, it is probably where did the new baby, this particular intruder, come from? Eventually, when he has overcome some of his self-consciousness, he will ask his parents, or whoever is in charge of him and who, in his eyes, knows everything and is the source of all knowledge. The answers usually given are either evasive, or standard myth such as ''the stork brought him.''

> I have reason to believe that far more children than their parents suspect are dissatisfied with this solution and meet it with energetic doubts, which, however, they do not always openly admit....It

> seems to me to follow from a great deal of information I have received that children refuse to believe the stork theory and that from the time of this first deception and rebuff nourish a distrust of adults and have a suspicion of there being something forbidden which is being withheld from them by the "grown-ups," and that they consequently hide their further researches under a cloak of secrecy.
> (Ibid. 213)

We have here the beginning of a "psychical conflict." Based on intuition, theories have been developed by the child, theories that he senses are not "right" from the grown-ups' viewpoint. In addition, new information which comes his way he knows to be unmentionable and he suppresses it. "The nuclear complex of a neurosis is in this way brought into being."

> I now know that the change which takes place in the mother during pregnancy does not escape the child's sharp eyes and that he is very well able before long to establish the true connection between the increase in his mother's stoutness and the appearance of the baby....This precocious discovery, however, is always kept secret.
> (Ibid. 214)

Based on his observations of people and animals, the child knows that babies grow inside the mother's body. He is on the right track, but a single piece of ignorance stymies him. His theories are false but are imposed on him by his incomplete state of sexual development.

In the first place the little boy attributes to everyone, including females, a genital similar to his own. This leading erotogenic zone and chief auto-erotic object, is valued so highly by the boy, that he cannot imagine any living being not having one. When he does see a little girl's genital he denies what he sees and says: "Hers is small, but when she gets bigger it'll grow." Why the distorted perception? Because the fact that anyone could be without a penis, or could possibly lose it, is too frightening for him to bear. He distorts his perception to protect himself from anxiety. He clings to this idea to protect himself from his dread of losing his highly prized organ. Should he become fixated, should he not outgrow this idea—this fear—then, when older, he will seek a love object with genitals similar to his own. He will make a homosexual object choice. Women, as he comes to know them later, cannot possibly be sexual objects for him because they lack the essential organ. Indeed they may even become abhorrent to him. On more than one occasion, when observed by his parents or a nurse pleasuring himself, he was threatened with having it cut off unless he gave up this socially unacceptable practice. If he remains fixated, he will not have outgrown this "threat of castration." The woman's genitalia will then be regarded as a mutilated organ and will arouse horror rather than pleasure in him.

> Anatomy has recognized the clitoris within the female pudenda as being an organ that is

> homologous to the penis; and the physiology of the sexual processes has been able to add that this small penis which does not grow any bigger behaves in fact during childhood like a real and genuine penis—that it becomes the seat of excitations which lead to its being touched, that its excitability gives the little girl's sexual activity a masculine character and that a wave of repression in the years of puberty is needed in order for this masculine sexuality to be discarded and the woman to emerge.
>
> (Ibid. 217)

When women suffered from frigidity, Freud noted, it was only the vagina that was anaesthetic; the clitoris remained extremely sensual. An obstinate clinging to the monopoly of sensation by the clitoris has to be modified and extended to the vagina if the frigidity is to be overcome. So one might say there is some truth in the infantile sexual theory, that women, like men, possess a penis.

Returning to the problem of how babies are made, the knowledge that the baby grows inside the mother is not sufficient. How does the baby get inside? It is obvious that the father has something to do with it, but what? The excitations in the child's penis impel urges to press in, push, penetrate, insert, but these impulses are thwarted by his ignorance of the vagina. Even when he senses that the father's penis has something to do with the mystery, he is still hopelessly perplexed. He still insists that mother possesses a penis just like a man's; the existence of the female cavity remains undiscovered.

Freud believed that the intellectual efforts made to solve this problem, the brooding and the doubting, became the prototype of all later intellectual pursuits.

Ignorance of the vagina gives rise to one infantile theory: if the baby is growing inside the mother's body, how does it come out? The awareness of only one opening provides the answer: the baby is evacuated like feces. This conclusion takes place before the development of a reaction of disgust to the movement of the bowels. By the time the child is old enough to discuss the matter with his friends, the anal birth has given way to a navel birth, or to the idea that the abdomen is cut open to allow the baby to come out. If babies are born through the anus, then women no longer have the exclusive prerogative of giving birth to children. A man can too. In the fantasies of male analysands, the wish to have a baby from the father is recalled again and again.

The theory of the anal birth contains the solution to how does the baby get inside the mother; one has but to eat some special thing and a baby will grow.

> This infantile theory of birth is revived in cases of insanity. A manic woman, for instance, will lead the visiting doctor to a little heap of feces which she has deposited in a corner of her cell, and say to him with a laugh, "That's the baby I had today."
>
> (Ibid. 220)

Sooner or later the child learns what his parents' sexual intercourse is. Whether they witness the act by chance or hear it from an adjoining room, children always arrive at the same conclusion: that it is a painful, sadistic act.

> I have not been able to ascertain that children recognize this behavior which they have witnessed between their parents as the missing link needed for solving the problem of babies; it appears more often that the connection is overlooked by them for the very reason that they have interpreted the act of love as an act of violence.
> (Ibid. 220)

A number of things may come together to give children this impression. A wife whose husband's embraces bring her no pleasure, but the risk of a fresh pregnancy, may communicate her reluctance to her husband. The child who is pretending to be asleep, may get the impression that the mother is resisting and defending herself from an act of violence. Some marriages offer a child the spectacle of ceaseless quarreling, loud arguments, and unfriendly remarks and gestures; we need not be surprised if the child believes that this goes on at night also, and that his parents settle their disputes as he does his with his siblings or playmates. Blood, discovered on a bedsheet or mother's underclothes confirms his view. No question about it, father made another assault on her last night. (Many a neurotic's "horror of blood" can be traced to this origin.)

Another question engages the child: what is the nature and substance of "being married"? All the answers have in common the idea of pleasure and a disregard for modesty. Some of the more frequent notions are that each member of the married couple urinates in front of the other. (A variation is that the man urinates into the woman's chamber pot, or that the two show their behinds to each other without being ashamed.) These seem to be the most frequent theories that children produce to explain the mysteries. These are others: for example, the idea that a baby comes from a kiss. This theory seems to be exclusively a feminine concept.

At about the tenth or eleventh year, children discuss sexual matters among themselves. An older child, or a child who has learned something the others don't know yet, enjoys a feeling of superiority as he informs his friends about the facts of life. What the children learn this way is mostly correct. The existence of the vagina and its purpose is revealed but the explanations are incomplete and get confused with the older infantile theories. Until now it was ignorance of the vagina that prevented the boy from understanding the process; now it is something else: it is ignorance of the semen. No child can guess that a substance other than urine is excreted by the penis.

The game is not yet over; the whole process is not yet understood. New theories grow but lack the creativity of the primary fantasies which were linked to the child's own sexual components and his libidinal development. Some of the later theories include: a girl explains to her friends that the husband gives his wife an egg, and she hatches it in her body. A boy who heard of the egg theory identified it with his testicle which in German is vulgarly called by the same name. He racked his brain trying to figure out how the scrotum could be constantly renewed. Another girl reported that intercourse takes place only once and lasts for twenty-four hours. All successive babies come from that one event.

Freud was not particularly interested in these ideas; he was pursuing the child's thoughts as they changed with his psychosexual stages: oral theories, anal theories, and so on. However widely children's later ideas may vary, Freud assumed that in the first years of childhood their attitudes are absolutely uniform. "We may feel certain that at that time all of them tried most eagerly to discover what it was that their parents did with each other so as to produce babies."[1]

[1]Ibid. 226

CHAPTER XXIX

■ *Diminishing Returns*

In 1908 Freud took a brief excursion into sociology; he published *Civilized Sexual Morality and Modern Nervous Illness.* The paper expresses his notion that the demands of society on the individual, especially on his sexual life, are oppressive, and make modern man anxious and neurotic.

Freud quotes several writers who are also concerned about the increase of nervousness in the general population and who attribute it to conditions at the beginning of the century. How strange it seems to us that they felt the essential trouble to be the speed of modern communication! He quotes W. Erb (1893):

> The original question, then, is whether the causes of nervous illness that have been put before you are present in modern life to such a heightened degree as to account for a marked increase in that form of illness....The extraordinary achievements of modern times, the progress in the face of increasing competition—these things have only been gained, and can only be held by great mental effort. The demands made on the efficiency of the individual in the struggle for existence have greatly increased and it is only by putting out all his mental powers that he can meet them. At the same time, the individual's needs and his demands for the enjoyment of life have increased in all classes; unprecedented luxury has spread to strata of the population who were formerly quite untouched by it; irreligion, discontent and covetousness have grown up in wide social spheres. The immense extension of communications which has been brought about by the network of telegraphs and telephones that encircle the world has completely altered the conditions of trade and commerce. All is hurry and agitation...political, religious and social struggles, party politics, electioneering, and the enormous spread of trade-unionism inflame tempers, place an ever greater strain on the mind, and encroach upon the hours for recreation, sleep and rest. City life is constantly becoming more sophisticated and more restless. The exhausted nerves seek recuperation in increased stimulation

> and in highly spiced pleasures, only to become more exhausted than before. Modern literature stirs up all the passions, and encourages sensuality and a craving for pleasure and contempt for every fundamental ethical principle and every ideal. It brings before the reader's mind pathological figures and problems concerned with psychopathic sexuality, and revolutionary and other subjects. Our ears are excited and overstimulated by large doses of noisy and insistent music. The theatres captivate all our senses with their exciting performances. The plastic arts, too, turn by preference to what is repellant, ugly and suggestive, and do not hesitate to set before your eyes with revolting fidelity the most horrible sights that reality has to offer....Let me now fill in the picture with new details.
>
> (Civilized Sexual Morality and Modern Nervous Illness, 1908, S.E. IX, p. 183)

Freud does not disagree with the above, but rather feels it insufficient. He presents an aspect of harm done by civilization that is seldom mentioned, namely, the restrictions on our sexual drives that society imposes on the individual. This factor alone can produce neurosis. In this view, civilization is based on the suppression of instincts and he raises the question whether or not we have reached the point of diminishing returns, whether the benefits we get from society are worth the dues we pay.

He describes the different phases of psychosexual development. The pregenital, the genital phase that leads to reproduction, and then the restriction of this to legal reproduction in marriage. There are many who have difficulty enduring even early restrictions and the results are neuroses or perversions. He believes that only a minority can suffer social restrictions without harm. Total abstinence, he feels, cannot be borne by most people without affecting their energy, self-confidence, or mental health. He was far from convinced that only marriage provided a satisfactory solution.

> This brings us to the question whether sexual intercourse in legal marriage can offer full compensation for the restriction imposed before marriage. There is such an abundance of material supporting a reply in the negative that we can give only the briefest summary of it. It must also above all be borne in mind that our cultural sexual morality restricts sexual intercourse even in marriage itself since it imposes on married couples the necessity of contenting themselves as a rule, with a very few procreative acts. As a consequence of this consideration, satisfying sexual intercourse in marriage takes place only for a few years; after three, four or five years, the marriage becomes a failure in so far as it has promised the satisfaction of sexual needs.
>
> (Ibid. p. 194)

Freud complains about the inadequacy of the devices invented for preventing conception. "They hurt the fine susceptibilities of both partners and even actually cause illness." Fear of the consequences of sexual intercourse first brings the married couple's physical affection to an end. And then it usually puts a stop to the mental sympathy between them, which should have been the successor to their original passionate love. The spiritual disillusionment and bodily deprivation to which most marriages are thus doomed returns both partners to the state they were in before their marriage, even the poorer by the loss of an illusion, and they must once more have recourse to their fortitude in mastering and deflecting their sexual drive.

> We need not enquire how far men, by then in their maturer years, succeed in this task. Experience shows that they very frequently avail themselves of the degree of sexual freedom which is allowed them—although only with reluctance under a veil of silence....
> (Ibid. p. 195)

The "double standard" which allows men sexual license not permitted women, is more than unfair; it is the plainest admission that society does not believe in the possibility of enforcing its own prescription: "Experience shows, I repeat, that women, when they are subjected to the disillusionment of marriage, fall ill of severe neuroses which permanently darken their lives."[1]

Freud felt that under the cultural conditions of the day, a woman could no longer turn to marriage as the panacea for her frustrations. "A girl must be very healthy if she is to be able to tolerate it (marriage)."[2]

The cure for the disappointment and nervous illness that marriage itself induces would be marital infidelity. But the more moral her upbringing, the more she sees herself as a respectable person, the less likely she is to turn to marital unfaithfulness as an alternative. "In the conflict between her desires and her sense of duty, she once more seeks refuge in a neurosis. Nothing protects her virtue as securely as an illness."[3] What our culture promises, that in marriage one will find gratification, proves to be incorrect. The deprivation imposed on premarital states, is not compensated by marriage.

Freud makes the point that frigidity in women and a diminished potency in men is much more common than is generally admitted, and until we develop more efficient and satisfactory means of contraception, this condition will continue. As things are, only a woman with a good ego can successfully endure a marriage.

Our civilization and our education aim to retard sexual development and sexual activity. "It is seen to be a necessity, when one considers the late age at which young people of the educated classes reach independence and are able to earn a living."[4] However, Freud believes that abstinence in young adults leads to other damage, even though it may not produce a neurosis. In his experience, abstinence does not bring about energetic and self-reliant persons, or creative thinkers, or bold

---

[1]Ibid. p. 195
[2]Ibid. p. 195
[3]Ibid. p. 195
[4]Ibid. p. 196

imaginative reformers, but more often it produces "well-behaved weaklings" who get lost in the general population that follows, unwillingly, the directions given by leaders.

Civilized education, in an attempt to maintain itself, tries to suppress the sexual drive only temporarily until marriage. Afterwards it intends to give it free rein.

> When the drive is set free it turns out to be permanently impaired. For this reason complete abstinence in youth is often not the best preparation for marriage for a young man. Women sense this, and prefer among their suitors those who have already proved their masculinity with other women.
>
> (Ibid. p. 197)

The harmful effects of the strict demands for abstinence in women before marriage are apparent. An education that forbids sexual intercourse and sets a high premium on female chastity, that attempts to protect the young woman from temptation as she grows up by keeping her ignorant of the role she is destined to play, and by finding intolerable any impulses of love in her which cannot lead to marriage, produces feelings of insecurity and confusion.

> The result is that when the girl's parents, authorities, suddenly allow her to fall in love, she is unequal to this psychical achievement and enters marriage uncertain of her own feelings....I do not know whether the anaesthetic type of woman exists apart from civilized education....But in any case such education actually breeds it.
>
> (Ibid. p. 197)

Thus the preparation for marriage frustrates the aims of marriage.

> When, later on, the retardation in the wife's development has been overcome and her capacity for love is awakened at the climax of her life as a woman, her relations to her husband have long since been ruined; and as a reward for her previous docility, she is left with the choice between unappeased desire, unfaithfulness, or a neurosis.
>
> (ibid. p. 197)

Freud goes on to state that our sexual behavior determines our pattern for dealing with other aspects of life. If a man pursues his love object energetically, we are confident that he will pursue his other aims with similar ardor. The man who refrains from gratifying his sexual drive, will tend to be conciliatory and resigned in other spheres of life as well. A special application of this concept can easily be recognized in women.

> Their upbringing forbids their concerning

> themselves with sexual problems though they nevertheless feel extremely curious about them, and frightens them by condemning such curiosity as unwomanly and a sign of a sinful disposition. In this way they are scared away from any form of thinking, and knowledge loses its value for them....I do not believe that women's "physiological feeble-mindedness" is to be explained by a biological opposition between intellectual work and sexual activity as Moebius (1903) has asserted....I think that the undoubted intellectual inferiority of so many women can rather be traced back to the inhibition of thought necessitated by sexual suppression.
> (Ibid. p. 199)

Our civilized morality reduces our capacity for love and for sexual satisfaction by making us more or less inhibited. As a result, a husband's weak potency frustrates his wife and she remains anaesthetic, even in cases where her frigidity could have been overcome by a powerful sexual experience. A couple like this has more difficulty preventing the birth of children because the husband's diminished potency suffers when contraceptives are employed. In this embarrassing perplexity, sexual intercourse is given up, "and with this the basis of married life is abandoned."

The neurotic, frustrated wife may turn to her child for libidinal expression that is absent with her husband. The result is an over-anxious, over-tender, over-protective mother, who, as she transfers her need for love to her child, awakens within it a sexual precocity. However, our mores do not tolerate sexual activity that has been aroused so early, and the suppressing force that follows contains everything necessary for the bringing about of a life of nervous illness.

In view of the sacrifices that civilized morality imposes upon us, Freud asks is it worth it and have we, in fact, reached the point of diminishing returns?

Freud seemed to be in favor of basic changes in society, though he understood that it is difficult to bring about radical reforms in any one sphere. As a physician it was out of his province to make detailed suggestions as to what reforms should be effected. However, he believed that his experience of the neuroses demonstrated the need for revolutionary changes in our society.

One thing is certain. The man who has come to understand that women suffer more than men from conventional morality is a long way from the idealistic medical student.

CHAPTER XXX

■ *Poltergeists*

Jung's admiration for Freud did not extend to the latter's group of followers. He described them as mediocrities and was upset that Freud was so surrounded by them. The bad feelings between the Viennese group and the Swiss group were mutual. Freud saw Jung as creative and original, but the Viennese complained that his thinking was "muddy."

Karl Abraham, a practicing psychoanalyst in Berlin, had spent three years studying at the famous Burgholzli Clinic under Bleuler. He was familiar with their religious convictions, their quasi-mysticism, their vegetarianism, and teetotalism. He felt that their beliefs were not compatible with those held by Freud and his followers. He tried to open Freud's eyes to the alien characteristics of the Zurich group that did not bode well for the future. But Freud's hopes were too high for him to give them up. The Swiss would put psychoanalysis on the scientific map and assure its future.

Freud felt that the great Burgholzli Clinic would provide the answer to psychoanalysis' greatest deficiency: lack of laboratory observation and measurement. Brucke had left a stamp upon him that was indelible. His Viennese followers had explored the dynamics of the ever-present unconscious, but their scientific standards left much to be desired. Now Zurich would provide a scientific experimental base for the new psychology.

As it happened, Jung's laboratory work, his "associations experiments" were not very psychoanalytic. It was Jung who got involved with "complexes," and there were as many complexes as there were emotional experiences. People "had" complexes, and health meant "getting rid of them." It was not like the "Oedipus Complex," the only Freudian concept which employed the term. According to Freud, one didn't have an Oedipus Complex which one then got rid of—it was an infantile conflict which all men without exception experienced. No lab can measure it, but with an understanding of one's Oedipal feelings, neurotic behavior patterns based on this infantile conflict can be resolved and one can live a more normal and gratifying life.

Freud did not take Jung's deviations from psychoanalytic theory seriously. Had he been less involved with his hopes for the future of his work, he would have seen how Jung's understanding of behavior was unrelated to infantile origins, and therefore decidedly opposed to analytic theory. Even when his Viennese friends clear-sightedly pointed this out, he defended Jung. After all, Jung's background, as a minister's son raised in a conventional religious tradition, meant that he had more to overcome. An optimistic Freud saw Jung as courageous.

Looking back, it is surprising how long it took Freud to accept the fundamental differences in theory between himself and Jung. Freud kept encouraging him, despite Jung's wavering on the critical point of sexuality in the etiology of emotional disturbances. Furthermore, Jung's identity was more that of a heretic son than of a leader. As President of the newly formed International Association for Psychoanalysis, he soon showed himself remiss in fulfilling the responsibilities of the leader of a large organization. But the Swiss were now associated with psychoanalysis, which meant that international acceptance had become a real possibility. For the sake of the "cause" Freud denied or rationalized what was apparent to others.

Freud was candid about his aspirations:

> Dear Friend
> ....I gladly accept your invitation to stay with you....I have various plans in mind....My selfish purpose, which I frankly confess, is to persuade you to continue and complete my work by applying to psychoses what I have begun with neuroses. With your strong and independent character, with your Germanic blood which enables you to command the sympathies of the public more readily than I, you seem better fitted than anyone else I know to carry out this mission....Besides, I'm fond of you; but I have learned to subordinate that factor.
>
> (Freud, Jung Letters, Princeton University Press, Princeton, N.J., 1974, p. 168)

Jung continued his own researches, but it became increasingly clear that he was involved in mystical preoccupations and convictions: extrasensory perception, poltergeists, and the occult in general. Concerned about Freud's attitude toward precognition and parapsychology, Jung tackled him on the subject. According to Jung, Freud characterized these concepts as "nonsense." He added, however, that this was based on his "materialistic prejudice." Jung claimed that while they were discussing the subject, he had a "peculiar sensation." His diaphragm felt that it was made of iron and was starting to get red hot, "a red-hot diaphragm vault." At that very moment there was a crash in a bookcase beside them that was so loud that both men were startled. Jung explained to Freud that it was a "catalytic exteriorization phenomenon." Freud would not hear of such an explanation, whereupon Jung predicted that another explosive crash would follow, and according to Jung it did. He stated that he didn't know why he was so sure of his prediction, adding that Freud looked at him in horror. He never spoke further to Freud about the incident.[1]

> To Jung from Freud, April 16, 1909
>
> Dear Friend
> Thinking that you were already on your bicycle

---

[1]Is it prejudice on the author's behalf to suspect that Freud's horrified look was directed more to Jung's utterances than to athe crackling sounds in the bookcase?

> tour of Northern Italy, I wrote your wife a card from Venice...an early taste of spring and some relaxation.
>
> It is remarkable that on the same evening on which I formally adopted you as my oldest son...you simultaneously divested me of my paternal dignity....Now I am afraid of falling back into the role of the father for you by speaking of my reaction to the "Poltergeist." Nevertheless I must do so because it is different from what you might think. Now I do not deny that your communications and experiment made a strong impression on me. I decided after you left to make some observations, and here are the results. In my first room there is a constant cracking on the spot where the two heavy Egyptian steles rest on the oak boards of the bookcases. So this one is too transparent. In the second one where we heard it, there is very seldom any cracking. At first I would have considered it as evidence if the noise, which was heard so frequently in your presence, never made itself heard again after your departure. However, it has since recurred repeatedly but never in connection with my thoughts and when I was preoccupied with you or with this special problem of yours (not now either, I might add as a further challenge)....
>
> Thus I again put on the horn-rimmed paternal glasses and warn the dear son to keep a cool head and rather not understand something than make such great sacrifices for the sake of understanding. I also shake my wise head over the psychosynthesis and think: "Yes, that's the way they are, the young ones; they really enjoy only those things where they do not have to take us along where we, with our short breath and weary legs, cannot follow.

The letter continues with a description of Freud's superstitious obsession with the date of his death.

> ...a few years ago I discovered in myself the conviction that I would die between the ages of 61 and 62, which at that time seemed to be a long way off....It was absolutely uncanny how the numbers 61 and 62, in conjunction with 1 or 2, kept cropping up under all kinds of circumstances.

Freud gives examples of the number appearing in various guises and places such as his hotel room in Athens. But, he adds, since there are aspects of his personality that are avid for knowledge and not at all superstitious, he attempted an analysis of his conviction.

> Two events coincided at that time; first I wrote "The Interpretation of Dreams"...and secondly, I was assigned a new telephone number, which I have to this day—14362. It is easy to establish a link between these two facts; in the year 1899, when I wrote "The Interpretation of Dreams," I was 43 years old. What then was more natural than that the other numbers should signify the end of my life, namely 61 or 62. Suddenly there was a method in the madness. The superstition that I would die between 61 and 62 turned out to be the equivalent to the conviction that with "The Interpretation of Dreams" I had completed my life work, needed to produce no more, and could die in peace. You will admit that with this knowledge, it no longer sounds so nonsensical....I therefore shall be able to hear about your further investigations of the spook-complex with interest one has in a lovely illusion which one does not share oneself.
>
> Your Freud

One can enjoy this letter as an example of Freud's talent as a letter writer, but it has a very special meaning. He described his superstitious preoccupation with death dates in order to show Jung that one's own superstitions must be analyzed.

CHAPTER XXXI

A Matter For The Police

The growth of interest in psychoanalysis was counterbalanced by a growing opposition. In fact, active steps were being taken to stop this dangerous Freudian Movement. This storm of opposition particularly in the years before World War I had to be endured by Freud. Later it subsided, but it was something he had to face to a certain degree all his life.

It is difficult to describe the quality and the extent of the opposition. Much of it was so obscene that it never found its way into print. In the process of an analysis, infantile feelings, positive and negative, are brought to the surface. Unknowingly, the analysand "transfers" these feelings to the analyst. During the phase of negative transference, the patient unconsciously may try to hurt the analyst and treat him the way he wished to, or actually did, treat the early frustrating persons in his life. In all innocence, in the name of "free association," Freud's patients kept him abreast of the latest insults.

> The strength of the hostility was exemplified by the man who accosted him in the street and attacked him with: "Let me tell you what a dirty-minded filthy old man you are." Freud, inured to attack, smiled and turned away. He was well aware of the situation and would later say that people treated him like a freshly painted wall; they never dared to touch him. He believed that silence was often the best defense and once wrote: "I know that my work is odious to most people. So long as I behave perfectly correctly, my opponents are at a loss."
>
> (Clark, p. 191)

In Viennese society, at social gatherings, one had but to mention Freud's name, and there would be laughs. The mention of his name in the presence of a lady was considered bad taste.

But the most vicious attacks took place unrecorded, at scientific meetings and the private conversations that followed. He and his followers were regarded as evil, sexual perverts, and a real danger to civilization. His theories were interpreted as a direct incitement to the masses to throw off all restraints and indulge in primitive savagery. The panic his work induced led his critics to lose all sense of objectivity and values that they themselves held dear. Ferenczi remarked that "they may deny Freud's theories, but they certainly dream them."

At a meeting of professionals trained in scientific methodology, the Congress of German Neurologists and Psychiatrists in Hamburg (1910), a Professor Wilhelm Weygandt was so alarmed when Freud's theories were mentioned, that he banged his fist on the table shouting: This is not a topic for discussion at a scientific meeting, it is a matter for the police.[1] Ferenczi read a paper before the Medical Society of Budapest. He was told that Freud's work was a moral disgrace and that the proper place for a psychoanalyst was in prison.

The first actual victim was as Presbyterian minister, Donald Fraser, in far-off Australia. He was forced to leave the ministry because of his "Freudian ideas" (1908). That same year Ernest Jones had to resign a neurological appointment in London; his association with psychoanalysis had become known. Two years later, the Government of Ontario closed down a periodical for publishing papers that Jones had written. Psychoanalysis was unfit for even a medical journal.

The antagonism to Freud's work entered a new phase. Originally, his medical colleagues tried to ignore him. At the Congress of Mid-German Psychiatrists and Neurologists at Halle (1900), a symposium on hysteria was conducted. Freud's name was not even mentioned. Then they verbally attacked him. Now, 1910, they took direct action; doctors who were suspected of "Freudian views" were discharged from their posts. Or, if that were not possible, they were publicly vilified.

Professor Oppenheim, a famous neurologist, at the Neurological Congress in Berlin (1910) proposed that any institution that even tolerated psychoanalytic views should be blacklisted. The directors of sanitoria, present in the audience, immediately stood up, declared their purity, and took the loyalty oath. Freud had to be stopped.

No one was immune from a crusading anti-Freudian. Even the venerated J.J. Putnam, Professor of Neurology at Harvard, whose distinction as a scientist was only surpassed by his high ethical repute, was not exempt from persecution for being a "Freudian." At the meeting of the American Neurological Association in Washington (May 1910), a New York neurologist, Joseph Collins, in an after-dinner speech, made an outrageously insulting personal attack on Putnam. He angrily criticized the Association for allowing Putnam to read his paper which was nothing more than "pornographic stories about pure virgins." He urged the Association to take a stand against Christian Science, Freudianism, Transcendentalism, and "all that bosh, rot, and nonsense." The next day someone got up in the meeting and said the Association should be thankful that a man of Dr. Putnam's stature should have examined and tested this new work. (Incidentally, the moral Dr. Joseph Collins was well known for his dirty jokes in private).

M. Wulff, who had been trained in Berlin, was discharged from his position on account of "Freudian views." He emigrated to Odessa, Russia, established contact by correspondence with Freud and Ferenczi, and continued his work. Schneider, director of a seminary, was dismissed for being "too Freudian." Even Hans Sperber, the distinguished Swedish philologist, had his career ruined. He had written on the sexual origin of speech and was therefore denied access to the university. The list would grow tedious.

Ostwald Bumke published an attack on Freud, based on quotes from a review that had assailed Freud's ten-years-earlier position on paranoia. According to the review, no one could read Freud's allusions to sexuality without feeling a sense of

---

[1] Jones II, 109

horror. Such nonsense could only lead to "gruesome old-wives psychiatry." The quotation enjoyed some popularity and Bumke expanded his vituperation into a book which became the standard reference work on the subject during the Nazi period.

One last example of the opposition. Professor Ziehen was president of the Berlin Psychiatric Association. When Abraham presented a paper on "Dream States," President Ziehen forbade any discussion. The profession felt it was its urgent duty to wage war against this psychopathic theory and its perverse consequences.

Ziehen's evaluation of analytic theory may be estimated from the following anecdote. A patient came to the Berlin Psychiatric Clinic, of which Ziehen was the Director, complaining of a compulsion to lift women's skirts. Ziehen was delighted: "This is an opportunity to test the supposed sexual nature of such obsessions. I will ask him if it applies to older women as well, in which case it evidently cannot be erotic." The patient replied: "Oh yes, to all women, even my mother and sister." Ziehen triumphantly turned to his pupils, raised his arms and ordered the entry into the records of the case as "definitely non-sexual."[1]

The criticism we have discussed may be reduced to two charges: Freud's views were irrational and unnatural, and since his conclusions were unpleasant, they must be untrue.

Freud thought it useless to engage the opposition. The American poet Hilda Doolittle in her poignant account of her experience with Freud wrote: "The Professor is standing in his study....He is asking something of me....Of course, you understand is the offhand way in which he offers me, from time to time, some rare discovery, some priceless finding, or perhaps you may feel differently as if my feelings, my discoveries, were on a par with his own. He does not lay down the law, only this once—this one law. He says, Please never—I mean never at any time, in any circumstance, endeavour to defend me, if and when you hear abusive remarks made about me and my work....You will do no good to the detractor by mistakenly beginning a logical defense. You will drive the hatred or the fear or the prejudice in deeper. You will do no good to yourself, for you will only expose your own feelings.[2] Freud likened the hostility of the public to the resistance one finds in patients, and wasted little time and energy on the matter. His chief reply to acrimonious colleagues was either silence, or the publication of more evidence in corroboration of his theories. He may not have taken the resistance to heart, but he despised the stupidity and bad manners the opposition displayed.

> But fancy that, when the history of the phase we have lived through comes to be written, German science will not have cause to be proud of those who represented it. I am not thinking of the fact that they rejected psycho-analysis or of the decisive way in which they did so; both of these things were easily intelligible, they were only to be expected and at any rate they threw no discredit on the character of the opponents of analysis. But for the degree of arrogance which they displaced, for their

---

[1]Jones I, p. 115

[2]Tribute to Freud by H.D., Pantheon Books, N.Y. 1956, p. 130-131

> conscienceless contempt of logic, and for the coarseness and bad taste of their attacks there could be no excuse.... Years later, during the World War, when a chorus of enemies were bringing against the German nation the charge of barbarism, a charge which sums up all that I have written above, it nonetheless hurt deeply to feel that my own experience would not allow me to contradict it.
>
> (Autobiography, 1925, S.E. XX, p. 49)

Fortunately, he never knew that his sisters were murdered at Ausschwitz.

CHAPTER XXXII

■ *Strange Love*

"Love and the necessary conditions for loving" has always been the province of writers, and especially poets. Knowledge gained from experience is molded into a form that is in harmony with artistic considerations. "Poetic license" allows artists to change reality and remove disturbing aspects, in order to provide aesthetic pleasure. On the other hand, a strictly scientific treatment of human love cannot be concerned with the feelings of the reader or his aesthetic experience. "Science is, after all, the most complete renunication of the pleasure principle of which our mental activity is capable."[1]

Freud observed that some men require special conditions in order to be romantically attracted to a woman. In fact, four prerequisites have to be fulfilled before the man can fall in love. At first glance they seem to be quite diverse:

1. The woman has to belong to another man. The precondition is the presence of "an injured third party." This type of man finds a woman attractive only when she is engaged or married.
2. She must not be seen as entirely pure: her fidelity must be open to doubt. A woman whose reputation is irreproachable is never the object of his passionate feelings. Any point along the continuum may serve to excite; anthing on her part from flirtatiousness to promiscuity. But such feelings of mistrust and jealousy although necessary for this type of lover are not directed against her legitimate partner. It is a stranger with whom the loved one can be linked with suspicion who becomes the target of his jealousy. It is also common with this syndrome that the lover show no wish for exclusive possession of the object of his passion; he seems quite accepting of a triangle.
3. She is experienced as unique, a rare and precious prize. It is of himself that the lover demands fidelity. The woman is the only one in the world he can love, and although he may break his pledge of faithfulness in reality, he repeats and believes in his own promises. These feelings may shift from one woman to another, indeed to a series of them if they meet the conditions.
4. The man has a favorite daydream: he rescues his beloved from a variety of dangers. He is indispensable. She needs him. Without him her life is in jeopardy.

A certain number of men require only one or a few of the features of this model.

Men who have an early and intense fixation on the mother that lasts beyond the time of puberty, are frequently victims of this syndrome. The exalted feelings

[1]A Special Type of Choice of Object Made by Men, 1910 S.E. XI p. 165.

from one woman to another, seeing each in turn as the only woman in the world, are merely substitutes for the one irreplaceable image in the unconscious: mother. The desired lack of purity surprisingly, arises from the same source and dates from the discovery of her forbidden acts, her unfaithful betrayal of her son—parental intercourse. At the time in the boy's life when he could no longer doubt his parents' sexual activity, he cynically felt that the differences between a mother and a "whore" are not much, since they do the same thing. The other man she belongs to is easily recognized as the rival of the owner of the desired woman—the father, who, in the triumphant fantasy of the lover, is the injured third party.

The rescue fantasy can be accounted for by conscious reasons, but the study of patients' dreams and fantasies reveal also an unconscious motive. In the mind of the child, the woman's propensity to be unfaithful under the force of her sex drive, leads her into dangerous situations. Our lover, then, makes her dependent on him, as he protects her from herself, and thereby guarantees that she will not leave him. In addition, the "rescue motif" has a history of its own. The child hears that his parents "gave him life," that "he owed his life to his parents." Fantasies of rescuing a king, or a famous man, obvious father substitutes, a theme that is familiar to creative writers, expresses the boy's defiance. Rescuing father not only pays his debt, it also reverses the roles: he becomes the father and enjoys the privileges of the father.

> His mother gave him life—his own life—and in exchange he gives her another life, that of a child which has the greatest resemblance to himself. The son shows his gratitude by wishing to have by his mother a son who is completely like himself, in other words, in the rescue phantasy he is completely identifying with his father. All his drives, those of tenderness, gratitude, lustfulness, defiance and independence, find satisfaction in the single wish: TO BE HIS OWN FATHER.
> (Ibid. p. 173)

It is unrealistic. It is primary-process thinking. It is unconscious.

> Under the laws governing the expression of unconscious thoughts, the meaning of rescuing may vary, depending on whether the author of the phantasy is a man or a woman.
> (Ibid. p. 174)

In the legend of Moses, the Pharaoh's daughter rescues the baby Moses from the river and raises him as her own son. The myth makes real a fantasy and the dream of rescuing. A woman who dreams she rescues someone from water is expressing a wish to make him her child. A man's fantasy dream of rescuing a man expresses a wish to make one's father a son. The old wish to possess the mother is carried out in the dream. He and mother have a son, his father.

The rescue motif is an important feature of the type just described. Not having sufficiently outgrown his original involvement with his parents, he dreams of gratifying his infantile wishes of reversing roles and enjoying the adult privileges he has been denied. In his rescue dreams, myths, and fantasies, his taboo wish is fulfilled.

Freud drew no particular conclusions from these observations. He believed that a proper appreciation of this kind of man would not be possible without further observation and study.

At a meeting of the Vienna Society in 1906, Freud casually mentioned to a few colleagues that he was considering writing on the ''love life'' of man. There was no further mention of the project. Two years later, ''A Special Type of Choice of Object Made by Men,'' the first in the series, was published.

CHAPTER XXXIII

■ *To Save The World From Sexuality*

Freud's main preoccupation during the year of 1911 was his break with Alfred Adler. It was a painful episode and it's a difficult topic to present. The nonanalytic world, naturally, tries to understand the differences between Freud and his dissenters on the objective merits of their respective theories. Unavoidably, it is bound to overlook or not fully appreciate an essential element in the situation.

A psychoanalysis, an investigation of the unconscious, can be carried out only by recognizing and overcoming "resistances." When this occurs, the patient gains an insight into his personality that he had no idea of, as though he had been blind to himself and to how he had been conducting his life.

Freud originally expected that once a resistance had been overcome, it would remain so, once and for all. His expectations were not corroborated by the facts. The mind is not static, but dynamic. It shifts and varies in the most unexpected ways. Many insights are only partial and are therefore not permanent, can in fact be lost. Clinical experience arrived at the concept of "working through," which implies that most resistances are deep-rooted, complex, and adhesive. One does not surrender one's defenses easily.

Unfortunately resistance to the unconscious affects the analyst as well as the patient. The public simply presumes, that having studied the necessary literature on the subject, the analyst's insights and personal emotions are steadfast, not subject to fluctuations. Indeed, the profession itself was slow to appreciate this point and "training analyses," which attempt to remove the resistances within the analyst's mind, was a late development in psychoanalytic training. None of the pioneers had much insight into their own unconscious, though theoretically it should had been predicted that there would be relapses similar to those observed in patients. But no one thought of it, and when it did take place, it was unexpected, difficult to understand, and in some cases painful.

> The disappointments that they caused me might have been averted if I had paid more attention to the reactions of patients under analytic treatment. I knew very well of course that anyone may take to flight at his first approach to the unwelcome truths of analysis....But I had not expected that anyone who had reached a certain depth in his understanding of analysis could renounce that understanding and lose it. And yet daily experience with patients had shown that total

> rejection of analytic knowledge may result whenever a specially strong resistance arises at any depth in the mind...one may see him, under the domination of the very next resistance, throw all he has learnt to the winds and stand on the defensive as he did in the days when he was a carefree beginner. I had to learn that the very same thing can happen with psychoanalysts as with patients in analysis.
>
> (On the History of the Psycho-Analytic Movement, 1914, S.E. XIV, p. 48-49).

When a patient loses an insight he had achieved and again feels resistant, he usually decides to leave treatment. The patient attempts to make sense of his feelings. The most common "reasons" offered are: "I'm cured now," "I can't afford it anymore," "I need a vacation from treatment," or "I'm really too busy and don't have the time." Usually it is a cue for the analyst to focus on the resistance.

In the early days, when an analyst similarly lost insight, he explained the recurring resistance in a pseudo-scientific manner. He rationalized it by producing a "new theory." Since the source of the new theory was unconscious, logical argument was of little avail.

Freud told Jung that he himself was not suited to the role of leader, but as founder of the new theories and methods, he could only play a dominant role within his little circle of Viennese followers.

> From the year 1902 onwards, a number of young doctors gathered round me with the express intention of learning....The small circle soon expanded, and in the course of the next few years often changed its composition. On the whole I could tell myself that it was hardly inferior, in wealth and variety of talent, to the staff of any clinical teacher one could think of....I had every reason to be satisfied, and I think I did everything possible to impart my own knowledge and experience to the others. There were only two inauspicious circumstances which at last estranged me inwardly from the group. I could not succeed in establishing among its members the friendly relations that ought to obtain between men who are all engaged upon the same difficult work; nor was I able to stifle the disputes about priority for which there were so many opportunities under these conditions of work in common.
>
> (Ibid. p. 25).

Freud exacerbated the situation by clearly and perhaps unwisely favoring the foreigner, Jung. This led the Viennese to band together in a common cause. It may be that the former jealousies developed into a rebellion against him. His attempts to appease the disgruntled Viennese were only partially successful.

Finding the bickering a strain he unburdened himself in a letter to Ferenczi:

> The tactlessness and unpleasant behavior of Adler and Stekel make it very difficult to get along together. I am chronically exasperated with both of them, Jung also, now that he is President....I am having an atrocious time with Adler and Stekel, I have been hoping that it would come to a clean separation, but it drags on....I am continually annoyed by the two...who are rapidly developing backwards and will soon end up by denying the existence of the unconscious.
> (Ferenczi, April 6, 1911)

Freud and Adler were very different personalities. Adler was short, pudgy-stout, sightly unkempt in appearance. He took pride in identifying with the "common man." He was very sociable although at times raucous and garrulous. Freud, on the other hand, was not particularly fashionable, but always correct and neat. He said that his conventional dress and manners confounded his critics. He loved words and spoke meticulously. Physically he was strong and vigorous; his mountain-climbing ability was the envy of his colleagues and friends. Adler had a long history of illness. Due to a severe case of rickets he had been unable to walk until the age of four. He suffered from respiratory illnesses and was what today would be called "accident prone."

Freud was born a Jew, and despite his atheistic convictions, had remained a Jew. Adler converted to the Christian religion. He felt that Orthodox Jewish faith and identity with one religious group constricted one's spiritual growth.

Adler believed that hostility is a reaction to frustration. He did not accept Freud's theory that hostility is is an expression of an inherent drive. Today, Adler's view is accepted by the academic world where Freud's theories have few adherents.

Adler's view of man's anger has social applications. It is based on everyday logic and fits in well with the Marxist philosophy. The basic frustration in society stems from the conflict between the haves and the have-nots, the propertied and the unpropertied. Eliminate the class struggle, the clash between those who own the means of production and those who do not, and you eradiate the cause of man's destructiveness to man. In response to the Socialist argument, Freud would point out that men were hostile to one another long before the advent of private property.

Adler and Freud were never intimate friends although Freud apparently thought highly of him in the early days. Jones described Adler as a morose person, very ambitious, constantly quarreling with others over the issue of the priority of his ideas. "When I met him many years later, however, I observed that success had brought him a certain benignity of which there had been little sign in his earlier years."[1]

Adler's theoretical differences with Freud were so basic that one can only wonder at Freud's patience in accepting him as an important colleague for so long. Freud as we know understood the neuroses as a product of sexual maladjustment. Not so Adler; he desexualized the illness. He saw neuroses as a compensation for physical and psychic inferiority. Human beings, he insisted, are driven by the wish for power

---

[1]Jones II, p. 130.

which begins with the helpless infant's striving to overcome its biological limitations. The "Masculine protest," the will to power, are particularly important in the economy of the psyche. Self-assertion compensates for feelings of inferiority and plays a dominating part in the conduct of life, in character formation, and neuroses. The different solutions to this problem of an inferiority complex account for individual behavioral variations. The role of psychosexual development and the Oedipus Complex were at best of secondary importance in the formation of a neurosis. Even sexual intercourse was at root a desire for power.[1]

It has been suggested that Adler's philosophy and psychology, that human behavior is based on feelings of organ inferiority, was a reflection of his own feelings about himself. Riddled with sickness and weaker than most boys when he was a child his own drive to compensate for his organ inferiority was projected into a belief system for all human behavior. The concepts of repression, infantile sexuality, and the unconscious itself were of little account. Indeed, little was left for psychoanalysis.

Freud and Adler related to patients in dramatically different ways. They had different aims. Freud worked deep; his aim was to make the unconscious conscious, to uncover unknown forces that might be determining neurotic behavior. Adler, on the other hand, stayed on the surface. He tried to mobilize the patient toward constructive, socially useful behavior. Reassurance is essentially not a psychoanalytic technique, but Adler and his followers gave it a prominent role. Freud felt that the analyst should maintain a professional distance and objectively analyze the manifestations of the patient's unconscious. Adler gave encouragement and advice, became friends with his patients, and saw no reason not to socialize with them.

Freud was bent on the recognition of his discoveries; they had not come easily, he had had to overcome much resistance, he had paid dearly for them. Further, he knew that if his work was to be accepted and established as a valid study, the distinction between what is psychoanalysis and any other psychology must not be muddled, the uniqueness of psychoanalysis must be crystal clear. Adler felt that Freud's concern with the dangers and trials that psychoanalysis had had to contend with was the result of Freud's own neurosis. He claimed that Freud was projecting his own sense of inferiority and insecurity, and that he greatly exaggerated the hazards that lay ahead for psychoanalysis.

The inevitable showdown took place. Adler was invited to present his views to the Viennese Society and several Wednesday evenings were put aside for this purpose. He presented three papers, (Adler was so convinced of his own insights that he actually hoped to convert Freud) in which Freud saw that Adler was trying to prove that psychoanalytic theories were basically wrong. (Indeed, many years later, Adler referred to Freudian theory as being concerned with filth and fecal matter.)

> Dear Frau Andreas
>
> I am so busy that it is best for me to answer you without delay....That you should have permitted me to see your correspondence with Adler I take

[1]Note that the psycholcgy of women was not yet an issue. The prevailing view was that psychologically, male and female were similar. Later when women became psychoanalysts their work brought the psychological differences between the sexes into focus.

> as a sign of great trust on your part. The letter shows his specific venomousness, and it is very characteristic of him. I don't believe that it belies the picture which I have given of him. Let us speak frankly (it will be easier then to continue): he is a loathsome individual.
>
> (Sigmund Freud and Lou Andreas-Salome Letters, Harcourt Brace Jovanovich, Inc., N.Y. 1972, p. 19)

> ...it was intended to prove that psychoanalysis was wrong in everything and that it had only attributed so much importance to sexual motive forces because of its credulity in accepting the assertions of neurotics. I may even speak publicly of the personal motive for his work, since he himself announced it in the presence of a small circle of members of the Viennese group: "Do you think it gives me such great pleasure to stand in your shadow my whole life long?" To be sure, I see nothing reprehensible in a younger man freely admitting his ambition, which one would in any case guess was among the incentives for his work. But even though a man is dominated by a motive of this kind he should know how to avoid being what the English, with their fine social tact, call "unfair"—which in German can only be expressed by a much cruder word.
>
> (History, S.E. XIV, p. 51)

At the last meeting of the Society allotted to Adler, Freud was infuriated. He regarded Adler's challenge as presumptuous, a betrayal, and a desertion. His words were incisive. He was unsparing in his evaluation of the "masculine protest." Lou Salome was present at the meeting and took notes in her journal:

> Wednesday Discussion: Freud on Adler
>
> Practically a debate on Adler. Freud discoursed at length....Adler's treatment comes to a halt before it reaches the neurosis itself, while Freud's exposes resistances instead (offering no quick relief)...
> Freud and Adler actually differ with regard to therapeutic method as the knife differs from salve....The plane whence the personality arises to become ego, from whose unconscious layers the personality derives the broad reality underlying its conscious interpretations—this plane of Freud's real achievement is ignored and bypassed.
>
> (Salome Journal, p. 62)

A few days later the Society lost both its President and Vice-President; Adler and Stekel resigned. The social Democrats, a quarter of the membership, left with them. Adler formed "The Society for Free Psychoanalysis." Freud remarked that the name was tasteless in that it implied that he was fighting for the freedom of science. Adler must have thought so too; later he changed it to "The Society for Individual Psychology."

The feud between Freud and Adler involved feelings that were not confined to professional scientific disagreement; they spilled over into social relationships. Friendships of long standing were broken. Awkward situations occurred at dinner parties, where couples, formerly friendly, were now cool to one another. It has been reported that, for the most part, the children of those involved weathered the adult feuds and remained friends. But part of Viennese society was never the same again.

Despite the basic differences between Adler's (and Jung's) theories and Freud's, all three referred to those theories as "psychoanalysis." In 1914, "fuming with rage," Freud wrote "On the History of the Psycho-Analytic Movement." The aim of the paper was to present the fundamental differences between the theories and to show that the "three schools of psychoanalysis" were incompatible.

After fifty pages of analysis of the differences between his and Adler's views, Freud wrote:

> There is room enough on God's earth, and anyone who can has a perfect right to potter on it without being prevented; but it is not a desirable thing for people who have ceased to understand one another and have grown incompatible with one another to remain under the same roof. Adler's "Individual Psychology" is now one of the many schools of psychology which are adverse to psycho-analysis and its further development is no concern of ours....The view of life which is relfected in the Adlerian system is founded exclusively on the aggressive instinct; there is no room in it for love. We might feel surprise that such a cheerless Weltanschauung should have met with any attention at all; but we must not forget that human beings, weighed down by the burden of their sexual needs, are ready to accept anything if only the "overcoming of sexuality" is offered them as a bait.
>
> (History, S.E. XIV, p. 52-58)

In later years Adler would say that he never understood the Freudians when they talked about the unconscious, and that he had never been a psychoanalyst. He believed in common-sense psychology and that proper education of the people could change the world. His wife, a Russian, was a close friend of Trotsky and other political emigres, who frequently visited their home. One can readily understand that he leaned toward the view that the basic human problem, socially and individually, is the struggle for power.

Freud heard that Stanley Hall had invited Adler to lecture in America. He was disappointed in Hall. His comment was: "Presumably the object is to save the world from sexuality and base it on aggression."[1]

Adler's Individual Psychology enjoyed a moderate success, particularly in America, and especially among social workers and educators. in 1937 he died suddenly of a cerebral hemorrhage, while attending a meeting of the British Association for the Advancement of Science. He was sixty-seven.

Arnold Zweig wrote that he was sorry to hear of Adler's death. Freud replied: "I don't understand your sympathy for Adler. For a Jew-boy out of a Viennese suburb a death in Aberdeen is an unheard-of-career in itself and a proof of how far he had got on. The world really rewarded him richly for his service in having contradicted psychoanalysis.[2]

Freud received a long letter from Stanley Hall. He had just learned that Freud regarded his invitation to Adler as a refutation of psychoanalysis. Yes, he had found something useful in Adler's psychology and also in Jung's, despite his mystical and obscure writing. But:

> The world knows that both these men owe their entire impulsion to you and I also think that both illustrate the revolt against the father which you have so well explained...
> ...Your own achievements are far and away beyond those of any psychologist of modern times...history will show that you are (to be compared with) Darwin in Biology. It seems to me you can well afford to be magnanimous toward these revolting children....
>
> For me, your work has been the chief inspiration of most that I have done for the last fifteen years. It has given me a totally new view of psychic life, and I owe to you more than to anyone else, living or dead.
>
> (Clark, p. 444)

[1]Ferenczi, May 10, 1924

[2]Jones 3, p. 208.

CHAPTER XXXIV

■ *Coming Storm*

The 1911 International Congress was indeed international: analysts from all over the world attended. The papers presented were very professional, the atmosphere was friendly, all in all it was a successful congress. Otto Rank gave an excellent paper on "The Motif of Nudity in Poetry and Legends." The next day the local newspaper reported that "interesting papers were read on nudity and other current topics." Everyone found it amusing, but it tended to discourage invitations to newspaper reporters at subsequent meetings.

Freud was still taken with Jung. Someone commented that Jung's jokes were rather coarse, whereupon Freud sharply replied: "It's a healthy coarseness."

In October, Emma Jung sent Freud a letter that contained a mild warning:

> Dear Professor Freud: 30 October 1911
>
> I don't really know how I am summoning the courage to write you this letter, but am certain it is not from presumption; rather I am following the voice of my unconscious which I have so often found was right and which I hope will not lead me astray this time.
>
> Since your visit I have been tormented by the idea that your relation with my husband is not altogether as it should be, and since it definitely ought not to be like this, I want to try to do whatever is in my power. I do not know whether I am deceiving myself when I think you are somehow not quite in agreement with "Transformation of Libido." You didn't speak of it at all and yet I think it would do you both so much good if you got down to a through discussion of it. Or is something else? If so, please tell me what, dear Herr Professor; for I cannot bear to see you so resigned and I even believe that your resignation relates not only to your real children (it made a quite special impression on me when you spoke of it) but also to your spiritual son; otherwise you would have so little need to be resigned.
>
> Please do not take my action as officiousness and do not count me among the women who,you once told me, always spoil your friendships. My

husband naturally knows nothing of this letter and I beg you not to hold him responsible for it or to let any kind of unpleasant effects it may have on you glance off on him.

I hope nevertheless, that you will not be angry with your admiring

Emma Jung

(Freud, Jung letters, Princeton Univ. Press, 1974, p. 452)

This perceptive and courageous woman's warning seemed to have little effect upon Freud. His aspirations made him oblivious to any signs of the coming storm.

In the meantime, the second part of Jung's "Transformations and Symbols" had been completed. The paper widened the rift between Jung's thinking and Freud's. The libido, which for Freud meant the mental representative of the sex drive, underwent a new definition. Jung defined it as psychic energy per se, something like the force of life. In other words, under Jung, the libido had no sexual connotation. He even quoted passages from Freud, who had attacked the problem of paranoia some fifteen years earlier and linked repressed homosexuality to paranoia. Jung offered an alternative theory. The long and painful battle for the recognition of the role of the sex drive in the formation of character structure and personality was being lost from within.

In "Psycho-Analytic Notes on an Autobiographical Account of a Case of Paranoia" (1911), Freud reasserted the role of sexual conflict in psychopathology and the libido as the representative of sexual energy. The case study is remarkable in that Freud never met the patient, Dr. Daniel Paul Schreber, and the patient had nothing to do with psychoanalysis. Jung introduced Freud to Schreber's autobiography, "Memoirs of my Nervous Illness," which had been written seven years earlier, in 1903. Freud's analysis of the case was based entirely on this autobiography, written after Schreber recovered from an attack of paranoia.

Schreber, an intelligent man of a distinguished family, was a judge on an Appeal Court. The theory that Freud applied to understanding Schreber's condition was not derived from this particular case but based upon Freud's own clinical experience. In fact Freud said that he had learned the secret of paranoia from his friend Wilhelm Fliess. Jung had his own views of Schreber's illness which Freud's analysis did not corroborate. It was the first serious scientific difference between Jung and Freud. Freud still believed that the differences between him and the Swiss psychiatrist would be resolved and there was nothing contentious in his presentation of the Schreber case.

Freud considered psychoanalysis a very limited therapeutic instrument for psychotics, so his present incursion into psychiatry was in his own words, "the boldest he had yet undertaken."[1] He anticipated that his analysis of Schreber would bring scornful laughter or immortality or both."[2]

Schreber's friends had begged him not to publish his memoirs because of their bizarre content: God has chosen him to restore blessedness to a world that had lost its way. Schreber's response was: "I have been at no pains to close my eyes to the

---

[1]Letter to Ferenczi December 16, 1910

[2]Ibid.

difficulties that would appear....On the other hand I am of the opinion that it might well be to the advantage both of science and of the recognition of religious truths if, during my lifetime, qualified authorities were enabled to undertake some examination of my body and to hold some enquiry into my personal experiences. To this consideration all feelings of a personal character must yield.''[1]

Schreber described himself ''a man of superior mental gifts and endowed with an unusual keenness alike of intellect and of observation.''[2] His self-portrait was accurate. He also possessed great personal charm and inspired confidence in those who knew him. In fact, during his hospitalizations he dined with the staff and was frequently sought after and consulted for advice.

While a candidate for President of the Senate of the Dresden Superior Provincial Court, he had had an attack of a ''nervous illness.'' After six months in a clinic under the care of Professor Flechsig of Leipzig he was discharged as completely cured, feeling appreciative and beholden to his doctor. The diagnosis was hypochondria.

For the next nine years there were no reports of illness. Then, three weeks after assuming his position as *Senatspraesident* he again fell ill, but with a far more serious condition. He was hospitalized for six years.

In the first phase of his illness Schreber imagined that he was the victim of dreadful homosexual assaults masterminded by his former physician and friend, Flechsig. Flechsig's co-conspirator was God. In the second phase God himself was carrying out the homosexual assaults and Schreber was voluptuously surrendering to his fate.

Schreber believed that he had been chosen to be the Divine Mother; therefore he had to be transformed into a woman. As the female savior impregnated by God he would beget a new race of human beings. This time, during his incarceration he had to be placed in a padded cell, forcibly fed, and when outside the cell attended to by three men. Schreber was acutely paranoid. Nevertheless, his powers of persuasion convinced the authorities that he should be discharged in a perfectly normal mental state, except for the presence of certain fixed delusions.

Schreber's ideas revolved around complicated religious concepts. He experienced miracles and thought he could communicate with birds and the wind—evidence that God had chosen him to redeem the world and restore it to its lost state of bliss.

Freud sought to understand how Schreber, a man of experience and intelligence, could undergo such an astonishing metamorphosis.

In his paper to the Weimar Congress Freud discussed the dynamics of paranoia in rich detail, emphasizing its chief features: projection and repressed homosexuality. Furthermore he was able to show a complete picture of the genesis of Schreber's complex cosmology. Many of Freud's findings led to theoretical investigations by others.

Such patients are usually institutionalized, which makes it difficult for a practitioner in private practice to study symptoms of delusion. Freud's previous work had given rise to doubts about the reliability of his material. In this case he was able to use biographical data which was also available to the general public. Such an idependent document, written without an influence from psychoanalysis, led to greater acceptance of his theories than would a confidential exchange in the seclusion of his private consulting room have done.

---

[1]Roberts 259

[2]Ibid.

The seminal "Psycho-Analytic Notes on an Autobiographical Account of a Case of Paranoia"[1] and its delineation of the basic structure of mental illness was a triumph for Freud.

Jung's extensive studies in religion and mysticism revived Freud's own early interest in the subject. That same year, Freud wrote a work on religion and anthropology, "Totem and Taboo." Characteristically, he arrived at different conclusions from Jung. Freud's views concerning incest and the Oedipus complex were confirmed. Jung, on the other hand, regarded these complexes not in the literal sense of sexual desires, but as symbols of esoteric tendencies in the mind. Incest for Jung meant a need to return to one's ground, to one's source of certainty and strength.

While Freud was coming to terms with the divergent views between him and the man he had hoped would protect and preserve psychoanalysis, Jung accepted an invitation to visit the United States to give a course at Fordham University, a Jesuit college. Ernest Jones had previously refused a similar invitation on the grounds that a Catholic university was not a suitable setting for discussions on psychoanalysis. The timing of Jung's acceptance was bad. It meant postponing the International Congress for a year. Freud was displeased. He felt it was improper for Jung, as president of the Society, to go to New York at that time. Later, when asked why he had not arranged to preside over the meeting himself, he replied that it had not occurred to him and anyhow it was Jung's responsibility to make such a suggestion.

Early in 1912 Jung wrote to Freud to tell him that Swiss newspapers were angrily attacking psychoanalysis. Further, Oskar Pfister, a clergyman and a very dear friend and colleague of Freud's had been called to account by his superiors for his "views," and it looked as if he might be expelled from the ministry. (Fortunately he survived the inquisition.) Riklin, a Swiss psychiatrist, told Freud that the campaign had a disastrous effect on the Swiss analysts; that their private practices were suffering and urged Freud to send them patients. Freud believed that the attack from the community was an important reason for the change in attitude towards psychoanalysis among the Swiss analysts, a change that occurred soon after. Freud observed that there is something about the Swiss that makes it very difficult for them to stand against their fellow countrymen.

Ludwig Binswanger, a Swiss psychiatrist who had earlier published a paper supporting Freud, accompanied Jung and his wife on their first visit to Vienna in 1907. Despite a twenty-five year difference in age, Binswanger and Freud developed a friendship that only ended thirty years later on Freud's death. Feelings of mutual respect, intimacy, and cordiality were maintained in a running correspondence long after Binswanger drifted away from Freud's theories into what is now referred to as "Existentialism."

In 1912 Binswanger had to undergo surgery that might have resulted in an early death. A malignant tumor had been discovered and the survival rate for such surgery was low. He confided the facts of his illness to Freud alone.

Freud answered (April 14, 1912)

> I, an old man, who will have no right to complain if his life ends in a few years...am particularly pained when one of my flowering young men..tells me

---

[1]S.E. 12, 1911

> that he has become uncertain of his life. I have gradually composed myself and recalled that despite the present doubts you still have every chance, and that you have only been reminded more forcefully of the uncertainty which keeps all of us in suspense and which we so readily forget...we shall hope for what our present knowledge permits us to think of without any self-deception. Naturally I shall keep the secret, in accordance with your wishes. But it is natural that I should desire to see you as soon as I can do so without inconveniencing you. How about Whitsun? You will write to me whether this is all right with you...

A few weeks later Freud spent two days as Binswanger's guest in Kreuzlingen. The fatiguing train journey from Vienna and back consumed as much time as the visit. Fortunately the tumor had been detected early, the surgery was successful, and Binswanger lived for another fifty years.

The testimony that scientific differences were no hindrance to Freud's friendships is eloquently expressed in the following exchange. In 1926 Binswanger's eight-year-old son died. He wrote to Freud:

> At a time when my life was most gravely threatened you stood by me in a way that, aside from all other ties, binds me to you forever...one of my children, a lovely eight-year-old boy, who showed promise of developing into an energetic personality, died suddenly after a fourteen days' illness, amidst great suffering. He succumbed to a tubercular meningitis....I could not bring myself to inform you about the death of my boy by way of a printed announcement, nor could I write to you directly, particularly to you. Now it is done. I know you went through a similar experience....
>
> I expect no letter from you dear Herr Professor, but a line from you would give me and my wife more pleasure than anything else.

Freud, seventy-three years old at that time, answered his young friend with an extraordinarily moving expression of sympathy:

> Even though you don't expect it, I must write to you—not a note of superfluous sympathy, but in fact I am writing out of an inner urge....Correct—I lost a beloved daughter when she was twenty-seven, but I bore this remarkably well. That was in 1920, when we were crushed and miserable, after years of war, during which we had steeled ourselves against hearing that we had lost a son or even three sons....But two years later I brought the younger child of this daughter, a little boy

> of three or four, to Vienna, where my childless oldest daughter took him into her home, and this child died—on June 23—from an acute miliary tuberculosis....To me this child had taken the place of all my children and other grandchildren, and since then, since Heinele's death, I don't care for my grandchildren anymore, but find no joy in life either. This is also the secret of my indifference—it was called courage—toward the danger to my own life....
> (Max Schur p. 360)

In the following years, in spite of the above letter, Freud's interest and concern for his friends and family, particularly children, showed no signs of diminishing. He did not simply make polite gestures; his ablility to take an interest in others before his own needs was genuine.

Since Jung's home was only forty miles from Kreuzlingen, Freud had written to Jung inviting him to join them. There was only time for a weekend visit, but it would be an opportunity to see each other. However, to Freud's surprise and disappointment, there was no word from Jung. Oddly, the reverberations from the visit to Binswanger intensified a crisis that was developing between Jung and Freud. Jung's letters to Freud reproachfully referred to the "Kreuzlingen gesture" or made sarcastic references to "understanding your gesture at Kreuzlingen," which left Freud completely puzzled. The puzzle was not solved until their next meeting six months later, but it remained decisive in their personal separation.

CHAPTER XXXV

■ *Ach Du Lieber Augustin*

Freud's practice included people from all over Europe; many were well known. He was the last resort when all other attempts at cure failed. He never mentioned his patients by name and it is from their writings that we learn about them. In *Theme and Variations:* An Autobiography by Bruno Walter, we read that Walter suffered from a paralysis of the arm, a symphony conductor's nightmare. He describes how one prominent doctor after another failed to help him. After submitting to a variety of techniques, from mud baths to magnetism, he decided to consult Professor Freud.

The meeting with Freud did not go as Walter expected, with Freud's searching for connections between the symptom and early experiences in his life. Instead Freud ordered him to leave for Sicily immediately, for a few weeks, with explicit instructions to forget about his arm and concentrate on using his eyes. He carried out Freud's instructions and returned a few weeks later with little improvement in his arm. Freud then ordered him to resume conducting:

Walter:	But I can't move my arm.
Freud:	Try it at any rate.
Walter:	And what if I should have to stop?
Freud:	You won't have to stop.
Walter:	Can I take upon myself the responsibility of possibly upsetting a performance?
Freud:	I'll take the responsibility.

(Clark, p. 193)

The concert was a smashing success.

Gustav Mahler, the composer, was having difficulties with his wife. Dr. Nepallek, a psychoanalyst and a relative of Mahler's wife, recommended that he consult Freud. Mahler suffered from the "folie de doute" (compulsive doubting). On three occasions he telegraphed Freud for an appointment and three times canceled at the last minute. Finally, in 1910, he kept an appointment in Leyden, Holland, where Freud was vacationing. The "analysis" consisted of a four-hour stroll through the town. Freud was impressed with Mahler's capacity for psychological understanding even without previous contact with psychoanalysis. At one point Freud, in a puzzled voice, asked Mahler why he married someone with the name Alma. He would have expected Mahler to marry someone named Marie. Mahler replied that his wife's name was Alma Marie, and that he called her Marie. A name may have played an important part in Mrs. Mahler's psychology also. She was the daughter of a famous painter, Schindler, whose statue stands in the Stadtpark in Vienna. "Painter" in German is "Mahler."

In the course of their talk, Mahler suddenly said that he now understood why his work didn't reach the highest rank. His father apparently was given to a brutal temper and treated his wife badly. When Mahler was a young boy there was a painful scene between his parents. Unable to bear it he rushed into the street. At that very moment a hurdy-gurdy organ in the street was grinding out the popular Viennese air "Ach Du Lieber Augustin." The admixture of the tragic with the light became fixed in his mind and the expression of one mood inevitably brought the other also. Freud said that he had never met anyone who so quickly grasped the role of the unconscious.

CHAPTER XXXVI

■ *A Dwarf, A Giant, And A Louse*

Wilhelm Stekel, in 1900, read a witty but critical review of The Interpretation of Dreams. He was a practicing psychiatrist in Vienna and himself an excellent writer. Perhaps because he was a journalist, he mistrusted reviews of scientific works. He decided to call upon Freud.

"He lent me his new book. I was enraptured....The books and my talks with Freud were like sunshine after rain. At last I had learned the right method of curing neurotics. Many obscure cases in my practice ceased to be enigmas....I wrote numerous articles about Freud and was one of the first to recognize the greatness of this genius....I was the apostle of Freud who was my Christ!"[1]

They became colleagues and Stekel suggested that they form a Society from which came later the Vienna Psycho-Analytical Society. But Stekel although very talented was also neurotic and undisciplined. Freud felt that he relied more on intuition than on careful research and did not trust his work.

> Regard for scientific criticism forbids our returning to the arbitrary judgment of the dream-interpreter, as it was employed in ancient times and seems to have been revived in the reckless interpretation of Stekel....This author's lack of a critical faculty and his tendency to generalization at all costs throw doubts upon other of his interpretations or render them unusable....
> (Dreams, p. 353-357)

The difficulty Stekel presented was very different from that of Adler; they were very different personalities. Unlike Adler, Stekel was amusing and cheerful. Whereas Adler felt uneasy with the concept of the unconscious, Stekel was at home with it. He was a naturally gifted psychologist with an unusual flair for recognizing repressed material, and it was he who, as early as 1908, suggested the existence of the death instinct. In the field of symbolism he displayed more intuition than Freud. In fact Freud said he often opposed Stekel's insight into a symbol only to discover, on further study, that Stekel had been right.

> Stekel's writings, and in particular his *Die Sprache des Traumes* (1911), contain the fullest collection of interpretations of symbols. Many of these show

The Autobiography of Wilhelm Stekel, Liverright Publishing Co., N.Y. 1950, p. 105.

> penetration, and further examination has proved them correct: for instance, his section on the symbolism of death.
> (Ibid. p. 357)

But his intuitiveness was combined with poor judgement. He had little interest in theory and all too often his intuition degenerated into sheer guessing. "I think it is worthwhile remarking that in my experience Stekel's generalization cannot be maintained in the face of the greater complexity of the facts."[1]

When Stekel published his book on dreams, Freud's comment was, "mortifying," Ferenczi's, "shameful and dishonest." when it was proposed that Putnam review the book, Freud objected. He said that we ask so much of Putnam that we cannot expect him also to deal with our own dirty linen. Actually Putnam did express an opinion of the book: "frivolous and base."

The problem with Stekel was not in his scientific speculations. It was that he had no scientific conscience. The man was a liar. No one gave any credence to his word. At Society meetings, whatever the topic of the day happened to be, it was his custom to remark: "Only this morning I saw a case of this kind." Stekel's "Wednesday patient" became an "in" joke.

He wrote a paper, "The Obligation of the Name," which pointed out the psychological significance of people's surnames. He claimed to have discovered a connection between a person's name and his choice of a career, his pathology, and his general interests. For example, he reported a patient whose business involved mailing packages. " 'I have the compulsion to count these packages again and again, and I am never sure.' 'What's your last name?' 'Sure....' "[2]

Freud was impressed with the number of examples he cited but also questioned the ethics of mentioning patient's names in print. Stekel replied with a reassuring smile, not to worry, he made them up. Freud refused to publish the paper in the Zentralblatt. Stekel had it published elsewhere.

He would make startling assertions. But when asked for substantiation he answered, "I am here to discover things, other people can prove them if they want to."[3]

Stekel had a practice that particularly upset Freud. After deliberately lying he would gaze at Freud defiantly, knowing that Freud was too much of a gentleman to expose him. Once when Freud was asked if he believed that the ego-ideal (conscience) were universal, he replied "Do you think Stekel has an ego-ideal?"[4]

It was something indirect however that brought about the break. Stekel and Victor Tausk, a young psychoanalyst, hated each other, and got into a ugly row in regard to Tausk's writing articles for the Journal. Stekel declared that he would not permit a single word of Tausk's to appear in print. Freud reminded him that personal vendettas were out of place in an association organ. Stekel obstinately refused to concede. His success in the field of symbolism had convinced him that he now surpassed Freud. He said that a dwarf on the shoulder of a giant could see further than the giant. Freud grimly replied: "That may be true, but a louse on the head of an astronomer does not."[5]

---

[1]Ibid. p. 358
[2]Stekel, p. 131
[3]Jones 2, p. 135
[4]Ibid. p. 136
[5]Ibid. p. 136

Finally, at the November meeting, Stekel's resignation was announced and Freud wrote to Abraham: "I am so glad that now Stekel is going his own way. You cannot imagine how I have suffered from the labor of having to defend him against the whole world. He is an unbearable fellow."[1]

Stekel was not one to hold a grudge and over the years he pleaded with Freud to forget their old differences and accept his offer to fight the enemies of psychoanalysis. Freud would have none of it. In a letter to Stekel, Freud made clear that their break had nothing to do with scientific differences, but was entirely personal. He throughly disapproved of Stekel's ethics and saw no reason why they should resume a relationship. Freud was unforgiving, but he did not sound bitter; if anything he seemed indifferent.

> Vienna IX Berggasse 19 January 13, 1924
> Dear Dr. Stekel
> I acknowledge receipt of your letter of December 31, 1923, and thank you for your good wishes regarding the improvement of my health. But I cannot refrain from contradicting you on a few important points.
>
> You are mistaken if you think that I hate you or have hated you....I had reason for many years to be annoyed with you while at the same time having to defend you against the aversion of everyone around me, and that I broke with you after you had deceived me on a certain occasion in the most heinous manner....It was exclusively your personal qualities...which made collaboration with you impossible for my friends and myself....It will not annoy me to learn that your medical and literary activities have earned you success, I admit that you have remained loyal to psychoanalysis and have been of use to it; you have also done it great harm....

In 1938, both men found refuge from the Nazis in England. Stekel wrote warm-hearted letters to Freud urging that they let bygones be bygones, that they were both old men living in a foreign country, had been through a lifetime together, and that they should see each other for old times' sake. Freud never answered his letters.

In the last two pages of Stekel's autobiography we read rather unexpectedly,

> I had just finished this book when I received the news of Freud's death....I told myself that Freud's integral character had only one goal, to serve the truth, his truth. It was the work of fate that I could not see my truth through the same glasses....The fact that after the rape of Austria, Freud had to leave the land of his birth will one day be regard-

[1]Abraham, Nov. 3, 1912

> ed as one of the blackest crimes of the Nazis. I can imagine, nay more, it is my conviction that in days to come his coffin will be brought in triumph to Vienna, and that an immense crowd of mourners will pay him the honor that was denied him during the reign of "the master race." Ideals cannot be destroyed by political movements. Our work will last longer than this epidemic of hatred....
>
> (Stekel, p. 285-287)

Stekel became ill with diabetes and began to have delusions that the Nazis were trying to kill him. On June 25, 1940, at the age of seventy-two, he took his own life.

CHAPTER XXXVII

■ *Impotence, The Love Of Civilized Man*

Freud said in 1912 that he intended to write a book or a series of essays on the "love life of man." Two years later, he published the first of the essays on the subject: "Special Object Choice." It was followed by "On the Universal Tendency to Debasement in the Sphere of Love."

Freud begins with a discussion of male impotence. This disorder is a principal reason why males come to doctors for help. The patient usually reports that he fails sexually only with certain persons, whereas with others he functions normally.

> He now becomes aware that it is some feature of the sexual object which gives rise to the inhibition of his male potency, and sometimes he reports that he has a feeling of an obstacle inside him, the sensation of a counter-will which successfully interferes with his conscious intention. However, he is unable to guess what this internal obstacle is and what feature of the sexual object brings it into operation.
>
> (On the Universal Tendency to Debasement in the Sphere of Love, 1912, S.E. XI, p. 179)

The determinants of the inhibition are indeed unconscious. The most prominent dynamic, and it's practically universal, is that the lack of sexual feeling is a defense against incestuous fixations which have never been overcome. In addition, there may be other distressing factors connected with infantile sexuality. Further, the privations of adolescence may contribute to the condition of psychological impotence.

The basic difficulty has been to blend sensual urges and tender feelings toward mother. Part of what the infant feels is an idyllic tenderness. The sweet sensations he in fact receives from mother's breast makes her into a nurturing sensual angel—his primary object choice. Any disapproval on his angel's part is tantamount to banishment from the Garden of Eden and condemnation to death. When sensual feelings towards her arise, he learns, sooner or later, that they are not acceptable; incest and incestuous feelings are taboo. For his own self-preservation he must split off the sexual longings from his angel and try to divert them elsewhere. He comes to associate loving but respectful feelings with a different object from that of his sensuality. The two currents, affectionate and sexual, seem to be incompatible. "Where they love they do not desire, and where they desire they cannot love."

Freud boldly states that the inhibition which results from this conflict between love and sex is universal, varying in degree in different cultures and individuals. One manifestation of it is that many men feel potent with a woman from a socially inferior class. They psychologically debase the sexual object. Normally the sexual object is overvalued, but in these cases the overvaluation is reserved for the incestuous object and its surrogates. Once debasement has taken place, a high degree of pleasure and sensuality can be set free and expressed. Going back to the former paper, 'A Special Type of Object Choice," we can readily see that debasing the mother to the level of a whore serves a purpose. It fuses the two currents and enables her to be felt as an object of sexuality.

The startling point Freud makes is that one cannot be civilized and completely potent. One cannot love and respect the partner and also enjoy maximum sexual pleasure. Feelings of love inhibit sexual potency.

> ....I shall put forward the view that psychical impotence is much more widespread than is supposed....If, however, we turn our attention not to an extension of the concept of psychical impotence, but to the gradations in its symptomatology, we cannot escape the conclusion that the behavior in love of men in the civilized world today bears the stamp altogether of psychical impotence. There are only a very few educated people in whom the two currents of affection and sensuality have become properly fused; the man almost always feels his respect for the woman acting as a restriction on his sexual activity, and only develops full potency when he is with a debased sexual object; and this in turn is partly caused by the entrance of perverse components into his sexual aims, which he does not venture to satisfy with a woman he respects....This is the source of his need for a debased sexual object, a woman who is ethically inferior, to whom he need attribute no aesthetic scruples, who does not know him in his other social relations and cannot judge him in them.
> (Ibid. p. 184)

In our culture, women who are denied their sensual longings in the years before marriage, are often frigid when the prohibition no longer exists. These women can enjoy sex with a forbidden lover, but not with a husband.

> In the case of women there is little sign of a need to debase their sexual object. This is no doubt connected with the absence in them, as a rule, of anything similar to the sexual overvaluation found in men.
> (Ibid. p. 186)

Denial in the erotic life of such women can be compared to the debasement of the object in men. It is a consequence of our education which for cultural reasons demands a long delay betwen the sexual drives and the social acceptance of sexual activity. The damage done by early sexual frustration is demonstrated when marriage does not result in full sexual gratification.

Would we do better if we were raised in a climate of sexual license? A study of unrestricted sexual freedom shows no better results: where sexual plesure is easily available, the value of the erotic experience is diminished. In order for the drive to be intense, and the pleasure of the release maximum, where no difficulties were in the way of sexual satisfaction, love practically disappeared. It became empty and worthless. The instinct was glorified as we today glorify the object. During the orgies in ancient Rome, the satisfaction of the instinct was more important than who was the recipient. We today consider that our sexual feelings are only acceptable if we "love and revere" the object. Pagan religions were never able to bestow as much love upon an object as Christianity, with its stress on asceticism, was able to do. The records of ascetic monks show that they were obsessed with their struggle against sexual temptation. "The psychical importance of an instinct rises in proportion to its frustration."

Freud raises the awesome possibility that the sexual drive in its very nature may be: "unfavorable to the realization of complete satisfaction." The course of sexual development in humans is unique. Only in man do we see two distinct phases: infancy and puberty. In all other mammals sexual development proceeds from infancy to maturity without interruption. Only in humans is the course of development interrupted by a "latency phase."

> ....two fundamental biological facts: the long period of the human child's dependence, and the remarkable way in which its sexual life reaches a first climax in the third to fifth years of life, and then, after a period of inhibition, sets in again at puberty.
>
> (The Ego and the Id, 1923, S.E. XIV, p. 208)

Freud ascribed to Fliess the first use of the terms "latency" and "sublimation." If the latency period, which Freud saw as determined by heredity, escapes trauma and follows a normal course, we would experience the repression of the Oedipus, a lessening of sexual and aggressive drives, and an increased concern with reality and activity. The interruption of libidinal development lays the groundwork for sublimation and also plays an important role in the child's eventual freedom from neurosis.

Added to the circumstance of a latency phase is the suppression of components of the sexual drive which are incompatible with cultural standards, such as exhibitionism, sadism, voyeurism, coprolalia, etc. The imposition of the incest barrier prevents the final object of the drive from ever being the original love object, but invariably a substitute. It may be that something is lost in the repression and Freud wonders if this phenomenon prevents the possibility of full sexual gratification. Another possible inhibitor may be the anatomical proximity of the exremental organs to the genitals. Further, the genitals themselves have retained their "animal cast" and by our aesthetic standards are not beautiful.

We may be forced to accept the fact that it is impossible to reconcile the claims of the sexual drive with the needs of civilization, not to mention the possibility that the human race may become extinct. The incapacity of the sexual drive to submit to all the demands of culture leads to sublimation. Sublimation of course means changes in the original instinctual form of gratification into socially acceptable activities. The urge to smear transformed into a desire to paint, sadism transformed into a study of surgery, are examples of sublimation. Under the influence of the ego the conversion of primitive wishes into socially useful activities plays a decisive role in scientific and artistic creativity. Hence the noblest acheivements of a culture often rest on the renunciation of sexual satisfaction. It would seem that the plight of civilized man is unavoidable repression; and inhibition the source of our proudest accomplishments.

Appreciation of the role of the unconscious in a culture made Freud wary of recommending social reforms. An analyst should confine himself to seeking explanations and avoid advice, because he cannot predict the outcome of such counsel nor be assured that social changes will not bring new problems in their train. Like other kinds of research, psychoanalytic investigation must avoid partisanship. It has no other aim than to shed light on the impulse hidden behind manifest phenomena, and to point out the role of that impulse. However, it registers no objection if others wish to make use of its findings to initiate reforms.

Freud concludes the paper:

> It is not the aim of science either to frighten or to console. But I, myself, am quite ready to admit that such far-reaching conclusions as those I have drawn should be built on a broader foundation, and that perhaps developments in other directions may enable mankind to correct the results of the develpments I have here been considering in isolation.
>
> (Debasement, p. 190)

CHAPTER XXXVIII

■ *A Bouquet For A Sagacious Eagle*

In November 1912, an incident occurred that led to a false rumor about Freud. He was supposed to have fallen in love and had an affair with a student. The matter would not be worth recounting had it ended there, but the rumor grew and Freud was accused of being jealous of her lover, which finally made him responsible for the man's suicide. As we digress to lay the rumor to rest, we will see still another aspect of Freud's personality.

The story was based on Freud's sending flowers to a student and seeing her to her hotel at 2:30 a.m. An exchange of notes followed. The "student" was Lou Andreas-Salome, probably the most distinguished woman in Europe. She was a prodigious writer on a wide range of topics, literary, philosophical, and scientific (seventeen books and one hundred ninety-nine articles). Among her friends she counted the oustanding personalities of the day: Tolstoy, Schnitzler, Turgenieff, Strindberg, Rodin, to mention a few. She and Nietzsche met in Rome when she was twenty-one years old. His first words to her were "From what stars have we fallen to meet here?"[1] They lived together for about six months. No other woman before or after her could make that claim. Nietzsche said of her that she was "sagacious as an eagle and courageous as a lion."[2] Long after they were separated and without hope of reconciliation, he said of her "I have never known a more gifted or understanding creature." It should be added that she was friends also with some of the outstanding women of her day.

At the age of twenty-six Lou married Friedrich Carl Andra Andreas, an older man who was an expert on Near-Eastern languages. Her autobiography describes a most unusual marriage. It was not a sexual union. Although she had had her share of passionate affairs, she was usually attracted to men of exceptional creative talents who needed her care.

She achieved world recognition for her talent as a writer, but that did not gratify her need for the devotion of men. She was a rare woman, with whom into her sixth decade men still fell in love.

Lou Andreas-Salome possessed an exceptional mind. She transcended the prevailing morality, despising hypocrisy but paying dearly for her freedom. She was often the object of the severe criticism of her contemporaries. Since her death, her diaries and autobiographical papers have revealed far less promiscuity than the gossips attributed to her. For example, she and Nietzsche never had a physical relationship.

[1]Freud, Journal of Lou Andreas Salome, Basic Books, N.Y. 1964, p. 6.
[2]Talent and Genius, Eissler K.R. Quadrangle Books, N.Y. 1971, p. 25.

In 1911 she attended a psychoanalytic convention at Weimar. She wrote that meeting Freud and his colleagues was the "turning point" of her life.

> Ever since I was permited to attend the Weimar Congress last autumn, the study of psychoanalysis has had a constant hold on me. The deeper I get into it, the more it grips me....
>
> (Freud, Journal of Lou Andreas Salome, Basic Books, N.Y., 1964, p. 31)

> From 1912 on Freud was her hero—probably the only man whose path she crossed who was never afraid of her and who did not ever fall in love with her. He also seems to have been the only man who never wrote or said a bad word about her. For curiously enough, no one—neither man nor woman—who becomes familiar with her life story seems to have a good word for her; almost everyone reproaches her, sometimes with a mild rebuke, more frequently with harsh words. It seems to me that no one is ready to forgive her for the fact that she succeeded in doing what women so rarely succeed in—namely, achieving a synthesis of a free, proud, indeed almost uninhibited sexual life (without submitting to the required concealments of the Victorian period) and high intellectual productivity.
>
> In Freud she found the man strong enough to cope with her, and a conflict-free relationship covered the period from their first meeting in 1912 up to her death in 1937.
>
> (Talent, p. 26)

In reply to her request for a personal meeting with him, Freud wrote:

> If I understand you rightly, you would like a personal exchange of ideas...I do not know whether a discussion after ten o'clock at night conforms with your daily routine, but I have no free time earlier than that. If you will do me the honor of a visit at such a late hour, I shall gladly engage to see you safely home.
>
> (Freud, Salome Journal, p. 44)

In accordance with Viennese custom, Freud brought a bouquet to their late supper at a local restaurant. He was fascinated by her. Her profound insights, her passionate and honest quest for understanding, her remarkable originality* made him feel that he had met someone unique. That their first meeting would last until the early hours was inevitable.

---

*For example, when Lou later became an analyst, she would lie on the couch and the patient would sit in a chair behind her.

The third member of the triangle which formed, and the victim of Freud's alleged jealousy, was Victor Tausk. Thirty-one years old, talented, even brilliant, he made his way into the psychoanalytic circle. The gossip claims that Freud, who was fifty-six years old, was jealous of Tausk's "affair with Lou." Supposedly also Tausk was getting ahead of Freud in psychoanalytic matters, his extreme originality being a problem for the latter. According to the rumor, Lou "made" Freud fall in love with her, though in a "sublimated way." He welcomed the triangle situation since she could give him information about Trausk. She could keep the potentially troublesome student under control.

The scandal raises questions about Freud's character and his professional integrity. Freud was seen as being threatened by Tausk and wanting him out of the way. He could have rescued Tausk but for selfish, unethical reasons, he maneuvered Tausk's suicide.

Tausk's father was an internationally known journalist whom he disliked so much that "he was forever embarrassed to be called by his father's name." At the age of eighteen years, he had gone to Vienna to study law. Three years later, he married a girl whom he had made pregnant. Before his marriage he was baptized, but concealed the fact whenever possible. To Gentiles he did not reveal that he was a Jew, and to Jews he did not reveal that he had been baptized. Because of a conflict with a court authority, he gave up his law practice, left his wife and two sons, and moved to Berlin. In Berlin he started a new career, directing plays, writing poetry, practicing the violin, and drawing charcoal sketches. At the age of twenty-eight he was hospitalized: "My whole past appears to me to be nothing but a preparation for this terrible collapse of my personality....The patients all look like poisoned rats and mules....Life has not shaped me, and I have had enough of this life."[1] A diagnosis may be difficult to make, but there is the suggestion here of a schizophrenic process.

Later, in Berlin, he fell in love with an actress, had a "very happy love affair," then abandoned her and went to Italy. From there, he wrote a letter to Freud, who, sufficiently impressed and thinking that Tausk was a physician, invited him to Vienna to study psychoanalysis. The little group that gathered around Freud acknowledged his talents and made him welcome. He decided to go to medical school and Freud and some members of the group supported him financially.

His psychoanalytic career was spectacular. Even as a student, he wrote papers that were well received and he participated vigorously in the affairs of the Society. He was frequently quarrelsome and got into conflict with individual members, but this was confined to theoretical disputes.

His private life was distinguished by liaisons with women, all of which he was the one to end. In medical school he organized a group to study hypnosis. While under hypnosis, a female participant would be asked whom, among those present, she might have an affair with. If he himself were named, he would subsequently ask her for a date. (Incidently, Ernst Pfeiffer, owner and administrator of Lou Andreas-Salome's literary estate, believes he has found evidence that Lou did not have a physical relationship with Tausk.)

From Lou's Journal we read that as a child "...in an unbridled rage that demanded action, he went to the room where there was a picture of his mother in her youth and pierced it through the heart with a needle—so that for a long time he hardly

[1]Talent, p. 70

dared enter the room, as if it were the scene of an actual murder.''[1] This rare behavior in a child, acting out his matricidal impulse, suggests a guarded psychiatric prognosis. There is the likelihood that, given his pathology, he would not be accepted in a psychoanalytic training institute today. There is also a question to what extent he would benefit from undergoing a classical analysis. Just as he never outgrew his conflict with his father, so did he find expression for his matricidal impulses in his relationship with women. The above throws some light on his turbulent relationships with men also.

After Tausk's suicide, Dr. Paul Federn wrote to his wife: ''....Whenever I approached him (Tausk) in a friendly way, I found only vanity, envy, and lack of interest.... He made enemies for himself everywhere and always.''[2]

The history is of a man who uses people, particularly women, selfishly and destructively. He lacked responsibility, as is seen by his desertion of his two sons. His conflict about his ancestry indicates a lack of moral fiber. His relationships with men show rivalry, envy, ambition, and ingratitude.

Could Freud have saved him? According to the story, the answer was simple: Freud should have taken him into analysis. After all, Tausk had demanded this with great insistence. Freud, apparently with equal insistence, refused. The story accuses Freud of refusing Tausk in order to carry out a personal vendetta. What is implied is that Freud's behavior was unethical by any human standards, and of course an abuse of his professional position.

It should be noted that the rumor ignores the timing of these events: the suicide took place in 1919, seven years after Lou Andreas-Salome had broken off her relationship with Tausk. In the meantime, there had been the difficult four years of World War I. Freud had two sons in the army and feared for their lives. His life savings vanished—a revolution changed the world in which he grew up. New scientific ideas were boiling inside him in such a way that they distracted him from fully mourning the death of his daughter Sophie. Is it possible that, at the age of sixty-three, he was still reacting to the affair seven years earlier of a young man with a woman eighteen years his senior? When Freud met Lou Andreas-Salome she was fifty-one years old, the same age as his wife. He himself was fifty-six. Both of them were old enough to have outgrown the demon, Passion, who seduces us into irrational behavior.

It was a policy of Freuds' not to take his students into analysis but rather to refer them to other analysts. He was not rigid about his own policy, but only rarely did he break it, and then it had to be his own decision. One can imagine what the situation would have been had Freud taken all his colleagues and collaborators into analysis with him. (And if he took Tausk as an analysand, could he refuse the same privilege to others?) However, there was a clinical reason that would have ruled out Freud's analysis of Tausk. Tausk had formed ideas and illusions about Freud. For about six years, Tausk had been complaining that Freud was assimilating his ideas. In short, Tausk had been openly accusing Freud of plagiarism. Freud said to Dr. Sarasin that if he had taken Tausk into analysis, ''he would never be able to publish another line without Tausk thinking Freud had stolen it.[3] Of course, one must ask

---

[1]Lou Andreas-Salome Journal, 107

[2]Talent, p. 78

[3]Ibid. p. 84

the question: if Tausk believed his own complaints, why would he want Freud to be his analyst? If Tausk were not a disturbed person, would he insist on help from the man who plagiarized his work?

Freud recommended that he go into analysis with Hitschmann or Federn, both experienced analysts. Tausk refused to go to a male colleague and chose Helene Deutsch. Tausk talked to her of nothing but his distrust of Freud, and after three months Dr. Deutsch discontinued the treatment. He did not protest but accepted Deutsch's decision with equanimity.

At the time Tausk was desperate. A young woman, sixteen years his junior, had consulted him as a patient. He had seduced her during the first visit. She was a virgin at the time, and she became pregnant. After efforts to interrupt the pregnancy failed,[1] he proposed marriage. This time it was impossible for him to repeat his pattern of breaking an engagement. To find himself in such a situation must have been a narcissistic injury: he who could conquer and dismiss women was now trapped. The young woman had come to him for help, trusting his professional integrity. He had failed. He had failed as a physician, as a psychoanalyst, and as a human being.

In the early morning of July 3, 1919, Victor Tausk decided to kill himself. He wrote a will containing a careful inventory of his possessions. Two sealed letters were found on his desk, one to Hilde Loewi, the unfortunate girl who expected to marry him, the other to Freud. While writing he drank the Yugoslav national drink, slivovitz. His hangman's rope was a curtain cord which he tied round his neck. He put a pistol to his right temple, and pulled the trigger. He blew off part of his head and strangled himself as he fell.

Freud's obituary (written in consideration of Tausk's sons) praised his talent and his contributions to psychoanalysis. However in a letter to Lou he admitted how little he had liked the man, how useless Tausk had been, for some time even a threat to the future of the psychoanalytic cause.

The unfortunate Victor Tausk was expressing in his suicide his rage against the young woman and the fetus who were responsible for his shame, guilt, and failure, indeed his rage against the world.*

Lou Andreas-Salome will be especially remembered for her friendships with famous men; however, she possessed a splendor all her own. The great minds of her day were attracted to her mind. She keenly appreciated the creative process and her gift lay in her ability to arouse creativity in others and to help them articulate their art. Her own writing remains relatively undiscovered.

The Nazis found her suspect although she was Aryan in every sense of the word—her father had been a general in the Russian Imperial Army, and both parents were descendants of German Protestants. After her death, they purged her library. A little red loose leaf notebook escaped their attention. It proved to be her personal journal which enables us to share some of her impressions of well-known personalities.

Although she had been early acquainted with Freud's writings, it was not until Lou was fifty years old that she made a personal contact with psychoanalysis. She spent the remaining years of her life as a psychoanalyst, treating patients at her home

---

[1]*Victor Tausk's Suicide,* K.R. Eissler, N.Y. Int. Univ. Press, 1983.

*The Tausk story is far more complicated than what is presently here. Whoever may be interested in a detailed study of this tragic man should read Roazen's *Brother Animal* (Alfred Knopf, N.Y. 1969) and above all *Talent and Genius* for a comprehensive view from an astute psychoanalyst, K. Eissler.

in Gottingen, and writing on a wide range of subjects. She once said to young Anna Freud that the only "sin" was to be untrue to one's nature.[1]

When Lou first arrived in Vienna she was met by Anna Freud. Since it was a Wednewday evening, the two women went directly to the Vienna Society meeting. Anna was seventeen and Lou was fifty-one, nevertheless Lou became one of the few intimate friends in Anna's life. They visited each other and maintained a correspondence which lasted until Lou's death. When Anna was studying to become an analyst, Lou was one of her training analysts.

On Sundays Lou would visit Freud and his family. "Anna and I used to sit with him in the evenings....I always spent the mornings in Anna's room; she would wrap me up in a wonderful rug and squat down herself by the stove....(Freud's) attitude of serene well-being struck me as characteristic of the whole family..."[2] The preface to Anna Freud's first manuscript "Beating Fantasies and Daydreams" reads: "This paper was written on the basis of several discussions I had with Frau Lou Andreas-Salome, to whom I am very grateful for her interest and participation."[3]

In Lou's descriptions of Freud we get to know his confidence and his humor, but also his pessimistic bent. He was by no means always hopeful about the human species. She on the other hand appears as someone who is "intoxicated with life."

Freud always feared that Anna might suffer a father fixation, especially since he knew his feelings toward her. He turned to Lou to help Anna tear herself loose. "Lou would not: she deemed Anna's incestuous setup more blissful than any alternative within normalcy."[4]

Abraham Kardiner once asked Freud why he thought so highly of Lou. His reply was, "There are some people who have an intrinsic superiority. They have an inborn nobility. She is just one of those people."[5]

Freud and Lou Andreas-Salome remained dearest friends from their first meeting until she died twenty-five years later.

---

[1]Journal p. 5
[2]*Anna Freud* U.H. Peters, Schocken Books, N.Y. p. 45
[3]Ibid. 46
[4]Ibid. p. 254
[5]*My Analysis with Freud* A. Kardiner, W.W. Norton N.Y. 1977 p. 77

CHAPTER XXXIX

■ *In The Beginning Was A Murder*

Freud's views on religion have evoked controversy second only to his writings on sexuality. The opposition has expressed itself chiefly in three main areas.

In the first place, Freud had no business in a field that was not his own. (This criticism was also leveled at him when he intruded into other fields: anthropology and art.) Although religiousness is part of the mind of man, it is not scientific and Freud, as a scientist, should keep hands off. Freud's response to this criticism was that contradition was not always refutation.

The second criticism, closely connected with the first, was that Freud ignored the mystics and the saints. Only through the profound experiences reported by uniquely committed and devout persons, can the truth of religion be understood or even approached. Freud's response was that his interest lay in what religion meant to humanity in general. In a later publication, *Moses and Monotheism,* he did however explore the question of why religion, more than any other human subject, evoked sublime emotions in the believer.

The third criticism was that Freud took the position that only infantile experience can explain religious emotions. In this Freud's view is misunderstood. He never claimed that religious beliefs had no connection with the supernatural. Who is in a position to say there is no God? Freud's premise is that religious beliefs can be understood on the basis of historical and psychological factors and do not require an external supernatural explanation.

Freud was raised in a Jewish family, but one in which, for the most part, the customary rituals and observances were ignored. The reader may recall how indignant Freud was when Martha restricted herself to a kosher diet (a practice he would not tolerate after they were married), and how much he disliked the ancient rites of a Jewish marriage ceremony. On the other hand, he had begun to read the Bible when he was seven and was always ready with a quotation from either the Old or New Testament. Later, he studied the cultures of Egypt, Rome, and Greece, as well as other Eastern religious of antiquity, and so came to know a great deal about diverse religious beliefs.

One gets the impression that Freud spent his life as a ''natural'' atheist, that for him the world of nature comprised everything and there was nothing outside of it. Religious people would probably say of him that he lacked a religious sense. And, in fact, he always observed in wonderment the religious beliefs of others and was curious about them.

The rituals and observances of both the Jewish and Christian faiths he regarded as antiquated nuisances. On the other hand, he held their ethical teachings in high esteem. He felt that monotheism was superior to the previous forms of worship.

> The race that first succeeded in thus concentrating the divine qualities (into a single figure) was not a little proud of this advance. It had revealed the father nucleus which had always lain hidden behind every divine figure; fundamentally it was a return to the historical beginnings of the idea of God. Now that God was a single person, man's relations to him could recover the intimacy and intensity of the child's relations to the father.
> (Jones, Vol. III, p. 352)

Even Catholicism, with its many saints and archangels, and its absorption of earlier pagan beliefs, represented to him a regression from rather than an advance on Judaism.

His letters to Pfister, a Protestant clergyman and psychoanalyst who worked chiefly with adolescents, urged him to make use of his Christian faith in therapy:

> ...people who over a long period have been severe sufferers do not come to a physician expecting moral elevation....You on the other hand have young people with recent conflicts who are attached to you personally, and who are in a suitable state for sublimation and indeed for its most convenient form--religious sublimation...you are in a fortunate position of leading them on to God...fortunate at least in one respect that religious piety stifles neuroses....Thus our patients have to seek in people what we are not able to promise them from the Land Above and what we have to refuse them personally. Naturally, therefore, it is much harder on us....
> In itself psychoanalysis is neither religious nor the opposite, but an impartial instrument which can serve the clergy as well as the laity when it is used only to free suffering people. I have been very struck at realizing how I had never thought of the extraordinary help the psychoanalytic method can be in pastoral work; probably because wicked heretics like us are so far away from the circle.
> (Pfister, Feb. 9, 1909)

Incidentally, Oskar Pfister, whom Freud called "my dear man of God," never had any difficulty defending his beliefs with a lusty enthusiasm. When Freud published "The Future of an Illusion," which presents the view that religion is a universal obsessional neurosis, Pfister fought back by writing "The Illusion of a Future." But the debate between the two friends never took on an inelegant tone: their mutual respect lasted until the end of their lives.

It was in his *Psychopathology of Everyday Life,* 1904, that Freud presented his naturalist views. He stated that man projects mythologies which touch on modern religions onto the outer world, and these mythologies are based on unconscious dynamics.

> ....It is hard to put it otherwise; one has to use here the analogy with paranoia in the construction of a supernatural reality, which science has to retranslate into the psychology of the unconscious. One could venture in this manner to resolve the myths of Paradise, the Fall of Man, of God, of Good and Evil, of Immortality, and so on, thus transforming Metaphysics into Metapsychology.
>
> (Determinism, S.E. VI, 259)

When he was invited to contribute a paper to the newly founded *Zeitschrift fur Religionspsychologie,* Freud submitted an original work, "Obsessive Acts and Religious Practices."[1] In it he pointed out the similarity between ritual acts in religious observances and the behavior of the obsessive-compulsive neurotic. Both experience a sense of compulsion, which gives way to anxiety if the act is not performed. The believer, in harmony with his religious community, finds it as necessary to kneel, pray, fast, cross himself, in the same way as the compulsive must step on every line on the pavement, or rapidly count to ten before doing something important. Whereas the neurotic carries out his ritual privately, the religious believer performs his in public along with others of the same persuasion.

Early in 1919, Dr. Hugo Heller presented before the Vienna Society a paper entitled "The History of the Devil." In his comments Freud discussed at length the varying images of the devil throughout the ages. In the Middle Ages he was a tempter and his influence had been used as an attempt to justify the performance of forbidden acts. Freud connected the latent fear and guilt aroused by the wave of syphilitic infection that was "bedeviling" Europe and the increased repression of the Reformation, with a transformation to the figure of a purely evil demon.

Freud's main contribution to the source of religious beliefs was summed up in his "Study of Leonardo da Vinci," in 1910.

> Psycho-analysis has made us aware of the intimate connection between the father complex and the belief in God, and has taught us that the personal God is psychologically nothing other than a magnified father; it shows us every day how young people can lose their religious faith as soon as the father's anthority collapses. We thus recognize the root of religious need as lying in the parental complex; the almighty and just God, and kindly Nature, appear to us as grand sublimations of father and mother, or rather as revivals and restorations of the young child's ideas of them. Biologically speaking, religiousness is to be traced to the small human child's helplessness and need of help; and when at a later date he perceives how truly forlorn and weak he is when confronted with the great forces of life, he feels his condition as he did in childhood, and attempts to deny his

[1]1907, S.E. IX

> own despondency by a regressive revival of the forces which protected his infancy.
> (Leonardo da Vinci, 1910, S.E. XI, p. 123)

Freud's serious investigation of the sources of religion was incorporated in his *Totem and Taboo*, 1913. Although the study was primarily concerned with the origins of religion, it turned out to be as much a search for the origins of civilization, and the beginnings of communal life to man's reactions to the confilicts aroused by the primordial Oedipus complex.

The book was badly received. It was dismissed as another of Freud's singular fantasies. The criticism did not present serious arguments, but expressed incredulity of the kind that met the publication of *The Interpretation of Dreams.* Freud himself, at that time, ranked the *Totem* work among the best and most daring he had written.

Even a brief summary of Freud's conclusions in this book makes it sound incredible. But the reader is again warned that Freud's logic can be very compelling, and that when his hypotheses are granted it's very hard to disagree with his conclusions. Based on Darwin's work, Freud hypothesizes that in man's early history the social organization consisted of a dominant male and a small group around him. Darwin referred to it as the "primal horde." If it were organized similarly to the many primal hordes among animals today, then we can see that only the dominant male would have access to the females. Any young male who showed an interest in the females would be driven off. The incest taboo has not yet made its appearance.

Freud speculates that in the course of time, in many different small family groups, the sons would reach a level of communication whereby they could join forces with the purpose of overthrowing and slaying the father.

> ....Darwin's primal horde. All that we find there is a violent and jealous father who keeps all the females for himself and drives away his sons as they grow up....
>
> One day the brothers who had been driven out came together, killed and devoured their father and so made an end of the patriarchal horde. United, they had the courage to do and succeeded in doing what would have been impossible for them individually. (Some cultural advance, perhaps command over some new weapon, had given them a sense of superior strength.) Cannibal savages as they were it goes without saying that they devoured their victim as well as killing him. The violent primal father had doubtless been the feared and envied model of each one of the company of brothers: and in the act of devouring him they accomplished their identification with him, and each one of them acquired a portion of his strength. The totem meal, which is perhaps mankind's earliest festival, would thus be a repetition and a commemoration of this memorable and criminal deed, which was the berginning of so many things—of social organization, of moral restrictions and of religion.

(Totem, p. 141-142)

Two things then take place in our reconstruction: chaos, as the brothers fight among themselves for the females, and remorse as they realise they have slain and eaten the admired model, the loved one. Guilt enters human history! The brothers unite again, and this time they renounce the females of the group they won, and idealize the memory of the all-powerfull father. Their feelings are unconsciously displaced onto an animal (which is exactly what the neurotic does in animal phobia) and the animal, the totem, thus becomes a sacred object.

Those who have no knowledge of the unconscious would naturally consider the above as more of Freud's nonsense. A characteristic of all totem religions is that while the totem animal is protected by taboos, he is slain once a year and every member of the totem clan must share in a ceremonious feast—mankind's first holiday. It is absolutely necessary that everyone literally eat and devour the totem animal. The ritual repeats the original deed, the original sin.

Why this deep involvement on Freud's part with primordial man? Jung had been exploring the literature of comparative religion and mythology, and the two men had engaged in lively talks and letters on the subject.

> Dear Professor Freud, 14. November 1911
>
> Many thanks for your very nice letter which I just received. However, the outlook for me is very gloomy if you get into the psychology of religion. You are a dangerous rival—if one has to speak of rivalry. Yet I think it has to be this way, for a natural development cannot be halted, nor should one try to halt it. Our personal differences will make our work different.
>
> With best regards,
> Jung

(Freud/Jung, p. 460)

But Freud had begun to feel uneasy about the direction that Jung's researches were taking him. Jung was drawing uncertain conclusions from man's distant past, man's sagas and myths, and using this data to explain clinical problems. Freud's approach was from the opposite direction. His method was to see how conclusions drawn from clinical experience and reports from contemporary primitives may be used to throw light backward on the problems of man's distant past.

There was also a political reason for Freud's new departure. The hopes of a happy alliance with the Swiss group of psychiatrists had come to an end. The Swiss analysts were hearing recriminations from the press and were seeking a dignified way of confessing their error and separating themselves from the "sensual" Viennese. All hopes that the Crown Prince Jung would lead the psychoanalytic movement into the future had ended. The views that Jung had already expressed in New York were incompatible with Freud's views. Jung said that incest wishes should not be taken literally but as symbols of other tendencies. The separation between the two groups was inevitable and it was merely a question how it should take place without causing major repercussions in the International Association.

Freud wrote to Abraham that his new essay on religion would be given before the Munich Congress and "would serve to make a sharp division between us and all Aryan religiosity. For that will be the result of it."[1] The same day he wrote to Ferenczi, "Since *The Interpretation of Dreams,* I have not worked at anything with such certainty and elation. The reception will be the same: a storm of indignation except among those near to me. In the dispute with Zurich it comes at the right time to divide us as an acid does a salt." Two weeks later: "Jung is crazy, but I don't really want a split; I should prefer him to leave of his own accord. Perhaps my Totem work will hasten the break against my will."[2]

Freud did not follow Jung into the areas of Greek mythology and comparative religions, even though he was familiar with the literature; instead, he turned to the unexplored realm of the Australian aborigines. Why? In 1910, Frazer's four-volumes *Totemism and Exogamy* had appeared, and it stimualted Freud's own interest in the symbolic significance of animals, which he equated with the unconscious father.

Freud submerged himself in the vast material he felt he had to master before being able to recognize connections between primitive beliefs and the unconscious fantasies of his neurotic patients.

> The Totem work is a beastly business. I am reading thick books without being really interested in them since I already know the results; my instinct tells me that. But they have to slither their way throught all the material on the subject. In that process one's insight gets clouded, so there are many things that don't fit and yet mustn't be forced. I haven't time every evening, and so on. With all that I feel as if I had intended only to start a little liaison and then discovered that at my time of life I have to marry a new wife.
> (Ferenczi, Nov. 30, 1911)

In the first section of the book "Horror of Incest," Freud tells us that he has chosen the most primitive, backward and "miserable of savages" for comparision with the fantasies of his neurotic patients. The Australian aborigines do not cultivate the soil, build houses or permanent structures, nor keep domesticated animals; they are not even acquainted with the art of pottery. They have no leader. There is no evidence that they worship anything resembling a higher being; they live entirely by hunting and digging edible roots.

> We should certainly not expect that the sexual life of these poor naked cannibals would be moral in our sense or that their sexual instincts would be subjected to any great degree of restriction. Yet we find that they set before themselves with the most scrupulous care and the most painful severity the aim of avoiding incestuous sexual relations. Indeed, their whole social organization seems to serve that purpose, or to have been brought into relation with its attainment.

---

[1]Abraham, May 13, 1913
[2]Jones 2, p. 350

(*Totem and Taboo,* 1913, S.E. XIII, 2)

Freud goes on to describe the extraordinarily varied precautions these people take to avoid the remotest possibility of incest, or even a relationship that might in any way resemble it. It is strictly forbidden to have sexual relations with a member of the same totem. A totem is usually an animal (rarely it may be a plant or a natural phenomenon like rain), and is considered the common ancestor of the clan. Members of a totem are under a sacred obligation not to kill or destroy their totem and to avoid eating its flesh. The penalty for the violation of the prohibition is death. Once a year the totem animal is slain and it is mandatory that every member of the clan partake of the totem feast.

Some of the precautions taken against incest may strike us as extreme. In New Mecklenburg, brothers and sisters, and cousins too, may not come near each other. They may not shake hands, may not give each other gifts, and may speak only at a distance of some paces. The penalty for sex with a sister is death by hanging. Among the Battas of Sumatra, who are also primitive people, a father may never remain alone in the house with his daughter, nor a mother with her son. If a man and a woman from the same totem find that they are approaching each other on the same path, one of them, depending on local custom, leaves the path and turns his back until the other has passed. "These people assume as a matter of course that a solitary meeting between a man and a woman will lead to an improper intimacy between them...." Among the A-Kamba of British East Africa, a girl between the age of puberty and marriage may not sit next to her father; if they meet on the road, she hides while he passes. On the other hand, after her marriage, she is not obliged to avoid her father in any way.

> Among the Basoga, a Bantu people who live in the region of the sources of the Nile, a man may only speak to his mother-in-law when she is in another room and out of sight. Incidentally, these people have such a horror of incest that they punish it even when it occurs among their domestic animals.
>
> (Ibid. p.13)

These people are much more sensitive about the matter of incest than are civilized peoples, and punish infractions of the prohibitions with instant death. Freud inferred that the primitive has no organized defenses against his temptations and, therefore, cannot rely upon the repressions that civilized man has organized. "In that respect they may be compared with the neurotics who often have to establish complicated phobias and other symptoms that serve the same purpose as the primitive taboos."[1]

"Taboo and the Ambivalence of Feelings" is the title of the second section. Four times as long as the first, in it Freud offers evidence from man's early history that supports one aspect of psychoanalytic theory. He shows us that neurotic pro-

---

[1]Jones 2, p. 355

hibitions are strikingly similar to the taboos of primitive peoples, and that an investigation of this phenomenon may shed light on the origins of man's morality. Freud ranges over what seems to be an infinite variety of taboos. Interestingly, no reasons or rationalizations are offered for the taboo. To the believer a taboo is automatic, autonomous, it requires no explanation. For example, if a member of the tribe hunts or eats a totem animal, the tribe immediately destroys him. There is nothing to question. Perhaps the nearest we can come to this phenomenon in modern times is the existence of the conscience. If we transgress our own moral code, we immediately, with unquestioning certainty, feel the discomfort of guilt, even if no one else knows about the transgression.

To illustrate how a taboo may be very easily displaced, that whoever, or whatever touches the taboo object becomes in turn taboo, Freud relates the following:

> A Maori chief would not blow a fire with his mouth; for his sacred breath would communicate its sanctity to the fire, which would pass it on to the pot on the fire, which would pass it on to the meat in the pot, which would pass it on to the man who ate the meat, which was in the pot, which stood on the fire, which was breathed on by the chief's breath conveyed through these intermediaries, would surely die.
> (*Totem,* p. 28)

A common characteristic of an obsessional neurotic is a fear of touching, or being touched. The feeling is that something terrible will follow if the touching occurs. In a taboo too the essential prohibition is contact. Freud proceeds to demonstrate parallels between characteristics of primitive taboos and those of obsessive-compulsive neurotics, and he draws the conclusion that the taboo represents a renunciation of a former temptation which is now forbidden.

He discusses the different kinds of taboo and shows that they are characterized by ambivalence as are the obsessive neuroses. On the island of Timor, when a warlike expedition has returned in triumph and offers a display of the heads of the vanquished, the leader of the expedition is submitted to severe restrictions. A special hut is prepared for him where he must live for two months, during which time he undergoes rituals for bodily and spiritual purification. He is not to touch his wife, nor feed himself; the food must be put in his mouth by another person. (It strikes us as hardly an appropriate reward for a victory over an enemy.) Meanwhile, the others are taking part in a ceremony that consists of dances and songs in which the death of the slain is lamented and their forgiveness entreated.

> "Be not angry," they say, "because your head is here with us; had we been less lucky, our heads might now have been exposed in your village. We have offered the sacrifice to appease you. Your spirit may now rest and leave us in peace. Why were you our enemy?Would it not have been better that we should have remained friends? Then your blood would not have been spilt and your head would not have been cut off."
> (Ibid. p. 37)

What emerges is that primitive peoples have a more intense feeling of ambivalence than modern man, who is better defended against his unacceptable impulses.

The third essay is "Animism, Magic and the Omnipotence of Thoughts." Freud describes the many ways that man uses magic to influence his enemies, his neighbors, and indeed the world itself. Sticking a pin into a wax image with the intention of harming the person represented by the image is among the most common forms of magic.

> In some parts of Java at the season when the bloom will be on the rice, the husband and his wife visit their fields by night and there engage in sexual intercourse to encourage the fertility of the rice by their example.
>
> Or again, while a Gilyak hunter is pursuing game in the forest, his children at home are forbidden to make drawings on wood or on sand; for they fear that if the children did so, the paths in the forest would become as perplexed as the lines in the drawings, so that the hunter might lose his way and never return.
>
> In these last examples, as in so many other instances of the working of magic, the element of distance is disregarded; in other words, telepathy is taken for granted.
>
> (Ibid. p. 80)

Freud adopted the term "omnipotence of thoughts" from the case of a patient who suffered from obsessional ideas. The patient became well-known in the literature as the Rat Man (see Charpter XXV) because of one of his specific obsessions. (S.E. X)

Freud saw that the basis of magic lies in man's exaggerated belief in the power of his thoughts, "or more exactly his wishes." It resembles the omnipotence of thought that we find in the mental life of young children and in the fantasies of neurotics.

The fourth section, the one to which the rest of the book led up, and the most important of all, he called "the Infantile Return of Totemism." Each clan traces its descent from its totem. Not only is it strictly forbidden to kill one, but that kind of animal must be protected and must in its turn protect the clan. Also, members of the clan are forbidden sexual contact with other members, which is the beginning of exogamy.

Psychoanalysis had found that the animal that appears in an animal phobia is an unconscious symbol of the father who is both loved and hated. Freud drew the conclusion that the totemic "ancestor" of the clans of primitive people had the same significance. From that point of view the various features of the taboo, ambivalence of feelings and so on, are easy to understand.

It was easy for Freud to see the connection between exogamy and totemism: exogamy was insurance against the possibility of committing incest. Totemism and exogamy represent the two halves of Oedipus Complex: the child's attraction to the mother and his death wishes against the rival father. Seen in the context of the

Oedipus Complex, everything falls into place.

At this point, Freud drew heavily on Robertson Smith's* writings on the subject of sacrifice and sacrificial feasts. During the most solemn ceremony of the year, the totem animal is slain and eaten. This deed is followed by a ceremony of mourning. When the mourning is over, triumphant rejoicing is felt and wild excesses take place. In this way the totem members maintain a permanent connection with their ancestor whose virtues they have absorbed.

Thousands of years later, the totem becomes a god and the complicated story of the various religions are set in motion. Freud does not pursue the subject, but, fortunately, he does touch on it.

> When Christianity first penerated into the ancient world it met with competition from the religion of Mithras and for a time it was doubtful which of the two deities would gain the victory. In spite of the halo of light surrrounding his form, the youthful Persian god remains obscure to us. We may perhaps infer from the sculpture of Mithras slaying a bull that he represented a son who was alone in sacrificing his father and thus redeemed his brothers from their burden of complicity in the deed. There was an alternative method of allaying their guilt and this was first adopted by Christ. He sacrificed his own life and so redeemed the company of brothers from original sin.
>
> (Ibid. p. 153)
>
> ....There can be no doubt that in the christian myth the original sin was one against God the Father. If, however, Christ redeemed mankind from the burden of original sin by the sacrific of his own life, we are driven to conclude that the son was a murdered. The law of Ialion, which is so deeply rooted in human feelings, lays it down that a murder can only be expiated by the sacrifice of another life: self-sacrifice points back to blood-guilt.**And if this sacrifice of a life brought about atonement with God the Father, the crime to be expiated can only have been murder of the father.
>
> In the Christian doctrine, therefore, men were acknowledging in the most undisguised manner the guilty primaeval deed, since they found the fullest atonement for it in the sacrifice of this one son. Atonement with the father was all the more complete since the sacrifice was accompanied by a total renunciatin of the women on whose account the rebellion against the father was started. But at that point the inexorable psychological law of ambivalence stepped in. The very deed in which

*A Scottish semitic scholar

**We find that impulses to suicide in a neurotic turn out regularly to be self-punishments for wishes for someone else's death.

> the son offered the greatest possible atonement to the father brought him at the same time to the attainment of his wishes against the father. He himself became God, beside, or, more correctly, in place of the father. A son-religion displaced the father-religion. As a sign of this substitution the ancient totem meal was revived in the form of communion, in which the company of brothers consumed the flesh and blood of the son—no longer the father—obtained sanctity thereby, are identified themselves with him. Thus we can trace through the ages the identity of the totem meal with animal sacrifice, with the anthropic human sacrifice and with the Christian Eucharist, and we can recognize in all these rituals the effect of the crime by which men were so deeply weighed down but of which they must nonetheless feel so proud. The Christian communion, however, is essentially a fresh elimination of the father, a repetition of the guilty deed.
>
> (Ibid. p. 154)

At the end of the book, *Totem and Taboo,* Freud makes this memorable statement: ''At the conclusion, then, of this exceedingly condensed inquiry, I should like to insist that its outcome shows that the beginnings of religion, morals, society and art converge in the Oedipus complex.''[1] So, Freud concludes, ''In the beginning was the deed.''

[1]Ibid. p. 156

CHAPTER XL

Who's Got The Neurosis?

Freud had a pet peeve: any delay in an answer to a letter from him upset him. An avid correspondent himself, he enjoyed receiving letters and answered promptly and profusely. Jung, on the other hand, was an erratic correspondent. Freud told him that the delays reminded him of the relationship with Fliess: the first sign of his friend's cooling toward him was his tardiness in answering his letters. On that occasion and others, Jung had sworn that he would never desert Freud; but by this time Freud was facing the situation. He resigned himself to the fact that a personal, friendly contact with a colleague was coming to a close.

Freud saw that even without a break in their personal relationship, Jung's revision of the the concept of the libido brought them to a fundamental disagreement, a professional parting of the ways. Since the publication of his "Transformations and Symbols," Jung could no longer be considered a psychoanalyst.

The suspicions the Viennese group felt about Jung were much more personal than objective. Abraham was perplexed at Jung's belief in mysticism, astrology, and occultism, but he had no impact on Freud. Freud's hopes were too high to listen to disparaging criticisms of the swiss group. (He told himself that Abraham had motives of competition.) There clearly was an antipathy between the two groups, but Freud's hope was that common interests would smooth over the feelings of mistrust.

It was during the trip to America, when Freud found his porcupine, that Jung startled Jones by saying he thought it unnecessary to go into unsavory details with his patients. He added that it made him feel uncomfortable when they met at dinner parties. To anyone committed to psychoanalytic psychology, such an avoidance is truly startling. A little later it became known that ignoring sexual details was a regular part of Jung's teaching. By contrast, note the letter Freud wrote concerning an analysis that Pfister was conducting:

> Your analysis suffers from the hereditary weakness of virtue. It is the work of an over-decent man who feels himself obliged to be discreet. Now these psychoanalytical matters need a full exposition to make them comprehensible, just as an actual analysis can proceed only when one descends to the small details from the abstractions that cover them. Discretion is thus incompatible with a good presentation of psychoanalysis. One has to become a bad fellow, transcend the rules, sacrifice oneself, betray, and behave like the artist who buys paints

> with his wife's household money, or burns the furniture to warm the room for his model. Without some such criminality there is no real achievement.
> (June 6, 1910)

Jung felt that stressing the sexual factors was unwise and even dangerous:

> We should do well not to burst out with the theory of sexuality in the foreground. I have many thoughts about that, especially on the ethical aspects of the question. I believe that in publicly announcing certain things one would saw off the branch on which civilization rests; one undermines the impulse to sublimation....Both with students and with patients I get on further by not making the theme of sexuality prominent.
> (Letter from Jung to Jones, May 15, 1909)

Bleuler, Jung's chief at the Burgholzli, had been expressing reservations about psychoanalysis and Freud had a talk with him in Munich that seemed to have been very successful.

> I came to a complete understanding with him and achieved a good personal relationship. After all, he is only a poor devil like ourselves and in need of a little love....It is almost certain that he will join the Zurich society and then the division there will be healed. The day after he left, Jung came. He was magnificent and did me a power of good. I opened my heart to him, about the Alder affair, my own difficulties and my worry over what to do about the matter of telepathy....I am more than ever convinced that he is the man of the future. His own investingations have carried him far into the realm of mythology, which he wants to open up with the key of the libido theory. However, agreeable all that may be, I nevertheless bade him return in good time to the neuroses. There is the motherland where we have first to fortify our dominion against everything and everybody.
> (To Ferenczi, Dec. 29, 1910)

During the two distressing years with Adler and Stekel, trouble was brewing in Zurich. Articles began to appear in the daily press denouncing Viennese psychoanalysis. They declared the hope that Swiss analysts would not be corrupted by the wickedness from Vienna. As mentioned earlier, there is an outstanding peculiarity of the Swiss. They feel a bond of "Swissness." Few outsiders ever succeed in becoming Swiss. The need to conform to the prevailing morality of the community, may be stronger there than in any other part of the civilized world. Could the Swiss psychiatrists withstand the recriminations against Freud's sexual theories? Within two years practically all Swiss analysts, with two or three exceptions, had renounced their former ways.

Despite Freud's fondness for Jung and admiration for his qualities, he was less deeply involved emotionally in the relationship than was Jung. It is not unusual in such circumstances for the more involved member of a partnership to be the first to withdraw. For a year or two there had been indications that this is what Jung was doing. Toward the end of 1909, he announced his intention of going deeply into a study of all branches of occultism and mythology. Freud suggested that he concentrate on a narrow theme and not spread himself over the whole field. Jung did not take his advice. Before long, he sent out vague warnings that something surprising pertaining to the libido might come out of his studies.

Freud was not concerned about Jung's hints of theoretical modifications. What did bother him was that Jung was neglecting his responsibilities as President of the Association. Freud had thought of Jung as the one to relieve him of duties he himself did not relish; be a liaison officer between various societies, supervise the administrative work of the meetings, do editorial work, and so on. Jung on his part did not relish such tasks either. He was unsuited for the position that Freud had planned for him. Jung was not cut out to be President of an Association, or leader of a movement.

Freud was disappointed when there was no news from Jung during Freud's visit to Binswanger so near to Jung's home. Following that incident, Jung made sarcastic references in letters to Freud about "understand his gesture of Kreuzlingen," which left Freud completely puzzled. Freud noted that Jung no longer addressed his letters to "Lieber Freud" reverting to the more formal "Lieber Herr Doktor."

While Jung was in New York, reports kept coming back that he was antagonistic to Freud's theories, called Freud out-of date, and claimed to be able to expose and correct Freud's errors. Indeed, Jung told his audiences that recent observations indicated that Freud had exaggerated the role of the sexual disposition in mental health. The Oedipus complex, the unconscious wish to commit murder and incest, also came under Jung's scrutiny. Jung revised the Oedipus complex into a formula for a child's jealousy, defending his love of his parents. He presented his conclusion that the incest wish itself is not to be taken as a concrete sexual wish but as a symbol of a higher need. The "cleaning up" of psychoanalysis was well received by his American audience.

At the time, Freud barely knew what Jung was doing in America and didn't take the rumors seriously. Had he known more, he would have been more upset. Jung was gaining a lot of publicity and was putting his ideas before large audiences with considerable success. When he returned, he sent Freud a long account of his experiences and how he succeeded in making psychoanalysis popular by omitting the sexual themes. His letter showed no discomfort concerning the positions he had taken. He seemed in fact confident and even bent on modifying and expanding psychoanalytic theory.

1003 Seestrasse, Kusnach-Zurich
11 November 1912

Dear Professor Freud,

I have just got back from America and hasten to give you my news. Of course, I should have

> done so from America weeks ago but was so busy that I had neither the inclination nor the leisure to write....
>
> Altogether, the psychoanalytic movement over there has enjoyed a tremendous upswing since we were last in America. Everywhere I met with great interest and was favorably received. Thus I had rich soil to work on and was able to do a very great deal for the spread of the movement....
>
> Naturally I also made room for those of my views which deviate in places from the hitherto existing conceptions, particulrly in regard to the libido theory. I found that my version of psychoanalysis won over many people who until now had been put off by the problem of sexuality in neurosis.
>
> As soon as I have an offprint, I shall take pleasure in sending you a copy of my lectures in the hope that you will gradually come to accept innovations already hinted at in my libido paper.

The next line calling into question Freud's ability to be objective is practically an insult:

> I feel no need to let you down provided you can take an objective view of our common endeavours. I regret it very much if you think that the modifications in question have been prompted solely by resistances to you. Your Kreuzlingen gesture has dealt me a lasting wound. I would prefer a direct confrontation.
>
> (Freud/Jung Letters, p. 515)

Freud was annoyed that Jung did not have the courtesy to discuss with him in advance his modifications of psychoanalytic theory. His reply omitted his usual "My friend" :

> Vienna, IX Berggasse 19
> 14 November 1912
>
> Dear Dr. Jung,
>
> I greet you on your return from America, no longer as affectionately as on the last occasion in Nuremburg--you have successfully broken me of the habit--but still with considerable sympathy, interest, and satisfaction at your personal success....You have reduced a good deal of resistance with your modifications, but I shouldn't advise you to enter this in the credit column because, as you know, the farther you remove yourself from what is new in psychoanalysis, the more certain

> you will be of applause and the less resistance you will meet....
>
> You can count on my objectivity and hence on the continuance of our relations; I still hold that personal variations are quite justified and I still feel the same need to continue our collaboration....
>
> I must own that I find your harping on the "Kreuzlingen gesture" both incomprehensible and insulting, but there are things that cannot be straightened out in writing.
>
> (Freud/Jung, p. 517)

The rest of the letter discussed the problem of Stekel's refusal to relinquish his position as editor of the *Zentrablatt*, even though he had resigned from the Society. Freud suggested that they found a new journal and simply ignore the *Zentrablatt*.

Jung called a meeting to settle the matter of the journal. His invitation to Jones was sent to the wrong address, and also, contained the wrong date for the meeting. Jones in the meantime heard the correct date from Vienna and so arrived in time. He said that the look of astonishment on Jung's face told him it was a "parapraxis" (Freudian slip). When Jones mentioned the slip to Freud, he replied, "A gentleman should not do such things even unconsciously."[1]

The problems of the journal were settled amicably and the meeting ended early. Freud and Jung went off for a walk before lunch. Freud took the opportunity to find out about the mysterious "gesture of Kreuzlingen." Jung explained that he was very angry that Freud notified him too late for Jung to join them. He claimed he had received Freud's letter the day Freud had to return to Vienna. Freud agreed that this would have been a disturbing action but he was certain that he mailed the two letters, to Binswanger and Jung, at the same time. Jung suddenly remembered that he had been away for two days that weekend. Freud had indeed notified Jung in time. Freud asked him why he had not looked at the postmark before attacking him' that obviously his anger was displaced from another source, and this a thin excuse to justify it.

Jung, of course, did not know the reason for Freud's visit to Binswanger and he was jealous. He felt slighted because Freud had not arranged a visit with him also. Jung contritely admitted difficult traits in his personality, but Freud did not let him off easily and unleashed some of his own anger. Jung accepted the criticisms. He promised to reform.

Freud was in a good mood at the ensuing luncheon, doubtless because Jung seemed to have returned to the fold. After some discussion of Abraham's recent paper on the Egyptian Amenhotep IV, Freud turned to Franz Riklin, a Swiss analyst, and Jung. He reproached the two for recent publications in Zurich which ignored his work and even his name. He declared that this was a sign of Swiss withdrawal from the psychoanalytic movement. He seemed to be taking the matter personally, when suddenly, to everyone's alarm, he fell to the floor in a dead faint. The stalwart Jung swiftly carried him to the lounge where he soon revived. "How sweet it must

---

[1]Jones 2, p. 145

be to die'' were Freud's first words when he awakened.[1]

The incident was similar to one that had happened when Freud, Ferenczi, and Jung were in Bremen setting out for their American voyage. At the time Freud had succeeded in a small victory over Jung: he overcame Jung's attitude toward alcohol, but then fell to the ground in a faint. It would seem that Freud himself was a mild example of a type he described as ''those wrecked by success''; in this case, overcoming Jung's resistance to psychoanalysis.

Later, Freud analyzed his fainting. He traced it to the death of a younger brother when he himself was a year and seven months old. His death wish toward his brother Julius had been successful, which resulted in a neurotic conflict, a fear of gratifying unconscious wishes. Confirming his interpretation is the fact that on both the occasions with Jung there had been an argumentative discussion of death wishes. On both occasions Jung admonished him for attaching too much importance to them.

In Bremen Jung had been carrying on at length about the significance of some prehistoric cemeteries that had recently been discovered in the neighborhood. Freud became impatient and suggested that Jung's continuing the theme must indicate the presence of some unconscious death wishes. Jung denounced the idea and heatedly asserted that Freud was too ready to jump to such conclusions. On this occasion in Munich, in the discussion of Amenhotep, Abraham traced the revolution against the religious establishment to hostility to the father. Jung protested that just because Amenhotep erased his father's name and inscriptions wherever he found them was making too much of death wishes. He felt that the important deed was the establishment of monotheism and that death wishes as such were trivial. It seems the combination of a victory over Jung and the theme of death wishes forced Freud to protect himself from anxiety by giving up his consciousness. Fainting removed the irritating stimuli.

On returning to Zurich, Jung wrote a humble letter assuring Freud of his loyalty and expressing his desire to reform.

26 Nov. 1912

Dear Professor Freud,

I am glad we were able to meet in Munich, as this was the first time I have really understood you. I realized how different I am from you. This realization will be enough to effect a radical change in my whole attitude. Now you can rest assured that I shall not give up our personal relationship. Please forgive the mistakes which I will not try to excuse or extenuate. I hope the insight I have gained will guide my conduct from now on. I am most distressed that I did not gain this insight much earlier. It could have spared you so many disappointments....I hope all is well with you personally and with your family, with kind regards,

Yours sincerely,
Jung

(The Freud/Jung Letters, Bollingen 329)

---

[1]Jones 1, 317

Ferenczi expressed the hope that from now on things would go smoothly with Zurich, but Freud had been hurt too often, and did not share the optimism. The next week something must have happened in Zurich, for Freud received a letter for which the word "brazen" would be apt.

3 Dec. 1912

Dear Professor Freud,

My very best thanks for one passage in your letter, where you speak of a "bit of neurosis" you haven't got rid of. This "bit" should, in my opinion, be taken very seriously indeed because, as experience shows, it leads "usque ad instar voluntariae mortis."* I have suffered from this bit in my dealings with you...if these blinkers were removed you would, I am sure, see my work in a very different light. As evidence that you--if I may be permitted so disrespectful an expression--underestimate my work by a very wide margin, I would cite your remark that "without intending it I have solved the riddle of all mysticism, showing it to be based on the symbolic utilization of complexes that have outlived their function." My dear Professor, forgive me again, but this sentence shows me that you deprive yourself of the possibility of understanding my work by your underestimation of it....One thing I beg of you: take these statements as an effort to be honest and do not apply the depreciatory Viennese criterion of egoistic striving for power or heaven knows what other insinuations from the world of the father complex....

With kind regards,

Jung

(Ibid. 330)

Some time before, Freud had pointed out to Jung a certain resemblance between his ideas and Adler's. They both believed that the mind artificially created things like the incest complex to cover impulses of another kind. Jung resented the comparison. Being said to resemble Adler in any way was "a bitter pill." Freud received another angry note: "not even Adler's companions think that I belong to your group." This was a slip of the pen for "their group." Since all along Jung had been insisting that Freud be objective, Freud could not resist asking him if he could be objective enough to analyze his slip of the pen. Jung was a very sensitive man and this kind of insinuation was almost an insult. He wrote an angry reply:

18 Dec. 1912

Dear Professor Freud,

....If you doubt my word, so much the worst

*"To the semblance of a voluntary death" Apuleius, *The golden Ass.* This may serve the reader as a sample of Jung's learning.

> for you. I would, however, point out that your technique of treating your pupils like patients is a blunder. In that way you produce either slavish sons or impudent puppies (Alder-Stekel and the whole insolent gang now throwing their weight about in Vienna). I am objective enough to see through your little trick....You go around sniffing out all the symptomatic actions in your vicinity, thus reducing everyone to the level of sons and daughters who blushingly admit the existence of ther faults. Meanwhile you remain on top as the father, sitting pretty. For sheer obsequiousness nobody dares to pluck the prophet by the beard and inquire for once what you would say to a patient with a tendency to analyze the analyst instead of himself. You would certainly ask him: "Who's got the neurosis?"
>
> You see, my dear Professor, so long as you hand out this stuff I don't give a damn for my symptomatic actions; they shrink to nothing in comparision with the formidable beam in my brother Freud's eye. I am not in the least neurotic--touch wood!....Adler and Stekel were taken in by your little tricks and reacted with childish insolence. I shall continue to stand by you publicly while maintaining my own views, but privately shall start telling you in my letters what I really think of you....
>
> (Freud/Jung, p. 535)

Freud felt humiliated and wrote Jung a letter which he never sent. a few weeks later, writing in regard to a business matter, he added:

> I can answer only one point in your previous letter in any detail. Your allegation that I treat my followers like patients is demonstrably untrue. In Vienna I am reproached for the exact opposite....In building your construction on this foundation you have made matters as easy for yourself as with your famous "Kreuzlingen gesture"....
>
> It is a convention among us analysts that none of us need feel ashamed of his own bit of neurosis. But one who, while behaving abnormally, keeps shouting that he is normal, gives ground for the suspicion that he lacks insight into his illness. Accordingly, I propose that we abandon our personal relations entirely.
>
> (Ibid. 538)

And so eneded Freud's correspondence with the man who was to protect psychoanalysis from the accusation that it was the expression of a Jewish ghetto.

The situation was very awkard. After all, Jung was still President of the International Psycho-Analytical Association and Editor of the *Jahrbuch.* He still had the responsibility of holding the many societies together and arranging Association business. But the increasing divergence of Jung's outlook from Freud's led to the question of how long there would be any point to collaboration.

Maeder wrote to Ferenczi that the scientific differences between the Swiss and the Viennese was really a difference between Aryans and Jews. In a letter to Ferenczi, Freud advised answering Maeder along the following lines:

> Certainly there are great differences between the Jewish and the Aryan spirit. We can observe that every day. Hence there would assuredly be here and there differences in outlook on life and art. But there should no be such a thing as Aryan or Jewish science. Results in science must be identical, though the presentation of them may vary. If these differences mirror themselves in the apprehension of objective relationships in science, there must be something wrong.
> (June 8, 1913)

In a series of lectures to the International Congress of Medicine in London (August 1913), Jung presented the system of his thought. He used the name "Analytical Psychology" to distinguish it from Freud's psychoanalysis. In the matter of dream theory, he disagreed with psychoanalysis, rather, he found himself in agreement with Adler's Individual Psychology. He introduced a concept of an "energetic" factor in neuroses. Finally, he described a "collective unconscious" and gave it great importance. Each person was born with an imprint of man's myths and a sense of the mystery of eternal life, and the spirit peculiar to his racial culture. The collective unconscious had within it a profound mystical understanding of human behavior, and in fact of all life. Whereas Freud's unconscious is a chaotic, asocial, primitive urge for instinctual release and gratification, the collective unconscious contains a wisdom based on mankind's experiences through history. Jung's disagreement with Freud was now complete.

There was considerable apprehension about the upcoming Congress to be held in Munich in September 1913. The strategy for the Vienna group was to avoid a split with the Swiss group. It was felt that the International Association was too new and weak to survive the break. They even made a point of staying at the same hotel as the Swiss so as to avoid the appearance of strained relations.

The scientific level of the papers was banal. One of the Swiss papers was full of statistics and so tedious that Freud whispered to Jones: "All sorts of criticisms have been brought against psychoanalysis, but this is the first time that anyone could have called it boring."[1]

Jung conducted the meeting in a way that many considered offensive. He was prejudiced in his comments concerning the papers that were presented and his manner was officious and highhanded.

Lou Andreas Salome wrote:

---

[1]Jones 2, 102

> At the congress the Zurich members sat at their own table opposite Freud's. Their behavior toward Freud can be characterized in a word: it is not so much that Jung diverges from Freud, as that he does it in such a way as if he had taken it on himself, it is misconstrued to mean that he cannot show scientific tolerance, is dogmatic, and so forth. One glance at the two of them tells which is the more dogmatic, and the more in love with power. Two years ago Jung's booming laughter gave voice to a kind of robust gaiety and exuberant vitality, but now his earnestness is composed of pure aggression, ambition, and intellectual brutality....
>
> (The Freud Journal of Lou Andreas Salome, Basic Books, 1964,168)

Some of the members present felt that, at the very least, a gesture of protest should be made.

When Jung's name came up for re-election as President of the International Association, Abraham suggested that those who disapproved should abstain from voting. Jung accepted his re-election with fifty-two votes for, twenty-two votes against. Jones wrote: "He came up to me afterwards, observing that I was one of the dissidents, and with a sour look said: 'I thought you were a Christian' (i.e. a non-Jew). It sounded irrelevant but presumably it had some meaning."[1] In view of Jung's subsequent involvement with the German government during the Hitler period the remark was not irrelevant.

In a letter to Ferenczi, Jung reproached him for not supporting his candidacy at the Congress. Ferenczi replied in his characteristic direct fashion.

> It is altogether untrue when you ascribe our attitude to Freud's reaction to your "own scientific views." So little is the case that in spite of our deep differences we had decided in accord with Freud's own suggestion, to vote again in favor of your being President. It was only the absolutely improper way in which you as Chairman of the Congress dealt with the suggestions we put forward, the quite one-sided and partial comments you made on all the papers read, and also the personal behavior on the part of your group,that caused us to protest by voting with blank cards.
>
> (Ferenczi to Jung, Nov.13, 1913)

In October Freud received a letter from Jung complaining that he had heard from Maeder that Freud doubted his bona fides, therefore no further coorperation and collaboration with Freud was possible and he was resigning from his editorship of the *Jahrbuch*. Jung wrote to Jones that the situation was "absolutely incurable."

Soon one was hearing that there are three schools of psychoanalysis: Freud, Adler, and Jung. Academics concluded that since they could not agree over their own

[1]Jones 2, 102

findings there was no need for anyone to take the subject seriously: it was a mixture of uncertainties.

The claim that there are conflicting kinds of psychoanalysis impelled Freud to write "On the History of the Psycho-Analytic Movement." There he stated that he alone was best qualified to know what psychoanalysis was. It had its own characteristic methods and theories that distinguished it from other schools of thought and other psychologies:

> Alder's secession took place before the Weimar congress in 1911; after that date, the Swiss begin theirs....
>
> Of the two movements under discussion, Adler's is indubitably the more important; while radically false, it is marked by constancy and coherence. It is, moreover in spite of everything, founded upon a theory of the instincts. Jung's modification, on the other hand, loosened the connection of the phenomena with instinctual life; and further...it is so obscure, unintelligible and confused as to make it difficult to take up any position upon it....
>
> It must be admitted, however, that the exponents of the new theory find themselves in a difficult position. They are now disputing things which they themselves formerly upheld, and they are doing so, moreover, not on the ground of fresh observations which might have taught them something further....For this reason they are unwilling to give up their connection with psychoanalysis, as whose representatives they have become known to the world, and prefer to give it out that psycho-analysis has changed....
>
> The truth is that these people have picked out a few cultural overtones from the symphony of life and have once more failed to hear the mighty and primordial melody of the instincts....
>
> Every analysis conducted in a proper manner, and in particular every analysis of a child, strengthens the convictions upon which the theory of psycho-analysis is founded....
>
> In conclusion, I can only express a wish that fortune may grant an agreeable upward journey to all those who have found their stay in the underworld of psycho-analysis too uncomfortable for their taste. The rest of us, I hope, will be permitted without hindrance to carry through to their conclusions our labours in the depths.
>
> (History, p. 58-66)

Ferenczi called "On the History of the Psycho-Analytic Movement" a bombshell. Three weeks after the bombshell burst, June 1914, Jung resigned. He added that no Swiss analyst would attend the 1914 Congress. Four days later, the Swiss group submitted their resignation from the International Association.

Freud wrote in delight to Abraham: "So we are at last rid of them, the brutal, sanctimonious Jung and his disciples."[1]

The Freud-Jung alliance was over. Freud regained control of the International Association and the "Committee" was there to protect him.

In a letter to Jones he wrote; "Anyone who promises to mankind liberation from the hardship of sex will be hailed as a hero, let him talk whatever nonsense he chooses."[2]

As early as January, The British Medical Journal hailed Jung's secession from Freud as a return on his part to a saner life.

---

[1]Clark, p. 336
[2]May 17, 1914

CHAPTER XLI

■ *He's Wonderful, Aren't We?*

"Fuming with rage," Freud wrote "On the History of the Psychoanalytic Movement," to expand the basic tenets of psycho-analysis and to show that the theories of Jung and Adler were incompatible with them. Freud's next paper, "On Narcissism: An Introduction," continued to deal with the scientific differences between Adler, Jung and himself.

The controversy revolved around the concept of the libido. Adler had denied the importance of the libido: he did not consider infantile sexuality and the unconscious mental life to be significant motivating forces in human behavior. In his view, the "masculine protest," the will to power, was the dominant factor in man's actions. The particular way that man deals with his self-assertion determines his neurosis, his character, the style in which he conducts his life. In other words, Adler replaced the libido theory with a theory of aggresion. Jung, on his part, extended the meaning of libido to make it synonymous with psychic energy in general. He "de-libidinized" the libido. Freud wanted to make it clear that he himself always used the libido in its strict sense: the mental representation of the sexual drive.

The "Narcissism" paper was completed early in 1914 and published in the same journal as the "History" paper. In the "Narcissism" essay, Freud made a radical revision of his instinct theory which caused considerable bewilderment among his followers. The psychoanalytic theory of instincts went back to Freud's first attempt to understand human behavior when he hypothesized that behavior serves two purposes: self-preservation and species preservation. The first he called the ego instincts, the latter the sexual instincts (drives would be a more accurate translation of the German word *Trieben*). A neurosis was an unconscious conflict between the two drives. This was standard psychoanalytic theory until the publication of the "Narcissism" paper, when Freud declared the theory inadequate.

He described cases in which the patient was apparently in love with himself. The patient was clearly neurotic, but where was the conflict? The two drives seemed to be gratifying each other. Paranoia, the megalomania of insanity, hypochondria, the desperation of the very ill and the aged, are all examples of the conflict between the two drives which is resolved by the libidinal interest in the self. It is as though the self-preservative drive is only a narcissistic part of the sexual drive. So, the theory of instincts was inadequate; it did not explain narcissistic disorders and it had to be changed.

This attack on classic theory threw the practicing analysts of that time into confusion. On of the mainstays of their work, the theory concerning instincts, was pulled out from under them.

Freud hypothesized that the original love is self-love, but when it flowed out to others he called it object love. Here he drew a new distinction between ego-libido and object-libido; between libido invested in the self and libido invested in others. Conflict arises between these two alternatives. This theory came to be known as the Object-Relations theory. Pathology is an inhibition of emotional involvement in others and an over-investment in the self. When the patient is capable of entering a loving, cooperative relationship with another person, the basis for health has been established. Today, the majority of practicing analysts base their clinical work on the object-relations theory. It is interesting that Freud, within a few years, radically modified his instinct theory once more, but practicing clinicians, with few exceptions, do not follow this last step.

Freud explores how we choose our love objects. As the first satisfactions are experienced in connection with normal bodily functions (feeding, cleaning, eliminating, cuddling, and so forth), it is from these bodily pleasures that the first love objects are derived. The child's love attachment is to persons who are concerned with his care, his protection, and his well-being. This choice of a caring, giving person was termed "anaclitic," which means nurturing. Those who are libidinally attracted to persons who seem to be capable of loving and caring for others make what we call an anaclitic choice. Such a choice allows for the possibility of a relationship that is cooperative, supportive, sympathetic, and loving. The original model, of course, is the nurturing mother.

Analysis of patients revealed another type and one that was quite unexpected. Among those whose libidinal development suffered difficulties which led to fixations and regressions, a type of patient appeared who had taken as a model for his object love, not a nurturing mother, but his own self. This type of object choice was termed "narcissistic."

This personality is attracted sensually, not to a person who is loving, but rather to a person whom he admires. He sees his choice of a lover as beautiful and talented. He feels that if he is in a relationship with his wonderful one, then he too, by identification, will acquire these characteristics. That is his aim. He fantasizes that if he had these qualities he would never suffer again. He would be forever the world's favorite child, free from the demands of life free from the laws of nature, from aging and dying. (The analysts might well say "she's wonderful, aren't we?") Needless to say, these thoughts and feelings are quite unconscious. It doesn't matter that in the course of the analysis it becomes clear that Ms. Wonderful never cared about him, that his chosen love was not interested in his feelings, that she was not loving. All that mattered was her admirable qualities (which invariably existed only in his imagination). Such relationships tend to be exploitative, characterized by submission and dominance. Many a puzzling relationship can be understood by the dynamics of the narcissistic choice.

Analysis has since shown differences in the outcome of the two different choices. Anaclitic love objects can lead to lasting and gratifying relationships. When they come to an end, for whatever reasons the partner in question goes through a period of grief, even of heartbreak, has an overwhelming sense of the loss of a loved one. However, after a reasonable time depending on individual variation, he comes out of it, he recovers. He feels that he has something of value to offer someone else, and that there is someone who will desire it. His depression is then replaced by a feeling of hope that he can once again enter a loving relationship.

The person who is attracted to a narcissistic love object experiences something very different. He, too, suffers and becomes depressed when he loses her. But, his depression is deeper and he does not come out of it. He feels he has lost the only opportunity he will ever have to transcend life. One hears talk of suicide. The unique opportunity to become the world's favorite child through an osmosis with his blessed one has been lost forever.

Narcissistic choices are often seen in homosexual relationships. One form they take is the attraction of an older person to a very young one. In such cases, the older lover treats the young partner in the way he wanted his mother to treat him. Hence the "dirty old man" is usually gentle and kind to his young sweetheart. He identifies with his mother; his young partner represents himself. His choice is the ultimate in narcissism; he takes himself as his love object.

Freud proceeds to draw an interesting comparison between the sexes in this regard. He suggests that overvaluation of an object, falling in love with the object choice, is more characteristic of males. Women tend to differ in that their need does not lie in the direction of loving, but of being loved. The man who fulfills this condition, who deeply adores her, is the one who finds her favor: she will find his love for her irresistible.

> ...another person's narcissism has a great attraction for those who have renounced part of their own narcissism and are in search of object-love. The charm of a child lies to a great extent in his narcissism, his self-contentment and inaccessibility, just as does the charm of certain animals which seem not to concern themselves about us, such as cats and the large beats of prey....It is as if we envied them for maintaining a blissful state of mind—an unassailable libidinal position which we ourselves have since abandoned. The great charm of narcissistic women has, however, its reverse side; a large part of the lover's dissatisfaction, of his doubts of the woman's love, of his complaints of her enigmatic nature, has its root in this incongruity between the types of object choice. I am ready to admit that there are quite a number of women who love according to the masculine type and who also develop the sexual overvaluation proper to that type.
>
> (On Narcissism, 1914, S.E. XIV, p. 89)

There is a road open for complete object love even for a narcissistic woman. The child she bears may become the complete recipient for feelings of love that were only infrequentlly directly to the husband.

Narcissistic involvement may apply to men or women and neither sex can claim a monoploy of types of object choices.

CHAPTER XLII

■ *Secret Service*

Freud said of himself that he was not a good *menschenkenner.* That is, he was not a good judge of people. Although it has its own complicated dynamics, this inability has been observed in people who have generous natures. Jones was concerned that Freud had elevated Adler and Stekel, and even more Jung, to important positions in the association, only to suffer the consequences of his bad judgment. He discussed the situation with Ferenczi, and proposed that a small group of trustworthy analysts form a sort of "guard" around Freud. This would give Freud a body of friends to talk over critical decisions with; it would give him a sense of assurance, and the guard could even help with suggestions, respond to criticisms, and so forth. Ferenczi heartily agreed to the proposition and the two of them discussed the matter with Rank. Jones also wrote to Freud about it. There would be only one stipulation: if anyone wished to depart from any of the basic tenets of psychoanalytic theory, he should promise to alert the other members of the guard before stating his views publicly. Oddly, during the discussion with Rank, Ferenczi, with his characteristic directness, asked Rank if he thought he would remain loyal to Freudian theory. Jones wrote later that Rank regarded the question as offensive and was at a loss to find a proper reply. In years to come, only Ferenczi and Rank did not remain faithful to the original agreement.

Freud himself warmly accepted the suggestion. He spoke of the group taking care of the psychoanalytic movement long after he was no longer on the scene. He suggested that the committee be "strictly secret," and mentioned friends he considered likely candidates for the guard: Sacks and Abraham, "but only under the condition of all of you consenting. I had better be left outside of your conditions and pledges; to be sure I will keep the utmost secrecy and be thankful for all you communicate to me...."[1]

The following summer, the committee of five members held their first meeting. To celebrate the event, Freud presented each member with an antique Greek intaglio which was mounted on a gold ring. He himself had long had such a ring, a Greek-Roman intaglio with the head of Jupiter. "Don't be misled by the boyish business of the rings," he warned. "They didn't amount to anything, and at least two members of the committee were embarrassed to wear them...."[2] Although formed in 1912, the "Committee," as it came to be called, was of most help to Freud after the 1913-18 War. In a letter to Eitington, announcing his membership, Freud wrote: "The secret of this Committee is that it has taken from me my most burdensome care for the future, so that I can calmly follow my path to the end."[3]

---

[1]To Jones, August 1, 1912
[2]Clark 321
[3]To Eitington, Oct. 22, 1919

In a later letter he wrote:

> The care that weighs me down about the future I can best convey to you genetically. It comes from the time when psychoanalysis depended on me alone, and when I was so uneasy about what the human rabble would make out of it when I was no longer alive. In 1912, when we saw an example of these possibilities, the Committee was formed and took on the task of continuation along the right lines. Since then I have felt more light-hearted and carefree about how long my life will last.
>
> (Eitington, Nov. 23, 1919)

CHAPTER XLIII

■ *Unfortunate Morbid Idea*

A young woman engaged a lawyer to protect her from the threats of a man with whom she had had an affair. She told him how this man had abused her confidence: he had had unseen witnesses photograph him and her while they were making love. Now he was in a position to ruin her. The lawyer was experienced and recognized the questionable nature of the accusation. He knew that what is reported is often not the whole story. He decided, therefore, to consult Freud, and shortly thereafter he brought the client in person to him.

The woman was a most attractive person who looked younger than her thirty years. She somewhat resented the introduction of a doctor into the case but the persuasion of her lawyer and the urgency of the matter made her cooperate. She told her story without the slightest hesitation or trace of embarrassment.

For some time she had been in a responsible position with a large business firm. She derived a great deal of satisfaction from her work, and felt appreciated by her superiors. She lived with her elderly mother, of whom she was the sole support. He father had died many years before, and she had no brothers or sisters. She had never sought love affairs with men, but she found herself attracted to an employee in her office. He was a very attractive man, highly cultivated, attentive and was obviously very attracted to her. He could not marry her but refused to give up their relationship on that account. He pleaded with her that they had an indisputable right to enrich their lives with each other, and that it was senseless to sacrifice what they both longed for, and what was beautiful, for the sake of social convention. After listening to his pleading and to his promises that he would not expose her to any risks, she consented to visit him in his bachelor apartment. They kissed, they embraced as they lay side by side, and he admired her charms, now somewhat more visible. Suddenly, in the midst of this idyllic scene, she heard a click. She felt frightened. The click seemed to come from behind a heavy curtain which hung between a writing desk and the window. In response to her questions, her lover told her it probably came from a small clock on the desk.

As she left the apartment, she met two men on the stairs, who seemed to be whispering to each other. One of them was carrying a package that looked like a small box. This meeting upset her further and, on her way home, she tried to figure out what had happened. the box could easily have been a camera, one of the men could be a photographer, the click could have been the click of a shutter. The photographer could have been hiding behind the curtain, waiting to catch her in a compromising position. She became obsessed with suspicion. She kept after her lover for an explanation and reassurance when they met again and wrote him also, between times. His efforts to convince her that her mistrust was entirely without foundation were in vain. Finally, she called on the lawyer, told him everything, and handed over the letters which her lover had written to her about the incident. Later, Freud had an opportunity to read the letters and was impressed with his sincere expressions of regret that such a beautiful and tender relationship should suffer by this "unfortunate morbid idea." "I need hardly justify my agreement with this judgment."

Aside from the fact that the case had an interest in its own right, a beautiful woman suffering because of her paranoid delusions, it had a special meaning for Freud. Psychoanalytic psychology had taken the view that patients suffering from paranoia are struggling against an intensification of their homosexual trends. As the theory adds that the persecutor represents someone whom the patient loves or once loved, the persecutor must be one of the same sex. It was not insisted on that without exception paranoia always had a homosexual base. After all psychiatric literature contains many cases in which the patient imagines himself to be persecuted by a person of the opposite sex. Nevertheless, it is one thing to read of such cases, and quite another to come into personal contact with one of them. Psychoanalysts had yet to report a case of paranoia that contradicted their theory; even their apparently heterosexual case examples could be seen as defenses against homosexuality.

The present case clearly conflicted with the theory. No influence of another woman was present; the one woman in the case was transforming the man she loved into an enemy.

The theory should therefore be abandoned and Freud should assume that the woman is correctly interpreting her experience. Either that or the case had to be studied more thoroughly. Freud said that he could not form an immediate opinion, and asked the woman to call on him a second time, when she could relate her story again at greater length and with more detail. Thanks to the lawyer's influence, the woman agreed although reluctantly to visit him again, this time without the lawyer's presence.

The second visit did not contradict the previous one, but additonal details proved to be very important. In the first place, she had visited the young man in his apartment not once,but twice. She didn't mention the first visit because it seemed unimportant to her. (The camera click occurred on the second visit.) Nothing of any significance happened on the first rendezvous, but something suspicious happened the day after it. The person in charge of her department was an elderly lady whom she described as, "She has white hair like my mother." She and her elderly boss enjoyed a friendly relationship.Though at times the lady would tease her, the girl felt herself to be her boss's particular favorite.

The day after the first visit, the young man had come into the office to discuss some business with the elderly lady. The patient noted that they were speaking in low tones and she felt that they were talking about her. She was mortified in case he would tell her boss about her visit. Probably he was telling her that they had been having an affair for a long time. The motherly white-haired lady would now know everything. What convinced our client that she was right was the way her boss conducted herself after the conversation with him, and the way she spoke to her. No question about it; although she was very subtle, the elderly superior was obviously disapproving of her. The patient felt dismay.

She confronted the young man. He protested vigorously against what he called her senseless accusations. After much pleading he succeeded in re-establishing her confidence. A few weeks later she visited him again. The rest we know from her first report.

For Freud the new information removed any doubts about the pathological nature of her accusations. She had created a triangle. In the mind of the child, all triangles are the same: mother, father, and child. In the triangle fantasy, one person is invariably excluded, the origin and meaning of jealousy takes place in this context. It was obvious that the elderly white-haired lady was a substitute for her mother. The father's role is played by the lover, despite his youth. She is attracted to her mother-like boss, but because such impulses are unacceptable to her, she projects her feelings onto the young man. We must remember that it is irrelevant to the unconscious that in reality the pair are ill-matched. She fantasizes a liaison between her mother substitute and her young lover.

Here we find a homosexual basis for her paranoia. Very simply, the psychoanalytic formulation for paranoia is as follows: "I love her," "I hate her," "she hates and persecutes me." "I love her" is the original feeling for the object. However it is homosexual, therefore it is unacceptable and induces anxiety. The person in question attempts to protect herself by turning her feelings into their opposite. "It's not true that I love her, I really hate her." This represents the first line of defense, turning the feeling into its opposite, but if that does not work, if the person still feels anxiety, then another defense is necessary. The next defense is projection. The paranoid spits out onto the original object her still unacceptable feelings, even though they no longer seem to be sexual. "It is she who hates me and it is she who persecutes me, I have to defend myself."

This confused woman was unconsciously sexually attracted to her superior who was then seen as the original persecutor. She knows about the girl's love affair and she shows her disapproval by subtle hints in voice and conduct. The client's libidinal attachment to her mother and to her own sex has all along prevented her from turning to men for love-objects.

All girls go through the mother-complex stage, the time when they are libidinally attracted to the mother. The developmental task is to outgrow this phase and then decide for herself what her share of sexual enjoyment should be. To the extent that this phase is not outgrown the girl will fall victim to a neurosis. Whatever the choice of the neurosis, based on the subject's disposition, the neurotic reaction will always be determined, not by her current relation to her mother, but by her infantile relations to her earliest image of her mother.

This patient until the age of thirty had stayed away from men. We may assume that having been fatherless for years, she had made a powerful attachment to the mother. What was originally a source of comfort and security, became a burden when her libido began to turn to a man in response to his persistent wooing. She tried to undo her homosexual attachment, but her homosexual feelings for her mother retained enough power to keep her at a safe distance from men. Thus, at the first stage of the conflict, although she becomes estranged from her mother, she still cannot move close to a man. In fact, both of them become the enemy. Her mother substitute becomes the hostile, jealous watcher and persecutor, and her father substitute joins her mother in plotting her ruin.

However, once again the young man's vigorous wooing succeeds in attracting her libido and this results in her second visit. One thinks that her mother-attachment has been overcome and the girl is at last free to love a man. Instead, a new delusion appears; by making use of accidental circumstances, her homosexuality successfully destroys this new love. It still seems strange that a woman should employ a paranoiac defense against loving a man, but the explanation is at hand. Her young lover, in her unconscious, is still the father, but now she herself has taken her mother's place. She has identified with her mother: "If mother does it, I may do it too because I am just like her." It is unusual for paranoids to substitute identification for their primary defense, namely projection. In this case it seemed as though through identification she advanced from a female to a male love-object. But due to her feelings of anxiety, she employed projection again, this time against the new object, her young lover. From the woman's account, the burst of anxiety took place before there was genital contact, and projection carried out the intention of her mother-complex to ensure that there would be none.

Freud published an account of the case in 1915 under the title, "A Case of Paranoia Running Counter to the Psychoanalytic theory of the disease."[1] He concluded the paper with a detailed discussion of the ramifications of the psychoanalytic theory of paranoia.

[1]S.E. XIV

CHAPTER XLIV

■ *Imperishable Savage*

The war within psychoanalytic ranks broke out in 1914. Jung resigned as President of the International Psychoanalytic Association, left the organization, and was followed by most of his compatriots. But as meaningful as the conflict within the psychoanalytic world was to those concerned, their dissension shrinks to insignificance in comparison with the conflict that was tearing Europe apart.

World War I had a powerful effect on Freud's views of life, his scientific formulations, and the whole psychoanalytic movement. At a time when "German" police dogs and Wagner were suspect, psychoanalysis was seen as an alien import.

Freud read the daily newspapers and was abreast of current events and the mounting international crisis. But, clearly, he did not appreciate its gravity. His correspondence was filled with references to the reorganization of the International Psychoanalytic Association and the aftermath of the split with Jung. He was concerned with his health and with his summer vacation. He even allowed his daughter Anna to leave for England as late as July 18, less than two weeks before Austria-Hungary launched an attack on Serbia.

Given Freud's peaceful temperament, his scepticism about the real motives for behavior, his distrust of popular causes, and his devotion to intelligence over chaotic passions, his reaction to the outbreak of war was quite unmexpected. Rather than feelings of alarm at the coming slaughter, as one would expect, Freud, age fifty-eight, felt a surge of patriotic spirit. He connected the fate of the Jewish people with their only tie to a national life--Austria-Hungary. To Karl Abraham (July 26) he wrote, "Dear Friend,....so we are at last rid of them, the brutal sanctimonious Jung and his disciples...for the first time in thirty years I feel myself to be an Austrian and feel like giving this not very hopeful Empire another chance...." No doubt the primitive anti-Semitism of the the enemy contributed to his belief in fighting for the Austrian fatherland. It should be added, that, like most Europeans, he expected the war to be brief. And what regret did he voice? That England and its wonderful democracy was on the "wrong side."

In the second week of the war, Martin his eldest son volunteered for the army. His other sons, Oliver and Ernst, enlisted a few days later. Ernst was received with the reprimand, "You enlist now when the war is nearly over!"(On hearing of this Freud remaked that the officer should be immediately transferred to the High command.) Martin gave his family and friends his reason for enlisting as a wish to visit Russia without having to change his religion. (At the time, Russia was closed to Jewish visitors.) Oliver, a qualified engineer, did not pass the army physical examination but served in an engineering capacity throughout the war.

Freud soon recovered his common sense. As early as November his letters show that his patriotic fervor had subsided. Characteristically, he illustrated his recovery by means of a Jewish anecdote. An old grandfather was upset that his grandson seemed to have given up his Jewish identity and adopted German dress, style, and manners. However, when he saw the youth's underwear, he realized that the German part was only a veneer.

By December, Freud was feeling low. His half-bother Emanuel, whom he had always loved, had been killed in a train accident in England. And to add to the bewilderment of the times, two steadfast colleagues were not around: Ferenczi was serving as a medical officer, a major in a Hungarian Hussar regiment, and Abraham had had to return to Berlin. Hans Sachs had been turned down by the army for nearsightedness, and Otto Rank was doing his best to avoid conscription, "fighting like a lion against his fatherland."[1]

Like people of good sense, Freud was not only distraught by events at the onset of the war, but deeply disappointed. Why couldn't the highest civilization mankind had achieved settle its differences peacefully without resorting to barbarism? To clear his own mind about what attitude to adopt in the war situation, and to help others in a similar quandary, he wrote "Thoughts for the Times on War and Death." Typically, he did not offer reassurances nor any denial of reality; rather, he tried to achieve the clarity which comes from facing the truth, no matter how unpleasant. Neither did he triumph at the corroboration of the psychoanalytic conclusions about the nature of man. In a letter to Dr. Friederich van Eeden, an old acquaintance, he expressed some of his thoughts and feelings:

> Vienna, December 28, 1914
>
> Dear Dr. van Eeden,
>
> ....I venture to remind you of two assertions psychoanalysis has put forward which have assuredly contributed to its unpopularity.
>
> Psychoanalysis has concluded...that the primitive, savage and evil impulses of mankind have not vanished in any individual, but continue their existence, though in a repressed state--in the unconscious...and that they wait for opportunities to display their activity....Our intellect is...a plaything and tool of our impulses and emotion.
>
> And now just look at the cruelties and injustices for which the most civilized nations are responsible, at the different way in which they judge of their own lies...and those of their enemies, at the general loss of clear insight; then you must confess that psychoanalysis has been right with both assertions.
>
> ...many thinkers and students of mankind have said similar things, but our science has worked them out in detail and employed them to unravel many psychological riddles.
>
> I hope to see you again in better times,
>
> Yours very sincerely,
>
> Sigmund Freud

[1]Ferenczi, Dec. 2, 1914

(S.E. XIV, p. 301)

The wanton destruction of the war, the cruetly, the lies, the hatred, had shattered illusions we had had about the ethical advances civilized man and nations had achieved. He realized that his own objectivity had been influenced by propaganda and the feelings it had roused in him. The time had come to do away with illusions.

It took courage to publish "Thoughts for the Times on War and Death," when overheated partriotism was the temper of the day. The essay is written philosophically, with a tinge of sadness. There are, of course, inevitable horrors that go with a bloody war, but what was especially unsettling was the way in which the war was being conducted. International treaties and obligations were disregarded; prisoners and the wounded were ill-treated. The involvement of the civilian population signified a regression from the standards associated with a highly developed civilization and a level of ethics men had hoped was permanently reached. The opening sentences go right to the heart of the matter.

> In the confusion in which we are caught up, relying as we must on one-sided information, standing too close to the great changes that have already taken place or were beginning to, and without a glimmering of the future that is being shaped, we ourselves are at a loss as to the...value of the judgments which we form. We cannot but feel that no event has ever destroyed so much that is precious in the common possessions of humanity, confused so many of the clearest intelligences, or so thoroughly debased what is highest. Science herself has lost her passionless impartiality; her deeply embittered servants seek for weapons from her with which to contribute towards the struggle with the enemy. Anthropologists feel driven to declare him inferior and degenerate, psychiatrists issue a diagnosis of his disease of mind and spirit....
>
> (Thoughts for the Times on War and Death, 1915, S.E. XIV, p.275)

Freud reminds us that we were cherishing an illusion if we believed that wars, even though possibly inevitable, would be conducted by the rules of international law.

> When I speak of disillusionment, everyone will know at once what I mean....We have told ourselves, no doubt, that wars can never cease so long as nations live under such widely differing conditions....But we permitted ourselves to have other hopes. We had expected the great world-dominating nations...the artistic and scientific standards of civilization...to succeed in discovering another way of settling misunderstandings and conflicts of interest. Within each of these nations high norms of moral conduct were laid down for the individual....It was to be assumed, therefore,

> that the state itself would respect them, and would not think of undertaking anything against them which would contradict the basis of its own existence...the great nations themselves...would have acquired so much comprehension...that "foreigner" and "enemy" could no longer be merged, as they still were in classical antiquity, into a single concept....
>
> (Ibid. 275-277)

Freud offered some hope for the future of mankind. He maintained that the continuance of civilization even with its vacilations, offers the possibility, in each new generation, of the transformation of drives, a transformation which could become the basis for a more stable civilization.

> We saw it as an opportunity for demonstrating the progress of comity among men since the era when the Greek Amophictyonic council proclaimed that no city of the league might be destroyed, nor its olive-groves cut down, nor its water supply stopped...as far as possible avoiding acute suffering...granting complete immunity for the wounded who had to withdraw from the contest, as well as for the doctors and nurses who devoted themselves to their recovery. There would, of course be the utmost consideration for the noncombatant classes of the population--for women who take no part in war-work, and for the children who, when they are grown up, should become on both sides one another's friends and helpers. And again, all the international undertaking and institutions in which the common civilization of peace-time had been embodied would be maintained...
>
> (Ibid. p. 278)

Freud believed that truth, no matter how unpleasant, is a protection: it enables one to prepare for and adjust to reality. Illusion, on the other hand, exposes one to the pain of disillusionment, and leaves one helpless.

> Then the war in which we had refused to believe broke out, and it brought disillusionment. Not only is it more bloody and more destructive than any war of other days...it is at least as cruel, as embittered, as implacable as any that has preceded it. It disregards all the restriction known as International Law, it ignores the prerogatives of the wounded and the medical service, the distinction between civil and military service, sections of the population, the claims of private property. It tramples in blind fury on all that comes in its way....
>
> (Ibid. 278-279)

Freud pointed out that there are two kinds of moral conduct that look alike: one is displayed by those whose love instinct has mastered the underlying hostile one; the other is the result of a fear of punishment and of rejection by the community. The latter easily relapses when external control is removed. And the hypocritical moral behavior is much more common than the genuine type of goodness.

Once we come to understand the dynamics of our fellow citizens, our expectations will be more modest and we shall more easily endure the disappointments which nations and individuals cause us.

> Civilization has been attained through the renunciation of instinctual satisfaction, and it demands the same renunciation from each newcomer in turn....
>
> Generally speaking, we are apt to attach too much importance to...the total susceptibility to culture in comparision with the portion of instinctual life which has remained primitive--that is, we are misled into regarding men as "better" than they actually are....
>
> we may already derive one consolation from this discussion: our mortification and our painful disillusionment on account of the uncivilized behavior of our fellow-citizens of the world during this war were unjustified. They were based on an illusion to which we had given way. In reality our fellow-citizens have not sunk so low as we feared, because they had never risen so high as we believed....
>
> The primitive stages can always be reestablished; the primitive mind is, in the fullest meaning of the word, imperishable.
>
> What are called mental diseases inevitably produce an impression in the layman that intellectual and mental life have been destroyed. In reality, the destruction only applies to later acquisition and developments. The essence of mental disease lies in a return to earlier states of affective life and of functioning....
>
> (Ibid. p. 282-286)

It seems as though individual acquired moral qualities vanish when people become a collective. Communities, cities, states, nations, can express what the individual has renounced: the crudest, most primitive, mental attitudes.

> It would seem that nations still obey their passions far more readily than their interests....It is, to be sure, a mystery why the collective individuals should in fact despise, hate and detest one another--every nation against every other--and even in times of peace. I cannot tell why this is so.
>
> (Ibid. 288)

The final part of the essay, entitled, "Our Attitude Towards Death," Freud described as "an audacious lecture, containing much grim humor."[1] He stated that modern man does not truly believe that death is a necessary outcome of life; he does not believe that death is natural, unavoidable, and undeniable, he does not believe that everyone "owes God a death." In our daily life, we are accustomed to live as though life goes on forever. We cannot imagine our own death. whenever we attempt to, we become spectators at our own funeral. In the unconscious everyone is convinced of his immortality. News of the approach of death almost always comes as a surprise. Our habit is to "blame" death on some fortuitous circumstance: an accident, disease, advanced age. Thus we betray our wish to reduce death from a necessity to a chance event.

> Towards the actual person who has died we adopt a special attitude--something almost like admiration for someone who has accomplished a very difficult task. We suspend criticism of him, overlook his possible misdeeds, declare that *de mortuis nil nisi bonum* (say nothing bad about the dead) and think it justifiable to set out all that is most favorable to his memory in the funeral oration and upon the tombstone. Consideration for the dead, who, after all, no longer need it, is more important to us than the truth and certainly, for most of us, than consideration for the living.
> (ibid. p. 290)

Freud believed that our attitude toward death affects the quality of our lives. When the highest stake in the game, life itself, may not be risked, something is lost. Our emotional investment in life is less and may become shallow and empty.

> It is evident that war is bound to sweep away this conventional treatment of death. Death will no longer be denied; we are forced to believe in it. People really die; and no longer one by one, but many, often death is no longer a chance event. to be sure, it still seems a matter of chance whether a bullet hits this man or that; but a second bullet may well hit the survivor....Life has indeed recovered its full content....
> (Ibid. p. 291)

What Freud may have had in mind when he spoke of the "second bullet" was his son Martin. Martin had been wounded several times in combat and once had a Russian bullet pierce his hat when he raised his head above his trench.

Freud presumes that for primitive man death was as unimaginable as it is for us today. "On the one hand, he took death seriouly, recognized it as the termination of life...he also denied death and reduced it to nothing....He had no objection to someone else's death; it meant the annihilation of someone he hated."[2] Primitive

---

[1]To Ferenczi, April 8, 1915
[2]Ibid. P. 292

man did not have a conscience. He was far less repressed than we are today, and therefore, a more passionate creature. His cruelty was unrestrained; he was more malignant than other animals.

> He liked to kill, and killed as a matter of course. The instinct which is said to restrain other animals from killing and devouring their own species need not be attributed to him....Hence the primaeval history of mankind is filled with murder. Even to-day, the history of the world which our children learn at school is essentially a series of murders of peoples. The obscure sense of guilt to which mankind has been subject since prehistoric times, and which in some religions has been condensed into the doctrine of primal guilt, of original sin, is probably the outcome of a blood-guilt incurred by prehistoric man....If the Son of God was obliged to sacrifice his life to redeem mankind from original sin, then by the law of talion...that sin must have been a killing, a murder.
>
> (ibid. p. 292-293)

Loving someone is psychologically like being a part of that someone. When primeval man saw someone die whom he loved, he not only felt pain but was forced to learn that he too could die. His whole being revolted against this admission.

> But on the other hand, deaths such as these pleased him as well, since in each of the loved persons there was also something of the stranger. The law of ambivalence of feeling, which to this day governs our emotional relations with those whom we love most, certainly had a very much wider validity in primeval times...
>
> Man could no longer keep death at a distance...but...he could not conceive of himself as dead. So he devised a compromise:he coincided ed the fact of his own death as well, but denied it the significance of annihilation....His persisting memory of the dead became the basis for assuming other forms of existence and gave him the conception of a life continuing after apparent death....
>
> (Ibid. p. 294)

The representation of afterlife as more desirable than our present existence, the concept that life here is only a preparation for some heavenly paradise that awaits us, is a much later development, far removed from our primeval ancestor. We may recall the answer made to Odysseus by the soul of Achilles:

> For of old, when thou wast alive, we Argives honoured thee even as the gods, and now that thou art here, thou rulest mightily over the dead.

> Wherefore grieve not at all that thou art dead, Achiles.
>
> So I spoke, and he straightway made answer and said: "Nay, seek not to speak soothingly to me of death, glorious Odysseus, I should choose, so I might live on earth, to serve as the hireling of another, of some portionless man whose livelihood was but small, rather than be lord over all the dead that have perished."
>
> (Odyssey XI, p. 484-91, Ibid. p. 294)

The loved one's death awakened our conscience and brought into existence two concepts: the doctrine of the soul and the earliest ethical commandment: "Thou shalt not kill." Eventually, it was extended to strangers and even to enemies.

> This final extension of the commandment is no longer experienced by civilized man. When the furious struggle of the present has been decided, each one of the victorious fighters will return home joyfully to his wife and children, unchecked and undisturbed by thoughts of the enemies he has killed....It is worthy of note that the primitive races which still survive in the world, and are undoubtedly closer than we are to primeval man, act differently in this respect....Savages--Australian Bushmen, Tierra del Fuegans--arc far from being remorseless murderers; when they return victorious from the war-path they may not set foot in their villages or touch their wives till they have atoned for the murders they committed in war by penances which are often long and tedious.
>
> (Ibid. p. 295)

Freud speaks of the pious who point to our prohibition of murder in order to demonstrate the strength of ethical impulses. They would like to believe that our nature is remote from any contact with what is evil and base. Freud points out that it is unnecessary to prohibit that which no human desires.

> So powerful a prohibition can only be directed against an equally powerful impulse....
>
> What, we ask, is the attitude of our unconscious towards the problem of death?....What we call our "unconscious," the deepest strata of our minds, made up of instinctual impulses know nothing that is negative...does not know its own death, which dominates us oftener than we know, is...something secondary and is usually the outcome of a sense of guilt....
>
> On the other hand, for strangers and for enemies we do acknowledge death and consign them to it quite as readily and unhesitatingly as

> did primeval man....In our unconscious impulses we daily and hourly get rid of anyone who stands in our way, of anyone who has offended or injured us....
>
> And so, if we are to be judged by our unconscious wishful impulses, we ourselves are, like primeval man, a gang of murderers.
>
> (Ibid. p. 296-297)

War removes the veneer of civilization and brings the primal man in each of us to the surface. To the extent that we deny the primitive man in us and believe that civilized attitudes govern our life, to that extent we are living, psychologically speaking, beyond our means. War and other stresses of life cannnot be abolished. Sonner or later there must be a reckoning.

What is one to do? Accept our ambivalence? Regard hating as being as natural as loving? Should we adapt ourselves to war? Is psychologically denying our primal state living beyond our means? It would seem that to bow to the primitive in us is to take a backward step, to accept what we have long labored to outgrow. But, said Freud, taking the truth into account has advantages: it minimizes the pain of disappointment and thereby makes life more tolerable. Freud concluded: ''To tolerate life remains, after all, the first duty of all living beings. Illusion becomes valueless if it makes it harder for us. We recall the old saying: *Si vis pacem, para bellum*. If you want to endure life, prepare yourself for death.''[1]

[1]Ibid. p. 300

CHAPTER XLV

■ *Ubiquitous Enemy*

The basis of all Freud's work was the exploration of psychoneuroses. He was aware that access to the deep layers of the mind had greater significance than clinical application. Taking soundings of mental processes, tracing the innermost pathways without resorting to metaphysics, was the aspect of his work that primarily interested him. He wanted to know how the workings of the mind came to be expressed in folklore, custom, myth, legend, as well as in mental pathology. In fact, after his neurological period, he wrote two books devoted to an investigation of two nonmedical subjects: the psychology of dreams, and the psychology of "slips," that run counter to normal mental functioning.

However, his writings on nonmedical subjects were invariably followed by a report of a clinical nature. "Thoughts for the Times on War and Death" was followed by "Some Character-Types Met With in Psycho-Analytic Work." The subject is the formation of character traits.

When psychoanalytic treatment begins, neither the patient nor the doctor directs interest to the patient's character. Both are more concerned with symptoms, their meaning, and above all, what they are concealing. Behind every symptom lies an unacceptable instinctual wish, and the analyst, if not the patient, is interested in the mysterious path that has led from the repressed wish to the outbreak of a symptom. Soon, however, both the analyst and his patient find that the latter is resisting investigation. Resistances now become the analyst's main interest, and objectives other than the symptom proper come within the scope of the analysis. Putting up resistance is one of the ways by which a patient protects himself against painful feelings. The particular form the resistance takes may be considered part of the patient's character structure.

In "Character Types," rather than attempting broad generalized statements (since he felt analytic theory was not yet ripe for a grand synthesis), Freud chose three particular types that he had come across in his work.

1. *The exceptions*:

There are people who feel that they should be above the vicissitudes of life. These persons expect a "special dispensation." They feel they have transcended ordinariness, and should not be expected to accept life on its own terms. When such a self-image inhibits one's normal functioning a person may be forced to resort to a psychoanalysis to resolve the dilemma.

Psychoanalytic work has the problem of inducing the patient to give up an infantile pattern of behavior. The neurotic (or infantile and unrealistic) pattern is unconscious and its discovery by the patient is often accompanied by surprise, sometimes by embarrassment, occasionally amusement. The consequences of childlike behavior are readily seen, and a resolve to change the pattern usually follow. The change involves feeling some temporary discomfort in exchange for greater subsequent pleasure. The modification of a neurotic pattern stirs up old anxieties rooted in childhood when we were dependent, and it takes some analytic "working through," but the wish, the resolve to make life better, the energy to make the change, is in evidence. If the analytic work goes well, the analysand gains the strength to renounce the immediate pleasure of childish patterns for the pleasure in being free.

There are however patients who, after discovering an infantile behavior pattern, refuse to give it up. They refuse to submit to the necessities of reality. They will not tolerate the anxiety that is the prelude to growth. They feel that the laws of nature should not apply to them. They know that society demands a certain standard of conduct, but they claim to be free of such rules. Even when it is discovered that some of their behavior is unreasonable and contrary to their best interests, they still cling to the belief that such reasoning does not apply to them. They are "exceptions" and intend to remain so.

All of us would like to consider ourselves exceptions and to enjoy special privileges, but when someone actually proclaims himself to be above the demands of life there must be a reason.

In the cases Freud studied, he found a common characteristic in the early life of the "exceptional" patients. It was some experience of suffering in early childhood in which they felt themselves to be guiltless. The suffering imposed upon them was unjust and as a result of this injustice, they claimed immunity: they felt that society owed them restitution, while they owed society nothing. Their rebelliousness intensified their unconscious conflict and developed into a neurosis.

Rather than offer analogies between sickness in childhood and defects in character, Freud turned to a figure created by Shakespeare. In "Richard III," Gloucester, who subsequently becomes king, claims to be an "exception" because of his congenital deformity: a hunchback.

> I that am rudely stamp'd....
> cheated of feature by dissembling Nature,
> Deform'd, unfinish'd, sent before my time
> Into this breathing world, scarce half made up..
> ..since I cannot prove a lover....
> I am determined to prove a villain.
> (Some Character Types Met With in Psycho-Analytic Work, 1916, S.E. XIV, p. 314: Richard III, Act I, scene 1)

Freud expresses his appreciation of Shakespeare as a psychologist and his admiration for the skill and the subtlety with which he presented the character so as to win some degree of sympathy from the audience. He then sums up what he thinks is the meaning of the soliloquy:

> Nature has done me a grievous wrong in denying me the beauty of form which wins human love. Life owes me reparation for this, and I will see that I get it. I have a right to be an exception, to disregard the scruples by which others let themselves be held back. I may do wrong myself,

since wrong has been done to me.
(ibid. p. 314)

We have learned from psychoanalysis that many neurotic women tend to regard themselves as damaged, as having been treated unfairly in infancy, as born with a defect. One of the basic reasons for the bitterness that so many women feel toward their mothers is that they resent having been brought into the world female rather than male. Many of them feel like "exceptions," and claim exemption from many of the importunities of life.

2. *Those Wrecked by Success*

A man who taught in a university cherished a natural wish to succeed the old master who had introduced him to his field. When the old man died, the younger was chosen as the successor, much to his surprise. He at once grew hesitant, declared himself unworthy of the position, made light of his real merits, and, poor man, went into a depression which left him unfit for any work.

We know that unconscious frustration may cause illness. How surprising then to discover cases where the contrary appears to hold: people who seem well and happy until a wish, an improtant goal that they had striven toward all their lives, is achieved. They then fall seriously ill. The connection between their success and their neurosis suggests that they cannot tolerate their own happiness.

A woman raised in a comfortable upper-middle-class setting possessed an apparent zest for life. When still quite young she ran away from home, and traveled around the world seeking adventure. She met an artist who appreciated her spirit, her intellect, her cultivation. They fell in love and lived together for many years. She was a faithful companion to him and both of them were quite happy except for her relationship with his family. Finally, after years of trying, he succeeded in getting his family to accept her and he began preparations to make her his legal wife. From that moment on she went into a decline, fell apart, and neglected household responsibilities. She senselessly accused her lover of unfaithfulness, refused to share his bed, complained that his relatives were plotting against her, prevented him from working. shortly afterwards the unfortunate woman succumbed to an incurable mental illness.

This is a puzzling phenomenon. We know that the ego is not afraid of a wish it considers harmless. So long as a wish is confined to fantasy alone and seems remote from fulfillment, there is no conflict to speak of. Such a person is permitted to keep well and to function efficiently. The outbreak of the conflict is triggered by some external change.

Analytic work has provided us with an answer to this puzzle. In some cases, the conscience, known as the superego, forbids the subject to gain pleasure from the long-hoped-for change. It is as though the superego says: "You may enjoy the wish and play with it, but you must not gratify it in reality." Discovering the origins of this punishing, judging superego is often difficult.

Lady Macbeth, after striving for success with single-minded purpose, collapsed when she attained it. Prior to achieving her goal nothing could stand in her way. she was determined to overcome the conscience of her tender-minded but equally ambitious husband. For her murderous intentions she was even willing to sacrifice herself sexually if necessary; and renounce her womanliness:

Come, you spirits

> That tend on mortal thoughts, unsex me here
> ...Come to my woman's breasts
> And take my milk for gall, you murdering ministers!
> (Act I, Scene 5)

Just before the deed, there is a moment of reluctance;

> ...Had he not resembled
> My father as he slept, I had done it...
> (Act II, Scene 2)

When she does become queen, through the murder of Duncan, she experiences disillusionment.

> Nought's had, all's spent,
> Where our desire is got without content:
> 'Tis safer to be that which we destroy,
> Than by destruction dwell in doubtful joy.
> (Act III, Scene 2)

Freud analyzes the underlying dynamics that result in Lady Macbeth's disappointment on attaining her ambition, and in her death shortly afterwards. For our purposes it is enough she who relentlessly, with no sign of internal conflict, aimed at her cherished goal, should break down, suffer, and die shortly after achieving her aim.

Analytic work teaches that illness following success is a product of guilt. The superego punishes the subject for the success of a taboo wish. Further analysis connects the guilt to the Oedipus complex. The present-day success represents the unconscious fulfillment of an earlier wish, the elimination of the parent of the same sex, and sexual gratification with the parent of the opposite sex. The successful instinctual wish of childhood overwhelms the ego. The subject falls ill.

3. *Criminals From a Sense of Guilt*

Patients in analysis, who appear highly respectable, often report that in youth they did things that were forbidden--stealing,lying, and even setting fires. Freud, when he first heard these reports, did not attribute much significance to them. He tended to dismiss them with some reference to moral weakness at that period in life. But when patients who were no longer youthful reported misdeeds while they were in treatment, he took the phenomenon more seriouly.

It is natural to assume that a guilty conscience is the consequence of wrongdoing. Analytic work brought the surprising discovery that it was often the other way around: wrongdoing was the result of guilt feelings. The patients reported that after the misdeed, which they themselves disapproved of, they felt less anxious--they experienced relief. In fact these law-breakers may be considered to have become criminals out of a sense of guilt.

"But scientific work is not satisfied with the establishment of a curious fact." Two questions immediately present themselves: What is the origin of unconscious guilt before the deed? And how important a role does it play in human crime? The invariable outcome of analytic investigation shows that this obscure guilt is derived from the Oedipus complex. The unconscious wish to kill the parent of the same gender and have sexual relations with the parent of the opposite gender results in feeling "I deserve to be punished, and the punishment is imminent." "I feel tense and frightened and I don't know why." Only after doing something that is forbidden does the patient feel relief. It's as though compared to being guilty of murder and incest, having committed a mere theft, or a fraud, or even arson, is trivial. The patient displaces his guilt onto consciously committed acts so as to make that guilt more bearable.

Children at times persistently provoke us to punish them. After the punishment the child seems quite relaxed and cheerful; there are practically no signs of remorse. The phenomenon is known as "testing limits." It's as though the child says, "Something in me is dangerous, please stop me so that I will not do anything really bad." Analysis enables us to understand the guilt that led them to demand punishment. Note, however, that it is punishment for a far lesser crime than parenticide and incest.

No doubt among adult criminals we will find some who have developed no moral inhibitions or any sense of guilt. For these people the only crime seems to be getting caught. But in many other criminals, the motivation for a need to be punished. The Boston Strangler left notes pleading "please stop me."

Freud's findings have been called outrageous, absurd, untrue. But he was a cautious research scientist. All of his published formulations were preceded by, literally, years of observation. He knew that psychoanalytic psychology was contrary to common sense, and rather than insist on the originality of his conclusions, he found solace in discovering other thinkers who had made observations similar to his own. "A friend has since called to my attention the fact that the "criminal from a sense of guilt" was known to Nietzsche too..."[1]

"Some Character-Types Met With in Psycho-Analytic Work" was published in 1916, and laid the basis for most of the modern work on the psychology of criminals and delinquents.

---

[1]Character-Types, p.333

CHAPTER XLVI

■ *Childish Facts Of life*

As a *Privatdocent,* Freud had been lecturing on an introduction to psychoanalysis since 1900. But in 1915, to his surprise, he was greeted by an audience of seventy. Quite a contrast to the audience of three when he had first offered his class fifteen years earlier. The next month his audience had grown to a hundred. Freud them made up his mind to publish his lectures in book form. Otto Rank at once saw that these lectures were to be the last Freud would deliver as a *Privatdocent.*

The book appeared in 1917, known in English as *A General Introduction to Psychoanalysis.* It proved to be his most popular book, and deservedly so. In a few years it was translated into sixteen languages, including Serbian, Hungarian, Hebrew, and Chinese. It was also printed in Braille.

The book, as its title suggests, is the one most apt to be recommended as a first introduction to Freud's views. He makes the best use of his faculty for explanation. He leads his reader gently along, with full and fair discussion of possible objections. At the same time he warns the reader to be careful, because he knows he can be very persuasive.

In a style that is almost conversational, Freud raises the question to what is to be understood by the term ''sexual.'' If the sexual act and reproduction are the nucleus of sexuality, which is the popular view, quite a number of things not aimed at reproduction are excluded. Yet they are certainly sexual—kissing and masturbation, for instance. One attempt after another at a definition of ''sexual'' proves inadequate. There are individuals whose sexual lives deviate quite strikingly from what we are accustomed to think of as average. Homosexuals do not regard members of the opposite sex as sexual objects; in some cases, they are objects of disgust. Aside from their one deviation, homosexuals are frequently people irreproachable in other respects. Freud reminds us that they are often, though not always, persons of high ethical and intellectual development.

A description follows of those whose sexual activity diverges even more from the accepted view of sexuality. There are people who substitute other parts of the body for the genitals, but are only interested in their excretory function. Still others abandon the genital altogether and take some other part of the body as the object they desire--a breast, or a foot, or a braid of hair. Some are no longer interested in the body, but are satisfied by a shoe, or an article of underwear. Some prefer a defenseless corpse. ''But enough of this kind of sorrow.''[1]

The above examples show how the *object* of the sex drive changes, and Freud then turned his attention to the alteration of the sexual *aim*. Here he included voy-

[1]Introductory Lectures on Psychoanalysis, 1916, S.E. XVI, p. 306

eurs, exhibitionists, sadists, etc. "Now there cannot be the slightest doubt that all these crasy, eccentric and horrible things really constitue the sexual activity of these people."[1]

Unless we can understand these pathological forms of sexuality and give a complete account of how these perversions are formed, and what their connection to normal sexuality is, we cannot understand normal sexuality.

We have seen how one can eroticize nongenital parts of the body. This is precisely what the hysteric does. Some part of the body takes on a symbolic sexual meaning, the feeling is then repressed, and a symptom is the consequence. The symbolism never represents adult intercourse, but is a pregenital impulse belonging to childhood. In a similar way Freud links the obsessional neuroses to repressed sadism. For example, the obsessive-compulsive-neurotic is defending against the pleasure he would receive through sadistic acts. On the other hand, the pervert, who accepts and indulges in sexual activities, does not require neurotic, obsessive, compulsive symptoms. Neurosis is the negative side of the perversion. Furthermore, history teaches us that these perversions have occurred in all periods, and among all peoples, the most primitive and the most civilized.

Psychoanalytic researches led Freud to the sexual life of children.* The memories and associations of adults, during the analysis of their symptoms, regularly pointed back to the early years of childhood. "What we inferred from these analyses was later confirmed point by point by direct observation of children."[2] All inclinations to perversion have their roots in childhood. "In short, perverse sexuality is nothing else than a magnified infantile sexualtiy split up into its separate impulses.[3]

An important task of education is to socialize and civilize the child. This requires taming and restricting the child's instinctual life, developing within him self-controls, so that he can conform to the community's will. "Otherwise, the drives would break down every dam and wash away the laboriously erected work of civilization."[4]

Let us re-examine what is known about the sexual life of children. The first impulses of sexuality, of pleasure, are attached to vital functions. Although the infant's main interest is in nourishment, which involves sucking, we notice that he repeats the sucking action without making a demand for further food--the sensual sucking in itself brings him satisfaction. So we learn that infants do things which have no purpose other than pleasure.

No doubt the most important early event in life is sucking mother's breast. In this single act, the child gratifies his two most vital needs. Freud believed that this is the prototype of every later sexual satisfaction. The first transformation involves his giving up his object and replacing it with a part of his body, usually his thumb. The sucking action is retained, only the object changes. The erotogenic zones are not of equal intensity in yielding pleasure. Sonner or later, in the course of self-

---

[1]Ibid. p. 306

*Strangely enough, those who do not accept the existence of infantile sexuality, are not the milder in their educational pursuits. They seem to oppose what psychoanalysis considers to be manifestations of infantile sexuality with considerable severity. What they call "childish naughtiness" they recognize as the child's pursuit of pleasure and they do their best to compel him to abandon it; causing him distress until he complies.

[2]Ibid. p. 310 [4]Ibid. p.311-312

[3]Ibid. p. 311

exploration, the especially exciting genital is discovered. The infant makes his way from sucking to masturbation.

There are two decisive characteristics of infantile sexuality: it is attached to vital organic needs, and it is auto-erotic. It seeks and finds its objects in its own body. What applies to taking nourishment is repeated with other major bodily functions--the excretory processes.

Freud concluded that infants take pleasure in the process of evacuating their feces and urine and soon contrive ways to bring about the greatest yield of pleasure from there erotogenic zones. For the first time, they experience the external world as hostile to their desire for pleasure; they get a glimpse of later conflicts, internal and external. They soon learn that they can no longer enjoy the excretory experience whenever and wherever they choose. They are taught that these functions are disgusting, improper, and must be kept secret, private. At first the child's production delighted mother, and he would offer them to her to please her. He clings to this and

> ....carries on his high valuation of feces in his estimate of ''gifts'' and ''money.''
> (Ibid. p.315)

> I know you have been wanting for a long time to interrupt me and exclaim: Enough of these atrocities! You tell us that defacating is a source of sexual satisfaction, and already exploited in infancy, that feces is a valuable substance, and that the anus is a kind of genital! We don't believe all that--but we do understand why pediatricians and educationists have given a wide berth to psychoanalysis and its findings! No, Gentlemen. You have merely forgotten that I have been trying to introduce the facts of infantile sexual life to you in connection with the facts of the sexual perversions. Why should you not be aware that for a large number of adults, homosexual and heterosexual alike, the anus does really take over the role of the vagina in sexual intercourse. And that there are many people who retain a voluptuous feeling in defecating all through their lives and describe it as being far from small? As regards interest in the act of defecation and enjoyment in watching someone else defecating, you can get children themselves to confirm the fact when they are a few years older and able to tell you about it. Of course, you must not have systematically intimidated them beforehand, or they will quite understand that they must be silent on the subject. And as to the other things that you are anxious not to believe, I will refer you to the findings of analysis and of the direct observation of children and will add that it calls for real ingenuity not to see all this or to see it differently.

> Nor do I complain if you find the kinship between infantile sexual activity and sexual perversions something very striking. But it is in fact self-evident; if a child has a sexual life at all it is bound to be of a perverse kind: for except for a few obscure hints, children are without what makes sexuality into the reproductive function. On the other hand, the abandonment of the reproductive function is the common feature of all perversions. We actually describe a sexual activity as perverse if it has given up the aim of reproduction and pursues the attainment of pleasure as an aim independent of it. So, as you will see, the breach and turning point in the development of sexual life lies in its becoming subordinate to the purposes of reproduction. Everything that happens before this turn of events and equally everything that disregards it and that aims solely at obtaining pleasure is given the uncomplimentary name of "perverse" and as such is proscribed.
>
> (Introductory Lectures on Psychoanalysis, 1916, S.E. XVI, p. 315-316)

A child's sexuality is made up of a number of component drives, which, independently of one another, seek pleasure in part from an external object and in part from his own body. The erotic zone that is most intense, and yields the highest pleasure, is the genital. There are people who obtain pleasure from their own genital, without help from any other source, and maintain this pleasure for an indefinite length of time. "The topic of masturbation is not one that can be so easily disposed of; it is something that calls for examination from many angles."[1]

When the little boy discovers the anatomical differences between the sexes, he tries to deny what he has seen: he cannot imagine anyone without such a precious organ as he has. Later he is frightened by the possibility of losing his organ, a fear based on earlier threats when he took much interest in his little member. He suffers the castration complex. The form the complex takes plays a major part in the construction of his character, if he remains normal, and in his neurosis, if he falls ill. If he undergoes analytic treatment, his castration complex will be the basis for his strongest resistances.

> As regards little girls, we can say of them that they feel greatly at a disadvantage owing to their lack of a big, visible penis, that they envy boys for possessing one and that, in the main for this reason, they develop a wish to be a man--a wish that emerges later on, in any neurosis that may arise if they meet with a mishap in playing a feminine part. In her childhood, moreover, a little girl's clitoris takes on the role of a penis entirely: it is characterized by special excitability and

[1]Ibid. p. 317

> is the area in which auto-erotic satisfaction is obtained. The process of a girl's becoming a woman depends very much on the clitoris pasing on this sensitivity to the vaginal orifice in good time and completely. In cases of what is known as sexual anaesthesia in women, the clitoris has obstinately retained its sensitivity.
> (Ibid. p. 318)

The child's curiosity turns to the problem of where babies come from. The story of the stork is believed even by the youngest children far less often than adults realize. But the child cannot solve this problem by himself. His undeveloped sexual constitution sets limits to his imagination. At first, he thinks that babies come from eating something special, nor does he know that only women can have babies. Later he senses that he the father has a role in producing babies, but he cannot guess what it is. If he witnesses a sexual act, he experiences it as a fight, an attempt at subjugation: he has a sadistic misunderstanding of coition. Should he find traces of blood on mother's bed or her underwear, his suspicions are confirmed. He believes that she has been injured by his father.

The theory of special food and anal birth gives way to the idea that the navel comes open or that an area between the breasts is where birth takes place. He comes nearer to the facts about sex, but it is not until puberty that "he is given what is as a rule a depreciatory and incomplete explanation, which often produces traumatic effects."[1]

Before we leave the subject of perversions, there is something to add. Calm consideration will show that some perverse trait is to be found in the sexual life of normal people. A kiss can be described as perverse since it brings two erotic zones together instead of the two genitals. Yet kissing does exist as a perversion: there are those who achieve orgasm, genital discharge, through this act alone. Perversity pertains not to the extension of the sexual aim, or the replacement of the genitals, but solely in the exclusiveness of these deviations. So long as "perverse actions" are in the service of the normal sexual act, so long as they prepare and intensify the sexual union of lovers, they are not perversions at all.

From the third year of life on, there is a similarity between the sexual life of a child and an adult. There are differences of course, particularly in establishing the primacy of the genitals, but from a theoretical point of view, the pregenital phases of libidinal development belong to an earlier period. This early period develops so rapidly, that it is easy to understand why it usually escapes direct observation except by experts. The oral phase, with its emphasis on sucking mother's breast, and the replacement of the breast with a part of the infant's own body, is followed by a stage which has been identified as anal-sadistic. The terms "masculine" and "feminine" play no part here. The contrast is between "active" and "passive." What appears to be active turns out to be an expression of a drive for mastery, which may easily pass over into cruetly, in pleasure in dominating the other. Passive aims get attached to the anal orifice. This anal-sadistic organization is the immediate predecessor to the stage of genital primacy. Detailed study shows how characteristics from the anal-sadistic phase may be retained in the new genital organization.

---

[1]Ibid. p. 319

The important point Freud tried to establish is that sexual life does not emerge as something ready-made, but passes through a series of successive phases. The turning point of this development is the subordination of all the component sexual instincts to the primacy of the genitals, and along with this the subjection of sexuality to the reproductive function.

Further development involves the abandonment of auto-eroticism, the replacing of one's own body by an outside object once more. Once more mother is chosen as the love object, but this time it becomes part of an important drama. We come now to the "Oedipus Complex" which, at that time, Freud considered the nucleus of the neurosis.

> Listen to this episode which occurred in the course of the present war (World War I). One of the stout disciples of psycho-analysis was ststioned as medical officer on the German front somewhere in Poland. He attracted his colleagues' attention by the fact that he occasionally exercised an unexpected influence on a patient. When he was questioned he acknowledged that he was employing the methods of psychoanalysis and declared his readiness to convey his knowledge to his colleagues. Every evening thereafter, the medical officers of the corps, his colleagues and his superiors, came together in order to learn the secret doctrines of analysis. All went well for a while; but when he spoke to his audience about Oedipus Complex, one of his superiors rose, declared he did not believe it, that it was a vile act on the part of the lecturer to speak of such things to them, honest men who were fighting for their country and fathers of a family, and that he forbade the continuance of the lectures. That was the end of the matter. The analyst got himself transferred to another part of the front.
>
> (ibid. p. 330)

What is this terrible, unspeakable Oedipus Complex? In the Greek legend, Oedipus is destined by fare to kill his father and take his mother for a wife. He does everything possible to escape the oracle's decree, but years later he learns that he has unwittingly committed both of these crimes. For punishment he blinds himself.

Freud believed that every member of the audience of Sophocles' Oedipus recognized Oedipus in himself and that the will of the gods and the oracle are disguises of his own unconscious. As though each of us remembers two wishes: do away with the parent of the same sex, marry the parent of the opposite sex, and yet be horrified at the thought. And the audience understands the dramatist's voice: "You are guilty because these wishes still persist in your unconscious." What our simple-minded army doctor did not understand was that "unconscious" means what was in the mind of the very young child--boys and girls alike. It is not to be taken any more seriously than their belief in Santa Claus. It is the taking of it seriously, the failure to give up the wish, the conflict with what seemed like a perfect solution to an infant's problems--union with an idyllic mother--that produces illness, neurosis.

> In 1913 under the title of *Totem and Taboo*, I put forward a suggestion that mankind as a whole may have acquired its sense of guilt, the ultimate source of religion and morality, at the beginning of its history, in connection with the Oedipus complex. I should be very glad to tell you more about this, but I had better leave it on one side. Once one has begun on that topic it is hard to break off; and we must go back to individual psychology.
> (Ibid. p. 332)

As was the custom, and for the most part still remains the custom, Freud used male pronouns in connection with psychological happenings. He asked what direct observations of prelatency children reflect the presence of the Oedipus. It is easy to see that the little man wants his mother all to himself. He feels that his father's presence is a nuisance, and he is delighted when father goes away. It is not at all unusual for a little boy to declare his intention of marrying his mother when he grows up. This may not seem like much compared to Oedipus' crime, but at root it is the same thing. Observations get confused because there are times when the boy displays great affection for his father. This ambivalence, which does not seem to upset the child, can lead to a neurotic conflict in adults. The little boy may show a blatant sexual curiosity about his mother. He tries to be present when she is dressing and may insist upon sleeping beside her at night. She is his love-object.

> As you see, I have only described the relation of a boy to his father and mother. Things happen in just the same way with little girls, with the necessary changes; an affectionate attachment to her father, a need to get rid of her mother as superfluous and to take her place, a coquetry which already employs the method of later womanhood--these offer a charming picture, especially in small girls, which makes us forget the situation. (This viepoint was revised by Freud eight years later.) We must not omit to add that the parents themselves often exercise a determining influence on the awakening of a child's Oedipus attitude by themselves obeying the pull of sexual attraction, and that where there are several children the father will give the plainest evidence of his greater affection for his little daughter and the mother for her son. But the spontaneous nature of the Oedipus complex in children cannot be seriously shaken even by this factor.
> (Ibid. p. 333)

When other children, brothers and sisters, appear on the scene, they are perceived as competition: the Oedipus complex expands to include them. As a rule it is easier for children to express feelings of hatred toward their siblings than toward the rival parent. On more than one occasion an Oedipal son permanently turns away from his mother because she has proved her unfaithfulness with the birth of a new baby.

One cannot but be amused at some of the explanations for the prohibition of incest. It has been said that sexual attraction is blunted in members of the same family because they have been living together since childhood; or that there is an innate biological horror of incest to avoid inbreeding. If such natural barriers existed, prohibition of it in law and custom would not be needed. But the opposite is true. Our very first choice of a love-object is an incestuous one, and the severest prohibitions are necessary to deter this persistent infantile wish. What does the analysis of adults tell us about the Oedipus complex? Simply that in the legend is a truth within us all. Every patient in his childish, primitive mind, is an Oedipus

At puberty, the sexual demand is experienced at full strength. The repressed, unconscious, incestuous objects are reinvested with fresh libido. From this time onward every person, male and female, faces the important task of detaching himself from his parents. Until this is achieved, he never fully experiences himself as an adult, a peer among authority figures, an adult among adults. He suffers an Oedipus complex; he is neurotic.

Clinical observation makes us aware that people who experience neurotic anxiety are frequently those whose intense sexual excitation meets with an insufficient discharge, or an unsatisfactory conclusion. Men, for example, while they are engaged to be married and do not enjoy complete sexual release, will exhibit anxiety. Women, whose husbands are insufficiently potent or who as a precaution against pregnancy perform in an incomplete or abridged fashion, show signs of an anxiety neurosis. In such circumstances, the libidinal excitation seems to disappear and is replaced by anxiety. A regular practice of interrupted sexual intercourse is a common cause of anxiety neuroses in men, but even more in women. The more passionate a woman, the more inclined she is to this condition, the more certain she is to react to a man's sexual restraints, whether they be impotence or coitus interruptus. In the case of women who are anesthetic or frigid, however, such ill-treatment has far less effect. "So far as I know, the connection between anxiety states and sexual restraint, is no longer disputed even by physicians who have no contact with psycho-analysis."[1]

---

[1]Ibid. p. 402

CHAPTER XLVII

■ *Bitterness Toward Men*

Freud's anthropological studies initiated by *Totem and Taboo* were continued in "The Taboo of Virginity." In a letter to Ferenczi he joked: "You see, nothing is too small for me."[1]

Krafft-Ebing has described cases where a wife completely merges her personality with that of her husband. He used the terms "sexual bondage" and extreme "thralldom," and added that these feelings were necessary if the tie to her husband were to last for any length of time. There is a common notion that whoever is the first to satisfy a woman's desire for sexual love, which she has held in check since the beginning of her life, will be the one whom she takes to her heart. She will feel a bond between herself and her man that guarantees possession of her and that enables her to resist temptation from others. Since the essence of monogamy is the exclusive possession of a woman, perhaps the high value we place on virginity is an extension of this monopoly to include the past, and also a means of guaranteeing the female spouse's fidelity.

Freud found that in analytic experience this explanation of the high value placed on virginity was too simple. Psycho-analytic investigation revealed that the decisive factor in creating a state of bondage was the amount of sexual resistance that the man was able to overcome, and once done it is consolidated. These feelings are much more common and intense in women than in men; however there are cases where a man has overcome his impotence with a particular woman, and a similar state of sexual bondage may result. "...it occurs more often nowadays than it did in ancient times." Many strange relationships, and even tragic events, owe their explanation to this source.

Freud then turned his attention to a strange custom of some primitive people where it would appear the opposite holds. Paradoxically, every precaution is taken to prevent the future partner from performing the defloration. It is not because the act is regarded as unimportant; on the contrary it is highly significant and has even become the subject of a religious ceremony. The rupturing of the hymen is carried out by an appointed person, accompanied by rituals which vary from tribe to tribe.

> ....In the Portland and Glenelg tribes this is done to the bride by an old woman; and sometimes white men are asked for this reason to deflower maidens....The artificial rupture of the hymen sometimes takes place in infancy, but generally at puberty...this defloration is performed by the

[1]Ferenczi, September 24, 1917

> father of the bride amongst the Sakais (Malay), Battas (Sumatra) and Alfoers of Celebes....In the Philippines there were certain men whose profession it was to deflower brides, in case the hymen had not been ruptured in childhood by an old woman who was sometimes employed for this....The defloration of the bride was amongst some Eskimo tribes entrusted to the angekok, or priest....
>
> (The Taboo of Virginity, 1917, S.E. XI p. 195)

Freud reviewed some of the sociological and anthropological explanations for the defloration ritual. They involve the horror and symbol of blood among primitive races, the mystery of menstruation, anxiety associated with new undertakings, and so forth. The question that presents itself is—what danger is the taboo designed to protect against?

> We consider it to be the normal reaction for a woman after intercourse to embrace the man, pressing him to her at the climax of satisfaction, and we see this as an expression of her gratitude and a token of lasting bondage. But we know it is by no means the rule that the first occasion of intercourse should lead to this behavior; very frequently it means only disappointment for the woman, who remains cold and unsatisfied, and it usually requires quite a long time and frequent repetition of the sexual act before she too begins to find satisfaction in it. There is an unbroken series from these cases of mere initial frigidity which soon vanishes, up to the cheerless phenomenon of permanent and obstinate frigidity which no tender efforts on the part of the husband can overcome. I believe this frigidity in women is not yet sufficiently understood and, except for those cases which must be blamed on the man's insufficient potency, calls for elucidation, possibly through allied phenomena.
>
> (Ibid. p. 201)

An understanding of normal behavior is often made clear by an examination of an extreme, pathological form of conduct. There are cases where women are angry after intercourse, nor do they hesitate to express it. They abuse their partner by ridicule, complaints, even by actually striking him.

> In one very clear case of this kind, which I was able to submit to a very thorough analysis, this happened although the woman loved the man very much, used to demand intercourse herself and unmistakably found a great satisfaction in it.
>
> (Ibid. p. 201)

Whatever may give rise to this hostile reaction, the husband would surely have every reason to want to avoid it.

What is the explanation of the woman's wrath? Freud thought that the pain which defloration causes is not the important determinant in *the establishment of the ritual*. He considered narcissistic injury which follows the destruction of an organ, but to this neither did he give much weight. In some cases the defloration rite falls into two phases: the breaking of the hymen, by hand or with some instrument, and the ceremonial act of mock intercourse which follows with the representative of the husband. This would suggest that the purpose of the taboo is not to avoid anatomical pentration, but rather to protect the husband as well as the woman's reaction to the trauma.

Freud went back to the beginning; he re-examined the development of the sex drive. The sexual wishes of the little girl are usually directed toward the father, or a brother who takes his place. We know from analytic research how universal and powerful these earliest sensual investments are, and that fixations do result. The husband is never really the right man; he is a substitute for the earlier choice, the father. The substitute will be rejected in proportion to the strength of the fixation of the first love. Given sufficient investment in the father, a degree of frigidity will be the consequence. The more powerful and psychological the woman's fixation on the earlier object choice, the greater will be her resistance to the upheaval of her first sexual intercourse, and the less overpowering will be the effect of her body's being possessed. Primitive peoples who turn the task of defloration over to an elderly man, or a priest, seem to grasp intuitively the motif of the early sexual wish.

> It agrees with our expectation, therefore, when we find the images of gods included among the father-surrogates entrusted with defloration. In some districts of India, the newly married woman was obliged to sacrifice her hymen to the wooden lingam, and according to St. Augustine's account, the same custom existed in the Roman marriage ceremony (of his time), but modified so that the young wife only had to seat herself on the gigantic stone phallus of Priapus.
>
> (Ibid. p. 204)

Freud went still deeper to find reasons for the paradoxical reaction toward the husband, which contributes to female frigidity. He stated that the first act of intercourse activates feelings in a woman other than the old sexual longings already mentioned. These other feelings are in opposition to her role as a woman.

From the analysis of many neurotic women, we have learned that they go through an early age in which they envy their brother his emblem of masculinity and they feel at a disadvantage and are humiliated because they lack it:

> During this phase, little girls often make no secret of their envy, nor of the hostility towards their favoured brothers which arises from it. They even try to urinate standing upright like their brother in order to prove the equality which they lay claim to.

This masculine phase, in which she envies the boy for his penis, occurs earlier than her object choice of the father. In analysis there comes to light behind her penis envy a hostile bitterness toward men which never completely disappears.

After exploring some of the motives for women's paradoxical reactions and the traces of it that result in frigidity, Freud summed up his conclusion. The man who first acquaints her with intercourse becomes the recipient of the residues of her infantile frustrations, her anger. *Now the defloration ritual makes sense*; the man she is to share her life with thereby avoids the danger of her hostility.

At higher levels of civilization these dangers become more subtle.

> I think it must strike the observer in how uncommonly large a number of cases the woman remains frigid and feels unhappy in a first marriage, whereas after it has been dissolved she becomes a tender wife, able to make her second husband happy. The archaic reaction has, so to speak, exhausted itself on the first object.
> (Ibid. p. 206)

So, in trying to understand the nature of the danger which the ritual is designed to avoid, he traced it to the woman's infantile sexuality. Forced to give up her masculine hopes, she is also forced into the adult feminine position. The clitoric phase must now include the vagina. The archaic, infantile part her mentality rages against the situation, and the man who brings it about becomes of the object of her hostility. It is from this hostility that the primitive custom we are exploring protects the future husband.

Freud added an observation of some women who have fallen out with their husbands but are unable to leave them. "They cannot get away from them, because they have not completed their revenge upon them, and in pronounced cases they have not even brought the impulses for vengeance to consciousness."[1]

---

[1]Ibid. p. 208

CHAPTER XLVIII

■ *Gigantic Hypocrisy*

The war continued. In Vienna there was little food; there was little work; ordinary pleasures were curtailed. For example, the closed borders prevented the holidays away from home and visits to his daughters that Freud much enjoyed.

Freud had always had an immense respect for artists like Lou Salome; her grasp of the intricate problems of psychoanalysis amazed him. He wrote a postcard to her asking for a word of cheer. Lou rose to the occasion and wrote him a moving and optimistic letter. Freud replied:

> I do not doubt that mankind will surmount even this war, but I know for certain that I and my contemporaries will never again see a joyous world. It is all too hideous. And the saddest thing about it is that it has come out just as from our psychoanalytical expectations we should have imagined man and his behavior. Because of this attitude I have never been able to agree with your blithe optimism. My secret conclusion was: since we can only regard the highest civilization of the present as disfigured by a gigantic hypocrisy it follows that we are organically unfitted for it.
> (Jones 2, p. 177)

Freud was now sixty years old. An old superstitition in regard to the date of his death convinced him he had only a few years to live. No doubt his mood was determined by the anticipation of a long war which he might not survive. His practice had become minimal and, rare for him, he had time to study. As often happened when his spirits were low, his productivity was at its height. He decided to write a synthesis of his psychological theories and to add whatever he still felt he had to offer the world. In a letter to Ferenczi he said: "I know I am writing for only five people in the present, you and the few others." (Abraham, Rank, Sachs and Jones)[1] The book was to be published after the war and entitled "Introduction to Metapsychology." Within six weeks, he had written five essays that are among the most important of his works. The penetration into his previous concepts are so novel that they require careful study.

Naturally, Freud was concerned about his two sons who were at the front: Martin at the Russian (where he had already won a medal for gallantry) and Ernst, who had enlisted in April, at the Italian. Oliver at home was engaged in the construction of tunnels, barracks, and so forth. Freud had several dreams about his sons be-

[1]Ferenczi, Dec. 15, 1914

ing wounded. He interpreted them as the envy that an old man feels toward youth.

In the Autumn of 1917 he felt convinced the war was already lsot.

> I judge the situation with extreme pessimism and believe that unless there is a parliamentary revolution in Germany we must expect the war to go on until a complete downfall. I think we should take seriously the assurances of the English about their intentions, and we also have to admit the failure of the submarine war.
>
> (Ferenczi, Oct. 9, 1917)

Toward the end of the year Freud had lost all sympathy for Germany. "The only cheerful news is the capture of Jerusalem by the English and the experiment they propose about a home for the Jews."[1]

Rose, his favorite sister, lost her only son, killed on the Italian front. But it was the only loss the family suffered in the war. Despite many close calls, adventure, and hardships, his two sons came through unharmed.

Life in Vienna continued to be very difficult. There was not enough food to keep nourished and Freud had to stop writing simply because he couldn't heat his study and it was too cold to hold a pen. Ferenczi and von Freund, from time to time, managed to smuggle in flour, bread, and a few luxuries from Hungary; such help was precious but precarious. Nevertheless, Freud could say: "Curiously enough, with all that, I am quite well and my spirits are unshaken. It is proof of how little justification in reality one needs for inner well-being."[2]

At the end of the year something happened which was a sinister omen of things to come.

> Yesterday I smoked my last cigar and since then have been bad-tempered and tired. Palpitation appeared and a worsening of a painful swelling in the palate....Then a patient brought me fifty cigars, I lit one, became cheerful, and the affection of the palate rapidly went down. I should not have believed it had it not been so striking. Quite a la Groddeck. (Groddeck had a remarkable gift of connecting physical conditions with emotional motivation.)
>
> (Ferenczi, Nov. 6, 1917)

Six years later cancer attacked his palate. The connection with smoking is indisputable.

In October, correspondence with Pfister was resumed on the occasion of his old friend's publishing a new book, *What does Psychoanalysis Offer the Pedagogue*? Freud praised it, but disagreed with his views on ethics:

> I don't rack my brains much about the problem of good and evil, but on the whole I have not found much of the "good" in people. Most of

[1]Abraham, July 13, 1917 [2]Ferenczi, Feb. 16, 1917

> them are in my experience riff-raff, whether they proclaim themselves adherents of this or that ethical doctrine, or none at all.... Your experiences in life can hardly have been different from mine. If there is any question of ethics I avow I have high ideals, from which sad to say most people I have known diverge.... From a therapeutic point of view I can only envy you the possibility of sublimation that religion affords. But the beauty of religion certainly does not belong to the domain of psychoanalysis. Naturally our ways part at this point in therapy; and it may stay so. By the way, how comes it that none of all the pious people discovered psychoanalysis; why did they have to wait for a quite godless Jew?
>
> (Pfister, Oct. 9, 1918)

To Freud's last question Pfister replied:

> In the first place you are not a Jew, which my endless admiration for Amos, Isaiah, Jeremiah, with the men who composed Job and the Prophets, makes me greatly regret; and in the second place you are not so godless, since whoever lives for the truth lives in God and whoever strives for the freeing of love "dwelleth in God." If you would fuse your own contribution with the great world harmony, like the synthesis of notes in a Beethoven symphony into a musical whole, I could say of you: There never was a better Christian.
>
> (to Freud, Oct. 29, 1918)

At the time three valuable new members joined the Psychoanalytic society: George Groddeck, a wildly creative physician, Otto Potzl, a lecturer at the University, later to become Professor of Psychiatry, and Anton von Freund. a Hungarian industrialist and doctor of philosophy.

George Groddeck, who worked in a military hospital in Baden-Baden, wrote to Freud that he had successfully treated a patient with methods that might be considered psychoanalytic. However, he would not call himself a psychoanalyst if Freud rejected his ideas. He explained that he saw no separation between bodily and mental illness. He tried to treat the inaccessible "it" in the person, and to find a way to reach the unexplored region of his patient.

Freud was impressed. The treatment of organic illnesses by psychological methods opened up staggering possibilities. He answered:

> I note that you urge me to confirm to you officially that you are not a psychoanalyst, that you don't belong to the flock of disciples, but that you may be allowed to consider yourself as something apart and independent. I evidently would be doing you a great favour by rejecting you and relegating you

> to the place where Adler, Jung, and others stand. But this I cannot do! I must lay claim to you, but must insist that you are an analyst of the first order who has grasped the essence of the matter once for all. The man who has recognized that transference and resistance are the hubs of treatment belongs irrevocably to the "wild hunt."
> (Roberts, p. 174)

Freud attended Potzl's lecture. He could hardly believe that his theories were not only being defended but actually taught at the University.

The great German offensive of March 1918, which the British called the "Ludendorf push," aroused hope in Germany of another victory, but not of peace itself. Like so many Austrians, Freud resigned himself to being dragged along by Germany to the bitter end. In a letter to Abraham he apologized for being pessimistic and not more heartening.

The deprivations brought on by war increased. The Freuds wer better off than most Viennese families due to the efforts of Ferenczi and von Freund, who used, or misused, their positions to get food to the Freud family. Freud was extremely grateful and pleased that he had such loyal friends. Unfortunately, in October, Hungary separated from Austria and all communications were cut. The precious help came to an end.

That February a patient he had cured left him a fortune in his will: ten thousand Kronen. Freud enjoyed "playing the rich man"[1] and distributed the money among his children and relatives.

He had always been superstitious about the date of his death, changing it each time death didn't take place. At the moment the date he had in mind was February 1918. Three months later he wrote: "My mother will be eighty-three this year and is no longer very strong. I sometimes think I shall feel a little freer when she dies, for the idea that she might have to be told that I have died is a terrifying thought."[2] This haunting thought sometimes almost reached the point of an obsession.

That summer gave Freud the feeling that there was something in the future to live for. Dr. Phil. Anton von Freund had recently had a sarcoma of the testicle removed. Naturally he was apprenhensive about recurrences and uncertain of his life. He made plans to dispose of his vast fortune and decided to devote it to the cause of psychoanalysis. With help from Ferenczi and Rank he was arranging the founding of an independent publishing firm to be put at Freud's disposal. Freud joyously began to busy himself with all sorts of plans for future psychoanalytic publications.

Unfortunately, von Freund's generous gift had been deposited in Hungary. The transfer of the funds to Vienna involved complicated administrative arrangements. The result was that hardly a quarter of it was sent to Vienna, the rest being appropriated by the Hungarian authorities. The International Psychoanalytical Association did indeed have its own publishing house, but from the begining it was beset with discouraging financial problems. It managed to hold together for twenty years and published psychoanalytical literature in a way no commercial firm could have

[1]Ferenczi, Feb. 27, 1918
[2]Abraham, May 29, 1918

done. To its credit were some hundred and fifty books, including Freud's *Complete Works* in eleven volumes.

Despite the war, the Fifth International Psycho-Analytical Congress was held in Budapest, September 28, 1918. The mayor and officials of the town outdid themselves in generosity, because of the success that psychoanalytic treatment had with the "war neurosis," today the condition is known as battle fatigue. It was the first Congress at which official representatives from the Government were present. The military authorities were impressed with analytic treatment and wished to learn more about it. There was talk of building psychoanalytic clinics at various centers for the treatment of war neuroses. (There was no realization that the loss of the war was imminent, an event which, of course, changed the situation altogether. A special steamer down the Danube was placed at their convenience, and receptions and dinners were planned for the members of this now august body of psychoanalysts. In the following month more than a thousand University students petitioned that Ferenczi give lectures on psychoanalysis.

At last came the downfall followed by the breakup of the Austro-Hungarian Empire. Freud was delighted: "I shall not weep a single tear for the fate of Austria or Germany."[1]

In the northwest of Austria a new republic was formed, Czechoslovakia, and in the south, a new nation came into being, Yugoslavia. Revolution broke out in Austria. It was very brief. Hans Sachs parodied it by describing imaginary placards: "The Revolution will take place tomorrow at two-thirty; in case of unfavorable weather it will be held indoors."[2] This was the one occasion in Freud's life when he was actually under fire. He and Mathilde, his daughter, were strolling in the Horlagasse when shots rang out. They took to their heels and were soon out of danger.

On the last day of the year, Jones informed Freud of the death of J. J. Putnam. Freud's obituary for Putnam was published in the International Journal of Psychoanalysis.

> He was universally respected for his unimpeachable character, and it was recognized that he was influenced only by the highest ethical considerations. His closer personal acquaintances could not escape the conclusion that he was one of those happily compensated people of the obsessional type for whom what is noble is second nature and for whom any concession to unworthiness has become an impossibility.
> (S.E. XVII p. 271)

After the defection of Adler, Stekel, and the Swiss, Freud had felt that only a handful of adherents could be counted on to continue his work. The events of 1918 revive his spirits. The enthusiastic official reception of his work at the Budapest Congress and the von Freund's magnificent donation charged him with a brighter outlook. The Hungarian government also promised to arrange for lectures on psychoanalysis at a special department in the University and, futher, to organize a Psychoanalytical Insititute. It seemed as though Budapest would be the main center

[1]Ferenczi, Nov. 3, 1918
[2]Jones 2, p. 201

for their work.

But two events changed the new vision. Hungary became independent of Austria and soon afterwards it came under a Bolshevist government. The new regime cut off its previous close contact with Austria and for months no mail could pass between Budapest and Vienna, and so no word from Ferenczi. Also the availability of the fund became doubtful.

Bela Kun's Bolshevist government saw psychoanalysis as revolutionary (it had not yet been designated as a degenerate bourgeois psychology), and they appointed Ferenczi as the first University Professor of Psychoanalysis.

Ferenczi was to pay dearly for this honor. Four and a half months later, in August, the Roumanians entered Budapest. Their regime was reactionary. "Jew" and "revolutionary" were synonymous terms; they were violently anti-Semitic. To his mortification, he was expelled from the Medical Society of Budapest. In fact, he had to hide away for weeks to escape Bela Kun's successors and the police. For a long time he was afraid to show himself in the street.

On the other hand, news of interest in psychoanalysis from London, Berlin, and New York made Freud feel that the world was getting ready to recognize his work as a valid subject for investigation. Despite everything, the outlook seemed bright.

CHAPTER XLIX

■ *He Beats Me And Loves Me*

Whoever studies Freud is taken on the one hand with the boldness of his imagination, and on the other with his scientific objectivity. How odd that the man who explored so brazenly the labyrinths of the mind was, in actuality, cautious. From his earliest days he would not publish his findings before critically examining them for at least four years.

Quite unexpectedly Freud presented a paper that was reminiscent of his earlier days: a purely clinical study, a technical work, that runs over thirty pages, and is entitled "A Child is Being Beaten." It is a detailed inquiry into a particular perversion, and it throws some light on the general problem of masochism.

The paper may also serve to reveal how Freud worked. Psychoanalytic technique entails a patient, known as the analysand, lying on a couch and pledged to say everything that comes into his mind—regardless of how embarrassing, trivial, even apparently crazy. He must censor nothing. This is known as "free association." At first patients usually find this exercise very difficult, and in the beginning the analyst helps; but after a while, the patient learns how to freely associate. The analyst can gauge the degree of resistance by the nature of the associations.

Freud had treated patients who reported masturbating while compulsively thinking "a child is being beaten." The patient felt shame and guilt at having to report this, and it was difficult to obtain any further details about the fantasy. It was even hard to find out the identity of who was being spanked or who was administering the punishment.

A deeper examination of the fantasy found that both the origin and the fantasy differed between men and women.

In women, Freud uncovered three stages of the fantasy. The first, which is nonsexual, expressed the wish that the patient's father would beat, or show that he was displeased with, another child, frequently a brother or sister. Further exploration revealed that the patient had once been jealous of this sibling. In the second phase, which was difficult to get at because it was unconscious, the wish had changed into herself being beaten by her father. This was accompanied by feelings of intense pleasure. The third phase had been conscious from the beginning: the father was replaced by a teacher or some other authority figure, and the child being beaten was now a stranger, often a boy. This third phase evoked intense, unambiguous, sexual excitement, thus providing a strong stimulus for masturbatory relief. Freud concluded that a boy appeared because the woman's incestuous wishes were repressed, and a regression to her masculine phase had taken place. Thus the beating was a punishment for incestuous genital wishes toward the father, and a regression to the pregenital sexual substitute.

Male patients did not seem to be involved with the first, nonsexual stage. They began with a wish to be beaten by their fathers, which wish a deeper exploration proved to be a distortion of the patient's simple desire to be loved, sexually, by him. This then changed into a fantasy of a "boy being beaten by a woman" (a substitute for the mother).

Note a difference between the males and the females. The men were passive throughout the entire fantasy; the women, on the other hand, enjoyed some sadistic pleasure within the imaginary situation.

Women analysands who produced these fantasies discovered, as the analysis proceeded, that they still had unconscious sexual feelings for their fathers, and also feelings of sibling rivalry that they had not outgrown. The second stage in which she herself is being beaten, is a direct expression of her guilt for her Oedipal feelings, and therefore has become masochistic. Her forbidden genital wishes for her father induce a regression to an earlier anal-sadistic phase, where psychically the sexual gratification takes place.

People who harbor "beating" fantasies develop a special sensitiveness toward anyone whom they feel is in the class of fathers. They are easily offended by a "father" of this kind, and in that way, to their own sorrow and cost, re-experience a beating by their father.

The following quotation is typical of Freud's writings in that, in a throw-away line, he reveals a depth of insight: "I should not be surprised if it were one day possible to prove that the same phantasy is the basis of the delusional litigious of paranoia."[1]

Male patients who enjoy the "a-child-is-being-beaten" fantasy show, with few exceptions, serious impairment of their sexual potency. They either obtained sexual satisfaction exclusively from masturbation, accompanied by their fantasies, or they were only able to carry our normal intercourse if they were first subjected to physical pain (beatings, etc.), or to some other form of humiliation. The masochistic masturbator, when he attempts intercourse with a woman, finds that he is impotent. This type of man, who manages a sexual performance with a woman with the secret help of a masochistic fantasy, will inevitably discover sooner or later that after a while the secret inventions no longer work, and he suffers impotence. In analysis, the fact emerges that not only in their fantasy do they assume a feminine attitude (passive) but that the one who administers the punishment is always a woman. Although it may be disguised, the fantasy is: "I am being beaten by my mother." But deeper analysis reveals that this is not the primary fantasy. From the unconscious, which the treatment brings to the surface, emerges: "I am being beaten by my father."

> In the male phantasy—as I shall call it briefly, and, I hope, without any risk of being misunderstood—the being beaten also stands for being loved (in a genital sense), though this had been debased to a lower level owing to regression. So the original form of the unconscious male phantasy was not the provisional one that we have hitherto given: "I am being beaten by my father" but rather: "I AM LOVED BY MY FATHER." The phantasy has been transformed by the pro-

[1]A Child is Being Beaten, S.E. 17 p. 195, 1919

> cesses with which we are familiar, into the conscious phantasy: "I am being beaten by my mother." The boy's phantasy is therefore passive from the very beginning, and is derived from a feminine attitude towards his father. It corresponds with the Oedipus complex just as the female one (that of girls) does; only the parallel relation which we had expected to find betwen the two must be given up in favor of a common character of another kind. In both cases the beating-phantasy has its origin in an incestuous attachment to the father.
>
> (Ibid. p. 198)

So, the same fantasy "a child is being beaten" is for females at root heterosexual and for males homosexual.

Freud added some important considerations concerning the nature of sexual perversions. They are a product of the Oedipus complex, which explains why manifest perversions rarely show themselves before the age of five or six.

This techincal paper also includes a discussion of a problem that had puzzled Freud since the early days of psychoanalysis: the motive forces which cause repression. Here he states that the sexual instincts break through the repressive forces and become the chief determinants in the formation of symptoms.

CHAPTER L

■ *Wolf-Man*

In 1910 Freud acquired a patient of a very different stamp. He was the heir to a large estate in Russia and he came to his first interview accompanied both by his physician and his valet. He was so incapacitated physically that he could not take care of his simplest needs. During the interview he expressed the wish to have Freud as a doctor and, in order to show his appreciation, he offered to have anal intercourse with him and promised that afterwards he would defecate on Freud's head. Freud was fascinated with the workings of the young man's mind and, though he had no office hours open, he arranged to treat him at the local sanitarium.

The patient had a long history of treatment, including hydro- and electric therapy, had spent much time in hospitals in Germany, and had consulted well-known psychiatrists such as Kraeplin and Ziehen. Everything had failed and he was on his way to Switzerland, accompanied by his doctor, for yet another treatment when, in Vienna, they heard by chance about Freud.

He was to become Freud's most famous patient, the Wolf-Man.

The analysis which followed ran from 1910 to 1914, the very period during which serious differences were growing up between Freud, Jung, and Adler. The case entitled "From the History of an Infantile Neurosis," (S.E. XVII, 1918) emphasized once more the importance of infantile sexuality in the aetiology of a neurosis. It was published after the rebels had left Freud and organized independent schools, and it was, of course, an argument against these rebels.

> The case history known as that of the "Wolfman" is assuredly the best of the series. Freud was then at the very height of his powers, a confident master of his method, and the technique he displays in the interpretation and synthesis of the incredibly complex material must win every reader's admiration.
>
> (Jones 2, p. 274)

The published case report is far from complete. Four years of analysis produced such a quantity of material as to make a complete account impossible. In addition, the young man was well known and his privacy had to be guarded, even though he himself urged Freud to publish the case in all its details.

Freud preferred to use the case exclusively to expose the falsity of the ideas put forth by Jung and Adler. Consequently little is known about the patient's later and adult symptoms. At the age of four he suffered from a wolf phobia which gave way to an obsessional neurosis. The obsession lasted until he was ten years old.

> There was a particular picture-book, in which a wolf was represented, standing upright and striding along. Whenever he caught sight of this picture he began to scream like a lunatic that he was afraid of the wolf coming and eating him up. His sister, however, always succeeded in arranging so that he was obliged to see this picture, and was delighted at his terror. Meanwhile he was also frightened at other animals as well, big and small...he went through an easily recognizable attack of obsessional neurosis...he was very pious. Before he went to sleep he was obliged to pray for a long time and to make an endless series of signs of the cross...he used to make the round of all the holy pictures...taking a chair with him, upon which he climbed and used to kiss each one of them devoutly...blasphemous thoughts...used to come into his head....He was obliged to think "God-swine" or "God-shit"....
>
> (S.E. SVII p. 16-17)

At seventeen he contracted gonorrhea and regressed to the condition he was in at the time he met Freud.

In their rejection of psychoanalysis both Jung and Adler replaced with cultural factors and personal experiences the role of infantile sexuality in the development of a neurosis. If Freud could demonstrate that his patient's illness dated back to early childhood, he had a compelling argument against that of pathogenic factors arising later in life. The paper therefore concentrated on the patient's infantile neurosis and little on the adult neurosis which actually brought the patient into treatment.

Freud himself found the material from the patient's early life astonishing.

> A...peculiarity of the analysis which is to be described in these pages has only increased my difficulty in deciding to make a report upon it. On the whole its results have coincided in the most satisfactory manner with our previous knowledge, or have been easily embodied into it. Many details, however, seemed to me myself to be so extraordinary and incredible that I felt some hesitation in asking other people to believe them....I myself am only reporting what I came upon as an independent experience, uninfluenced by my expectation.
>
> So that there was nothing left for me but to remember the wise saying that there are more things in heaven and earth than are dreamed of in our philosophy. Anyone who could succeed in eliminating his pre-existing convictions even more thoroughly could no doubt discover even more such things.
>
> (S.E. XVII p. 12)

The patient reported having witnessed parental intercourse, (since then known as ''the primal scene'') when he was eighteen months old. He could not directly recall the incident, nor at that age could he fully grasp what he was seeing. Freud assumed that after the original sight, subsequent information such as stories the child heard, or family gossip, or the watching of animals copulating enabled him to understand it. In fact the associations and memories of this particular patient suggested that his perception of the primal scene occurred when he was only six months old! This gave Freud pause: he did not wish to repeat a mistake like that about the early seduction of hysterics.

> I will now turn...to a consideration of the problem....I should myself be glad to know whether the primal scene in my present patient's case was a phantasy or a real experience....These scenes of observing parental intercourse, of being seduced in childhood, and of being threatened with castration are unquestionably an inherited endowment, a phylogenetic heritage, but they may just as easily be acquired by personal experience. With my patient, his seduction by his elder sister was an indisputable reality; why should not the same have been true of his observation of his parents' intercourse?
>
> All that we find in the prehistory of neuroses is that a child catches hold of this phylogentic experience where his own experience fails him. He fills in the gaps in individual truth with prehistoric truth; he replaces occurrences in his own life by occurrences in the life of his ancestors.
>
> (Ibid. p. 97)

The mass of material supporting the observation of the primal scene was so compelling that in Freud's judgment a fantasy or reconstruction could reach the same degree of verisimilitude as an actual memory and have a similar effect on the patient. This is a very fundamental and important conclusion for psychoanalysis.

Throughout his life Freud grappled with the problem of phylogenic or racially inherited knowledge. Was it possible that something mental could be inherited? Could there be something similar to the ''instinctive'' knowledge of animals at work in the mind of children, prior to the development of the mental apparatus?

The patient returned to Russia after his analysis, fully recovered. But the Bolshevik Revolution had completely wiped out his family fortune and he escaped from Russia in 1919 to return to Vienna. For six years Freud collected money from pupils and colleagues for the patient and his sick wife, so that they might survive in post-war Vienna where earning a living, especially as a foreigner, was impossible. The patient was suffering from hysterical constipation and Freud treated him for another four months* without a fee. Finally the illness yielded permanently.

This case is unique. The patient underwent four separate analyses; two with Freud, and later two with Ruth Mack Brunswick, a pupil of Freud. In 1952 the

---

*recent research has revealed that Freud terminated his analysis of Helene Deutsh in order to make room for him.

patient published his memoirs and his recollection of Freud.

> (The Wolf-Man by the Wolf-Man, Baisc Books Inc., N. Y. 1971)

> I, who am now a Russian emigre, eighty-three years of age, and who was one of Freud's early psychoanalytic patients, known as "The Wolf-Man," am sitting down to write my recollections of my childhood. (p. 4)

> ...the very next day we visited him. Freud's appearance was such as to win my confidence immediately. He was then in his middle fifties and seemed to enjoy the best of health. He was of medium height and figure. In his rather long face, framed by a closely clipped, already graying beard, the most impressive feature was his intelligent dark eyes, which looked at me penetratingly but without causing me the slightest feeling of discomfort. His correct, conventional way of dressing, and his simple but self-assured manner, indicated his love of order and his inner serenity. Freud's whole attitude, and the way in which he listened to me, differentiate him strikingly from his famous colleagues, whom I had hitherto known and in whom I had found such a lack of deeper psychological understand. At my first meeting with Freud I had the feeling of encountering a great personality. (p. 137)

> Although Freud certainly did not underestimate the neurotic in his patients, he attempted always to support and strengthen the kernel of health, separated from the chaff of neurosis. (p. 138)

> The rooms themselves must have been a surprise to any patient, for they in no way reminded one of a doctor's office, but rather of an archeologist's study. Here were all kinds of statuettes and other unusual objects, which even the layman recognized as archeological finds from ancient Egypt....Freud himself explained his love for archeology in that the psychoanalyst, like the archeologist in his excavations, must uncover layer after layer of the patient's psyche, before coming to the deepest, most valuable treasures. (p. 139)

> ...in my analysis with Freud I felt myself less as a patient than as a co-worker, the younger comrade of an experienced explorer setting out to study a new recently discovered land. This new land is the realm of the unconscious, over which

the neurotic has lost that mastery which he now seeks, through analysis, to regain. (p. 140)

Freud's memory was absolutely astonishing, he retained everthing in his mind, noticed the smallest details, and never mixed up family relationships or anything of the sort. (p. 141)

As an analysis requires a great deal of time, it raises difficulties for those not well-to-do. "We have made it a rule," Freud once said to me, "always to treat one patient without remuneration." He added that such an analysis often meets with greater resistance than one that is paid for, as feelings of gratitude appear with special strength and hamper the treatment....(p. 142)

Freud told me that he had originally sat at the opposite end of the couch, so that analyst and analysand could look at each other. One female patient, exploiting this situation, made all possible—or rather all impossible—attempts to seduce him. To rule out anything similar, once and for all, Freud moved from his earlier position to the opposite end of the couch. (p. 142)

I was occupied with the idea of becoming a painter. Freud advised me against this, expressing the opinion that although I probably had the ability, I would not find this profession satisfying. He believed that the contemplative nature of the artist was not foreign to me but that the rational (he once called me a "dialectician") predominated. He suggested that I should strive for a sublimation that would absorb my intellectual interest completely. (p. 144)

Modern art in general had no great appeal for him. He had no affinity to music either. World literature, as one might expect, claimed Freud's interest in the highest degree. He was enthusiastic about Dostoevsky, who more than any other has the gift of piercing the depths of the human soul and searching out the most hidden stirrings of the unconscious, to give them expression in a work of art....Freud had less appreciation of Tolstoi...as a psychologist he did not penetrate as deeply as Dostoevsky. And Freud must have had little sympathy for Tolstoi's sharply critical stand against sexuality. (p. 146)

In the weeks before the end of my analysis, we often spoke of the danger of the patient's feeling

> too close a tie to the therapist...it soon becomes evident that the original neurosis has been replaced by another. In this connection Freud was of the opinion that at the end of treatment a gift from the patient could contribute, as a symbolic act, to lessening his feeling of gratitude and his consequent dependence on the physician....As I knew of his love for archeology, the gift I chose for him was a female Egyptian figure, with a miter-shaped headdress. Freud placed it on his desk. Twenty years later, looking through a magazine, I saw a picture of Freud at his desk. "My Egyptian immediately struck my eye, the figure which for me symbolized my analysis with Freud. (p. 150)

For twelve years after his first analysis, the patient was free of any serious neurosis. Then, in 1926, he developed an entirely different illness: paranoia. He was referred to Ruth Mack Brunswick who treated him for several years. Her published studies enriched our appreciation of the dynamics of the case. Her last paper, published in 1940, states that the patient was enjoying good health.

While in his first analysis with Freud, the patient reported a dream he had had at the age of four. The dream and its analysis is the central theme of the case history.

> I dreamt that it was night and I was lying in my bed. (My bed stood with its foot towards the window; in front of the window there was a row of old walnut trees. I know it was winter when I had the dream, and nighttime). Suddenly the window opened of its own accord, and I was terrified to see that some white wolves were sitting on the big walnut tree in front of the window. There were six or seven of them. The wolves were quite white, and looked more like foxes or sheep-dogs, for they had big tails like foxes and they had their ears pricked like dogs when they pay attention to something. In great terror, evidently of being eaten up by the wolves, I screamed and woke up.
>
> My nurse hurried to my bed to see what had happened to me. It took quite a long while before I was convinced that it had only been a dream; I had had such a clear and life-like picture of the window opening and the wolves sitting on the tree. At last I grew quieter, felt as though I had escaped from some danger, and went to sleep again.

At Freud's request the patient made a drawing of the dream. The sketch showed five, not six or seven, white wolves staring in front of them. His associations to the different elements of the dream led him to recall stories like "Little Red Riding Hood," "The Wolf and Seven Little Goats," and the story of the tailor who cut off the wolf's tail in Grimm's fairy tale.

...let us return to its immediate interpretation. I may remark that this interpretataion was a task that dragged on over several years. The patient related the dream at a very early stage of the analysis and very soon came to share my conviction that the cause of his infantile neurosis lay concealed behind it....He had always emphasized the fact that two factors in the dream had made the greatest impression on him: first, the perfect stillness and immobility of the wolves, and secondly, the strained attention with which they all looked at him. The lasting sense of reality, too, which the dream left behind it, seemed to him to deserve notice.

Let us take this last remark as a starting-point. We know from our experience in interpreting dreams that this sense of reality carries a particular significance along with it. It assures us that some part of the latent material of the dream is claiming in the dreamer's memory to possess the quality of reality, that is, that the dream relates to an occurrence that really took place and was not merely imagined....

If it was to be assumed that behind the content of the dream there lay some such unknown scene—one, that is, which had already been forgotten at the time of the dream—then it must have taken place very early.......If we put together as the result of the provisional analysis what can be derived from the material produced by the dreamer, we then find before us for reconstruction some such fragments as there:

A real occurrence...dating from a very early period...looking...immobility...sexual problems...castration...his father...something terrible....

One day the patient continued suddenly with the interpretation of the dream. He thought that the part of the dream which said that "suddenly the window opened of its own accord" was not completely explained...."It must mean: "My eyes suddenly opened." I was asleep, therefore, and suddenly woke up, and as I woke I saw something....

What, then, if the other factor emphasized by the dreamer were also distorted by means of a transposition or reversal? In that case instead of immobility (the wolves sat there motionless; they looked at him but did not move) the meaning would have to be: the most violent motion. That is to say, he suddenly woke up, and saw in front of him a scene of violent movement at which he looked with strained attention....(p. 29-35)

The dream material contained the themes of murder, copulation, castration, and cannabalism; all in the mind of the four-year old dreamer.

The chief mechanism of the "dream work" was reversal. The fixed stare of the wolves was the little dreamer's own fixed attention. The big tails on the wolves represented the absence of tails: castration. The immobility of the wolves signified strange movement which terrified him. The analysis of the dream suggests a very young frightened child watching his parents in intercourse. The link between his wolf phobia and his infantile sexual interests and drives was established.

Alder and Jung represented the view that life's later experiences are responsible for pathology rather that infantile sexuality. The link between the Wolf Man's early libidinal involvements and his neurosis emphatically validates Freud's theory of the etiology of neuroses.

CHAPTER LI

Fur Alle Falle

Unvictorious on the battlefield, both the German and Austro-Hungarian empires were disintegrating. The Central Powers sued for peace. Armistice was signed November 11, 1918.

Austria and Germany paid heavily for their role in the war and for their defeat. The economic situation in both countries was bleak and little hope for improvement lay in the near future. In Vienna life was very hard. Shortages of food and fuel were scarcely bearable. The diet was monotonous—mostly thin vegetable soup. Malnutrition, hunger, cold, and poverty were everywhere.

Freud treated patients hour after hour wearing an overcoat and gloves. In the evenings he tried to maintain his correspondence, correct proof, and edit new editions of his books, all with half-frozen fingers.

Once again he was in a precarious financial position. The inflationary prices were greater than his earnings and he was forced to live on savings. These were rapidly running out. He had saved 150,000 Crowns for his old age, but inflation had wiped that out. He had insured his life for 100,000 Crowns so that Martha would be provided for, but now it was scarcely enough for a taxi fare.

From Berlin came a letter from Eitingon announcing that he had deposited 3,000 Swedish Crowns in Freud's account in the event that he ran short of money. At dinner Freud read the letter aloud to his family. The two sons present thought it good news, but Martha and his daughter Anna felt that it was an insult to Freud, implying that he could not provide for them. So Freud had to send a telegram to Eitingon refusing his generous offer. He assured him that if he needed help, he would indeed call upon him.

However, before the year was out, budding analysts from England and America began to come to study psychoanalysis, and paid him in foreign currency. Soon he was solvent again. But working with English-speaking analysands presented a new difficulty. He found it hard to follow the different accents and complained that Americans do not speak clearly. Now in his middle sixties, he had to limit his day to six patients because the effort left him exhausted.

Jones found that he couldn't get permission from the English authorities to visit Freud in Vienna. It was as though they expected Germany to renew the war any minute and looked with suspiciom at anyone who wished to travel abroad. He tried the Ministries of War, Health, and Trade, and wrote that he would always remember what bureaucracy can accomplish when working at full efficiency. Finally, he succeeded in getting the Ministry of Education to vouch for a visit to Switzerland. In Bern he met Rank, accompanied by a new wife, and Hans Sachs.

Jones was surprised to see the change in Rank. From an obsequious youth, timid and deferential, he had become a tough, wiry man. His first act was to take out a large revolver and deposit it on the table. The astonished Jones asked what it was for. Rank replied, "Fur alle Falle," (for any eventuality). How did he mangage to get it past the customs officers at the frontier? He had calmly announced to the inquiring official that the bulge in his pocket was "bread." Later it became clear that the gesture was a manic reaction to three severe attacks of depression he had suffered while in the army in Krakow.

Sachs announced that he was changing his profession from law to psychoanalysis, since he couldn't make a living in Vienna anyway. He was the wittiest member of the group. His fund of Jewish jokes and anecdotes was endless. In fact, when years later he moved to America and found that he was treating more Gentile patients than he had in Eurpoe, he was concerned about whether he could analyze without resorting to Jewish stories. He solved the problem: he baptized the stories. He replaced the rabbi with a minister. He was a typical Viennese Jewish intellectual, very intelligent and informed. He seemed to know everything about everything. Short, plump, articulate, he was a frequent visitor at the cafes, where he delighted in good food, wine, and delicious conversation. He had been married briefly, hardly ever spoke about it, and lived the life of a carefree bachelor. He loved beautiful women and it is said that there were many women in his life. When he moved to America he loved the movies and burlesque shows.

In 1920 Sachs moved to Berlin and became a training analyst in the Psychoanalytic Training Institute. Many of his analysands became well-known psychoanalysts. Among them were Erich Fromm, Franz Alexander, Gregory Zilborg, and Karen Horney.

Freud was fond of Sachs and took a personal interest in him. Feeling as he did that psychoanalytic psychology could throw light on human behavior in general and not be limited to treatment of the emotionally troubled, he welcomed nonphysicians from different fields to practice analysis. They could, he felt, apply the psychoanalytic method to different aspects of the humanities. However, such men should give up their previous careers. He believed that psychoanalysis could not be practiced part-time.

Sachs's interests were primarily literary. Of all the Committee members, he was the least interested in the political and administrative aspects of the psychoanalytic movement. He wrote papers applying psychoanalysis to cultural problems and a book on the Roman emperor, Caligula. With Otto Rank, he was a founding editor of "Imago," a periodical devoted to nonmedical applications of analysis. He was invited to Boston and guaranteed eight patients a day and a teaching appointment at Harvard Medical School. To the very end, he held Freud in reverence. His own book, *Freud: Master and Friend*, written shortly before his own death, is a tribute of appreciation and devotion.

Unfortunately, Rank, Sachs, and Jones were unable to visit Freud. Official barriers could not be overcome. Germany and Austria were still considered enemy-occupied territory. They presented papers to a newly constituted Swiss Psychoanalytic Society in March and returned home. Among the new Swiss members was Hermann Rorschach who later became know for the projective test he devised.

Jones tried to see Freud again in August. Again he managed to get as far as Bern, but there he had more success. Although the Austrian ambassador expressed surprise that anyone would wish to go to so dismal a place as Vienna, and supposed "It's a matter of taste," he granted Jones and his assistant, Eric Hiller, passage.

> It did not take long to confirm Freud's hints of the desolate situation of his country. The starved and ragged officials were evidence enough, nor shall I forget the vain efforts of the emaciated dogs to stagger to the food I threw to them. We were the first foreign civilians to reach Vienna and were joyfully received at the Hotel Regina, where visiting analysts always stayed.
> (Jones 3, p. 16)

After not having seen each other for nearly six years, Jones and Freud finally met. Freud appeared grayer and thinner; in fact he never regained his former plump figure. They had not been together long when Ferenczi burst into the room. To Jones's surprise, Ferenczi effusively kissed both of them. He and Freud had not seen each other for more than a year. It was the first of many talks; there simply wasn't time to catch up with everything. Freud startled both of them by saying that he had been half-converted to communism by an ardent believer. His interviewer had informed him that with the advent of Bolshevism (communism), there would be some years of misery and chaos, and that would be followed by universal peace, prosperity, and happiness. Jones and Ferenczi were reassured when Freud added, "I told him I believed the first half."[1]

The next day Jones invited the Freud family, with Rank and his wife, to dine at the beautiful Hotel Cobenzl outside Vienna. He reported that it was a moving experience to see what a good meal meant to them. That night they celebrated Martin's engagement; the wedding was to follow in a few months.

In October 1919, Freud was granted the title Full Professor. Since it brought no seat on the Board of the Faculty or special teaching responsibilities, he referred to it as an "empty title." However, he received so many congratulations on the occasion that he remarked that the establishment of a republic in Austria had made no difference to the Austrian respect for titles.

During the war something had been happening in military hospitals: army doctors were discovering that with the shell-shock patient only psychoanalysis was effective. "Shell shock" was the name given to a condition that was also known as nervous breakdown. It had nothing to do with the presence of bursting shells. Neurologists looking for organic lesions were of no help. Treating these war casualties as malingerers did not help either. Psychoanalysis grew out of an attempt to help patients deal with inner conflicts which were interfering with their living a full life; paradoxically it had been used to send soldiers back to the front lines.

At the end of the war, there had been so many complaints about harsh treatment of war neurotics in the Psychiatric Division of the Vienna General Hospital that a special commission was instituted to investigate the matter. Freud and Emil Rainmann (Wagner-Jauregg's assistant) were invited to submit a memorandum on the situation, which indicates what Freud's status as a scientist was in Vienna at that time (February 1920).

Freud began by describing the division of opinion within the medical profession concerning traumatic neuroses. For example, "railway spine" and similar conditions that result from minor accidents give rise to much controversy in courts of law. There are those who insist that it is due to organic lesions in the nervous sys-

---

[1]Ibid. p. 16

tem, even when this cannot be demonstrated. On the other hand, there is a school of thought that views the matter as functional, that is, psychological. The experiences of war, in which soldiers who are far removed from bursting shells, break down without any physical trauma, had decided the question in favor of the latter. Psychoanalysis traces a neurosis to an emotional conflict. The soldiers who broke down were suffering from a conflict between self-preservation and their sense of duty. The German army had devised a treatment for this condition. They applied electric shock in such large doses as to make the treatment more disagreeable than returning to the front. Wagner-Jauregg was the director of the Psychiatric Divison of the Vienna General Hospital, and therefore responsible for the Austrian military doctors who were being investigated.

Professor Julius Wagner-Jauregg, a Nobel Prize winner for his discovery of the malaria treatment for general paresis, was the most celebrated psychiatrist in the Austro-Hungarian Empire. His clinic was a bulwark of traditional psychiatry. He had to oppose psychoanalysis. He and Freud had known each other since schooldays. He respected Freud and he made the auditorium of the hospital available for Freud's Saturday night lectures. But he personally considered psychoanalysis nonsense. Helene Deutsh, who had recently become a student of psychoanalysis, and had been Wagner-Jauregg's psychiatric assistant during the war, described him as a warm fatherly man. He was a sensitive clinician and took a personal interest in his patients. But he also had a coarse side. He enjoyed making jokes about Freud and teasing members of his staff who showed any interest in psychoanalysis.

Freud's memorandum remarked:

> As to its use (electricaql treatment) in the Vienna Clinics, I am personally convinced that Professor Wagner-jauregg would never have allowed it to be intensified to a cruel pitch. I cannot vouch for other doctors whom I do not know. The psychological education of doctors is in general pretty deficient, and many of them may well have forgotten that the patient he was seeking to treat as a malingerer was not really one.
>
> (Ibid. p. 22)

Freud went on to report that the successes of electrical treatment were not long-lasting. Soon after the soldier returned to the front, the immediate fear was stronger than the fear of electric shock and there would be a fresh relapse.

> In these circumstances some gave way to the characteristically German inclination to achieve their aims quite ruthlessly. Something happened which never should have: the strength of the currents, as well as the severity of the treatment otherwise, were increased to an unbearable point in order to deprive war neurotics of the advantage they gained from their illness. The fact has never been contradicted that in German hospitals there were cases of death during the treatment and suicides as a result of it. I have no idea at all, however, whether the Vienna Clinics also passed

> through this phase of the therapy.
> (Ibid. p. 22)

Eight months later Freud had the disagreeable task of testifying before the Investigating Commission. All the Viennese neurologists and psychiatrists were present; the press too, had been invited. The complaints about the treatment of war neuroses centered on Wagner-Jauregg, the person ultimately reponsible. Freud read aloud from his memorandum. He intended to be as friendly as possible to Wagner-Jauregg, who was not personally responsible for what had happened. Wagner-Jauregg, of course, did his best to defend himself. Freud maintained that not only were a small number of such cases malingerers, but that in a conflict between a doctor's duty to his patient and demands of military authorities, his patient's interests came first. In the debate that followed, the entire Commission violently attacked Freud and said the usual unfair things about psychoanalysis. Afterwards, Freud said that the meeting confirmed what he knew so well, "the insincerity and hatefulness of the Viennesse psychiatrists."[1] The Commission exonerated Wagner-Jauregg.

Two years after the investigation of the treatment of German soldiers, Wagner-Jauregg rejected a proposal for a low-cost psychoanalytic clinic. His opinion carried weight in official circles and petition was denied.

Some years later, Wagner-Jauregg wrote his autobiography, which was published posthumously. In this book he bitterly attacked Freud. He accused him of being intolerant of criticism and charged that Freud's memorandum for the Commission was a personal attack upon himself.

At about this time there was a rumor that Freud had committed suicide because of the hard conditions in Vienna. He said he regarded it as an unkind thought.

In the American press, reports ran the gamut from Freud as a wizard, who could cure all the ills of the American working man, to Freud as a sexual pervert come to debauch the helpless. What Freud had always feared was taking place: a field day for quackery. Self-styled analysts were going into business by making glowing claims. On the other hand, professional societies were trying to set high standards and rigorous training for their members.

Important journalists treated the subject of psychoanalysis seriously. Walter Lippmann, who had studied with William James at Harvard, wrote of Freud: (2/17/15)

> When I compare his work with the psychology that I studied in college, or with most of the material that is used to controvert him, I cannot help feeling that for his illumination, for his steadiness and brilliancy of mind, he may rank among the greatest who have contributed to thought. I know how easy it is to be deceived, but I take it that this is a small risk in comparision with the necessity for recognizing in his own lifetime a man of outstanding importance....He has set up a reverberation in human thought and conduct of which few as yet dare to predict the consequences.
> (Clark, p. 379)

---

[1]Ibid. p. 24

298. *Fur Alle Falle*

A New-York-Times editorial stated: (2/14/16)

> Belief in (psychoanalysis) has not more to do with regularity or irregularity of life than has the "belief" that quinine is a remedy for malaria, or that early operation for cancer is to be commended. The fervent psychoanalyst, like the fervent scorner of Freud, can have good morals or bad, as he or she pleases, can follow any religion or none, can pick any philosophy of life that seems sound, but in no case will these decisions be affected, one way or the other, by his or her judgment of Freud and Freud's contentions as to the origin and cure of hysteria.
> (Ibid. p. 373)

On the other hand, in a New York court a suit was brought against a woman to deprive her of her child. Her crime? She was living with a man out of wedlock and therefore unsuited for the custody of her child. The final proof of unsuitability was that she was living with a man who had studied under Jung.

One must remember that the sinking of the Lusitania in May 1915 with the loss of eleven hundred lives, one hundred of them American, had turned America's sympathies against the Germans. "German" became synonomous with savage. Psychoanalysis was now considered to be part of "German Kultur." For years the charge against Freud's creation was its "Jewishness." Now his baby was accused of being German, the very thing Vienna and Berlin claimed it was not.

In Britain the situation was similar, though not so extreme (more than likely due to Jones's excellent work). David Eder, among the first to practice analysis in Berlin, presented a paper to the British Medical Association. In simple terms he described psychoanalytic theory and technique for treatment of hysteria and obsession. At the conclusion of his presentation, he was shocked to see the chairman and the audience of about nine walk out without a single comment. On the other hand, Jones took part in a debate at the Psycho-Medical Society. After the meeting, Sir James Crichton-Browne, the President, thanked Jones and said it was "a much needed protest against these misrepresentations" and went on to speak highly of psychoanalysis. Other members did the same; the atmosphere reflected cordiality and English "fair play."[1]

In October 1920, encouraged by the thought of American royalties, Freud offered to write four popular articles for a good magazine in New York. His first article would be entitled "Don't Use Psychoanalysis in Polemics." Cosmopolitan Magazine offered him $1,000 for the first article, and if that proved a success, they would want more. They also suggested acceptable topics : "The Wife's Mental Place in the Home," "The Husband's Mental Place in the Home," and others. Freud sent a sharp letter of refusal. It was the first time he had ever attempted to depart from his own standards in order to earn money. One may suspect that he was ashamed. He never did anything like it again.

---

[1]Ibid. p. 373

CHAPTER LII

■ *To Punish A Father*

Whereas Freud's earlier publications of case histories of women dealt with the problems of hysteria, by 1920 he was considering more seriously the whole question of female sexuality. His investigations led to "The Psychogenesis of a Case of Homosexuality in a Woman."

The case is remarkable in that the patient, an attractive and intelligent girl of eighteen, had no intention of giving up he sole "symptom." Her resistance was not against the analysis itself, but against its having any effect. She, therefore, was able to allow the analysis to proceed freely and fully, enabling Freud to gain complete insight into the origins of her condition.

Freud often observed how much more conspicuous a role male homosexuality plays, socially and legally, than female homosexuality. Perhaps for that reason, not only has the law ignored homosexuality in women, but so had psychoanalytic research.

The patient was desperately in love with a woman about ten years older than herself. The patient's parents, particularly her father, were alarmed at her admiration for this "society lady." The lady was married, carried on promiscuously with a number of men, was living with a woman and having intimate relations with her. Despite her distinguished name, in the parents' opinion she was nothing but a "cocotte" (prostitute). The girl did not contradict their accusations, but neither did she allow them to interfere with her infatuation for her beloved. She would wait outside her door for hours or at a trolley stop where she might alight; she would send her flowers, and so on. Her parents saw this as a continuation, in a more extreme degree, of feelings she had recently displayed toward other members of her own sex, which had already aroused her father's suspicion and led to his fury.

She seemed indifferent to her own reputation; she appeared everywhere with her "friend." In some ways she was too open. On the other hand, she would use any means of deception, or lies, or excuses to be with her beloved.

One day the inevitable happened: her father met her on the street in the company of the lady. He passed them without speaking, but with a furious glare. Shortly thereafter she threw herself over a wall above a railway line. She paid dearly for this effort at suicide: she was confined to bed, on her back, for a considerable time. After this, the parents no longer opposed her wishes, and the lady, who up until then received her advances somewhat coldly, was moved by such a display of passion and began to treat her more warmly.

The father was a good person, even tender-hearted, but he estranged his children by being a strong disciplinarian. When he first learned about his daughter's homosexual tendencies, he flew into a rage. He saw her as vicious, or mentally unbalanced and he tried to suppress her homosexuality with threats. Something about his daughter's homosexuality aroused the deepest bitterness in him, and he was determined to overcome this nonsense with every means at his disposal. In his desperation, he even took her to a psychoanalyst, a breed who at the time was held in low esteem in Vienna.

The mother's attitude is harder to understand. She was a youngish woman who still claimed to be attractive. At the time her youngest son was three years old. She gave the impression that she was over-indulgent toward him and her two other sons. She was not nearly as incensed by her daughter's infatuation as was her husband. She did not take it tragically, and even enjoyed her daughter's confidence regarding her passion. She was mostly concerned about her daughter's reputation, since the girl made no effort to hide her feelings when in public. Furthermore, the girl was not ill in any way. Her genital chastity was preserved; she and her lover had not enjoyed anything beyond a few kisses.

Freud accepted the case with misgivings and expressed his reservations to the parents in regard to the success of the treatment. In the first place, the patient was not neurotic and she did not regard her condition as pathological. She entered analysis only to please her parents. She herself did not experience any conflict and did not wish to change. She said that she would honestly try to assist the therapy for her parent's sake, for it pained her to cause them so much grief, but she could not conceive of any other way of being in love. Secondly, Freud knew that converting one variety of genital formation into another, such as homosexuality into heterosexuality

> ...is in my experience never an easy matter. On the contrary, I have found success possible only in specially favourable circumstances, and even then the success essentially consisted in making access to the opposite sex (which had hitherto been barred) possible to a person restricted to homosexuality, thus restoring his full bisexual functions. After that it lay with him to choose whether he wished to abandon the path that is banned by society, and in some cases he has done so....In general, to undertake to convert a fully developed homosexual into a heterosexual does not offer much more prospect of success than the reverse, except that for good practical reasons the latter is never attempted.
>
> (Psychogenesis of a CAse of Homosexuality in a Woman, 1920, S.E. XVIII, p. 147)

A more favorable prognosis is possible only when the homosexual fixation has not yet become strong enough or where there is evidence of rudiments and vestiges of a heterosexual object choice "...in a still oscillating or in a definitely bisexual organization."

Analysis did not uncover anything unusual in the young woman's history. She passed through a normal Oedipal complex, and later turned to a brother, slightly older than herself, as a substitute. She compared her brother's genitals with her own, and this left a strong impression on her and some after-effects. The birth of a second bother when she was between five and six years old seemed to have had no special effect upon her development. She learned about the facts of sex during her prepubertal years at school from her peers, in a way that might be called normal and in no way seemed exaggerated. The amount of information gathered seemed meager and the analysis was broken off after a short time. Furthermore, the girl had never been neurotic and she came to analysis without ever having had a hysterical symptom, making it difficult for an investigation of her early life.

At about fourteen years old she developed a tender, exaggeratedly strong affection for a small boy whom she would see in a children's playground and in consequence she enjoyed a lasting friendship with the boy's parents. Freud deduced from this that at this time she felt a strong desire to be a mother herself and to have a child. However, shortly after that she grew indifferent to the boy and began to take an interest in mature, but still youthful women. This led to severe chastisement from her father.

The change in her occurred simultaneously with a particular event within the family which, beyond all doubt, provides some of the explanation for the change. At a time when her Oedipus complex was at its height, when all her desires were directed at her father, her mother, her rival, became pregnant and gave birth to her third brother.

> The position of affairs which I shall now proceed to lay bare is not a product of my inventive powers; it is based on such trustworthy analytic evidence that I can claim objective validity for it. It was in particular a series of dreams, inter-related and easy to interpret, that decided me in favour of its reality.
>
> (Ibid. p. 156)

Analysis revealed that her lady love was a substitute for her mother. The especially intense bond she felt for her had still another basis. The lady's slender figure, exceptional beauty, and even her manner, reminded her of her older brother. Therefore, her object choice combined satisfaction of both her homosexual and heterosexual tendencies.

> It is well known that analysis of male homosexuals has in numerous cases revealed that same combination, which should warn us not to form too simple a conception of the nature and genesis of inversion, and to keep in mind the universal bisexuality of human beings.
>
> (Ibid. p. 156)

The information gathered so far is puzzling. At a time whe she herself was mature (she was sixteen years old) enough to have strong wishes to be a mother, why would she give up desires for a man to bestow her passion on the woman who had given birth—her own mother? Adolescent girls usually feel embarrassed if their mothers get pregnant; many feel a mixture of contempt, envy, and compassion, but not an increased tenderness. Why should her passion for her mother flare up at this time?

It was just when the patient was re-experiencing her infantile wishes to have a child, a male child, and from the FATHER, that her unconsciously hated rival, her mother, gave birth to a boy child from HIM. This information came directly from the patient in analysis. Resentful, embittered, she turned away from her father and from all men. She would never be betrayed again. She renounced womanhood and redirected the aim of her libido; its original course was diverted.

Hers was an extreme case: it was as though she changed into a man and took her mother in place of her father, as her lov object. Another dynamic emerged from the analysis: revenge. She had an overpowering wish to displease, frustrate, and defy her father. "Since you betrayed me, I will make you suffer." She would walk in the streets near her father's business in the company of her beloved, as if openly to defy and embarrass him. The father behaved as though he understood his daughter's unconscious; he would become enraged, as if he knew he was the target of her revenge.

She had adopted a characteristically masculine attitude toward a love object: idealization. She experienced bliss if she were allowed to accompany her lady a little way or to kiss her hand. Far from being repelled by the bad reputation of her sweetheart,she found that reputation a necessary prerequisite for her love. When she learned that her loved one made a living by giving her body to men, her reaction was compassion. She formed plans for "rescuing" her lover from these circumstances. To complete the pattern, when she found that her beloved belonged to and lived with someone else, this did not arouse feelings of jealousy.

On the day of the suicide attempt (which Freud regarded as seriously intended), she was walking with her lady at a time when she was likely to meet her father returning from his office. And so it happened. He glowered at her and her companion but kept on walking. She confessed to her friend that the man who had cast the furious look at them was her father, and that he strongly opposed their friendship. The lady got angry and insisted that the girl leave her immediately and never try to see her again, to cease waiting for her, nor ever address her on the street. The girl was crushed. She had lost her loved one. There was no point in living. Further investigation, as one might expect, uncovered two other motives besides the loss of her loved one: the fulfillment of a punishment and the fulfillment of a wish. The latter, the wish, takes us deep into the unconscious, to a depth where anyone unacquainted with the workings of the unconscious would doubt the plausibility of the analysis. It was the one that had been frustrated and driven her to homosexuality in the first place: to have a child by her father. Psychoanalysts have long known that various methods of suicide can represent the unconscious fulfillment of a sexual fantasy. In Freud's original test there is a play on the word *niederkommen*, which means both "to fall" and "to be delivered of a child."

In the unconscious, in the primary process, no distinction is made between the symbol and the thing the symbol represents, just as no distinction is made between a thought and a deed, a word and an action, reality and nonreality. In fact, the origin of all guilt is the taboo, the unacceptable wish, not a deed or an action, merely a thought. The original sin is an unconscious fantasy that did not reach consciousness.

The lady spoke to her just the way her father did, angrily and voicing similar prohibitions. This provided the connection between the girl's superficial, conscious reason for leaping onto the railway tracks and the much deeper unconscious motive. The girl had developed strong unconscious death wishes concerning her parents.

> For the analysis had explained the enigma of suicide in the following way: probably no one finds the mental energy required to kill himself unless, in the first place, in doing so he is at the same time killing an object with whom he has identified himself, and in the second place, is turning against himself a death-wish which had been directed against someone else. Nor need the regular discovery of these unconscious death-wishes in those who have attempted suicide surprise us...since the unconscious of all human beings is full enough of such death-wishes, discovery that several quite different motives, all of great strength, must have cooperated to make such a deed possible is only in accordance with what we should expect.
> (Ibid. p. 162)

In the girl's conscious explanation her father was not even mentioned. In the motives uncovered by analysis, however, he played the principal part. Her feelings for her father had the same importance for the ineffectiveness of her analysis. For, behind her pretended consideration for her parents, lay a determined effort to take revenge and punish her father. The analysis proceeded without any resistance, without emotional commitment in the treatment; in short, it was for her an intellectual exercise. Freud saw that she had transferred her repudiation of her father and all men to himself, and that his "negative transference" could manifest itself by her rendering all his efforts futile.

> As soon, therefore, as I recognized the girl's attitude to her father, I broke off treatment and advised her parents that if they set store by the therapeutic procedure it should be continued by a woman doctor. The girl had in the meanwhile promised her father that at any rate she would give up seeing the "lady" and I do not know whether my advice, the reasons for which are obvious, will be followed.
> (Ibid. p. 164)

A psychoanalysis passes through two clearly distinguishable phases. In the first phase, the analyst is the more active one. He makes the patient familiar with the rules and procedures of the treatment. He seeks necessary information from the analysand, he informs him of some of the postulates and premises of psychoanalysis, he interprets material and calls to the patient's attention the meanings of some of his conflicts. In the second phase, it is the patient who takes charge of the work. He recalls what he can of long forgotten memories, he tries to re-experience early events in his life, he confirms and adds to inferences made by the analyst and eventually he attains the convictions necessary to make him independent of the analyst's authority. He finally experiences himself as an adult. Freud gave as an analogy the two stages of a journey. The first one comprises the complicated preparations—passports, visas, tickets, etc. Even when the traveler has finally taken his seat on the train, he is not one step nearer his destination. Nevertheless, he has done what is essential in order for the trip to take place. The journey itself may well be compared to the second phase of the analysis.

In the above case, the first stage was successfully carried out. Both the patient and Freud obtained clear information and insight into the nature and genesis of her condition. It was not continued beyond the beginning of the second phase.

In discussing the analysis, Freud made some interesting comments on a limitation of psychoanalysis. In this case, as with many others, he was confident that he could understand the steps that led to the final condition. Provided, however, he could start with the end product and trace back the determining events. He was very clear that were he to proceed in the opposite direction, from the beginning to the end product, he would enjoy no such certainty. Again and again one can see that important aetiological events might have led to several different outcomes. (As he mentioned in the above paper, not all adolescent girls, re-experiencing their infantile Oedipus, turn to homosexuality if they suffer a bitter frustration.) Why one solution is chosen rather than another is usually far from clear. Understanding the problem is simple enough. We have difficulty predicting the outcome of a conflict, because we have no way of measuring, no way of quantifying the strength of psychological "forces." In short, our understanding of psychology is qualitative rather than quantitative.

There is no record of whether this patient ever sought further psychoanalytic treatment.

CHAPTER LIII

Mute Submission

In the first month of 1920, Freud was struck by two heart-breaking blows: the death of a friend and the death of a daughter. He was prepared for one, though not resigned; the other came as a complete shock. Anton von Freund, philanthropist, doctor of philosophy, and a charming, well-liked man, developed, at the age of thirty-nine, a cancerous tumor. This made necessary the removal by surgery of a testicle. The trauma was too much for him and he developed a severe neurosis. He moved to Vienna, underwent an analysis with Freud for a year, and was apparently completely cured.

Freud and von Freund and their families became warm friends and spent a holiday together. But in March 1919 suspicious signs reappeared in the abdominal region. This time the fear was cancer. For months his friends hoped for the best, but an exploratory surgical operation left no doubt: the condition was malignant. The patient's state speedily grew worse. Abraham, who was fond of von Freund, asked Freud whether von Freund knew of his condition and the approaching end—so that Abraham would know in what terms to write to him. Freud replied that von Freund knew everything.

Von Freund was one of the people to whom Freud had given a ring—he was a member of the "Committee." Von Freund gave orders that after his death the ring be returned to Freud so that he in turn could give it to Eitingon who was to take his place. Later, when the widow refused to return the ring, Freud gave Eitingon the one that he himself always wore.

When he became convinced that he faced death soon, van Freund turned his thoughts to philanthropic plans for disposing of his fortune, and decided that a portion should go to the furthering of psychoanalysis. Freud visited the dying man every day and with pain saw "Toni" wasted by the devouring cancer. The end came on January 2, 1920. Freud said that von Freund died heroically, but he himself felt the death as a severe personal blow. He said it was a contributing factor to his own aging.

Three days after the death, on the very evening of von Freund's funeral, came news that Freud's daughter Sophie, age twenty-five, had fallen seriously ill with influenza. In 1918 a flu epidemic was ravaging a malnourished Europe, claiming almost as many lives as the war had. Sophie was living in Hamburg with her husband and two children, but since no trains were leaving Vienna for Germany, it was impossible to reach her. Her brothers, Oliver and Ernst, who lived in Berlin, left for Hamburg immediately, along with Eitingon. They arrived too late—Sophie was already dead. It was two days before a telegram to Freud announced the death. Before the disease, she had been in perfect health and happy with her family. Freud had once described her as "a china doll."

> We had been worried about her for two days, but were still hopeful.... We could not, as we wished to, go to her at once when the first alarming news came, because there were no trains.... The undisguised brutality of our time weighs heavily on us. Our poor Sunday child is to be cremated tomorrow....
>
> Sophie leaves behind two boys, one aged six and the other thirteen months, and an inconsolable husband who will have to pay dearly for the happiness of these seven years. The happiness was only between them, not in external circumstances, which were war and war service, being wounded and losing their money, but they remained brave and cheerful....
>
> (Pfister, Jan. 27, 1920)

Postwar Austria barely functioned, even the postal service was uncertain. Freud wrote to his son-in-law Max, gave the letter to a friend who took it to Berlin and there posted it to Hamburg.

> It seems to me that I have never written anything more superfluous than this.... But I won't try to comfort you, just as you cannot comfort us. I need not tell you that this misfortune does not change anything in my feelings towards you and that you remain our son as long as you wish to do so. It goes without saying that this follows from our earlier relationship.... It is a senseless brutal act of fate which has taken our Sophie from us, something that one cannot wrack one's brain about, a blow under which we have to bow our heads, poor helpless human beings that we are. I think she was happy as long as she was with you, despite the difficult times of your short seven year marriage, and her happiness was due to you.
>
> Mama is completely broken. She wants to visit you as soon as possible but the nearest date would be the 29th. She wants to know what your plans are regarding the children and your household in the immediate future. I would prefer it if Math(ilde) and Robert (her husband) came to you instead of her as I am not too confident of her strength.... I am also glad that Oliver and Ernst can be close to you and most of all that we all met in the autumn.
>
> Kiss both the boys for their grandfather. Take courage. With the most heartfelt greetings from Papa.
>
> (Clark, p. 402)

The day after receiving the telegram about beloved Sophie, Freud learned that Jones's father had cancer.

> Poor unhappy Toni Freund was buried last Thursday....Sorry to hear your father is on the list now, but we all must and I wonder when my turn will come. Yesterday I lived throught an experience which makes me wish it should not last a long time.
> (Jones 3, p. 19)

Freud wrote to Ferenczi and Pfister using phrases like, "She was blown away as if she had never been"; "It is such a paralyzing event"; "Blunt necessity, mute submission"; "For years I was prepared for the loss of my sons, now comes that of my daughter. Since I am profoundly irreligious there is no one I can accuse."

Two weeks later, he heard of the death of Jones's father: "So your father was not to hold out until he got devoured piece-meal by his cancer as poor Freund was. What good fortune. Yet you will soon find out what it means to you. I was about your age when my father died and it revolutionized my soul. Can you remember a time so full of death as this?"[1]

Prior to these two grievous blows that fate delivered to Freud, he had been working on theoretical questions. His period of mourning was finally ended by a return to work. The hypotheses that he was then to submit for serious consideration stunned the world of psychoanalysis.

---

[1]Shur, p. 318

CHAPTER LIV

■ *Death, The Aim Of Life*

As the law of gravity was supposedly inspired by Newton's seeing an apple fall from a tree, so the pleasure principle was dramatically modified by the observation of a child's game. The child was Freud's daughter Sophie's eldest son. At the time of the observation he was eighteen months old. Though he was a pleasant, untroubled child, he baffled everyone by his habit of throwing toys under his bed. This pastime was accompanied by a long-drawn-out "o-o-o-" with an intense expression of interest and satisfaction.

> His mother and the writer of the present account were agreed in thinking that this was not a mere interjection but represented the German word "fort" (gone). I eventually realized that it was a game and that the only use he made of any of his toys was to play "gone" with them. One day I made an observation which confirmed my view. The child had a wooden reel with a piece of string tied round it. It never occurred to him to pull it along the floor behind him, for instance, and play at its being a carriage. What he did was to hold the reel by the string and very skillfully throw it over the edge of his curtained cot, so that it disappeared into it, at the same time uttering his expressive "o-o-o-." He then pulled the reel out of the cot again by the string and hailed its reappearance with a joyful "da" (there). This, then, was the complete game—disappearance and return. As a rule one only witnessed its first act, which was repeated untiringly as a game in itself, though there is no doubt that the greater pleasure was attached to the second act.
>
> (Beyond the Pleasure Principle, 1920, S.E. XVIII, p. 14-15)

What did it all mean? Freud thought the real represented mother, and its disappearance and reappearance represented her departure and return. Since her departure was always painful, the game, with its emphasis on the disappearance, involved deliberately choosing a painful event. The recurrent game made an important impression of Freud; so much so, that four years later when he wrote "Beyond the Pleasure Principle," he made it the starting point of his arguments.

Of all that Freud has written, "Beyond the Pleasure Principle" is the only publication that met with resistance in analytic circles. Nothing else compares with it in this respect. The book deals with ultimate questions: the origin of life and the nature of death. It seems as though Freud had no audience in mind beyond himself; his hope was to clarify some long-standing problems. He covers a wide range of subjects and proceeds to a conclusion through reason to the concept of the death instinct.

> I am writing the new essay...and count on your understanding which has never failed me. Much of what I am saying in it is pretty obscure, and the reader must make what he can of it. Sometimes one cannot do otherwise. Still I hope you will find much in it that is interesting.
> (Ferenczi, Mar. 31, 1919)

Freud made a curious request of Eitingon. After he had read the manuscript, Freud asked him to bear witness that it had been half completed while his daughter Sophie was still in good health. Freud had anticipated that many people would draw the inference that the essay was inspired by his mourning for Sophie and, indeed, its critics do point to the connection.

In this work, Freud departed from his usual method of observation and inductive reasoning. The "often far-fetched" speculations in "Beyond the Pleasure Principle," despite their hypothetical character, try to wed psychoanalysis and experimental biology. The essay led as we have said, to the theory of the death instinct. He presented his startling ideas in a highly tentative fashion. Later, however, he came to accept them entirely.

He begins by restating the unpleasure/pleasure principle: tension within the organism is experienced as unpleasure, pain; the release of tension is experienced as pleasure. The unpleasure/pleasure mechanism is unconscious. According to this theory, the aim of the organism is to reduce tensions whether induced by internal or external stimuli. The wish to eliminate tension is in the service of the "nirvana principle."

The concept is in accord with the whole theory of wish fulfilment: impulses seek discharge and gratification, then recede. However, the correlation between increased tension and unpleasure, and between relief and pleasure is not as close as had been assumed. The experience of the war neuroses was a flagrant violation of the rule. Also, the pleasure obtained from an increase in sexual tension raised fundamental questions.

Freud describes the child's game referred to above and reminds us of the fondness children show for the repetition of stories and games, without consideration of whether they are pleasurable or not. He then makes one of his startling inductive leaps: maybe there is a principle independent of the unpleasure/pleasure principle and maybe it is something like a "repetition compulsion"? He offers a number of phenomena which seem to fit this conception—the recurrent nightmares of war neurotics, in which the original trauma is revived and relived again and again; the repetitive self-injuring behavior that can be traced through the lives of some people, and the tendency of patients to re-experience, again and again during analysis, the painful moments of childhood.

The early blossoming of infantile sexual life is doomed to failure: its wishes are incompatible with reality. The experience of failure and loss of love is accompanied by the most painful of feelings. The consequence may be a narcissistic scar, a "sense of inferiority," so common in neurotics. The patient's complaint: "I can't accomplish anything; I can't succeed in anything" is frequently the residue of the above process. The child's affection for his parent of the opposite sex leads to disappointment. The birth of a new baby is unmistakable proof of the infidelity of the child's object of affection. His own wish to make a baby fails. Increasing demands and occasional punishments show him the full extent to which he has been scorned. The question that forces itself upon us is why we unconsciously repeat our painful history? Why does one still cling to infantile wishes that make one feel inferior, inadequate, a failure? True, neurotics suffer from reminiscences, but why re-experience the anguish? Why not forget about it? Or outgrow it? Why not adopt an attitude that says (to paraphrase St. Paul): when I was a child I needed childish things, but now that I'm an adult....?

Patients revive these painful emotions in the transference, sometimes with remarkable ingenuity. They try to accomplish with the analyst what they failed to achieve with their parents. Of course it fails again.

The compulsion to repeat can be observed in the lives of normal people. Often one gets the impression that some people are victims of fate. The woman whose love affairs always turn out badly. The man whose friendships always end in betrayal. The person who never achieves economic security.

A woman patient was married to an alcoholic. He was her third husband; the other two had also been alcoholics. She insisted that prior to marriage, she had had no idea that they were addicts. After her analysis she married a fourth time, a nonalcoholic.

> If we take into account observations such as these, based upon behaviour in the transference and upon the life-histories of men and women, we shall find courage to assume that there really does exist in the mind a compulsion to repeat which overrides the pleasure principle.
>
> (Beyond the Pleasure Principle, p. 22)

Freud freely admits that what follows is speculation, often far-fetched. It is an attempt to pursue an idea consistently, out of curiosity to see where it will lead.

> At this point we cannot escape a suspicion that we may have come upon the track of a universal attribute of instincts and perhaps of organic life in general which has not hitherto been clearly recognized or at least not explicitly stressed. It seems, then, that an instinct is an urge inherent in organ life to restore an earlier state of things which the living entity has been obliged to abandon under the pressure of external disturbing forces....
>
> (Ibid. p. 36)

Freud offers examples from animal life which seem to confirm the view that instincts are historically determined. Certain fish undertake laborious migrations at spawning time, and the migratory flights of birds suggest the same principle.

> but we are quickly relieved of the necessity for seeking for further examples by the reflection that the most impressive proofs of there being an organic compulsion to repeat lie in the phenomena of heredity and the facts of embryology. We see how the germ of a living animal is obliged in the course of its development to recapitulate (even if only in a transient and abbreviated fashion) the structures of all forms from which it is sprung, instead of proceeding quickly by the shortest path to its final shape.
>
> (Ibid. p. 37)

This drive—to return to an earlier state, whether pleasurable or not—Freud now considered as more fundamental than the pleasure principle. If the instinct aims at the past, why should it stop before reducing matter to its previous inorganic state?

> If we are to take it as a truth that knows no exception that everything living dies for internal reasons—becomes inorganic once again—then we shall be compelled to say that "the aim of life is death" and looking backwards, that "inanimate things existed before living ones."
>
> (Ibid. p. 38)

A force, whose nature we can hardly conceive, once acted somehow upon inanimate matter to create the features of life. It may have, perhaps, been similar to the process that later caused the development of consciousness in a particular stratum of living matter.

> The tension which then arose in what had hitherto been an inanimate substance endeavored to cancel itself out. In this way the first instinct came into being; the instinct to return to the inanimate state. It was still an easy matter at that time for a living substance to die....For a long time, perhaps, living substance was thus being constantly created afresh and easily dying, till decisive external influences altered in such a way as to oblige the still surviving substance to diverge ever more widely from its original course of life and to make ever more complicated detours before reaching its aim of death. These circuitous paths to death, faithfully kept to by the conservative instincts, would thus present us today with the picture of the phenomena of life. If we firmly maintain the exclusively conservative nature of instincts, we cannot arrive at any other notions as the origin and aim of life.
>
> (Ibid. p. 38-39)

Freud did not limit his concept to mental phenomena but extended it to the whole of living nature and indeed to the whole universe as well. Sooner or later, all matter decays and dissolves, and all systems eventually run down. His concept is cosmic. Imagine his scorn when a communist announced that the death instinct was merely a by-product of the degenerate capitalistic system?

The instinct for self-preservation—does that oppose the death instinct? Freud says no. The only function of self-preservation is to ensure that the organism will die according to inner law and not through any avoidable circumstances. In this sense, the instinct for self preservation proves to be the servant of the death instinct. Is Freud slipping away from a dualistic to a monistic view of life? Even the famous pleasure principle, the need to reduce tension and excitation, is a handmaiden of the death instinct, the extinction of all stimuli and excitation—death.

The sexual instincts—do they oppose the death instinct? True, they are conservative and obey the repetition compulsion and the nirvana principle, but they do so in a way peculiar to themselves. Like the death instinct they return life to its earliest forms of being. As male and female gametes, they unite and start the process of organic development all over again. They thereby have the merit of indefinitely postponing the goal of the death drive. By warding off the latter they give the organism time to develop multicellular organisms which are better able to withstand threats from external destructive forces.

So Freud dexterously re-established his dualism. The sexual instinct constitutes a second, independent driving force in life. His final instinct theory postulates two opposing forces in the mind: the life instincts, called Eros, and the death instincts. Freud used the terms "death instinct" and "destructive instinct" synonymously (though later in his discussions with Einstein about war he made a distinction.) The destructive drive is the death instinct directed outward. A man preserves his life by directing the self-destructive tendencies outward toward other people, much as a government may deflect rebellious or revolutionary impulses toward a foreign power. The signs of the death instinct are to be found in the cruelties of life.

> It may be asked whether and how far I am myself convinced of the truth of the hypotheses that have been set out in these pages. My answer would be that I am not convinced myself and that I do not seek to persuade other people to believe in them. Or, more precisely, that I do not know how far I believe in them. There is no reason, as it seems to me, why the emotional factor of conviction should enter into this question at all.
>
> (Ibid. p. 59)

Very few psychoanalysts today are adherents of the death instinct theory. And Freud? "In the course of time they have gained such a hold upon me that I can no longer think in any other way."[1]

---

[1]*Civilization and Its Discontents*, 1930

CHAPTER LV

■ *Helpless Horror*

Freud was now sixty-five years old and he grew increasingly conscious of age and death. He said that seven of his internal organs were fighting to have the honor of bringing his life to an end. Yet, during his vacation, when he played host to many visitors, including the entire Committee, he impressed others with the energy of his daily walking expeditions in the mountains. He seemed as swift and tireless as ever.

In April 1921, a son was born to Martin and in July came Ernst's first son. Freud now had four grandsons. He was heard to express a wish for granddaughters.

An incident occurred in New York that was a scandal within the profession and threatened to spread to the public. Of all the Americans who had come to study with him, Freud considered Horace W. Frink the most brilliant and promising. His *Morbid Fears and Compulsions* was at that time the best psychoanalytic textbook in English. Frink was a man of charm and culture as well as being an excellent clinician. He served two terms as president of the New York Psychoanalytic Society.

Then he fell in love with one of his patients. Both he and the patient were unhappily married and they made plans to get divorced so they could marry each other. But the patient's husband was outraged that his wife had fallen in love with her analyst and threatened a scandal that would have ruined Frink. Freud, whom Frink consulted, took the position that it was always a mistake to fall in love with a patient, but since it had happened, it had to be accepted. Then while Frink was in Vienna, his lover's husband died, and shorftly thereafter Frink's own wife died. Wild rumors circulated in New York, including one that Freud himself was planning to marry the lady. Frink was married for only a short time when he broke down with a serious mental illness. He put himself under the care of Adolph Meyer, a famous psychiatrist at Johns Hopkins. But he never recovered and died in the Chapel Hill Mental Hosptial, a victim of a manic psychosis. To Freud the loss of Frink and of Putnam was very serious to the psychoanalytic movement in America.

The latter part of 1922 Freud devoted to attempting to integrate his new theory of instinctual drives, as formulated in "Beyond the Pleasure Principle." He postulated there were three "provinces" of the mind: the id, the ego, and the superego. How they functioned in relation to the death instinct and the life instinct was presented in *The Ego and the Id*. The book was published in April 1923, the very month that Freud's cancer was diagnosed.

In February Freud, now sixty-seven years old, had become aware of a growth on his jaw and palate. He did nothing about it, and mentioned it to no one, neither family or friends. Although many of his friends were physicians, there was no one whom he saw on a regular basis. About mid-April he finally consulted Max Steiner.

Steiner must have recognized the lesion for what it was, because he recommended an excision. However he told Freud it was only a leucoplakia and advised him to give up smoking. That was the first of a long series of deceptions that had far-reaching effects. Abstinence from tobacco was much more threatening to Freud than surgery. He suspected that he had an epithelioma.* That week when Felix Deutsch visited Freud to discuss some private matters, Freud said to him: "Be prepared to see somthing you won't like." Deutsch, at the very first glance, recognized a lesion in an advanced stage of cancer. He was shocked. Freud upset him further by expressing misgivings about dying before his mother who was then eighty-seven years old. He said that she would find the news of his death unbearable. He then added that he wished to "disappear from the world with decency," and that he might require Deutsch's help. Deutsch later said that he didn't regard Freud's request as a suicide threat, rather as a plea for help in sparing him the suffering of a painful and hopeless cancer.

Deutsch was caught by surprise. He decided not to mention cancer and pronounced it as a simple leukoplakia which should be removed, the sooner the better. Freud suggested that Professor Marcus Hajek do the surgery, even though he felt that the man had mixed feelings toward him. Deutsch left the decision in Freud's hands.

After much urging from Duetsch not to delay consulting a surgeon, Freud arranged to see Hajek. He too said the trouble was a leukoplakia, but when Freud asked a question, he evaded him and answered, "No one can expect to live forever."[1] He advised Freud to come to his out-patient clinic one morning because the growth should be removed. It is unknown to what extent Freud believed in the benign diagnosis he kept hearing.

After thinking about the matter for a few days, Freud quietly turned up at Hajek's clinic. It was not a private hospital, but part of a general teaching hospital attached to the University. It had no private wards; in fact facilities were as wanting as in the out-patient wards of old New York hospitals. Characteristically, Freud said nothing of his visit to anyone at home. Deutsch accompanied him to the clinic, but did not stay. This was to be the first of thirty-three operations.

The operation did not go well, the loss of blood was so serious that it was inadvisable to let the patient go home. The family was notified by a telephone call from the clinic requesting that someone bring night clothes for Freud, because he had to stay in the hospital overnight. A Stunned Martha and Anna rushed over and found him sitting on a kitchen chair in the out-patient department covered with blood. A bed was "rigged up" for him in a small room in which the other bed was occupied by a cretinous dwarf. At lunch time visitors were not allowed, so the two ladies left after being assured that the patient would be all right.

Shortly after they left, Freud had an attack of profuse bleeding. He rang for help, but the bell was out of order. He couldn't speak or call out. The dwarf (who had been labeled imbecilic) saw that Freud was choking on blood, rushed to secure a nurse, and stayed with him until a doctor arrived. After much difficulty the bleeding was stopped. The dwarf had probably saved Freud's life. Once again, when visiting hours were over, the nurses assured Martha and Anna that the patient would be all right, but this time Anna refused to leave. She spent the night at her father's

---

*cancerous tumors on the skin

[1]Jones 3, p. 90

side. He was very weak from loss of blood, heavily drugged, but nonetheless in great pain. During the night, the nurse and Anna became alarmed at his condition and called the house surgeon, who refused to get out of bed. The next morning Hajek demonstrated the case before a class of students. That afternoon Freud was allowed to go home. It must be mentioned that the Low Sanatorium, a luxurious private hospital, was just one block away. When one of Freud's patients, Frau Emma, had hemorrhaged, Freud had taken her there.

Three puzzles immediately present themselves to the mind: Hajek's behavior, Deutsch's behavior, and Freud's.

Dr. Hajek's perfunctory attitude is hard to understand. He knew the seriousness of the case, yet he acted with complete irresponsibility. It is possible that he thought he had done everything that could be done and that the growth would not recur; or perhaps he believed that the case was hopeless and he was just going through the motions. But he neglected procedures which would have made it easier for Freud to bear. How could he perform such surgery on an ambulatory basis, then leave Freud without proper medical and nursing care? Such behavior is inexcusable even for a patient who is not a personal friend, and incidentally a world-famous figure.

Hajek also neglected the scar. It shrank and reduced Freud's ability to open his mouth, thereby creating serious obstacles for further treatment. Max Schur, who later became Freud's personal physician, claimed that because the patient was Sigmund Freud, revealer of the uncivilized animal in all of us, an ambivalence arose in Hajek and that this contributed to his treatment of Freud. Another episode may be added to the Hajek dossier. A year after the Freud incident, Franz Kafka was suffering from tubercular laryngitis. He was sent to the hospital by Hajek and the treatment he received outraged the literary world. Franz Werfel, in particular, fought for better treatment for Kafka a separate room, more consideration. "Professor Hajek answered: 'A certain Werfel writes to me that I must do something for a certain Kafka. I know Kafka, he's patient number twelve, but who is Werfel?'"[1]

The hospital incident also raises the issue of Deutsch's decision not to tell Freud what he saw when he examined his throat. Much later Deutsch said it was because he felt Freud was not prepared to face the reality of his condition. There is little evidence to support this. Even if it were so, why did he not share his responsibility with a member of Freud's family, or one of Freud's friends, many of whom were prominent physicians? It has been suggested that it was actually Deutsch who could not face reality. Freud was regarded with reverence by his followers, including Deutsch. Unconsciously, they responded to Freud as to an omnipotent father. To see him as merely human was too threatening; just as a little boy in a particular phase of development cannot see his father realistically. So Deutsch denied what his eyes saw because of his own unconscious conflicts.

And lastly, how can one explain Freud's own behavior? Why did he wait for two months before having his lesion examined? It is easy to see why he did not mention it to his family: whenever he was ill he tried to protect them from worry. But why did he not ask his physician friends for advice in the choice of a surgeon? Could the answer be as simple as what is called fatalism?*

In a letter to two dear friends, Freud wrote:

---

[1]Roberts, p. 341

*Max Schur in *Freud, living and Dying* attempts an exhaustive exploration of the question.

> About my operation and affliction...there is nothing to say....The uncertainty that hovers over a man of sixty-seven has now found its material expression. I don't take it very hard; one will defend oneself for a while with help of modern medicine and then remember Bernard Shaw's warning: "Don't try to live for ever, you will not succeed."
>
> (Eissler/Pctrs, p. 225)

The pathology report of the excised specimen revealed maligant epithelioma. Two X-ray treatments followed and then Freud was turned over to Hajek's assistant for local radium applications. Two uncomfortable facts stand out here: X-ray treatment for this type of malignancy is usually unsuccessful, and radium treatment, outside of Paris and especially in Vienna, was haphazard. The doses must have been too strong, for Freud suffered from toxic effects. Four months later he wrote that he had not known an hour free from pain. The radiation caused tissue damage accompained by acute pain. Still neither Freud nor anyone else had been told the truth.

While recovering from the treament Freud received another blow, the hardest of all, and which had a profound effect upon him for the rest of his life. Sophie's second child, Heinerle (Heinz Rudolf), who was thirteen months old when his mother died, had been taken to Vienna to his aunt Mathilde. No one could overstate the amount of love that his child generated. Mathilde and her husband wanted to adpot him. Freud was in love with him. He said that his love for this delightful, gifted child was greater than any he had ever felt for another person. To Freud he was more than a grandson; Heinerle seemed to stand for all children. He called this elfin boy the most intelligent child he had ever encountered. Heinerle had his tonsils removed at about the same time as Freud's first operation. When the two patients met after their operations, Heinerle said to his grandfather with great interest: "I can already eat crusts. Can you too?"[1] Unfortunately, Heinerle had contracted tuberculosis a year before the surgery and was very delicate, "a bag of bones," weak, never entirely without a temperature. Freud described him as one whose mental development seems to grow at the expense of his physical strength.

The joy that Freud received from this wonderful child was short-lived. Slowly but surely came the realization that Heinerle had a miliary tuberculosis; the enchanting little elf was doomed. Doctors said that at best he would last a week. Freud stood by in helpless horror waiting for the death of his beloved grandson. Heinz Rudolph Haberstadt died on June 19, 1923, at the age of four-and-a-half years. This was the only occasion that Freud was known to have shed tears. Afterwards, on more than one occasion, he said that whereas other tragedies in his life brought him dreadful pain, this loss destroyed something in him for good. Later he told Marie Bonaparte that after the death of Heinerle, he retained feelings for old attachments but he could not feel deep affection for anyone. The blow was more unbearable than his own cancer. Three years later in a letter of condolence to Binswanger, who had lost his eight-year-old son, he said that since Heinerle's death he had lost interest in people and no longer enjoyed life: "It is the secret of my indifference—people call it courage—toward the danger to my own life."[2] Those who knew Freud well said

---

[1]Jones 3, p. 92
[2]Binswanger, Oct. 15, 1926

that he remained intensely fond of his family, his old friendships grew even richer, and he could not have lived without them.

Freud saw Hajek a few times during the months that followed and his reservations about his doctor increased. Hajek was inconsistent. First he raised no objection to Freud's leaving Vienna for the summer; later he startled Freud by requesting that he send him fortnightly reports of his condition. Finally, just when the cancer was reapearing, Hajek said he could go away for the entire season.

While on vacation, recovering from Hajek's operation, Freud received a letter from a young jew, a Mr. Leyens. Leyens had fought in World War I, was an ardent German nationalist, and a follower of Hans Buhler. He was bewildered by the fact that Hans Buhler, a passionate anti-Semite, was at the same time an admirer of Freud. He asked Freud to help him understand this paradox. Freud answered July 4, 1923, that mass psychoses are immune to argument and that he would not waste his time and energy in a fruitless struggle against the current political tide. He added what he personally thought of Buhler. What the Germans might have learned from the World War, they seemed unable to—so let them alone. He suggested that the young man devote himself to things that raise the Jews above all this foolishness, and finally, not to join up with the Germans. Thirteen years later he heard from Leyens again. When the Nazis came, he had fled to America and was writing to tell Freud how right he had been. Freud replied modestly: "You don't really think I am proud at having been right? I was right as a pessimist against the enthusiasts, as an old man against a young one. I wish I had been wrong."[1]

Freud's general discomfort and pain made Anna insist that he invite Deutsch to Lavarone where the family was vacationing. Deutsch, although he was quite uncomfortable with his role in the deception that was still going on, came at once. He recognized the recurrence of the growth and the need for further radical surgery. Once again Deutsch, despite an earlier agreement with Freud, did not explain the situation candidly. He was uncertain. Freud was still in mourning for his grandson; perhaps Freud would not consent to a major operation and would prefer to die. Also, Freud was looking forward to a trip to Rome with his daughter Anna, which Deutsch was most reluctant to spoil. Deutsch decided to consult the Committee, and say nothing to Freud or Anna. At the time the Committee was meeting a half-mile away at San Cristoforo on the same lake. The Committee convened. Rank had already been informed, but the rest were dismayed to learn of the dire situation. The questions discussed were how to convince Freud to undergo an operation and whether an attempt should be made to interrupt the impending trip to Rome. It was at this meeting that Rank attacked Jones and called for his dismissal from the Committee. (See Chapter LVII "His Estate")

While they were discussing Freud's situation, according to Jones's report, Rank broke out in a fit of maniacal laughter. The others looked on in horror at his inability to control himself. A point to be mentioned is that of all the Committee, Rank was by far the most vulnerable, because he was the most dependent on Freud. Rank was not a physician; furthermore, he was so clearly from a lower class, that it was out of the question in class-conscious Vienna for anyone from the middle-class to consult him. His colleagues, who were physicians, were embarrassed to refer patients. Only Freud, who made practically all the referrals anyway, referred patients to him for consultation and therapy. One can see that the effect of Freud's illness would fall more heavily on Rank than on any of the others.

[1]July 25, 1936, Ibid. p. 98

The Committee joined Anna for dinner after the meeting. On the walk back to Lavarone, Anna remarked that if she and her father were enjoying their stay in Rome, they might prolong their visit. At this news, Duetsch became upset and made Anna promise not to lengthen the trip. It was a very broad hint concerning the true state of affairs; it did not escape Anna's attention.

Many years later in London, Jones referred to the meeting and what the Committee had discussed and decided. Freud angrily snapped: "Mit welchem Recht?" (with what right?) As early as 1924, Freud told Ferenczi that from the beginning he was sure his condition was cancerous.

The decision of the Committee not to mar Freud's visit to Rome was both humane and constructive. Freud had already decided after his first operation in April that he would go, as this might be his last opportunity to show his daughter Rome. A terrifying episode took place. During breakfast on the train, a sudden stream of blood squirted from Freud's mouth; a piece of tissue had probably been torn by a hard crust. The looks they gave each other left no doubt in each of their minds of its significance.

In spite of this episode the trip was a success. Freud delighted in showing Anna his favorite places and she responded enthusiastically. To Eitingon he wrote: "Anna was splendid. She understood and enjoyed everything and I was very proud of her." (September 26, 1923)

While Freud was in Rome, Duetsch persuaded the distinguished oral surgeon, Professor Hans Pichler, to take charge of Freud's case. Freud was always to be grateful to him for his excellent choice. And now finally he was told the truth.

During World War I, Pichler had operated on many seriously injured soldiers. Too often he had had to improvise procedures that had never been attempted before. He built up a record of results. He was an ideal choice for Freud's case since a novel plan had to be approached for him. Although unaware of Freud's status in the scientific world, he treated him for fifteen years with kindness, tact, and profound consideration. When Hitler invaded Austria, Pichler did everything he could to protect his patient.

Pichler found Freud's case so difficult that he experimented on a corpse before he made his decision. The surgery on the jaw was performed in two stages: the "minor" one on October 4, and the major one week later. The second operation lasted seven hours. Finally, those parts of the mucous membranes which could not be sutured, were replaced with skin grafts. Pichler then fit a prosthesis in place. This frightful surgery was carried out under local anaesthesia only. For days the patient could not talk nor eat. All this was before the development of antibiotics and intravenous feeding. Nourishment was supplied by nasal tube, fluids through the rectum.

Pichler found that the malignancy had spread to neighboring tissues, including the lower jaw and cheek. He had made careful preparations, including several different models for the prosthesis that the surgery would require. The whole upper jaw and the affected palate had to be removed—a very extensive operation which made the nasal cavity and the mouth into one cavity. A metal prosthesis would serve as an artificial roof for Freud's mouth. For the rest of his life the "monster," Freud's name for the prosthesis, had to be taken out then replaced regularly. Unfortunately, it caused inflammation so the removals had to be frequent. But, if it were out for more than a few hours, the scar tissue would shrink and the monster would no longer fit. It almost always involved pain. Too often Dr. Pichler had to be summoned to reinsert or remove it.

Pichler's notes about the operation concluded with "The only mistake is that perhaps more of the internal pterygoid muscle should have been removed." His professionalism is awesome. He kept his eye on the spot where he felt enough tissue might not have been removed. Ten days after the operation, his suspicions were confirmed: on that very spot he noticed a tiny necrotic part of the graft. It proved malignant. At this point most surgeons would have given up, but both Freud and Pichler showed their mettle. Pichler told Freud that whole truth and recommended immediate further surgery. The operation was performed the same afternoon, again under local anaesthesia. "There was a further resection of the mandible and the soft tissues, with considerable blood loss. Only now was Pichler satisfied."[1] Thirteen years would pass before the appearance of new malignant cells.

Freud made, on the whole, a good recovery. On October 28 he went home. Awaiting him was the news that Maria, the wife of his half-brother Emanuel, had died. He had known her since childhood days in Freiberg. In a letter to Samuel he wrote that "the distressing news does away with another part of the cherished past."[2]

For the next sixteen years, Freud would know pain, discomfort, and distress interrupted only by further operations either to remove precancerous tissue or to adjust the prosthesis. "There were sixteen entries in Pichler's notes for the remainder of 1923 and seventy-four in 1924."[3]

Those who know German tell us of the beauty of Freud's style of his mastery of the language. In fact, the only international award he received was the Goethe prize for literary achievement. His delivery of the spoken word was "an equally unique experience."[4] But from this time on his speech was defective and he never again spoke in public. Eating was difficult and he preferred to take his meals alone. Damage done to the Eustachian tube, plus the infection of the area, made him almost deaf on one side, the side on which he was accustomed to listen to patients. The position of his chair had to be reversed.

From now to the end, Freud would have no other nurse than his daughter Anna. They made a pact that there was to be no sentimental nonsense. She was to perform her duties with all the professionalism characteristic of a surgeon. Despite the most agonizing situations, Anna never broke the pact.

Some years later, Deutsch assured Freud that, given the same circumstances, he would have done things similarly. Freud did not agree. He did not doubt that Deutsch had acted from the best motives and in good faith, but the implication was that Freud couldn't stand a painful truth. This was a trait he counted among his virtues. Characteristically, their disagreement did not stand in the way of friendly feelings toward each other.

Freud had been unable to work for six months. Now, due to the expenses of his illness (he insisted on paying all his doctors their full fee), Freud returned to work as soon as he felt able. Starting on January 2, 1924, sixty-eight years old, he resumed his routine of six patients a day. But his difficulty in talking made this tiring. In March he suffered an attack of influenzal nasal catarrh. For the first time in his medical career, he did not work that Saturday and Sunday. He was permitted

---

[1]Schur, p. 363
[2]Clark, p. 445
[3]Schur, p. 366
[4]Ibid. p. 365

to smoke and it was a source of comfort to him. However, in order to get the cigar between his teeth, he had to pry his mouth open with a wooden clothespin.

Although Freud's illness was cutting down his daily work as a psychoanalyst, interest in psychoanalysis itself was growing. Freud and psychoanalysis were coming to the attention of professionals, scientists, and intellectuals as well as the popular press. "L'Encephale," the leading French neurological journal, requested photographs of Freud to be published with a full exposition of his work. Andre Gide as one of the directiors of the Nouvelle Revue Francaise sought permission to publish his writings. A French journalist interviewed him and described him as an old rabbi straight from Palestine, who played with ideas the way the Oriental plays with his beads.[1] A weekly magazine in London, The Sphere, actually published photographs of him. The *Verlag* was busy negotiating for various translations of his work. In Moscow two thousand copies of the "introductory Lectures" were sold in one month. When an offer came from China, Freud wondered whether his theories would prove more intelligible in that language than in the original. He complained that his increasing popularity was becoming a burden. Keeping up with his correspondence and writing to decline offers from periodicals to write on a variety of subjects, took away time and energy from scientific work.

Popularity is frequently accompanied by vulgarity. For example, Freud received several offers from the United States to pyschoanalyze two youths from Chicago: Leopold and Loeb, who were being tried for what they described as "the perfect murder." Of course Freud refused. Hearst offered him any sum he would name, and when he heard that Freud was ill, offered to charter a private liner so he could travel undisturbed by others.

Freud was particularly pleased and interested in a message from New York reporting that John Barrymore was basing his performance of Hamlet on psychoanalytic insights. One might guess what some of Freud's thoughts were when he heard that an idea about Hamlet that had occurred to him more than twenty years ago, during his self-analysis, was now actually being portrayed on the stage.

When Freud's serious illness became known around Vienna, gestures of friendliness were not lacking. A laudatory article on him was published in the *Neue Freie Presse*. A Social Democratic majority dominated the City Council and bestowed upon him on his birthday the Burgerecht of Vienna, an honor similar to the British "Freedom of the City."

After receiving congratulations for his sixty-eight birthday from Lou Andreas-Salome, he wrote to her (May 13, 1924):

> I have admired your art work more than ever this time. Here is a person who, instead of working hard into old age...and then dying without preliminaries, contracts a horrible disease in middle age, has to be treated and operated on, squanders his hard-earned money, generates and enjoys discontent, and then crawls about for an indefinite period of time as an invalid. In Erewhon (I trust you know Samuel Butler's brilliant phantasy) such an individual would certainly be punished and locked up....And still you can praise me

[1]Jones 3, p. 97

> for bearing my suffering so well. Actually, it isn't quite like this; although I have weathered the awful realities fairly well, it is the possibilities that I find hard to bear; I cannot get accustomed to life under sentence....
>
> Six hours of psychoanalysis, this is all I have retained of my capacity for work; everything else, especially social contact, I keep at bay. (Of course, Romain Rolland, who has announced himself for tomorrow, I cannot refuse....)
>
> Well, I have written this off my chest because we both seem to be prevented from meeting. The number of things one has to renounce! And instead one is overwhelmed with honors (such as the "Freedom of the City of Vienna"), for which one would never have lifted a finger.
>
> (Schur, p. 380)

One consequence of becoming well-known is that one becomes the subject of all sorts of rumors. One story told about Freud is that he had a sex operation. The various versions usually include a trip to Switzerland and "monkey glands." Steinach, an endocrinologist, was the discoverer of the interstitial cells of the testicles which produce the male sex hormone. He hypothesized that tying off the sperm ducts would result in a relative hypertrophy of the hormone-producing cells and result in a "rejuvenation." Since, at the time, cancer was considered part of an aging process, the duct ligation known as "Steinach's rejuvenation operation" was believed to prevent a recurrence of the disease. The operation, which was a very minor procedure, was performed on Freud November 17, 1923. Two years later he told Ferenczi that he perceived no benefits from it.

In addition to his involvement with the psychoanalytic movement and some of its members, and his daily practice, Freud continued to write. "The Economic Problem of Masochism" appeared in April. The revision of his theory of instincts into a life and death instinct had left some serious clinical problems. The masochism paper was his resolution of what he had stirred up in "Beyond the Pleasure Principle." It is a non-clinical, highly theoretical work, and because so much is predicated on the death instinct, it is still controversial.

CHAPTER LVI

■ *The Enemy Is Me*

It is easy enough to understand that human beings seek pleasure. But what is one to say about those who seem to seek pain? The contradiction between the wish to suffer and the pleasure principle seems incomprehensible.

Analytic experience shows that many people are unconsciously compelled to do things contrary to their best interests; indeed a large class of people, known as masochistic, unconsciously cling to a pattern of suffering. If pain and unpleasure actually become aims, some mysterious force is at work.

Are there people who really enjoy pain, suffering, humiliation, self defeat? Analytic examination reveals that sought after pain is not experienced as pleasurable, but as necessary; as an alternative to anxiety. Over-simplified the masochist formula reads: success leads to anxiety; failure leads to relief.

Prior to the paper "The Economic Problem of Masochism" (economic refers to the quantity of the drives in question), masochism was understood as sadism directed towards the self. Hostile-erotic energy originally aimed at an object is redirected; what was once sadism is inverted and is experienced as masochism. The dynamics of hurting the self depended on the particular individual in question, but the condition always relates to feelings of guilt; a need for punishment.

A woman entered analysis at the advice of her physician who recommended psychotherapy rather than anti-depressant medication. In analysis she recognized a pattern. She was surprised to find that she was attracted to men who had hostile feelings toward women and a need to exploit them. Further analysis revealed that when she was four years old, her parents separated and divorced. The patient blamed herself for her parent's marital difficulties. At the same time, she learned in treatment that she was very angry with her father for leaving her and wished to hurt him. Her guilt for her wish to punish a male was assuaged by being punished by a male. Her unconscious had no difficulty in recognizing men who have a need to be punitive toward women. It is not that she enjoyed the mistreatment by her lovers, but without periodic punishment she would experience anxiety. If things were going well her anxiety would grow and she would automatically, unconsciously create a situation in which she would be humiliated. She hated the suffering, but without recurrent setbacks she would become anxious.

Freud opens the paper with a re-examination of the pleasure principle in light of the new theory of instincts: the life instinct and the death instinct. Once again he radically changed accepted psychoanalytic theory. At the age of 68 years he boldly overturned the classic view of the pleasure principle.

The early theory stated that relaxation of tension was experienced as pleasurable. The libidinal aim of the mental apparatus was to keep excitation or tension as low as possible. The tendency to reduce excitation was known as the nirvana principle and was identified with the pleasure principle.

The new theory views the nirvana tendency as no longer in the service of pleasure, the libido, but rather as an expression of the death instinct, whose aim is to eliminate stimuli, reduce the restlessness of life and regress to an inorganic state.

Freud makes an interesting set of connections: the nirvana principle represents the drive of the death instinct; the pleasure principle expresses the libido, the life instinct; and the influence of the external world modifies the pleasure principle into the reality principle. As a rule the three principles do not exclude one another and exist side by side, although because of their different aims conflicts are bound to arise.

Freud concluded that the energy for masochistic behavior is a derivative of the death instinct. Masochism, self-destructiveness, is a failure of sadism; a failure of the libido, the life instinct, to merge with the destructive drive and direct it outward.

The following concepts were based on Freud's analytic experience with men, "to whom I shall restrict my remarks." (The Economic Problem of Masochism, 1924, S.E. XIX, p. 161)

Masochism can be observed in three forms: erotogenic, feminine, and moral. Erotogenic masochism refers to that condition in which the person cannot experience sexual excitement unless it is accompanied by physical pain. Such persons require whipping, spanking, binding and so forth, in order to function sexually. This condition is difficult to understand theoretically and Freud used phrases like: "if one is prepared to overlook a little inexactitude" or "the inadequacy of this explanation" in his attempt to fit erotogenic masochism into his theory of instincts. (Ibid, 164) Incidentally erotogenic masochism is rarely seen in women.

In a sado-masochistic relationship it is the masochist who is in control. He tells his sadistic partner exactly what he wishes him or her to do. He usually says: "Stay away from my eyes," "don't do it too hard," "don't really hurt me, only pretend," etc. If the sadistic partner loses control and inflicts too much pain, the masochist gets angry and calls it off, usually accompanied by the sadist's plea that he be given another chance. Pain, in erotogenic masochism, is essentially symbolic.

The second form of masochism Freud called feminine. Since his paper was based on experience with men, why call this phenomenon feminine?— because of the fantasies the men created to induce potency. The fantasies are those of being castrated, being copulated with, or giving birth to a baby.

> "For this reason I have called this form of masochism, a potiori as it were (i.e. on the basis of its extreme examples), the feminine form." (Ibid, 162)

Erotogenic masochism accompanies the libido through all stages of psycho-sexual development. The self-destructive drive in the oral phase is expressed by a fear of being devoured by the angry parent; the wish to be beaten originates in the anal-sadistic stage; and castration enters the masochistic fantasies as a precipitate of the phallic phase. Finally, in the genital stage we find the fantasy of copulation and giving birth to a baby.

> "It is instructive too, to find, contrary to all theory

> and expectation, that a neurosis which had defied every therapeutic effort may vanish if the subject becomes involved in the misery of an unhappy marriage, or loses all his money, or develops a dangerous organic disease.''
>
> (Ibid, 166)

In such instances, one form of pain has replaced another. All that matters is that the person experience a certain amount of suffering.

> ''(We) speak of a 'need for punishment'....The course of childhood development leads to an ever-increasing detachment from parents....To the images they leave behind there are then linked the influences of teachers and authorities....The last figure in the series that began with the parents is the dark power of Destiny which only the fewest of us are able to look upon as Impersonal....but all who transfer to guidance of the world to Providence, to God, or to God and Nature, arouse a suspicion that they still look upon these ultimate and remotest powers as a parental couple, in a mythological sense, and believe themselves linked to them by libidinal ties...
>
> In order to provoke punishment from this last representative of the parents, the masochist must do what is inexpedient, must act against his own interests, must ruin the prospects which open out to him in the real world...''
>
> (Ibid, 168-170)

A man rose from rags to riches. Starting as a laborer, through intelligence, skill, pluck, and unusually good business sense, the man became a minor industrial baron. His business decisions were based on his own judgment, but not until he discussed the matter carefully with his lawyer and accountant. Then, after many years of spectacular success, he began to make deals in different parts of the country without informing his consultants. He made investments a schoolboy would not have made. Of course he never mentioned them to his loyal and wise business friends; they would never have permitted him to throw away millions of dollars. The final episode of this story was his taking his family on a trip in his own plane and flying into a mountain killing all of them. Those who knew said that he was an excellent pilot and there was absolutely no reason why the plane should have crashed. Afterwards, his lawyer and accountant were stunned to discover the irresponsible business deals he had made. His physician declared that he had been in good health. This obvious self-destructive behavior exemplifies the extreme moral masochist, who willy-nilly, unconsciously, is bent on destroying himself.

A patient needed an agent to handle a book she had written. She brought to the analyst's attention the fact that the agent she had chosen had un unimpressive track record. When asked why she overlooked two well-known competant agents to choose an obvious loser: ''I don't know, he seemed nice, I really didn't think about it.'' She could be awarded the moral-masochist-of-month.

The socialization process insures that we inhibit our sadistic desires. The unacceptable drive doesn't go away, rather it turns against the self and contributes to what is known as our conscience. The sadism of the conscience (super-ego) and the masochism of the ego compliment each other. Paradoxically the more one refrains from aggression against others, the more severe his conscience. It might be expected that the less one expresses hostility to others the less he would experience guilt, the more his conscience would be benign and less suspicious. However, psychoanalysis shows that it is the other way around: passivity and the suppresion of aggression form the harshest conscience which demands even further renunciation of instinct gratification.

Popular notion holds that in a society ethical requirements are primary and give rise to conscience and instinct renunciation. Freud's view is the opposite. He concluded that originally instinctual control is enforced by external powers and the repressed drive forms an ethical sense which is represented by conscience and further repression of our instinctual life.

No civilized person fully escapes the process. In everyone's life there are many examples of acting contrary to one's best interests.

CHAPTER LVII

■ *His Estate*

Two predominant themes ran through Freud's dreams (as related during the voyage to America with Jung and Ferenczi): care and anxiety for his family and care and anxiety for the future of psychoanalysis. Freud felt that he had made great discoveries and his responsibility was to cherish and promote them, "rather as a conscientious hereditary landowner might feel about his estate."[1] His attitude toward the "Committee" transcended his personal feelings of warmth and friendship toward individual members; it was the agency entrusted to guarantee the welfare of psychoanalysis. He was concerned that harmony should exist among the members. Any difficulty that arose among them made him anxious about that welfare. But the differences among the members, coming as they did from five different countries, and with limited opportunities to meet and exchange views, raised doubts concerning how long their harmony could last.

After ten good years, ominous signs of dissension arose. Freud took them as a calamity. His distress was augmented by the onset of what he knew to be a fatal illness. The blame at first fell on Jones and Abraham; a few years later the true source of the difficulties became clear—the gradual mental disintegration of both Rank and Ferenczi.

Rank and Jones were the two who had been given the task of running the *Verlag,* the publishing house set up by von Freund. The problems they encountered deserve a chapter of their own. For example, the depreciation of the Austrian currency offered what seemed like a good idea: produce the International Journal and the books in Austria, where money was almost worthless, and sell them in England, where money was appreciating. What they didn't anticipate was that, as the currency fell, the costs would rise to keep abreast with the world market. Paper and type were hard to come by, labor disputes seemed a daily occurrence, and communications were exasperatingly slow. Rank worked like a beaver. He had to buy his own string, wrap the packages, and carry them himself to the post office. Foreign printers, not knowing, interlarded the text with German words and phrases. In England a strong dislike of everything German prevailed, and psychoanalysis was disdained as a product of German decadence. The result of all this was that the proofs had to be returned to Vienna for correction.

Communication between London and Vienna was unreliable and slow, and sending shipments back and forth added to the misunderstanding and frustrations. In the name of expedience, Rank, who knew very little English, took to correcting the proofs himself, without informing the Englishman, Jones. Furthermore, the type itself was obviously foreign, there being no English type available in Austria.

---

[1]Jones 3, p. 44

Anti-German feeling was only part of a more general problem for psychoanalysis. Scores of quacks had sprung up and their misdemeanors was laid at the door of the Freudians. The press delighted in recounting stories of rape, blackmail, all said to be part of the daily life of an analyst. An English Psycho-Analytical Publishing Company ran the following advertisement:

> Would you like to earn a thousand pounds a year as a psychoanalyst? We can show you how to do it. Take eight postal lesson from us at four guineas a course.
>
> (Ibid. p. 48)

The Archbishop of Canterbury appointed a committee to investigate psychoanalysts; so did the General Medical Council and the British Medical Association. The list of difficulties and humiliations mounted to the point of tedium.

Jones was like an army fighting on two unguarded fronts. In America and England he fought valiantly, often successfully, for psychoanalysis's right to respectability; and in Vienna, in the face of actual material and technical difficulties, he fought, though less successfully, for sympathy and cooperation.

In the meantime, Rank's treatment of Jones went from over-bearing to harsh and dictatorial. Jones didn't want the English Journal to be a duplicate of the German edition but to give English and American analysts an opportunity to publish their contributions. Rank refused to accept what he called "trans-Atlantic rubbish," putting Jones in an awkward position. Although it was not his responsibility, Rank kept sending Jones sharp criticisms of his editing of the Journal. Such behavior, of course was exceedingly offensive, especially from an old friend. Eventually, Rank came to ignore completely Jones's suggestion and decisions. Within a couple of years, it became evident that Rank was in a manic phase of a cyclothymia (manic-depression), which was gradually intensifying.

Otto Rank had been born in Vienna in 1884, on a social level distinctly lower than that of the others on the Committee. His father was reputed to be an irresponsible drunk, though Rank's family suffered more from the father's indifference than from his brutality. In his teens, Otto threw off his father's authority and changed his name from Rosenfeld to Rank, supposedly inspired by the character of that name in Ibsen's "A Doll's House." At an early age, he had worked as a mechanic to support his family because he had been trained in a technical school to handle tools expertly. He was timid and deferential in the presence of the other members of the Committee, and his accent clearly revealed his social origins. But somehow he had found the time and energy for scholarship and was widely read. When he first came across Freud's writings, he had been spellbound. Alfred Adler, whose Marxist-Socialist leanings made him available to the working class, was Rank's family physician. During a physical examination, Rank referred to his fascination with Freud and, much to his surprise, Adler offered to introduce him. So at the age of twenty-two he met Freud and presented him with an essay he had written, "The Artist." Freud was impressed with the quality of his thinking, and soon took him under his wing. He became his protector, mentor, and patron. Freud describes Rank in "The History."

> a number of young doctors gathered round me with the express intention of learning....Regular meetings took place on certain evenings at my house....One day a young man who had passed

> through a technical training college introduced himself with a manuscript which showed very unusual comprehension. We persuaded him to go through the Gymnasium and the University and to devote himself to the non-medical side of psychoanalysis. The little society acquired in him a zealous and dependable secretary and I gained in Otto Rank a most loyal helper and co-worker.
> (S.E. XIV, 25)

Since Rank was a full-time student, it was not clear what he lived on, and the general suspicion was that Freud, at least in part, supported him. Freud would often say that if any of the group became rich they should provide for Rank. He once said to Jones that if Rank had been born in the Middle Ages he would have found a patron, because he was so clever. On the other hand, "It might not have been easy since he is so ugly."[1]

Freud became the father that Rank had never had; a father who had faith in this most gifted son, an inspiring model. Rank was an ideal secretary and served Freud in this way. He was a tireless worker, extraordinarily resourceful, and never complained, whatever the burden put upon him. He was quick-witted and extremely intelligent. With Freud's help he earned a PhD from the University of Vienna.

Rank's specialty was mythology, and he had a flair for interpreting legends, myths, and dreams. According to Jones it was "quite mysterious how Rank found the time to read all that he did. One of the compliments I treasure in my life was when he asked me wherever I had found all that material in one of my non-medical essays, that the omniscient Rank should be impressed signified much."[2] Rank's work on creativity and the psychology of the artist is a classic, and "The Myth of the Birth of the Hero" has become standard literature for the analytic student. For years Rank enjoyed daily contact with Freud; naturally he was the envy of other pupils.

This unattractive man, who was intellectually gifted but who lacked personal charm, married a beauty. Beata Tola Mincer in her early twenties fell in love with and married him. Freud and his family accepted her as their own daughter and she went on to have a career of her own in psychoanalysis.

Rank was dependent on Freud for a livelihood; on the other hand Freud was dependent on Rank's loyalty and devotion, as well as on his ability to relieve Freud of a mountain of paperwork.

Jones did his best to conceal from Freud his difficulties with Rank in order to protect him. Rank, on the other hand, poured his troubles into Freud's ear. He complained that Jones interfered with the publishing process. In fact all Freud heard was what an impossible colleague Rank had to deal with. Although Jones kept reassuring Freud that he should not trouble himself about the matter and that things would work out, Freud's opinion of Jones diminished.

Freud was not as concerned with the Journal as he was with the books that the *Verlag* had promised to publish. obsessed by the idea that he had not long to live, he was eager to see some of the promised volumes appear during his lifetime, and grew increasingly irritated over the delays. He accepted Rank's word that Jones was solely to blame. Not only was the printing a problem, but there were disagreements

---

[1]Jones 2, p. 60
[2]Ibid. p. 60

concerning the arrangement of material that was to make up the "Collected Papers." Rank, Eric Hiller the translator, Freud, and Jones all had different views, and to make matters worse, each kept changing. For example, Rank sent Jones "final instructions" that the order of the papers was to be "the same as in the enclosed list just like that of the publication in German, i. e., chronological."[1] Jones wrote back that the two lists did not correspond and that, further, neither of them were chronological. It took months to get this simple matter straightened out.

Freud himself complicated the problem. He would causally give copyrights of his translations to the English, then would give his nephew copyrights for publication in America, and then he would turn to Rank to take care of the difficulties he had caused.

Jones had not realized how ignorant Freud was of the complications, nor that the little he knew was based entirely on what Rank told him. He was therefore shocked ro receive the following letter:

> Dear Jones:
> ....This last year brought a disappointment not easy to bear. I had to find out that you had less control of your moods and passions, were less consistent, sincere and reliable than I had the right to expect of you and that was required by your conspicuous position....You know it is not my habit to suppress my true judgment in relations of friendship and I am always prepared to run the risk of attaching to that behavior.
>
> You are quite right in asking that friends should treat each other as unrelentingly as fate does, but just imagine how much more satisfactory it is to a friend to acknowledge, or praise or admire the other man than to forgive him....Wishing for complete restoration of faith and friendship in 1923.
>
> affectionately yours,
> Freud
>
> (Ibid. p. 51)

Of course such a letter was painful to Jones but what puzzled him was the allusion to his "passions." What could Freud possibly mean? Could this allusion have emanated from Rank? Later letters from Freud alluded to Jones's "adventures," and how they must distract him from work. To a psychoanalyst such "adventures" could only mean erotic ones. Several months later the mystery was cleared up. Jones had referred to Freud a woman whom he had partially analyzed and had sent Freud a short account of the case. The patient had taken Jones's kindness to her as personal affection. In his letter Jones had written, "It came to a declaration of love." Freud misunderstood the meaning, assumed that Jones had had sexual relations with his patient. When the woman herself appeared for analysis, Freud was pleased to find himself mistaken.

Finally, it was Jones's answer to the following letter from Freud that got him off the hook and enlightened Freud as to what was really happening between them.

[1]Jones 3, p. 50

> Dear Jones:
> Another wheel in the machinery seems to be wrong and I imagine it is your position in the middle of it and the ceremonial that prescribes your personal interference in every step of the process....I don't see where you want to do it all alone and suffer yourself to be crushed by the common drudgery of the routine work....It would do if you got a glimpse of the last Korrektur, make it the final one and leave the intermediate phases to others....many months could be spared if you could be moved to throw down part of the burden....
> Pardon my meddling with your affairs but they are ours and mine too and Rank is too meek to oppose you in these quarters. My broad shoulders are as you say better to lift this weight....
> With best love to you, wife and children
> affectionately yours,
> Freud
> (Ibid. p. 52)

Given the situation, Freud's describing Rank as meek was testimony to his innocence. Jones grasped at once that Freud had never seen the arrogant letters from Rank that Jones was receiving. In his reply, he said:

> As you say, we must also see what can be done to hasten matters at the London end, and there I shall be very grateful for any definite suggestions. The only one you make, of leaving all but the final proof corrections to Vienna, I have already put into force some eighteen months ago....
> (Ibid. p. 52)

Jones went on to describe in detail the complexities and slowness of the communication between London and Vienna that they were attempting to straighten out. "I am sorry to trouble you at such length, but the matter concerns us all, and I wanted to put the true situation before you since you have been so good as to take deep interest in it all...."[1] A postcard from Freud followed: "Thank you so much for your kind letter. Afraid I am growing old and moody. You spared me all criticism." In the next letter he went on:

> My first suspicion that the fault lay with you I had to take back and to apologize to you....Now I am getting sick of this translation business. I was deeply stirred by your saying that you considered the bringing out of my English books as one of the foremost tasks of your work....I still appreciate your words as an expression of an unfailing kindness towards me which as you know I always in-

[1]Ibid. p. 54

tend to return.
(Ibid. p. 54)

Abraham now enters the scene and was soon to supplant Jones as the target of Rank's hostility. The arrangements for the Berlin Congress were Abraham's responsibility, and Rank began to interfere with them. He circulated memos among the various Societies, without letting Abraham or Jones know—matters that concerned the Central Executive Committee. Abraham's natural response was anger. Soon a letter from Freud arrived, defending Rank. Both Abraham and Jones disagreed with Freud's version.

The entire matter was discussed at a Committee meeting held after the Berlin Congress. There it was decided that the English publications should lead an independent existence.

The last Committee meeting ever held was in August 1923. Freud had suggested that they meet without his presence in order to achieve harmony among themselves. Rank accused Jones of unfriendliness. Jones apologized for having hurt his feelings, but Rank would not accept the apology and demanded that Jones be expelled from the Committee. Naturally, the other members would not agree to this and a painful scene ensued, with Rank in an uncontrollable rage and Jones staring in "puzzled silence." It was after that that Jones receded as Rank's target and was supplanted by Abraham.

Toward the end of the year, Ferenczi and Rank published a book called *The Development of Psychoanalysis* that took the Committee by surprise—it had never been mentioned although Freud knew about it. The members of the Committee considered it an inauspicious sign, since it departed from custom and, indeed, promises.

The aim of the book was to show how patients live out their unconscious impulses in action, and how the analysis of the acting-out can be effective therapeutically. Moreover, there were suggestions in the book that anlayzing such tendencies might be sufficient without reaching the origins of the neurotic patterns in the distant past. Freud accepted this modification of his former technique. But Jones, on opening a symposium at the Innsbruck Congress, voiced his concern that ambitious analysts might exploit this technique. Freud concurred, but expressed his certainty that the authors themselves would not do so. The Berlin representatives were not so sure and time has corroborated their uncertainty.

Freud later told Ferenczi that at first he had been quite taken by the work, but now had his doubts. He found it "not honest;" that behind the new suggestions was the aim of shortening analysis in line with Rank's ideas about the birth trauma and Ferenczi's "active method." Neither of these were mentioned in the book.

On January 2, 1924, Ferenczi presented a paper to the Vienna Society based on the book. Freud wrote to him that his presentation omitted some important features of the book. In addition, he stated that he himself did not entirely agree with some of the concepts put forth. Ferenczi responded with a ten-page letter. He said that he had been "shattered" by this statement and went on to say that he would never deviate in the slightest from Freud's teaching. Freud did not see the significance of Ferenczi's over-reaction to his mild statement. Instead he focused on the unscientific attitude implied:

> As for your endeavor to remain completely in agreement with me I treasure it as an expression of your friendship, but find this aim neither necessary nor easily attainable.... Why shouldn't you therefore have the right to try if things won't work in another way from that I had thought? If you go astray in so doing you will find that out yourself sometime or other, or I will take the liberty of pointing it out to you as soon as I am myself sure about it.
>
> (Ferenczi, Feb. 4, 1924)

The situation was made more complicated by the appearance of Rank's own book. *The Trauma of Birth*. Though both Freud and Ferenczi knew he was writing it, neither had seen it, and it came as a complete surprise to the rest of the Committee. The members of the Committee had agreed that they would not publish anything without informing the other members beforehand. Sachs was particularly perturbed. He and Rank had been vacationing at the same resort that summer and had seen each other daily. Rank had never mentioned that he was writing a book.

Freud had long believed that the prototype of fear was the painful experience of being born. The infant, taking his first breath, was on the brink of suffocation and in mortal peril. Rank used the word "trauma" and developed to a logical conclusion the concept that the fundamental determinant in a person's psychological growth was the separation anxiety experienced at birth. Man's aim was to undo and overcome this trauma; as his fundamental wish and fear in life was to return to his mother's womb. He partly succeeded through coitus, which aims at fusion with the mother, partly through sublimation. The unconscious motivation of artistic and religious creativity was to re-establish unity with mother. There lay the deepest root in the aetiology of psychopathology. It was failure in his complicated endeavors to surmount his birth trauma that resulted in neurosis. Rank presented no data which could be tested; rather the whole book was written in a hyperbolical style more suited to philosophic or religious thinking than to scientific. It was a disturbing book; the deviations from standard psychoanalytic psychology were glaring. The Oedipal complex was of secondary concern; the essential conflict concerned the child and his mother.

It followed that it was clinically unnecessary to let the patient's neurotic patterns unfold or to trace them back to their origins; all that was required was that the patient re-experience in the transference the drama of birth. The consequent rebirth would constitute a cure. A psychoanalysis could be completed in a few months.

Freud's response to Rank's theory was mixed. After all, he himself, as early as 1901, in a footnote to the second edition of *The Interpretation of Dreams*, had stated that the source and the prototype of anxiety is the act of birth. And, as recently as 1923, in "The Ego and the Id" he had related the first anxiety state to the experience of birth. So he was not exactly dealing with a dissenter who challenged orthodoxy. Nevertheless Freud felt alarmed. Was the whole of his life's work on the aetiology of neuroses to be reduced to the one trauma of birth? On the other hand, Freud was pleased that his young disciple should make a discovery of such fundamental importance. His interest now turned to the problem of how Rank's bold theory was to be woven into previous discoveries, discoveries that had been hard won over a long painful period.

Many analysts, especially Abraham, were critical of Rank's work. They saw the human condition as a conflict between the individual organism and the outside world—the world of father, the author of the ban on incest—and the control over, even the resignation of, instinct. They had been alarmed at the Ferenczi-Rank book. *The Development of Psychoanalysis*. Now *The Trauma of Birth*, like its predecessor, shifted the center of neuroses from the Oedipal conflict with the father to an even earlier mother-child complex. They urged Freud to take a critical stance in order to restore the theory to its true foundations, and to give up his tolerant attitude toward Rank and Ferenczi.

It was not easy for Freud to take a hard line with his two "sons." He seemed to cling to the high hopes he had of them, which were inextricably bound up with the future of psychoanalysis. It was much easier for him to withdraw sympathy from Jones and Abraham. Their realism and practical sense at times made them seem less than generous, and this irritated Freud.

Sachs visited Freud at Christmas 1923 and Freud expressed some misgivings he had about the new theory. Sachs reported this to his colleagues in Berlin and the prevailing critical attitude was reinforced. Eitingon then informed Freud about the storm brewing in Berlin and urged him to do something. Freud decided that a circular letter to all members of the Committee might help calm things down.

> Liebe Freunde, 15 February 1924
>
> I have heard from various sides...that the recent publications of our Ferenczi and Rank...have evoked considerable disagreeable and agitated discussion....I should prefer...each of you follow his own way.
>
> The fact of the matter is this: neither the harmony among us nor the respect you have often shown me should hinder any of you in the free employment of his productivity. I do not expect you to work in a direction to please me....Complete agreement in all scientific details and on all fresh themes is quite impossible among half a dozen men with different temperaments, and is not even disirable....I do not find it easy to feel my way into alien modes of thought....So if you wanted to wait with every new idea until I can indorse it you would run the risk of getting pretty old.
>
> My attitude towards the two books in question is as follows. The joint work I value as a correction of my conception of the part played by repetition or acting out in the analysis....In my opinion their description has the shortcoming of not being complete; i. e., they give no account of the changes in technique with which they are so concerned, but only hint at them....I find the experiment of the two authors entirely justified. We shall see what comes of it....All the same, we need not suppress certain misgivings....Three months have passed since my last operation, and

I am still suffering from the changes in the scar tissue. So I find it hard to believe that in only a slightly longer time, four to five months, one can penetrate to the deepest layers of the unconscious and bring about lasting changes in the mind. Naturally, however, I shall bow to experience....I am of the opinion that we still have very much to investigate....

Now for the second, and incomparably more interesting book, *The Birh Trauma* by Rank....I have not yet come to a definitive judgment about it. We have long been familiar with womb phantasies and recognized their importance, but in the prominence Rank had given them they achieve a far highter significance....To repeat it in my own language: some instinct must be associated with the birth trauma which aims at restoring the previous existence....

Now comes the point where I find the difficulties begin. Obstacles, which evoke anxiety, the barriers against incest, are opposed to the phantastic return to the womb: now where do these come from? Their representative is evidently the father, reality, the authority which does not permit incest. Why have these set up the barrier against incest?....I derived the barrier against incest from the primordial history of the human family, and thus saw in the actual father the real obstacle, which erects the barrier against incest anew. Here Rank diverges from me. He refuses to consider the phylogenesis and regards the anxiety opposing incest as simply a repetition of the anxiety at birth....I find it very hard to decide here, nor do I see how experience can help us, since in analysis we always come across the father as the representative of the prohibition. But naturally that is not an argument. For the time being I must leave the matter open....

When I add that it is not clear to me how the premature interpreting of the transference as an attachment to the mother can contribute to shortening the analysis, I have given you a faithful picture of my attitude to the two works in question. I value them highly, already accept them in part...look forward to a clarification from further reflection and experience, and would recommend all analysts not to form too quickly a judgment, least of all a disapproving one, about the questions that have been stirred.

Forgive my discursiveness. Perhaps it will keep you from provoking me to express opinions over matters which you can just as well judge for yourselves.

Freud

This mollifying letter failed to allay Abraham's suspicions. Perhaps Freud might see the new theories as based on genuine research; not so Abraham. The memory of Jung and Adler was too fresh. Abraham's position was that whatever was discovered through the psychoanalytic method would not be cause for concern; quite the contrary, it would stimulate more investigation. But Rank's book was something else. It was not based on experience with patients but came from an intellectual leap. However brilliant it might seem, it was an ominous harbinger of the development of issues in psychoanalysis. Abraham believed that a warning should be issued to Freud and the Committee. To reply to Freud in a circular letter would disturb the two men concerned, so he wrote privately to Freud. He saw the works in question as a scientific regression similar to Jung's of twelve years ago. The one hope lay in arranging a Committee meeting where the entire matter could be discussed frankly.

A flaw in Freud's personality caused him to agitate the very waters he wished to calm. The flaw was his occasional lack of social judgment. For instance he would sometimes reveal something told to him in confidence, much to the chagrin of all parties involved.

Now he very unwisely related to Rank what Abraham had written him, especially the analogy with Jung. Rank in turn naturally repeated it to Ferenczi. One can guess which of the two was angrier. Ferenczi wrote a vicious attack on Abraham. He spoke of the "limitless ambition and jealousy" that lay behind his "mask of politeness." Furthermore he declared that Abraham had forfeited his right to become President of the International Association. The fate of the Committee was sealed. Sigmund Freud had unwittingly put his foot in his mouth. Rank sent a circular letter to the Committee announcing its dissolution.

Freud was resigned. And whom did he blame?—Abraham. It reminds one of the old custom of punishing the bearer of bad news. He wrote to Abraham that although his reaction to the Ferenczi-Rank problem was justified, his attitude had been unfriendly and how could the Committee survive in the face of such an attitude? Freud was clearly being unfair to a colleague whose steadfastness in his work had never been challenged. He even urged Abraham to desist in his destructive behavior and not jeopardize the International Association.

Abraham fought back. He boldly told him that it was the painful truth that Freud was reacting to. A few weeks later at the Salzburg Congress at Easter 1924, Abraham and Jones tackled Ferenczi head on. Abraham submitted that Ferenczi was on a path that would lead away from psychoanalysis altogether. His manner this time was so direct and yet sincere and friendly that Ferenczi could only respond softly with "You can't really mean that."[1] A friendly and calm discussion followed.

Rank, on the other hand, was unreachable; in fact, he left the Congress on the second day. The New York Society had booked him for a six-months lecture tour and he had decided this would be a good time to go. Later he told Freud that he had left because he could not stand by and witness Abraham's election to the Presidency.

In the meantime Freud had been trying to apply Rank's theory in his daily work with patients, and had little success. The responses in no way supported Rank's theories. In a congratulatory letter to Abraham he wrote that his enthusiasm for Rank's position was rapidly waning, that in effect he was finding the importance of the birth trauma less and less convincing.

---

[1]Jones 3, p. 67

Rank, who had been known as Freud's right-hand man, was acclaimed in the United States and lectured before the leading neurological societies in New York. After about three months, however, startling rumors began to reach Europe. The "old" psychoanalysis was superseded by a new one. The creator of this new theory and its revolutionary technique was telling his audiences that a psychoanalysis now could be completed in three to four months.

Most American analysts practiced in New York and they all flocked to work with Freud's famous colleague. He was taking on many patients for short-term analysis and charging unusually high fees. The analysts in training with Rank looked forward to his elucidating Freud's theories. They were bewildered to discover that Rank was critical of some of the theory. Rank tried to organize an analytic association under his leadership, but this did not sit well with the established figures in the Society who had invited him. Rank also took to addressing nonmedical groups and thus opened the door to all comers.

Young analysts were fascinated by Rank's apparent improvements, but older ones were cautious. Brill, who has been described as tough-minded, was puzzled but took a wait-and-see attitude until he heard from Freud. Freud, for his part, hoped that the reports he was hearing were exaggerated. And upon receiving a letter from his nephew in America (Edward Bernays), which described Rank's behavior as high and mighty, Freud found himself once more defending his former pupil. He began to describe Rank's activities as the result of his not having been analyzed himself. Freud decided to be friendly and supportive when Rank returned.

He couldn't give up on Rank and continued to maintain his friendly attitude. By letter he wished Rank well and hoped he was doing well in the United States. He ended one of his letters jocularly: "Give my regards to all the squirrels and also feed them with peanuts in my name. The real zoo to be visited is in the Bronx."[1]

Freud was sorry that Rank had left in a state of agitation and mistrust, but glad that there was no animosity between him and the psychoanalytic community. As far as Rank's new theories were concerned, only good could come of them. Furthermore, scientific creativity is no reason to sever an intimate relation of so many years. The test of time would allow everyone to make a proper judgment.

But Rank had already written a devastating letter to Freud which was soon to arrive. The time had now come when he was to attack his old benefactor directly. After scolding Freud for being partial to Abraham and influenced by him, he continued: "Do not let us forget that the psychoanalytic movement as such is a fiction, and for people who are now eager to work at a psychoanalytic movement, I confess, I have no sympathy."[2]

Freud couldn't believe what he read. The malice was so unlike the Rank he knew that it bewildered him. He answered by stating that all of this would not have arisen if Rank had been analyzed. To this Rank angrily replied that from what he had seen of Freud's analysands, he was lucky not to be among them.

Still Freud hoped for the prodigal's return. He felt that Rank had been carried away by his discovery and that when he came to his senses he would be different. Then it would be time to recall his extraordinary services to psychoanalysis and to forgive him his neurotic flight. But Freud was not entirely hoodwinked: in a letter to Ferenczi he stated that in his experience, once the devil takes over, he carries

---

[1]Taft. p. 96
[2]Clark, p. 454

the day to the very end. He expressed surprise that Ferenczi had joined Rank. And it is true that when Freud passed the rude letter on to him, Ferenczi broke with Rank.

When Rank returned to Vienna in October, odd as it may seem, Freud still hoped that fences could be mended. They met and talked for three hours. The meeting was not very satisfactory. There was much evasion and denial, which left a confused impression. Rank claimed that Abraham's provacation had made Freud wish to drop him which forced Rank to look elesewhere to make a living. The talk ended with Rank declaring his intention to return to America.

A few weeks later Rank called on Freud to say goodbye. Freud saw at once that he was troubled, depressed, and giving the impression that there were things on his mind he was unable to express. The farewell was uneasy, embarrassing on both sides and Freud had little hope of seeing him again. That same day he had received a letter from Brill describing in vivid terms Rank's behavior and the confusion he had created. His pupils were blithely stating that they were relieved of the unpleasant task of exploring their patient's sexual activities, that it was no longer necessary to learn how to interpret dreams. The interpretation of the birth trauma solved all. The Rank episode seemed to have come to an end. In the correspondence between Jones and Freud, discussing the recent events, neither man expressed any resentment toward Rank, rather they felt the loss of a valuable colleague.

Then a most unexpected thing happened. In Paris, Rank was overcome by so severe an attack of depression that he returned to Vienna to see Freud. After many hours of treatment he emerged once more a changed man. He seemed to have a clear understanding of all that had transpired. He saw that he had undergone a "acting-out" that almost ended in tragedy. Now his wish was to undo any harm he had caused. He wrote a circular letter to the Committee explaining what he had gone through. His hostility to Freud had been part of a neurosis that was aggravated by the news of Freud's illness. He apologized to Jones and Abraham for the wrongs done to them and asked the Committee for forgiveness. He also announced his intention of returning to America to rectify any wrong he might have done to the cause of psychoanalysis.

Freud was at once overjoyed and deeply touched., He had found again his old friend and loyal comrade. This relief may have been responsible for his overlooking two facts that he knew well. First, he knew that Rank suffered from a cyclothymic condition; therefore, his manic phase was bound to recur. It did so six months later. Secondly, Rank still seemed to be adhering to the very heresy that had caused the trouble in the first place. Freud knew that a condition like cyclothymic could not be cured with anything less than a long-term, deep psychoanalysis. Could he really believe that his talks with Rank had effected a cure?

Rank left for America again in January 1925. Freud wrote to Brill, explained the situation, and asked him to help Rank face the difficult tasks ahead. The generous Brill informed Freud that he was doing all he could but that Rank was nor faring well at all. In a few weeks Rank returned to Vienna, depressed, in a pitiable condition. More talks with Freud seemed to help. Nevertheless, after another round of trips between the United States and Europe, depressions, and talks with Freud, Rank returned to the United States and disassociated himself from psychoanalysis. In April 1926, he and Freud saw each other for the last time. To Sachs Freud was to say: "Now, after I have forgiven everything, I am through with him."[1]

---

[1]Sachs, p. 148

Helene Deutsch visited Freud specifically to invervene on Rank's behalf. Her plea was that Rank was so distraught by Freud's illness that he was not fully accountable for his behavior. But Freud disposed of her efforts with a jest: ''Then why isn't he kissing the hot stove?'' He was referring to a Jewish anecdote about a rabbi who discovered his young wife being kissed by one of his students. The wife's plea that the young man didn't know what he was doing was met with ''Then why isn't he kissing the hot stove?[1]

As in the case of the earlier dissidents—Adler, Stekel, and Jung—others perceived their divergencies long vefore Freud recognized them. Freud tried as best he could to bring about reconciliations, but when he failed he relegated the matter to oblivion.

A month after Freud's death in 1939, Rank also died suddenly. He had an allergic reaction to medication for a throat infection.

[1]Helene Deutsch, Roazen. Anchor Press N. Y. 1985, p. 257

CHAPTER LVIII

■ *Only The Bad And The Unworthy*

Whatever activity Freud was involved in, political, personal, social, or professional, one activity was practically a constant: that of seeing patients. He was working in his "lab" until the last few weeks of his life, and always reviewed theories and hypotheses in the light of incoming data from patients. When his ideas no longer fit the new facts, he would modify those ideas, bring them into harmony with the data, and share his new formulations with the public in a paper.

In 1923, Freud published a very short and highly technical addition to his theory of sexual development, "The Infantile Genital organization of the Libido." It was to rectify a concept submitted eighteen years earlier in the "Three Essays." That two decades of continual observation could have overlooked features of such general occurrence highlights the difficulty of research in psychoanalysis.

Freud had by this time learned that the differences between children of both sexes were less than he thought. He believed that between the ages of two and four years, only one genital phase existed for both sexes, the male one. He called this phase the phallic, and he inserted it between the anal-sadistic and the genital psychosexual development of both girls and boys. The existence of the vagina remained undiscovered.

> Unfortunately we can describe this state of things only as it affects the male child; corresponding processes in the little girl are not known to us.
> (The Infantile Genital Organization of the Libido, 1923, S.E. XIX p. 142)

It is not that the little boy fails to recognize the difference between men and women; it is that it never occurs to him that their genitals might be different. He presumes, if he thinks about it at all, that everybody possesses a genital similar to his own. This part of the body, so rich in sensation, arouses in him a high degree of interest. He wants to observe it in others and he always behaves as though he has a vague idea that his should be bigger. At this stage, much of his aggressiveness and exhibition is an expression of sexual curiosity.

When he finally discovers that there are people without a genital similar to his, he reacts at first with complete disavowal. He mentally insists that they do indeed have one. He tells himself that it may be very small but it will grow. Then he slowly comes to the conclusion that there had been a penis there, but it was taken away. This line of thinking develops into a "castration complex," and it comes into being during the phallic phase: "The significance of the castration complex can only be rightly appreciated if its origin in the phase of phallic primacy is also taken into account."[1]

The young boy's conviction that females do not possess a penis gives rise to a belittlement of women, even a horror of them, and this can result in his finding a refuge in homosexuality. The child believes that only bad and socially inferior women are without a penis, only those guilty of unacceptable impulses like his own. Their lack is a punishment. Women whom he likes and respects have, in his mind, a penis. When he approaches the problem of where babies come from, and begins to realize that only women can give birth, he at last accepts the reality that the female genitals are different from his own.

> I learnt from the analysis of a young married woman who had no father but several aunts that she clung, until quite far on in the latency period, to the belief that her mother and her aunts had a penis. One of her aunts was feeble-minded; and she regarded this aunt as castrated as she felt herself to be.
>
> (Ibid. p. 145)

Thus, not until puberty does psychosexual development reach its completion for both sexes. It is then that sexual polarity becomes clear and coincides with "male" and "female." Only then, does the vagina come to be highly valued as the shelter of the baby, and part of the heritage of femininity.

---

[1]Ibid. p. 144

CHAPTER LIX

■ *Ceaseless Obligations*

A survey of the events of 1926 gives us a glimpse of Freud's life as he approached his seventieth birthday.

Since his major operation, Freud didn't like to appear in public. Nevertheless, January 6, when the Vienna Society met to honor Karl Abraham, he attended the ceremony. With Abraham's death psychoanalysis had lost one of its ablest and most courageous voices. Also, it left political problems: Who should replace him on the Committee? Who should take over the Presidency of the International Association? Who should be the new President of the German Society? Needless to say, these matters kept Freud busy with correspondence, discussions, and meetings.

Early in February during a stroll, Freud suffered a mild heart attack. Two days later, a second attack occurred just a few steps from the home of his friend Dr. Ludwig Braun. Braun's diagnosis of myocarditis made Freud decide to slow down and reduce the number of his patients to three a day. That lightening of his load didn't satisfy Braun, who insisted that Freud spend at least a month in a sanatorium. Freud resisted, then reluctantly gave in. In March, from the sanatorium, he wrote a long letter to Eitingon which indicated that he was taking his condition seriously.

> I intend to give up my work from May 6 to May 10 in order to devote myself exclusively to my guests (the Committee)....It may easily be the last meeting with my friends....Renouncing the sweet habit of smoking has resulted in a great diminution of my intellectual interests....The only real dread I have is of long invalidism with no possibility of working...no possibility of earning. And just that is the most likely thing to happen. I do not possess enough...to fulfill my ceaseless obligations. It is those serious and personal consideration that matter in the last resort....
>
> I regard it as a triumph to retain a clear judgment in all circumstances, not like poor Abraham to let oneself be deceived by a euphoria....Were it not for...possibly not being able to work I should deem myself a man to be envied. To grow so old; to find so much warm love in family and friends; so much expectation of success in such a venturesome undertaking, if not the success itself; who else has attained so much?
>
> (Eitingon, March 19, 1926)

Freud had been reluctant to follow Braum's advice to leave Vienna, because he wished to work with Marie Bonaparte who could only stay there briefly. She had previously requested that Freud analyze her and he had accepted. Freud deduced from the analytic content that she had seen her nurse and groom having sex when she was about a year old. Upon inquiry, the old groom confirmed Freud's deduction. Both Marie and Freud were excited by this confirmation by a living participant of a psychoanalytic reconstruction. Freud has written that he was able to hold out against scorn and disbelief without getting bitter because of the certainty he had always felt about his discoveries.

Princess Marie Bonaparte was a mebmer of one of the reigning families in Europe. Her husband, Prince George, was a brother of the King of Greece and a member of the royal family of Denmark. Her aspirations, when she was still a young girl, to be a physician, were considered unsuitable to her rank.

Although a member of the international "set" and a direct descendant of Napoleon's brother Lucien, she was not invulnerable. Her maternal grandfather, the founder of the gambling casino in Monte Carlo, had been a Jew. She was very rich, but her money was therefore somewhat "tainted." Her personality was grand; she was a queen in Parisian society. A lively, attractive, even seductive woman, she was, like a number of other beautiful women, facinated by Freud.

Meeting Freud at the age of forty-three had changed her life. She became an analyst herself, a loyal friend to the Freud family, and a confidante of Freud himself. Years later, Jones expressed surprise at what Freud had disclosed about himself to her. For the rest of her life she was deeply involved in the fortunes of the psychoanalytic movement, and in applying psychoanalytic theory to the study of literary works, mythology, anthropology, and psychopathology. In addition to her more than one hundred publications, she traslated into French Freud's basic writings. Her own best know works were *Female Sexuality*, *Myth of War*, and *The Life and Work of Edgar Allan Poe*. Freud and Marie corresponded to the end of his life.

Freud returned from the sanatorium free of heart symptoms, but continued to work on a reduced schedule. Each morning before work, he would take a drive to the green suburbs of Vienna to enjoy the early spring weather. To Marie Bonaparte he wrote: "What a pity that one had to grow old and ill before being able to make this discovery."[1]

As May 6, his birthday, approached, Freud expressed mixed feelings about the celebration. He considered escaping to a sanatorium to avoid uninvited guests, but that would also mean excluding dear friends and loved ones he longed to see. He decided the courageous thing to do was to stop work, and to make himself available to his well-wishers. He wrote to his nephew Samuel in England:

> I have continued to do some work. I give 5-6 hours treatment daily....I am considered a celebrity, writers and philosophers who pass through Vienna call on me to have a talk, the Jews all over the world boast of my name, pairing me with Einstein. After all, I have no reason to complain and to look with fright at the near end of my life. After a long period of poverty...I dare say I have pro-

[1]Marie Bonaparte, April 27, 1926

vided for my wife.
(Clark, p. 480)

Freud's seventieth birthday brought a deluge of telegrams and letters of congratulations. Articles appeared in magazines, newspapers, and journals from all over the world, recognizing his work. There was one notable exception: the official academic world of Vienna. The University, the Academy, and the *Gesellschaft der Aerzte* (Society of Phsicians) completely ignored the occasion. "I should not have regarded any congratulations from them as honest."[1]

During the celebration the Committee and several analysts gathered in Freud's drawing room to pay a special tribute to him. His response was practically a farewell speech. He emphasized that the future of the psychoanalytic movement lay with them, that they would someday testify he had had loyal and loving friends, and above all, that despite the apparent successes of the movement, they must never underestimate the resistance to the acceptance of the unconscious.

The B'nai B'rith Lodge published a commemoration issue of its periodical and held a meeting at which Professor Braun made a moving speech. Freud's family attended, but he himself stayed away.

> It would have been embarrassing and tasteless to attend. When someone abuses me I can defend myself, but against praise I am defenseless....Although the Jews are treating me like a national hero, although my service to the Jewish cause is confined to the single point that I have never disowned my Jewishness.
> (MB, May 10, 1926)

To the B'nai B'rith he responded:

> I thank you for the honors you have paid me today....It happened that....I gained my first insight into the depths...of the human instincts....I felt as though I were despised and universally shunned. In my loneliness I was seized with a longing to find a circle of picked men of high character who would receive me in a friendly spirit....Your society was pointed out to me as the place where such men were to be found...at a time when no one in Europe listened to me...you gave me your kindly attention. You were my first audience.
> (Eissler, p. 238)

The following anecdote illustrates how well-known Freud had by this time become. An American writer, J. W. Drawbell, published a book containing a story about Dorothy Thompson, the well-known journalist.

> One night at a concert someone told her that trouble would break out in Warsaw. Pulling on a wrap

---

[1]Jones 3, p. 123

> she rushed to her office and there the news tapes were already ticking out the news that revolution had broken out in Poland and that Pilsudski was marching on Warsaw. She packed quickly, borrowed one hundred pounds from her companion at the concert, none other than Dr. Sigmund Freud, the great psychologist, and dashed to the station.
>
> (Jones 3, p. 125)

Knowing that Freud practically never attended musical concerts, Jones contacted Dorothy Thompson to have the story verified. She informed him that first, it was an opera not a concert; nor was her companion Freud. In the emergency, however, it occurred to her that in Vienna the most likely person to have foreign currency was Freud. She boldly called at his house and explained her situation. He graciously helped her.

Another American journalist, George Sylvester Viereck, interviewed Freud and published some of their conversation in *Glimpses of the great* (Lodon; Duckworth, 1930). The following quote reflects Freud's outlook at that time:

> Seventy years have taught me to accept life with a cheerful humility.... I prefer a mechanical jaw to no jaw at all. I still prefer existence to extinction.... Perhaps the gods are kind to us in making life more disagreeable as we grow older. In the end death seems less intolerable than the manifold burdens we carry....I have no aspirations to posthumous glory. My modesty is no virtue....
>
> I am not a pessimist. I permit no philosophic reflection to spoil my enjoyment of the simple things in life.

In October Freud met the Indian guru Rabindranath Tagore, and a few weeks later the Professor of Philosophy in Calcutta, Gupta. Both men seemed to have made little impresion upon him. To Ferenczi he wrote; "My need for Indians is for the present fully satisfied."[1]

Binswanger, an old friend, and President of the Swiss Psychiatric Society, notified Freud that he had been unanimously elected to an honorary membership. He added that had the honor been bestowed upon him twenty years ago it would have given Freud pleasure, but now it would hardly make an impression upon him. Freud wrote: "You are right."

Freud and Martha visited Berlin at Christmas to see his two sons and four grandchildren. It was his first journey since his operation three years ago.

On this occasion Freud and Albert Einstein had their first meeting. Freud was staying with his son Ernst, and Einstein and his wife paid them a visit. They enjoyed a friendly hour-long chat, after which Freud wrote: "He is cheerful, sure of himself and agreeable. He understands as much about psychology as I do about physics, so we had a very pleasant talk...."[2]

---

[1]Ferenczi, December 13, 1926

[2]Ibid. p. 131

CHAPTER LX

Unparallel Lines

Freud had been complaining since the early days of psycho-analysis, that the sexual life of women was obscure: "The sexual life of men alone has become accessible to research. That of women...is still veiled in an impenetrable obscurity,"[1] And the same sentiment was expressed by him many times: "We know less about the sexual life of little girls than of boys. But we need not feel ashamed of this distinction; after all the sexual life of adult women is a 'dark continent' for psychology."[2] One consequence of this obscurity was that it led Freud to assume that the psychology of women ran parallel to that of men.

He had not focused his interest on the psychology of women since 1900, when he published the case of "Dora." In fact he did not publish an important case dealing with female psychology for fifteen years. Then a case of female paranoia, "running counter to psychoanalytic theory," made its appearance. The dynamic of the case lay in the patient's relationship with her mother. Five years later, in 1920, he published a study of female homosexuality. Once more the dynamic was the relationship between mother and daughter. Between these two cases came the study of "beating fantasies" in 1919, which concerned itself primarily with the sexual development of girls. This investigation led Freud to say: "The expectation of there being a complete parallel was mistaken."[3]

Years of experience in analyzing neurotics had led him to stress the need to deal with the remotest periods of childhood. It lit up realms where no signposts existed. And these explorations assured that the work could not become mechanical and lose its interest.

The farther Freud advanced the more father's importance was crowded out by mother's. Fresh clinical observations supplied grounds for a modification of psychoanalytic theory. Indeed, Freud believed there was much pioneering to be done, at least for the next few decades.

In boys, what makes the Oedipus easy to understand is that the male retains his original love object, the object chosen when he was being suckled. The consequence is straightforward: he would like to get rid of his rival, the father, and take his place with the mother. The Oedipus complex is resolved by the boy's fear of castration. What complicates the matter is that the Oedipus complex has a double orientation, active and passive. In accordance with our innate bisexuality, a feminine posture is observable: the boy wants to replace his mother and be the love object.

[1]Three Essays, p. 151
[2]"The Qestion of Lay Analysis," p. 212
[3]S.E. XVII, p. 196

of his father.

In little girls the Oedipus is more complicated. Her original object is the same as the boy's but at some point a girl abandons her first choice and takes her father as an object. Every little girl is destined to make a momentous discovery.

> Usually it is from women that the threat emanates; very often they seek to strengthen their authority by a reference to the father or the doctor, who, so they say, will carry out the punishment....It happens particularly often that the little boy is threatened with castration, not because he plays with his penis...but because he wets his bed every night....Those in charge of him behave as if this nocturnal incontinence was the result and the pro-of his being unduly concerned with his penis, and they are probably right.
>
> ("The Dissolution of the Oedipus Complex," 1924, S.E. XIX, p. 174)

Then he remembers his observation of the difference between himself and girls, and he no longer denies it. There are people alive who do not possess a penis and it could happen to him. He is horrified.

His reactions at this time may determine his future feelings about women. There are men who view women as mutilated creatures and unconsciously fear them. Other see women as inferior, enjoy a triumphant contempt for them, and so forth. Although these developments belong to the future, this future is not very remote. The unspeakable danger of losing his penis makes him give up rivalry with his father and desire for his mother. He resolves to preserve his penis at any cost.

The male's belief in the possiblity of suffering the grand narcissistic injury of the loss of his penis has a historical basis. He has already suffered the loss of his mother's breast, and has daily surrendered a part of himself, his bowel content. His belief in the reality of castration is based on these earlier experiences. In the mind of the little boy, and later in his unconscious, lives the horror of the possibility of such a castration.

Men never fully recover from their fear of castration. The need to be "a big man," powerful, successful, and respected has, at its base, a concern with masculinity. Certainly men who can love and work, who function within normal limits, are not considered neurotic. Nevertheless, the fears of childhood, the awesome comparisons with father, the feelings of insecurity and inferiority persist in the unconscious. Much normal activity of men and many of their interests can be understood as symbolic triumphs over their unconscious castration complex.

All male patients feel some anxiety in regard to the functioning of the penis, even under the best conditions. Men have a universal fear that perhaps this time the penis will not be strong enough, it will not perform. Fear of inadequacy and failure is one of the sources of Venus envy. Commonly, on the analytic couch, men express the wish to be a woman. They complain that women cannot fail sexually: their mere presence is sufficient; they don't have to worry about their performance. Also, they are capable of multiple orgasms, while men are limited to a precious few. Furthermore, these men feel that care of children and household responsibilities are easy and anxiety-free and women are envied because they do not have to fight the daily battle for survival in the jungle of business.

No male ever quite gets over father's giant omnipotent penis in comparison with "Johnny's little tassle." Therefore, lodged in every man's unconscious lies envy for father's omnipotence. Many homosexual males are fixated at this point in their development and devote their energy to the search for the mythical giant penis, the magic wand, the possession of which would end all suffering forever.

The universal wish to possess a super-penis takes many forms—from the homosexual who walks the streets literally hoping to find a man who has one, to the "normal" man who tries to achieve it symbolically. Nevertheless, the outcome of the Oedipus complex that a psychoanalyst today is called upon most often to deal with is sexual impotence. Sexual impotence, the "modern epidemic," merits a detailed account.

A professional man in his mid-thirties, sought an appointment with an analyst. He was attractive, tall, slender exuding boyish charm. Yet, obviously anxious, he was pale, and spoke in a subdued voice. His wife had just left him for a younger man, probably because he was not very good in bed. Whenever he thought that he was expected to perform sexually, he would drink, and lately he had turned to marijuana, but he could not rely on these supports. He was still unable "to be a man." "Maybe this time I won't even have an erection. But what's worse I ejaculate too fast, sometimes even before I enter." He was a successful attorney and earned a good living. "I'm really talented, Doc, but when I feel pressure, I turn the work over to one of my partners."

In high school, on dates, he had marveled that his friends seemed to be fearless in their pursuit of sex. "Necking" was as far as he would go. He met his wife when he was in law school, at a weekend fraternity party. He was not particularly attracted to her, but she was clearly interested in him. She boldly took him to bed, ignoring his protests. He barely had an erection, there was a partial entrance, and he immediately ejaculated. To his surprise she was more than pleased and practically claimed ownership of him. Further attempts at sex were much the same. He was very grateful that she did not tell anyone about his shoddy performance. She would even brag to others how great their sex was. And he on his part felt that like other men, he had a girlfriend. Within the year she decided that they should get married. He panicked. He pleaded with her, but she was adamant. He felt that he had to go through with it or she would tell everyone the truth—reveal his impotency. If his secret came out, he would kill himself.

When his wife left him he was afraid to consult a lawyer, because she would tell everybody the truth. He wanted her back. They had two young daughters, a big house, and respectability. All he wanted was the facade, his wife and daughters and the two cars that he had taken refuge behind. He knew that his life was miserable, but what choice did he have?

Why should a young man well endowed with a first rate intelligence and a handsome body, find himself in such painful circumstances? Why should he suffer ejaculation praecox (premature ejaculation)?

Among his earliest memories was the joy of walking down the street with his father, proudly holding his hand. He loved to feel his father's muscles as he was tossed into the air and caught and tossed again. He loved to look at his father's body; it seemed so big and powerful. On the other hand, his father would severely spank him when he misbehaved.

His mother, a soft-spoken, formal lady, took him everywhere and he loved it.

He said that he remembered sexual feelings toward her. On one occasion, he saw her change a sanitary pad. The sight of the blood on the pad frightened him. He claimed that it remained a conscious memory.

He was three-and-a-half years old when a baby brother was born. He was shattered. Whenever his parents picked up the little one, he would get frightened and angry. He hated the child. Any hostile expression toward his brother resulted in his being spanked. However, when no one was in sight, he would punch, kick, and make fun of his brother.

From puberty onward, he was selfconscious and timid, compared to the other boys. He was an ordinary student and just managed to enter college and law school.

He always was attracted to girls; his masturbatory fantasies were built around the pretty girl of the day. However, from high school until the present, he found himself attracted to "macho"-looking men. "I think I'm queer, Doc, because I picture making it with those guys."

His case was classic: jealousy toward his father's possession of his mother, wishes to attack him, desire to steal his giant penis and get mother. His fear of retaliation from father, the "eye for an eye" of the primitive unconscious, made him retreat from the Oedipal to the anal-sadistic stage of development. Much of his anger at his father and mother for their betrayal and his feelings of frustration were directed at the new arrival and competitor, his brother. Lastly he feared success and adulthood because unconsciously, success and adulthood meant the success of his instincts: of his wishes to murder and commit incest. The picture gets more complicated when one realizes that accompanying his rage toward his father was love and a wish to surrender to him.

His castration complex was of such proportion that for years the very word "cut" would make him anxious. On the other hand, thoughts of cutting others, ripping them apart, were so exciting that they became part of his masturbatory ritual.

Investigation revealed that the patient's ejaculations were not accompanied by pelvic thrusts, but rather by a passive flow of semen. The similarity between the premature emission and the process of urination is striking.

Most males who suffer this condition have been difficult to train in habits of cleanliness. They describe the physical sensation of premature ejaculation as identical with loss of bladder control. The patient's account of his own sensation during premature emission was similar, but despite his embarrassment, there was something very pleasurable about the passive flow. He reported that after his wife left, he wet the bed several times. The manner in which he related this was without the shame one would expect from an incontinent adult. He reported that urinating was one of the great pleasures in life and he surprised himself when he discovered that excitement of any kind stimulated a desire to urinate. Consciously he wished to perform the sex act normally; his premature ejaculation left him ashamed, anxious, and depressed. During masturbation he functioned normally. This condition appeared only when he was with a woman.

The question that presents itself is: what is the attitude of such men toward women? This patient repeatedly expressed contempt for women. He looked upon them as inferior, was disdainful of their intelligence, and suspicious of their motives. The feminist movement angered him and he would hold it up to ridicule. His unconscious urination might be a gift, but it was also an expression of the strongest contempt. It was an expression of both love and hate for women. He first excited expectations of pleasure in a girl, then disappointed her (and unconsciously deprived her of having a baby). Thereby he took revenge on every woman who had ever disappointed him.

Women were the object of his sadistic wishes. He felt that his penis was a sadistic weapon and copulation was a double act: it was both defecating on her and killing her. He employed projection: he would attribute to others what he wished to do himself, a mechanism which, like all defense mechanisms, is unconscious. Thus, he saw women as sadistic creatures whose chief aim was to castrate men. His fear of the female genital overwhelmed him. Not only was it an ugly mutilated organ; it also contained knives and razors, which would cut off his penis if he were to enter. Consciously all he knew was that he would "get scared" when he "had to put it in." The reader must remember that neurotic behavior is unconsciously determined by what is in the mind of the child.

Some men suffer from the fact that the slightest contact with the female body is sufficient stimulation to cause an involuntary flow of semen. Actually the over-excitability of the genital is not indicative of its primacy: it is on the contrary an indication of weakness. A common condition among those who suffer ejaculatio praecox is that the most exciting zone of the penis is not the very tip, the glans penis, but rather the base. Frequently these men cannot tolerate the use of condoms, since the covering reduces even further an already weak excitability of the glans penis.

Premature ejaculators can be placed in one of two groups: those who are extemely passive and seem to lack energy, and those who are in a state of constant haste. A man who suffered this first condition expressed his reluctance toward activity in sexual matters: he would hire a prostitute, lie back, and have her do everything. "She should work for her money." His desire was to attain sexual gratification, indeed, all of life's gratifiations, without any effort. The other type, those who live in perpetual haste, find sexual intercourse a task, like all tasks, to be gotten over with a quickly as possible.

The manner in which a person seeks libidinal gratification characterizes his life style. For example, the inert type does not understand why anyone would wish to be active in any endeavor. The hasty one, on the other hand, approaches activities with excessive enthusiasm. However, as soon as he fails in any way, he tends to give the whole thing up.

Analysis of both the above types reveals a defense against sadistic impulses. These men tend to be quarrelsome, have bursts of anger, and would commit acts of violence if they were not fearful of retaliation. Their passive manner serves to hide their wish to harm everyone, and they consciously indulge in fantasies of doing so. The lawyer patient so feared that others would see what he wished to do to them, that at times his hands would shake.

Ejaclatio praecox is not difficult to understand. The male genital is made safe from its sadism by being robbed of its powers and thereby able to avoid danger. And father is unconsciously expected to interfere during sex. Now we reach the familiar ground of castration anxiety.

The history of premature ejaculators indicates that they had set an even higher value on the penis than is usual. As a consequence, they cling to narcissism long after other boys are developing normal love objects. The high estimation of the penis as the organ for urinating pleasure becomes fixed, so that when the time comes for the penis to fulfill its normal sexual function and give up some of its narcissism, it refuses to do so. The compromise is ejaculatio praecox, an attempt to be sexual and enjoy the pleasure of giving via his bodily product, and of experiencing the grand pleasure of urinating at the same time. Just as the small child wets for his mother, so he wets for his partner.

The patient reported that mother used to assist him by holding his penis when he urinated. He has since learned that for him, unconsciously, ejaculating and urinating were the same thing. Once again it became obvious that the woman was transformed into the mother. Analysis of men with this neurosis teaches us that they endeavor to restore the situation of early childhood.

It was mentioned that this patient was a very handsome man. He was also quite vain. He wished to be admired and would resent the slightest criticism. His analysis brought to light an abundance of narcissism which is standard for premature ejaculators. "The fact is, Doc, I really don't like anybody." His true love object was himself.

The dread of the female genital in such men may go beyond projected sadism. The fact that there is no penis present makes it seem to them uncanny. And now we recall that it was the lack of the penis in women which originally gave rise to castration anxiety. Physical proximity to a woman always brings out this fear, the early horror is re-awakened.

A little girl reacts very differently to the discovery of the anatomical differences between the sexes. "She has seen it and knows that she is without it and wants to have it." She makes her judgment and her decision immediately. How she deals with this problem is important for her development toward femininity. In some girls the hope of one day possessing a penis may persist to an extremely late age. Strange and unaccountable actions may be traced to this persistent wish. Or, a process may set in by which the girl refuses to accept her lack of a penis. Such a disavowal is not uncommon in the mental life of a female child. But in an adult it could mean psycho-pathology. She may harden herself in the conviction that she does possess a penis, and subsequently behave as though she were a man. She develops a masculinity complex.

Even if the envy of the penis does not develop into a masculinity complex, the psychological consequences are various and far-reaching. In any event her narcissism has been wounded and she develops a sense of inferiority, like a scar. Afterwards, she no longer feels that her lack of a penis is a personal punishment, but rather a natural, universal, sexual characteristic. She begins to share with men a contempt for women.

The female is caught in a dilemma: either she denies there is any difference between her and men; or she continues to wish and hope for a male organ. If she accepts the reality of the situation, she feels inferior. "Even after penis envy has abandoned its true object, it continues to exist: by an easy displacement it persists in the character trait of jealousy."[1]

Jealousy, of course, has a wider foundation than penis envy and is not limited to one sex. Nevertheless, Freud was of the opinion that it played a far larger part in the mental life of women than of men, because it was reinforced by the displacement of an earlier penis envy.

Another consequence of penis envy is that it loosens the girl's bond to her mother. She who brought her into the world with inferior equipment is almost always held responsible for her lack of a penis.

---

[1]Anatomical Distinction, p. 254

> There is yet another surprising effect of penis envy, or of the discovery of the inferiority of the clitoris, which is undoubtedly the most important of all...in general women tolerate masturbation worse than men...they are unable to make use of it in circumstances in which a man would seize upon it as a way of escape without any hesitation. Experience would no doubt elicit innumerable exceptions to this statement, if we attempted to turn it into a rule...both sexes are of course made up of masculine and feminine traits...the solution of the problem could be assisted by the reflection that masturbation...of the clitoris, is a masculine activity....Analysis of the remote phallic period...in girls...an intense current of feeling against masturbation makes its appearance, which cannot be attributed exclusively to the educational influence of those in charge of the child....This impulse...at puberty will do away with a large amount of the girl's masculine sexuality in order to make room for the development of her femininity.
>
> (Ibid. p. 255)

Masculine and feminine, for Freud, does not mean male and female, but active and passive—clitoral activity in that sense for Freud is masculine.

The girl's libido now undergoes a change: she establishes an equation between penis and baby. She gives up her penis envy; its place is taken by a wish for a child. With that purpose in mind, she takes her father as a love object. Mother, whom she fantasized about during clitoral masturbation, is now a rival, the object of her jealousy. The little girl is now a little woman. She wants her man and will brook no rivals. Yet, when her attachment to her father and her wish for a baby by him is disappointed, her new libidinal position has to be abandoned. If, at that time, she persists in identification with him, she may return to her masculinity complex and perhaps remain fixated in it.

Thus, there is a fundamental difference between the two sexes in regard to the Oedipus and castration complexes. The boy's Oedipus comes to an end when he believes that he might lose his valuable organ. The little girl, however, is attracted to father and wishes to eliminate mother only after she experiences the "inferiority" of her genital. In girls, the Oedipus follows the castration complex. The castration complex always inhibits and limits masculinity and encourages femininity.

The Oedipus is so important that its resolution, the way one enters and leaves it, cannot be without effect. In boys, the threat of castration smashes the Oedipus to pieces. They abandon libidinal investment, and seek substitute desexualized avenues, in other words sublimation. Important psychological changes take place: father is no longer someone they compete with, but someone they idenify with. Father now becomes a psychological part of themselves; indeed, the nucleus of their conscience, their superego.

Girls, of course, cannot be threatened with castration, thus the motive for ending the Oedipus complex is not nearly as strong as it is in boys. It may be slowly given up, or repressed; or its effects may persist into the mental life of the grown woman. They do not psychologically incorporate the father, and they do not develop a severe superego. Therefore, we can expect women to be more in touch with their feelings than men are.

> I cannot evade the notion (though I hesitate to give it expression) that for women the level of what is ethically normal is different from what it is in men. Their super-ego is never so inexorable, so impersonal, so independent of its emotional origins as we require it to be in men. Character traits which critics of every epoch have brought up against women—that they show less sense of justice than men, that they are less ready to submit to the great exigencies of life, that they are more often influenced in their judgments by feelings of affection or hostility—all these would be amply accounted for by the modification in the formation of their super-ego which we have inferred above. We must not allow ourselves to be deflected from such conclusions by the denials of the feminists, who are anxious to force us to regard the two sexes as completely equal in position and worth; but we shall, of course, willingly agree that the majority of men are also far behind the masculine ideal and that all human individuals, as a result of their bisexual disposition and of cross-inheritance, combine in themselves both masculine and feminine characteristics, so that pure masculinity and femininity remain theoretical constructions of uncertain content.
> (Ibid. p. 257)

Early in Freud's career, he formed the habit of holding back conclusions based on the observations of only a few patients. He instead accumulated evidence to the point where his ideas could be applied universally. For example, he withheld publication of *The Interpretation of Dreams*, and its extension "fragment of an Analysis of a Case of Hysteria," for five years because he wanted to be sure the ideas expressed therein were correct.

> ...In those days I had unlimited time before me...material poured in upon me in such quantities that fresh experiences were hardly to be escaped. Moreover, I was the only worker in a new field, so that my reticence involved no danger to myself and no loss to others. But now everything has changed. The time before me is limited.
> (Ibid. p. 249)

Since he had become ill, he worked less and therefore had fewer opportunities for fresh observations.

> If I think I see something new, I am uncertain

> whether I can wait for it to be confirmed. And further, everything that is to be seen upon the surface has already been exhausted; what remains has to be slowly and laboriously dragged up from the depths. Finally, I am no longer alone. An eager crowd of fellow workers is ready to make use of what is unfinished or doubtful, and I can leave to them that part of that work which I should otherwise have done myself. On this occasion therefore, I feel justified in publishing something which stands in urgent need of confirmation before its value or lack of value can be decided.
> (Ibid. p. 249)

Freud felt that the considerations which he had brought forward on the psychical consequences of the anatomical distinction between the sexes, which were based on a handful of cases, could only be maintained if his findings proved to have general validity. "If not, they would remain no more than a contribution to our knowledge of the different paths along which sexual life develops."[1]

When the castration complex takes the form of ejaculatio praecox, the character traits of the men who suffer this syndrome are so strikingly similar, that we were justified in labeling the case as "classic." We cannot claim such a classic condition for the women who suffer a castration complex or penis envy. The forms and manifestations in women are so varied that even a detailed description cannot do full justice to them or present the condition in all aspects.

Psychoanalysis of women shows that a great number have a repressed wish to have a penis. The extraordinary frequency of these observations of women patients, suggests that this wish may be common to all women. The fact that they have been born female has caused many a woman to suffer in childhood or as adults. Many of these patients were consciously aware that they felt disadvantaged and they disliked being women.Most were quite unaware of the motives for the aversion.The arguments that these women presented to explain their feelings were stereotyped. They would say that even in childhood girls are at a disadvantage. Boys are allowed greater freedom, and later in life, as men, they have far more alternatives than women. They are permitted to choose their profession, can extend their interests and activities in many spheres, and especially, are subjected to far fewer restrictions in their sexual life. Correct as these reasons may be, analysis shows that they are rationalizations, that there are underlying, unconscious motives. Direct observaion of little girls shows, without question, that at the recognition of the anatomical differences between boys and girls, they feel inferior to boys because their genitals seem inferior. The analysis of adult women confirms this phenomenon.

Originally, girls do not feel inferior in regard to their own bodies, do not perceive themselves as defective in comparsion with boys. *Later*, we hear from them, "I had one and I was robbed." The defect is perceived as resulting from castration.

The non-possession of a male genital may have such an effect on a woman's mental life that we could call it a "genital complex." However, since males suffer the same condition, we can speak of it as a "female castration complex" or "penis envy."

---

[1]Ibid. p. 258

Actions, neurotic symptoms, and fantasies indicate, in many women, a hostile attitude toward males. The feeling that they have been damaged gives rise to the wish to avenge themselves. Their aim, though unconscious, is to castrate men.

A husband discovered that his wife was having affairs with amputees from a nearby army hospital. A confrontation took place and they decided she should undergo an analysis. In treatment she expressed strong feelings of inferiority. She had a younger brother: "He was a prince and I was the ugly duckling." She loved her husband but she was not attracted to him. Further sessions uncovered that she was more comfortable with men "who had something wrong with them." She felt a particular erotic interest in men who had lost an arm or a leg by amputation or in an accident. They were mutilated as she was. They could be comrades in suffering; she did not need to hate them as she hated men she admired.

Another patient said that she preferred Jewish men because they were more exciting and better lovers. Analytic exploration revealed that she regarded circumcision as a partial castration. She could enjoy herself because "he's a cripple too."

Psychoanalysts are familiar with patients who have attacked their lovers after being deflorated. One patient fell asleep beside her husband after their first intercourse, then awoke and attempted to strangle him. Only gradually was her husband able to bring her to her senses. There was no mistaking the meaning of her action: she was avenging herself for the injury done to her physical integrity. As in all such cases, her defloration had ended all attempts to deny the functional differences between male and female sexuality. Her revenge was retaliation for the injuries she had suffered because her father never gave her the gift she longed for. She transferred her anger from father to husband.

Some women seem less inclined to seek substitute gratification for their masculine wishes. Their symptoms reflect an attitude toward the male organ of its unimportance, even superfluity. For instance, most patients appreciate and eagerly seek the analyst's interventions and interpretations. One particular woman showed irritation when the analyst interrupted. He might be pointing out something she had overlooked, or suggesting that she further explore a statement she had just made. Her irritation became clear after the analysis of a dream. In the dream she had identified with the Virgin Mary, and the Immaculate Conception. What was repressed became conscious: "I can do it myself, without a man. I don't need anyone, I am able to do it alone." Her need in her analysis to uncover everything without the help of her therapist then became intelligible. And this woman had paid heavily for the neurosis: her obstinacy, overestimation of self, ana envy had destroyed more than one relationship that had been valuable to her. The symptoms described above bear a common characteristic: a possible wish fulfillment. The women are all gratifying an infantile desire to be like a man. An immaculate conception does indeed imply the uselessness of the male organ; it expresses castration in a sublimated form.

A patient compulsively drew her thighs rigidly together whenever her husband approached her. When treatment overcame the symptom, a fresh symptom developed to take its place, vaginismus. Vaginismus is a painful muscular contraction of the vagina that makes intromission of the penis impossible. This symptom reflects the unconscious fantasy of castrating a man. Its function is to protect the woman from impulses which frighten her. Once upon a time, when she was a little girl, vulnerable, helpless, frighened, the possession of a magic wand would have solved all her problems. The patient had a strong libidinal fixation on her father. Shortly before marriage she had a dream in which her father appeared. In the dreamhe had been run over. "He lost a leg or something like that and his money." Castration is here expressed, both by the loss of a limb and of money.

In the eyes of child, love and gifts are synonomous. The first proof of love and the first gift is mother's breast. The child gives mother a gift in return—the regulation of its bodily evacuations. In a particular psychosexual phase, the child considers its feces as a part of its own body and the girl hopes to obtain a penis by making one the way she makes feces. The boy too "identifies" feces and penis. But, he is afraid that his penis will be detached from his body in the same way feces are.

Of course the girl's hopes that a penis will grow remains unfilled. But there is a solution to her problem. To complete the eqution feces-gift-penis, she adds baby. The new hope is to get a baby from father as a substitute for the penis that was never granted her. This is also a substitute for the penis that was never granted her. This also is a gift, but at last there is an approximation to reality. At the Oedipus stage an identification with her mother and the development of maternal impulses takes place. Thus: the hoped-for possession of a child acts as compensation for her physical defect as a woman. If this process takes a "normal" course, the adult woman becomes reconciled to the facts of male and female anatomy and she longs for a child. Her castration complex produces no disturbing effects. Analytic observation shows how seldom this favorable outcome is attained. Much of a woman's normal physiological processes—menstruation, defloration, and childbirth—involve blood, which is a continuous reminder of her "wound" and "castration." As a consequence, there is some trace of a castration complex in every female. The degree is paramount. In normal women there are occasional indications from dreams of male tendencies. Beginning with these very mild signs of unconscious, normal penis envy there are many stages, leading in some cases to severe and complicated pathologies.

The normal attitude toward love of the other sex in both men and women is desire for mutual gratification. Psychosexual development that does not reach this level is always involved with a hostile-sadistic attitude toward the partner. A woman's desire to be masculine only occasionally succeeds in breaking through in a primitive sense. On the other hand, a considerable number of women, due to unconscious conflicts, are unable to fully adapt to the female sexual role. One alternative that is possible, in virture of the bisexual disposition in all humans—is homosexuality.

There are women who exhibit their masculinity in dress, hair style, and general behavior. In erotic relations with other women, they tend to adopt the male role. In many other women, the wish to be male remains repressed and takes sublimated form. These women do not consciously deny their femininity, rather they extend the areas traditionally associated with males. They believe that gender has nothing to do with capacities, especially in professional and intellectual spheres, and that these areas should be open to all who are interested and capable. This type ilustrates the successful sublimation of a woman's castration complex.

The neurotic transformations of the female castration complex fall into two groups. One group has a strong unconscious investment in the male role, retaining the fantasy of possessing a male organ. The other group, unconsciously, refuses to play the female role. This group exhibits an unconscious wish for revenge on the penis bearer. There is no sharp line of demarcation between the two groups: one does not preclude the other. Nevertheless, the preponderance of this or that attitude can often be recognized so that we may refer to a "wish-fulfillment type" or a "revenge type."

The wish-fulifillment type abounds in dreams, symptoms, and idiosyncracies which convert the fact of female anatomy into its opposite. A woman related a conscious memory from her youth. Her sister had just menstruated for the first time and was talking secretly with her mother. What occurred to the patient was, "Now she's going to get a penis." The implication was that in time she too would get one.

A patient reported that while in the waiting room she had the fantasy that a big black man would walk in and force her to suck on his enormous penis. When the analyst asked her to imagine the same thing with a midget, she giggled "Who wants that?" This woman sought help because her anger intruded on her career and on her social life. Analysis revealed that she considered women weak and passive and that anger was strength, meriting respect. "My mother was a castrated *shmota* (rag). My father had the balls in our family, he was king. He didn't take shit from anybody and I don't either." To the analyst's "You and your father are similar?" she replied, "You bet your ass." This attractive woman unconsciously clung to the idea that she had a penis; she took a special delight in talking like un uncultured male. Although she was approaching forty, she had no wish to have children, despite her husband's protestations.

A mildly obese woman in her mid-thirties went into analysis because she suffered from depression. A good working alliance developed and treatment proceeded favorably. The depression lifted, she lost weight, became more active socially, and was quite pleased with her progress. At this point in the treatment, she began to show more and more resistance: subtle signs of defiance toward the analyst, less productive free association, and a decrease in the dreams brought to the treatment sessions suggested the presence of a negative transference. A plateau had been reached and for a time very little progress was made. The patient expressed the wish to leave analysis. Then one day she began to describe some dreams she had had during the week. They were very vague, something about an older man, something about getting something. She left the session feeling disappointed and angry. The next day she reported that no sooner had she stepped into the street, then she caught herself thinking: "I will not be well until I have a penis." The idea that had been resisted suddenly appeared from her unconscious. The following sessions dealt with her expectation that the analyst, (as a substitute for her father) should provide her with the magic male genital longed for since childhood.

There seems noend to the variey of forms that penis envy may take. As in other neurotic conflicts, it is in the unconscious that compromises between impulses and repression occur. In many cases the unconscious is content with a substitute gratification. In such instances the libido may get displaced onto a part of the body other than the genital. A patient spoke of her pleasure in responding to certain "inferior people" with "fixed stare." She felt that taxi drivers and doormen would behave themselves if she looked at them in this way. Her problem was that later she would feel uncomfortable. Free associations led to the discovery that she associated her fixed stare with an erection. Just as male exhibitionists attempt to terrify women with the sight of their genitals, so she was trying to frighten these men with her unconscious phallus. Another patient recalled how she and her sister fought for the privilege of using a hose to water the garden. She found that activity "thrilling" and would continue until her father insisted that the garden had had more than enough water.

The symptoms described above bear a common characteristic: a positive wish fulfillment. The women are expressing their early desire to have what they felt was missing.

The second type, the revenger, is characterized by a desire to steal the precious organ, to take revenge on the privileged fellow. Most women who suffer envy of the penis—the wish fulfillment and the revenge type—disapprove of such feelings. Unconsciously they fear loss of control and that they will act out their primitive wishes. Their fear may lead to inhibition in the sexual act, to frigidity.

The complexities of frigidity are due, among other things, to ambivalence. In many cases, the woman consciously wishes to assume the female role and to accommodate the man, but unconsciously she strives to disappoint him. Moreover, she has a need to demonstrate to her partner and herself that his sexuality is of no importance to her. A deeper penetration into the unconscious of the frigid woman uncovers a very strong desire to be male. The analogy with ejaculatio praecox in the male is unmistakable. In cases of frigidity the pleasurable sensation is concentrated in the clitoris (her active, masculine organ), the viginal zone has none.

It is an old wives' tale but also a demonstrated fact of medicine that some women obtain pleasure from sex only after they have had a child. It would seem as though maternal feelings pave the way to femininity. In the light of the castration complex one can make deeper connections. Now that the woman has received the "gift" that compensates her for her defect, her "wound" is healed at last. Anger no longer gets in the way of her sensuality. What are we to say about those women who wish to get a child from a man against his will? We cannot fail to see in this an act of aggression; an unconscious tendency to take the penis from him in the form of a child. The other extreme among these women are those who refuse to have a child at all costs. They refuse any kind of "substitute"; further, they would be reminded of their femininity constantly if they became mothers.

It might be expected that men who are "lover types" would be most able to excite a frigid woman. This is not necessarily so; there are many women who need to debase a man as condition for love, like the neurotic men who are attracted only to debased women. For example, a young woman deeply distressed her family because she was attracted to men who were vulgar and rough and belonged to a lower economic class. In fact, the man she was planning to marry had a criminal record and had spent time in jail. "He's really sweet but they don't see that." Her choice of a love object was complicated, but debasement was one of the threads in the design.

One of the rules when an analysis begins, is that the analysand should make no major life decisions without first examining them in the analytic sessions. Such decisions include getting married or divorced, leaving a job, and so on. Because the young woman discussed above had an opportunity to explore the underlying motives for her object choice, she was in a better position to understand her true feelings and make a choice more in harmony with her own value system.

Another patient was seeing several men. She discovered, in analysis, that, if she picked a quarrel with her date and succeeded in forcing him to give in to her, her frigidity disappeared.

Cases of these kinds show that if a woman is to have a normal and gratifying love life, she must acknowledge and accept the male genital rather than need either to control it or surrender to it. Similarly, if a man is to enjoy a normal, loving relationship with a woman, he has to accept and acknowledge the reality of the vagina and its functions, and not see it as a child sees it: a ugly mutilated organ.

The Don Juan type of man has constantly to change partners. Compulsively he seduces, conquers, and rejects. This "lover" is really a "hater." He is avenging himself for the pain and disappointment he received from his very first love object—pain and disappointment he is no longer conscious of.

The experience of full sexual gratification binds a woman to a man. Only when complete satisfaction is not taking place, do we see a tendency toward promiscuity. This is particularly true of prostitutes. The frigid prostitute avenges herself on every man for the gift she never received. When a prostitute and a "John" (customer) get together, we have a meeting between a woman hater and a man hater. Prostitution is commonly associated with frigidity.

To repeat again, penis envy takes many forms. A woman who was very depressed complained that her life was utterly useless because she had been born a girl. A patient who came into treatment because she had been arrested in a department store for stealing a worthless trinket, discovered that unconsciously her kleptomania, which she had suffered from for years, was in the service of stealing the "magic organ."

There are women who feel horror at the sight of wounds; every wound re-awakens in their unconscious the idea of the "wound" they received in childhood. One woman refused to undergo surgery. Exploration revealed that "whoever is operated on is a cripple for life." In her unconscious an operation had made her a "cripple" in early childhood. Another patient desired sexual relations as long as her "wound" was avoided. She displaced her libido "upwards" to mouth and breasts and thereby softened the feeling of displeasure which originated from her castration complex. Oral and anal perversions in women are, to a considerable extent, effect of their penis envy.

Some women who reject their femininity mention a certain proviso all analysts are familiar with: "I could be content with being a woman if I were absolutely the most beautiful woman in the world." The fantasy envisions handsome men lying at her feet. The narcissism of these women considers this scenario not a bad compensation for the defect of being a woman. One woman added that she would give all the men the cold shoulder.

The castration complex of most women is not extreme. They can satisfy themselves with relatively harmless expressions of repressed hostility. A familiar trait in many women nowadays is a bit easier to understand. There are those who feel that they have gone through life waiting. They waited for "a tassle like Johnny's," They waited for a baby from Daddy. They waited for a man to find them attractive and lovable. And now they anxiously wait for their husbands to respond to them sexually. In their married lives they get their revenge on men: they keep them waiting on every possible occasion.

The multiplicity of manifestations of penis envy becomes tedious, but one aspect should be mentioned: the effect that such women have on their children. Where the mother herself has retreated to the anal-sadistic stage, she tends to reinforce this route. Consciously or unconsciously, she expresses feelings of disgust at the male body. Her aversion to men could have a permanent effect because it tends to undermine the heterosexuality of the growing girl.

Anal-sadistic women also produce negative effects on their sons, without any awareness of what they are doing. A little boy, proud of his genitals, loves to exhibit them to his mother for her admiration. If she responds negatively, no matter how subtly, he experiences a narcissistic blow. Such women feel a disgust reaction and anxiety to his touching himself, which leaves him confused and frightened. On the other hand, though they avoid his genital, they make a fuss over his bottom. They teach him cute words for it and take an excessive interest in his anal productions. The boy may be encouraged into a regressive orientation for his libido from the genital to the anal zone. Thus the woman who rejects her own femininity may create a boy who will grow up to be a woman hater.

One consolation for the limited number of analysands that an analyst has time to treat, is that when the work is successful, the children benefit too!

CHAPTER LXI

■ *More Freudian Than Freud*

Karl Abraham, perhaps the most loyal and certainly the most dogmatic of Freud's disciples, planned to visit in Easter. Freud was eagerly looking to the meeting. But "the monster" got in the way. Pichler (whose notes for 1925 show sixty-nine entries and one surgical intervention) was undertaking a major remodeling of the prothesis because it was causing Freud such discomfort and depriving him of the ability to speak. He had to put off the visit. The new plan was to see each other in the summer—it would have been their last chance to meet. Abraham contracted what was to prove a fatal illness and could not keep their summer date.

Josef Breuer, Freud's old friend and mentor, died at the age of eighty-four on June 20. Freud wrote an obituary for the *Zeitschrift,* and sent condolences to the family.

"Inhibitions, Symptoms and Anxiety" was completed in July. Whoever accuses Freud of rigidity and dogmatism has clearly never read this paper. Freud attacks his old theories, not so much for their incorrectness as for their incompleteness. He overhauled his basic concepts concerning symptom formation and the function of anxiety, both in normal and abnormal development. Difficult and abstruse as parts of "Inhibitions" are, it was well received by the psychoanalytic community.

In a letter to Pfister (January 3, 1926) he wrote:

> A new pamphlet of mine, "Inhibitions, Symptoms and Anxiety," is now being published. It shakes up so much that was established and puts things which seemed fixed into a state of flux again....But it would be rash to believe that I have now succeeded in finally solving the problem with which the association of anxiety with neurosis confronts us.

That month Freud also wrote an amusing note to Abraham. A mornig paper had run a lead article on psychoanalysis. The joke was that the morning paper was in Port-au-Prince, in Haiti, "a place that one does not correspond with every day."

Abraham presided over the Hamburg Congress, September 2-5. He was obviously ill and under the influence of medication aimed at controlling a chronic cough. The reason given was that during a lecture tour in Holland he had swallowed a fishbone that pierced the bronchus. Evidently the condition refused to heal and it was thought that it had led to a chronic bronchiectasis, dilation of the bronchial tubes that results in a chronic cough.

The Hamburg Congress was a success even though the scientific presentations were not quite as outstanding as at the previous Congress. What did merge, however, were some differences over the question of lay analysis between the many Americans present and the European groups. Lay analysis in this context meant nonmedical analysis. Should persons who are not trained physicians be permitted to practice psychoanalysis? Those who were against lay analysis took the position that opening the door to "anyone" would admit the chance of "wild analysis" (Freud's term for the treatment given by analysts who were not sufficiently trained). The profession would fill up with quacks and this would make the struggle for acceptance and respectability, already difficult, more arduous. If physicians seemd to be practicing wild analysis, they would be more readily controlled by medical colleagues and medical societies. Furthermore, since the lay analyst was untrained in medical diagnoses, he was incompetent to decide for which patients analysis was suitable. This problem could be solved if the patient had first to consult a physician, who would then make the recommendation. However, the law farbade any therapeutic measures to be carried out by nonmedical persons and members of the medical profession were forbidden by law to cooperate with nonmedical personnel. More important, if prospective students werc told that studying medicine was unnecessary, how many would submit to the toil and expense of medical school? The whole thing would lead, sooner or later, to the majority of psychoanalysts being nonmedical.

Freud had very strong feelings about training nonmedical people to practice analysis. Even though psychoanalysis had originated in the field of psychopathology, he knew that the discoveries he had made had significance far beyond the field of psychiatry. The insights and the understanding of human nature that analysis afforded made it inevitable that it should make valuable and crucial contributions to all fields of human endeavor. If the medical profession had exclusive domain over analysis, the latter risked becoming a mere chapter in medical textbooks on psychiatry, alongside those on electrotherapy, hypnosis, and so on. He desired that psychoanalysis should have a broader outlook than could be expected from physicians alone. On the other hand he would have been grieved if medical doctors stayed aloof from his work, because he knew that research had to come from the analysis of suffering people.

Although a practicing analyst could make suggestions and offer leads, valuable contributions would have to come from the experts in diverse fields, experts who had acquired a professional knowledge of psychoanalysis. Not only would representatives from other fields have to acquire suitable training, but they would have to carry out analysis of actual patients who had come for help. They would have to acquaint themselves with the deepest layers of the mind, and that could only come by working with people who were suffering.

Freud therefore warmly welcomed suitable candidates, men and women, from all walks of life into the therapeutic field. For him it was a matter of indifference if a student possessed a medical degree, or indeed, any academic degree—he welcomed persons of intelligence, sensitivity, responsibility, and integrity who showed a lively interest in the study of psychoanalysis.

The conflict over lay analysis was so emotionally charged that some delegations, including the American, threatened to withdraw from the International Association if nonmedical people were accepted. The vast majority of the members were physicians who stood against lay analysis. Jones urged Freud to drop the subject or face the dissolution of the Association. Freud described his position to Eitingon:

"I am a Commander-in-Chief without any army."[1]

By this time Freud had become the drawing card of Vienna. Eminences who visited there did their best to meet him. In December 1925, two of the visitors were Emil Ludwig and Stefan Zweig. Freud and Zweig became dear friends. Of Ludwig he said that he had no special impression. More than twenty years later Ludwig wrote, *Dr. Freud, An Analysis and a Warning* (N. Y. Hellman, Williams, 1947). From what Ludwig said about Freud he was obviously "returning the compliment."[2]

Regrettably, the last months of Abraham's relations with Freud were clouded by disagreement and misunderstanding. It all began when Samuel Goldwyn, the well-known movie director, conceived of a film depicting love stories of history. The first was to be Antony and Cleopatra. And whom did he have in mind as a consultant? Dr. Sigmund Freud of Vienna. He offered Freud $100,000 for his cooperation. Although Freud found the idea amusing, particularly the ingenious way of exploiting the association of love and psychoanalysis, he refused. Hans Sachs, who was in New York, reported that Freud's telegram of refusal caused a greater sensation than his most important work, *The Interpretation of Dreams.*

Goldwyn was not a man to be easily put off; he decided to go to Europe to see if the matter couldn't be resolved. He was interviewed by the New York *Times* aboard ship.

> So I thought I would go and see Freud and at least have a talk with the greatest love specialist in the world.... The finished picture produced with Professor Freud as collaborator will have audience appeal far greater than any productions made today, because these love revelations and psychological truths will strike fire with the deepest thoughts and feelings of the people who unquestionably react more strongly to the genuine in pictures.
> (Clark, p. 461)

Freud's reaction: "I do not intend to see Mr. Goldwyn."[3]

Six months later, the largest film company in Germany, *Universum Film Aktiengesellschaft*, decided to do a documentary on psychoanalysis and sought advice from Abraham and Sachs. Abraham contacted Freud and suggested that it would be better if they supervised the film than let some "wild analyst" do it. Freud refused to give his approval, but he did not actively oppose Abraham's involvement with the film company. In a letter to Ferenczi he wrote: "The film will be as unpreventable, it seems, as bobbed hair, but I'm not having mine cut, and neither will I have any personal connection with any film."[4]

Freud wrote to Abraham that his main objection was that abstract ideas and theories could not be adequately presented by the movies. However, if he were proved wrong, he would reconsider and give his own authorization. Actually, it was his name the film company sought and for which they were offering the money. Freud added that any money that he was paid he would give to *Verlag*.

---

[1]Eitingon, April 3, 1928
[2]Jones 3, p. 114
[3]Ibid. p. 462
[4]Eissler/Pictures, p. 224

The film, "Secrets of a Soul," was made and released in early 1926, with an explanatory monograph written for the audience by Sachs. This paper descirbed an actual case, naturally with some details altered to protect the anonymity of the patient. It was the case of a compulsive neurotic who also suffered a knife phobia.* The monograph traced the origin of the symptoms and the events that brought them to the surface. "Secrets of a Soul" was an honest attempt to present to a mass audience some of the basic concepts of psychoanalysis and, all things considered, did it fairly well. Nevertheless, it caused a good deal of trepidation throughout the profession, especially because it was endorsed by Abraham, the President of the International Association. It was a time when psychoanalysis was in disfavor (which occurs in waves, then recedes again). The press took full advantage of the story. It was said that having failed to find acceptance in scientific circles, Freud was now using theatrical techniques to advertise his ideas among the populace.

In a letter to Abraham (August 10, 1925) Freud complained that the film company was announcing that the film had been made "with Freud's cooperation" though without his consent. In New York, the film was entitled "The Mystery of the Soul," and claimed that "every foot" had been scrutinized and edited by Dr. Freud.

Abraham's health was continuing to decline, which threw more and more of the responsibility for the film onto Sachs. Doubts continued about how much psychoanalysts should sponsor film-makers. In the meantime two analysts from Vienna, Bernfeld and Storfer, were courting movie companies with their own material and invited Abraham to join them. Abraham pointed out that he had signed a contract and that he wouldn't get involved with another film project, nor should any other film be supported by members of the profession. This led to a dispute in the course of which Abraham came to feel that the two Viennese analysts were untrustworthy. Freud thought that Abraham's judgment was harsh, but Abraham stuck to his guns, reminding Freud how wrong he had been in the earlier case of Rank and Jung. Freud answered sharply that there was no reason why Abraham should always be right, but if he proved to be right in this case, Freud would be willing to agree with him again. Freud's letter ended with his wish for a speedy recovery for his colleague.

After the Hamburg Congress, where Abraham's sickness became public, he returned to Berlin to be treated by Fliess, Freud's one-time friend. The cynical, scientific Abraham was astonished to find how closely his mysterious ailment coincided with Fliess's mathematical computations. However, despite optimism, he was not improving and no one was able to diagnose the condition. Freud found this very unsettling and grew anxious. In the light of later medical knowledge, a diagnosis of lung cancer seems likely. Yet Abraham took some of the symptoms to be gall bladder infection and insisted on an operation. He turned to Fliess's calculations to decide the date of surgery. The operation did more harm than good. A letter from Abraham brought Freud regards from Fliess. Freud's response was "This expression of sympathy after twenty years leaves me rather cold."[1] He had always admired Abraham's scientific attitude, his display of practical judgment. All the more does one suspect that Freud was irritated that Abraham should come under Fliess's spell.

---

*Kine phobia refers to a person's experiencing extreme anxiety at the sight of or even the mention of the word "knife". The dynamic pertains to unconscious hostility and fear of loss of control.

[1]Jones 3, p. 116

Abraham's condition continued to deteriorate. On December 18, Sachs sent a telegram: "Abraham's condition hopeless." The end came on Christmas day; he was forty-eight years old.

Karl Abraham had come from a modest background. He was the younger of two sons of a teacher of religion. His mother, a cousin of his father, was warm, devoted, and unusually well educated. It was said she had literary and linguistic talents. They lived in a large, old-fashioned, rambling house, where a tradition of hospitality reigned. Karl was an excellent student, but an academic career in a German university held out little prospect for a poor Jewish boy. An affluent, eccentric uncle offered to pay his school fees if Karl would consent to become a dentist. He accepted but found that he did not like the profession and transferred to the school of general medicine. He married at twenty-nine and had a daughter and a son. He felt little need for social contact outside his family; he would arrange his contacts with colleagues during office hours. It was common knowledge that domestic ties took first priority. His wife and he shared common cultural interests and she was to play an active role in the organization of the Berlin Psychoanalytic Society. Abraham was known for his views on marital equality of the sexes.

His essay "Iknaton," an Egyptian Pharoah who lived over three thousand years ago, was the first attempt by a psychoanalyst to study the character of an historical person. After its publication in 1912, one of its readers said that more was known about the determining forces of Iknaton's character than about Abraham's.

His interest in psychiatry landed him on Bleuler's staff at the Burgholzli, where he met Jung but did not like him. At the Burgholzli he also became familiar with Freud's work. Personal contact with Freud led him into psychoanalytic practice and later into founding the Berlin Psychoanalytic Society. His love of philology found expression in his writing, fluent but precise and economical. In the course of his career he made extremely important contributions to psychoanalytic theory and technique. One reason his clinical results were so outstanding was his own optimism, a quality he held almost to the very end.

Jones once remarked that "the secret of Abraham's life and character was that he was so divinely normal."[1] Just under average height, of slight build, Abraham's attire was self-conscious, correct, almost dapper. He possessed considerable charm and was easy and friendly in his approach.

He was more Freudian than Freud himself. In his correspondence with Freud he emerges as the more dogmatic of the two in the cause of psychoanalytic psychology. He was a courageous man, in fact possessing such strong integerity that at times he seemed fearless. Yet Freud was not as sympathetic with him as he was with, say, Ferenczi. In a letter to Jung in December 1907, he wrote "...but there is something inhibited about him, no dash. At the crucial moment he can't find the right word."

Freud also disliked his formality. In reading some of his long letters to Freud, one does get the impression of someone pedantic, pedestrian, a hint of his being a bore.

But if Freud was not taken with Abraham's personality, there was no lack of appreciation for his importance to the psychoanalytic movement. Since his operation, Freud had given up attending the meetings of the Vienna Society. However, when the Society announced it was holding a memorial meeting for Abraham, Freud made a point of being present. The *Zeitschrift* was planning to devote the whole

[1]Eidelberg, p. 7

of his next edition to a commemoration of Freud's seventieth Birthday, but Freud instructed the editor to devote the issue instead to Abraham's memory.

In referring to the obituary he wrote for Abraham he said, "Exaggerations on the occasion of a death I have always found specially distasteful. I was careful to avoid them, but I feel this citation to be really truthful."[1] The citation was a quotation from Horace: "Integer vitae, sclerisque purus" (A man of upright life and free of stain). In 1908 at the unveiling of a memorial tablet to Fleischl, Professor Exner had quoted that same line about his old friend. Of all the men whom Freud had met, no two merited that description more than Fleischl and Abraham.

---

[1]Jones 3. p. 116

CHAPTER LXII

■ *The Voice Of The Intellect Is A Soft One*

After the death of Karl Abraham, Freud declared that no one was indispensable to the growth of the psychoanalytic movement. His own physical condition, however, was a matter of concern: how long would he be able to continue his work? The Pichler notes show seventy-seven entries for the year 1927. Among these is a personal reference to Freud: "The patient has made interesting self-observations about the ingratitude of patients and about the revolt against dependency."[1]

The note reminds us of Freud's suffering, but also that he was practically a semi-invalid. He did what he always did under adverse conditions, he worked and wrote. *The Future of an Illusion* appeared late in 1927. The book takes matters up where *Totem and Taboo* and "Thoughts for the Times on War and Death" had left off; it reflects Freud's development since the war. He was reluctant to publish his latest thoughts on religion because of his friendship with Oskar Pfister, the Swiss clergyman who employed psychoanalytic psychology in his counseling. On more than one occasion Pfister had come under sharp criticism for spreading that "dirty Viennese philosophy." Freud's genuine concern for his friend's feelings and his unwillingness to embrarrass him are revealed in a letter:

> In the next few weeks a pamphlet of mine will be appearing which has a great deal to do with you. I had been wanting to write it for a long time, and postponed it out of regard for you,but the impulse became too strong. The subject matter—as you will easily guess—is my completely negative attitude to religion, in any form and however attenuated, and though there can be nothing new to you in this, I feared and still fear, that such a public profession of my attitude will be painful to you. When you have read it you must let me know what measure of toleration and understanding you are able to preserve for the hopeless pagan
>
> Always your cordially devoted
> Freud (October 16, 1927)

Pfister's response was no surprise; nothing could change his devotion and loyalty

[1]Schur, p. 395

to Freud. He answered with vigor and enthusiasm.* Freud had used Pfister's arguments, which he attributed to a "discussant," in the final two chapters of the book.

"Illusion" aroused angry controversy that continues to this day. Until 1927, Freud had been concerned merely with the origins of religion; now he was examining its very nature and its future. In 1923 he had published "A Seventeenth Century Demonological Neurosis, " primarily a clinical work in which he had shown that in earlier centuries repressed impulses could be projected onto imaginary figures such as demons and devils. Today however these impulses were internalized and gave rise to pathology, physical and mental. This case had confirmed Freud's conviction that ambivalent feelings toward the father were the genesis of religions. He suggested that originally God and the Devil were one figure; with time they split into two opposing entities.

Freud had a good sense of which theories in his work would lead to criticism and he went out of his way to make particular positions clear, though it rarely helped. He is frequently charged with stating in this book that religious beliefs are an illusion, in the sense that they are false or nonexistent. These charges continued despite his care in explaining what he ment by the term "illusion."

> An illusion is not the same thing as an error,nor is it necessarily an error. Aristotle's belief that vermin are developed out of dung was an error, so was the belief of a former generation of doctors that *Tabes dorsalis* is the result of sexual excess....It would be incorrect to call these error illusions. On the other hand, it was an illusion of Columbus's that he had discovered a new sea-route to the Indies. The part played by his wish in this error is very clear....What is characteristic of illusions is that they are derived from human wishes....Illusions need not necessarily be false—that is to say, unrealizable or in contradiction to reality. For instance, a middle-class girl may have the illusion that a prince will come and marry her. This is possible; and a few such cases have occurred. That the Messiah will come and found a golden age is much less likely....Thus we call a belief an illusion when a wish-fulfillment is a prominent factor in its motivation, and in doing so we disregard its relations to reality, but just as the illusion itself sets no store by verification.
>
> (*The Future of an Illusion*, 1927 S.E. XXI, p. 31)

In previous writings, Freud had laid stress on the necessity of coming to terms with the child's complicated feelings toward the father, and with the role these feelings play in the history of religious beliefs. In his new book he focused on the helplessness of mankind in coping with the outer world, with himself, and with his relation to his fellow man. This last is a difficult, dangerous, and at times an

---

*and a book of his own:*The Illusion of a Future*

almost impossible task. Freud believed that the principle function of civilization was to protect mankind against the terrors of nature—the elements, illness, and of course death.

> ...nature rises up against us, majestic, cruel and inexorable; she brings to our mind once more our weakness and helplessness, which we thought to escape through...civilization....Life and the universe must be robbed of their terrors, nature must be humanized....If the elements have passions...if death itself is...the violent act of an evil will...we can deal by psychical means with our...anxiety.
>
> This process is the repetition of an infantile prototype. For once before one has found oneself in a similar state of helplessness: as a small child....Here too wishing played its part....
>
> (Ibid. p. 16)

Mankind personalizes nature, endows the force of the elements with the characteristics of a father and turns them into gods. He assigns to the gods three tasks:

> ...they must exorcize the terrors of nature, they must reconcile men to the cruelty of Fate, particularly as it is shown in death, and they must compensate them for the sufferings and privations which a civilized life in common has imposed on them....
>
> (Ibid. p. 18)

Our better understanding of the laws of nature has somewhat lessened the first demand: for instance knowledge of irrigation control of epidemics, and so on. The second, the fear of death, on the other hand, is as strong as ever, and offers the solution, an ever-protecting father, for the third demand—protection from our fellows and from the restrictions and constrictions imposed upon us by civilization itself. Today, religion's chief concern is to ally itself with ethics; modern religions endeavor to regulate relations among people. For example, religious issues have come to include the question of capital punishment, the right of abortion, women's right to be priests, and so on. Those who have a normal superego, require less supernatural sanction for their behavior. Religion, originally, represented a prohibition of murder and incest. Today, its insistence on regulating morality and life's daily tasks has not given it a more important role in the conscience of men.

Freud raises the interesting question: is it possible for man, someday, to face the hardships of life without the consolations offered by religion? His life work had been to reveal the power of emotions over reason, and one would expect a "no" to the question. But he doesn't say no, he says "maybe," and admits that perhaps he is now indulging in an illusion. He offers two major considerations: if we no longer conditioned our youth by the teachings of religion, and at the same time liberated them from the sexual restrictions society imposes on them, would it be possible for the intelligence thus released to be more effective than heretofore?

> they will have to admit...their insignificance in the machinery of the universe; they can no longer be the center of creation...the object of tender care on the part of a beneficent Providence....Men cannot remain children forever; they must in the end go out into "hostile" life. We may call this "education to reality." Need I confess to you that the sole purpose of my book is to point out the necessity for this forward step?....Their scientific knowledge has taught them much since the days of the Deluge, and it will increase their power still further. And, as for the great necessities of Fate, against which there is no help, they will learn to endure them with resignation....By withdrawing their expectations from the other world and concentrating all their liberated energies into their life on earth, they will probably succeed in achieving a state of things in which life will become tolerable for everyone and civilization no longer oppressive to anyone...they will be able to say without regret:
>
> "We leave Heaven to the angels and the sparrows."
>
> (Heine, Deutchland, Caput 1)
>
> (Ibid. p. 50)

Another consideration is that religion is to be regarded as a phase in the development of man. Just as individuals go through phases—childhood, adolescence, adulthood—so perhaps does man. It may turn out that just as earlier mythologies belong to man's earlier development, religion may represent his, let us say, adolescent phase. Every child has to learn to distinguish fantasy from reality, to separate his ideas and wishes from the facts of the external world, and eventually to learn independence, no longer turning to his parents for protection. Could it be that the same process applies to mankind as a whole? One could certainly make the case: animism gave way to to the religious phase which leads in turn to the scientific phase.

Freud would not admit that intuition, mysticism, and religious faith deserve the same place as science does, as avenues to knowledge.

> In the long run nothing can withstand reason and experience and the contradiction religion offers to both is only too palpable. We may insist as often as we like that man's intellect is powerless in comparision with his instinctual life, and we may be right in this. Nevertheless, there is something peculiar about this weakness. The voice of the intellect is a soft one, but it does not rest till it has gained a hearing. Finally, after a countless succession of rebuffs, it succeeds. This is one of the few points on which one may be optimistic about the future of mankind, but it is in itself a point of no small importance. And from it one can derive yet other hopes. The primacy of the intellect lies, it is true, in a distant, distant future, but

probably not in an infinitely distant one.
(Ibid. p. 55)

Freud concludes: "No, our science is no illusion. But an illusion it would be to suppose that what science cannot give us we can get elsewhere."[1]

Dour, tragic, pessimistic, Freud however ends The Future of an Illusion on a triumphant note: "The primacy of the intellect, Logos, reality, will prevail."

[1]Ibid. p. 56

CHAPTER LXIII

■ *Vaginal Father (?)*

The seed of psychoanalysis was planted when Anna O, Breuer's patient, was able to overcome her complex symptoms by recalling the events associated with their origin. For the next forty-five years, until his death, Freud's clinical experience led him to evolve what came to be known as psychoanalytic psychology. Psychoanalysis was rooted in, and was a product of clinical psychopathology. And yet, surprisingly, Freud considered the application of his theories to nonclinical fields even more important than their clinical aspects.

His foremost interest during his life was the problem of how man came to be what he is. He recognized that his own discoveries could lead to an understanding of the mystery of human nature. Manifestations of human activity, cultural elements, could then be understood in psychological terms. He believed that the scientific psychological study of anthropology, sociology, art and esthetics, religion, mythology, folkways and folk tales could bring us closer to understanding human enterprise than could the study of medical procedures. To take an example—one cannot appreciate the differences between an aborigine and a twentieth century person through the study of anatomy. In fact, Freud believed that eventually biochemical means would encompass therapy. "The man with the syringe is at our heels."

Freud raised questions: Did human beings who lived thousands of years ago have the same mental structure as we have today? Are psychoanalytic theories universal, or are they culture-bound? Are these real questions? Are answers possible, beyond mere speculation?

The "official" position of anthropology at that time was that psychoanalytic theory is not universal. Bronislaw Malinowski's work among the Trobriand Islanders was referred to as "proof" of the cultural relativity of such a theory. The Trobrianders, according to Malinowski, never manifested an Oedipus complex. After all, how could they develop one when the husband spent the night in his original family's hut, while his wife and children lived with the wife's brother? In fact, the Trobrianders seemed to remain ignorant of the father's role in procreation. Psychoanalysts were unconvinced. But they had no facts and so remained silent.

Even though Malinowski is still associated with "anti-psycho-analysis," in his published findings he paid warm tribute to Freud. He emphasized the stimulation psychoanalytic concepts brought to the field of anthropology, and he acknowledged the correlation between much of the theory and "human nature" as observed in various cultures.

Then at last, an opportunity arose to test the universality of psychoanalytic theory by direct observation. In 1928, Geza Roheim, a well-trained analyst and a professor of anthroplogy (he had been analyzed by Ferenczi), organized a two-to-three year expedition to Normanby Island off New Guinea, and to Central Australia to investigate at first hand the lives of people who had not yet been subjected to modern civilization: the Trobrianders and the Somalis. The project, which stirred up much excitement in the world of psychoanalysis, was made possible through the generosity of Marie Bonaparte.

Even in the days when critics were saying that psychoanalysis was ''Viennese,'' Freud was convinced that the basic theory should apply to all human beings, regardless of their culture. In other words, all societies would manifest an incest taboo, prohibition against murder, the Oedipus complex, and so on. If valid, this view would blend anthropology with psychoanalysis.

> Roheim is burning with eagerness to ''analyze'' his primitive natives. I think it would be more urgent to make observations concerning the sexual freedom and the latency period of children, on any signs of the Oedipus complex, and on any indications of a masculine complex among the primitive women. But we agreed that the program would in the end follow the opportunities that presented themselves.
>
> (Marie Bonaparte, January 16, 1928)

Roheim's findings corroborated Malinowski's, but his conclusions were different. It is the difference between one who has knowledge of the unconscious dynamic in human affairs, and one who accepts at face value the appearance of things. Roheim clearly demonstrated that classic Oedipal feelings were present among the Trobrianders, but were displaced onto the maternal uncle. Furthermore, that ''ignorance'' of the father's role in procreation is evidence of denial, a defense mechanism that is familiar to all psychoanalysts.

Roheim's conclusions are summed up in *Psychoanalysis and Anthropology* (1950): biology is basic to the fate of the species. All humans are subject to a long dependency as compared to other species, and a rapid growth of intelligence. And they all pass through the classic psychoanalytic developmental stages. Cultural controls are necessary to govern instinctual drives and ensure social conformity and survival. Separation anxiety and castration anxiety are basic to all cultures. ''When we are children we wish to be adults, and when we are adults we wish to be children.'' Roheim published many papers; they all corroborated the universality of psychoanalytic psychology.

For the reason that the unconscious is timeless and universal, study of the myths and rites of primitive peoples help us to understand the fantasies of ''civilized'' neurotics. To cite one example, psychoanalysts had become familiar with male patients who dreamed that they had vaginas, or that both they and their male analyst had breasts. Some would even dream of having intercourse with other men. Yet these men were in no overt way homosexual; rather they were maternal to their wives and children, and felt a constant need to be loved. Analysis deduced a strong identification with the pre-Oedipal and the Oedipal mother. This very situation was reflected in an initiation ritual of the Ngallunga tribe that Roheim observed and reported on. The function of the ritual was to separate the young men from their mothers. At the ceremony an older man would show his subincision hole (a slit in the underside of the foreskin) to pubertal boys and ceremoniously welcome them into the fathers' group. In other words the ritual offered the youngsters an artificial vagina in place of a real one. Psychoanalysts derived the term "vaginal father" from Roheim and applied it to males with the symptoms described above.[1]

Until after the second World War, Roheim was practically the only anthropologist who supported Freud. Since then psychoanalytic theory has gained a more sympathetic hearing among the profession. Margaret Mead, for example, discusses at length the links between social anthropology and Freud's theories. And Clyde Kluckholm, a leading American anthropologist, wrote:

> The facts uncovered in my own field work and that of my collaborators have forced me to the conclusion that Freud and other psychoanalysts have depicted with astonishing correctness many central themes in motivational life which are universal. The styles of expression of these themes and much of the manifest content are culturally determined, but the underlying psychological drama transcends cultural difference.
>
> (Zilborg G. One Hundred Years of American Psychiatry, Columbia Univ. Press, N.Y. 1944)

Today most scholars agree that there may be varieties of personalities, but there is only one unconscious.

Freud's contribution to anthropology and humanity was well summed up by Thomas Mann:

> And no less firmly do I hold that we shall one day recognize in Freud's life-work the cornerstone for the building of a new anthropology and therewith of a new structure...which shall be the future dwelling of a wiser and freer humanity. This physician-psychologist will, I make no doubt at all, be honored as the pathfinder towards a humanism of the future...
>
> (Mann T. Essays on Three Decades, N.Y. Alfred Knopf, 1947 , p. 427)

Roheim G. "The Eternal Ones in Dreams" IUP, p. 155-177, 1945

CHAPTER LXIV

■ *A Name For Dessert*

Despite the enthusiasm and excitement engendered by the Roheim expedition, Freud was living through a difficult time. The physical suffering had increased, which led to desperate attempts to alleviate it. Pichler saw him for the last time that year on June 15, 1928, the forty-ninth visit in five and a half months. There was the familiar misery of the prosthesis and Pichler tried building one after another. At times Freud couldn't tolerate wearing the lower one at night, but leaving it out would cause shrinkage and more difficulty next day. For the past year his son Ernst had been urging him to see a famous oral surgeon in Berlin, a Professor Schroeder, but Freud's loyalty toward Pichler made him delay this plan. Pichler then confessed that he had come to the end of the road; he could do no more. Schroeder was sent for and came to see Freud. He felt sure that he could help and arrangements were made for Freud to spend some time in Berlin. Pichler behaved like the perfect gentleman he always was. He was cooperative in regard to the Berlin project and when, eventually, Freud had to return to him, he treated him with the same devotion he had always shown.

Freud and Anna spent two months in Berlin. At Freud's request, the reason given to his public was that he and Anna were visting his children and grandchildren. By this Freud avoided any reflection on his Viennese surgeon, Pichler. Old friends came to visist—Ferenczi, Marie Bonaparte, Lou Andreas-Salome, and of course, family. It was during this visit that he enjoyed his first ride in an airplane: "I found the sensation startling and rather pleasant."[1]

Many years of correspondence had formed a strong bond between Lou Andreas-Salome and Freud. Now, during this visit, they were able to walk together in the parks along the Tegelsee. Flowers grew there in abundance and Freud picked a bunch of pansies for her. Although his cancer made talking difficult, they reminisced for hours. Almost twenty years earlier Lou had shown him a poem, "Prayer to Life," which he thought had been written by Nietzsche:

> "Millenia to be, to think to live,
> Hold me in both your arms with might and main.
> If you have no more happiness to give,
> Give me your pain."

Freud had found it offensive. "No, no. I could not go along with that. A good head cold would cure me of all such wishes." In truth it was she, not Nietzsche, who had written the poem. "Suddenly," says her biographer, "Lou asked Freud

[1]Clark, p. 472

whether he still remembered her 'Prayer to Life,' the poem which he thought Nietzsche had written. Freud did remember. 'And then,' Lou wroter later, 'something happened that I did not understand myself, but no power in the world could have stopped me; my trembling lips in revolt against his fate and martyrdom, burst out: "You have done what I , in my youthful enthusiasm, only raved about." ' Startled by her own words, Lou burst into tears. Freud did not answer. 'I only felt his arms around me,' she wrote."[2]

Freud returned to Vienna with a less bulky prosthesis which he claimed was "seventy per cent" better than the previous one.

Psychoanalysis had now come into vogue in Paris and Dr. Gilbert Robin, former chief of the Paris Psychiatric Clinic, visited Freud. He later published an account of his impressions:

> the most incorruptible savant in a time of corruption....Have we ever known a psychologist, a philosopher or a physician attain such a height of fame in his life-time? Has so much noise ever emerged from so much silence? Psychology, pathological medicine, literature can no longer dispense with him; the salons know no other conversation; there is no dinner party at which his name does not turn up during the dessert.

When told that a French translation of his "Autobiography" was soon to appear accompanied by his photograph Freud commented: "adding pictures of an author seems to me a bad habit, a nuisance, a concession to the bad taste of the public. What the author looks like has nothing to do with the reader...."[2]

That year Ernest Jones and his wife suffered the loss of their young daughter.

> My painful sympathy draws on my own experience. I recognize that the potion you had to take in one drain was set before me in two doses. To be sure, Sophie was a beloved daughter, but not a child. Only when three years later, in June of 1923, little Heinele died did I become weary of life for good. There is a very peculiar point of agreement between him and your little one. He, too, was of superior intelligence and indescribable spiritual grace, and he repeatedly said that he would die soon. How do these children come to know these things?
>
> You and your dear wife are of course young enough to regain your attachment to life.
>
> Jones, March 11, 1928

[1]Ibid. p. 472
[2]MB July 28, 1928

CHAPTER LXV

Dear Max

For some time Marie Bonaparte had been urging Freud to engage a personal physician, to have someone to watch over his daily health and to be in contact with the surgeons and specialists as they were needed. She recommended Max Schur, an excellent internist who had the rare attribute of being psycho-analytically trained. Freud agreed.

Schur was only thirty-one years old and naturally viewed Freud with awe. The initial meeting went very well with Freud insisting upon the basic conditions of their relationship: he was to be told the truth always, and nothing but the truth. "He then added, looking searchingly at me: 'Promise me one more thing; that when the time comes, you won't let me suffer unnecessarily.' All this was said with the utmost simplicity, without a trace of pathos, but also with complete determination. We shook hands at this point."[1]

Freud ended the interview by saying that he did not expect any professional courtesy and that he must be charged a normal fee. When he received Schur's bill at the end of the year, as was customary, he considered it inadequate.

> My Dear Doctor Schur:
>
> I am in a quandary as to how to react to the bill you sent me for the past year. If I submitted it to a professional medical organization, you would probably be called upon to account for an unprofessional disregard of medical accomplishment. I feel that you have backed away from the contract upon which our formal relations are based. I do not want to pay this bill and suggest you send me a more appropriate one.
>
> with cordial devotion
> Your
> Freud
> (January 10, 1930)

"Dear Max" was a perfect choice: his resourcefulness, his consideration, his untiring patience were unsurpassed. He and Anna were ideal guardians. They became expert at evaluating the slightest change in Freud's condition and this watchful care and skill in detecting the earliest signs of danger prolonged Freud's life by years. Anna, with a characteristically low profile, played many roles. She was a nurse, a

[1]Schur, p. 40

companion, a truly "personal" physician, secretary, co-worker, and a shield against the intrusions of the world.

All Freud's physicians attested to his being a model patient. He was touchingly appreciative for relief and, in all the years of suffering, there was never any complaining or sign of irritability or annoyance. His gratitude, consideration, and politeness to doctors never wavered. He had a favorite expression; "It is no use quarreling with fate."[1]

In January 1929, a professor of philosophy at Harvard University invited Jones to edit a source book of Freud's writings. He was to take one ninth of the writings and arrange and edit them for a single volume. Jones wrote to Freud for advice; the answer was typical Freud:

> Dear Jones 4.1. 1929
>
> I do not find it easy to answer your question, and shall not be able to get beyond a for and against. Fortunately I don't have to decide.
>
> Fundamentally the whole idea is very repellent to me, typically American. One can be sure that when such a "source" book exists no American will ever touch the original writings. But perhaps he will not do so anyhow, and will go on getting his information from the muddy popular sources. So that speaks in favor of your doing it. On the other hand, if you undertake it, it would be a tedious and laborious task, one not quite worthy of you. Now that you are fifty you should employ your working powers for more original work. Speaking as your friend I can only advise you not to undertake it.
>
> Against this, however, is the fact that when the publisher fancies he has found something that will pay him he will not desist because of your refusal. He will hand over the task to someone else, and heaven knows what he will make of it. Most certainly he wouldn't do it as well as you.
>
> That is how the considerations balance each other. Beyond them all an inner voice tells me that the world will go on very much the same whether the Americans get a good or a bad source book for my writings.
>
> I believe I have been sincere. And I shall not be offended at hearing that you have refused the offer.
>
> Herzlicht
> Ihr
> Freud

Jones replied that Freud's amusing letter was exactly what he had expected in the first place and he did not know why he had bothered Freud with the question.

---

[1]Jones 3, p. 245

CHAPTER LXVI

Banal Truths

Freud felt that clarity of thought was the most precious thing he owned and he refused to take any opiates or barbiturates that might interfere with his thinking. The only general sedative which he accepted was aspirin or an occasional Pyamidom for migraine. He maintained this attitude up to the end. At a time when his health was troubling him a great deal he resumed his literary activity. In November 1929, he sent to press *Civilization and its Discontents.*

> Dear Lou July 28, 1929
>
> You will have guessed with your usual perspicacity why I have taken so long to answer you. Anna has already told you that I am writing something, and today I wrote the last sentence, which—as far as is posible here without a library—finishes the work. It deals with civilization, guilt feelings, happiness, and similar lofty matters, and it strikes me, no doubt rightly, as quite superfluous in contrast to earlier works, which after all always derived from some inner urge. But what else should I do? One cannot smoke and play cards the whole day! I no longer walk very much, and most of what there is to read does not interest me anymore. I wrote and the time passed quite pleasantly that way, I have discovered the most banal truths in the course of writing this work.

Freud felt that *Civilization and its Discontents* was nothing more than psychology applied to the field of sociology. The book is eaiser to read than to summarize. Writing in a conversational style, Freud lets his thoughts wander, and drops sharp insights along the way. Even when the content is not very original, it is expressed in his personal style.

The book begins in the widest area possible, man's relation to the universe. Romain Rolland had described to him mystical feelings of oneness with the universe, feelings which Freud himself had never experienced. Freud called it an "oceanic" feeling and traced it back to the earliest stage of infancy, to a time when the infant made no distinction between the self and the outer world. He then raised the question which everyone, sooner or later, asks, what is the purpose of life? Freud stated that in his opinion the question has no meaning. He pointed out how rarely this is raised in regard to animal life. He turned to the more modest question: if we study human behavior what does it reveal as its aim? Indisputably, the answer is happiness; the term is used in the very broadest sense and includes pleasure, bliss, contentedness, peace of mind—the satisfaction of all desires. Life is in fact dominated by the pleasure-pain principle. In its most intense form the feeling is only temporary; any continuation of the pleasure principle assumes a milder quality. The possibility of unhappiness lies more readily at hand. It does not seem that human happiness is the purpose of the universe. Unhappines, he said, has three sources: dangers from the outer world, bodily suffering, and what is probably the most painful of all, our relation with our fellow man.

Freud discusses at length this subject of social relations, the beginning of civilization. Men discovered that if they banded together, even if it meant restricting their own immediate impulse gratification, they would be stronger than any single man, however strong he was, who was accustomed to gratifying his impulses unrestrainedly The strength of any individual was condemned as "brute force." The first requisite of a culture, therefore, is the assurance that a law once made will not be broken in favor of any individual.

This first requisite of a culture led to conflict between the wish for personal gratifications and the demands of society. A vital question presents itself for the future of civilization: is the conflict between the individual and the group reconcilable or not? In this regard Freud presents an awesome list of the restrictions imposed on man's sexual life.

> The sexual life of civilized man is notwithstanding severely impaired; it sometimes gives the impression of being in process of involution as a function, just as our teeth and hair seem to be as organs. One is probably justified in assuming that its importance as a source of feelings of happiness, and therefore in the fulfillment of an aim in life, has sensibly diminished. Sometimes one seems to perceive that it is not only the pressure of civilization but something in the nature of the function itself which denies us full satisfaction and urge us along other paths. This may be wrong; it is hard to decide.
>
> (*Civilization and its Discontents*, 1930, S.E. XXI, p. 105)

Society makes great demands on the individual—for example, "Thou shalt love thy neighbor as thyself"—to counteract the aggressive cruelty inherent in man. It is not necessary to go far back into history to confirm this.

> The element of truth behind all this, which people are so ready to disavow, is that men are not gentle creatures who want to be loved and who at the most can defend themselves if they are attacked; they are, on the contrary, creatures among whose instinctual endowments is to be reckoned a powerful share of aggressiveness. As a result, their neighbour is for them not only a potential helper or sexual object, but also someone who tempts them to satisfy their aggressiveness on him,

> to exploit his capacity for work without compensation, to use him sexually without his consent, to seize his possessions, to humiliate him, to cause him pain, to torture and to kill him. *Homo homini lupus*. (Man is a wolf to man.)
>
> Civilization has to use its utmost efforts in order to set limits to man's aggressive instincts....In spite of every effort, these endeavors of civilization have not so far archived very much.
>
> The communists believe...if private property were abolished, all wealth held in common, and everyone allowed to share in the enjoyment of it, ill-will and hostility would disappear among men. Since everyone's needs would be satisfied, no one would have any reason to regard another as his enemy; all would willingly undertake the work that was necessary....Aggressiveness was not created by property. It reigned almost without limit in primitive times, when property was still very scanty, and it already shows itself in the nursery almost before property has given up its primal, anal form. It forms the basis of every relation of all affection and love among people....
>
> It is clearly not easy for men to give up the satisfaction of this inclination to aggression. They do not feel comfortable without it....It is always possible to bind together a considerable number of people in love, so long as there are other people left over to receive the manifestations of their aggressivenes.
>
> (Ibid. p. 114)

Thus, if civilization imposes too great sacrifices on man's sexuality and aggressivity, it will make it difficult for man to be happy.

Freud reminds us that when he assumed the existence of a death instinct, he raised a worldwide outcry even among those in analytic circles. Although originally he had presented the concept tentatively, in the course of time he became convinced of its validity.

> I can no longer think in any other way. To my mind, they are far more serviceable from a theoretical standpoint than any other possible ones; they provide that simplification, without either ignoring or doing violence to the facts, for which we strive in scientific work.

He however admitted that his view of a life and death instinct reflects how things appear in our present state of knowledge, and that future research and reflection may shed further light on the matter.

Freud maintained that the tendency to aggression, the externalization of the death instinct, was the most powerful obstacle to civilization and "is an original, self-subsisting instinctual disposition in man."[1]

---

[1]ibid. p. 122

Freud ended the book with an examination of that part of the self called the superego, or conscience. The conscience does to the individual what he wishes to do to others. Tension between the conscience and the forbidden wishes gives rise to guilt. In adult life this is experienced as fear of public opinion or "social anxiety." There are many who would do "wicked" things if they could get away with it, but when the superego is firmly established, its disapproval causes fear stronger than that of the disapproval of other people.

At this point Freud put forward the idea that the sense of guilt is the response to repressed aggression. Further, since guilt is to a large extent unconscious, its manifest form is a general feeling of discontent, of uneasiness, of an underlying unhappiness. "The intention is to represent the sense of guilt as the most important problem in the development of civilization and to show that the price we pay for our advance in civilization is a loss of happines through the heightening of the sense of guilt."[1]

If we compare *The Future of an Illusion* and *Civilization and its Discontents*, we are struck by the change in attitude. The triumphant note of the former gives way to pessimism. Many have suggested that the state of the world looked bleak, the captialist economics of the West had collapsed, and Freud had no faith in the communist revolution. His bodily suffering, which was depleting his capacity to enjoy life, has of course also been suggested as a determinant of his deeply pessimistic mood. Freud himself preferred to believe that his conclusions were based on ojective not subjective reactions. It had been ten years since he proposed the death instinct in "Beyond the Pleasure Principle," and since then he had had ample time and opportunity to test his new theory in his private laboratory, the analyses of his patients.

The book ends with the following paragraph:

> The fateful question for the human species seems to me to be whether and to what extent their cultural development will succeed in mastering the disturbance of their communal life by the human instinct of aggression and self-destruction. It may be that in this respect precisely the present time deserves a special interest. Men have gained control over the forces of nature to such an extent that with their help they would have no difficulty in exterminating one another to the last man. They know this, and hence comes a large part of their current unrest, their unhappiness and their mood of anxiety. And now it is to be expected that the other of the two "Heavenly Powers," eternal Eros, will make an effort to assert himself in the struggle with his equally immortal adversary.

Four years later, when Hitler came to power, Freud added another sentence: "But who can predict his success and the final outcome?" What might Freud have added after Auschwitz and Hiroshima?

---

[1]Ibid. p. 134

CHAPTER LXVII

■ *Bible Of The Ungodly*

In july, 1930, Freud received a letter announcing that he had been awarded the Goethe Prize for literature. He was greatly pleased by the honor of association with Goethe.

> Dear Dr. Zweig, 21.8. 1930
>
> Of the many congratulations which the Goethe Prize brought me none has touched me so deeply as the one which you extorted from your poor eyes (though there is no evidence of this in your handwriting) and this is obviously because I feel with you as with scarcely anyone else that my friendship meets with a real response. I do not deny that I was pleased about the Goethe prize. The thought of a closer connection with Goethe is very tempting, and the prize itself is more an act of deference to the person than an appraisal of his achievement....As I read your letter I discovered that I would have been not much less pleased had they given you the prize, and it would really have been more appropriate, but no doubt many similar things lie in store for you.
>
> My wife and daughter send warm regards to you, and to your wife whom I would like to thank especially for her congratulations. My daughter will represent me at the Goethe celebration in Frankfort.
>
> With every good wish
>
> Yours
>
> Freud

A few days later he began to compose his address to the Goethe Foundation and, in his own masterly way, he brought psychoanalysis into relation with Goethe and his works. In this way he was justifying his psychological studies of great men such as Leonardo and Goethe: "So that if his spirit reproaches me in the next world for adopting the same attitude toward him, likewise I shall simply quote his own words in my defense." He could not travel to Frankfurt, let alone address an audience, because of his prosthesis.

> Unfortunately I cannot come to the celebration in Frankfurt; my health is not reliable enough for

> such an undertaking. The audience will lose nothing by my absence; my daughter is certainly more pleasant to the eye and ear than I am. She is going to read a few lines dealing with Goethe in relation to psychoanalysis and defending the analysts against the reproach of having impugned the veneration due to the great man by their analytical invertigations.
> (Roberts, p. 367)

He received many letters of congratulations, but at the same time a number of newspaper articles appeared "regretting" that Freud was on the point of death. Freud felt that these were expressions of veiled hostility, and observed that it would keep new patients away. Mostly, however, he was amused by the number of cures for cancer that seemed to exist all over the world.

In September, Freud's mother died from gangrene of the leg at the age of ninety-five. Whatever Freud's relation to his mother had been in his earlier years, it had been one of cordial filial duty during the last. To his nephew Samuel he wrote, "Mother died peacefully this morning in her bedroom in Vienna. The funeral may be on Saturday. At ninety-five she well deserved to be relieved."[1] There was no apparent grief at her death.

> I will not disguise the fact that my reaction to this event has because of special circumstances been a curious one. Assuredly, there is no saying what effects such an experience may produce in deeper layers, but on the surface I can detect only two things: an increase in personal freedom, since it was always a terrifying thought that she might come to hear of my death; and secondly, the satisfaction that at last she has achieved the deliverance for which she had earned a right after such a long life. No grief otherwise, such as my ten years younger brother is painfully experiencing. I was not at the funeral; again Anna represented me as at Frankfort. Her value to me can hardly be heightened.
> (E. J. Sept. 15, 1930)

1931 was Freud's seventy-fifth year. He had an intense dislike of ceremonies and he braced himself for the unpleasant eventualities.

> Last week there also began the threat of another calamity....The *Gesellschaft der Aerzte* have nominated me and Landsteiner (the Nobel Prize man) for the Honorary Membership of the Society, and it will soon be ratified. A cowardly gesture at the appearance of success....It won't do to refuse; that would only mean creating a sensation. I shall cope with the affair by a cool letter of thanks. (Eitingon, March 20, 1931)

---

[1]Clark, p. 482

How else could he respond to such a gesture from people who for years had done nothing but discourage, persecute, and insult?

And Freud's strength was taxed from another source. The particularly difficult surgery he had undergone the past October was a harbinger of things to come: after a spring of misery, more surgical procedures were deemed necessary. The operation, April 24, removed "at the twelfth hour" tissue that was becoming malignant. The hope had lasted for eight years that the first radical jaw operation had brought about a permanent cure; now that hope was gone. The future must consist of watching out for further recurrences and dealing with them as they arose.

More blows were to follow. Professor Guido Holzknecht was a leading radiologist in Vienna, one of the pioneers of that science. But like other pioneers in that field he had become a victim of it. An amputation of his right arm failed to arrest the cancer and he lay dying. He had been a patient of Freud's and Freud and Schur visited him in the hospital. Of course, none of them were under any illusion. On parting Freud said, "You are to be admired for the way you bear your fate." Holzknecht replied, "You know I have only you to thank for that."[1]

Freud returned from his own convalescence at the sanatorium in May. His family was delighted to have him home for his birthday but there was no question of any celebration. Nevertheless he received letters and gifts from all over the world, "Not to mention a forest of splendid flowers."[2] Marie Bonaparte sent him a Grecian vase. In thanking her, he added, "It is a pity one cannot take it into one's grave."[3] (As it happened, his wish was to be fulfilled: his ashes now repose in that vase.) An ivory statue of Vishnu arrived from India accompanied by a poem in Sanskrit (with an English translation). From New York came a cablegram: "Men and women recruited from the ranks of psychoanalysis, medicine and sociology are assembling in New York to honor themselves by honoring on his seventy-fifth birthday the intrepid explorer who discovered the submerged continents of the ego and gave a new orientation to science and life." Among those present were Clarence Darrow and Theodore Dreiser.

That year, 1931, was a bad one: the Austrian economy was collapsing and Hitler's aggressions were gaining strength in Germany. In contrast, as though a reminder of Eros, the creative instinct, and the human spirit, the year was also marked by the publication of Freud's Complete Works. The literary and political journal *Die Weltbuhne* published an extraordinary tribute to him under the signature of Kurt Tucholsky:

> Freud's Complete Works have been published. Eleven volumes which shook the world....According to Schopenhauer it is the fate of truth to appear at first paradoxical, then tirvial. Freud is a good example of this....But one can be sure that it will continue to be an active force....Parts of these eleven volumes, particularly in the early ones, are like thrilling detective stories. You can see how the theories slowly germinate, emerge from their broken covering, see the light of day

---

[1]Jones 3, p. 157
[2]Ibid. p. 158
M.B. May 6, 1931

> and suddenly make their appearance with power and assurance. Freud's art is everywhere unvarying; in the fundamental works and in the short essays....The childish joy which Americans and other nations warped by puritanism feel in at last being able to speak publicly of sex is not Freud's fault. The great renewer of old, buried truth—of the truth that the will of man is not free—will remain. Freud's limitations are obvious in his books. He is not God, but he has taught us to discern the part played by illness in the criticisms leveled against him. let it be said for the benefit of semi-educated Catholics: his work is the Bible of the ungodly. Ignorance of his work means failure to understand the world. Sigmund Freud will be seventy-five on May 6th. We greet him in love and respect.
>
> (Roberts, p.369)

The editor of *Die Weltbuhne*, Carl von Ossietzky, was to be one of the first victims of the Nazis.

CHAPTER LXVIII

■ *Why Stop At A Kiss?*

The accumulation of honors went on. That year, 1931, the town of Freiberg placed a plaque at his birthplace. In a letter to his nephew Samuel he wrote, "Think what a treat it would have been for grandfather and for your father to witness the ceremony, but of course grandfather would have had to be one hundred sixteen years old at the time."[1] The University of London invited Freud to deliver the annual T.H. Huxley lecture. For years he had been an admirer of Huxley and being chosen for the occasion pleased him. Unfortunately he had to decline the honor.

He felt strong enough however to leave for his usual summer vacation, although only as far as a suburb of Vienna. (In fact he was never to leave Vienna again until his flight from the Nazis in 1938.) He found a delightful spot in Polzleinsdorf with a jewel of a park. His surgeon visited him every day. In July he told Eitingon that in his leisure he had composed a "hate list" of seven or eight people. Naturally curiosity is aroused as to what names "made" the list. Only one was mentioned, a certain Theodore Lessing. Lessing had recently dedicated a book, *Jewish Self-Hatred,* to Freud with the words "In devotion from an opponent."

A few years later the whole story came out. In 1936 a certain Kurt Hiller had written a book that contained a biographical essay on Theodore Lessing. He sent the essay to Freud who replied in the following letter:

> I have read your essay on Th. Lessing with great interest and I believe understanding....To me he was to the depths of my being antipathetic...long before the War....It was the time when every day or...every week, brought me an abusive article about my psychoanalysis. One day a newspaper article reached me which ridiculed it in the most hateful manner as a lucubration of the Jewish spirit. It was signed by a Theodore Lessing who was then quite unknown to me....In my innocence I assumed he must belong to the family of the great critic and dramatist, so I wrote him a letter recalling the memory of his revered ancestor. To my astonishment he told me he was himself a Jew and mentioned the Old Testament name of his daughter. You know that Jewish families have out of their respect for Lessing, Schiller and others adopted their names. I turned away from him in disgust.

[1]Quoted by Clark, p. 482

Freud ended the letter with a discussion in general terms of the nature of self-hatred:

> It may come about through someone hating his father intensely and nevertheless identifying himself with him; that results in the self-hatred and the splitting of the personality. Don't you think that the self-hatred as shown by Th. L. is an exquisitely Jewish phenomenon? I really think it is.
>
> (Jones 3, p. 160)

Later, Lessing met his death at the hands of the Nazis.

In September Ferenczi sent Freud a copy of a paper he intended to read before the upcoming Congress. He felt he had discovered a second function of dreams—to deal with traumatic experiences. Freud dryly answered that this was actually their first function, which psychoanalytic theory had expounded many years before.

In October Ferenczi spent a couple of days in Vienna, and he and Freud discussed the theory and technique that Ferenczi was developing. Five weeks later Ferenczi wrote that he had thought the matter over carefully and he had not changed his mind.

Freud had always regarded the psychoanalytic method as a means of investigating the human mind. The process itself, the overcoming of resistances, the examination of defense mechanisms, the uncovering of unconscious conflicts, brought relief from suffering to the patient. In fact Freud warned against "furor therapeuticus." He observed that the therapist's need to cure was a repetition of parental need and parental demands made upon the child, and that it was countertherapeutic.

Ferenczi concentrated entirely on curing the patient and he questioned the effectiveness of the "passive" style associated with classical analysis. The conclusion he had reached was that there are no bad children, only children who are the product of a harsh upbringing by unsympathetic parents. Further, he believed that it was the analyst's task to undo the errors of inadequate parents. In effect he was separating psychoanalytic theory from technique. He had changed his technique in order to counteract the early unhappiness of his patients. He played the part of a loving parent, allowing patients to analyze him as well. The role of the dreaded father was kept in the background. Ferenczi's interest was in therapeutic success and at the same time in shortening the therapy. Therefore, any improvement in technique would lead to the analyst's being more "active" than was the case in the technique of that time. Freud later described the method as reducing the analytic situation to a game between mother and child, with interchangeable roles.

At the time Freud sent Ferenczi an important letter:

> Lieber Freund 13, XII. 1931
> ....If by now you cannot bring yourself to change your attitude at all it is very unlikely that you will do so later. But that is essentially your affair....I see that the differences between us come to a head in a technical detail which is well worth discussing. You have not made a secret of the fact that you kiss your patients and let them kiss you....When you decide to give a full account of your technique and its results, you will have to choose between two ways: either you relate this

> or you conceal it. The latter, as you may well think, is dishonorable. What one does in one's technique one has to defend openly....
>
> With us a kiss signifies a certain erotic intimacy. We have hitherto in our technique held to the conclusion that patients are to be refused erotic gratifications.
>
> Now picture what will be the result of publishing your technique. There is no revolutionary who is not driven out of the field by a still more radical one...why stop at a kiss?....Soon we shall have accepted in the technique of analysis the whole repertoire of demiviergeries and petting parties...and God the Father Ferenczi, gazing at the lively scene he has created, will perhaps say to himself: maybe after all I should have halted in my technique of motherly affection before the kiss....
>
> In this warning I do not think I have said anything you do not know yourself...and now you have compelled me to be quite blunt.
>
> I do not expect to make any impression on you....The need for definite independence seems to me to be stronger in you than you recognize. But at least I have done what I could in my father role. Now you must go on.
>
> With cordial greetings
> your
> Freud

Ferenczi was dependent on Freud's approval and did not take the letter well. Nevertheless, he did not give up his active therapy. He said that this was the first time that he and Freud had really disagreed. There was no break in their relationship, although their correspondence suggests that Ferenczi withdrew somewhat. Freud's affection for him never wavered.

CHAPTER LXIX

■ *This Sounds Absurd*

Within psychoanalytic circles female sexuality was never a controversial subject. That is not to say that there were no lively disagreements with current theory, but it never became an emotional issue. Oddly enough, the most controversial subject was that of nonmedical analysts, over which issue the American analysts actually threatened to leave the International Association. Nor did the question of female sexuality reach the pitch of controversy aroused by Freud's pronouncements on the death instinct. The general attitude toward the psychology of women was that we know a little and we have more to learn.

It is therefore not surprising that "Some Psychical Consequences of the Anatomical Distinction Between the Sexes" caused a stir in psychoanalytic circles. Analysts from Britain and Germany in particular, took issue with Freud in important respects, all quite technical. For example, Karen Horney felt that Freud greatly overestimated the girl's primary penis envy, and that the strength for the masculine trend she develops later is a defense against her feminine impulses toward her father. It is therefore a "secondary" penis envy. Opposition papers mounted and finally, it was essentially for fellow professionals that, six years later, at the age of seventy-five, Freud wrote "Female Sexuality." It is hard to believe that burdened as he was by physical suffering and loss of energy not to mention the demands that came from a myriad sources, he found time and strength to write a work that so sharply criticized and revised what he had previously written on the subject.

Originally, Freud worked alone. An analogy can be drawn with the mythological King of Cyprus, Pygmalion, whose statue of his loved Galatea came to life. Freud trained others to be analysts, among them women, who made discoveries that surprised the master. Abraham, Fenichel, Horney, Jones, Klein, Lampl de Groot, Deutsch, to mention some of the better-known names, had now written on the pre-Oedipal phase of females, reporting findings that corroborated some of Freud's conclusions and questioned others. One thing was clear: there was still a great deal to learn about the early stages of development and more research was necessary before firm conclusions could be reached about the prehistory (pre-Oedipal) of both girls and boys.

Freud opened the paper with a review of the classic Oedipus complex. There is no difficulty in understanding this in the case of the boy. As his erotic drives become stronger, he is bound to see father as a rival. The situation is different with the girl. Why, when, and how does she detach herself from mother to find her way to father? It had been long understood that her psychosexual development was complicated by the fact that she had to give up her leading genital zone and her original object, in favor of a different zone and a diferent object. But, it was not yet clear how these two tasks were connected.

Many women who are in no way neurotic have a strong attachment to their fathers. Observation showed that where the woman's attachment to her father was particularly intense, it had been preceded by an equally intense and passionate attachment to her mother. Furthermore, the duration of the original attachment had been greatly underestimated: it might last until puberty. This suggests that the pre-oedipus phase in women is more important than has been appreciated thus far. After all, it is to the pre-oedipal phase that all the fixations and repressions, the origins of the neurosis, can be traced. Indeed, the possibility exists that, due to a protracted pre-oedipus, a number of women remain arrested in their original attachment to their mothers, never achieving a complete changeover toward men. "It would seem as though we must retract the universality of the thesis that the Oedipus complex is the nucleus of the neurosis."[1] So here was Freud, at the age of seventy-five, having to modify the very bedrock of psychoanalytic theory.

> We can extend the content of the Oedipus complex to include all the child's relations to both parents; or...we can take due account of our new findings by saying that the female only reaches the normal positive Oedipus situation after she has surmounted a period before it that is governed by the negative complex.
>
> (Ibid. p. 226)

During the stage when the little girl is attached to her mother, her father is not much more than a troublesome rival, although her hostility does not approach that which is characteristic of the little boy's. "We have, after all, long given up any expectation of a neat parallelism between male and female sexual development."[2]

Freud suggests that he had difficulty getting at his female patients' earliest attachments to their mothers because during analysis they clung to a transferred attachment to him as father, and took refuge from the early stages in question.

> It does indeed appear that women analysts—as for instance, Jeanne Lampl-de Groot and Helene Deusch—have been able to perceive these facts more easily and clearly, because they were helped in dealing with those under their treatment by the transference to a suitable mother-substitue. Nor have I succeeded in seeing my way through any case completely, and I shall therefore confine myself to reporting the most general findings and shall give only a few examples of the new ideas which I have arrived at.
>
> (Ibid. p. 227)

Two facts had struck him as new: that a woman's strong dependence on her father merely takes over from an earlier equally strong attachment to her mother,

---

[1]Female Sexuality, 1931, S.E. XXI, p. 226
[2]Ibid. p. 226

and that this earlier phase lasts for an unexpectedly long time. He attempted to graft these new findings onto the former picture of female sexual development.

Bisexuality, which is an innate characteristic of human beings, is seen much more clearly in women than in men. There is a physiological substrate for this. A man has only one leading sexual zone, one sexual organ, whereas a woman has two, vagina and clitoris. While there may be sensations in the vagina in early childhood, the main genital events of childhood take place with the clitoris. Thus female sexuality is divided into two phases: first the clitoral, active, masculine phase, and then the pasive, feminine, vaginal. There is a transition from an active to a passive phase, to which there is no analogy in the male. Complications arise from the fact that the clitoris continues to function and play an important role in the later sexual life of the woman.

Parallel to this difference in the sexes, there is the mother-as-a-love-object phase. In the male, the mother is his first choice, and remains so until she is replaced by another female. A girl's first object, too, must be her mother. In fact the primary conditions for the choice of an object are the same for all children. But by the end of her psychosexual development, the girl's father, a man, should have become her love object. How does this change come about?

Another difference between the sexes, related to the Oedipus complex, occurs because the male child, when the sight of the female genitals reveals to him the possibility of castration, gives up his oedipal complex, and develops a superego, a conscience, through identifying with his father. This remarkable development is due precisely to his narcissistic interest in his genitals; he curtails his infantile sexuality in order to preserve his precious penis.

The effects of the Oedipus are quite different in the female. She acknowledges the superiority of the male, and her own genital inferiority, but she rebels against this unwelcome state of affairs. Three choices are open to her. Frightened by the comparison with boys, dissatisfied with her clitoris, she may give up her phallic activity and, with it, sexuality in general. Or she may develop a "masculinity complex," and cling, unconsciously, to the hope of acquiring her own magic wand. This defiant wish may result in a manifest homosexual choice of object. Only if her development follows a third, more circuitous path does she reach the normal female attitude. She takes father as her love object and develops a feminine form of the oedipus. In women, the Oedipus is not destroyed by castration but created by it. Mother is seen as castrated and devalued and the child turns toward father. She does not feel strong hostility to the parent of the same gender which in the male was smashed out of existence, as it were. In women the Oedipus is frequently not surmounted at all, so that the social consequences of its breakup are less significant than in men. Men display strong superegos, severe consciences, and tend to be less in touch with their feelings and more concerned with their "duty." Women are more in touch with feelings and in that sense more realistic. Therefore, they tend to be less extremist than men in political-social-religious movements. For example, most of the Christians in the Coliseum were men. Generally, it is the men who fight to the death on the barricades for the "cause," for flag and country, whereas the women tend to gather the children and cooking utensils, and march off with the conquerors. A less severe superego allows them to put reality above "duty."

The stage of exclusive attachment to mother, the pre-oedipus phase, is much more important for women than for men, and much of what formerly was not understood about female sexuality can be explained by reference to this experience.

The married woman whose choice of a husband was modeled on her father presents one example. In her married life, she repeated toward her husband her bad relationship with her mother. This puzzled her analyst—the husband was not meant to be the inheritor of this. The pre-oedipal explanation solves such puzzles. Her relation to her mother was the original one; her relation to her father was built on it; and now in marriage the original relation re-emerges from repression.

The impression is created that the maturity of many women is spent in conflict with their mothers. The hostility toward mother can be understood not as originating in the rivalty of the Oedipus phase, but in a previous one, reinforced it is true by the Oedipus situation. Direct analytic observation confirms this view. In the light of our question concerning how the girl finds her way to the father, we must investigate the mechanism that turns her away from her original object, the mother.

Childhood love is boundless and demands exclusive possession. The jealousy of rivals—brother, sister, as well as father, is therefore inevitable. This unbounded love has no aim and is incapable of obtaining complete satisfaction. It is doomed to disappointment and must give way to hostile feelings. Under the stress of disappointment, in the process of development, the libido abandons its unsatisfying position and seeks a new one.

A more specific reason for turning away from mother arises from the contempt felt toward one who possesses an inferior genital. At some time the girl discovers her organic inferiority and mother's too. It is not easy to determine the exact timing or even the typical course of events. Much depends on the girl's phallic activity, its timing, and how much interference it is subjected to. Little girls discover their characteristic phallic activity, clitoral masturbation, for themselves. The part played by nursery hygiene is reflected in the fantasies of mother or nurse as a seducer. Actual seduction, in fact, is fairly common. Those charged with caring for children have been known to teach the child to masturbate in order to soothe him, or encourage sleep, or other children may teach the activity. Where apparent seduction intervenes, it invariably disturbs the natural course of development and may leave extensive and lasting consequences.

The prohibition of masturbation becomes an impetus for giving it up, but it also evokes feelings of rebellion against the person who does the prohibiting. Thus, the mother or mother-substitute elicits feelings of opposition. Even where the girl does not give up masturbation, the effect of the prohibition is seen in later efforts to suppress sexuality and to free herself from what has been spoiled for her. Her resentment at being prevented from the enjoyment of free sexual activity plays a major part in her detachment from mother, and it may influence her choice of a love object. At puberty the girl discovers that mother has assumed the duty of guarding her child from its own sexual drive. The same dynamic applies to boys and provides them, too, with a strong motive for rebellion against mother.

This account of how girls respond to the implication of castration and the prohibition of masturbation may:

> very probably strike the reader as confused and contradictory. This is not entirely the author's fault. In truth, it is hardly possible to give a description which has general validity. We find the most different reactions in different individuals, and in the same individual the contrary

> attitudes exist side by side.
> (ibid. p. 233)

The revelations offered by patients make it difficult to distinguish the mental processes of the first phase from those of later ones by which the earlier are distorted in memory. Girls frequently construe the fact of castration as a punishment for masturbation, carried out by the father. Boys also fear castration by the father, although the actual threat usually comes from the mother. However, we learn from women patients that the strongest reproach against mother and the strongest motive for turning away from her is that it was mother who brought her into the world as female. Mother brought her into the world, but did not give her a proper penis.

A second reproach against mother caught Freud by surprise—patients complained that mother did not give them enough milk, did not suckle long enough. Under conditions of modern civilization this might be true, but certainly not as frequent as patients report. Perhaps it stems from a general dissatisfaction all children have, who, in our culture, are weaned after six or nine months. In some primitive societies, the mother devotes herself exclusively to her child for two or three years. It may be that our children remain forever unsated. "But I'm not sure whether, if one analyzed children who had been suckled as long as children of primitive peoples, one would not come upon the same complaint. Such is the greed of a child's libido."[1]

Analysis brings to light a whole range of motives for turning away from mother: she failed to provide the girl with a magic penis, she did not feed her sufficiently, she compelled her to share love with her rivals, she never fulfilled her daughter's expectations of love, and, finally, she seduced and rejected—she aroused sexual excitement and then forbade it. Yet all these reasons do not seem to justify the girl's final hostility. It may be that the attachment to mother is bound to perish:

> ...precisely because it was the first and was so intense; just as one can often see happen in the first marriages of young women which they have entered into when they were most passionately in love. In both situations the attitude of love probably comes to grief from the disappointments that are unavoidable and from the accumulation of occasions for aggression. As a rule, second marriages turn out much better.
> (Ibid. p. 234)

No doubt normal adults do succeed in separating love from hate; they do not find themselves obliged to hate their love objects, while they love their enemies. This, however, seems to arise from later developments. In the first phase of erotic life, ambivalence is the rule. The little girl's intense attachment to her mother is highly ambivalent and, because of this (with the assistance of the other factors discussed above) her attachment is forced away from her mother.

How is it then that boys are able to keep their object choice intact? Their first attachment is no less strong than that of girls. Freud's answer is:

> Because boys are able to deal with their ambivalent feelings toward their mother by directing all their hostility on to their father. But in the first place,

> we ought not to make this reply until we have made a close study of the pre-Oedipus phase in boys, and, in the second place, it is probably more prudent in general to admit that we have as yet no clear understanding of these processes, with which we have only just become acquainted.
> (Ibid. p. 235)

What does a little girl want from her mother? What is the nature of her libidinal aim? The answer from patients is just what one would expect—it depends on the psychosexual phase the child is in, and it is both active and passive.

The relation of activity to passivity is an interesting one. Generally speaking, there seems to be a preference for an active over a passive position in every field of experience. When a child experiences something passively, it tends to produce an active reaction. When a child's throat is being examined he may resist at the time; but he will shortly thereafter introduce his friends to the "doctor game." This time he is the active one. This swingover from passivity to activity does not occur with the same regularity and intensity in all children; in some it does not take place at all. In fact, from a child's relative activity and passivity, conclusions may be drawn about the relative degree of masculinity and femininity that will manifest itself in the child's sexuality.

The first experiences a child has with its mother are of a passive character—it is suckled, fed, cleaned, and dressed by her. A part of the libido enjoys these experiences and clings to them; another part strives to turn them into an active experience. Being suckled gives way to active sucking. Mother herself becomes an object and the child behaves as the active one toward her, the love object. On occasion, one hears a child say, "You be the baby, and I'll be the mommy." Usually it is considered a sign of awakened femininity when a girl displays a fondness for dolls. However, we must not overlook the active, masculine side of femininity. The child behaves toward a doll the way mother does toward her. A preference for dolls is probably an indication of a girl's exclusive attachment to mother, neglecting the existence of father.

A basic need felt by the child is to undo the separation between herself and mother. It is the aim of oral erotism. Thus, the child sucks, not only for nourishment, and not only for sucking pleasure, but also to take mother into herself. Naturally the wish and effort are doomed to failure. Then what oral erotism has failed to do, anal erotism tries to accomplish. It too fails, and so do the attempts of phallic erotism to achieve the same thing, namely to undo the separation from mother. Eventually, the longing for some kind of union becomes directed to the father, turning him into a love object.

Freud was able to study the pre-oedipus phase in women patients who showed strong attachment to their mothers. All of them told him that when their mothers gave them enemas, they screamed with rage and put up the greatest resistance.

> I only came to understand the reason for such a specially violent opposition from a remark made by Ruth Mack Brunswick, who was studying these problems at the same time as I was, to the effect that she was inclined to compare the outbreak of anger after an enema to the orgasm following gen-

> ital excitation. The accompanying anxiety should, she thought, be construed as a transformation of the desire for aggression which has been stirred up. I believe that this is really so and that, at the sadistic-anal level, the intense passive stimulation of the intestinal zone is responded to by an outbreak of desire for aggression which is manifested either directly as rage, or in consequence of its suppression, as anxiety. In later years this reaction seems to die away.
>
> (Ibid. p. 238)

What Freud and Brunswick hypothesized was that, just as the peak experience following genital stimulation is an orgasm, the peak consequence of the passive stimulation of the intestinal zone (via the enema) is rage. During the enema, the child is indeed passive. In harmony with the need to convert a passive experience into an active one, a desire for active aggression mounts. However, the child's dependency inhibits his expression of rage.*

Early in Freud's career he had been shocked to hear from his woman patients that their introduction to sexual life was seduction by a father. Subsequent analytic information revealed that when a girl turns away from her mother, she transfers her feelings to the father. Then further analysis elicited that mother too had seduced them. By necessity they received their first genital sensations (and in accordance with the concept of the all-or-nothing of infancy therefore, their strongest genital sensations) when being cleaned and cared for by their mother, or mother surrogate. Mothers frequently report that daughters of two and three years enjoy these sensations and try to intensify them by repeated touching and rubbing. Unavoidably, mother initiates the child into the phallic phase. Years later, in fantasy, this initiation is attribured to the father.

During the phallic phase, intense active wishes are directed toward the mother. For girls, the phallic stage is the clitoral stage, which culminates in clitoral masturbation. If a baby brother or sister arrives, the little girl wants to believe that she has given her mother the new baby. This is exactly what the boy also wishes, and her reaction and her behavior are the same as his. "No doubt this sounds quite absurd, but perhaps that is only because it sounds so unfamiliar."[1]

The turning away from mother is an important step in the course of a girl's psychosexual development. More than a change of object, a marked lowering of the active sexual impulses and an increase in the passive ones may be observed. Active trends are abandoned because they have proved unrealizable. Passive trends have not escaped disappointment either. With the turning away from mother comes a decrease in clitoral masturbation. However, too often, when the small girl gives up her active sexuality, (the masculine, clitoral), a portion of her sexuality is permanently impaired. Insofar as she escapes this catastrophe, the transition to the father object is accomplished with the assistance of passive trends. To the extent that she is not restricted by the remains of pre-oedipal attachment to her mother, the path to the development of her femininity is open.

---

*Many primitive peoples refer to an enema as "anal rape."

[1]Ibid. p. 239

For a period the libidinal forces in the male and female child follow the same course. Then, in the girl's case, subsequent biological factors deflect those libidinal forces from their original aims and lead active (in every sense of the word masculine) trends into feminine channels. She changes her love object and her principal sex organ.

The child does not get what she needs from the mother, and turns to the father. What she wishes from the father is also not forthcoming and again she is frustrated. She turns away from him and back to mother. This going back and forth between father and mother makes it difficult for the analyst to understand the dynamics in question. Discovery that the pre-oedipal phase for girls frequently lasts until puberty has made this somewhat more intelligible.

Freud believed that it was plausible that biochemistry might one day discover a substance for the male libido and another for the female libido. However, for psychology it is a matter of indifference how many chemical substances in the body contribute to sexual excitation.

In this paper the girl has at last made her contribution to analytic research. From the beginning, it was the boy who had lent himself for study, particularly for an understanding of the Oedipus complex. An appreciation of the role of the pre-oedipus in the life of children arose out of the study of the female.

The discovery of the pre-oedipal stage occurred during the final phase of Freud's career. It came to him as a surprise; he compared it to the discovery of the Minoan-Mycenean civilization, which served as the foundation for the Greek civilization. Practically all psychoanalytic material had to be re-examined in the light of pre-oedipal factors. The mother was now assuming a role that had been attributed to the father, which opened up an area for new investigations. Freud thought that there were advantages in this for a female analyst. "It does appear that women analysts...have been able to perceive these facts more easily and clearly because they were helped in dealing with those under their treatment by the transference to a suitable mother-substitute."[1]

Today's male analysts, due to Freud's work and that of many other authors, are able to detect a "mother transference" as readily as are his female colleagues.

[1]Ibid. p. 227

CHAPTER LXX

■ *First Love, First Hate*

Now we are ready to examine the puzzle of why women are universally degraded and why they concur with and participate in their own debasement.

We have covered the motives for rejecting mother which succeed each other: she seduces, rejects, and later forbids sexual pleasure; she compels us to share her love with others; she does not feed us enough, and she has failed to provide her daughter with a magic genital. Moreover, mother herself is seen as a castrated and therefore devalued figure.

Is then the universal degradation of women a biopsychological phenomenon? Contempt is directed toward the possessor of the mutilated organ by female children who blame her for their own "genital deficiency," and by male children whose castration anxiety hides behind feelings of superiority.

We protect ourselves. We degrade her. We render her powerless. We punish her. Regardless of what she may do in reality, in our unconscious psyche we relegate the possessor of the inferior organ to an inferior position. Castration anxiety and the narcissistic injury that the vagina represents are so pervasive that no one and therefore no society escapes it. The universal devaluation of women is indeed a biopsychological fact! This conclusion was challenged by many of Freud's most important colleagues—in particular, the British psychoanalytic school led by Ernest Jones.

The pregenital phase is the world of mother and child. Every child lives in a matriarchy. Mother is the primary source of gratification, and for that reason the first source of frustration. The child's first love is his first hate. The child feels that mother has an unlimited supply of milk and love and comfort which she terrifyingly withholds. An infant cannot wait. The object that causes the first frustrations, the first narcissistic injuries, the first forced waiting, evokes primary rage and envy. Melanie Klein, in *Envy and Gratitude*, defines envy as an angry wish to take from another person something desirable, and failing that, to spoil the desired object. If mother is the first to be envied, then mother must be the first to be spoiled. If I devalue her, and she is less, then she frustrates me less. I am in less pain. I am avenged. After all, who would long for something that has been spoiled?

All infants are helpless and in the course of history more than one has been abandoned. Oedipus's parents were warned by the Oracle at Delphi that their son would grow up to slay his father and marry his mother. They took the infant, bound his feet, and left him exposed on a mountain. Through a series of circumstances Oedipus survived to carry out the Oracle's prophecy. The horrifying fact remains that Jocasta, his mother, did actually abandon him.

The child's helplessness gives rise to feelings of fear, rage, and envy. No one is comfortable with weakness and the tendency within the organism to convert a passive experience into an active one is brought to bear. "The activity is put into operation by the instinct for mastery through the agency of the somatic musculature."[1] What parent has not heard her child say, "Let me be Mommy"?

A child meets the world with his mouth. What tastes good he swallows, what testes bad he spits out. And he does the same psychically: he gets rid of intolerable thoughts and feelings by "projecting" them. In the pre-oedipal world of the child there is only mother. When he employs projection it is upon her.

Klein reported that in the course of her analysis of patients she had been able to trace penis envy to the oral stage: to envy of the mother's breast. Klein considered that the wish to internalize and to identify with the power and magic of the breast, was a basic determinant in human character formation. Both sexes indentify with mother.[2] (We are referring only to the first indentification among many that make up a person's character.) Identification is a defense against loss of a love object. "I cannot lose you if I am you." "You can love, I'm like you."

Society exerts enormous pressure upon its members to conform to its values and mores. We raise our children to conform to cultural stereotypes.

A strong man providing for and protecting a weak, dependent woman is one of our cultural stereotypes. He is the active one: he courts her. He is experienced and worldly; she is innocent. He is attracted to her and he calls her his "baby" or his "doll." She is fragile, helpless, and lost without him. In fact, were she to be otherwise—practical, bright, ambitious, and capable of better judgment than he, she would be considered as "castrating." Is there a more bitter insult for a woman?

Our society expects the "feminine" woman to be shorter than her man and not as physically strong. If he and she enjoy athletic activities together, of course he performs better. A robust woman, who can beat men at sports, is hardly considered feminine. In fact she is not expected to surpass him in any area of achievement. If a woman becomes a professional or achieves an intellectual superiority, she may be admired, but both sexes would regard her as unfeminine and maybe unlovable. She is supposed to "think like a woman," while "he" comes to the rescue with cold logic, to make the proper decision and solve the problem for the "little" woman.

The man who chooses her (she may have learned tricks to attract him) is expected to be older and wiser than she. The reverse, an older woman with a younger man, is a cultural outrage: "They're both sick," "He is after her money," "There is something strange going on there."

One stereotype finds passivity and dependency in men unattractive. A real man is muscular, big, reliable, never whiny or petulant, and he has a good head on his shoulders. Short men and physically delicate or sensitive men may be acceptable, but we would not consider them to be a model for our sons. He-man actors, the manly John Waynes and the confident Charlton Hestons, are just as popular with men as they are with women.

Once she succeeds in getting him to marry her, what stereotype does she adopt? In the world of entertainment it is "Take my wife, please." A wife is portrayed as silly, quickly moved to tears, sentimental, dependent on her level-headed husband to rescue her and her gossipy, fickle girl friends from the foolish problems they create. However, her aim in life is clear: to look eternally adolescent.

---

[1]Three Essays, S.E. VII, p. 198

[2]Klein, *Envy and Gratitude*, N.Y. Basic Books, 1957

In describing the stereotypic woman, we have been depicting a child, The "little doll" is immature, naive; a baby. She is incapable of assuming real responsibility.

Always and everywhere, the mother-child dyad consists of an omnipotent parent and a totally dependent child. Inevitably the child's frustrations reach intolerable proportions. The wish to reverse roles, to convert a passive experience into an active one, for revenge, is very strong, but the child is physically helpless. His only resources are psychological mechanisms. *The child projects onto the mother his own dependence, his weakness, and his helplessness. Then he identifies with her strengths*! Thus, in the unconscious, the female is a helpless baby. Moreover, the complicated psychology of women involves identification with a debased object. Men, on the other hand, tend to identify with the active mother who is big, dominant, and knows why the sky is blue (in fact she knows everything). They identify with the fruitful provider who protects from pain.

In a nutshell this is the solution to why women are universally debased. The male is the powerful parent who took care of me, and the female is the baby I once was. Ironically, in order for the girl to become a woman, she must identify with the female she herself had to depreciate.

There is an additional quality our stereotypic woman must have that contrasts sharply with the fatuous person we have been describing. She must be soft and nurturing. She is expected to care for us, offer emotional support and sympathetic understanding. We wish that she be the good mother. Her servitude is associated with another, more subtle stereotype: behind every successful man there is an alert woman whose wisdom made it possible. Her loyalty, understanding, intuition, and strength of character were essential to his success.

How has our culture created its stereotype notion of women? Simply stated, we overthrew the feared matriarchy and we retained our slave. The good mother has everything but power. She serves and smiles and asks for nothing.

In this universal condition modifiable? When Freud said "Anatomy is fate" was he saying that nothing can be done to alter a biopsychological fact?

Psychoanalysis is essentially an empirical science. Its conclusions, always provisional, are based on observed data. Prophesying and speculation, however tempting, have no official place within the discipline. Nevertheless, the question is provocative: shall anatomy always be fate?

There is not sufficient data as yet to answer the question with certitude. What changes might take place if the image of the primordial mother were defused by the presence of the father? Would shared parenting, which is conceivable, alter our identifications? Who can predict the outcome of a child's projecting its weakness onto the father too?

Is it possible that the steep curve that seems to chart the differences between the sexes, the superior-inferior, active-passive, masculine-feminine dichotomy, may be flattened out? If that were to happen, the cultural stereotypes might make way for reality. Appreciation of the individual and of individuality might in some measure replace stereotype.

Such a change would alter the way people relate to one another. If I do not have to play a stereotyped role, if I can relate to you more realistically and honestly, maybe we could discover parts of me that no longer require suppression. Greater freedom, mutuality, and intimacy must result from a less fearful exchange between partners. After all, as I discover myself, I discover you.

Can we analyze the projections and identifications our society makes use of and thereby cure it of its neuroses? Perhaps. It is not entirely inconceivable.

CHAPTER LXXI

■ *Why War?*

The year 1932 brought no new honors. Rather, severe stresses were added to Freud's life: his physical condition was worse, and his beloved publishing house, the *Verlag,* was in financial straits.

Freud's health was in fact failing and much effort was spent trying just to reduce his discomfort. In Pichler's notes we find ninety-two entries for 1932.

Martin, Freud's eldest son, had given up his postiion at a bank to manage the precarious business of the *Verlag*. He did what he could: he called upon his creditors and asked for moratorium, he tried to reduce expenses, and so forth. However, economic conditions were very bad. Eitingon's generous contributions and the sale of Freud's books (he took no royalties) were the mainstay of the *Verlag*. Unfortunately, the Eitingon family business in the United States did not survive the economic depression. Eitingon for the first time in his life could hardly support himself. The sale of Freud's books was reduced to a minimum. This left the *Verlag* on the brink of bankruptcy. The economic situation was even worse in Europe than in the United States and Freud's practice and income shrank accordingly.

> I must write something, since I shall have few analyses...there are no fresh applications whatever. They are of course quite right. I am too old, and working with me is too precarious. I should not need to work any longer. On the other hand it is pleasant to think that the "supply" has lasted longer than the "demand."
>
> (M. B. Aprial 14, 1932)

In an effort to keep the *Verlag* alive Freud agreed to colloborate with W. C. Bullitt, the American Ambassador to Germany, on a psychoanalytic study of President Wilson. When it became clear that the Wilson book would not provide the needed financial assistance, Freud decided to write *New Introductory Lectures*, which cover the developments in psychoanalysis since the time of the original lectures, fifteen years before. Freud had no intention of actually delivering them as lectures.

The new material covered dream theory, occultism, communism, telepathy, religion, education, and elements from *The Ego and the Id.*

"Progressive" education believed that a child should not be "repressed," his creativity and free expression should not be inhibited. Freud's statements on the subject must have come as a surprise and a disappointment to such educators:

> Let us make ourselves clear as to what the first task of education is. The child must learn to control

> his insintcts. It is impossible to give him liberty to carry out all his impulses without restriction...life would be impossible for the parents and the children themselves would suffer grave damage....Accordingly, education must inhibit, forbid and suppress, and this it has abundantly seen to in all periods of histoy. But we have learned from analysis that precisely this suppression of instincts involves the risk of neurotic illness....Thus education has to find its way between the Scylla of non-interference and the Charybids of frustration...an optimum must be discovered which will enable education to achieve the most and damage the least....Hitherto education has fulfilled its task very badly and has done children great damage.
> (S.E. XXII p. 149)

Freud felt that one of the tasks of education was to enable the child to live in harmony with himself and his society.

The last lecture was "The Question of a *Weltanschauung*." He started by saying that the German word *weltanschauung* is untranslatable. In English it is usually translated as philosophy of life. Freud raised the question of whether there is a world view peculiar to psychoanalysis. His answer was no. The only commitment psychoanalysis could make was to science, not philosophy. He proceeded to mount an energetic defense of the scientific outlook on life. He saw religion as its chief opponent and sharply contrasted the purpose and aim of these two modalities. He insisted that no area is off limits to scientific investigation, including religious beliefs. He vehemently opposed the view that religions are concerned with a different sphere of truth.

Like other intellectuals throughtout the world, Freud had closely watched that grand social experiment, the Russian Revolusion. He was an interested if somewhat puzzled observer. He was struck by the complete insensitivity of its leaders "to the suffering of anyone who stands between them and their goal."

> Theoretical Marxism, as realized in Russian Bolshevism, has acquired the...exclusive character of a *Weltanschauung*, but at the same time an uncanny likeness to what it is fighting against. Though originally ...built...upon as science and technology, it has created a prohibition of thought which is just as ruthless as was that of religion in the past. Any critical examination of Marxist theory is forbidden...in the same way as heresy was once punished by the Catholic Church. The writings of Marx have taken the place of the Bible...though they would seem to be no more free from contradictions...than those older sacred books.
> (Ibid. p. 179)

The question has to arise—why did Freud add his new credo, or non-credo, to the Lectures? Perhaps the rapidly approaching threat of a new disaster for the world (Hitler came to power a year after the Lectures were written) inspired Freud to tell the present and future generations that there was still an articulate and passionate voice that spoke on behalf on Reason, Objectivity, and Science.

> Ladies and Gentlemen—Allow me in conclusion to sum up what I had to say of the relation of psycho-analysis to the question of a *Weltanschauung*....It does not need one; it is a part of science and can adhere to the scientific *Weltanschauung*....Scientific thought is still young...there are too many of the great problems which it has not yet been able to solve. A *Weltanschauung* erected upon science has...submission to the truth and rejection of illusions. Any of your fellow men...who calls for more than this for his momentary consolation, may look for it where he can find it. We shall not grudge it him, we cannot help him, but nor can we on his account think differently.
>
> (Ibid. p. 182)

The League of Nations founded the International Institute of Intellectual Cooperation. This elite body spoke for the many who had experienced disappointment at the conduct of major nations during World War I. They were puzzled that the highest civilizations that man has reached were unable to settle their differences without resort to war. After all, the major nations shared the same value system, and the means for peaceful settlement of disputes, such as the World Court, were available. Einstein suggested that he write to Freud about the matter; the Institute of Intellectual Cooperation enthusiastically concurred.

> Dear Professor Freud 30 July, 1932
> ....This is the problem: is there any way of delivering mankind from the menace of war?....Every attempt at its solution has ended in a lamentable breakdown....
> ...my thought affords no insight into the dark places of human will and feeling ...bring the light of your far-reaching knowledge of man's instinctive life to bear upon the problem....I am convinced (you) will be able to suggest educative methods lying more or less outside the scope of politics, which will eliminate these obstacles....
>
> The ill-success, despite their obvious sincerity, of all the efforts made during the last decade to reach this goal leaves us no room to doubt that strong psychological factors are at work, which paralyze these efforts ...The craving for power....I have specially in mind that small but determined group, active in every nation, composed of individuals who, indifferent to social considerations and restraints, regard warfare...simply as an occasion to advance their personal interests and en-

> large their personal authority.
>
> ....How is it possible for this small clique to bend the will of the majority, who stand to lose and suffer by a state of war, to the service of their ambitions?....How is it...(they) succeed so well in rousing men to such wild enthusiasm, even to sacrifice their lives?....Here, lies...an enigma that only the expert in the lore of human instincts can resolve....
>
> To conclude: I have so far been speaking only of wars between nations....But...other forms and in other circumstances. I am thinking of civil wars, for instance, due in earlier days to religious zeal, but nowadays to social factors; or, again, the persecution of racial minorities...
>
> ...it would be of the greatest service to us all were you to present the problem of world peace in the light of your most recent discoveries, for such a presentation well might blaze the trail for new and fruitful modes of action.
>
> Your very sincerely,
> A. Einstein
> (Why War?, 1933, S.E. XXII, p. 201)

Freud found the League of Nations project tedious and referred to the so-called "discussion" with Einstein as "tiresome and sterile." Earlier he had told a League official that all his life he had had to tell truths that people did not wish to hear; now that he was old he still did not wish to deceive them. Nevertheless, he replied to Einstein's letter at length.

He appreciated the fact that Einstein had written as a philanthropist rather than as a natural scientist and physicist. Essentially he was in agreement with what Einstein had to say.

> You begin with the relation between Right and Might...may I replace the word "might" by a bolder and harsher word "violence"? Today right and violence appear to us as antitheses. It can easily be shown, however, that the one has developed out of the other.
>
> (Ibid. p. 203)

Right—law—is the might of the community. Any individual who resists soon discovers that law still is violence, it employs the same methods and follows the same purposes. The violence of an individual has historically given way to that of the community. The true source of the community's strength lies in the emotional tie between its members. Therefore the community must be permanent. It must be organized; it must draw up regulations to anticipate rebellion; and it must institute authorities to see that regulations and laws are obeyed. We need authorities to superintend the execution of legal acts of violence. The recognition of shared interests leads to the growth of emotional ties, uniting groups of people.

> Here I believe, we already have all the essentials;

> violence overcome by the transference of power to a larger unity, which is held together by emotional ties between its members. What remains to be said is no more than an expansion and a repetition of this.
> (Ibid. p. 205)

Actually, communities comprise elements of unequal strength: parents and children, men and women, victors and vanquished, who turn into masters and slaves. Laws then tend to be made by, and for, those in power. The rights of those subjected find little expression. Then, within the community, a power struggle takes place. Oppressed members struggle to obtain more power, although it will be historical circumstances that determine the outcome. In some societies, there is no recourse other than violence; in others, the ballot may succeed in bringing about significant change.

> Yet a glance at the history of the human race reveals an endless series of conflicts between one community and another or several others, between larger and smaller units—between cities, provinces, races, nations, empires—which have almost always been settled by force of arms.
> (ibid. p. 207)

Freud agreed with Einstein that in our time wars will only be prevented if humankind can unite to create a central authority, one with the right of judgment and endowed with necessary power. "One without the other would be useless. At the moment there seems very little prospect of this."[1] An attempt to replace actual force by the force of ideas would be doomed to failure.

In referring to Einstein's astonishment that men are so readily available for violence, and that there seems to be an instinct for destruction which falls in with the efforts of warmongers, Freud reminded him that psychoanalysis has always postulated the existence of such an instinct and has been occupied in the study of its manifestations.

> According to our hypothesis human instincts are of only two kinds: those which seek to preserve and unite which we call "erotic," exactly in the sense in which Plato uses the word "Eros" in his Symposium, or "sexual," with a deliberate extension of the popular conception of "sexuality"—and those which seek to destroy and kill and which we group together as the aggressive or destructive instinct. As you see, this is in fact no more than a theoretical clarification of the universally familiar opposition between Love and Hate.
> (Ibid. p. 20)

He added that we must not be hasty in introducing judgments of good and evil. Life requires both instincts. Further, they never exist in a pure form—one is

[1]Ibid. p. 207

always allied with the other. No doubt the instinct for self-preservation is of an erotic sort, but it must have aggressiveness at its disposal to overcome obstacles and fulfill its aim.

> So, too, the instinct of love when it is directed towards an object, stands in need of some contribution from the instinct for mastery if it is in any way to obtain possession of that object. The difficulty of isolating the two classes of instincts in their actual manifestations is indeed what has so long prevented us from recognizing them.
> (Ibid. p. 210)

Rarely is an action the work of a single instinctual impulse. No doubt when human beings are incited to war a number of motives operate, with lust for destructiveness among them. The cruelties of history vouch for the existence and the strength of such aggressive impulses. Sometimes it seems that idealistic motives serve only as vehicles for destructive appetites. The cruelties of the Inquisition offered idealistic motives to allow the destructive ones to find expression.

> I fear I may be abusing your interest, which is after all concerned with the prevention of war and not with our theories. Nevertheless I should like to linger for a moment over our destructive instinct, whose popularity is by no means equal to its importance. As a result of a little speculation, we have come to suppose that this instinct is at work in every living creature and is striving to bring it to ruin and to reduce life to its original condition of inanimate matter. Thus it quite seriously deserves to be called a death instinct, while the erotic instincts represent the effort to live.
> (Ibid. p. 210)

Freud explained that the death instinct turns into a destructive one when it is directed outward. The organism then preserves its own life by destroying one extraneous to it. This would serve as a biological justification for all the ugly and dangerous impulses against which men struggle.

> For our immediate purpose then, this much follows from what has been said: There is no use in trying to get rid of men's aggressive inclinations. We are told that in certain happy regions of the earth, where nature provides in abundance everything that man requires, there are races whose life is passed in tranquility and who know neither coercion nor aggression. I can scarely believe it and I should be glad to hear more of these fortunate beings. The Russian Communists, too, hope to be able to cause human aggressiveness to disappear by guaranteeing the satisfaction of all material needs and by establishing equality in other respects among all the members of the community. That,

> in my opinion, is an illusion.
> (Ibid. p. 212)

Then he changed to a less pessimistic tone: Theory suggests that the antagonist of the destructive instinct, Eros, be used to deal with it. Whatever fosters emotional ties between peoples operates against war. These ties are of two kinds: love, in the sense of "Thou shalt love thy neighbor as thyself" and *identification*. Whereas the first is easier to pronounce than to achieve, whatever leads men to share important interests produces a community of feeling and identification. Human society is to a large extent based on these.

At this point Freud raised a question:

> Why do you and I and so many other people rebel so violently against war? Why do we not accept it as another of the many painful calamaties of life? After all, it seems to be quite a natural thing, to have a good biological basis and in practice to be scarcely avoidable. There is no need to be shocked at my raising this question. For the purpose of an investigation such as this, one may perhaps be allowed to wear a mask of assumed detachment.
> (ibid. p. 213)

The Freud-Einstein correspondence was published under the title *Why War?* It was translated into French and English, and at Freud's request, printed in German. But by that time Hitler had come into power and *Why War?* was banned throughout the Third Reich.

CHAPTER LXXII

■ *More Intelligent And Livelier Than Boys*

Two years after "Female Sexuality" Freud devoted a chapter of his "New Introductory Lectures" to the subject of women. It makes pleasant reading. It was not written for professionals and is couched in his friendly and candid style.

He opens with an expression of the difficulty he has with his presentation to a lay audience:

> ...for analysts I am saying too little, and nothing at all that is new, but for you I am saying too much and saying things which you are not equipped to understand and which are not in your province.
> ("New Introductory Lectures," 1932, S.E. XXII, p. 112)

The riddle of what femininity is has puzzled the best minds since the beginning of history. And what constitutes masculinity and femininity is an unknown quantity which even science has not been able to make clear.

A comparison with what happens to little boys would indicate that the development of little girl's into women is more difficult and complicated. It involves two extra tasks, which have no parallel in the life of males. From the beginning there are differences: that which lies in the structure of the genitals is accompanied by others. It would seem that as a rule, the girl is less assertive than the boy. She seems less contentious, more cooperative. She appears to be more dependent and pliant and has a greater need for affection.

> One gets an impression, too, that little girls are more intelligent and livelier than boys of the same age; they go out more to meet the external world and at the same time form stronger object-cathexis. I cannot say whether this lead in development has been confirmed by exact observations, but in any case there is no question that girls cannot be described as intellectually backward.
> (Ibid. p. 117)

Boys and girls seem to pass through early psychosexual phases in the same way. Though less assertiveness and defiance might be expected in girls during the anal-sadistic stage, experienced women analysts report the contrary. The little girl shows abundant violent and aggressive impulses. In the phallic phase, in which for both sexes the love object is the mother, there is a higher degree of resemblance than difference. The little girl is a little man. The vagina, that exclusively female organ, is as yet unknown to the girl. There may be a few isolated sensations in the vagina, but these play no important role. One of the steps that the woman has to take in the course of her development, is to transfer, wholly or in part, the sensitivity of the clitoris to the vagina. This is the great step toward femininity. The more fortunate male has only to continue the activity of his early efflorescence to reach sexual maturity.

Psychologically, males are simpler than females. The boy's first love object is his mother. She remains so, in essence, all his life. With maturity, he will simply transfer his early feelings, from mother to a socially acceptable woman. The story is different for a female. She initially chooses her mother for a love object, but in the Oedipus situation, her father becomes her object. In the normal course of development, she must find her way from her father object to a suitable final object. In other words, a girl has to change both her erotogenic zone and her object.

Through laborious psychoanalytic investigation, we have learned that a great number of women retain to a late age, tender, dependent feelings on the father, or at least on a paternal object. We had known that there was a preliminary stage of attachment to mother, but it came as a surprise that it could be so long-lasting and so rich in content, allowing many opportunities for fixations and neurotic tendencies. During this phase the father is only a bothersome rival. Whatever we find directed toward the father was already felt and experienced toward the mother. We cannot understand women until we understand their pre-oedipal attachment to the mother.

As libidinal relations persist through all three stages of infantile sexuality, they express themselves by oral, sadistic-anal, and phallic wishes. These wishes represent active as well as passive impulses; in short, they are masculine and feminine. They are ambivalent, at once affectionate and hostile. It is not always easy to formulate these wishes—those belonging to the phallic stage are clearest: to impregnate the mother and to bear her a child. Startling, but established analytic observation. Deeper investigation brings many surprisingly detailed disclosures. Fears of being murdered or poisoned prove to be already present in pre-oedipus relations to mother. It must not be forgotten that in the early history of psychoanalysis, all Freud's women patients revealed to him that they had been seduced by their fathers.

> I was driven to recognize in the end that these reports were untrue and so came to understand that hysterical symptoms are derived from phantasies and not from real occurrences. It was only later that I was able to recognize in this phantasy of being seduced by father the expression of the typical Oedipus complex in women. And now we find the phantasy of seduction once more in pre-Oedipus prehistory of girls; but the seducer is regularly the mother.
>
> (Ibid. p. 120)

Here we have a fantasy with a base of reality: for it is the mother who by her activities over the child's bodily hygiene invariably stimulates and arouses for the first time pleasurable sensations in the genitals.

The child's desire for the breast is insatiable. In treatment, women analysands reproach their mothers for not giving enough milk—which is construed as a lack of love. Or the complaint may be that mother sent away the nurse, who was feeding and caring for the child, too early. (Among primitive people children remain at the breast for two or three years.) The frequency with which this complaint is heard makes it suspect. Freud speculated that if one could analyze a primitive child, we would still hear the same reproach about insufficient nourishment. And the fear of being poisoned may also be connected with withdrawal of the breast: "Poison is nourishment that makes one ill."

And so it follows that a child's demand for love knows no limits; it makes exclusive claims and tolerates no sharing. And we hear again and again complaints against the mother because of a new baby. Of course it is not only the suckling that the child begrudges the new baby, but all other signs of maternal care. The child feels dethroned. Her Majesty, the child, hurls jealous hatred at the faithless mother. Not infrequently the child becomes "naughty." The angry child regresses in toilet training, is irritable and disobedient. The tenacity is some cases of these jealous impulses, and their magnitude, may influence later development.

The child's sexual wishes toward the mother cannot be satisfied: the strongest occur at the phallic period. Even the most indulgent of upbringing cannot avoid some restriction of the child's freedom to enjoy gratifications, and this provokes aggressiveness and rebelliousness. So it turns out that mother herself first stimulates genital sensations, then forbids them. This alone would be reason for the girl's turning away from her. The more passionate the child's love for the object, the more sensitive it is to disappointment and frustration. The original love must succumb to accumulated hostility. The daughter must leave the mother.

All of the above—the slights, the disappointments, the jealousies, the seductions followed by prohibitions—are also in operation between a boy and his mother, yet he does not turn away from her. The above reasons don't alienate him from his first object choice. In order to understand the severing of the attachment between girls and their mothers, we have to find something specific about girls that is not present in boys, or we have not explained the phenomenon.

Psychoanalysis has found the specific factor, though in a surprising form. It is the female castration complex: girls hold mother responsible for their being born without the highly prized penis. They do not forgive her for putting them at a disadvantage.

The recognition of the anatomical difference between the sexes has psychical consequences. The castration complex in girls begins with the sight of the genitals of the other sex. They feel aggrieved, mistreated, injured. They often declare that they want a "tassle like Jonny's," they fall victim to penis envy. Envy of the penis will leave lasting traces on the formation of character and personality. Even in the most favorable cases, surmounting this envy calls for a huge expenditure of psychical energy. The recognition of the truth does not mean that the girl accepts the reality of her anatomy easily. Analysis shows that long after knowledge has extinguished the hope of acquiring the magic penis, the wish for it persists in the unconscious.

> You may take it as an instance of male injustice if I assert that envy and jealousy play an even greater part in the mental life of women than of men. It is not that I think these characteristics are absent in men or that I think they have no other

> roots in women than envy for the penis; but I am inclined to attribute their greater amount in women to this later influence.
> (Ibid. p. 124)

The recognition of the anatomical differences is a turning point in a girl's growth. It may lead to a sexual inhibition or neurosis, or to a masculinity complex, or to normal femininity.

Until she discovers the differences between girls and boys, the little girl has been enjoying the excitation of her clitoris. Her fantasies concerning her mother were active, masculine. Penis envy brings an end to her enjoyment of her phallic, masculine, clitoral pleasure. At first she regards her castration as an individual misfortune; only gradually does she realize that it is a universal phenomenon for her sex. Her love was directed toward her phallic mother, and when she discovers that her mother is castrated too, her hostility, which has long been accumulating, gains the upper hand. She drops her mother as a love object. Women are debased in her eyes because they lack the penis, just as they are debased for boys and later "perhaps for men."

With the renunciation of clitoral masturbation, the girl repressed a certain amount of activity. Passivity is ascendant, and the girl's turning to the father is accomplished with the help of passive impulses. As phallic activity recedes, the way is paved for femininity. What she did not get from her mother, a penis, she now hopes to get from her father. Only if the wish for a penis is replaced by the wish for a baby, is the feminine situation re-established. If her development proceeds along normal lines, the desire for the penis-baby from father becomes the most powerful feminine wish. If later she has a baby in reality, she will feel great happiness, especially if the baby is a little boy, who brings the desired genital with him.

After displacing the penis-baby wish to her father, the girl enters the Oedipus phase. Mother, who seems to receive everything she needs from father, becomes her hated rival. The girl's sense of castration introduces the Oedipus rather than destroying it. She rejects the castrated mother, envies the penis bearer, and enters the Oedipus as though it were a refuge. She does not fear castration and therefore the motive the male has for surmounting the Oedipus is lacking. Thus girls remain in the Oedipal situation for an indeterminate length of time; they end it late, and even then, incompletely.

> In these circumstances the formation of the superego must suffer; it cannot attain the strength and independence which gives it its cultural significance, and feminists are not pleased when we point out to them the effect of this factor upon the average feminine character.
> (Ibid. p. 129)

A possible reaction to the discovered differences between boys and girls, may be the development of a masculinity complex. The girl refuses to recognize the unwelcome fact and persists in her clitoral activity. Rebellious and defiant, she even exaggerates her previous activity, her masculinity. She takes refuge in identifying with her father or her phallic mother. The extreme of a masculinity complex would appear to be a manifest homosexual object choice. Female homosexuality is seldom or never a direct continuation of infantile masculinity. It was necessary that she enter the Oedipus situation, but after the inevitable disappointments from her father, she is driven to regress to her early masculinity complex. All girls suffer these disappointments, but those destined to become feminine react differently. "The predominance of the constitutional factor seems indisputable." Two aspects of female homosexuality are reflected in the practice of homosexuals: they play the roles of mother and baby as often and as unmistakably as those of wife and husband.

We have been discussing the prehistory of women. It is a recent product of analytic investigation and has been carried out by women analysts. To mention by name a few who have made valuable contributions to our knowledge, there is Dr. Ruth Mack Brunswick who was the first to describe a case of neurosis that went back to a pre-oedipus fixation and never reached the Oedipus at all. The case took the form of jealous paranoia and proved to respond well to analytic therapy. The incredibly strong phallic activity of girls toward their mothers was established by Dr. Jeanne Lampl-de Groot, based on direct observations. That erotic actions of homosexual women reproduce the relationship between mother and baby was demonstrated and explained by Dr. Helene Deutsch.

The point to be emphasized is that the development of femininity can be disturbed by the residues of infantile masculinity. When the child alternates between mother and father, experiencing disappointment from both, changing from mother to father and back again (which goes on much longer than our early theory appreciated), an alteration is also taking place between the polarities of passivity and activity, in other words, between masculinity and femininity. Regression to the pre-oedipal phases, and fixation there, frequently occurs. Some of what is referred to as the "enigma of women" may be explained by this evidence of bisexuality, in which at different times masculinity or femininity gains the upper hand.

The sexual frigidity of women is still insufficiently understood. Sometimes it appears to be psychological and accessible to therapy. But in other cases, it seems to be constitutional, as though nature can disregard the feminine libido because the woman can peform her biological function, namely reproduction, independent of her consent. Whereas the male must perform satisfactorily, the female could fulfill her biological role even if she were in a coma. This difference in "responsibility" for the reproductive act gives rise to different attitudes to sexuality in men and women.

Analytic experience attributes greater narcissism to femininity, which also affects women's choice of a love object. Overstating the case for the sake of clarity, one could say that whereas men have a need to love an object, women have a greater need to be loved. Men fall in love in order to have sex, and women have sex so that they will be loved.

During the phallic phase, the little girl experiences genital inferiority. Thus the unconscious of women, where the mind of the child is still alive, has a share in the physical vanity of women: women value their charms as a compensation for their original feelings of sexual inferiority. Shame also seems to be a strictly feminine characteristic. This affect is partly a matter of culture and convention; nevertheless, women exhibit it far more than men. Analytic investigation traces shame to a wish to conceal genital deficiencies. Those women who do not experience their genital as a mutilated organ are thus not so prone to neurotic shame. Of course, there are other dynamics that lead to feelings of shame, particularly with regard to behavior that we feel we should have outgrown.

Women have been accused of making few contributions, discoveries, or inventions to the course of civilization.

> ...there is, however, one technique which they may have invented, that of plaiting and weaving. If that is so, we should be tempted to guess the unconscious motive for the achievement. Nature itself would seem to have given the model which this achievement imitates by causing the growth at maturity of the pubic hair that conceals the genitals. The step that remained to be taken lay in making the threads adhere to one another, while on the body they stick into the skin and are only matted together. If you reject this idea as fantastic and regard my belief in the influence of lack of a penis on the configuration of femininity as an *idee fixe,* I am of course defenseless....
> (Ibid. p. 132)

Why a woman chooses a particular man as her object is often difficult to determine, because of social circumstances. Where one can disentangle the determinants of her choice, one can see that it is often made in accordance with an idealized image of the man whom the girl had wished to become. If her Oedipal choice has persisted, an unconscious attachment to her father, she chooses according to paternal type. At the time she turned to her father, her hostility was directed to her mother. A choice of this kind should encourage a happy marriage, but very often the woman's object choice shows ambivalence. Hostility follows in the train of the positive attachment and spreads to the new object. The woman's husband, who inherits the attachment to the father, after a time becomes the heir to the hostility to the mother as well.

> So it may easily happen that the second half of a woman's life may be filled by the struggle against her husband, just as the shorter first half was filled by her rebellion against her mother. When this reaction has been lived through, a second marriage may easily turn out very much more satisfying.
> (Ibid. p. 133)

Change in a woman's "nature," for which their husbands are unprepared, may occur after the first child is born. Entering the state of motherhood may revive an identification with her own mother, which she had resisted up to the time of her marriage. The revived identification may lead to a compulsion to reproduce her mother's behavior and duplicate an unhappy marriage between her parents. A husband caught in such a situation "won't know what hit him."

> The difference in a mother's reaction to the birth of a son or a daughter shows that the old factor of lack of a penis has even now not lost its strength.

> A mother is only brought unlimited satisfaction by her relation to a son; this is altogether the most perfect, the most free from ambivalence of all human relationships.
> (Ibid. p. 133)

The aspirations which she has been forced to suppress in herself, she can transfer to her son, and she can expect from him the satisfaction of all the unfinished business that is left over in her from her masculinity complex. "Even a marriage is not made secure until the wife has succeeded in making her husband her child as well and in acting as a mother to him."[1]

In order for a woman to be a woman she has to make an identification with her mother. However, analysis distinguishes two layers of identification: the pre-oedipal layer, during which her feelings for her mother are affectionate, and the later oedipus complex, where she seeks to get rid of mother and to take her place with father. Neither layer is adequately disposed of in the course of development; both find expression in future relationships. But the most decisive phase is the affectionate pre-oedipus attachment. Preparations are made during it for those characteristics with which she will play her social role as an adult. It is in this identification that she acquire her attractiveness to a man. After all, during his own Oedipus phase his attraction to mother was kindled into passion. Too often it is only his son who gets the love he himself aspired to from his wife.

Freud felt that in comparison with men, women had little sense of justice. He atributed this to two factors. Since they do not suffer a fear of castration, their superego, their conscience, is not as strong as a man's. Also the role of envy plays a greater part in the mental life of women than of men. The demand for justice requires that envy be put aside. Since women are more in touch with their feelings, less bound by the superego and therefore less compulsively involved with duty and tradition, they are more inclined to respond subjectively than men. (The reader should be reminded that everyone contains within himself both masculine and feminine characteristics; in every individual it is always a matter of more or less.)

Freud also felt that women were weaker in their social interests and had less capacity than men for sublimating their selfish instincts. In that sense, women may be more realistic than men. Where a man may dedicate his life to an abstract cause or to a flag, a woman focuses on life. Do the children have enough to eat? Is she pregnant? Once again, we may be dealing with a derivative of a less severe superego. When a man refers to a work of art or a bridge he has designed as "that's my baby," we understand. But if a woman refers to a bridge as "that's my baby"?

> That is all I have to say to you about femininity. It is certainly incomplete and fragmentary and does not always sound friendly. But do not forget that I have only been describing women in so far as their nature is determined by their sexual function. It is true that that influence extends very far; but we do not overlook the fact that an individual

---

[1]Ibid. p. 133

woman may be a human being in other respects as well. If you want to know more about femininity, enquire from your own experience of life, or turn to the poets, or wait until science can give you deeper and more coherent information.

(Ibid. p. 135)

CHAPTER LXXIII

■ *Assuredly No Advantage*

Homosexuality? What is it? Is it a disease? Is it inherited? Is it neurosis? Should it be made illegal? Are lesbians different from male homosexuals? How about latent homosexuality?...what does it mean? What has Freud to say on the subject?

The above questions reflect the confusion and anxiety that attend the subject. A current concern in fact is whether homosexuals should be excluded from certain professions: the education system, the government, and so forth. Imagine what the situation was like a century ago, in Freud's time!

If you were to hear that a lesbian was in the next room, what would you know about her? She could be short or tall, a person of ordinary intelligence or a genius, an altruist or a scoundrel, etc. There is only one thing you could be certain of: her love object must possess a genital similar to her own.

Freud's focus was psychobiological. He recognized that as the sexual drive accumulates tension, its aim becomes discharge of that tension and the satisfaction that follows. The "object" is the means through which the drive achieves its aim. If the object is conventional, for example if a woman chooses a man and he in turn chooses her, and a reasonable amount of gratification is experienced (if in a sense biology is served), then the person is seen as functioning normally. However, if there is a conflict within the mind as to either the aim or the object, then neurotic symptoms may develop. Again, if the object is an unconventional one, then the drive is diverted from its normal course and the diversion is considered a perversion. It is important to remember that Freud attached no moral judgment to the term. He even considered a perversion as a superior solution to a neurosis, because the drive achieves its aim of discharge; whereas in a neurosis the drive finds expression in "symptoms."

Pyschoanalysis is neither anti- nor pro-homosexual; its interest lies in understanding the determinants of an object choice.*

The best illustration of Freud's attitude on the matter is revealed in the following incident. In April, 1935, he received a letter from a mother in America asking for his advice. His answer is one of many examples of his unfailing kindness, despite his own suffering at the time from a painful cancer. (He was seventy-nine years old.) Years later the letter was sent to Dr. Kinsey with this note: "Herewith I enclose a letter from a great and good man which you man retain. From a grateful Mother."

Dear Mrs.... April 9, 1935

*The focus in psychoanalytic literature on the subject of homosexuality is on the complexity of the determinants of the object choice.

I gather from your letter that your son is a homosexual. I am most impressed by the fact that you do not mention this term yourself in your information about him. May I question you, why you avoid it? Homosexuality is assuredly no advantage, but it is nothing to be ashamed of, no vice, no degradation, it cannot be classified as an illness; we consider it to be a variation of the sexual function produced by a certain arrest of sexual development. Many highly respectable individuals of ancient and modern times have been homosexuals, several of the greatest men among them (Plato, Michelangelo, Leonardo da Vinci, etc.). It is a great injustice to persecute homosexuality as a crime, and a cruelty too. if you do not believe me, read the books of Havelock Ellis.

By asking me if I can help, you mean, I suppose, if I can abolish homosexuality and make normal heterosexuality take its place. The answer is, in a general way, we cannot promise to achieve it. In a certain number of cases we succeed in developing the blighted germs of heterosexual tendencies which are present in every homosexual, in the majority of cases it is no more possible. It is a question of the quality and the age of the individual. The result of treatment cannot be predicted.

What analysis can do for your son runs in a different line. If he is unhappy, neurotic, torn by conflicts, inhibited in his social life, analysis may bring him harmony and peace of mind, full efficiency, whether he remains a homosexual or gets changed. If you make up your mind he should have analysis with me! I don't expect you will! He has to come over to Vienna. I have no intention of leaving here. However, don't neglect to give me your answer.

Sincerely yours with kind wishes,

Freud

P.S. I did not find it difficult to read your handwriting. Hope you will not find my writing and my English a harder task.

CHAPTER LXXIV

■ *Burning Of The Books*

During World War I, Freud had feared that the rampant anger and the forces of destruction let loose might diminish the interest in psychoanalysis or even bring it to an end. After January 1933, with Hitler in power in Germany, that fear was fulfilled, at least as far as the homelands of psychoanalysis were concerned: Austria, Germany, and Hungary. The Psychoanalytic Society and Training Institute had to stop functioning; all Jewish analysts had to flee.

From the beginning many feared that Austria could not withstand the impact of Hitler and would succumb to it. Freud received invitations to settle elsewhere, first from Marie Bonaparte and then from Binswanger and Pfister, among others.

Oddly enough, for some time Freud ignored the mounting terror of Nazism which eventually was to lead to World War II, and the concentration camps. He wrote to Marie Bonaparte:

> How fortunate you are to be immersed in your work without having to take notice of all the horrible things around. In our circles there is already a great deal of trepidation. People fear that the nationalistic extravagences in Germany may extend to our little country. I have even been advised to flee already to Switzerland or France. That is nonsense; I don't believe there is any danger here and if it should come I am firmly resolved to await it here. If they killed me—good. It is one kind of death like another. But probably that is only cheap boasting.
>
> (M.B. March 16, 1933)

The next letter to her, written ten days later, had a curiously optimistic tone. He thanked her for her invitation to St. Cloud and went on to say that the brutalities in Germany were diminishing:

> The way France and America have reacted to them has not failed to make an impression, but the torments, small but none the less painful on that account, will not cease, and the systematic suppression of the Jews, depriving them of all positions, has as yet scarcely begun. One cannot avoid seeing that persecution of the Jews and restriction of intellectual freedom are the only features of the

> Hitler program that can be carried out. All the rest is weakness and utopianism.
> (M.B. March 26, 1933)

It has been said that Freud, who had uncovered the destructive drive in the human species, had himself difficulty in recognizing it even when it was right in front of him. It had taken him a long time to recognize the growing hostility of Jung and Rank; in the same way he refused to believe that the Nazi destructive force could be unleashed on an entire nation.

On his seventy-seventh birthday he suffered from a sudden attack of dizziness. Schur as usual examined him and reported:

> At that time my wife was expecting our first child, by then a few days overdue. Freud was certainly feeling miserable that day when I arrived, yet he greeted me with the question: Nothing yet? I examined him and was able to reassure him about the cause of his attack; he urged me to leave at once, saying: "Go now, you should be with your wife." Then he looked at me, yet not really at me, and remarked in a deeply meditative tone while holding on to my hand, "So gehen Sie von einem alten Mann, der noch nicht sterben will, zu einem Kind, das noch nicht auf die Welt kommen will." ("So you go from an old man who does not yet want to die to a child who does not yet want to come into the world.")
>
> I was deeply touched then by the poignancy of this simple sentence with its recognition of the oneness of life and death. Many years later...I recognized the continuity in Freud's thinking and what he called "the immortality of the unconscious."
> (Schur p. 445)

Freud had a great fondness for children and took a lively interest in the news of any fresh arrival. When Jones told him that his wife was expecting he wrote: "The lovely news of your expectation in May deserves a hearty congratulation without any delay in the name of us all. If it proves to be the youngest child, you may see from my own family that the last is far from being the least."[1]

Jews were now leaving Germany in large numbers. Analysts who remained faced a bleak future. The emigrants found temporary rest in Switzerland and in the Scandinavian countries, but ultimately the majority reached America. Freud's son Ernst left Berlin and settled in London. Freud still held to unrealistic hope:

> ...but we all think that special laws against Jews are out of the question in Austria because of the clauses in our peace treaty which expressly guaran-

[1]E. J. Jan. 13, 1933

> tee the rights of minorities....Legal persecution of the Jews here would lead to immediate action on the part of the League of Nations. And as for Austria joining Germany, in which case the Jews would lose all their rights, France and her Allies would never allow that. Furthermore, Austria is not given to German brutality. In such ways we buoy ourselves up in relative security. I am in any event determined not to move from the sopt.
> (E.J. April 7, 1933)

The first signal of the "liquidation" of psychoanalysis in Germany was the "Bur-ing of the Books." On May 10, 1933, five thousand Nazi students, bearing swastikas, burned the books of all Jewish and many non-Jewish but anti-Nazi authors. The bonfire took place in front of the Berlin Opera House, cheered on by about forty thousand Berliners. Included were the works of Thomas Mann, Einstein, Stefan Zweig, Freud, and many others. The buring of a particular author or group of authors was preceded by a special speech from an announcer. In Freud's case the announcer proclaimed: "Against the soul-destroying overestimation of the sex life and on behalf of the nobility of the human soul, I offer to the flames the writing of one Sigmund Freud!" A Viennese newspaper reported the event and Marie Bonaparte kept a copy of the paper.[1] "The Burning of the Books Bonfire" was presided over by Goebbels, who ended the ceremony with an impassioned speech. Freud's comment to a friend was : "What progress we are making. In the Middle Ages they would have burned me; nowadays they are content with burning my books."[2] Even in this comment Freud was optimistic—there is little doubt that ten years later they would have burned his body as well. In fact there was something ominous about his remark: four of his five sisters were to burn in extermination camps.

After their last meeting in the previous September, Freud and Ferenczi continued to exchange letters. They did not discuss their differences, the principal subject was Ferenczi's health. Medical treatment seemed to be containing the anemia, but in March the disease attacked the brain and spinal cord. For the last few months of his life he was unable to stand or walk. Jones reports that this exacerbated his latent psychotic tendencies. On May 24, 1933, Sandor Ferenczi died. This brilliant, lovable old friend of Freud's had come to a tragic end. The following are excepts from Freud's obituary:

> ....Since the days when he was led to me by his interest in psychoanalysis, still in its youth, we have shared many things with each other....For many successive years we spent the autumn holidays together in Italy and a number of papers that appeared later in the literature under his or my name took their first shape in our talks there....The feeling of a secure common bond, which grew up between us from so many shared experiences, was not interrupted when late in life

---

[1]Schur, p. 446
[2]Jones III, p. 182

> unfortunately, he was united to the outstanding woman who mourns him today as his widow.
>
> Ten years ago...he had already published most of the works which have made all analysts into his pupils....The need to cure and to help had become paramount in him. He had probably set himself aims which, with our therapeutic means, are altogether out of reach today....Signs were slowly revealed in him of a grave organic destructive process which had probably overshadowed his life for many years already. Shortly before completing his sixtieth year he succumbed to pernicious anemia. It is impossible to believe that the history of our science will ever forget him.
>
> (Sandor Ferenczi, 1933, S. E. XXII, p. 227)

Slowly Freud allowed the terrible truth of events around him to sink in. In a letter to Marie Bonaparte he described the world as an enormous prision. "Germany is the worst cell." He humorously remarked to a friend, "Look how poverty stricken the poet's imagination really is. Shakespeare in "A Midsummer Night's Dream" has a woman fall in love with a donkey. The audience wonders at that. And now, think of it, that a nation of sixty-five million have......, and he ended the sentence with a wave of the hand.[1]

In June the German Society for Psychotherapy came under Nazi control. Reichsfuhrer HermannGoering announced that all members were expected to study *Mein kampf*, which was to serve as the theoretical base for their work. Kretschmer, the president, resigned. His place was promptly filled by C. G. Jung.

Jung had also become editor of the Society's journal, the *Zentralblatt fur Psychotherapie*, and in 1936 was joined by a cousin of Hermann Goering, a psychiatrist, as co-editor. However Jung servered his connections with the Nazis in 1940. He has been severely criticized from many quarters, nonetheless, for his conduct. For the rest of his life he was contiunally asked to explain his collaboration with the Nazis. In a letter in 1951 he defended himself.

> ...my German colleagues were afraid that the Nazis would wipe out psychotherapy in Germany altogether and they wanted a non-German authority to help them. Well, I stepped in and made it possible for the cast-out Jewish doctors to become immediate members of the International Society....Soon the Nazis put Goering in. I wanted to withdraw, but my colleagues insisted that I should stay, in the hope that I could do something for them....From 1937 on I tried to withdraw but representatives of the Dutch and of the recently founded British group begged me not to give up and to hold the connection....I would not disavow my colleagues and friends. Thus I had to play the game and tread softly (much against

[1]Clark, p. 490

> my grain) knowing very well that I was a black sheep on account of my Wotan essay which only a complete ass can misunderstand as a pro-Nazi sentiment. I have never changed my view about the Nazis, nor have I ever been an anti-Semite, but I am convinced of the psychological differences between Jew and Gentile as between French and English and so on.
>
> (Roazen, p. 293)

Jung is said to have assisted Jewish refugees to reach Switzerland during the Nazi ascendancy in Europe, and to have helped Jews enter England. Perhaps what is most significant is that Nazis later put his name on their "black list." Jung's works were suppressed in Germany and occupied countries.[1]

The criticism against Jung goes beyond his collaboration with the Nazis. His writings seemed to corroborate the anti-Semistism that Freud had long accused him of. He wrote in the *Zentralblatt fur Psychotherapie* of January 1934:

> The Aryan unconsciousness has a higher potential than the Jewish; that is the advantage and the disadvantage of a youthfulness not yet fully escaped from barbarism. In my opinion it has been a great mistake of all previous medical psychology to apply Jewish categories which are not even binding for all Jews, indiscriminately to Christians, Germans or Slavs. In so doing, medical psychology has declared that most precious secret of the Germanic people—the creatively prophetic depth of the soul—to be childishly banal mores, while for decades my warning voice has been suspected of anti-Semitism. The source of this suspicion is Freud. He did not know the German soul any more than did all his Germanic imitators....Has the mighty apparition of National Socialism which the whole world watches with astonished eyes taught them something better?....That is why I say that the Germanic unconscious contains tensions and potentialities which medical psychology must consider in its evaluation of the unconscious.

Similarities between Jung's views and those of the Nazis are puzzling but in order to understand his concept of different psychologies for different peoples one should read his "Civilization in Transition."

After his separation from Freud, Jung grew angry. He claimed that Freud and his followers were neurotic and that they had practically ruined his private practice. Many people wrote to him for an explanation of his criticisms of Freud. Typical was his reply:

> As you know, Freud previously accused me of anti-

---

[1]Ibid. p. 290

> Semitism because I could not abide his soulless materialism. The Jew directly solicits anti-Semitism with his readiness to scent out anti-Semitism everywhere....It is typically Jewish that Freud can forget his roots to such an extent....To (Freud) as to many other Jews, as I have seen with my own eyes, the re-establishment of the communication with the instincts means a true and vital find and source of satisfaction and joy.
> (Clark, p. 494)

Jung would repeatedly refer to his break with Freud:

> From this I must conclude that I had somehow trespassed against the Jews....This prejudice has stuck to me ever since and has been repeated by all Freudians, thereby confirming every time that psychoanalysis is in fact a Jewish psychology which nobody else can criticize without making himself guilty of anti-Semitism.
> (Ibid. p. 494)

When Ernest Jones was working on the biography of Freud he contacted Jung for his version of the controversy. Jung replied that it had happened many years ago and that he no longer wished to carry on the feud.

For the four years that preceded Hitler's invasion of Austria in 1938, Freud's correspondence shows a preoccupation with political events. Will Austria go Nazi? If they do, will they be brutal as the Germans? Was it a good thing that the Chancellor had put down a Socialist uprising? There was also Freud's concern for the well-being of psychoanalysis. Should there be international meetings and where? The president must not be a Jew. What could be done to keep the *Verlag* alive now that psychoanalytic books could not be sold in Germany? Was it better to stay under the control of the Third Reich and somehow manage, or should one run as far as possible beyond their control?

The impotence of the League of Nations as exposed by the Abyssinian crisis added to the general pessimism Freud felt about the future of Austria. He was particularly disappointed by England's appeasement of Mussolini and he foresaw that Hitler would continue to gain power. Despite his feelings of apprehension, his enervated physical condition, and his conviction that he was in no frame of mind to work on anything, he now, at the age of seventy-eight, found his next topic, his last, and one that turned out to be a tour de force, *Moses and Monotheism*. "Not knowing what to do with my leisure time I have been writing something, and against my original intention it so took hold of me that everything else was put aside."[1]

In January 1935 he wrote to Lou Salome a full account of his ideas on Moses and religion. "And now you see, Lou, one connot publish this formula, which has quite fascinated me, in Austria today without running the risk of the Catholic authorities officially forbidding the practice of analysis. And only this Catholicism protects us against Nazism."[2]

---

[1]A. Z. Sept. 30, 1934
[2]L. S. Jan. 6, 1935

Theoretical differences existed within the psychoanalytic movement, but with one exception, the question of lay analysis, they never reached an emotional pitch. For example, at this time (April 1935), the London school differed from the Viennese school on some basic issues. The Londoners had doubts about the theory of the "death instinct" and had a somewhat different conception of the phallic phase, particularly in the female. So Jones went to Vienna to present a paper clarifying the theoretical differences, and Robert Waelder expounded the Viennese views to the London group. The main emphasis fell on Melanie Klein's work. Klein saw the various psychosexual stages occurring at younger ages than did the earlier Freudians. "I do not estimate our theoretical differences of opinion as slight, but so long as there is no bad feeling behind them they can have no troublesome results...."[1]

In June Freud received a message from the American publisher of his "Autobiographical Study," requesting him to write a supplement to it. He responded promptly. He advised his friends never to publish the details of their private lives and he expressed his own regret at having done so.

The year 1936 brought a special hazard, his eightieth birthday. He knew that preparations for celebrations were in progress and he steeled himself for the occasion. Jones, who was president of the International Association, discussed the matter with Freud many times. Fortunately for Freud, Jones shared his feelings about ceremonial occasions being quiet. In fact, Jones remarked that it was a good thing that Eitingon was not president at the time of the birthday, since it was well known that Eitingon would make much of the occasion.

Jones suggested a volume of commemorative essays, but that would take time to organize and probably lead to jealousies. Freud suggested a photograph album containing photographs of all the members.

> I turn to my own suggestion of an album and confess that now it pleases me just as little; indeed it fundamentally displeases me. Leaving aside the two objections that it would mean a great deal of trouble and bring me no guarantee that I live to the date, now I am taking unbrage at the aesthetic monstrosity of 400 pictures of most ugly people of whom I don't at all know the half and of whom a good number do not want to know anything of me. No, the times are not suited to a festival, "intra Iliacos muros nec extra" (Let us keep it among ourselves). The only possible thing seems to me renounce any action in common. Whoever feels that he must congratulate me let him do so, and who does not need not fear my vengeance.

Freud continued the letter and explored the meaning of celebrating the big round numbers of one's life. It must represent, he goes on to say, a feeling of triumph over the transient nature of life. We never forget that life is ready to devour us. When one reaches sixty, seventy, or even eighty, it must tell us that we are not so frail and that we can indeed stand up to the hostile effects of life.

---

[1]E. J. May 26, 1935

> That one can understand and agree with, but the celebration evidently has sense only when the survivor can in spite of all wounds and scars join in as a hale fellow; it loses this sense when he is an invalid with whom there is no question of conviviality. And since the latter is my case and I bear my fate by myself I should prefer my 80th birthday to be treated as my private affair—by my friends.
>
> (E. J. July 21, 1935)

He of course knew that he could not prevent other anniversary celebrations; indeed many took place.

His birthday, May 6, turned out to be a lovely spring day. The house was full of flowers, telegrams, gifts, and letters from all over the world. A scroll containing an address written by Stefan Zweig and Thomas Mann arrived, and its list of signers reads like a *Who's Who* of the litery, artistic, and scientific worlds.[1] Thomas Mann also sent a handwritten copy of a speech he was to give in tribute to Freud at the *Akademischer Verein fur Medizinische Psychologie*, an organization formed by a young group of intelligent psychiatrists. Freud couldn't read Mann's handwriting, so he called on Max Schur to read it for him. Max couldn't read the handwriting either. Despite all his prior objections, Freud enjoyed the party. He was charming, gracious, altogether in fine form.

In New York the American Neurological Association was treated to a Freudian slip. Smith Ely Jellife presented "Sigmund Freud as a Neurologist." He told of the good old days, working in Meynert's laboratory. Somehow he had forgotten the name of one of the men he worked with; the audience roared at him: "Freud!" Marie Bonaparte delivered a eulogy at the Sorbonne in Paris; in London Freud was elected a Foreign Member of the Royal Society. He jokingly inquired whether that entitled him to write F.M.O.T.R.S. after his name.

At the *Akademischer Verin fur Medizinische Psychologie* two addresses in honor of Freud were delivered: one by Mann, as mentioned earlier, and the other by Binswanger. Mann, who was usualy formal, even detached, as a speaker, delivered a deeply moving speech. Schur wrote that it was more than a tribute to Freud, it was addressed to the power of the creative spirit in man, the rights of the individual, and it challenged the forces of unreasion and evil. On the way to the lecture Schur had passed a group of marching Brown Shirts, but, he said, Mann's speech made him feel that all was not lost. At the reception which followed Schur explained why Freud could not be present and asked Mann if he would be willing to read the speech to Freud personally. "Mann accepted gladly."[2]

The meeting between the two men, which Schur described as "an unforgettable experience," was attended by Freud's family, by Mrs. Mann, and by Dr. Schur and his wife.

> With obvious emotion Mann read the speech, which in the meantime he had given in several other places, all, of course, outside of Germany.

---

[1]Schur. p. 479
[2]Ibid. p. 480

> Freud, who never liked to listen to praise of himself, was profoundly impressed this time. To him it was a summary of his life's work, a vindication for the years of calumny and misunderstanding he had endured, and a confirmation that it had been worthwhile to have lived that long.
>
> (Ibid. p. 481)

There were many tributes in the foreign press; a particularly striking one by Selma Lagerlof, the distinguished Swedish writer. There were also many callers; Elisabeth Rotten asked him how he felt and he answered, "How a man of eighty feels is not a topic for conversation."[1]

And Vienna? How did his Viennese colleagues acknowledge his eightieth anniversary? Grudgingly:

> Viennese colleagues also celebrated the occasion, and betrayed by all sorts of indications how hard they found it to do so. The Minister of Education ceremoniously congratulated me in a polite fashion, but the Austrian newspapers were forbidden under pain of confiscation to mention this sympathetic action. Numerous articles here and abroad expressed plainly enough their rejection and hatred. So I had the satisfaction of observing that honesty has not quite vanished from the world.
>
> (A.Z. May 31, 1936)

Freud was deeply saddened when he heard shortly thereafter of Lou Andreas-Salome's death at the age of seventy-six. He learned of it in a letter from Ernst Pfeiffer, her friend and literary executor. She had died on February 5, 1937. Thus a correspondence that had covered twenty-four years came to a close. In a letter to Arnold Zweig he commented on how much he had admired and loved her.

In July, 1936, two exceptionally difficult and painful operations were necessary. The report of July 16 had noted a definite malignancy. For the past five years, frequent surgery had removed any precancerous tissue but now the dreaded enemy had to be faced and constant recurrences of malignancy were expected. Schur kept his word and told Freud the truth. "The frightening factor was that now each new lesion had a tendency to grow fast and be potentially malignant. Our vigil had to be even more strict."[2]

> On Saturday, December 12, Pichler told me he was obliged to burn a new spot that seemed to him suspicious. He did so and this time the microscopic examination showed only harmless tissue, but the reaction was frightful. Severe pain

---

[1]Jones 3, p. 206
[2]Schur, p. 484

> above all, then in the following days a badly locked mouth so that I could not eat anything and had great difficulty in drinking. I carry on with my analyses by changing a hot water bottle every half hour to hold my cheek. I get slight relief from short wave therapy, but it does not last long. I am told I have to put up with this existence for another week. I wish you could have seen what sympathy Jo-fi (his chow dog) shows me in my suffering, just as if she understood everything.
> (M.B. Dec. 17, 1936)

This operation was one of the few occasions when Freud reached the limit of his endurance. The local anesthesia had not taken full effect and wore off before the lengthy procedure was completed. Somewhat to Pichler's surprise Freud cried out: "Ich kann nicht mehr weiter." (I can't go on any longer.) Only Pichler's iron nerve enabled him to complete the operation. That was the only protest.

Jo-fi had to be operated on for two large ovarian cysts, and did not survive the surgery. Feeling that he could not get along without a dog, Freud asked Dorothy Burlingham to give him a chow named Lun, which four years earlier he had had to return because of Jo-fi's jealousy. On one occasion Dorothy Burlingham had asked Felix and Helene Deutsch to care for Lun while she left on a holiday. The following is a quote from Felix Deutsch:

> This dog is a psychosomatic case, indeed! She supposedly had too narrow a pelvis for ever having puppies without danger to her life. For this reason, she had to be watched carefully whenever she was in heat. At those times Helene and I alternated in the anti-baby-sitting service. Once, on a Sunday, sitting in our garden with the dog, I fell asleep, and when I awakened the dog had disappeared. Frantically searching for her, I found her finally in the neighbor's garden with a beautiful male poodle. The chow looked very sheepish, but no real evidence of a love act could be established. Nothing could be done at the moment more than to wait and see. Several weeks went by without any change in her behavior. At the end of the second month, however, the teats began to swell and colostrum appeared. She began to get fat rapidly. When on the street, she scratched and dug holes in the ground, altogether unmistakable signs of pregnancy. I resigned myself to the inevitable but nothing happened.
>
> On the contrary, in the fourth month, instead of increasing, these signs started to decrease. I rushed the dog to the veterinarian. Diagnosis: Pseudo-cyesis. Have you ever heard of a dog with a false pregnancy? I am almost inclined to say: "That can only happen to the dog of an analyst."
> (Jones 3, p. 212)

As a point of interest—it was at this time that Marie Bonaparte acquired the Fliess letters. "I should not like any of it to come to the knowledge of so-called posterity."[1] The story and the fate of these letters have already been described. In 1961 at St. Tropez, Marie Bonaparte told Max Schur how difficult it was for her to act against the wishes of her beloved mentor, but she was determined to preserve this material for posterity. For this we are all grateful.

The political situation in Austria grew steadily more somber. The appeasement policy of the West was increasingly apparent. "Mussolini seems now to be giving Germany a free hand."[2] The approach of Nazidom loomed as a daily threat. The blatant official anti-Semitism of the Third Reich and their official opposition to psychoanalysis could only have brought Freud great apprehension. Nevertheless, in June 1937, he published a very important technical paper, "Analysis Terminable and Interminable." It is probably the most important contribution he ever made to the practicing analyst. At the age of eighty-one Freud showed not the slightest impairment of his intellectual powers. The close thinking and the deep wisdom it evinces is remarkable. He began with the problems encountered in trying to shorten analysis. But he also raised the question of how complete an analysis can ever be and examined the forces that hinder such an ideal result. Then he explored the possibility of forestalling neurotic disturbances by dealing with conflicts before they are manifest. He concluded that we not only should let sleeping dogs lie, but that we actually lack the power to awaken them. He believed that the greatest resistance to therapy is the death instinct, and other deep constitutional factors such as the peculiar quality he termed "adhesiveness of the libido"—the resistance to change. All in all, it was hardly an optimistic view of psychotherapy.

---

[1]M.B. Jan. 3, 1937
[2]Ibid. p. 213

CHAPTER LXXV

■ *Two Centigrams Of Morphine*

In February 1938, Hitler confronted Kurt Schuschnigg, the Austrian chancellor, and served him an ultimatum: He must announce a plebiscite to determine whether the Austrian people wanted independence from Germany. The whole thing proved to be a gesture merely: in March Schuschnigg was forced to resign and the Germans marched into Austria. Freud's diary entry that day consisted of two words: "Finis Austriae."

The Austrian Nazi Seys-Inquart was appointed chancellor and his first act was to invite the German army into Austria. In fact, the Germans had already started to move. From early morning, tanks and soldiers packed the streets of Vienna, welcomed by cheering crowds. The next day, March 12, Hitler himself entered Austria and without even setting up a puppet government declared Austria a part of Germany.

Max Schur was making his rounds at the hospital when the news of Schuschnigg's resignation reached him. He called home, then left immediately to be with Freud. Marching storm troopers filled the streets; "Heil Hitler" could be heard everywhere. A number of friends had already gathered at Freud's home to convince him he must leave.

A great deal has been written about the ordeal of concentration and extermination camps; less is known about the state of mind that accompanies the realization that you are outside the protection of the law. Friends and relatives suddenly disappear, and it is abnormal not to fear a knock on the door. The Gestapo had moved in, established their headquarters, and news of outrages were beginning to circulate.

Ernest Jones, after discussing the situation by telephone with Dorothy Burlingham in Vienna and Marie Bonaparte in Paris, decided to go to Vienna and make a final effort to change Freud's mind about leaving. Flights to Vienna had been cancelled but Jones managed to complete the journey in a small monoplane from Prague. He has described the depressing sight of German planes stacked at the airport and filling the air, of tanks roaring on the streets, and of the constant shouts of "Heil Hitler."

Jones's first stop was at his sister-in-law's, where Anna Freud got in touch with him. On her advice he went to the office of the *Verlag* where he hoped his assertion of its international character would be useful. The stairs and rooms were full of "villainous-looking" youths armed with pistols and daggers; Martin Freud was sitting in a corner under arrest, while the Nazi "authorities" were counting the petty cash in a drawer. Jones declared that he was the British representative to the *Verlag* and was immediately put under arrest. That ended the hope that the *Verlag* would be spared. "The remarks made when I asked to be allowed to communicate with the British Embassy showed me how low my country's prestige had fallen after Hitler's successes.[1] An hour later he was released. He made his way directly to Freud's residence.

In the meantime Freud's home had been invaded by an SA troop. A sentry guarded the door and several others forced their way into the dining room. Martha responded with hospitality. She invited the sentry to sit down, remarking that she found it unpleasant to see a stranger standing up in her house. Then she took her household money, placed it on the table and said: "Won't the gentlemen help themselves?" Anna led them to the family safe and opened it. They helped themselves to 6,000 Austrian schillings. "They were debating their prospects of continuing their petty burglary when a frail, gaunt figure appeared in the doorway. It was Freud, aroused by the disturbance. He had a way of frowning with blazing eyes that an Old Testament prophet might have envied, and the effect produced by his lowering mien completed the visitor's discomfiture. Saying they would call another day, they hastily took their departure."[2] When Freud heard how much money they had taken he remarked that they got more for a house call than he did.

Immediately after the SA left, Jones arrived. As he feared, Freud was determined to stay in Vienna, arguing that he was too weak to travel, could not even climb the steps of the train. Jones simply rejected the argument. Freud then went on to say that no country would grant him entry. That argument carried some weight. Unemployment was so widespread that countries had revised their immigration policies to the point of ferocious inhospitality. Jone's reply was that he was asking Freud's permission to allow him, on his return to England, to arrange a possible exception in his case. Freud's last plea was that to leave Vienna now would be like a soldier deserting his post. Jones countered this argument by quoting the officer of the Titanic who claimed that his ship had left *Him.*

There were three hurdles to be got over before Freud could emigrate to England. The first was Freud himself, but Jones overcame that. The second was that of obtaining permission to live in England. The last was to persuade the Nazis to release Freud. But Freud had more friends in high places than he knew. Without their help his chance for survival would have been slim indeed.

William C. Bullitt was deeply impressed with Freud and with psychoanalysis. (In fact he and Freud had almost collaborated on a book about President Wilson.) While Bullitt was the United States Ambassador to Russia, he had been skeptical about Austria's ability to stand up to Hitler and had therefore arranged for the appointment of a Mr. Wiley as consul-general in Vienna. Mr. Wiley had a special assignment; he was to keep a watchful eye and a protective hand on Freud and his family. By the time the Nazis occupied Austria, Bullitt was American Ambassador to France, and he immediately called Wiley and requested that he "show his presence." Bullitt was a personal friend of President Roosevelt and cabled him asking for intervention. Roosevelt instructed his Secretary of State, Cordell Hull, to give the proper orders to his charge d'Affaires in Vienna, Mr. Wiley, to do whatever he could within diplomatic limits. Wiley conscientiously carried out his mission. That evening he visited Freud and the following plan was adopted: Dorothy Burlingham, who was by now practically a member of the Freud family and lived in the same building

---

[1]Jones III, p. 219
[2]Ibid. p. 219

with a house phone connecting the two apartments, was to call the American Embassy as soon as there was any sign of trouble, and within minutes an American official would "just drop in."[1]

Marie Bonaparte in the meantime left for Vienna and her presence there had its effect too.

Pichler, although an old member of the National Party of Greater Germany (a group who since World War I favored the unification of Austria and Germany), would have nothing to do with the Nazis. That courageous man used whatever influence he had behind the scenes to keep the Gestapo off Freud's back. He came to the house repeatedly, at the slightest sign of a medical problem. Bullitt, in Paris, called on Graf von Welczeck, the German Ambassador, and let him know in the strongest terms what a world scandal would follow any insult to Freud. Count Wilczeck, an aristocrat of the old diplomatic service, a man of culture and a humanitarian, needed no persuading. He took steps at once and brought the matter before the highest Nazi authorities.

In the meantime, ominous events were occurring daily. A copy of Freud's will that indicated that he had money abroad had been left at the *Verlag*. Martin had tried to destroy it along with other documents, but was caught. He was held for hours at bayonet point.[2]

Then, one day, omnipresent threat became reality. Anna Freud was summoned before the Gestapo and it was common knowledge that many who were summoned before the Gestapo never returned. Martin, since his arrest at the *Verlag*, expected to be summoned by the Gestapo at any moment. Anna and Martin went to Schur's house and asked for a drug they could take in the event of torture. He gave them a sufficient amount of Veronal and promised that he would take care of Freud as long as was possible. As it turned out, Martin was never called before the Gestapo and Anna kept her appointment alone. The only thing that Schur ever kept from Freud was that visit from Anna and Martin.

> That was the worst day. I went to the Berggasse and stayed with Freud. The hours were endless. It was the only time I ever saw Freud deeply worried. He paced the floor, smoking incessantly. I tried to reassure him as well as I could. Finally, late in the evening, Anna Freud returned. Freud, who was rarely demonstrative in his affection, showed his feelings that evening. This danger was over. Martin was never called in. I have never inquired of Anna what actually happened at the Gestapo.
>
> (Ibid. p. 498)

Edoardo Weiss, a psychoanalyst and a friend of Mussolini, made a plea on behalf of the Freud family and Mussolini sent Hitler a diplomatic note expressing his friendship for Freud.

> Some idea of the close attention that Roosevelt's

---

[1]Schur, p. 497
[2]Ibid. p. 497

> instructions had brought about was also given on the twenty-second, when Bullitt was advised: Anna Freud just arrested. Have informed Berlin and von Stein. The message was followed five hours later with the news: Anna Freud released.
> (Clark, p. 507)

In the meantime, Mr. Wiley had called the Gestapo in regard to Anna's arrest. His "presence" had been made known. Due to this pressure from the highest places, Freud and his family were not molested. The Nazis preferred not to risk the consequences.

Only later was it discovered that Anna had not been in quite the danger they had feared. The Nazi Commissar of the *Verlag* (every Austrian enterprise was assigned its "Nazi-Kommissar"), Dr. Sauerwald, knew about the incriminating will but kept it a secret from the Gestapo. The "Dr. Sauerwald Episode" was one of those strange incidents where "fate" may have saved Freud and those around him. When he was first assigned to the *Verlag,* Sauerwald behaved in typical SA manner: coarse, brutal bullying. He was contemptuous of Drs. Sterba and Hartmann, Gentiles, for getting mixed up with "Jewish swine." Soon, however, he found himself getting bored with his job and for distraction began to read Freud's works. He grew fascinated. His own background was a PhD in chemistry. The more he read the more he was impressed with psychoanalysis and with Freud as a person. He became extremely helpful and used his considerable influence with the Nazis on behalf of the Freud family. Later it was learned that he knew of the bank account abroad, but at great risk to himself withheld the information from the Gestapo. On one occasion when the Gestapo was disrespectful to Freud, he apologized to Anna: "What can you expect? These Prussians don't know who Freud is."[1] He personally took charge of the packing of Freud's belongings, including his art collection and books. After Freud's departure he visited Freud's sisters and kept a watchful eye on them. It was only after he was drafted into the German army that they were sent to extermination camps. Sauerwald was wounded and contracted tuberculosis. When the Austrian government brought him to trial as a war criminal, Marie Bonaparte and Anna Freud signed affidavits attesting to his help and cooperation at his personal risk. Their testimony helped bring about his acquittal.

Jones left for home with the urgent task of obtaining permits in England. He had a list of people whom Freud wished to bring with him: his own family of ten, including three inlaws, his physician (Schur) with his family of three, and the housekeeper' sixteen in all.

Typically, Jones delivered. He contacted the Royal Society which had honored Freud only two years before and asked them to help. As the Society rarely intervenes in social and political affairs, its requests were listened to with particular respect. At the time the president of the Society was the famous physicist Sir William Bragg. Jones was startled at how naive a distinguished scientist could be. "He asked me, 'Do you really think the Germans are unkind to the Jews?' He was shocked when I described to him the bodily marks I had seen on friends who had got away from concentration camps, but I daresay the impression I made was soon blotted out."[2]

---

[1]Schur p. 498
[2]Jones 3, p. 232

Then came the Home Office. Sir Samuel Hoare, the Home Secretary, displayed his usual humanitarian qualities and without hesitation gave Jones carte blanche to fill in permits, including permission to work, for Freud, his family, personal doctors, a certain number of pupils and servants.

There remained the final difficulty of securing permission to leave from the Nazis. Three very anxious months followed. Years later Anna was to tell Schur that when things were at their worst and all hope of escape was gone, she had asked Freud whether it wouldn't be better if they all killed themselves. To which he replied with characteristic irony: "Why? Because they would like us to?"[1]

During this period he did not leave his house; it was not safe to walk the streets of Vienna. He continued to see whatever patients were left, to work on his "Moses" book, and to prepare for emigration by sorting through stacks of manuscripts and correspondence. He and Anna completed their translation of Marie Bonaparte's book *Topsy*.

Marie Bonaparte and Anna joined Freud in sorting his papers. They burned masses that they felt not worth taking to England; they also rescued from waste baskets much that Freud had thrown away.

The final chapter in Vienna was the "ransom story." Nazi authorities demanded large sums of money under the guise of an income tax, and every emigrant had to pay this "Fugitive tax." As Freud's bank accounts, cash, and the *Verlag* had already been confiscated, he had no money to pay this tax. They threatened to confiscate his library and his art collection if he did not, so Marie Bonaparte advanced some Austrian schillings for the purpose. The Gestapo claimed that Freud owed his publisher thirty-two thousand schillings. Marie Bonaparte paid that blackmail as well. Freud was to repay her when he arrived in London.

The Nazi inquisition was conducted with great detail. When they discovered that a store of the *Collected Works* was in Switzerland, a neutral country, they insisted that Martin issue instructions for the books to be sent back to Vienna. When the books were returned, the Nazis burned them.

In May, considering their chances better, Freud wrote to his son Ernst in London: "I sometimes compare myself with the old Jacob whom in his old age his children brought to Egypt. It is to be hoped that the result will not be the same, an exodus from Egypt. It is time for Ahasuerus (The Wandering Jew) to come to rest somewhere."[2]

Minna Bernays, Martha's sister, whom Dorothy Burlingham brought home from the sanatorium, was the first member allowed to travel. Then Martin, Freud's eldest son, whose wife and children were already in Paris, left with their daughter Mathilde Hollitscher and her husband. A week later exit visas for Freud and Martha arrived. However, one of the conditions before official clearance was given, was that Freud sign a document for the Gestapo.

> I, Prof. Freud, hereby confirm that after the Anschluss of Austria to the German Reich, I have been treated by the German authorities and particularly by the Gestapo with all the respect and

---

[1]Schur p. 499
[2]Jones III, p. 225

> consideration due to my scientific reputation, that I could live and work in full freedom, that I could continue to pursue my activities in every way I desired, that I found full support from all concerned in this respect, and that I have not the slightest reason for any complaint.

Freud felt no compunction in signing. He then asked if he might add a postscript; they nodded in agreement. He wrote: "P.S. I can heartily recommend the Gestapo to anyone."[1]

The nightmare ended on June 4, 1938. Freud, Martha, and Anna left the city that had been their home for almost eighty years. With them went two maidservants and a member of the United States Legation staff to see that nothing went wrong before they reached the French border. At three o'clock the next morning, aboard the Orient Express, they crossed the frontier into France. They never had to see another Nazi.

Schur had suffered an attack of appendicitis at the last minute and his place was taken by Dr. Josephine Stross, a friend of Anna's. Marie Bonaparte, Ambassador Bullitt, Harry Freud (Freud's nephew), and Ernst met the train in Paris at ten in the morning. They spent twelve wonderful hours in Marie Bonaparte's beautiful home. She surprised Freud with several Greek terra cotta figures she had purchased for his collection. Having lived through the experience of total inflation which rendered currency worthless, Freud had wisely preserved some of his money in gold, as a protection against future disaster. Even Marie Bonaparte could not safely take gold out of the country, so she arranged for the Greek Embassy in Vienna to deliver it by courier to the King of Greece, who transferred it to the Greek Embassy in London. She informed Freud that his gold was safe in London.

> The one day in your house in Paris restored our good mood and sense of dignity; after being surrounded by love for twelve hours we left proud and rich under the protection of Athene. (Athene was a statuette on Freud's desk which Marie Bonaparte had smuggled to Paris and restored to him there.)
>
> (M.B. June 8, 1938)

That night they crossed the channel by ferry to Dover. Even there they were to feel the touch of Jone's devotion: he had arranged diplomatic privileges for them and none of their baggage was examined there or in London. He had also arranged that their train arrive at an unannounced platform to avoid the crowds and the battery of cameras. Waiting were Freud's eldest children, Mathilde and Martin, along with Jones and his wife. All were deeply moved at the reunion. They made a fast exit in Jones' car, so it was some time before the reporters caught up with them.

During the night crossing to London, Freud had dreamed that he was landing at Pevensey. When he related this to Ernst he had to explain that Pevensey was where William the Conqueror had landed in 1066. On the surface the dream does not express the feelings of a depressed refugee; in fact it foreshadowed the extraordinary

---

[1]Ibid. p. 226

honors with which he was greeted in London.

Their first stop was at the house Ernst had rented at 39 Elsworthy Road, while he continued his search for a permanent residence for his parents. On Freud's first stroll in the garden of his new house he said to Jones: "I am almost tempted to cry out 'Heil Hitler'."[1] "We are buried in flowers. Interesting letters....Finally and this is something special for England, numerous letters from strangers who only wish to say how happy they are that we have come to England and that we are in safety and peace."[2]

Newspapers were full of photographs and sympathetic accounts of his arrival. Medical and other professional journals published articles honoring him. The *Lancet* wrote:

> His teachings in their time aroused controversy more acute, and antagonism more bitter than any since the days of Darwin. Now, in his old age, there are few psychologists of any school who do not admit their debt to him. Some of the conceptions he formulated clearly for the first time have crept into current philosophy against the stream of willful incredulity which he himself recognized as man's natural reaction to unbearable truth.
>
> (Jones III, p. 229)

Taxi drivers were familiar with his address and the local bank manager greeted him with "I know all about you."

Ever since his youth Freud had looked upon England as the cradle of democracy, the country of freedom of thought. He thoroughly enjoyed his newly adopted home. Also he was made a member of the Royal Society in the company of Newton and Darwin. Freud was pleased.

Martha wrote to Freud's sisters in Vienna:

> If one's thought were not always with the dear ones one has left behind, one would be completely happy. You cannot imagine how honored this town feels at having our modest beloved old man in their midst. Every day we receive letters welcoming him. Although we have only been here two weeks, letters arrive without any indication of the street: simply, "Freud, London;" and they arrive without delay despite the great size and magnificence of this city of ten million people.
>
> (Clark, p. 515)

Freud had had to leave his four sisters in Vienna. Not certain of his earning ability in England, he had given them 160,000 Austrian schillings which would be enough for their old age, provided that the Nazis did not confiscate it. Marie Bonaparte tried to get permission for them to emigrate to France but could not

---

[1]Jones III, p. 229
[2]M.B. June 8, 1938

manage it. The persecution of Jews was still in its early stage and Freud had no special reason to be concerned about them. Fortunately, he never knew of their fate: they were burned in concentration camp ovens about five years later.

For a man in his eighties, in pain from a "monster" in his mouth which made speaking difficult, Freud was remarkably busy. An unending stream of visitors, from the most distinguished scientists, literary and artistic figures, down to Josef Breuer's granddaughter, paid calls. And the endless task of maintaining his correspondence and his writing kept him fully occupied. He completed *Moses and Monotheism* and began work on an *Outline of Psychoanalysis.*

In late June three visitors arrived who particularly pleased him. They were secretaries from the Royal Society who brought the charter book for him to sign. Bringing the book to the signer instead of the reverse was a privilege reserved for royalty. In view of the fact that Freud couldn't make the journey, the right of a king was granted him. To Arnold Zweig he wrote, "They left me a facsimile of the book, and if you were here with me I could show you the signatures of I. Newton and Charles Darwin. Good company'."[1] In a postscript he added that he had to change his signature to "Sigm. Freud" instead of "Freud." In that strange country only lords signed the surname alone.

Minna was seriously ill, confined to bed on the first floor. Freud could not visit her because of the stairs. Not long after, it was decided that she required a nursing home.

The British had strict regulations against rabies and Lun was kept in quarantine for six months. Freud missed her companionship and visited her four days after his arrival. He managed several more visits.

The Home Office graciously granted Schur permission to function as Freud's personal physician even before he passed the official British examinations. He saw Freud almost daily. Schur felt the enormous responsibility and sorely missed Pichler. When Exner, the English physician whom Pichler recommended, saw a lesion, he couldn't believe it could be significant. Schur was insistent and Exner listened in disbelief to this foreigner who was supposed to be an internist. Schur wrote urgent letters to Pichler asking if he would come to London if necessary. Pichler immediately expressed his willingness.

By September 1938 it was clear that the lesion was serious. Pichler arrived in London September 7 to perform the operation. Pichler's concern was not only the character of the lesion but also its location. Any further growth would make it even less accessible. Even now he would have to approach the area by a large external excision through the cheek and lips. Pichler asked Schur if Freud's heart could take the strain. Schur believed it could, but left the decision to Freud who decided that they should proceed. Freud's confidence in Pichler made it easier for all concerned. Jones visited Freud that evening and for the first time since he had known him, saw him shaven clean of his familiar beard, as part of the preparation for surgery. The technique of general anesthesia was more advanced in England than on the Continent, and Freud tolerated the operation, though extensive, quite well.

He seemed to be making a normal recovery, and Pichler left on September 9. Freud was recovering, but very slowly. "The area where the bone had been coagulated was partly necrotic, slow to heal, and very painful."[2] Actually he never fully re-

---

[1]A.Z. June 28, 1938

[2]Schur p. 510

covered from the effects of this operation. He became more frail.

Martha, Anna, Paula (the housekeeper), and Freud moved into their permanent home at 20 Maresfield Gardens in late September. All his books, furniture, and antiques had arrived safely from Vienna. Anna and Paula arranged everything so that his favorite objects occupied the same places that they had in their old surroundings. The new room was sunnier and bigger and had direct access to the garden, which was roomy, well stocked with shrubs and flowers, and bordered by high trees which secluded it from the neighbors. Freud said that it was beautiful and too good for someone who would not tenant it for long. He loved this home and spent as much time as possible in the garden.

He observed that Martha was the quickest to adapt to the new home. She continued her Viennese custom of doing all the marketing, a practice she went on with daily until the end of her life. Before long she was on friendly terms with the various shopkeepers. She always gave the impression that her chief function was to provide a comfortable background for her distinguished husband. In this she succeeded admirably. She was a charming companion, a capable and considerate mistress of the house, and a gracious hostess.

This old, sick, suffering man lived an active life until his last three days, three days in which he did not read anything. Until then he saw patients, guests, wrote, and continued his correspondence. The impressions he left on his guests we learn from their writings. None left unimpressed.

His continued interest in life, and his generosity, were shown when in December he read a book by Rachel Berdach, *The Emperor, the Sages, and Death.* As soon as he had finished he wrote:

> Dear Madam (or Miss?)
>
> Your mysterious and beautiful book has pleased me to an extent that makes me unsure of my judgment....I haven't ready anything so substantial and poetically accomplished for a long time.
>
> And with it such a diffident letter! Can it be that your modesty causes you to underrate your own value? Who are you? Where did you acquire all the knowledge expressed in your book? Judging by the priority you grant to death, one is led to conclude that you are very young.
>
> Won't you give me the pleasure of paying me a visit one day? I have time in the morning.
>
> Yours very sincerely,
>
> Freud
>
> (Schur p. 514)

Old friends and pupils who visited him were always taken aback by how frail and shrunken he had become. Others have described him in Olympian terms. Arthur Koestler: "...though small and frail...the dominating impression was not that of a sick octogenarian, but of the indestructible vitality of the Hebrew patriarchs."[1] In fact Koestler describes himself as feeling uneasy and confused as he approached the great man. His conclusions in regard to Freud's difficulty in speaking was that

---

[1]Arthur Koestler, *The Invisible Writing,* Boston, Beacon, 1955, p. 408

Freud had set up a taboo of his own in which the word "cancer" was never to be mentioned in his presence or referred to in a letter. "The man who knew more than any other mortal about the ruses of self-deception had chosen to enter the darkness with a transparent veil over his eyes."[1] Endless examples can be given to refute Koestler's statement: the following amusing one should do. In a letter to Marie Bonaparte, Freud said that it was odd that he should suffer from cancer since he was so fond of crabs. (The German word for crab and cancer is the same: *Krebs*).

Leonard Woolf, Freud's publisher in London, and his wife, Virginia, paid him a call. Leonard felt that Freud had "an aura, not of fame, but of greatness....There was something about him as of a half-extinct volcano, something sombre, suppressed, reserved....a formidable man."[2] By the end of the year Freud had sufficiently recovered to be able to see four patients a day and add the finishing touches to his "Moses" book.

Moses and Monotheism, written after he was eighty years old, is a magnum opus. It has been suggested that it was the persecution of the Jews in Nazi Germany that narrowed Freud's general interest in mankind down to the problem of the Jew. Freud was forced to reflect on what in his people evoked such horrible reactions throughout history and how Jews had become what they were. But a deep, reflective person like Freud would not require persecution to make him ponder the mysteries of life. In Freud's case, the questions "What is a Jew?," "How did I become a Jew?," "How did Jews become what they are?" must have crossed his mind countless times since he was very young. The "Moses" book deals with these questions.

Not surprisingly, Freud's study of the origins of the Jewish religion, and to some extent of the Christian religion, is essentially a historical-psychological study, and while it is not antireligious, it is certainly irreligious. In view of the fact that Austria's Catholic regime was the last bulwark against a Nazi takeover, Freud had been reluctant to publish his findings. And the timing was hardly propitious. Why offend the Church? It already had shown a horror of psychoanalysis. Edoardo Weiss, an Italian psychoanalyst who had direct access to Mussolini, had had to stand by helplessly while a ban was placed on the Italian psychoanalytic journal. The ban was said to come directly from the Vatican and could not be lifted. So why should Freud expose his colleagues to the risk of having psychoanalysis and its publications banned in Vienna?

> Were this danger confined to myself it would make little impression on me, but to deprive all our members in Vienna of their livelihood strikes me as too great a responsibility....So all in all it isn't quite the proper occasion for martyrdom.
> (A.Z. Sept. 20, 1934)

Moreover, at a time when Jews needed all the support they could get, when they turned to the consolation of the sacred letter of the Law and their prophet, why deprive them of their God and his spokesman? Only a few very close friends, Anna and Martin, had read the manuscript. No one else knew of its existence. Freud considered having it published posthumously. But he couldn't leave it alone—it

---

[1]Jones 3, p. 236

[2]Quoted by Roazan, p. 540

tormented him.

> I determined to give it up, but it tormented me like an unlaid ghost, and I found a way out by making two pieces of it independent and publishing them in our periodical Imago....Then, in March 1938, came the unexpected German invasion, which forced me to leave my home but also freed me from my anxiety lest my publication might conjure up a prohibition of psychoanalysis in a place where it was still tolerated. I had scarcely arrived in England before I found the temptation irresistible to make the knowledge I had held back accessible to the world....
>
> (*Moses and Monotheism,* 1939, S.E. XXIII, p. 103)

He was not surprised that the reaction to these articles in the *Imago* was critical. Orthodoxy everywhere was outraged. Jewish scholars visited, beseeching him not to publish the book.

But Freud had made the decision to publish. "Needless to say, I don't like offending my own people either," he wrote to Charles Singer. "But what can I do about it? I have spent my whole life standing up for what I have considered to be the scientific truth, even when it was uncomfortable and unpleasant for my fellowmen. I cannot end up with an act of disavowal."[1]

Freud believed that Moses was not a Jew but an Egyptian, perhaps a prince or a friend of the court, who was a believer in the new monotheistic religion founded by the Pharaoh Ikhnaton. The priests of the old cults rebelled at the time and overthrew Ikhnaton, forcing Moses to flee Egypt. Determined to preserve and propagate the new religion, Moses *chose* a Hebrew tribe that lived in slavery on the edge of the Empire and imposed monotheism on them. But the "chosen people" were too primitive to endure the suppression of their instincts demanded of them. They reverted to their primitive religion, worshiped the golden calf, revolted against Moses, and killed. Like their early brothers in *Totem and Taboo,* they never forgot their crime. Mosaic law is an expression of their remorse.

The book is very controversial. The first part lacks Freud's usual clear-flowing style, perhaps due to his fatigue and his ambivalence about the subject. To those interested in Biblical events, *Moses and Monotheism* is a tour de force.

The end was approaching. In the last two years suspicious lesions were no longer precancerous, but malignant recurrences of the cancer itself. In mid-January 1939, Schur was concerned about a new swelling close to the area of bone necrosis. Once again Exner made light of Schur's anxiety. The condition worsened and in February they consulted the world's leading authority on cancer, Wilfred Trotter (Jones's brother-in-law). This led to further disagreements, discussions, and frustrations. Schur and Anna were very uneasy. Their daily observations of Freud's condition gave them expertise that no outsider could match. Exner and Trotter were slightly indignant that this foreign internist and his amateur assistant should question their judgment.

---

[1]Clark p. 523

Dr. Lacassagne from the Institute Curie came from Paris for a consultation. Schur sent an SOS to Pichler. There were meetings to discuss radium treatment, electrocoagulation, and surgery. A biopsy performed on February 28 showed a typical malignant epithelioma. The lesion was so high that no further operation was feasible. "Inoperable, incurable cancer" was the fatal name given to the case. The end of the struggle was in sight. Radiotherapy was started immediately by Dr. Vinzi, but the treatment was only palliative.

Freud continued to live his busy life; patients, visitors, correspondence, reading and writing. The "Moses" had been published in German; now he was eager to see it published in English. Jone's wife, who was the translator, worked hard on the project and the book was published in March 1939. In a note to Hans Sachs, one of his guests, he wrote: "The Moses is not an unworthy leavetaking."[1] The publications led to a new avalanche of mail. Freud was destined to be a controversial figure to the end.

In April Freud received a hard blow: Max Schur had to leave for the United States. Freud had grown dependent on his personal doctor's daily ministrations. Although he tried to hide his feelings, he was deeply upset.

> I was now faced with an extremely difficult and painful decision. After Munich I had decided to remain in England only as long as Freud was still alive, and then to emigrate to the United States....I had previously applied for a visa while still in Vienna, but had forfeited it when I received a permit to go to England....I was notified by the American Consulate in London that I was now eligible for an immigration visa....Due to the complicated American quota regulations, I would have to take this visa or lose my quota number....and the quota was now filled for years to come. Yet I could not leave Freud in the condition he was in at the beginning of 1939.
>
> (Schur, p. 522)

If he did not accept this permit, Schur would endanger his family's future. "I decided to take the New York State Boards for my medical license, and return to London at the earliest possible moment."[2] Schur had trained Dr. B. Samet to take his place temporarily.

Freud had helped Schur. He had written letters to friends in the United States on his behalf and facilitated matters with the American consulate in London. At Schur's departure Freud seemed understanding and gentle. Freud "gave me his blessing."[3]

The reports Schur received from Anna and Dr. Samet were at first encouraging: Freud was feeling better and enjoying the spring. But by June the picture darkened—pain, severe X-ray reactions, a bone necrosis, and so forth.

---

[1]Jones 3, p. 242
[2]Ibid. p. 522
[3]Ibid. p. 523

> My dear Marie,
>
> The evening before last I was ready to write you a long letter of condolence on the occasion of our old Tattou's death (one of Marie Bonaparte's chows), and then to prepare you for the fact that on your next visit I would listen eagerly to whatever you might tell me about your new papers, and throw in a word here and there whenever I believed that I could supplement something. The two nights that followed again cruelly destroyed my expectations. The radium has once again begun to eat away at something, causing pain and toxic manifestations, and my world is what it was previously; a small island of pain floating in an ocean of indifference.
>
> Vinzi continues to assert his satisfaction. His answer to my last complaint was: "In the end you, too, will be satisfied." So he is luring me half against my will into continuing to hope and in the meantime into continuing to suffer.
>
> (M.B. June 16, 1939)

It proved to be the last letter he would write to Marie Bonaparte.

Schur returned to London early in July and found Freud much worse than when he had left him in April. He had lost weight and, compared to his usual mental vigor, he seemed apathetic. There was a cancerous ulceration slightly upwards of the old lesion, the bone was tender and exuded a foul odor.

Freud disliked taking drugs. "I prefer to think in torment than not to be able to think clearly."[1] He only consented to an occasional dose of aspirin, which made Schur's task of alleviating his suffering very difficult.

The downhill trend continued through August. All the symptoms became more marked and unfortunately, antibiotics were not yet available. The unpleasant odor from the wound became unbearable. The chow that he had become attached to could not tolerate the smell and would not go near him; when she was brought into the room she would shrink into the farthest corner. Freud, of course, knew what this meant. He would look at his pet with pained, knowing sadness.

One of the last visitors was Hans Sachs who came to take leave of the man he called "master and friend." Sachs reported two particular observations. Despite Freud's painful condition he showed no sign of irritability or complaint—only the full acceptance of his fate and his resignation to it. The other observation concerned Freud's unflagging interest in everything around him. He showed himself to be fully informed about recent events in analytic circles and the pesonalities connected with them.

War had started. Freud read the newspapers, fully aware of the impact of events. But there was about him an air of detachment. Schur had moved into Freud's house while his wife and children were evacuated to a "safe" place in the country. "Not once in all the time did I witness any impatient or angry reaction toward any person in his environment. He still asked how my children were reacting to evacuation, and suggested to me reading material from his library, recommending among other

---

[1]Jones 3, p. 245

things certain works by Albert Schweitzer whom he held in high esteem."[1]

It was very difficult for him to eat anything; he was suffering badly and his nights were uncomfortable. It was agonizing for Schur to be unable to alleviate such suffering. But he knew he had to wait for the word from Freud.

The final phase left Freud unable to read. His last book was Balzac's *La Peau de Chagrin* (The Fatal Skin). "That was the proper book for me to read; it deals with shrinking and starvation."[2]

On September 21, during Schur's daily ministration, Freud took his hand and quietly said: "Lieber Schur, Sie erinnern Sich wohl an unser erstes Gesprach. Sie haben mir es so weit ist. Das ist jetzt nur noch Qualerei und hat keinen Sinn mehr. (My dear Schur, you certainly remember our first talk. You promised me then not to forsake me when my time comes. Now it is nothing but torture and makes no sense anymore)."

Schur indicated that he had not forgotten his promise. Freud sighed with relief, held Schur's hand for a moment longer, and said: "Ich danke Ihnen (I thank you)"; after a moment's hesitation: "Sagen Sie es der Anna. (Tell Anna about this)"[3] Schur related that all this took place without a trace of emotion, with full consciousness of reality and no self-pity.

Schur gave him a hypodermic of two centigrams of morphine. Freud fell into a peaceful sleep, all expression of suffering and pain gone. Twelve hours later Schur repeated the dose. Freud was so close to the end of his reserves that he lapsed into a coma. He did not wake again. Sigmund Freud died at 3:00 A.M. on September 23, 1939.

---

[1]Schur, p. 527
[2]Ibid. p. 528
[3]Ibid. p. 529

Index